B

298

20th-Century Plays in Synopsis

20th-Century Plays in Synopsis

Edited and with an introduction by

E V E R T   S P R I N C H O R N

Thomas Y. Crowell Company   *[New York, Established 1834]*

NOTE. *Throughout the book the date given after a play's title, unless otherwise specified, is that of the first performance.*

The synopses were written by Harriet Blum, Betsy Cenedella, Joan Cenedella, Maureen Grice, Beverly Horowitz, Marian Houston, Arthur Hudgins, Frances Olan, Robert Snyder, Kristina Snyder, Edward Stewart, Rhoda Tripp, Dorothy Tuck, Mary Walter, and Ian Whitney.

Contents

Contents

Contents

Contents

Contents

20th-Century Plays in Synopsis

The Decline and Disappearance of Plot

Everybody likes a good story, and a good storyteller is always the center of attention whether he is holding forth in the men's room of a train, in a Third Avenue bar, on the political rostrum, in the church pulpit, or on the Broadway stage. The best stories are those that can be told over and over again, constantly satisfying our hopes and expectations. The details may change but the outline remains the same, and the outcome is altered only at the peril of the storyteller. When Bernard Shaw refused to let Professor Higgins marry Eliza Doolittle, the Galatea he had created with phonetics, the audiences accused the Irish author of being impish and perverse. They finally had their way when Shaw was dead and *Pygmalion* was set to music. A more illuminating example of the serious relationship that exists between the storyteller and his listeners is provided by Ibsen. When he allowed Nora to walk out of her doll house and abandon her husband and her three little children, the audiences of Europe rose up to protest, demanding that the author be silenced. They knew that the story had to end with the reconciliation of the respectable but thick-headed husband with the sacrificing but giddy wife, both of whom had erred in taking too much for granted, and, moreover, the audience had waited two hours for the happy reunion that would send them contentedly home to their bourgeois beds. When they did not get what they wanted, they accused Ibsen of being immoral. In this case they eventually had to yield to Ibsen and let him have his way with the old story. The public had to give women the same rights to come and go as a man and thus make Ibsen's immoral ending moral by changing their own standards and expectations.

Radical departures in the retelling of popular stories reflect the spirit of revolution, and Ibsen and Shaw were rather revolutionary spirits. Imagine the new order that will lie in the offing when someone composes an Adam-and-Eve story in which man and woman will remain in paradise and it will be God who learns how evil he has been, who grows ashamed at the knowledge, and who is cast out to toil and spin, while Adam and Eve let factories and robots do their work for them and treat sex as an inconsequential game played with pills. The fact that such a story has not already won popular acceptance shows how difficult it is to alter religious stories, deeply embedded, as they are, in the human mind.

To see how changing times and manners affect plot let us consider two plays popular in the 1890's. In Pinero's *The Second Mrs. Tanqueray*, a woman who

1

has had love affairs in the past and who cannot become a mother marries a respectable gentleman who has a daughter by a previous marriage. To overcome her past and recover her self-respect Paula Tanqueray wants more than social acceptance: she wants the daughter to accept her as a mother. This the daughter will not do. Being a teen-aged, convent-bred, nineteenth-century girl, she identifies motherhood with monogamy. She goes abroad, falls in love, returns with her boy friend, and introduces him to Paula. The confrontation of Paula and the boy friend provides Pinero with the climax for his play. The boy friend is Paula's former lover. The daughter guesses the truth and insults her stepmother, who kills herself, realizing that the past cannot be defeated. As the curtain falls the daughter begins to realize what Paula has gone through.

Pinero clearly makes Paula the center of his story. Had he written the play a half century earlier, he would have made Mr. Tanqueray the center and would have described the disaster that follows when a man of the upper classes marries into the demimonde. Such a play is Augier's *Le mariage d'Olympe* of 1854, with which Pinero's play was inevitably compared. In the middle of the twentieth century the daughter would almost certainly be made the central figure, and the play would show how a prim teen-ager is transformed into a sensual woman through the experience of love and is ready to understand and forgive Paula and, conceivably, accept the lover as her husband.

The Second Mrs. Tanqueray is rarely performed nowadays, but Shaw's *Candida*, written just a year after Pinero's drama, is still frequently revived. It presents the classic triangle of two men in love with the same woman. One of the men is her husband, strong, handsome, admired by men and adored by women. The potential lover is a callow youth, effeminate, physically weak, rejected by his family and by most of the world. As Shaw tells the story, the woman dallies with the poet without ever seriously thinking of giving herself to him. In the famous auction scene at the end of the play, when she is forced by the two men to commit herself to one of them, she chooses to stay with her husband on the ground that he is actually a weak little boy incapable of functioning unless he is constantly flattered, attended to, and cared for, whereas the poet has a soul of steel and needs no one to help him make his way in the world. The poet Marchbanks is, as a matter of fact, a portrait of Professor Higgins as a young man.

A half century later the same plot situation was handled on the American stage in Robert Anderson's *Tea and Sympathy* (1953) in which the married woman gives herself to a young man who is suspected of being a homosexual in order to prove to him that he is indeed a man. The athletic husband who sneers at the weak student turns out to be a latent homosexual. *Candida* and *Tea and Sympathy* represent the pre-Freud and post-Freud treatments of the same plot situation.

WELL-MADE AND PROPERLY MOTIVATED

By comparing plots, we can use them as cultural artifacts to tell us a great deal about changing mores. But in the present century even more enlightening than the change in audience response is a study of the playwright's attitude to the conception of plot itself. The classic view, as stated by Aristotle and maintained to the nineteenth century, held that plot was the most important element in a drama. By plot one meant the arrangement of incidents: the same story may be plotted in many different ways. When the Shakespearean theater disappeared and Paris became the cultural capital of Europe, Racine was recognized as the model playwright and the neoclassic drama as the ideal form. In the latter part of the eighteenth century the Shakespearean influence finally made itself felt on the Continent as German writers began a literary revolution that threatened to hurl Racine from his throne. Some French dramatists now turned to writing romantic and poetic plays; others wrote pure melodramas that pleased the mob. But the playwrights who catered to the middle class steered a middle course. Remaining faithful to the neoclassic rules in principle, they allowed the social and political revolutions that followed 1789 to make deep inroads into the drama. Seizing on the empiricist and positivist philosophy, which had acquired a firm basis during the Enlightenment and which was used to buttress the logical structure of the neoclassic drama, and exploiting the popular emotionalism and colloquial flavor of the melodrama, a group of young French playwrights led by Eugène Scribe perfected a dramatic form that came to be known as *la pièce bien faite*, the well-made play.

From the Racinian model Scribe learned that a good play has a tight cluster of characters involved in a single action that builds steadily to a climax, which is followed by a quick resolution. From the melodrama he learned to hold an audience by cutting the long speeches or *tirades* that only bored the tired shopkeeper, by adding physical movement, and by appealing directly to class prejudices, patriotic ideals, and bourgeois moral standards. In all this there was nothing new. But Scribe borrowed from the field of science an idea that constituted the technical novelty in his method. He made each event in his plays seem realistic and convincing by anticipating the audience's how and why. Like a scientist he explained and justified what happened by giving every effect a cause and by making all the causes consistent with one another. Racine had taken a set of human relationships and examined the different alternatives; Scribe constructed a complicated clockwork machine that produced surprises at carefully timed intervals.

The opposite of the well-made play (a term that I am giving a wider application than it generally receives) was not a badly made play but the Shakespearean kind of drama in which the action seems as often as not to be improvised. Iago's motives are strangely inconsistent, and none of them is exploited in the course of the play. Scribe would have given one or two strong motives and made use of them to create certain dramatic situations—or else he would not have mentioned them at all. Shakespeare does not bother to explain why the ghost in *Hamlet* is visible to one person and not to another at the same time. A realistic dramatist writing well-made plays could not allow such an anomaly. Another example brings us to the essential difference between the two methods. Hamlet's skill at swordplay would have had to be introduced early in a well-made play to justify the final scene. Far from preparing us for Hamlet's skill, Shakespeare lets us know in Act Two that Hamlet has "forgone all custom of exercises." On the other hand, Ibsen, the master builder of well-made plays, takes great pains to "plant" early in his drama the pistol with which Hedda Gabler shoots herself so that no one will be inclined to reply to Brack's curtain line, "People don't do such things!" with a skeptical "Of course not. Where did she get that pistol?" The fact that Ibsen was able to invest his "planted" properties with symbolic qualities shows how genius can make a virtue of necessity.

So important was this notion of explaining what happens in Act Three by referring to a minor point in Act One that drama was defined in the middle of the nineteenth century as the art of preparation. Like solid citizens and good students well-made plays were properly motivated. To Scribe a play was simply a machine designed to produce laughs, gasps, and tears. He regarded himself as a mere entertainer whose sole aim was to keep the *bourgeoisie* from yawning. The next generation of playwrights often had higher aspirations. They wrote with a reformer's zeal and sought to appropriate to the dramatist the functions of the journalist and the priest. Disdaining art for the sake of art, Dumas *fils* in 1868 called for a utilitarian theater serving social causes and wrote a series of plays dealing with women's rights and sexual morality. At about the same time the naturalist Zola ridiculed the cardboard characters and clockwork mechanism of the well-made play and urged dramatists to adopt the attitude of the scientist who dispassionately observes the world around him and ruthlessly draws his conclusions, regardless of what art and morality may dictate. In 1871 the Danish critic Brandes, swimming with the new intellectual currents, told his countrymen that in order to be significant modern literature must "submit current problems to debate."

It was under these pressures that Ibsen, who was living in Germany where it was impossible to escape the stimulus of the new ideas, and who had his poetic and national masterpieces *Brand* and *Peer Gynt* behind him, now turned to the realistic problem play and in so doing won international fame as the father of the modern drama. The young Ibsen had written plays that abounded in Scribean intrigue, in the plotting and counterplotting of hero against villain, but when he reached maturity, he banished these elements from his plays. Combining the German romantic conception of fate with nineteenth-century Darwinism and scientific determinism, he made the action of his plays consist in the working out of the forces of the past. The well-made play with its stress on preparation turned out to be perfectly suited to Ibsen's thought. Without radically changing the form of the well-made play, he revitalized it by cramming it with sociology, psychology, and symbolism. Not a borrower like Shakespeare, Ibsen with his extraordinary mythopoeic powers was able to invent stories that were capsule histories of his century. *Ghosts*, *The Wild Duck*, and *The Master Builder* became modern myths that could be subjected to a variety of interpretations and that have not lost their power to arouse the imagination and stir the intellect. While overhearing the subdued talk and suppressed whispers in Ibsen's Victorian parlors, one can hear the soft footsteps of history at one's back and the distant rumble of revolution on the horizon. Not only were whole lives compressed into Ibsen's plots; whole epochs passed in review.

No one believed a bourgeois entertainment could have such potential for transforming men's minds. Ibsen's triumph was so great that many critics were led to think that the whole history of dramaturgy had reached its culmination in *Hedda Gabler*, and the only way to preserve Shakespeare's greatness was to transform him, too, into an author of problem plays and psychological character studies. Playwriting manuals began to appear regularly, all based on the dramaturgy implicit in Ibsen's works. It seemed impossible to surpass the Norwegian genius; one could only imitate him or react against him.

Zola failed to accomplish his naturalistic reform of the stage because, though protesting against the artificialities of the well-made play (as everyone was doing after 1852 and the advent of Realism) and urging fidelity to nature as the only valid artistic principle, he worked within the structural pattern of the play form he despised. His own efforts in the drama were only badly made well-made plays. Strindberg, writing in the 1880's when Ibsen was bringing the well-made play to fulfillment, was the first to break the old plot pattern and create a new one. Instead of presenting three, four, or five acts forming exposition, rising action, climax, and denouement, Strindberg concentrated the action into one long, virtually uninterrupted act. *Miss Julie* and *Creditors*, both written in 1888, represented the first truly creative departure from the form of the well-made play.

But these one-act plays still had a great deal of action or story. A truly radical plotting innovation, the effects of which are being felt more strongly now than ever before, took place in the last decade of the century. Just as the realists had reduced the melodramatic intrigue of the well-made play to a minimum, so now action in general was reduced to a minimum. In the 1890's, the decade of symbolism, Maeterlinck came forward with the idea that the most deeply significant moments in life are precisely those in which nothing appears to happen. Protesting against the scenes of violence that authors inevitably make the focus of interest and reminding us that most lives are lived out without scenes of murder, poisoning, duels, and insane jealousy, Maeterlinck wished to put on stage the "tragedy of everyday life." The active life of the conventional hero of even the most realistic play inhibits the life of the spirit, said Maeterlinck. It is when the room is still and the body in repose that the mind blossoms and bends toward the source of silence to absorb the eternal forces and respond to the shy gods who play the major roles in our lives.

Although Maeterlinck's early plays were too unsubstantial to endure the coarseness and crudities of the stage, the theories he advocated have had an enormous influence on the modern drama. His most impressive efforts were in the area of the short one-act play. When he attempted full-length plays, he succumbed willy-nilly to the demons of plot and intrigue. Nothing much needs to happen in a twenty-minute sketch, but it is extremely difficult to hold an audience for two hours without having anything happen. Maeterlinck's solution was to follow Wagner into myth and legend for story material.

In 1898 Strindberg took the same course, up to a point. In *To Damascus* he created a drama in which he gave small events cosmic importance by drawing on the cultural storehouse of myths, legends, archetypes, and symbols. But there was a crucial difference between Strindberg's method and Maeterlinck's. When the latter resorted to legends to build a full-length play, he took them over whole, retelling them with new emphases here and there, a method followed by Giraudoux and a host of twentieth-century dramatists. Strindberg used them in bits and pieces and built his symbolic plays like mosaics, as he said, though it would be more meaningful nowadays to describe them as collages. Seeing his autobiographical protagonist as a hodgepodge of cultural potsherds, Strindberg was among the first, if not the very first, to give his antihero heroic significance by making him the sum of past and present history. Allusion replaced action in *To Damascus*, and thus the problem of how to hold the interest of the audience while avoiding intrigue and banal effects found one extremely fruitful solution.

Chekhov tried another approach. Though he is always classed among the realists, and rightly so, it should be remembered that his major plays were written from 1896 to 1903, when reaction against the naturalism of the 1880's had set in and the symbolist movement had spread throughout Europe. Chekhov distrusted conventional plot-making as much as Maeterlinck did. "In life," said Chekhov, "one dosen't fight duels, hang oneself, declare one's undying love, nor spout the most profound thoughts in one steady stream. No; more often than not, one eats, drinks, flirts, and says silly things. It is this that one should see on stage. A play should be written in which people come in, dine, talk about the rain or the good weather, and play whist, not because the author has willed it but because that is how things happen in real life."

Chekhov could admire Ibsen's craftsmanship but he felt oppressed by the Norwegian playwright's ever-present intellect shaping events. It has been remarked that the story of Madame Ranevsky's life, which she tosses off in a single speech in *The Cherry Orchard*, would suffice for a three-act play by Ibsen. But it is easy to tell that kind of story and insert it into a play. One can pick up a dozen like it in a single afternoon at a ladies' bridge party. The difficult thing is to plot such a story, that is, make a play of it; and it is infinitely more difficult to plot such a story and avoid all the stale situations that had been presented a thousand times on the nineteenth-century stage. Chekhov chose not to tell Ranevsky's story in the conventional way because in doing so he would have had to make the death of Ranevsky's little boy serve as a second-act climax and her abandonment by her lover and her subsequent attempt at suicide come as a fitting denouement. Her life would acquire a thrust and significance that Chekhov obviously felt it should not have. She was, in a word, not worth a play. Accordingly, Chekhov substitutes for action a number of excruciatingly banal situations, none of which is allowed to develop in the orthodox fashion. He has a number of people, all linked together in a daisy chain of triangular love affairs, drift on stage for a party or a homecoming and then drift off again. But the love affairs do not constitute the real plot or structure of *The Cherry Orchard* any more than do Gaev's imaginary billiard games. The plot of a Chekhov play shows how a sister-in-law usurps a house or how a beautiful ancestral estate is turned into a housing development. There is implicit in a Chekhov action ten times as much awkward intrigue as in an Ibsen play, but it is all off stage. Chekhov may say that fighting duels and killing oneself are not part of the ordinary day's routine, but his characters still do that sort of thing—off stage. The Greek tragedians kept on-stage violence to a minimum for technical production reasons (not for religious reasons, as one sometimes hears), but Chekhov banished it because he was tired of the conventional French boulevard drama that had overrun Europe and of everything associated with it: stereotyped acting, standard lines of business, interchangeable situations, cliché-ridden speeches, phony climaxes.

More important than these artistic reasons for his choice of technique was the fact that for him God did not exist, myths were mere superstitions, and at least part of him looked with skepticism on all programs and ideals, especially those of the middle class. It would have been dishonest of him, and temperamentally impossible, to cloak his plays with myths or adorn them with transcendental ideals. And he also knew that by shaping his plots like those of the well-made play he would be committing himself to the kind of thinking that created the form. Strindberg preferred to throw it out; Chekhov turned it inside out.

In less than a century the well-made play had undergone every vicissitude. As fresh and vivacious as an unspoiled ingenue at the beginning of the century, it looked by the end of the century like a tired character actor. Though the common man still liked his old favorite situations and asked for violence and intrigue in equally large doses, which the motion pictures were soon to give him, the intellectual vanguard looked for its aesthetic kicks in more ethereal realms. Or else made a shambles of the old-fashioned play by reducing it to the level of the comic strip, as Jarry did in *Ubu Roi*, staged in 1896—about the time, as a matter of fact, that the first comic strips did appear.

ABSTRACT, ABSURD, AB OVO

The period from 1887, when Antoine opened the Théâtre Libre in Paris, to 1922, by which time the expressionist fever had subsided and the first surrealist plays had been written, was an era of uninhibited experimentation in the theater, as in the other arts. A whole century of romanticism, of reaction against the neoclassic rules, had left the artist free to invent and create as he chose. Said Strindberg in the first decade of this century: "All forms are now permissible." The designer swept the stage clean of the cluttered realistic set and turned the newly perfected electric lights on a bare stage. The German expressionists got rid of realistic psychology along with the realistic sets. Getting down to fundamentals, they wanted to put on stage pure man and pure woman, stripped of those characteristics acquired in the process of becoming civilized. Wedekind, a forerunner of the expressionists, saw man as an animal driven largely by elemental passions, and modern morality as a monstrous deceit that would lead man to destroy himself under the delusion that he was bettering

7

himself. The heroine of Wedekind's *Earth-Spirit*, performed in 1898, is no longer a realistic human being; she is the sex drive incarnate, unintentionally destroying the men who cross her path. A quarter of a century later the young Brecht in his first play, *Baal*, converted Lulu into a man; and forty years after that, the type cropped up in plays and movies about beatniks. Sorge, the author of *The Beggar*, often called the first truly expressionist play, also pleaded for a new moral order, but of a different kind than Wedekind's atheistic one. Written in 1912 just before European civilization was shattered to its foundations in the First World War, *The Beggar* follows Strindberg in putting directly on stage the inner conflicts and visions of a man undergoing a religious conversion. Kaiser in *From Morn to Midnight*, first produced in the middle of the war, as was Sorge's play, viewed modern man as the crucified victim of dehumanizing greed, hypocrisy, and selfishness, and borrowed from Strindberg the technique of picturing the journey of discovery and enlightenment as a pilgrimage through the stations of the cross. The station drama, which has its origins in the religious drama of the Middle Ages, became a form preferred by expressionist playwrights.

The French avant-garde of this time, who disliked German expressionism for its vague abstractionism and embarrassing soulfulness, employed their own methods to dissolve the calcified deposits of thought and morals that gave the mind cultural arthritis. They wanted less philosophy and more fun. They wanted to capture the playfulness and waywardness of the pristine, childlike, dreaming mind. Just as the expressionists wanted to consider the essential man, man stripped of all his attributes, so these writers, generally known as surrealists, sought to capture man's thought processes before logic (meaning Western logic) and value judgments had imposed their patterns and limitations. The surrealist preferred to work with concrete images rather than with conventional symbols or signs, such as the cross. Symbols had become so encrusted with meanings and obscured by connotations that one could not apprehend them freshly. The surrealist technique was that of wit as Voltaire defined it: "a novel comparison, . . . a delicate relation between two common ideas, . . . the art of bringing together two objects separate from each other."

A horse tapping out a message is merely a clever circus horse. When it taps them out to a poet, as happens in Cocteau, the horse becomes Pegasus and a symbol of inspiration. All symbols are surreal at first. The Greek Pegasus had wings. Wings on a horse! That is surreal until one gets used to it. Becoming cultured or civilized is the process of becoming accustomed to strangeness and of accommodating oneself to symbols. The surrealists wished to remind us of that fact, and to find a form for their thought they went back to primitive types of theater, the revue skit, the vaudeville act, the circus. E. E. Cummings even invaded American burlesque for the "fairy" scene in *him*; and the three Weirds in his play are obviously the old Fates, but here they appear as vaudeville figures. The nine sketches or numbers of Act Two suggest pregnancy, and the whole play becomes a Joycean and Freudian picture of the mind of a woman reviewing her life while giving birth to new life.

By the mid-1920's nearly every line of development that led away from the well-made play had been explored. Many of the plays of the 1950's and 1960's that seem daringly original to students unfamiliar with the history of the modern drama are either variations of these earlier forms or instances of atavism in cultural evolution. The vitality of Strindberg's extended one-act form has been demonstrated in such mid-century plays as Sartre's *No Exit*, Genet's *The Maids*, and Albee's *The Zoo Story*. Whether existential, homosexual, or absurd, they have much more in common with Strindberg's naturalistic one-acts than may at first appear. Ionesco's first plays hark back to Jarry and the surrealists. And anyone who supposes that Maeterlinckism and the drama of inaction and silence died a generation ago should take another look at the plays of Beckett and Pinter. They represent the mid-century fulfillment of Maeterlinck's principles—dramas in which very little happens but in which we are led to feel that something of vast significance is being implied. Plotlessness becomes a virtue, and pauses the source of mysterious meanings, while words and phrases are repeated over and over again to suggest that active life is at a standstill.

The whole theater of the absurd is best explained with reference to the dramaturgical problem of finding a satisfactory substitute for motivation and intrigue. Scribe and Ibsen were obliged to motivate the actions of their characters, and in so doing they gave meaning to their plays. Today, if an action is not motivated, it becomes absurd. The easiest way to write an absurd play is to take a conventional plot and demotivate it. A typical beginning exercise in a course in playwriting is to write a fifteen-minute dialogue between two people, one of whom is kept relatively silent. Another slightly more advanced finger exercise is to write the dialogue for three people. If one has a good ear for colloquial speech, one can turn out these two exercises overnight. The difficult thing is to have something happen in the dialogue and to explain why it happens, but in fifteen minutes one is not expected to explain very much. The next thing to do is to paste the two sketches together and call them a play. Pinter's *The Room* illustrates this. Ibsen had so much to say that he could motivate on several levels; the absurdists have nothing to say and cannot motivate even on the simplest level without falling into clichés. When Ionesco wrote the full-length play *Rhinoceros*, he gave us a tendentious message play.

The great virtue of absurd plays is that they offer the spectator an opportunity to exercise his imagination. He supplies the motives and the meaning deliberately omitted by the playwright. In this respect absurd drama resembles nonobjective painting, where the viewer is free to read whatever he wants to into the pattern of line and color. Theoretically this is a valid artistic principle, at least as old as da Vinci in the visual arts, and reaffirmed by Strindberg at the end of the nineteenth century. But when it was a question of playwriting, Strindberg insisted that a play "that stands still is undramatic." Nothing would be of greater value to aspiring playwrights than to study the fourth and fifth acts of Strindberg's *Charles XII* to learn how a master of the drama of inaction fills out his play of a king waiting to die.

WHAT SYNOPSES FAIL TO DO

The recent attempts to write nonplays have also shown us that the theater is a complicated art in which story or plot is only one among several elements. Like the experiments of the 1910's, those of the mid-century remind us that the apparatus of the theater can be put together in different ways, that new axioms lead to new universes in the theater as well as in geometry. The well-made play with all its variants continues to dominate the popular stage because it accords best with the common man's preference for a relatively simple universe organized on rational principles. This kind of play can generally be summarized without too great a loss of meaning. But the inventive plays in which the dramatist is exploring new worlds or enriching his means of expression, plays distinguished by visual and aural effects, allusiveness, or the absence of rational motivation, cannot be reduced to a story line. In them texture is more important than pattern. In studying a playscript the reader is already at one remove from the play itself. In reading a synopsis he is at two removes and sees only the shadow of a shadow. A drama that reads badly may play well, and a drama that seems to make no sense when synopsized may be a powerfully coherent work when properly staged.

As an illustration, let us consider one of the most discussed plays of recent years, Peter Weiss's *The Persecution and Assassination of Marat as Performed by the Inmates of the Asylum of Charenton under the Direction of the Marquis de Sade*, first performed in 1964 in Berlin. The play has been censured by many critics, who feel that the author has tried to capitalize on recent and not so recent trends and fads in the theater without investing sufficient thought and talent. *Marat/Sade*, they say, is a compound of the absurd and the existential, of Pirandello and Genet, of Shaw's discussion play, of Brecht's epic theater, of Artaud's theater of cruelty, but with the whole adding up to less than the sum of its parts. Perhaps their perplexity has its roots in the fact that the play has no plot structure in the ordinary sense. Weiss has chosen to balance the entire action of his play on one point in history, the moment when the French revolutionist Marat was murdered by Charlotte Corday. From the begining to the end of the play Marat is sitting in his bathtub waiting to be stabbed, and throughout the play Corday is approaching through the streets of Paris, knocking on his door, and entering his apartment. A scene, a tableau from the French revolution (David's famous painting is referred to) is used by Weiss as a prism through which the various interpretations of the event can be refracted and broken down into their basic components. The playwright no longer wants to be seen as the clever intrigue maker, the off-stage God who pulls the strings, for then he will be accused of bias even before he has expressed his views. So Weiss has Sade take over the task of the playwright, and it is Sade who presents Marat's views gathered from Marat's writings. The play (both the outer play and the play-within-a-play) takes the form of a debate between the revolutionist Marat, who believes in progress even if it can be achieved only through the shedding of blood, and the nihilist Sade, who looks upon revolution as merely one of man's infinite ways of satisfying his lust for violence and cruelty. At least one critic has remonstrated that it is ridiculous to have Marat sitting in his bathtub throughout the whole play, and no doubt it appears ridiculous to anyone who reads the play in synopsis. But his bleeding skin is visual evidence of his suffering and a constant reminder to the audience that for a man like him the pain of giving birth to a new social order counts for very little when weighed against the alleviation of suffering it will bring to countless thousands. To give another dimension to the play, the author has the murder of Marat acted out by the inmates of a hospital for the mentally ill. The man playing Marat does suffer from a skin disease and need scarcely act at all. The part of Corday, the killer of the revolutionary spirit, is played by a woman suffering from sleeping sickness. It is with touches like this that Weiss can make his points without seeming to. The inmates as a group become representative of suffering humanity, ignorant and unthinking, whipped and subdued by guards indifferent to the pain and injustice that surround them. The play is put on in the shower room of the hospital so that the associations with German concentration camps is unmistakable. On stage throughout is the superintendent of the asylum and his family, representatives of the *bourgeoisie* who are in the political saddle after the French revolution and whose satisfaction with things as they are is ironically counterpointed by the wailing of the inmates. The issue between Marat and Sade is joined at the end after Corday has plunged her knife into Marat. Hailing Napoleon, who ended the revolution of the sans-culottes and restored order to France, the superintendent eulogizes the new age of prosperity and freedom. Identifying political with sexual satisfaction, the mob of inmates release their pent-up emotions by marching and chanting, "revolution, copulation." Roux, a revolutionary extremist, and probably the author's spokesman (he is played, significantly, by an inmate in a strait jacket), shouts through the noise and tumult, "When will you learn to see, when will you finally understand?" as the unheeding mob swallows him up. Sade stands up in his chair, laughing triumphantly. In the extraordinarily effective Stockholm production the inmates march forward en masse on the spectators gathered in the auditorium, which is fitted out like a shower room. Alarmed, the superintendent shouts for an iron net to be dropped across the stage. The mob storms ahead, climbs up the netting, reaching out to grab at the audience as darkness engulfs the theater.

THE MUSE OF HISTORY AND THE GODDESS OF CHANCE

Weiss's play represents one of the directions the theater of today is taking in its efforts to find a way out of the blind alley of nonaction and absurdity. Weiss has invited history to be his collaborator in providing story material and much of the commentary. The playwright stands on the sidelines and tries to seem as uninvolved as possible. Some playwrights have been even more self-effacing. They have let the historical records speak for themselves, up to a point, and given us documentaries like Kipphardt's *The Oppenheimer Case* (1964) and Martin

Duberman's study of slavery *In White America* (1964), plays that have their antecedents in the Living Newspaper productions of the 1930's and in the Russian theater of the 1920's. Other dramatists, like Nordahl Grieg in his magnificent play on the Paris Commune, *The Defeat*, have produced a powerful effect by adopting a clear and definite posture toward the events depicted.

One of the strongest advocates of the modern historical drama is the Russian Vishnevski, who was a young man at the time of the Bolshevik revolution. In 1933 he asked if "an art, however perfect it may be in form but whose inner spirit is nourished and limited by old traditions, can possibly be relevant to the social upheavals" of recent times. "One must break ruthlessly with the methods formerly employed in literature," he declared. "All possibilities for creating a great art stand before us." He wanted his plots to picture the world as Engels saw it—"not as a complex of finished things" but as a "complex of processes" in which material things as well as ideas are subject to change. His *Optimistic Tragedy* is "the representation of an historical process from the point of view of historical change."

The idea that man, his institutions, and even his personality are changeable appealed strongly to Brecht, although it informs his theoretical writings much more than his plays, which often convey a sense of despair that man will ever change. Like the naturalists of the nineteenth century he wanted to be as inquisitive and as dispassionate as a scientist; but whereas they were deterministic in their outlook (at least in their plays), Brecht affirms (at least in his essays) his belief in the potential for change in the human being.

The thought that the universe is open-ended and that nothing is predetermined suggests a second approach that the theater is taking at the present time. There is a growing trend to let chance reign in the drama both in the writing of the script and more especially in the performance. Already the epic theater is old-fashioned, and the vanguard is speaking of the dynamic theater. Says a Swedish critic, "We are breaking with all the different forms of epic and psychological theater; we are abandoning the peephole stage with its opposition of stage and audience." This sounds like an echo from the great period of experimentation, and indeed it is a throwback to the "Merz" Theater, which the artist Kurt Schwitters proposed in 1919, and to the antics of the Dadaists at the Cabaret Voltaire in 1916.

As examples of how the dynamic theater breaks down the dichotomy of actor and spectator and allows chance to dictate the plot, consider these two playlets. In one devised by Claus Bremer and Daniel Spoerri, each admission ticket is numbered and bears on its reverse side a series of words. During the performance, numbers appear at random on the stage. Thereupon the spectator whose ticket corresponds to the number must call out any one of the words on his ticket. These words are signals to the actors to begin a new activity, or to continue or to change the one they were engaged in. It all suggests a football game in which only half the players know the signals.

Ferdinand Kriwet's *drei* (1962) requires three simple sets, three costumes, three actors, and a director who writes nine key phrases on a blackboard—words like "pity," "feel like killing," "kleptomania." Then he places one of the sets on stage. Each performer now chooses a key word, selects one of the costumes, and the three then improvise a scene. The scene is repeated two more times with the remaining key words and sets. Once the actors are warmed up and the spectators understand the principle, it becomes the audience's turn to call out the key words and choose the set—and the play begins again.

With plays like these the playwright has virtually done himself out of a job and confirmed the bankruptcy of his art. It is not the theater that is dying but the plotted drama. If the present trend continues, thirty years from now a book of synopses like this one will be filled with descriptions of performances rather than summaries of playscripts. Each title will have its rubric; for example: *"drei* by Kriwet, as performed at Ulm, June 16, 1962."

Or do these experiments constitute a necessary prelude to the development of a new form for the plotted play?

In either case the playscripts summarized here convey some idea of the richness, variety, and desperate search for new forms of expression that have characterized the last half of the period 1860–1960, a century that ranks with the Greek, the Elizabethan, and the French neoclassic periods as one of the great ages of the drama.

EDWARD ALBEE

Who's Afraid of Virginia Woolf?

[1962]

ACT ONE. Fun and Games

It is two o'clock in the morning as the front door opens and Martha comes into the living room of a house in an Eastern college town, followed by her husband George, a history professor in his forties.

In an irritable mood Martha looks around the room. "What a dump!" she says, teasing George to tell her what movie she is imitating. Wearily, George protests he doesn't know. He grumbles about the Saturday-night parties instituted by her father, who is president of the college at which George teaches. Martha demands a drink, and George is astounded to learn that she is expecting guests: a new young teacher and his wife, whom Martha's father has said she and George should be nice to. George sulks, and Martha sings, "Who's afraid of Virginia Woolf, Virginia Woolf, Virginia Woolf?" She asks for a big sloppy kiss, which he refuses as too stimulating, and she demands another drink. George is appalled, and they quarrel. Martha observes that he is such a nobody he almost doesn't exist.

The doorbell chimes, and she orders George to answer it. Warning Martha not to talk about their kid, he moves with exasperating slowness. "Screw you!" she explodes as he flings open the door on Honey and Nick. Hesitatingly, they enter and sit down. Offered a drink, Honey asks for a little brandy. "Never mix —never worry," she giggles shyly.

The young couple are politely enthusiastic about the earlier party. Martha thinks her father is quite a guy, but George confides to Nick that there are easier things than being married to the president's daughter. Martha remarks loudly that *some* men would give their right arm for the chance.

Honey needs to powder her nose, so Martha takes her out. George plies Nick with disconnected questions and treats his puzzled replies with mocking humor. Nettled, Nick snaps at him. Asked if he has kids, Nick answers stiffly: not yet—he and Honey want to wait until they are settled. George tells him Martha's father expects his staff to stay forever, adding that the president is rumored to be over two hundred years old.

Honey returns, explaining that Martha is changing. She announces she has just found out that George has a son who will be twenty-one tomorrow. To her perplexity, George is angry.

Martha enters looking voluptuous and, beaming, turns her attention on Nick. Learning that he was a champion boxer in college, she observes that he must have a pretty good body. Nick smiles at her. She begins the story of how, twenty years ago, she knocked George down. George goes out and returns with a shotgun, which he aims at Martha's head. He pulls the trigger and out pops a Chinese parasol. Pleased, Martha draws his hand to her breast, but he breaks away.

Nick is in the biology department; George accuses him of plotting to rearrange chromosomes in order to make everybody exactly alike. Grimly, Nick humors his host. Honey, drunk, asks with a titter when their son is coming home, but Martha doesn't want to talk about it. Maliciously, George pursues the subject, and Martha, rising to the bait, lets out that he is unsure of his paternity. She argues that her son's eyes are green like hers and Daddy's. George says her father has tiny red eyes like a white mouse.

Then Martha tells how she grew up alone with her father, whom she worshiped. After he had built up the college from almost nothing, she looked among the staff for a presidential heir and fell in love with George (who interrupts, saying he was six years younger than Martha). They were married, Martha continues, but George was a flop, and the plan didn't work out; now she is stuck with this *bog* in the history department. Almost crying with rage, George breaks a bottle against the bar and, to drown out his wife, sings, "Who's afraid of Virginia Woolf?" Honey joins in drunkenly, then leaves the room to throw up. Exasperated, Nick goes after her. Martha gives George a contemptuous look, spits "Jesus!" and follows.

ACT TWO. Walpurgisnacht

On Nick's return, George remarks that it gets pretty bouncy around there. The young man replies coolly that he doesn't like to get involved in other people's affairs. George draws him into admitting that he married Honey because he thought she was pregnant; the pregnancy turned out to be only hysteria. They laugh, and George tells a story about a boyhood friend who accidentally killed his mother with a shotgun and his father in a car collision.

Losing his reserve, Nick confesses that he really married his wife for the money left by her father, who got rich preaching. George says Martha's money came from her stepmother. Suspecting his guest of power-grabbing intentions, George advises him to plow all the faculty wives.

Martha leads Honey in and accuses George of making the younger woman sick. She adds that he made their son vomit all the time. Honey insists, petulantly, on more brandy, then decides to dance. George puts on a Beethoven symphony, which Martha soon removes, substituting a slow jazz tune. She and Nick undulate to the music. Rhythmically, she says that her father refused to let George publish his novel about the boy who accidentally killed his mother and father and that George revealed that it was not a novel, but an autobiography. George rips off the record and grabs his wife by the throat. Nick tears him away and throws him on the floor.

George drags himself to a chair and regains his composure. They have played "humiliate the host," he says: the next game will be "get the guests." His second novel is about a nice young pair from the Middle West—and he narrates the story of Honey and Nick. Horror-struck at Nick's betrayal, Honey rushes off to be sick again, and her husband follows her, threatening George. In a fury of recriminations, Martha and George declare total war.

On his return Nick reports that Honey is lying on the bathroom floor: she finds it cooling. George goes out to get more ice. Martha urges Nick to come closer, and entering unnoticed, George sees them intertwined. He smiles, leaves, and re-enters with the ice, remarking that Honey is curled up sucking her thumb. Martha is suspicious of his cheerful manner. Moving to a chair that faces toward the wall, George takes up a book. Nick puts his arm around Martha. Nettled at her husband's indifference, Martha warns him that she is necking and hints at further acts. Without looking up, George tells her to go right ahead. Frustrated to fury, she follows Nick out of the room.

George hurls his book at the chimes, which ring and awaken Honey. She comes in, half-asleep, telling her dream of being naked and frightened. She begins to cry: "I don't want any children. I'm afraid. I don't want to be hurt!" Snapping awake, she asks who rang the bells. George tells her that it was someone with a message that his and Martha's son is dead. Talking to himself, laughing softly, and half-crying, he brings the news to Martha in an imagined scene.

ACT THREE. The Exorcism

Martha enters the empty living room, calling for George, who doesn't answer. She addresses Daddy White Mouse, who has red eyes because he cries all the time. She cries all the time too, Martha confides, but deep inside, and Georgie cries all the time.

Nick watches her from the doorway, then enters, saying that everyone is crazy. His wife is curled up on the bathroom floor peeling the label off the brandy bottle. Martha informs Nick he is no better than the others and that he is definitely a flop in some departments. She ridicules him mercilessly. Only one man has ever made her happy, she tells him, and that is George. Nick is disbelieving.

The doorbell rings and Martha makes him answer it. George appears with a bunch of snapdragons. He throws them spearlike at Martha, saying, "Snap go the dragons." There is one more game to play, he announces: "bringing up baby." He orders Nick to get Honey. Martha pleads not to have the game, but George insists soothingly, then jerks her head back and tells her roughly that this game will make her performance look like an Easter pageant.

Nick returns unhappily, supporting Honey, who is still holding the brandy bottle. "Hip, hop," she says cheerfully. Prompted by George, Martha describes the happy, healthy life of their beautiful child. As she warms to her subject, he interjects phrases of the Requiem Mass. When the idyll comes to an end, he contradicts her. Things aren't so fine as she makes out: poor Martha is stuck

17

with a spineless husband, she can't get her fill of liquor, her father doesn't love her, and her son fought her all the way. "Lies!" Martha shouts. They blame each other bitterly for failure, and the quarrel rises to a climax, George reciting the Requiem. Then he breaks the news of their son's death. Martha leaps at him. He can't do that, she yells. George answers that he did it because she broke the rule of silence.

Nick comprehends at last that Martha and George have no children and asks Martha whether she was unable to produce any. "*We* couldn't," Martha and George reply. George tells the guests they must go home. Nick holds out his hand to Honey, and they leave. Sadly, Martha asks George if he had to do it, and he answers that it was time. He lays his hand gently on her shoulder, she puts her head back, and he sings softly: "Who's afraid of Virginia Woolf . . . ?" "I am," Martha says. George nods.

MAXWELL ANDERSON

Winterset [1935]

ACT ONE

Early on a December morning, Trock and Shadow appear on the bank of a river under a bridge. Flinging a series of bitter invectives at the sleeping city, Trock ascribes his own degenerate condition to his experiences in prison, from which he has just been released. Because the authorities want to return him to prison, he is here to discover whether, as he suspects, they have sufficient evidence to condemn him to death; he reveals that, in any case, the prison doctor has given him but six months to live. As Lucia, the street-piano man, and Pliny, the apple woman, appear, Trock and Shadow leave, ignoring Lucia's greeting. Lucia and Pliny discuss the strangers, Lucia calming Pliny, who is startled by their strange appearance and behavior.

In a basement apartment in the building next to the bridge, Garth sits alone, examining a violin, when Miriamne, his fifteen-year-old sister, joins him and begins to question him concerning the fear that has confined him indoors for three days and that has caused their father to behave so strangely. Speaking of the recent trial and execution of a man by the name of Romagna, she reveals that she has learned of Romagna's innocence; Garth, however, denies any involvement in the affair.

Their father Esdras, an old rabbi, enters, followed by Trock and Shadow. Left alone with Garth, Trock accuses him of turning state's evidence and reviving interest in the Romagna case. Insisting that the revived interest is due solely to the research of a professor, Garth maintains that a re-examination of the case could only prove injurious to himself. Trock informs Garth that Judge Gaunt, who presided in the Romagna case and condemned the man to death, has been publicly defending his decision and, suspected of insanity, has disappeared. Ordering Garth to stay home, Trock leaves with Shadow.

Summoning Miriamne and Esdras, Garth breaks down under Miriamne's questions and admits that he took part in a payroll robbery during which he saw Trock commit murder. Tired of living in fear of Trock and the police and disgusted with his own cowardice, he is ready to tell the truth, for which he will have to die. But Esdras, describing the crime and guilt of all men, begs Garth not to sacrifice himself to an idea of justice. Garth admits that he prefers to keep silent and live. After he leaves, Miriamne reflects that she would prefer to die.

That evening Miriamne sits alone under the bridge. Judge Gaunt appears and begins to argue his case to a tramp. Returning to his senses, he apologizes and leaves. Miriamne is about to go inside when Mio and Carr, boys of seventeen, enter. While Mio is bringing his friend Carr up to date on his activities, he sees Miriamne and inquires what is wrong. Replying that nothing is wrong, she leaves. Mio follows her, but she has disappeared. Mio describes to Carr his hopeless situation: his innocent father, Romagna, has been executed, his mother has died of grief, and he himself has been rejected by his home town. Hearing of a professor interested in the Romagna trial, he has come here to read the professor's work and to investigate on his own, all of which has led him to this particular tenement house. Carr cautions Mio that the state will never admit having committed such an error as executing an innocent man and that only money obtains justice. Mio, however, feels a responsibility to his father to bring the truth to light.

Lucia enters with his piano, followed by Pliny, who is indignant that the police have ordered Lucia not to play his piano on the street. As Lucia sadly begins to turn the crank, a crowd gathers, and some begin to dance. Mio dances with Miriamne, as Esdras and Judge Gaunt join the assembled throng. The merry scene is interrupted by a policeman, who orders Lucia to stop playing. As all protest, a young radical launches into a speech challenging the actions of the policeman. While the policeman tries to silence the radical, Judge Gaunt steps forward to defend him. His defense turns into a self-defense, and soon others are defending Judge Gaunt against the policeman. Mio directs a verbal attack against the policeman, who loses his temper and orders the crowd to disperse. Trock watches as Garth and Esdras take Judge Gaunt inside with them, the judge confessing that his madness is due to his inability to bear the burden of having condemned one man, Romagna, to die for the good of many.

Miriamne is left alone until Mio returns. He earlier asked her to wait for him, but now he tells her to go inside where she will be warm and safe, for he is of a different sort than she. When he speaks of his disillusion and loneliness, however, she instinctively offers to go with him. To her tender words he replies at first with bitterness, recalling his father. Then he admits his love for her, though still rejecting her youthful dreams. In describing his father's death, however, he reaffirms his loyalty to his father's love and once again attempts to send her away. But Miriamne has recognized the story as that of Romagna. Knowing that Mio is in danger, Trock having an interest in keeping Romagna's innocence secret, she urges him to go away, without explaining why. As Trock and Shadow enter, Miriamne pulls Mio into the shadows. Trock and Shadow argue, and Shadow, wary of Trock, takes a gun from him before leaving. Two young men appear and follow Shadow. Shots are heard. As Carr returns, he and Mio go to investigate, while Miriamne goes slowly inside. When Mio and Carr return, they part company, Mio continuing his quest alone.

ACT TWO

The same evening, Miriamne and Esdras are seated in the basement apartment as the sound of Garth's violin is heard. When Garth joins them,

Miriamne urges him to flee, but he refuses. Meanwhile they have awakened Judge Gaunt, who enters. Recognizing Garth's name as that of the witness he never called, he dismisses it, inquiring instead how he came to be in their company and asking to be directed home. He becomes involved, however, in explaining the Romagna case and in defending his part in it. As he is about to leave, a knock at the door sends Miriamne into the inner room. The caller is Mio, who has come to ask Garth whether he knows anything that would exonerate Romagna. Garth and Esdras deny possessing such knowledge, Esdras advising Mio to cease his efforts to convince the world of his father's innocence. Judge Gaunt interrupts to proclaim that Romagna was guilty. An argument ensues between the judge and Mio, who at length recognizes the judge as the man who condemned his father to die. Mio bitterly accuses the judge of willfully sentencing an innocent man to death. Judge Gaunt defends himself, but Mio remains unconvinced as Esdras and Judge Gaunt leave.

Miriamne returns as Garth leaves. Surprised to find her here, Mio rejects her loving words, crushed by the thought that perhaps he has been deceived about his father's innocence. Though Miriamne cautiously tells him never to believe the others, in his doubt he regards himself as unworthy of her. Her protestations are interrupted by Garth, to whom Miriamne confesses her love for Mio. As Mio is about to leave, Esdras and Judge Gaunt return, followed by Trock. Ascertaining Mio's identity, Trock is immediately suspicious of Garth. When Trock wants to take Judge Gaunt away, a heavy rainstorm intervenes. Mio begins to question Trock, who threatens his life.

At that moment the door opens to reveal the bloodstained figure of Shadow holding a gun and accusing the terrified Trock of trying to have him killed for refusing to kill Judge Gaunt. Before he can shoot, however, he drops the gun and is helped into the other room, where he soon dies. Mio frightens Trock with the story of the return of all Trock's victims seeking revenge. Judge Gaunt begins to conduct the proceedings like a trial. When Mio accuses Trock of killing the paymaster, Trock breaks down and shouts that it was Shadow. Mio now knows that Trock and Shadow were involved in the murder and that Garth was a witness. Questioned by Mio, Judge Gaunt admits that the judgment was delivered in anger at the common worker Romagna, who was a confessed anarchist. Though realizing Romagna's innocence, he let the decision stand, believing that justice is governed by opinion, that society is best rid of anarchists, and that the common good outweighs the small injustice. When Mio joyfully announces that he will spread this news far and wide, Trock threatens that the news will not get far. Mio, however, is ecstatic at the confirmation of his father's innocence.

The policeman and a sergeant arrive, seeking Judge Gaunt. Recognizing Trock, they warn him to stay out of trouble. Suddenly Mio accuses Trock of murder, inviting the police to look in the other room and proclaiming his father's innocence. No corpse, however, is to be found. The police dismiss Mio as a joker. At Miriamne's coaxing, he states that he is dreaming. After the police lead Judge Gaunt away and Trock departs, Miriamne urges Mio to flee immediately, as Trock will be waiting to kill him later. Mio denounces Garth's treachery, extending the blame to Miriamne, who despairingly replies that she could not condemn her own brother. Mio bitterly reflects that though he has uncovered the truth, she has ironically rendered his knowledge useless. Despite the danger, he goes out into the night.

ACT THREE

On the riverbank, Trock emerges from the tenement. After a few words to two young men lounging nearby, he leaves. Mio comes out of the tenement, tests the rain, and remains uncertainly next to the wall, ignoring Miriamne when she joins him. She offers to find him a hiding place or to go with him; he refuses both offers. Garth and the hobo emerge from the tenement carrying a door, upon which lies the body of Shadow. Mio's ensuing burst of cynicism is interrupted by the return of Garth and the hobo. Esdras joins Mio and Miriamne, offering to call the police to remove Mio safely from the scene. When Mio replies that he will reveal his story and thus implicate Garth, Esdras pleads for his son, at length entrusting his son's life to Mio.

Deeply moved by the old man's trust and goodness, Mio wonders how to spend his last minutes on earth, as Miriamne berates herself for not telling the truth and thus failing him. He replies that should he live, they will always be separated by her brother and his father. Carr appears with the news that two men are lurking by the bank and leaves without comprehending Mio's dangerous situation, for suddenly Mio no longer wants to publish the truth if it will hurt Miriamne. Suddenly he loses the desire to hate, realizing for the first time that his father would have forgiven. He draws Miriamne to him and speaks of being with her again and always.

Esdras appears, his face bleeding, having tried to pass Trock on the bridge in order to reach the police. Telling of Trock's determination to kill Mio and live out his six months, Esdras goes inside to seek a path of escape on the roof for Mio. Miriamne directs Mio to a path that she thinks is unwatched, but moments after he disappears, a machine gun is heard. Mio slowly returns and sinks down, repeating to her the declaration of undying love that his dying father had made to him. To show Mio that she would have died for him, Miriamne walks toward the path, shouting to the murderer that she will reveal the truth that Mio was to tell. The machine gun is again heard. The wounded Miriamne crawls toward Mio to show him that she is dying, but it is too late. Esdras speaks sadly, almost enviously, of their defiant death. Deeply touched, he is reminded of his own intimations of the meaning of life. Lucia and Pliny appear to help Esdras and Garth carry the body of Miriamne.

JEAN ANOUILH

Antigone [1943]

All the characters in the play are on-stage when the curtain rises on a stair, flanked by arches, in front of the palace of the king of Thebes. The chorus steps forward and announces that "these people" are about to act out the story of Antigone, then proceeds to introduce each of the characters as a historical person with a preordained role to play before the audience—who are not doomed as some of the characters are.

There is Antigone, a "tense, sallow, willful girl," who will stand up alone against Creon, king of Thebes, and will die for her action; Antigone's sister Ismene, who, in contrast to Antigone, is "gay and beautiful"; Haemon, son of Creon and Antigone's fiancé, who, in preferring Antigone to her more beautiful sister, is doomed to die. Creon is next introduced: he is Antigone's uncle and Oedipus' brother-in-law. Once he was a patron of the arts; now he is a consummate politician. Eurydice, Creon's wife and queen of Thebes, is described as a good, simple woman. The messenger, who has "a premonition of catastrophe," is introduced next. Finally, we are introduced to the palace guards, who are policemen and therefore "eternally indifferent."

The chorus briefly gives the background: Oedipus' sons, Eteocles and Polynices, were supposed to share the throne after their father's exile, each reigning in alternate years. But Eteocles refused to step down and so precipitated a civil war. The two brothers fought and killed one another. Creon then ascended to the throne and ordered that Eteocles, with whom he had sided, be buried with honors, while the corpse of Polynices be left to rot. Anyone defying his orders and daring to bury Polynices shall be put to death.

The chorus and characters leave the stage and the action commences. It is dawn. Antigone is caught returning indoors to the palace by the nurse. They bicker, Antigone teasing the old woman with the thought that she, Antigone, had met in the night with a lover. Though when she is with the nurse, Antigone generally feels and acts the part of a little girl, she announces that she must not be a little girl on this day.

Ismene enters and tells Antigone that she too wishes to bury Polynices, but doesn't want to die. Antigone insists that they are certain to die; nevertheless, they are bound to bury their brother. Ismene admonishes her sister for being impulsive and stubborn and says, moreover, that a girl cannot do such a thing. Antigone becomes angry, claiming that Ismene has spent her life cursing the fact that she is a girl; but she also pities Ismene for not being as willful as she.

After Ismene leaves, Antigone tests the nurse's love and then the love Haemon swears he feels toward her. She describes to him her love, which is in large measure sexual, then tells him that they can never marry, that he must leave her now. Stupefied, but completely dominated by her, Haemon retreats. Ismene returns briefly to suggest to Antigone that Polynices never cared for her and that she is a fool, always defying the world. Antigone says that Ismene's words come too late: she has already buried her brother.

Later in the day, Creon is told by one of the guards, who was out on watch, that the corpse of Polynices has been covered up. Creon insists that it was probably a child—one of Polynices' followers—who did it. He tells the guard to uncover the body once more and to keep this news quiet.

In midafternoon the chorus returns to the stage and offers a brief, sardonical definition of tragedy. Unlike melodrama, tragedy is "clean, restful, flawless": nothing is in doubt, everyone's destiny is known, there is no hope. The audience is told that from now on Antigone "is going to be herself," for she has been caught.

The guards, unaware of her identity, enter with Antigone. They joke among themselves and handle her roughly. They describe how she covered the body, digging into the earth with her fingernails and refusing to stop until she had finished burying Polynices. Creon enters and, seeing that it is Antigone who has been captured, sends the guards away, telling them again not to speak of what has happened.

Antigone insists to Creon that she will simply do it again if he should release her, for Polynices was her brother and she owes him burial; it would have been the same had she been a scullery maid and not Antigone. Creon reminds her that her brother was a rebel and a traitor. When she speaks of her father Oedipus' "headstrong pride," Creon suggests that she and her father both desired "torments," a "cosy tea party with death and destiny." Creon goes on to speak of a king's position, how he must not bother with private feelings, but must introduce a measure of order into "this absurd kingdom." Therefore Antigone will not die; it is more important that she marry Haemon and give him a healthy son.

Antigone counters, "What a person can do, a person ought to do." She admits that the religious connotations of burials are absurd; she is simply acting for herself. It is her job to die, just as it is Creon's to have her killed. Creon resents being cast as a villain, with Antigone as heroine: he calls her a "mischiefmaker" and declares his intent to save her.

The argument shifts to politics. Creon too would like to bury Polynices, but the people, the "featherheaded rabble," need this example. Antigone keeps shifting their talk back to an existential plane. Creon, she says, chooses something vile when he says "yes" to politics, whereas she says "no" to vile things. Creon speaks of responsibility, the importance of saying "yes"; Antigone invokes a higher order of things, where politics is transcended.

Creon admits to having had fantasies of assassin-children. He tells Antigone that burying her brother is meaningless, for Polynices was a "cheap, idiotic bounder . . . a cruel, vicious . . . voluptuary," who in fact once struck his father Oedipus and even plotted his assassination. Eteocles, too, was rotten. He reproaches Antigone for failing to deal with this "kitchen of politics" and suggests that she had a romantic attachment to her brother; she rejects the sordid insinuation as "an obscene story."

Creon then compares actual life, which is prosaic and humdrum, with Antigone's youthful and unrealistic thoughts of self-sacrifice. He seems to have her convinced, but when he speaks of "the happiness you get out of life," Antigone rejects him as a hypocrite: she sees happiness as "a stone step worn away by the tread of life," and hope as something "filthy, docile, female." She compares herself to her father—they are of a tribe that "asks questions"; in the end they are beautiful because nothing can save them. This is the beauty that she sensed when she was a little girl.

Ismene enters and states that she wants to die also, but Antigone claims it is too late—Ismene does not deserve death. Creon runs out of patience and calls the guards. The chorus warns Creon not to have Antigone killed, for they will "carry the scar of her death for centuries." But Creon insists he has no choice, that death is her purpose, that she finds life and happiness repellent. He will not condemn her to live. Haemon rushes in and begs his father to change his mind; if not Haemon will disown him. Creon refuses: he must remain a political person; he has chosen to do so.

The guards enter with Antigone, who expresses a fear of the crowd. She questions one of the guards and learns of the compromises he has made in his life. She bribes the guard to take a letter. At first she dictates that she does not know what she is dying for; then she recants and asks him only to write that she begs forgiveness. Antigone is taken away before the letter can be addressed to any particular person.

The messenger comes with the following news: while Antigone was being walled up alive outside the city, it was discovered that Haemon had gotten into the cave with her and that she had hanged herself; when the two were dug out, Haemon confronted his father, struck him, and then killed himself by falling on his sword.

Creon returns to the palace and learns that his good, pragmatic, loving wife, Eurydice, has cut her throat. Abandoned and alone, Creon falters but recovers to go off to do state business: there is a cabinet meeting at five. He warns his page not to grow up too quickly.

The chorus is left on-stage. They point out that the roles are played out, the dead are "stiff, useless, rotting," and the living will quietly forget them. The guards return and begin playing cards. Nothing matters to them.

JEAN ANOUILH

Becket, or The Honor of God

[*Becket, ou L'Honneur de Dieu,* 1959]

ACT ONE

Henry, wearing his crown and a cloak, enters the cathedral where Thomas Becket is entombed. He is naked under the cloak. Before Becket's tomb, he drops his robe and kneels.

He speaks to Becket, asking why it couldn't have been different. Becket, dressed as he was the day he died, comes from behind a pillar and admonishes Henry to pray. Henry muses how odd it is—Becket, now a saint, and he, humbling himself by accepting a beating to win over the Saxons. He remembers the happy days they had together.

The lighting changes, and Becket, now an elegant young nobleman, comes into Henry's room. Henry quizzes him about his Saxon background. Becket tells him his father amassed a fortune collaborating with the Norman conquerors and sent him to France to learn French. Together they enter the council chamber. There Henry appoints Becket Chancellor of England to help him force the clergy to pay the absentee tax. Becket, armed with authority and the triple lion seal, sets to work to enforce Henry's command. The bishops argue with him, then, when he and Henry leave, wonder together at this new opposition they face.

Henry and Becket, hunting on horseback, seek shelter in a miserable Saxon hut. The king discovers a girl hiding there and proposes to bring her back to the castle to make a whore of her. The girl's brother, defending his sister, gets into a scuffle with Becket and cuts his hand. The king promises Becket a gift for being wounded in his service. Becket asks for the Saxon girl. The king reluctantly agrees but exacts from Becket the promise to render "favor for favor." After the king leaves, Becket throws the girl's father a purse and tells him the girl will not be taken.

In Becket's castle, Gwendolen, Becket's mistress, is curled up on a low bed. In the background, behind a curtain, are shadows and sounds of a wild banquet. Gwendolen tells Becket he is her "Lord, God or no God." Becket moves away and says that he doesn't like being loved.

The king comes in and, after hearing Gwendolen sing a long lament, suddenly says to Becket, "Favor for favor," and asks for Gwendolen. Becket is stunned, but since he cannot say he really cares for her, agrees. The King leaves, and Becket tells Gwendolen she will have to go and that he will not take her back. She reminds him that even conquered people have one thing left. "Yes, I daresay I had forgotten. There is a gap in me where honor ought to be," Becket admits. After Gwendolen leaves, guards drag the Saxon girl in to Becket. The king stumbles in, terror-stricken: Gwendolen, he tells Becket, has slain herself. Becket has the Saxon girl taken away. The king throws himself down on Becket's bed. He falls into a troubled sleep as Becket ponders his own strange position as one of an alien race whose allegiance is confused. ". . . Where is Becket's honor?" he sighs, as he too lies down to sleep.

ACT TWO

Becket meets four English barons, retainers of the king, in a forest in France. He tells them there will be a triumphal entry into the French city they have been attacking. Becket wakes Henry and warns him that the English bishops are getting too powerful. He also informs him that he has managed to get the French to collaborate. They ride into the city to the cathedral. There, as the king waits to speak to the French bishop, word comes that the Archbishop of Canterbury is dead. Henry exults at having one enemy less, then conceives a "profound" idea. He discloses his wish that Becket be elected to the post. Becket speaks his dismay, for, he says, "If I become Archbishop, I can no longer be your friend." They leave, the king adamant.

In Becket's room, two servants pile costly clothes into chests. Becket, clad in a plain gray gown, enters to supervise the disposal of all his worldly goods. When the servants leave, Becket laughs at himself for giving away everything in a day, then prays, "I wish there had been something I had regretted parting with, so I could offer it to You. . . . It all seems far too easy."

ACT THREE

In a room in his palace, Henry quarrels with the queen and the queen mother, defending Becket against their criticisms. When he receives from Becket a letter returning the triple lion seal and telling him that Becket now has God's honor to defend, Henry, stunned, weeps like a child, "I loved you and you didn't love me," but resolves, "I shall learn to be alone."

At a church, Henry, dressed as a squire, approaches Gilbert Folliot, bishop of London, to confess his repentance of having forced the election of Becket, whom he now wants to be rid of. Folliot finally agrees to meet with him the next day to plot Becket's removal.

At his episcopal palace, Becket receives bishops who tell him he must appear before the king's assembled council on a charge that Becket states is trumped up. They try to persuade him that he was wrong openly to oppose the king by excommunicating three men who interfered with his jurisdiction over clerics. Becket smilingly reminds them that though he was a worldly man, they passed the burden to him and that he will not set it down.

The king, the queen and queen mother peer through a curtain to try to hear the proceedings as the council calls for Becket. A page comes and tells them

27

that Becket finally appeared, strode unchallenged and unharmed in and out of the council with no word of sentence spoken against him. The king cannot help but admire Becket's strength, but the queen mother warns him Becket will flee to France.

At the court of Louis, king of France, Louis promises Becket protection. Becket plans to see the Pope, but Louis warns him to be wary of the Pope: "He'll sell you for thirty pieces of silver."

The Pope and a cardinal, both in tawdry splendor and with atrocious Italian accents, speak from rostrums. The Pope says he has been offered three-thousand silver marks by Henry to discredit Becket. The cardinal spins a web of intrigue planned to please King Henry and the archbishop, too. Even the Pope cannot follow the maneuvers that end in a decision to relieve the archbishop of his titles and functions, then reappoint him, and send him to a French convent.

In the convent, Becket, praying before a crucifix, voices his resolve to leave the austerities of the convent, where it is "too easy," and to take up the mitre, the cope, and the silver cross and to face the king again.

ACT FOUR

In his court, Louis, when Becket tells him of his decision to return to England, offers to try to make peace between the king and Becket, for he fears for Becket's life.

Becket and King Henry meet on a cold plain, both on horseback. They trade commonplaces, the king veering over and over into cries to his old friend about his now unhappy life. There is an apparent agreement, but before they part, Henry cries out, "I should never have seen you again." Becket replies "Farewell, my prince. I know I shall never see you again."

At his palace in France, Henry flies into a rage when his scheme to have his son crowned king by the Archbishop of York strikes the queen mother as displaying a rancor that is "neither healthy nor manly." He drives her and the rest of his family from the room, then, turning to his barons, asks them news of Becket. When they tell him Becket is triumphant in England, acclaimed and protected by the Saxons, he hurls himself on his couch, tearing at the mattress with his teeth and moaning, "I can do nothing! . . . Will no one rid me of him?" Drumbeats sound and continue pulsing like a beating heart. The barons gird on their swords and leave.

In Canterbury Cathedral, a young monk helps vest Becket in his Archbishop's robes. The four barons come in, drawing their swords. Becket speaks to dissuade them, then turns to start vespers. The barons close in and hack him to death.

Their hacking motions fade, and the same motions are seen as monks whip Henry, kneeling at Becket's tomb.

The baron comes in to say that the crowd has turned and now acclaims Becket and Henry in the same breath. Henry ironically observes that the honor of God is on his side now and sends the first baron to seek out and banish the murderers, lest anyone doubt his royal desire "to defend the honor of God and the memory of our friend from this day forward."

JEAN ANOUILH

Ornifle [1955]

ACT ONE

Ornifle, an aristocratic poet, is pacing his study dictating a poem to his secretary, Miss Supo. She has worked for him for ten years and is deeply infatuated with Ornifle, an inveterate woman chaser. She reminds the poet that photographers from a popular newspaper are due at midday. He dictates his poem, then opens his dressing gown, revealing a string of pearls; they agree that the pearls have improved in color, and Ornifle says all the society women of Paris give him their pearls because he has a skin that refurbishes them. Ornifle goes off to bathe, and Nenette, the housekeeper, enters with coffee to find Supo weeping; Nenette tells her that she too loved Ornifle and was once his mistress, but that it is now over. The countess, Ornifle's wife, enters, hears her husband's new poem, and goes out.

Machetu, Ornifle's rich agent, arrives, followed shortly by the poet. Machetu asks for a minor alteration in the new poem and leaves. Nenette announces that a young man wishes to see Ornifle; the poet refuses, but hurries off when the housekeeper tells him that Miss Marie Pêche is waiting in another room. Father Dubaton arrives and finds Supo in tears: she knows that Marie Pêche is a prostitute and tells the priest he must save Ornifle's soul. Ornifle returns, and the father tells him his church would like him to write a carol for Christmas. Ornifle composes one on the spot; as he dictates, Nenette announces the photographers, who are shown in and take pictures as the poet works. They persuade him to reveal the pearls he is wearing and to pose in bizarre positions with his agent, who has returned to ask Ornifle to rewrite a song.

ACT TWO

Ornifle, bewigged and in seventeenth-century costume for a fancy-dress ball, is being examined by his doctor, Dr. Subites; the poet insists he has heart trouble, but Subites tells him he is mistaken and leaves to fetch Professor Galopin, a heart specialist. The doctors, both in fancy dress, return. After a perfunctory examination, Galopin, a foolish jokester, assures Ornifle his heart is in good shape; Galopin and Subites then leave for the ball. Nenette announces that the young man is back asking to see Ornifle, and the poet orders that he wait. When the countess comes in, Ornifle tells her to go to the ball without him; she refuses and says she will stay with him, since he is ill. She reminds him it is their tenth wedding anniversary and then tells him that Clorinde, a middle-class girl whom he seduced, has tried to commit suicide. She asks him whether he would like a divorce, since he apparently no longer finds her physically attractive. Ornifle laughs at the idea and says that Clorinde should simply have an abortion. He calls to Supo to telephone Machetu and explains to his wife that his agent has been in love with Clorinde for the past six months and can now have her; he then gaily sends his wife off to the ball.

When Machetu arrives, Ornifle tells him that Clorinde is ready to marry him. Machetu leaves, full of gratitude for Ornifle's kindness in passing the girl on to him. Supo enters and in tearful anger tells Ornifle that she habitually listens at the door and knows all his affairs; she says his treatment of women is horrible. Ornifle offers his love-sick secretary one sweet moment of love; she is on the point of accepting the thing she has been waiting ten years for when Nenette enters to remind the poet about the young man.

The young man, Fabrice, enters; when Ornifle fails to recognize his name, he reminds the poet of an affair he had twenty-five years ago: Fabrice is the result. The boy says that his mother never married, considering herself already married to Ornifle, and had a very hard life bringing up her son, who is a medical student; before she died she revealed the name of the boy's father, and now, Fabrice says, he has come to kill Ornifle to avenge his honor. He points a gun at Ornifle, who falls as the trigger makes a harmless click. Fabrice, muttering that his fiancée Marguerite must have removed the bullets, examines Ornifle, decides he is a victim of a heart condition called Bishop's disease, and runs to his car to get a hypodermic needle. Supo enters naked and tells the supine poet she is ready to accept one moment of love.

ACT THREE

Ornifle is lying in bed waiting for his doctor to arrive. He sends his new-found son to go and fetch his fiancée, who is waiting in Fabrice's car. The boy returns saying Marguerite has gone, leaving a note stating that she hates Fabrice. He explains that they had agreed to elope to avoid her being sent to South Africa by her father but that she threatened to do as her father wished if Fabrice insisted on killing Ornifle. Machetu remarks that a friend of his, Pilu, is also sending his daughter to South Africa, and they realize that it must be Marguerite. Ornifle sends Machetu to persuade Pilu to let the girl come to Ornifle's house. Fabrice starts to leave but faints in the doorway; when he recovers he says he has not eaten for two days. Ornifle, who has sprung from bed to help his son, orders food. He says he's a changed man; it's really quite pleasant being a father and he feels proud of his son. But Fabrice shows him a dossier compiled by a detective agency revealing all his father's affairs. Instead of being ashamed, as Fabrice wanted, Ornifle is delighted to be reminded of his forgotten love affairs; his son is disgusted.

Machetu arrives with the lovely Marguerite, who makes a great impression on Fabrice's amorous father. The girl tells Fabrice that they are finished and tries to leave, but Ornifle detains her and sends Fabrice out with Machetu. Asked why she fell in love with Fabrice, Marguerite says it was because, unlike other boys she knew, he was poor; together they romantically planned to live in poverty in Africa, treating the natives. The poet calls Machetu and tells him to stand back and watch. The old libertine then delivers a romantic speech saying that Fabrice is the girl's soul mate: they must remain together. His sentimental words make the stupid Machetu weep. Marguerite goes out to find Fabrice; they return together and kiss on Ornifle's orders. The kiss is prolonged, and Ornifle suddenly breaks down and jealously harangues his son for this "indecency" in the "death room."

Supo enters and announces that Father Dubaton has arrived at her request. The others go out, and the priest tells the poet that he is foolish in going from woman to woman. Nenette announces that the doctors have arrived, and Ornifle sends her out to buy all the roses she can find for his wife.

ACT FOUR

Supo and Machetu are awaiting the doctors' report on Ornifle. The poet comes in with the doctors, who angrily declaim against Fabrice: it was ridiculous of him to diagnose Bishop's disease; there is nothing seriously wrong with Ornifle. After they leave, Ornifle orders Machetu back to his dinner with Clorinde, with whom he has been making good progress. Ornifle then sends Supo to find Marguerite. Lying on the bed, he pretends to her that the doctors have confirmed Fabrice's diagnosis and are astonished that so young a student should be so medically advanced. He states that he has not long to live and that he wants Fabrice to look after him, since he is such a marvelous doctor. They will all go away to the south of France, Ornifle proposes, and Fabrice can continue his studies at Aix University. Playing the indulgent elderly father, he says he will keep the girl company till evening, when Fabrice returns from his studies. Marguerite agrees to the plan and goes off to talk to Fabrice about it; Supo enters, tells Ornifle she has heard everything, and angrily accuses him of planning to seduce his son's fiancée. Ornifle tells the raging woman that she is right.

Ornifle calls Nenette and tells her to pack; they will leave that night. Fabrice comes in and tells his father he is ready to devote himself to caring for him. Nenette enters and announces that Marie Pêche is waiting. Ornifle says she is to wait for him at the Montesquieu Hotel and leaves for his rendezvous with the prostitute. Supo hysterically screams that no one has ever seen her body, even though below her tasteless clothes she is beautiful. As she rages, the telephone rings, and the manager of the Montesqieu Hotel informs Supo that Ornifle has just had a heart attack in the hotel lobby; a doctor was called and mentioned Bishop's disease . . . he came too late to save Ornifle's life. The manager asks what he should do with "Mr. Ornifle's body."

Supo lets the telephone drop and staggers to the bed. She clutches a pillow in her arms, holding it tightly against her, repeating, "Mr. Ornifle's body!"

JEAN ANOUILH

Thieves' Carnival   [*Le Bal des voleurs,* 1932]

ACT ONE

A young man and woman are embracing in the public gardens of a French seaside town. She is afraid of being seen; they plan to meet later. Feigning passion for her hand, Hector is surreptitiously examining Eva's rings through a jeweler's eyeglass; when she leaves, he coldly assesses their value. During this vignette and others that follow, a clarinetist on stage plays appropriate background music tinged with irony.

The town crier warns the crowd of summer visitors that a dangerous band of pickpockets is loose; while he is delivering his speech, Hector robs him. A moment later Hector meets up with Peterbono, one of his accomplices. They decide to pull a job on a young woman, who turns out to be the third member of the group in disguise, Gustave. Peterbono, leader of the trio of thieves, is critical of the others' carelessness: it seems they often inadvertently rob each other. Gustave, like Hector, is taken with a girl he has met; he is unhappy when Peterbono decides that Hector, a professional seducer, should make up to the wealthy girl. They exit planning a "Three Musketeers Manoeuvre" to steal a nursemaid's gold chain.

Lady Hurf and Lord Edgard, two very English types, enter with Juliette, Lady Hurf's niece. She is none other than the girl Gustave has met. Lady Hurf dominates Lord Edgard with trivial directions. Eva and Juliette's suitors, Dupont-Dufort, Senior, and Dupont-Dufort, Junior, appear; though apparently men of means, they are actually fortune hunters, and Lord Edgard overhears their schemes.

Disguised as soldiers, Hector and Gustave perform a little ballet with policemen and the nursemaid, but are frustrated in their attempts to get the necklace.

Though fearful of the intrigues in which her highly eligible nieces are involved, Lady Hurf admits to Lord Edgard she is bored and thus excited by the danger. The lord suggests summoning a detective from Scotland Yard. When the thieves return, disguised as Spanish noblemen, Lady Hurf pretends to know them and invites them to her villa. Peterbono is forced to invent answers to Lady Hurf's questions regarding their supposed mutual acquaintances. The girls appear to recognize the young men, who cannot keep their eyes off them.

ACT TWO

In the drawing room in Lady Hurf's villa three days later, Juliette wonders why Gustave is so cold to her, although he has already professed his love; he tells her that their lives can never join. Between Hector and Eva the situation is reversed: she longs for the "real" Hector she met in the park, and he keeps changing disguises, trying to please her. Lord Edgard enters and mistakes Hector for the Scotland Yard detective.

Lady Hurf and Eva discuss love. Lady Hurf admits to a great loneliness after a full life. Eva, a recent widow, is unhappy; Lady Hurf tells her they are both alike. She hints again that she is planning an intrigue and speaks of the others as "puppets."

The thieves are left alone. Gustave wants to leave: he is ashamed of the game he has to play with the girl he loves. He is restless and despondent while Hector and Peterbono discuss plans for robbing the villa. Lord Edgard enters and faints; when revived, he tells all gathered that the Duke of Miraflores, whom Peterbono has been impersonating, died in 1904. But Lady Hurf insists he is mistaken and closes the incident by announcing that there will be a thieves' carnival that night at the casino: they are all going to go disguised as thieves.

Left alone, Juliette finds the news clipping referring to the duke's death, but refuses to have her romantic hopes shattered. Thieves won't hurt you, she tells a child who brings her flowers.

ACT THREE

A little later, examining objects in the drawing room, Gustave is startled by two dark figures who turn out to be the Dupont-Duforts dressed as apaches. He fires a revolver that they think is a toy—part of his thief's costume for the ball. Lord Edgard enters as a policeman; Lady Hurf and Eva are dressed as thieves in petticoats. Hector and Peterbono enter disguised ludicrously as comic-opera bandits. A little ballet by the characters precedes their departure for the ball.

Again examining the art objects, Gustave is confronted by Juliette, who wants to run away with him. He binds and gags her, then continues to loot the room. But her presence unnerves him; he frees her to hear that she loves him, thief or no, and she helps him to loot, unafraid of the consequences. He cannot shatter her illusions, and they go off together.

ACT FOUR

It is an hour later; the clarinetist plays the carnival theme. The characters wander in, vexed and dejected for having misread "Carnival of Leaves" as "Carnival of Thieves"; they were turned away. The thieves, however, are intent on not wasting the evening.

Left alone, the Dupont-Duforts realize that a burglary has been committed and that Gustave is the culprit, the other two acting as decoys. Since this gives them a chance to win the girls, they notify the police. Meanwhile, Hector is still trying to find the "face" that first pleased Eva. Lord Edgard again mistakes him for the detective.

Learning that the police have been called, Hector tries to warn Peterbono, who enters with Lady Hurf, but his accomplice fails to understand. Lady Hurf, far from upset, insists that she won't have the police in her house. The Dupont-Duforts are completely bewildered by her reluctance. When the thieves attempt to escape, father and son draw revolvers to hold them. The arrival of the police initiates a fanciful ballet, ending with the Dupont-Duforts mistaken for the thieves and taken away. Lord Edgard is terribly upset, but Lady Hurf is relieved to have finally gotten rid of them. Peterbono is convulsed with laughter until he learns that Lady Hurf knows they are the real thieves—for the real Duke of Miraflores died in her arms! At that moment Hector regains his original "face," but Eva claims it no longer appeals to her. Hector and Peterbono leave.

The others suddenly realize that Gustave has gone—presumably with Juliette. The clarinet strikes up a mournful tune as Gustave returns, carrying the sleeping girl. Lady Hurf is enchanted: Gustave will make a splendid fairy-tale husband for her niece; but she checks herself, remembering that he is a thief. Lord Edgard rushes out of the room and returns with mementos to prove that Gustave is his son; he collapses with sorrow when Gustave denies the possibility.

Juliette and Gustave go out to the garden. Lord Edgard confesses that he simply had a fancy to take Gustave off the hook. Lady Hurf commends him for the first time. Meanwhile Eva is sad, for she will remain the charming but unhappy widow. Lady Hurf consoles her, telling her that they are both "bobbing corks"; only those with a youthful romanticism can be truly happy, because they are serious—unconscious of the comedy of disguises and roles.

Lord Edgard's detective finally arrives, and the lord mistakes him for one of the thieves. When he realizes his mistake, he lets the man know his services are no longer needed. But the gentleman turns out to be the musician, who strikes up a quick-step on his clarinet—a signal for all the characters to return to the stage to dance a final pantomime of disguises.

JEAN ANOUILH

The Waltz of the Toreadors

[*La Valse des toréadors*, 1952]

ACT ONE

It is 1910. General St. Pé, writing his memoirs in his study, is being railed at by his invalid wife (unseen in an adjoining bedroom) for thinking about beautiful women; finally, in desperation, the general shuts the door on his wife's shrieks. The secretary, Gaston, enters, and the general begins to dictate his memoirs, but is interrupted by his immature and gawky daughters, who want new dresses for the Corpus Christi parade. The girls leave and the memoirs are resumed, interrupted again by the arrival of Dr. Bonfant, who has come to see Madame. The doctor reminds the general that his wife's paralysis is purely nervous in origin. While the doctor is with Mme. St. Pé, Mlle. Ghislaine de

Ste.-Euverte arrives; the general has been chastely in love with her since they danced the "Waltz of the Toreadors" together at a military ball seventeen years before. Ghislaine brings two love letters written by the general's wife to another man; the general believes that if he can find proof that his wife has wronged him, he will be able to divorce her and marry Ghislaine. However, when he learns that the letters are to Dr. Bonfant, the general becomes the epitome of the offended husband and insists on a duel; but the doctor persuades his friends that, though the letters may have been written to him, they were never received by him.

Calmed, the general confesses his love for Ghislaine and his inability to leave his wife, for he cannot bear to make her suffer. The doctor admonishes him for his ridiculous jealousy of his wife and for living in the past, but the general assures the doctor that his heart is still thirty years old and that he has found the woman of his dreams in Ghislaine. That being the case, the doctor persuades him to tell his wife that he is leaving her. After much hesitation and prodding, the general enters her bedroom, but there he finds that she is gone—having climbed out the window and down the wisteria. She has left a note that she has heard all and is going to kill herself.

The doctor and the general rush out. Ghislaine, convinced that the general still loves his wife, sits down to write a suicide note of her own. She pitches herself out a window and onto the head of Gaston, who is resting in a hammock below. Gaston carries her in and feels her all over for broken bones; Ghislaine, regaining consciousness, believes it is the general touching her and implores him not to stop. Thinking she is going to die, she begs him to kiss her, and Gaston, unable to refuse a dying woman, obliges. The general, carrying his wife, comes in on this scene. He exchanges burdens with Gaston, but Ghislaine, not recognizing the general, pushes him away; the act ends as the general carries Ghislaine out, and Gaston bears Madame, also imploring a kiss before she dies, to her room.

ACT TWO

The two women have been given sedatives and are resting; the general, talking with the doctor, admits his loneliness and the emptiness of his many amorous conquests. Gaston enters to take dictation on the memoirs, but is interrupted by the daughters and the dressmaker, Mme. Dupont-Fredaine. The general flirts heavily with Mme. Dupont-Fredaine and entices her out for a walk in the garden; inside, the two girls, who are both in love with Gaston, first accuse him of kissing Ghislaine and then get into a fight with one another, since each prevents the other from being alone with him. The others return and stop the battle, and Gaston confesses to the general that he has fallen in love with Ghislaine. The general refuses to take him seriously and gives him a cynical lecture on honor, idealism, and the necessity of acting at once when one has found one's love. Gaston takes the last part of his advice and, gathering up his courage, goes in to Ghislaine.

In Madame's bedroom. The general and his wife are talking things over,

Madame bewailing her state and accusing the general of every imaginable kind of philandering. The general finally brings up the subject of her letters to Dr. Bonfant, though she tries to turn his accusation by berating him for poking about her correspondence. She feigns a heart attack, recovers to attack him even more violently, and finally screeches that she has invalided herself to keep him attentive to her because he belongs to her. Horrified at this, her idea of love, the general protests that he does not belong to her, and their mutual accusations bring them to a pitch of open hatred. His wife, who believes he ruined her career as an opera singer, reminds him of the military ball seventeen years before and the "Waltz of the Toreadors": seeing how he flirted with his partner, she left the ball and was taken home by a young officer, who became her lover and who, when he was sent to another post, was succeeded by other lovers. She repeats that her reproaches and accusations and illnesses were simply a means of keeping her husband, because he is her object, her thing; she flaunts her certainty that she will always own him because he is too cowardly to hurt her by leaving her. She demands that he dance with her as she hums the "Waltz of the Toreadors"; horrified, he tries to evade her, but she pursues him into a corner. Then, suddenly, he stretches out his arms and yelling "Phantasmagoria!" grabs her by the throat.

ACT THREE

The general's study. The doctor comes in from Mme. St. Pé's bedroom and announces to the general that Madame is all right and is even rather flattered by his attack on her. Gaston and Ghislaine have disappeared for a walk, and the two plain daughters have left a note saying they are going to kill themselves because of their thwarted love for Gaston. Ghislaine and Gaston return, and Ghislaine confesses that they are in love and that he, at least, has not made her wait seventeen years, but has seized the moment and possessed her at once. The general, ranting and rattled, tries to get his swords in order to duel with Gaston for stealing the woman he loved, but he is sidetracked by the doctor on the matter of Gaston's youth: being only twenty, Gaston cannot marry without his guardian's consent. The general, triumphant, sends for Father Ambrose to have him tell Gaston's guardian to forbid his marriage to Ghislaine; but Father Ambrose reveals that he has just received the most remarkable news: Gaston is really the general's son. In exasperation the general finally surrenders and gives his consent to the marriage; the muddy daughters return, having swum out into the middle of the lake to commit suicide and then swum back. Amidst the rejoicing all but the general and the doctor go off to the nearby chapel to offer a prayer of thanksgiving. The doctor, having given his final words of wisdom ("You should have sown fewer wild oats and had the courage to hurt while there was still time"), departs. The general is left alone. His wife, about to take a nap, calls from the adjoining room, forbidding him to do anything while she is asleep. The new maid appears, a plump, pretty girl, and the general, putting his arm around her, persuades her to take a tour of the rose garden.

W . H . A U D E N A N D

C H R I S T O P H E R   I S H E R W O O D

The Ascent of F6 [1936]

Michael Ransom sits on a hilltop rock in England, reading Dante. He meditates about the poet's, and his own, disappointment and disgust with life.

In the box to the right of the stage Mr. and Mrs. A., speaking in verse, describe their meager lives as office clerk and housewife. They ask to be given something to be thankful for, something to live for.

On the wall at the Colonial office, where Michael's twin brother, Sir James Ransom, works, there is a large map showing British Sudoland and Ostnian Sudoland. The two Sudolands are separated by a chain of mountains, the highest of them marked F6. James is discussing the situation in Sudoland with Lord Stagmantle, a newspaper publisher; General Dellaby-Couch; and Lady Isabel Welwyn, daughter of a former governor of British Sudoland. Parts of the colony are in revolt against the British. General Dellaby-Couch urges that military force he used to quell the revolts. James describes the background of the situation and reveals the government's plan. The Sudoese believe that F6 is a haunted mountain, the home of a powerful demon. A legend has been fostered by the Ostnians that the first white man to reach the summit of F6 will rule over all of Sudoland. The Ostnians intend to send climbers up the mountain and, with the natives' help, oust the British from Sudoland. To forestall these plans, the British are sending climbers of their own to beat the Ostnians to the summit of F6. Michael Ransom, one of the country's best climbers, has been chosen to lead the expedition. General Dellaby-Couch disapproves of the scheme and withdraws. James, Lord Stagmantle, and Lady Isabel set off to ask Michael to lead the climbers.

In their home, Mr. and Mrs. A. are listening to a radiocast about the F6 venture that is to take place in faraway Sudoland. Mrs. A. complains that Mr. A. has never taken her on a trip abroad. She berates him for being only a dreary little clerk who does not make enough money. Mr. A. says that someday their luck will change and they will travel. Mrs. A. bitterly prophesies that they will always have only a two-week seaside vacation each year.

In a country inn, Michael and his fellow climbers are preparing for a climb the next day. The party consists of David Gunn, a carefree playboy; Ian Shawcross, a serious climber who idolizes Michael; Edward Lamp, a botanist passionately interested in his science; and Dr. Thomas Williams. James, Stagmantle, and Lady Isabel arrive. James asks Michael to lead the F6 climb. Michael, who clearly dislikes his brother, refuses. He wants to climb F6 but will do

37

nothing that might help James's career. James brings in their mother to persuade Michael. She says she knows that Michael is bitter because she always seemed to love James more. She hid her love for Michael, she says, because she knew he was stronger and had to develop on his own. She finally persuades Michael to lead the expedition. The scene changes to Mr. and Mrs. A.'s home where the radio and newsboys outside tell of the F6 climb by the British. Excited by the news, Mr. and Mrs. A. impulsively decide to go on a spree for the weekend. On the darkened stage, Michael's mother sits in a chair facing the audience. She talks to Michael, promising him that he will succeed in the climb because she will help him.

In a monastery on a glacier on F6, Michael and his party are preparing for the ascent. A monk appears in the room carrying a crystal that emits a bluish light. The men peer into it and see scenes of special interest to each of them. Dr. Williams sees himself, fatter and balder, sitting in a London Club. Gunn sees his married girl friend Toni, dressed in black, seated in his Alfa Romeo sports car. Lamp sees a rare five-leaved plant called *Polus Naufrangia*. Shawcross nervously refuses to look into the crystal. Ransom looks but does not reveal to the others what he sees: masses of people calling on him as their savior who can take away their own fears of life by his example of courage. The abbot of the monastery warns Michael against yielding to this temptation. To rule men in this way, he says, is wrong, because it leads to pride. Michael is convinced, but when word comes that the Ostnian climbers are already going up the mountain, Michael yields and prepares to lead the climb.

At home, Mr. and Mrs. A. are at breakfast. Their spree has left them with little money. Unhappy again, they seek vicarious satisfaction in the F6 contest. Ransom's team must win so that their England will again be a supreme power.

On F6, Ransom and his climbers proceed up the mountain. During a rest stop, Lamp crawls onto a ledge after the rare plant he saw in the monk's crystal. An avalanche sweeps him away. Michael says that his pride has claimed its first victim—Lamp.

At home, the A.'s listen to news of Lamp's death. Mrs. A. thinks it was a heroic one. Mr. A. disagrees, saying Lamp died only to satisfy their smug suburban pride.

Back on F6, the final climb to the summit is near. Michael decides to take Gunn with him, leaving Williams and Shawcross behind. Shawcross, crushed by disappointment, leaps over the precipice.

In the living room of Mr. and Mrs. A., the radio reports no news from F6. Bored, they claim to be tired of heroics anyway, and turn on dance music.

On F6, Gunn dies in a blizzard near the summit, thinking of his girl Toni and his sports-car racing. Ransom goes on alone and collapses at the summit. A chorus, dressed like the monks, appears and recites a verse chant about a dragon who wreaks havoc on the people and the land. When, the chorus asks, will the savior come to destroy the dragon? James enters in the guise of the dragon and, speaking in the glib half-truths of politicians, justifies himself to a figure seated on the summit of F6. Michael enters as the deliverer. The two men begin a chess game with life-size pieces. James's pieces are Stagmantle, Lady Isabel, and the general; Michael's are Shawcross, Gunn, and Lamp. Before the game begins, Mr. and Mrs. A. ask questions about their lives—why their work is dull, why their love life is not satisfying, why they have so little money. They are answered with platitudes by Stagmantle, Lady Isabel, and the general. Then they ask why they were born, and James answers them by quoting Michael— that the individual is born to serve a larger purpose than his own small existence. At the end of the chess game, James collapses, saying what Michael had said about Dante at the play's beginning—it was not virtue or knowledge, but power that was the motivating force. The victims of Michael's pride—Gunn, Shawcross, Lamp, and Williams—are called on-stage by the abbot. None say anything in his behalf. The chorus judges Michael guilty. Stagmantle, Lady Isabel, and the general shout the words "Honor," "Service," "Duty," and "Die for England," and Mr. and Mrs. A. shout "Die for us!" Thunder and an avalanche are heard as the lights go down on-stage, leaving only Michael and the draped figure on the summit illuminated. The draperies fall away, revealing Michael's mother. He falls at her feet with his head in her lap.

The lights fade, then brighten again as the sun rises on Michael, lying dead on the summit. A chorus chants about his weakness in yielding to the temptation of making the climb. The curtain slowly descends, and the box at stage left is lighted. James Ransom, Stagmantle, Isabel, the general, and the Ostnian climber Blavek take turns reciting clichés about Michael's great sacrifice, his strong character, and heroic qualities. The curtain rises, revealing Mr. and Mrs. A. looking at a monument to Michael. James, Stagmantle, Isabel, the general, and Blavek shout "Duty," "Service," "Sacrifice," and "England." Blavek shouts "Ostnia," but is drowned out by the others. Mr. and Mrs. A., looking at the monument, say, "He belongs to *us*, now!"

JACQUES AUDIBERTI

Quoat-Quoat [1946]

ACT ONE

Amédée, a young man, is unpacking his baggage in his cabin aboard the freighter *Mirmidon*, when the ship's Captain knocks at the door and enters to present his compliments. Amédée tells the Captain that he is an archeologist on his way to begin diggings at a site in Mexico. The Captain replies that he knows that Amédée is a secret agent for the French government and that he is being sent to recover the treasure hidden by Maximilian of Mexico before he died; the treasure consists mainly of loans made by France. Amédée admits that he is an agent but says that he is in fact an archeologist and a member of the Geographic Society; he has even written works on the Mexican god Quoat-Quoat, he says.

The Captain tells Amédée that they will arrive in Vera Cruz in five weeks, then reads a ship's order stating that if a secret agent of the French government clandestinely brings a woman aboard or if he imperils his mission through his relations with any female passenger, he is liable to be shot. The Captain also says that there are several beautiful women aboard, including his own daughter. Amédée replies that the order is incredible, and anyway he hasn't brought any woman aboard. The Captain warns him to be careful and says he has twelve policemen on the ship who will form a firing squad if necessary.

Clarisse, the Captain's lovely young daughter, appears, chasing her cat, and the Captain goes out. Amédée is astonished to see Clarisse, who is an old friend; not having seen each other for two years, they talk over their gay times with Amédée's sister. Clarisse tells Amédée that she is going to Martinique to stay with friends; Amédée talks of Quoat-Quoat and archeology and says Clarisse should go with him, for they will have wonderful adventures together; they embrace. Carried away, Amédée speaks of the fabulous trove of Maximilian and describes the contents; the Captain enters, stating that Amédée has revealed his mission. Amédée says that he loves Clarisse and that they want to get married; the Captain is unmoved and says that Amédée shall be shot at four o'clock the next day. Clarisse pleads for his life, but the Captain is adamant; Clarisse threatens to kill herself if Amédée is shot.

ACT TWO

Amédée is playing cards with the policeman sent to guard him; the young man persuades the policeman to go and find the Captain. There is a knock at the door; an exotic Mexican woman enters armed with a pistol and orders

40

Amédée to reveal where Maximilian's treasure is hidden. Amédée explains that he is sentenced to death and that he merely talked about the treasure to Clarisse and was overheard by the Captain. The woman says she needs the treasure to aid Mexican revolutionaries; the ship must not be allowed to reach Mexico, she says, fearing that the Captain will get the treasure. She shows Amédée a small piece of obsidian, which she says belonged to Quoat-Quoat and has magic powers: with the stone she can sink the ship, and she and Amédée can escape in a lifeboat; Amédée refuses to be a party to the plan. The Captain arrives, and the woman tries to seduce him. Amédée, who has been examining the obsidian, hands it to the Captain, who orders that the woman be taken to her cabin and locked in. Amédée tries to persuade the Captain to forget the comedy about having him shot, but the Captain says he is quite serious: Amédée shall be shot in a few minutes. Amédée seizes the pistol left by the Mexican woman and starts to leave the cabin, but the policeman, who has returned unseen, wrests the pistol from him.

All three head for the door to go on deck where the firing squad is waiting, but before they can leave, one of the passengers, Mme. Batrilant, a middle-aged wine merchant from Bordeaux, enters and declares that Amédée should not be shot, because he is innocent. She shows the Captain official papers and declares that *she* is the real French secret agent; Amédée is only a "front" to mislead any crooks or Mexican revolutionaries who might also be after the treasure.

Amédée, however, insists that he is the real agent and demands to be taken before the firing squad; everything has been arranged, he says, and his death is expected; there would be imbalance if he were not shot. The Captain calls him mad, but Amédée grabs the pistol and escapes from the cabin, locking the others in. As the Captain tries to break down the door, the firing squad on deck fires a salvo; the others realize that Amédée has been shot. The Captain says that he has had enough: he has been a captain a long time and always has the same trouble, the battle between his regulations and the passengers. He takes the obsidian from his pocket and says that the magic stone will blow up the ship when he throws it to the floor.

The Captain raises his arm, calling: "Hold tight!"

J . M . B A R R I E

The Admirable Crichton [1902]

ACT ONE

The family are gradually gathering for tea in the drawing room of the Earl of Loam. Lord Loam's nephew, the Honorable Ernest Woolley, a charmingly self-centered young man-about-town who fancies himself an epigrammatist, is soon joined by the three daughters of the house: Lady Agatha and Lady Catherine, exhausted by the mental strain of having had to select frocks for their impending yachting cruise, and Lady Mary, who has had a dreadfully tiring day trying on engagement rings. With the entrance of Mr. Treherne, a young clergyman, Lord Brocklehurst, Mary's mother-dominated fiancé, and the old earl, the monthly ritual of the servants' tea can begin.

During the course of the tea it becomes clear that the Earl of Loam has radical views about the equality of man, views shared neither by his family nor by his perfect butler Crichton, who feels that class distinctions are intended by Nature. Only the earl fails to share in the general discomfort as Crichton formally announces each of the servants; and everyone is determinedly equal among the teacups, the stilted conversation, and the earl's imperfectly memorized speech.

That ordeal over, another arises as the three ladies' maids, incensed that only one is to wait upon all three ladies on the yacht, give notice. Crichton solves the dilemma by presenting the between maid, Tweeny, who has found some favor in his eyes; he then solves another by reluctantly condescending to replace Lord Loam's resigning valet for the voyage.

ACT TWO

Two months and many miles later, the Ladies Mary, Catherine, and Agatha sit in shipwrecked dishevelment on a Pacific island, listening to Ernest's rousing, if somewhat inaccurate, account of yesterday's loss of yacht, crew, and Lord Loam, while Tweeny and Reverend Treherne help Crichton to hack out a home in the wilderness. Lady Mary admires Crichton's courage and willingness to adapt, but she is disturbed by his new qualities of leadership and manliness and asks whether he thinks that everyone will now be equal. Crichton assures her that he disbelieved in equality at home because it was against Nature, and for the same reason as utterly disbelieves in it here. "There must always, my lady, be one to command and others to obey." At first reassured, Lady Mary suddenly realizes the import of his words and hurries away.

Crichton and Tweeny are starting a cooking fire with his homemade lens when Ernest and the ladies rush to the hut with cries of alarm, evidently pursued by a tiger. The tiger turns out to be Lord Loam, washed up elsewhere on the island and delighted now to find not only his loved ones but an onion-scented pot over a fire. Lady Mary urges Lord Loam to assert himself as leader of the party; he does assert his ascendancy over the selfish Ernest, but only, to Mary's dismay, by appealing to Crichton for help. When Crichton immerses Ernest's head in a bucket as punishment for an inappropriate epigram, it is impressed upon the earl that it is Crichton's budding leadership he must abort, and he haughtily gives his butler a month's notice. Ernest points out that this tactic is ineffective on an island, and the family leaves instead. Crichton indicates to the apologetic Reverend Treherne that the wind is blowing across the cooking pot in the family's direction. "That pot is full of Nature," he says; and as night falls, all save Lady Mary return to fire and food and Crichton.

ACT THREE

In the two years since the shipwreck, Lord Loam has metamorphosed into a jolly, concertina-playing handyman called Daddy, who flirts with Tweeny as she prepares "the Gov's" dinner in the main hall of the yachting party's island home, fitted out by the ingenious Crichton with all modern comforts. A tanned, energetic Ernest displaces Daddy at Tweeny's side and soon confides to her his love. Treherne has told him that the Gov (who can be none other than Crichton) has expressed interest in Treherne's performing a marriage ceremony, and Ernest interprets this to Tweeny as the master's approval of their marriage. Tweeny heartbrokenly acknowledges that Crichton's heart has been stolen from her by Lady Mary and tries to pick a fight with her when she enters. But Polly (as Mary now is) is too happy to argue, elated that the Gov has asked for her to serve him.

Crichton enjoys a lordly dinner, waited on at table by Polly and in the kitchen by Kitty, Aggy (*nées* Ladies Catherine and Agatha), and Tweeny. Finishing his meal, Crichton urges the diffident Polly into conversation, and the two recall the unhappy days in England of Lady Mary Lasenby and her butler. The regal Crichton confesses that he has begun to believe that, in a previous incarnation, he was a king. Lordly but loving, he asks Polly to marry him and summons the rest of the "servants" to announce the news. After a quickly suppressed outbreak of feminine jealousy, all are celebrating the occasion with wine and dancing, when the gaiety is interrupted by the boom of a ship's gun.

As everyone rushes out, Polly and Crichton are left alone. He can insure their rescue by triggering his system of electric beacons; she implores him not to, but "Bill Crichton has got to play the game," he says. When Polly tells him she will never give him up, Crichton pulls away. His erect bearing becomes subservient as he says, "My lady."

ACT FOUR

In Lord Loam's London drawing room several months later, the family is happily reading the reviews of Ernest's just-published book recounting their island adventures. Ernest appears to have been the true hero, and one of the reviews mentions that "Mr. Woolley pays the butler a glowing tribute in a footnote." Only Crichton's occasional domestic intrusions somewhat mar their guilty pleasure.

Lady Mary enters (trying hard to remember to move and speak in ladylike fashion) and reminisces with her father about the insidious glamour of the island life. She believes that, at her insistence, the earl has told her fiancé about her romance with Crichton. She wants to "play the game" honorably—though she wishes Lord Brocklehurst had been less loyal during her absence so that she might not have to. When Brocklehurst is announced, Lord Loam leaves without having told Lady Mary that her fiancé is unaware of her indiscretion. Mary discovers his ignorance before she gives herself away, realizing at last that the flirtation he is speaking of is one of his own. She is relieved, she tells him, to find he is not quite perfect.

As Mary retires, her fiancé's formidable mother, Lady Brocklehurst, comes in and announces to her son that she suspects all was not proper on that island. As custodian of her son's future, she wants to know that Lady Mary is beyond reproach. To everyone's horror, she summons Crichton and Tweeny from belowstairs and, in front of the family, quizzes them about the intervening years. Always telling the exact truth, Crichton assures her that all social distinctions were preserved and that the servants had to keep in their place. There was nothing, Tweeny admits, between Lady Mary and Ernest, and the old lady is mollified.

Crichton announces his intention of leaving service. As everyone goes in to dinner, Mary lingers to tell Crichton he is the best man among them. On an island, perhaps, but not in England, he says. "Then there's something wrong with England," says Lady Mary.

J . M . B A R R I E

Dear Brutus [1917]

ACT ONE

Dinner over, five ladies, headed by sweet old Mrs. Coade, grope their way into the drawing room and switch on the light. Joanna Trout, a svelte young miss, rings for Matey, the butler, who soon appears. Immediately Alice Dearth, a sultry beauty, hands him a telegram that she has written and asks him to read it aloud. Obeying, Matey is dismayed to find that Mrs. Dearth is asking the police to arrest him for theft of rings. He produces the rings, returns them to their owners, and asks to tear up the telegram. The ladies, however, have another use for it. They warn Matey that it will be sent unless he tells them why they have been invited together to this country house by Lob, who scarcely knows them.

Matey protests that he doesn't know. The ladies discuss their host's strangeness, and the haughty Lady Caroline inquires of the butler how old Lob is. Matey replies that Lob considers himself all that is left of Merry England. That was in Queen Elizabeth's time, supplies Mabel Purdie, a soft little woman. The guests learn from each other that they were invited specifically for Midsummer week, and they realize that tonight is Midsummer Eve.

Alice Dearth waves the telegram warningly. Matey appeals to her mercy, declaring that when he went into domestic service he took the wrong turning, for if he had taken the clerkship offered him when young, he would be an honest man today. He vows that he would give anything to start over again. Lady Caroline coldly recommends that he be jailed. At last Matey cryptically warns his persecutors not to go into the wood that night—although, as Mabel Purdie observes, there isn't a wood within miles. Alice having torn up the telegram, Matey is permitted to leave.

The gnomelike Lob escorts his male guests into the drawing room, and Mr. Purdie suggests an outing to find a mysterious wood that is said to appear on Midsummer Eve. Lob declares that the wood is superstitious nonsense and suggests a round of cards, but when his guests drop the idea of a walk, he bursts into tears. To console him, they go to get their wraps, and Lob, left alone, chuckles.

Presently Mr. Purdie and Joanna Trout stroll in from the garden, and Lob departs. Joanna worries sweetly that she is being disloyal to her friend Mabel, but Purdie assures her that she is not. Taking her in his arms, he confesses that Mabel doesn't understand him, but that, through Joanna's elevating love, he is enabled to be kind to his wife. They are interrupted by the entrance of Mrs. Purdie, who asks Joanna to give back her husband. The lovers are shocked by Mabel's attitude, which they assert is ignoble, and she soon leaves them.

Now Alice Dearth enters, in search of her husband, and Purdie, offering to find him, goes out. Joanna drifts out too. On her husband's arrival, Alice asks him to keep an eye on their curious host during the outing, but Dearth plans to smoke in the garden. Alice reproaches him for being an alcoholic waster instead of the successful artist he once dreamed of becoming. Dearth suggests that it is a pity they didn't have children, but his wife replies that he would have been a poor father. She wishes she had married her former suitor Freddy Finch-Fallowe.

The other guests enter wearing wraps over their evening clothes. Pressed by Alice to tell what is in the wood, Lob discloses that in it they will get what nearly all of them are longing for—a second chance. Mr. Coade, an amiable old gentleman, remarks wistfully that if he had a second chance, he would be useful. Dearth draws back the window curtains, and in place of the garden a wood now stands. After a moment, Dearth passes into it. Mrs. Coade steals off to her room, calling her husband to follow. Mabel Purdie then steps through the window, and after her, Mr. Purdie and Joanna together. Lob warns Alice Dearth not to go, but, undaunted, she walks outside, followed by Lady Caroline and, finally, Coade. Matey, entering, peers out the window, and Lob pushes him into the wood.

ACT TWO

In a moonlit glade, two people recline in motoring attire. Lady Caroline, ecstatically happy to be married to Matey, carols that all she needed was a master. Touching his pocket, Matey replies that its contents is what fetches the ladies. Caroline says that she wishes she had known him when he was a poor clerk, but Matey answers that it doesn't matter how he began, for he would still have climbed to the top. He adds that there were nails in his boots for the people on the ladder below him.

Entering the glade, Joanna asks Matey whether he has seen her husband, Mr. Purdie. He answers no, and inquires of an old gentleman nearby, Mr. Coade, who is playing a whistle and capering. Coade has not seen Joanna's husband either. He dances off, and Matey and Caroline follow him gaily.

As Purdie and Mabel frolic into the glade, Joanna steps behind a tree. Purdie explains to Mabel that he was always different from other men and, not expecting any woman to plumb his depths, he married Joanna. It is his tragedy that he met Mabel too late. They wander off in the wood, pursued by Joanna.

A half-grown girl runs into the glade ahead of her father, Mr. Dearth. A successful artist now, he sets up his easel and paints the moon, while his fond daughter Margaret flirts outrageously with him. A vagrant woman wanders by, looking for scraps of food left by picnickers. Her name, she announces grandly, is The Honorable Mrs. Finch-Fallowe. Not having any food, Dearth gives her money, and she shuffles off. Dearth is unable to forget her and, seeing a lighted house in the distance, instructs Margaret to wait while he finds food for the poor woman. Although terrified to be left alone, Margaret waits dutifully for a short time and then, running after him, is lost among the trees.

ACT THREE

Feeling themselves trespassers, Purdie and Mabel steal into the drawing room, where a queer little man, a leer on his face, is sleeping curled up on a chair. Relieved to have escaped Joanna, the eloping couple are annoyed to see her step through the window. Presently the three intruders feel very strange, and as awareness dawns, they recognize the room and their host, Lob. Purdie is humiliated to perceive that he is nothing but a philanderer, and Joanna proclaims her joy at not being married to him; Mabel is not sure that she loves him any more. Ruminating that it is not Fate that shapes people's lives, but something inside them, Purdie quotes Shakespeare:

> The fault, dear Brutus, is not in our stars,
> But in ourselves, that we are underlings.

He is depressed to think that he hasn't the courage to change; but Joanna feels a challenge.

Ignorant of the wood's effect on the other guests, Mrs. Coade descends from her room, and is astonished when Matey and Lady Caroline arrive thinking themselves husband and wife. Joanna boldly asks Matey whether he is still a pilferer, and he, thinking of certain embezzlement scandals, replies stoutly that nothing was proved. Joanna observes that Matey would always take the wrong turning. His hands encountering a familiar-feeling tray with coffee cups and a cake, Matey comes to his senses and, after him, Lady Caroline. She is horrified and embarrassed, and Matey discreetly retires belowstairs.

When gay piping is heard, Joanna takes Mrs. Coade's hand comfortingly. Mr. Coade prances in. Having by this time caught on to the situation, his wife asks who was with him in the wood. Coade replies that he was a solitary bachelor. Very much taken with Mrs. Coade, however, he proposes marriage. After recovering, he is ashamed to discover that, given a second chance, he was just as lazy as before. Mrs. Coade is saddened to realize that her devoted husband would have been quite happy without her.

After a knock on the window, Alice Dearth enters defiantly. She gives her name and, asked where Mr. Finch-Fallowe is, says she isn't sure. She falls fiercely on the cake. Looking clear-eyed and hale, Dearth comes in, explaining that he and his daughter were distressed to meet a starving woman in the wood. He asks for the cake remains, then sees the beggar woman, now in evening dress. When the astonished pair recognize each other, Dearth is anguished to find that Margaret doesn't exist. Alice, knowing now that she is fortunate to be his wife, presses his shoulder convulsively and walks from the room. Dearth thanks the still-unconscious Lob for his hour in the wood.

The rather gloomy guests brighten when Matey announces breakfast, and all except Joanna go out. She asks Matey whether the Midsummer Eve experiment ever has a permanent effect. Once in a while, he believes, Matey answers. He adds that Lob could tell her.

When Matey goes to rouse Lob, the chair is empty. The butler opens the windows on the garden, and the little man is seen busily tending his flowers.

J . M . B A R R I E

Peter Pan [1904]

ACT ONE

As the cuckoo clock strikes six in the Darling nursery, Nana the dog springs into action, turning down bedcovers and running bath water. Disappearing into the next room, she returns with Michael, the youngest Darling, and carries him, protesting, to his bath. Mrs. Darling enters in her party dress and, glimpsing a face in the window, calls anxiously to her children. Wendy comes in with her younger brother John, and they play "Father and Mother," until Mr. Darling rushes in brandishing a recalcitrant tie, which his wife knots.

Emerging from the bathroom, Nana bumps into Mr. Darling, leaving hairs on his best trousers. He suggests crossly that it is a mistake to have a dog for a nurse, but is impressed when his wife tells of how she recently found a strange boy in the nursery. Nana sprang at him, and although he escaped, Nana closed the window on his shadow, which Mrs. Darling has kept.

Baths over, the dog approaches with Michael's medicine, and to persuade him to take it, Mr. Darling offers to drink his own medicine at the same time. As Michael gulps his spoonful, his father, to everyone's disapproval, hides his glass behind his back, then pours its contents into Nana's bowl. The unsuspecting dog laps, then retreats with hurt feelings into her kennel at one side of the room. Annoyed because of the poor figure he is cutting, Mr. Darling drags Nana out to chain her in the yard. Apprehensively, Mrs. Darling turns out the light and leaves.

Presently the nursery window is blown open, and a ball of light darts in, followed by Peter Pan, who calls, "Tinker Bell!" The fairy answers from the depths of a drawer, and, reaching into it, Peter pulls out his shadow. In his excitement he closes the drawer with Tinker Bell inside.

Peter tries to glue on his shadow with soap. Wendy awakens and, pleased to see an interesting stranger, sews it on for him. When he says that one girl is worth more than twenty boys, Wendy offers him a kiss. Peter holds out his hand and, realizing that he doesn't know what a kiss is, Wendy gives him her thimble. Peter gives her one of his acorn buttons, which she puts on a chain around her neck.

Plying the boy with questions, Wendy learns that he ran away from home the day he was born, because he didn't want to grow up. At first he lived with the fairies in Kensington Gardens, Peter says. This reminds him of Tinker Bell, whom he releases. She darts about in fury, tinkling insults, but Wendy is enchanted with her. Asked where he lives now, Peter tells Wendy that he stays in the Never Land with the lost boys, who fell out of their prams when their nurses weren't looking. He explains that he came to the Darling nursery to hear bedtime stories.

Wendy says that she knows lots of stories, and Peter begs her to come home with him. She awakens John and Michael, and Peter rubs the three children with fairy dust. They fly out of the window just as Mr. and Mrs. Darling return from their party.

ACT TWO

Waiting for Peter to come home, the six lost boys talk of "Cinderella" and of their mothers. At the sound of a pirate song they vanish down six hollow trees, which lead to their underground home in the Never Land forest.

Pirates appear, dragging a raft up the river. On it reclines Captain Hook, whose right arm ends in an iron claw. He orders his men to look for the boys, confiding to his boatswain Smee that he is particularly anxious to find their captain Peter Pan, who cut off his arm and flung it to a crocodile, which has followed him ever since, licking its lips. Luckily, Hook says, the beast once swallowed a clock. Suddenly a ticking sound is heard, the pirates flee, and the crocodile slides after them. Then Tiger Lily, the leader of the Indians, creeps from the silent forest with her Indian braves. They light a ceremonial fire, dance around it, and steal off after pirate scalps.

Emerging from their trees, the boys spy a great white bird flying toward them. It is pursued by Tinker Bell, who tinkles a message that Peter wants the boys to shoot it. One of them releases an arrow and brings the bird fluttering to earth; but, looking at it more closely, the boys realize their mistake. When Peter alights with the news that he has brought them a mother, they penitently show him Wendy. Pulling out the arrow, Peter finds that she is alive, having been saved by his button.

He commands the boys to build a house around the prostrate Wendy; John and Michael are made to help. The little house soon finished, Peter knocks politely on the door, and Wendy comes out to discover that she is the mother of nine children. They flock inside to hear the rest of "Cinderella."

ACT THREE

As mermaids splash in the lagoon, Peter and his band creep up to catch an especially beautiful one lying on Marooners' Rock. To Wendy's keen disappointment, the mermaid slips through their hands. Climbing on the rock, Peter tells Wendy how sailors, bound and left there by their captains, drown when the tide rises.

When the pirates' song is heard, the boys dive into the water, and Peter and Wendy hide behind a rock. Smee and his mate Starkey row up with Tiger Lily, tied hand and foot. Peter, imitating Hook's voice, tells the pirates to free her, and, puzzled, they obey. Tiger Lily swims away.

Hook swims to the rock. Sighing gloomily, he explains to the pirates that the boys have found a mother to protect them. Smee suggests that they capture her. Suddenly remembering Tiger Lily, Hook is bewildered to learn that he himself ordered her release. Peter than makes his presence known and orders his boys to attack the pirates. They struggle together in the lagoon until Hook is chased to land by the ticking crocodile.

Two boys appear with a dinghy, and the others climb in wearily. They call Peter and Wendy, but when there is no answer, they conclude that the two are swimming or flying home, and row off. Having fainted on the rock, Peter and Wendy rouse as the tide begins to rise. Because Peter is wounded, he can neither swim nor fly; Wendy refuses to try to do either alone. Fortunately a kite floats overhead, and Wendy, hanging to its tail, is carried shoreward. Just as Peter gives himself up for lost, a bird drops her nest on the rock. He climbs in and sails for land.

ACT FOUR

As the boys gobble a make-believe supper in their underground home, Wendy corrects their manners, and the Indians, grateful for Tiger Lily's rescue, keep watch above. Peter approaches from the forest with gun and game bag, descends a tree, and distributes imaginary nuts to the boys.

Soon in their nighties, the boys scramble into one large bed. Tonight Wendy tells them a story about Mr. and Mrs. Darling, whose three children flew away to the Never Land. She says that she, John, and Michael must go home, and invites the lost boys to come and be adopted. Refusing to go himself, Peter directs Tinker Bell to guide the party.

Shrieks are heard from above, and the boys realize that the pirates have attacked the Indians, who are soon routed. Hook beats the tom-tom and, hearing it, the boys think that the Indians have won. Bidding Peter goodby, they squeeze up the trees. The pirates seize and bind them and pile them into Wendy's house, which they carry off.

Peter has fallen asleep below, and Hook, struggling down a tree, poisons his medicine. As Hook walks away, Tinker Bell flashes past, darts down a hole, and tells Peter what has happened. He reaches for his medicine, but Tinker Bell snatches and drinks it. As her light grows faint, she murmurs that she could get well again if children believed in fairies. Concerned, Peter asks the children in the audience to clap their hands if they believe in fairies. They are counted on to do so, and Tinker Bell revives.

ACT FIVE

Captain Hook, on the deck of the *Jolly Roger*, orders his prisoners brought up. Wendy is tied to the mast to watch her children walk the plank, which is let over the ship's side. At the sound of ticking, Hook pauses as if under a spell, and the crew close their eyes. The ticking comes from Peter Pan, who climbs aboard, unseen by the pirates, and disappears into the darkness below.

Recovering, Hook capers and sings, and the children counter with the national anthem. Angrily Hook sends pirate Bill Jukes to get the cat-o'-nine-tails. Jukes descends to the cabin, and a screech is heard, then a crowing noise. Sent to investigate, Cecco returns with the news that Jukes has been stabbed to death. Cecco is dispatched to fetch the crowing cock, but this time his screech is heard. Hook descends with a lantern, returning to report uneasily that something blew out his light. He drives the boys down, and Peter removes their manacles; they arm themselves and creep up to the poop. Taking Wendy's place at the mast, Peter wraps himself in her cloak, and crows. The boys leap out of hiding and pursue the unnerved pirates to their doom.

Hook and Peter fence with swords, but as the pirate lashes about, the boy dances lightly around him. In desperation Hook tries to blow up the ship, but Peter tosses the bomb overboard. When Hook next sees him, the boy is sitting on a barrel playing his pipes. Hook strikes the barrel from under him, but Peter continues to play, sitting in mid-air. Broken-spirited, the captain lets himself into the water, where the crocodile lurks with open jaws.

Back at the nursery, Mrs. Darling waits by the open window for her children, while Nana stretches out on the floor. When the maid announces dinner,

Nana saunters off to the dining room. Presently the kennel is carried in, and Mr. Darling, dressed in office clothes, crawls out. Asked how his day has been, he proudly tells his wife how famous he has become since changing places with Nana. He retires into the kennel to nap, and Mrs. Darling goes to the next room to play a sad song on the piano.

Soon Peter Pan flies into the nursery and closes the window to prevent Wendy from coming home. Then, deciding that he doesn't want her as a mother after all, he opens it and flies out. The truants arrive and slip into their beds; when Mrs. Darling comes in, they jump into her arms.

A little later, Mr. Darling is seen romping outside with the lost boys, who have been adopted. Looking from the nursery window, Mrs. Darling offers to adopt Peter, but he refuses emphatically. Magnanimously she gives Wendy permission to go to the Never Land once a year to do Peter's spring cleaning. Waving a careless thanks, for he doesn't know what a spring cleaning is, Peter flies away.

In a dream a year later, Wendy stands at Peter's doorway, dressed for a journey. She is bigger and now flies so badly that she has to use a broomstick. Peter, unchanged, promises to come for her next year, so as to hear stories about himself. When Wendy has gone, he plays gaily on his pipes, and an admiring audience of Never birds and fairies gather around to listen.

J . M . B A R R I E

What Every Woman Knows [1908]

ACT ONE

The regular Saturday-night draughts game of old Alick Wylie and his son James is interrupted by James's elder brother David, who is worried about their unmarried, plain sister Maggie. The Wylies would do anything for their beloved Maggie, but they cannot buy her romance. When Maggie joins them, she soon discovers they propose to ambush a suspected burglar; for the past few nights they have heard someone prowling about the house, though nothing seems to be missing. Intrepidly she waits with them, and they catch the culprit red-handed, but discover he has come to steal only knowledge from the books in the Wylie library. He is John Shand, the young Glasgow University student who had made a fine speech at a political meeting that David had attended earlier that evening. He informs his host that he is a brilliant student with a great future but that lack of funds is keeping him from returning to the university. The Wylie men have a proposition, but they must put it to him in front of the suspicious Maggie, who refuses to be gotten rid of: they will subsidize his education on condition that in five years Maggie may claim him for her husband. The principals at first balk at this proposal—John on the ground that with three hundred pounds' worth of education he will be far above her, and Maggie because John is younger than she. Finally, however, the pact is made.

ACT TWO

Six years have passed; in the poster-filled headquarters of "Shand for Parliament" the four Wylies anxiously await election results. As Maggie rehearses her loyal consolation speech for John if the news is bad, the roar of the crowd rises outside, and there enters, weary but triumphant, John Shand, M.P. The joyful Maggie is picturing a thrilling future entertaining great lords and ladies when some real ladies arrive: the Comtesse de la Brière and her beautiful niece, Lady Sybil. Poor Maggie forgets her newly learned French and her poise, and leaves her father and brothers to entertain the ladies with proud recitals of John's climb to his exalted station.

Left alone briefly, the comtesse and Lady Sybil decide that John's boorishness could be refined by a properly elegant woman. Though Sybil professes indifference and even distaste, she is challenged by John's subsequent blunt request for her opinion of him, and invites him to call upon her in London.

Alone with John, Maggie wants to know when he will announce their marriage. Mortified by her awkwardness before the ladies, she alternately threatens to hold him to their agreement and indicates her willingness to release him from it. John is tempted by the glimpse of freedom she offers, but nobly refuses to consider it. She ends her outburst with the passionate declaration that she is essential to his career—and tears up the document that binds him to her.

A boisterous crowd of Shand supporters bursts in to cheer their hero. Not unconscious of the nobility of his behavior, he introduces to them "the future Mrs. John Shand!"

ACT THREE

Two years later, a meeting of John Shand's Ladies Committee is in progress at the Shand home as Maggie receives the comtesse in the next room. Spotting her niece among the committeewomen, the comtesse warns Maggie that John is seeing too much of Lady Sybil and wonders why Maggie doesn't take more of an interest in her husband's work. "I typewrite his speeches," says Maggie. John enters, and the comtesse twits him about his forthcoming speech on equal rights for women. He rehearses his peroration, in which he urgently calls upon the government to accept his bill but promises not to "press the matter to a division" at present. Maggie is doubtful about the hedging tone, but apparently accepts John's masterful assurance that his is the proper course.

As John goes to join his committee, the maid announces another visitor, Cabinet Minister Charles Venables. He admires John's "second thoughts" in Parliament and the characteristic touches of humor that have come to be known as "Shandisms." As John is notoriously humorless in conversation, Mr. Venables has wondered whether Mrs. Shand helps him, but his visit with the ingenuous Maggie allays his suspicions. He would like to consult John about the speech, but Maggie is loath to disturb him and offers to recite the peroration. To the delighted amazement of the comtesse, Maggie's peroration boldly promises to "press the matter now to a division." Venables is very pleased and says that if John had hedged, "We should have known that he was a pasteboard knight and have disregarded him." When John comes in, Maggie so contrives that John accepts Venables' congratulations on his forcefulness without giving away his original plan—and without either man recognizing her management.

Several days later, John and Sybil at last acknowledge their love. Maggie returns in time to overhear a bit of their impassioned dialogue, and when the visiting Wylie men present their anniversary gift to Maggie, she claims from John the ruby pendant he has just given Sybil. Angry but relieved, he now openly avows his love for Sybil. The Wylie men would deal with him and, failing that, would have Maggie come home with them, but she plans to fight.

Sitting down with John and Sybil to arrange things in a practical Scotch way, Maggie proposes that they wait till after John's big speech at Leeds and that John spend the intervening month at the cottage of the comtesse. John inquires whether she hopes to preserve their marriage by keeping him apart from Sybil. Maggie reminds him that she has promised to be different from other wives. On the telephone she asks the comtesse to invite Lady Sybil to the cottage with John and informs the lovers of the invitation without telling them it was at her suggestion. They protest, but nothing, she says, must be considered save the speech. "And with Sybil on the spot, John, *to help you and inspire you*, what a speech it will be!"

ACT FOUR

The month is almost up, and at her cottage the comtesse is suggesting to the miserable John Shand lover-like diversions for himself and Sybil. To her amusement, John dourly rejects her proposals and stumps out.

When Maggie arrives on a surprise visit, Mr. Venables readily acknowledges that he is unhappy with John's proposed Leeds speech. It seems that a minor cabinet post hangs on that speech, and though it is a powerful piece of work, it lacks the special Shand touch. Now alarmed, Maggie "remembers" that John is composing another speech. After Venables escapes from this uncomfortable situation, the comtesse forces Maggie to admit that she has brought another speech with her, but Maggie insists it is only a draft John had left at home. Alone for a moment with the speech in her possession, the comtesse dispatches it to Mr. Venables.

When Maggie sees John and Sybil together, she seems not displeased, especially when John admits that, despite Sybil's help and inspiration, his speech is a failure. Dismayed by Maggie's brisk practicality about living arrangements and such, the lovers at length confess that they are no longer in love. Maggie's scheme has worked, and John begins to recognize her canniness—perhaps without her realizing it she has somehow helped with the speeches too.

The comtesse interrupts them; Venables wants to see John about the second speech. Maggie, horrified, realizes that the comtesse has given it to him. To her furious husband she confesses she has inserted in his draft a few rough thoughts for him to polish, but she had never intended the copy to be ready. Venables' delighted appreciation and congratulations are like blows to John. Maggie has saved his career but destroyed his illusions.

Fighting to rebuild his shattered ego, she tells him there was nothing unusual about her help: "Every man who is high up loves to think that he has done it all himself, and the wife smiles, and lets it go at that. It's our only joke. Every woman knows that." Maggie knows too that only someone who can laugh at himself is completely human, and capable of love. She coaxes John to laugh. And at last, somewhere deep within him, the saving grace of humor is born.

PHILIP BARRY

Hotel Universe [1930]

NOTE: The action of the play, which is continuous, takes place in the course of about two hours.

Tom and Hope Ames, Lily Malone, Norman Rose, Alice Kendall, and Pat Farley are ending a three-day visit with Ann Field at her villa in the south of France. Pat, playing the piano on the terrace, mocks Ann's request for something gay and provokes her until she goes inside the house. Hope accuses everyone of taking their nerves out on Ann. Lily reminds Hope of the reason for their "nerves," though the others try to keep her from talking about it. Ignoring them, Lily goes on to describe the twenty-six-year-old acquaintance of theirs who, with the words, "Look, Farley, I'm off for Africa!" dived off a high rock to certain death. Hope again appeals to them not to dwell on such morbid subjects, and finally Tom reminds the others that they are here supposedly to dispense cheer to Ann, who for three years has been isolated in a strange country with a half-mad father.

Alice interrupts, saying that she saw Ann's father walking on the terrace late the previous night with a white rooster. Pat comments that Stephen Field is reputed to have some strange power over people, supposedly because he seems close to death. Tom remarks that Ann's house used to be a small hotel, called Hotel de l'Univers. Strange things supposedly happened in it: people came to resemble other people, and the pasts of the guests kept cropping up. Norman comments that there may be some truth in the story, for the terrace reminds him of something; Lily adds that it reminds her of a place she knew in childhood and begins to reminisce about her father.

Ann returns and begs them to stay on; she particularly addresses Pat, who refuses, saying he has a date with mountains. He then asks Tom to mail some letters for him in New York. Ann, talking about the accuracy of her hunches, reminds Pat that once she cabled him in London, having had the feeling that he was in some kind of trouble; exactly what the trouble was, however, he refused to tell her until the day before he was to die. Tom, meanwhile, has noticed the address on one of the letters, and asks Pat about it. Pat takes it back quickly and says he will explain it later. Lily announces that she wants to play Cordelia in *King Lear* and then, when Pat says he'll back her, hastily adds that she wouldn't dare. Norman makes a sarcastic remark, and Lily attacks him for his "damned Jewish superiority"; then Tom and Pat embark on a spontaneous parody of a day in the life of Norman Rose, the great financier.

Norman remarks that people expect too much from life, but Ann quickly

55

responds that life is infinitely rich in its possibilities. Tom wonders how anyone can believe himself important, knowing that in a few years he'll be dead and forgotten. Lily displays a scar on her wrist and in the repartee about suicide that follows makes a remark that Tom, raised a Catholic, objects to as blasphemous. Tom admits that he has abandoned his religion but protests that the only "real dope" on life he ever got came from an old priest named Father Francis. Ann compassionately says that a great emptiness has been left in Tom. When he asks what it could be filled with, Lily acidly remarks that cyanide would be quite satisfactory. Lily catechizes the others about their thoughts of suicide, and concludes that all of them but Ann and Alice have entertained the idea. Tom asks Pat why one of the letters was addressed to him. Pat replies that, since his foot might slip on an Alp, he was merely being foresightful. Tom begins to talk of his lost youth and the knowledge that all the brave things one dreamed of will never get done.

Pat, responding, imitates a small boy and cries that he wants to go to the South Seas like Father Damien. Tom takes the part of a boy who has been reading about Father Damien and who believes that a spot on his own wrist is the beginning of leprosy. Norman enters the game just as Pat calls Father Damien a "crazy old priest." When Tom objects that God wouldn't let a crazy priest exist, Norman recalls the monk Theophilus, who burnt the library at Alexandria. Norman insists that Theophilus was crazy, and Pat implies that Norman, as a Jew, would think any Christian holy man crazy. Tom peers at his wrist again and asks Pat what he would do if he had the "you-know." Pat decides that he would kill himself. Tom counters that Pat couldn't, since he would go to hell; and when Pat replies that he certainly wouldn't go around with leprosy, Tom claps his hand over Pat's mouth to keep him from saying the dreaded word with Norman there to overhear. Their struggles turn into a fight in dead earnest, and Hope, realizing that they are no longer playing, cries out for them to stop. Norman separates them. The butler comes in with a message for Ann, who goes off to see her father.

Norman reflects that he'd like to go all alone to Andorra and have time to think. He goes in to pack, followed shortly by Alice. Pat remarks that all of them are looking for an answer, when there isn't any answer—except perhaps "off for Africa." Tom, deeply disturbed, also goes to pack. Hope remarks that Tom is the worst of her children and that all she wants is to be at home taking care of her real babies. She leaves, and when Alice appears on the balcony, saying she feels awful, Lily goes to her. Ann returns and demands to know what is bothering Pat, reminding him that they have always been honest and direct with one another. He evades her and refuses to admit what is wrong.

Suddenly he feels that this place reminds him strangely of a house his mother had in Florida four years ago, when he came back from England. He begins to talk about his return, and Ann quickly slips into the part of his mother. He tells her that when he was at Cambridge he fell in love with an English girl, Mary Carr. He cabled his father, saying he wanted to get married, and his father came over and talked him out of it. Because his father was ill,

Pat went home with him immediately. Over a year later, after his father died and the estate was settled, he returned for the girl, only to find that she was lost to him. The illusion of his mother's house fades and Pat realizes he is confessing to Ann, who forces him to go on. Pat says that the girl is dead, having shot herself three days before he returned. Ann suddenly realizes that this was what Pat had said he would tell her the day before he died; then she remembers the letter to Tom, and becomes even more worried.

Just then Stephen Field speaks, having come onto the terrace unnoticed by either of them. He says that he wouldn't, if he were Pat, go to the mountains and to that strange accident. After first pretending not to know what Stephen is talking about, Pat finally bursts out that he should have done it three years ago. Tom and Hope enter; Tom finds that Stephen reminds him of Father Francis. Lily joins them; she stares intently at Stephen who, she says, reminds her so much of her father. Norman enters, and soon Alice appears on the balcony and comes down the outside stairway. She is in a kind of trance, and when she speaks, it is clear she is reliving several earlier experiences. The others are horrified as Alice confides to Ann her longings for Norman. Norman then tells the others that he loves Alice and takes her into the house. Stephen talks about his conception of the three states of existence: the life of action, the life one lives in his imagination, and the life past death, which contains the others. No matter in which state one exists, he says, winds from the other states blow upon one.

Hope complains that Tom is looking at her in a strange way. Stephen suggests that Tom may be seeing her, not as a mother, but as the woman he loves, and urges her not to discourage him. Tom tries to embrace her but she shakes him off. Lily's voice is heard calling goodby to her father in childlike tones. Telling Tom to stay where he is like a good boy, Hope goes off to help Lily. Tom addresses Stephen as if Stephen were Father Francis and he himself a boy; he confesses that he doesn't believe any more and that nothing has any meaning to him. Stephen persuades Tom that his life does have a meaning. Seeing that he is very white, Tom goes to get him a glass of brandy. Stephen goes to a chair in the shadow of the terrace wall; Tom returns and cannot find him. Tom goes toward the house and meets Norman, who is carrying a small fur rug, which he tries to sell Tom as a neckpiece. Tom pushes past him, and Norman mutters about quitting his job as a fur salesman, getting a job in a bank, and becoming rich.

Lily runs in from the garden and does a little ballet practice. Stephen gets up from his chair, and Lily cries with joy, welcoming her father home. He bullies her into drinking a glass of brandy, which she does not like, accuses her of lying about how long she practiced her ballet exercises, and threatens to leave her as he left her mother if she lies to him. He tells her to dance for him, and though she says she hurt her foot practicing, he bullies her until she tries to rise on her toes and falls. She turns on him, saying she hates him, accuses him of being a drunk and a bad actor, and leaves in a fury.

Stephen sinks into a chair. He finds that his left arm has gone limp and realizes that he must be having a cerebral hemorrhage. He calls Pat and Ann. They enter and re-enact their first meeting near the Westbury road, where Pat came upon Ann, lost and with a sprained ankle. Their fantasy shifts as Pat mixes it up with his return to Mary. Stephen rises and plays Mary's father, breaking the news to Pat that she is dead. Pat again shifts into the present and announces to Stephen that he is in love with Ann and doesn't intend to let her sacrifice her own life to take care of her father. Stephen says that these last three years he and Ann have needed one another but that now she does not need him any longer. Pat hears Ann's voice in the garden and rushes after her.

Stephen moves painfully toward his chair and slumps down in it, dying. Tom, Hope, Norman, and Alice enter; they remember that there were some strange doings on the terrace, but already they are not sure exactly what went on. Pat and Ann enter, hand in hand. Lily announces that next year she is going to play Cordelia in *King Lear*. Norman says that, in spite of his corporation meeting, he is not going to Paris but to Andorra; Alice asks to go with him, and he assents joyfully. The butler announces that the bags are in the car. Pat says that he is staying. All leave except Pat and Ann. In the distance a cock crows. Ann remarks that it is just one of her father's pets and then, with growing apprehension, turns in the direction of Stephen's chair. She and Pat echo his words that wherever there is an end, from it a beginning springs.

SAMUEL BECKETT

Waiting for Godot   [*En attendant Godot*, 1952]

ACT ONE

In the evening on a country road with one tree in sight, Estragon* is sitting on a mound, trying to take off his boot, when he is joined by his friend Vladimir. Estragon comments that he spent the previous night in a ditch and, as usual, was beaten by "them." Vladimir carefully inspects the inside of his hat and Estragon does the same to his boot when he succeeds in getting it off. Vladimir remarks that one of the two thieves was saved and, though Estragon is uninterested, goes on to tell the story, commenting that only one of the four Gospels includes the account of the saved thief and wondering which one of the four to believe. Estragon wants to leave, but Vladimir reminds him that they cannot, since they are waiting for Godot. Estragon wonders whether they have come to the right place, but Vladimir reassures him and points out the tree as a landmark. Estragon is certain that they were here the day before, but Vladimir is not so sure, and he becomes extremely agitated when Estragon prods him with his doubts about what day it is. Estragon, meanwhile, falls asleep. When Vladimir realizes that his friend is sleeping, he feels left alone and awakens him.

Estragon despairs at being awakened into the world again and tries to tell Vladimir his dream, but the latter violently refuses to listen. Estragon, put out, wonders whether it wouldn't be better for them to part; he begins to relate a joke to pass the time, but Vladimir, offended, stomps off stage. When he returns, Estragon makes placatory gestures, and they make up. They wonder what else to do to pass the time while waiting for Godot; Estragon suggests hanging themselves, though Vladimir is dubious that the bough of the tree would hold them. They argue over who should go first, and finally Estragon, reduced to baby talk, points out that Vladimir, the heavier, must go first, lest Estragon succeed in hanging himself and the bough break under Vladimir and leave him alive and alone. They finally decide not to do anything, since they are not sure Vladimir is really heavier after all. They agree to wait and see what Godot says, going on to comment on their uncertain recollection of something they asked him for and his heavily conditional answer that he couldn't promise anything but would see what he could do. Vladimir thinks he hears someone coming, and they are frightened and huddle together, but no one appears. Estragon, hungry, asks for a carrot; Vladimir mistakenly gives him a turnip but finally, having rummaged through his pockets, discovers a last carrot; Estragon eats it

* *Estragon* is the French word for tarragon, an aromatic herb.

while asking Vladimir whether they are tied down to anyone, particularly Godot, and Vladimir replies that they are not. Both go on to comment on the futility of struggle or of attempting to change. There is a terrible cry from off stage, and both run toward the wings where they huddle together, cringing.

Lucky enters, carrying a heavy bag, a stool, a picnic basket, and an overcoat; around his neck is a long rope, at the opposite end of which is Pozzo, carrying a whip. Vladimir and Estragon at first mistake Pozzo for Godot; Pozzo treats them and their confusion with curt contempt. Interspersed with his remarks to them are derogatory commands to Lucky to stop, turn, back up, etc., as if he were a performing horse; Lucky performs promptly. Pozzo demands the basket from Lucky and proceeds to eat a chicken and drink from a bottle of wine. Vladimir and Estragon inspect Lucky, wondering why he doesn't put down his baggage, commenting on the sore on his neck from the rope, speculating that perhaps he is a half-wit, but agreeing that in any event his condition is inevitable. Estragon begs the chicken bones from Pozzo, who replies that they usually go to Lucky; but Lucky does not answer when Pozzo demands whether or not he wants them, and Pozzo gives the bones to Estragon. Vladimir is scandalized at the way Pozzo treats Lucky. Estragon continues to ask why Lucky doesn't put down his bags, but Pozzo stalls, sprays his throat with a vaporizer, makes as if he is going to speak, but never answers the question. Estragon, again reduced to graphic gestures and baby talk, finally forces Pozzo to answer; Lucky, he claims, doesn't put down the bags because he wants Pozzo to keep him. Vladimir repeatedly asks Pozzo whether he wants to get rid of Lucky, and Pozzo finally admits that he is taking him to the fair, where he hopes to sell him. At this, Lucky weeps. Pozzo scorns him but offers his handkerchief to Estragon, telling him to comfort Lucky since he pities him. Estragon begins to wipe Lucky's eyes, whereupon Lucky kicks him in the shins. Pozzo then pronounces several lyrical platitudes, which he tenderly attributes to his Lucky, but for whom all of his thoughts would have been "common things." At Pozzo's command Lucky removes his hat (all four are wearing bowlers), and his long white hair falls about his face; Pozzo, claiming to look much younger, takes off his hat and reveals a completely bald head.

Vladimir again berates Pozzo for scorning such an old and faithful servant; Estragon joins him, and Pozzo grows violently agitated and cries that he is going mad because of the way Lucky is treating him. Vladimir then turns on Lucky and accuses him of crucifying such a good master. Pozzo regains control of himself, rummages for his pipe, begs to be asked to sit down again, carries on a platitudinous speech, and finally suggests that he have Lucky do something to entertain them. He orders Lucky to dance, and then Vladimir asks Pozzo to command Lucky to think for them. Pozzo replies that Lucky can't think without his hat, and Vladimir gives it to him. Lucky begins to recite a long and chaotic speech, during which Vladimir and Estragon make protests, from mild to violent, and finally Pozzo pulls on the rope and all three jump on Lucky, silencing him only when Vladimir snatches his hat. Pozzo dashes the hat to the ground and stomps on it. Vladimir and Estragon hold Lucky up while Pozzo places the bags in Lucky's hands, and he finally revives and manages to remain upright. Pozzo begins to depart, though at first goodbys are said but no one moves; finally he gets a running start and, urging Lucky ahead of him, leaves. Vladimir comments that the interlude helped to pass the time.

Estragon wonders what to do now and suggests that they go, but Vladimir reminds him that they can't, since they are waiting for Godot. Vladimir observes that Pozzo and Lucky have changed, but Estragon is not sure that he knew them before. Estragon suddenly realizes that his other foot hurts. A boy approaches with a message from Mr. Godot that he can't come this evening but will surely come tomorrow. The boy leaves and night falls. Estragon takes off his remaining boot and leaves the pair for someone with smaller feet. As they prepare to go to find a place to spend the night, they reminisce about earlier days grape-harvesting on the Rhone, and Estragon again wonders whether they wouldn't have been better off apart but agrees with Vladimir that nothing is certain. Though they agree to go, neither moves.

ACT TWO

The next day, Vladimir appears singing loudly, and soon is joined by Estragon, who peevishly rebuffs his attentions and complains that Vladimir is better off without him. Vladimir assures Estragon that he wouldn't have let "them" beat him and that Estragon doesn't know how to look out for himself. Vladimir questions Estragon about the events of the day before, but Estragon has already forgotten most of them. Estragon becomes exasperated with Vladimir's attempts to make him remember, and says again that it might be better if they parted.

Vladimir points out that the tree, bare yesterday, has four or five leaves, but Estragon insists that he and Vladimir weren't there yesterday but were in some other part of the void, blathering about nothing in particular. Vladimir asks Estragon where his boots are, but Estragon refuses to remember or know why he doesn't know. Vladimir points out the boots where Estragon left them the day before, but Estragon denies that they are his. Vladimir then reasons that someone must have taken Estragon's boots and left this pair. Estragon again wants to go, but Vladimir reminds him that they are waiting for Godot. Vladimir offers his friend a radish, but Estragon remarks petulantly that it is black and he only likes the pink ones, and gives it back. To pass the time Vladimir suggests that Estragon try on the boots; he staggers into them and remarks that they are too big. He sits down and goes to sleep and Vladimir covers him with his coat, though he is cold without it and swings his arms to keep warm. Estragon wakes violently and Vladimir rushes to him and soothes him.

Estragon again wants to leave, but Vladimir reminds him about Godot. Estragon complains until Vladimir loses patience and shouts at him, and Estragon petulantly threatens to leave. Vladimir ignores him, having spotted Lucky's hat; he puts it on and passes his own to Estragon, and there ensues a long round robin of hats, which finally ends with Vladimir wearing Lucky's hat and throwing his own down. Estragon again announces that he is going. To amuse him Vladimir begins to imitate Lucky and tells Estragon to act the part of Pozzo and curse him. Estragon repeats that he is going, leaves precipitately, but comes back almost immediately with vague alarms that "they" are coming and frightens himself and Vladimir into frantic and futile efforts to escape. Finally Vladimir urges Estragon to hide behind the tree but then realizes that the tree gives no protection. Estragon calms down and they establish a watch. Beginning to speak simultaneously, they first beg each other's pardon and then, growing angry, begin vigorous name-calling, from which Estragon emerges the victor, having delivered the killing shot of "critic!" They make up and again wonder what to do to pass the time. They try exercises, imitating a tree by standing on one leg.

Pozzo and Lucky enter, Pozzo blind and Lucky wearing a different hat. Estragon thinks it is Godot. Pozzo clutches Lucky, who falls, and both lie helpless under the pile of baggage. Pozzo cries for help; Vladimir suggests to Estragon, who wants to leave, that they should help him get up, but Estragon is cool and wants assurance of another bone before he helps Pozzo. When subtle persuasion has no effect, Vladimir delivers a vehement speech on the necessity of acting when the chance to act is there. Pozzo offers a hundred francs for help, but again Estragon refuses, and Vladimir rants that they have been bored to death and now that a diversion comes along they let it go to waste. He tries to help Pozzo up but falls himself and calls for help, while Estragon only says that he is going. Finally Vladimir remarks that he supposes in the end he will get up by himself; Estragon comes to him, worries about him, gives him his hand, and himself stumbles and falls. Estragon falls asleep, but is awakened by Pozzo; Estragon complains and Vladimir strikes Pozzo, who crawls away and collapses. Vladimir and Estragon call to him, Estragon trying other names after he does not answer to Pozzo, reflecting that it would pass the time and they'd be sure to hit on the right one sooner or later. He calls "Abel," to which Pozzo replies "Help," and then "Cain," to which Pozzo also answers. Estragon observes that Pozzo must therefore be all humanity. For lack of anything better to do, Estragon and Vladimir get up and finally help Pozzo to his feet. He falls. They get him up again and support him. Estragon complains that he is no diversion. Pozzo wonders where Lucky is, and Estragon goes to the fallen Lucky and begins kicking him furiously but hurts his own foot. Vladimir reminds Pozzo that he and Lucky were there yesterday, but Pozzo has no recollection of it. He orders Lucky up and they begin to leave; Vladimir asks to have Lucky sing or think or recite, but Pozzo says he is dumb. Vladimir wants to know since when, and Pozzo flies into a rage at being tormented by Vladimir's notions of time. He and Lucky leave; off stage they noisily fall again. Vladimir goes to Estragon and awakens him, and the latter complains that he is never allowed to sleep. Vladimir wonders whether Pozzo was really blind. Estragon asks whether Vladimir is sure Pozzo wasn't really Godot, and Vladimir is less sure the more he thinks about it.

Estragon's feet hurt him as he gets up, and he sits down and tries to take off his boots, while Vladimir speculates whether he himself is sleeping or waking, and what his future recollection of the day's events will have to do with truth. Estragon dozes off again, and a boy enters. He does not recognize Vladimir and gives a message from Mr. Godot saying he won't come this evening but will surely come tomorrow. The boy exits, and night falls. Estragon wakes, takes off his boots, and puts them in the center of the stage. He and Vladimir begin to leave, saying they cannot go far because they must be back tomorrow to wait for Godot. They contemplate the tree, and Estragon suggests they hang themselves. Estragon says they'll use his pants cord for rope, and takes it off; his trousers, much too big, fall about his ankles. To test the cord for strength, each takes an end and pulls. It breaks and they almost fall. Estragon remarks that when they return tomorrow they can bring a good piece of rope, and Vladimir says that they will hang themselves tomorrow—unless, of course, Godot should come. Estragon pulls up his trousers, and they agree to go. They do not move, and the curtain falls.

BRENDAN BEHAN

The Hostage [first performed in Gaelic, 1958; in English, 1961]

NOTE: The Irish Republican Army (I.R.A.) was a secret organization formed after the Easter Rebellion of 1916 and dedicated to the achievement of Irish independence. After the establishment in 1922 of the Irish Free State, the I.R.A. agitated against Ireland's dominion status and against the separation of Northern Ireland, resorting when necessary to assassination and terrorism on both sides of the Irish border. During the period of this play, popular sympathy with the organization was in decline, for the government of the Free State was taken over in 1932 by an ex-I.R.A. supporter, Eamon de Valera. Eventually, after the attainment in 1940 of full independence for Eire, the I.R.A. found itself outlawed by both Irish governments.

ACT ONE

The scene is a Dublin lodginghouse. Pat, the caretaker, more correctly describes it as a "brockel." The house's owner, Monsewer, is an aged, addled Anglo-Irishman who was once a captain in the Irish Republican Army. The house used to be a hideout for I.R.A. members fleeing from the British. Most of this activity has ended now, and Monsewer spends his time playing bagpipes with a complete lack of skill and imagining that the riffraff who frequent his place are I.R.A. heroes. Pat, who served in the I.R.A. with Monsewer, runs the house. Most of his time is spent in reminiscing, singing old songs, such as "There's No Place on Earth Like the World," and arguing with the whores and queers who inhabit the house. Pat's helper Meg is an old bawd who is "nearly" his wife.

The house is about to become an I.R.A. hideout again. An eighteen-year-old I.R.A. member who shot a British policeman is to be hanged in Belfast the next morning. In retaliation, the I.R.A. plans to kidnap a British soldier and hold him hostage, threatening to kill him if the hanging takes place. Pat, who has no respect for the new-type I.R.A., has nevertheless agreed to let them hold the hostage at the house.

Meg and Teresa, a young girl fresh from convent school who works as a maid in the house, discuss the Belfast hanging. To cheer themselves up, they turn on the radio and start to dance. The door is flung open and in come the I.R.A. men with the young British soldier. He is singing, "There's No Place on Earth Like the World."

64

ACT TWO

Teresa and the young British soldier, Leslie, are attracted to one another right away. Although both doors of the room are guarded, Teresa manages to get in to bring Leslie some tea. As they talk, a procession protesting the Belfast hanging marches past the house. The tenants rush in to look at it through the window. Miss Gilchrist, a social worker who is a friend of Mr. Mulleady, a lodger, tries to cheer Leslie by reading him items from the *Daily Express*. When this fails she and Mulleady sing him a song—"There's Nobody Loves You Like Yourself." Pat chases everyone out of the room, but Teresa returns to talk with Leslie. They sing a song, "The Golden Ball," with the refrain, "If you'll marry, marry, marry me." On the last verse, "But first I think that we should see/If we fit each other/Yes I agree," the lights go out, and they go to the bed. They are interrupted by Meg, who comes in and sings "Who Fears To Speak of Easter Week"—describing the famous Irish revolt.

Leslie, who has been fairly relaxed until now, becomes worried when he sees a newspaper with the story of his kidnaping and the threatened I.R.A. reprisal for the Belfast hanging. He sings "I Am a Happy English Lad."

ACT THREE

Pat, Meg, and Miss Gilchrist sit and drink while the I.R.A. guard watches Leslie. Pat claims that Leslie has nothing to fear; the I.R.A. threat is only a bluff. The I.R.A. guard leaves the room for a minute and returns just in time to prevent Pat from sending Leslie to the corner shop for more stout. Miss Gilchrist, who is as drunk as Pat by now, sings a plea to world statesmen, "Don't Muck About with the Moon." Nothing can dissuade Leslie from his worry. He continues to demand an explanation of why he should be shot. He knows nothing about British policies in Ireland, or in Cyprus, or Kenya, or Jordan, he says.

Princess Grace and Rio Rita, the two queers of the house, Mr. Mulleady, and the whores enter and protest the planned killing of Leslie. After everyone leaves, Teresa sneaks in to talk to Leslie. The hour for the Belfast hanging, and possibly his own death, is drawing near. Leslie is angry because he thinks Teresa is unwilling to help him. She is uncertain about what to do. She wants to help but believes that Pat is right when he says the I.R.A. is only bluffing.

Teresa says she will go and get Leslie some chips from the corner shop. As she is leaving, Pat and the I.R.A. officer enter. Leslie sits and wonders whether Teresa will go to the police or not. Just then a raid takes place. The British police are led into the house by Mulleady and Princess Grace. Pat, Meg, and Monsewer take refuge in the room with Leslie. In the confusion and shooting Leslie is hit by a bullet and falls. Mulleady, saying he is a secret policeman and he doesn't care who knows it, arrests Pat, Meg, and Monsewer. Teresa enters

65

and sees Leslie's body. She says she will never forget him. Leslie sits up and sings:

> The bells of hell
> Go ting-a-ling-a-ling
> For you but not for me.
> Oh death where is thy
> Sting-a-ling-a-ling
> Or grave thy victory?
> If you meet the undertaker
> Or the young man from the Pru,
> Get a pint with what's left over.
> Now I'll say goodbye to you.

S . N . B E H R M A N

End of Summer [1936]

ACT ONE

The scene is the living room of the Frothingham summer cottage in northern Maine, in the month of May. Will Dexter, a recent college graduate who espouses the radical ideas of his generation, is visiting his girl friend Paula Frothingham. Paula's wealth bothers Will. He is worried that her professed agreement with his radical views is only superficial. Paula assures him that she sincerely agrees with his ideas.

Paula's mother Leonie is more typical of the idle rich of whom Will disapproves. But Leonie's scatterbrained charm and vivacity captivate even Will. Leonie is still married to Sam Frothingham, but they have long lived separate lives. Leonie is never without a lover. Her latest interest, Dr. Kenneth Rice, a psychoanalyst, is due to arrive that afternoon. Leonie has invited him, she says, to examine her present lover, Count Boris Mirsky, a morose Russian émigré, the son of a famous Russian novelist and philosopher. Also coming for a visit is Will's friend Dennis McCarthy, who is trying to launch a new radical magazine.

Sam Frothingham stops by and Will leaves Paula alone with him. Sam tells Paula he has fallen in love with another woman and wants to divorce Leonie. He suggests that Paula come to live with him and his new wife.

Leonie returns with her guests and the discussion is interrupted. When told of Sam's plans, she is upset. Paula tells her father that she must remain with Leonie because her mother needs someone to look after her.

ACT TWO

It is now midsummer at the Frothingham cottage, late in the afternoon. Leonie's interest in Dr. Rice has irritated Boris. The Russian is no match for his rival, however. Rice leads Boris into admitting that he hated his father and that he has never written a line of the biography of the novelist on which he has supposedly been working.

Leonie, increasingly attracted by Rice, offers him money for a sanatorium that he wants to build. Rice says he cannot accept the money. He then advises Leonie against supporting the radical magazine that Dennis and Will hope to publish.

Will and Dennis, who had been job-hunting in New York, arrive for a visit. Will is having no luck finding work and is despondent. Paula proposes to him, urging him to overcome his resistance to living on her money. Will accepts the proposal.

Leonie's mother, Mrs. Wyler, calls Sam for a confidential talk. She is aging and expects to die soon. She asks Sam to be executor of her will and to look after Leonie and Paula. She knows of Leonie's offer of money to Rice and, distrusting the psychiatrist, believes that he will take the money. For Paula's sake, she asks Sam to keep an eye on Will, who she believes is still too young and impulsive to be trustworthy.

A few hours later, just before dinner, Leonie tells Boris that their affair is over. Rice enters in the middle of the quarrel. Boris bitterly bids farewell to both of them and stalks out.

Leonie proposes to Rice, but before he can answer, Paula enters, saying that Mrs. Wyler wants to see Leonie. Rice talks with Paula, who is fascinated by him against her will. He tells her of his hard climb from orphanhood to his present position. Then he criticizes Will as a false radical and a fortune hunter and urges Paula to give him up. Will enters and Rice expresses his opinion to him. Will is angered but knows there is some truth in Rice's words. He is also angry about Paula's interest in Rice.

When the guests assemble for dinner, Will can no longer contain himself. He denounces Rice as a man who plays on fear and chaos to gain power. Will leaves, pursued by Paula.

ACT THREE

The scene is the Frothingham cottage in late fall. Will and Dennis arrive from New York, at Leonie's invitation. Mrs. Wyler has recently died, and Sam is talking over the estate with Leonie.

Sam tries to talk with Will—to urge him to settle down and give up his radical ideas, for Paula's sake. He gets nowhere. Will is still bitter about Paula's attraction to Rice.

Paula and Rice come in. She is surprised and pleased at Will's visit. Rice is as antagonistic to Will as before.

Left alone with Paula, Rice declares his love for her. In answer to her questions, he says that he does not really love Leonie. She demands that he tell Leonie that and calls Leonie in. After Rice tells Leonie that he does not love her, Paula reveals that she led him to do this so her mother could see the kind of man he is.

Paula tells Will what she has done and asks him to take her with him to New York. He refuses. He cannot live on her money and does not want to subject her to his struggles.

Leonie advises Paula to follow Will anyway, to be near him so that she will not lose him forever. Rice makes an attempt to smooth things over with Leonie. She rejects him, even though she feels lost without love of some kind. Rice leaves.

Not wanting to be left alone, Leonie induces Dennis to postpone his return to New York. She offers to help him with the publication of his radical magazine. As the curtain comes down, they drink cocktails and chat happily.

U G O   B E T T I

The Queen and the Rebels

[*La Regina e gli insorti,* 1951]

ACT ONE

The hall-porter of the main public building in a hillside village is ushering into the hall a group of recently arrived travelers who have been prevented from continuing their voyage. Among them, unrecognized in the garb of a citizen, is Commissar Amos. The porter apologetically asks them to make themselves as comfortable as possible in the disorder of the hall. One of the travelers, an engineer, notes that they are already late and have had their papers checked three times. The others say they all have travel permits and important business to attend to, otherwise they would not be traveling about at a time like this; the porter, unable to do anything, tries to be reassuring. The engineer asks to speak to someone in authority, and the porter replies that the N.C.O.s are rather rough but that the interpreter is "an educated young man."

While the porter goes off to find the interpreter, the travelers discuss their situation. The engineer says that if anyone in the group knows himself to be the cause of the delay, he should speak out. Amos says it is quite likely that the revolutionaries are just being "stupid and awkward." The engineer says that the revolution has great possibilities, but the Commissar states that the revolutionaries are in difficulties and might not last another week.

Raim, the blustering, pompous interpreter, comes in and declares that the hostages are all foreign spies or loyalists and monarchists. The engineer tries to pacify him, saying they have the necessary papers and are sympathizers with the revolution. Raim brushes this aside and tells them that their truck has been requisitioned, they can go no farther, and probably won't be allowed to return home; he orders the porter to collect the group's travel permits.

Raim questions the travelers to discover their political affiliations and checks their hands to see whether they are calloused; there is a silence when Amos says he feels concerned about the Queen. Raim, disconcerted, checks a peasant woman, who disgusts him; he then turns to Argia, an attractive, well-dressed woman, who tells him she has always had servants. Raim is embarrassed; striving to recover his self-possession, he declares that the porter must send them into his room in small groups, to be inspected.

Two of the travelers follow Raim, and the others talk about the Queen, speculating that it is she whom the revolutionaries seek. Argia, calmly smoking, says she thought that the Queen died five years ago, but the others tell her that the Queen is believed to have escaped assassination in a cellar: she lay under the bodies of government officials and later courageously passed through the

rebel lines. Two more people enter Raim's room. The engineer declares the
Queen to have been an evil genius; the porter grudgingly says she is reputed to
have been sincere; Amos asserts that she stood for a "dignified and honorable
idea of the world."

Raim bursts in and orders everyone except Argia into his room; in conversation alone together, Raim and Argia drop pretense and talk to each other in
familiar terms. Argia tells Raim that things were getting difficult for her down
in the town; she narrowly escaped from a police check and decided to leave.
Raim candidly reveals himself an opportunist determined to come out of the
revolution on the right side; when Argia hints at her affection for him, he
laughs and tells her he won't let himself be burdened with her: as a woman she
will be able to get through somehow. He tells her she is cheap, petty, and a slut
and quickly reverts to his official role when Amos reappears. Raim sends Argia
into his room with the others.

Amos, still incognito, and Raim discuss the revolution in cynical terms;
Raim, pouring a drink for them both, says that a small group of bosses and
crooks always emerges at the top whatever happens; Raim says he doesn't believe in equality—only in money. At the sound of approaching steps Raim again
resumes his official voice. General Biante, hairy, bandaged, dressed in civilian
clothes, enters, and Raim rushes to usher him in.

Raim tells the general he has been interrogating the traveler, who in turn
states that Raim has been making "curious offers of help" to him. Raim says
that this was a subterfuge, that the traveler is a suspicious character who should
be turned over to Commissar Amos, but the traveler suddenly reveals himself as
Amos. Biante, who is afraid of getting gangrene from his stray bullet wound, furiously sends Raim to search for a doctor and, alone with Amos, tells him that
the Queen is in the vicinity. The group of travelers returns, and Biante tells
them they are all under arrest and will be closely questioned; the male travelers
are sent into another room.

Argia and the peasant woman are alone; as Argia prattles, she notices that
the other woman seems ill and goes to help her. Seeing her closely for the first
time, her eyes widen. She helps the woman to the sofa in the next room, then
thoughtfully walks about for a few moments. She runs to the door and calls
Raim; when he enters, she tells him she is now rich and worth marrying, because she has discovered the Queen: she points to the next room.

ACT TWO

A few minutes later, Raim and Argia are still discussing what to do about
their discovery; Raim says that Amos and Biante could easily have him killed in
order to claim the credit for themselves. He tells Argia they must get hold of
the bag that the Queen carries, for it must be full of gold and jewels. As they
talk, the Queen appears in the doorway; Raim leaves, and Argia begins by saying she is fond of country people: did the woman work the fields? The Queen
appealingly holds out rough, calloused hands. Argia insinuates that she can help

the woman, who in return could help her; Argia then directly asks whether the woman's name is Elisabetta. The Queen, terrified, denies this but, as Argia insists, suddenly tells her she can have the bag, which she has hidden in the rafters: it contains the remains of her fortune, hidden in three loaves.

Raim breaks in and tells Argia he wants the names of the Queen's friends. Alone again with Argia, the Queen says all her friends have been killed, but Argia pitilessly insists. Breaking down, the Queen passes her a slip of paper. Raim enters with blankets and takes the slip of paper; he and Argia study it, fixing the names in their memories, before Raim burns it. In whispers, Raim tells Argia that the Queen will have to be killed: if she contacts her friends it will make things difficult; if Amos and Biante question her, she will reveal everything and betray Raim and Argia. Raim leaves, and the Queen falls to her knees in front of Argia and begs for her life; she says she has never had any authority or responsibility and since the revolution started has lived in fear from enemies and friends alike; all she wants now is to live in peace.

Raim returns and, taking Argia to one side, tells her that he has a plan for getting rid of the Queen: he will guard one exit and Maupa, a bloodthirsty rebel, the only other one; Maupa, Raim says, has been trained to shoot on sight any suspicious person. Raim has arranged that when an owl-hoot signal is given, Argia will send the Queen forth; he counts on her being shot down by Maupa. Argia asks what will happen if the Queen is not killed; Raim answers that in that case he will have to finish her off himself. Raim leaves and Argia explains to the Queen that a man is waiting to take her to safety. The Queen, laughing and weeping in relief, falls on Argia with a flood of thanks and in a confused torrent of words tells of her sufferings and constant terror; she has even had to give herself to peasants and has given birth to a child; now, the Queen says, she thinks she is pregnant again. As Argia gently strokes her face in compassion, the signal is heard; the Queen kisses Argia, but before she can leave, Argia tells her to leave by the other door: she has thought of a better plan, Argia says—while the Queen escapes to the mountains without waiting for her supposed guide, Argia will create a diversion at Maupa's door.

Before leaving, the Queen gives Argia a ring; Argia pushes open the door with a pole and as machine-gun fire splinters the wood, the Queen escapes by the other exit. Maupa enters, gun in hand, followed by Raim, who guards Argia while Maupa goes to fetch Amos; Raim tells Argia she must get out of the mess herself. Amos comes in, followed by Biante, and Argia tells them that she wanted to go out because she was thirsty. They accept the explanation and say the incident was opportune, because they wanted to interview Argia anyway.

ACT THREE

The revolutionary officials begin interrogating Argia, the nature of their questions revealing that they believe her to be the Queen; Argia, by the insolence of her answers, adds to their belief. She claims, however, to be of low class and to be a prostitute and says she will reveal the name of someone who can identify her later. Voices are heard clamoring outside, and the porter comes in to say that peasants from the upper valley have heard of the Queen's capture; the officials go out to investigate, and the porter, alone with Argia, tells her it is comforting for cowards like himself that such courage and dignity as hers can still exist. Biante returns laughing and tells Argia that the people want to see her tried and hanged. A court is prepared, with Biante president, Amos accuser, and a group of peasants jurors. Amos rises and indicts the supposed Queen for oppression, massacre, persecution, bringing foreign armed forces into the country, and other crimes. The peasants, encouraged by Biante, rise and accuse the "Queen" of responsibility for their various sufferings; and Amos rounds off the accusations by saying she represents inequality, injustice, and tyranny.

Argia calls Raim to witness that she is not the Queen, that she is a mere prostitute; Raim denies ever having known her and disappears in the crowd. Argia then says that the peasant woman who was there earlier can prove Argia is not the Queen and asks them to search for her. Amos gives a sign and the Queen, who has been captured escaping, is brought in under guard; but she has swallowed a phial of poison that she carried and dies without revealing she is the Queen. Argia rises majestically and states, "Yes, I am the Queen!" Sentence of death is pronounced against her.

ACT FOUR

A short time after the sentence, Amos comes and asks Argia to sign a paper confessing the crimes of which she is accused; at the same time Amos tells her that her "accomplice," Raim, has been mortally wounded trying to escape and, in dying, confirmed the allegations against the "Queen." Argia says that even if she signs, the rebels will still kill her; but Amos says that the revolution has an interest in keeping her alive in disgrace and poverty. When he asks that the "Queen" divulge the names of her friends, Argia refuses. Amos goes to the door and makes a sign. Maupa enters with a three-year-old boy dressed in peasant clothes: Amos announces that it is the Queen's son. His life depends on the "Queen's" divulging the names of her friends. Argia, torn, runs to the little boy and hugs him; she hesitates, confused, saying perhaps she ought after all to tell Amos the names; but then, laughing, she whispers that she has forgotten them.

Amos declares that in this case the argument is over; Maupa comes in, followed by the porter, and goes to take the child. Argia holds the boy close. Amos orders that the boy be taken back to where he has been living, among people who are in ignorance of his true mother, and that the Queen's death sentence be carried out at once.

Maupa moves toward the door, followed by Argia; she turns and waves goodby to the boy; at the door she pauses, bewildered, takes out her lipstick, and puts rouge on her lips. She sees the dawn sky and the mountains and declares: "Unquestionably this is a seat for kings, and in it we must try to live regally." She goes out; suddenly the porter runs after her. Amos puts his hands over the child's ears, and a burst of gunfire is heard; Argia is dead.

BERTOLT BRECHT

Baal [written 1918; performed 1923]

Scene 1. The play opens with a chorale praising the riotous exploits of Baal, a deep-drinking, wild, amoral poet living in Augsburg circa 1911. Baal is then seen entering the home of Mech, a publisher and important businessman, with Mech, Mech's wife Emily, the idealistic youth Johannes, and Dr. Piller, a critic. All are fascinated by the Bohemian poet: Mech plies Baal with food and wine and tells him he will publish his poems. Piller says he can do a lot for the poet and offers to write an essay on Baal and make him known. But Baal is more interested in the wine and Mech's wife, whom he openly invites to visit him in his attic. Baal delivers calculated insults to Mech and Piller, rejecting their aid, and both men walk out, angry and scandalized; Emily goes with her husband, and Johannes follows, after asking Baal if he may visit him in his attic. Baal is left alone, still drinking.

Scene 2. In Baal's bare attic Johannes tells the poet about his fiancée Johanna, a seventeen-year-old innocent: they have never made love, the young man confesses, asking Baal to agree that the union of bodies is a "filthy thing." Baal, in unbridled licentious language, says that one becomes God with a woman clasped in one's arms. If it is so beautiful, Johannes replies, should he not go ahead and consummate his love for Johanna? The youth should "steer clear," Baal answers.

Scene 3. Baal is in a barroom with a gang of teamsters. He tells them of his visit to Mech's home and how, later, Emily Mech ran after him and they had "quite a time." Now, Baal tells the laughing men, he is sick of Emily but can't get rid of her. Johannes comes in with his fiancée, followed by Emily, who is horrified to find herself in such surroundings. Baal speaks bawdily of the joys of love, and there is a raucous outburst of crude language from the men. Johannes and the two women are shocked and embarrassed. Baal, angry and in a black mood, takes his guitar and sings a bawdy song describing the dearest, most peaceful place on earth—the "john." The teamsters roar with laughter and applause; tears of humiliation form in Emily's eyes. Ekart, a composer, enters and romantically invites Baal to join him and head for the open road, the forests, and the fields. Baal appeals to Louise, the waitress, to hold him back; and with the help of Emily, Louise, and Johanna he resists the temptation but then humiliates Emily still further by having one of the men kiss her. Johannes takes his fiancée away after more embarrassing language from Baal, who is left alone with the weeping Emily.

Scene 4. Baal and Johanna are sitting on Baal's bed in his attic after love-making; Baal says that what has happened is Johannes' fault for bringing her there and leaving her alone with him. Baal refuses direct answer when Johanna asks whether he loves her and tells the girl that if she hasn't got "anything out of it" she should go away; Johanna runs from the attic. At midday two sisters, obviously habituées of Baal's attic and bed, tell the poet that a girl called Johanna has just drowned herself in the river. Baal's landlady appears and orders the girls to go home to their mother; she angrily tells Baal he must leave: she is not running a brothel. That evening Baal, feeling lonely, goes out to find another woman; Johannes, distressed, enters the attic in his absence. Baal reappears with a woman, Sophie Barger; he roughly ejects Johannes and seduces the not-unwilling Sophie.

Scene 5. Baal meets a drunken, religious bum, who is worried by the trees which are set up outside the houses at Corpus Christi: he sees them as corpses. In drunken conversation the bum says Christ loved evil, and Baal replies, "As I do." Baal leaves, taking with him the bum's brandy flask.

Scene 6. Baal is lying with Sophie under some trees one May night. Sophie says that it must be three weeks since she met Baal, and that her mother, believing her to be dead, is weeping for her. Baal says he loves her, and she replies that it is good to be lying there "like some robber's loot." They make love.

Scene 7. Baal, now working in a sleazy nightspot, is arguing with Lupu, a fat, pale youth: Baal wants more brandy before going on-stage, but Lupu says that he has had his ration. Mjurk, the nightspot proprietor, enters, and Baal tells him, "No brandy, no poetry." A chanteuse, the other star of the program, comes in from the stage, and Mjurk tells Baal to go out and perform. Applause greets Baal, who begins a particularly shameless song about a child; protests lead to turmoil, and Baal runs from the stage and into a washroom. Mjurk is furious and orders him to carry on the performance; the audience, calling Baal a pig, shout for more songs. Lupu announces that Baal has fled through a washroom window, and Mjurk rushes out to call the police, while the audience rhythmically clamor for "Baal! Baal! Baal!"

Scene 8. Baal has rejoined Ekart, and together they wander through the fields in the month of July.

Scene 9. In a village tavern one evening Baal is telling a crowd of farmers that he will buy a bull—the bull with the strongest loins—for a large sum of money. The farmers leave, excitedly promising to return the next day with their bulls for Baal to choose among. Meanwhile, Baal is getting brandy on credit from the landlord for himself and Ekart. Ekart tells Baal they should leave quickly before they get into trouble, but the parson arrives, wanting to know why Baal is trying to swindle the people. Baal replies that it is for the pure spectacle: the sight of bulls trotting into the village from all the surrounding villages. The parson tells the two to make themselves scarce and takes the bill for the eleven brandies drunk by Baal and his companion.

Scene 10. Baal is sitting under some trees with six or seven lumberjacks; one of their comrades lies nearby, killed by a falling oak. The men sorrow for the dead Teddy, and one of them suggests they honor their fallen friend by drinking to his memory: they will drink Teddy's brandy ration, which he had been storing. Baal tries to dissuade them, but they rush off to seek the brandy; Baal talks to the dead man and tells him that the living will take over Teddy's cabin in the north since he will no longer need it. Returning empty-handed, the men accuse Baal of having got to the brandy first, before Teddy was even dead. Baal appeases the men.

Scene 11. Baal and Ekart are in Teddy's cabin; it is raining. Ekart asks why Baal has driven Sophie off, and Baal replies that she runs after them like one demented and is hanging round his neck. Ekart says Baal is sinking lower and lower. Sophie appears at the door and asks whether she may come in now.

Scene 12. Baal, Ekart, and Sophie are walking across the plains; Sophie is pregnant and can walk no farther. Baal, annoyed, calls her a millstone round his neck. Ekart says he will stay with the girl if Baal abandons her, and offers to take Sophie back to her mother if she will renounce "this animal." Sophie replies, "I love this animal." Ekart snarls that Baal is a "degenerate beast." They wrestle together, but the fighting stops when Baal suddenly looks up at the sky: "Now you can see the stars above the bushes, Ekhart," Baal says. He takes Ekart off with him, leaving Sophie alone in the dark shouting, "Baal!"

Scene 13. Baal and Ekart arrive at a poor inn where Googoo, Bolleboll, a beggar, and the beggarwoman Maja are drinking and playing cards. Maja opens the door to the wanderers after Baal announces that they have champagne with them. All begin getting drunk; Bolleboll, who says he has ulcers, grabs Maja and sits her on his knee, while Googoo declaims a speech in praise of Nothing, a state which "cures all bad habits" and in which one becomes free. Baal takes fright at his words and wants to leave. Maja sings in praise of drunkenness and moves closer to Bolleboll, to the annoyance of the beggar, who angrily tells Bolleboll to take his hands off her. Maja and Bolleboll are contemptuous of the beggar, who furiously tells Bolleboll that he has cancer, not ulcers, but backs down when Bolleboll challenges him. Baal moves over to look at Maja's baby, who is crying in a box, and Maja and the beggar, alarmed, tell him to leave the child alone. Baal, hurt, leaves with Ekart.

Scene 14. Baal and Ekart are sitting by a river. Ekart tells Baal that a woman has just passed, and Baal replies that he no longer needs women.

Scene 15. Ekart is sleeping on the grass near a highway when Baal disturbs him with a new poem about a girl who drowned and floated down rivers until "slowly God forgot her." Ekart tells Baal of a redhead who comes daily at noon to make love with him.

Scene 16. Baal is waiting for the young redhead to appear. When she comes, Baal tells her that Ekart is composing a Mass and drags her into the trees. . . .

Scene 17. Baal is reading Ekart a poem about a man who died and was buried under a tree. Ekart says Baal has been writing a lot lately and mustn't have had a woman for a long time. Baal laughs.

Scene 18. Ekart is in a barroom with Johannes, who has become a ragged, gone-to-seed drunk; they note that it is now eight years since Johanna died. Watzmann says that Baal's mother died the day before and that Baal is getting more and more disgusting. Ekart tells him not to say that; he loves Baal, who is "a child." Baal appears, and the waitress, who has the features of Sophie, brings brandy; Baal asks, "Is that still you, Louise?" Johannes speaks of his drowned love, and Baal springs up, smashes the light with his guitar, and begins singing. Ekart encourages him, but Baal stops to tune the instrument and asks, "Are you my friend, Ekart?" Ekart says with difficulty, "Yes, but go on playing." Watzmann puts on the light and Baal, seeing Ekart with his arm round the waitress, gets up. He crouches and leaps at Ekart, who shouts, "Why shouldn't I have women?" They fight, and the others see that Baal has a knife: Ekart falls dead.

Scene 19. On the run, Baal heads for the cabin in the north.

Scene 20. Two rangers on a highway, trailing Baal, talk about him; one of the men says that though Baal killed his best friend for a waitress, a registered prostitute, he is like a child and almost got caught carrying logs for an old lady. Baal, listening from nearby bushes, learns that Ekart is dead.

Scene 21. Baal lies dying in a forest cabin surrounded by lumberjacks. They are playing cards, and tell Baal to hurry up and die. They start to leave for work in the forest, mocking Baal's pleas that they stay with him for half an hour. Only one man stays behind briefly before following the others. As death closes in on him, Baal crawls to the door to get outside to the light.

BERTOLT BRECHT

The Caucasian Chalk Circle

[*Der Kaukasiche Kreiderkreis,* first performed in English, 1948; in German, 1954]

PROLOGUE

The members of two Soviet collective farms are meeting with a state planning expert amid the ruins of a Caucasian village destroyed during the Second World War. When they reach agreement on what shall be done with the village, one of the peasants says that in honor of the visiting expert they have arranged with the storyteller, Arkadi Tsheidse, to produce a play. Tsheidse enters with four musicians and announces they are going to perform a version of an old Chinese play called the "Circle of Chalk."

PART I

Tsheidse sets the scene of the play: long ago, a Caucasian city was ruled by a governor, Abashwili, who was rich and had a beautiful wife. The play opens with the governor on his way to church with his family one Easter Sunday;

crowds of beggars and poor people petition him, and soldiers whip the crowds back. At the rear of the procession, in an ornate carriage, is the governor's child and heir, who is heard to cough at the church door; the governor and his wife are immediately concerned, and the child's two doctors, who are constantly feuding, argue over who is responsible for the child's cough.

A dust-stained rider appears bearing a message from the capital, but the governor refuses to see him before the service and goes into the church with his retinue, joined by the fat prince who fawningly greeted him at the door. Standing guard at the door, Shashava, one of the palace guards, sees a girl, Grusha, walking by, and tells her he has seen her bathing in the river; she runs off. The fat prince emerges and makes a sign to two Ironshirts; they go off and muffled voices are heard: "To your posts!" The palace is surrounded. Later, the governor returns to the palace; a noise is heard, then the scream of a woman. The adjutant tries to get into the palace, but is stopped by Ironshirts and learns that the princes met last night in the capital: the war has been going badly, and they decided to overthrow the grand duke and his governors.

The governor is led out, gray-faced, and taken off for execution. The adjutant appears and orders panic-stricken servants to help with the packing. Shashava finds Grusha, and the girl tells him that if things go badly she can go to her brother in the mountains. Shashava asks Grusha to marry him and says he will return in two or three weeks after accompanying Mrs. Abashwili to the troops that have remained loyal to the grand duke. Grusha says she will wait for him.

Mrs. Abashwili appears in the courtyard, ordering servants to put her gowns in the carriage. Despite the adjutant's agitation she is stupidly more concerned with her dresses than with escaping and wastes minutes deciding which clothes she will take with her. She is finally jerked into reality by the sight of flames from the palace and runs after the adjutant, who has told her they have to travel by horse instead of carriage. The child, Michael, is left behind and accidentally falls into the keeping of Grusha. Despite the danger of being found with the child, Grusha finally takes him with her and leaves the city.

Heading toward the mountains, Grusha has to pay a peasant six times more than the usual price for a drop of milk for the child. Coming to another farmhouse, Grusha decides to leave Michael on the doorstep. The farm woman takes the child in, despite the protests of her husband, and Grusha hurries away. Soon afterwards she meets two Ironshirts on the road, and they tell her they are searching for the governor's child. Panicking, Grusha runs back to the farmhouse where she left the child; she tells the farm woman to hide the child from the soldiers.

The woman is scared, but agrees to tell the soldiers that the child is hers. But when the men arrive, she is terror-stricken and falls to her knees, pleading for mercy. The corporal, suspicions aroused, orders the other men to take the woman outside and bends over the child to inspect him. Grusha seizes a log and hits the corporal, who collapses; she grabs Michael and rushes off.

Grusha comes to a bridge over a glacier and finds several people standing undecided whether to chance crossing. She hears the two soldiers shouting to her and bravely decides she will have to risk the rotten bridge and the two-thousand-foot drop; she crosses the swaying bridge to safety, leaving the soldiers temporarily stranded on the other side. At last, fatigued and worn out by her journey, she arrives at her brother's house but doesn't receive the greeting she has been expecting. Her brother is fat and cowardly and dominated by his self-ish wife; he makes up a story about Grusha so that his wife won't worry about the strange situation.

Six months later, Grusha is living in a workroom at her brother Lavrenti's farm to avoid disturbing her sister-in-law. Lavrenti enters and tells Grusha that he has found a husband for her to legitimize the situation; he tells her that the man, a peasant, is dying and will only be a husband on paper. Grusha, who at first protests that she must wait for Shashava, admits that she ought to have a legal document for Michael's sake; Lavrenti hurries away to arrange the marriage.

Grusha arrives at the peasant's cottage and is married to the man, who is lying in bed and apparently dying. Lavrenti pays all the expenses, then hurries away. As Grusha sits with her new mother-in-law and wedding guests, she hears that the grand duke has got back into power, the war is over, and the soldiers are returning home. As she falls on her knees in prayer, Jussup, her "dying" husband, jumps from his bed and startles everybody with his appearance. The guests rush from the house.

That night the brutish peasant, fully recovered, forces Grusha to bathe him in the tub; he tells her that she is his wife and even if Shashava returns, it is too late. Some time later, Grusha is washing clothes in the river and sends Michael off to play with the other children. Shashava appears, and Grusha tearfully tries to tell him that although she is married and has a child, she still loves him, and the child isn't really hers. They are interrupted by two soldiers, who have seized Michael; they tell Grusha they are taking the child to the city on suspicion of his being the son of the dead governor. Grusha sadly follows them to the town.

PART II

Azdak, the village recorder, finds a fugitive in the woods and hides him from the police; later he learns that the fugitive was the grand duke, and goes voluntarily to the court to have himself tried. When he gets to the court, how-ever, he finds that the judge has just been hanged. The Ironshirts laughingly release Azdak. The fat prince enters and tells the soldiers that his nephew Kaz-beki will be the new judge; but, the fat prince says, it is for the people to decide. The soldiers decide to hold a trial that Kazbeki shall judge; then they will decide whether he is fit to be the judge.

Azdak pretends to be the grand duke, and after a mock trial the soldiers decide that Azdak, by his cleverness, is much more fitted to be the judge. They send the nephew away, and Azdak goes on to administer an ironical and rough-and-ready justice that is essentially based on wisdom. Later, yet another revolution returns the grand duke victorious to the city, and the fat prince is beheaded.

Mrs. Abashwili returns to the town seeking her child, and a trial is arranged to decide who shall have custody of him. Shashava tells Grusha he is ready to declare in court that Grusha's child is his. Azdak is led in, in chains, and the Ironshirts treat him roughly prior to hanging him. A messenger arrives from the grand duke to announce the latest appointments; Azdak, who earlier saved the duke's life, learns that he is once again the chief judge.

Azdac begins hearing the case against Grusha. Mrs. Abashwili's lawyers hand over a bribe to Azdac and present their case. Then Grusha declares simply that she had been looking after Michael all these years and has given him good care and attention. Shashava declares that the child is his. A lawyer for Mrs. Abashwili tells the judge that Grusha married in a mountain village, at which Grusha states that she married simply for the sake of the child. When the case appears to be going against Grusha, she indignantly scolds Azdak, who beamingly beats time with his gavel as the tirade continues.

Azdak orders a test to be made. He orders that a circle of chalk be drawn on the floor and the child put inside it; he then orders Mrs. Abashwili and Grusha to stand on opposite sides of the circle and each to take the child by one hand; the true mother, Azdak declares, is the one who can pull the boy out of the circle toward herself.

Mrs. Abashwili easily pulls Michael out of the circle: Grusha has dropped her hand and stands aghast. Again the test is performed, and the same thing happens: Grusha sadly says that she can't tear the child to pieces. Azdak triumphantly declares that Grusha is therefore the true mother; Mrs. Abashwili's estates will be seized and made into a playground for children. Azdak says he is quitting his job, but before doing so says he will write out the divorce decree for the aged couple who pleaded their case earlier. "By mistake," however, Azdak divorces Grusha from her peasant husband; the former judge then invites all the people to a dance outside and shortly afterwards disappears, never to be heard of again. Tsheidse sings that Azdak was long remembered for his justice.

B E R T O L T   B R E C H T

Galileo [*Das Leben des Galileo Galilei*, written 1938–1939; performed 1943]

Scene 1. Galileo is in his study in Padua in the year 1609. A boy, Andrea Sarti, the son of the housekeeper, enters carrying an astronomical model of the Ptolemaic universe, a present to Galileo from the Court of Naples. Galileo complains that he is never given money. Andrea asks how the model works. Galileo shows him the earth at the center and the eight rings around it that represents the sun and planets in their crystal spheres. Andrea says that it is like a cage. This pleases Galileo, who predicts a time when it will be taught that the earth spins around the sun. Andrea does not believe that the sun stands still; he says that he can see it move. In a simple demonstration Galileo shows Andrea that what appears to be true is not always so.

Mrs. Sarti, Andrea's mother, enters to announce Ludovico Marsili, a young gentleman of a fine Italian family. He wants to be Galileo's student, but he doesn't understand science. To prove this he explains how he was shown a telescope in Holland but didn't understand how it worked. Galileo makes notes while Ludovico describes the telescope. Galileo tells Ludovico to come back later for his first lesson. As Ludovico leaves, the curator, a bureaucrat, enters. Galileo borrows a scudo from the curator. He gives the money to Andrea and tells him to go to the spectacle-maker and buy lenses like those on the sketch he has made. Andrea leaves. The curator says that Galileo's petition for more money from the state has been rejected. Galileo offers him a paper on physics, but the curator says the state wants practical work from him that will bring in money. He says that if Galileo wants money and leisure he should go to Florence. Andrea returns with the lenses. As the curator leaves, Galileo fits the lenses together.

Scene 2. At the arsenal in Venice, Galileo's daughter Virginia presents the telescope, "the product of seventeen years patient research," to the merchants of the city. During the ceremony, Galileo is bored and talks with his friend Sagredo about looking at the sky through the telescope. He asks Sagredo whether he knows what the Milky Way is made of. "I do," says Galileo.

Scene 3. A few months later in Galileo's study, he and Sagredo watch the moon turn through the telescope; Sagredo is frightened by what he sees. Galileo says that he has discovered four small stars near Jupiter that seem to move around the planet. Galileo and Sagredo watch the four stars through the night. By morning both are convinced that they do move: there can be no crystal shell supporting Jupiter. Sagredo warns that they are approaching heresy, that there is no place for heaven or God in this new universe. Virginia comes in on her way to Mass with Ludovico. Galileo tells her that they are moving to Florence.

Scene 4. In his house in Florence, Galileo is about to show the four moons of Jupiter, named after the nine-year-old Prince Cosimo de Medici, to the boy. A philosopher of the court quotes the classical description of the heavens. Galileo invites the prince to look at the Medicean planets, but the philosopher intervenes, doubting the reliability of the telescope, no matter what it shows. All present refuse to look. The philosopher says that Galileo is trying to demonstrate the impossible: to disprove Aristotle. Galileo argues that Aristotle had no telescope. The prince's chamberlain says that the prince must leave for a state ball but that the chief astronomer of the papal college, Christopher Clavius, will be consulted.

Scene 5. In the Collegium Romanum in Rome, a group of scholars, churchmen, and monks are waiting for Clavius' decision on Galileo's theory that the earth turns around the sun. Galileo is alone in a corner. The monks ridicule the idea of the earth turning. An old cardinal approaches Galileo and tells him that he has degraded the earth and man, God's greatest effort. Clavius enters, muttering to himself that Galileo is right.

Scene 6. Galileo, Virginia, and Ludovico, now her fiancé, arrive at Cardinal Bellarmin's home in Rome for a ball. The cardinal enters with Cardinal Barberini. Galileo and Barberini spar with each other by quoting passages from the Bible, Galileo to champion newness and Barberini to caution against rashness. Bellarmin interrupts to tell Galileo that it is for the ministers of God alone to interpret the Bible. He says that the Holy Office has decided that Galileo's heliocentric theory is foolish, absurd, and a heresy. He charges Galileo to abandon these teachings.

Scene 7. In a garden in Rome, a monk, one of Galileo's followers, explains to Galileo why the Holy Office decided against the new theory: the little people of the world, in order to carry on their wretched lives, must think that they are in the center of God's world. They must not be allowed to think that the Scriptures are mistaken about anything; they cannot be frightened. He tells Galileo that they must remain silent for the sake of the inward peace of less fortunate souls. Galileo does not accept this; he says that truth must be pushed through.

Scene 8. After eight years of silence on the controversial subject, Galileo is at work in his study in Florence. Virginia and Mrs. Sarti are sewing bridal linen. The philosopher of the court enters, bringing Galileo a new book on the recent sunspots. Andrea Sarti, the monk, and Federzoni, Galileo's assistants, discuss current theories about the spots. Galileo ignores them. Ludovico enters. He has come from Rome and tells Galileo that the old Pope is dying and that Barberini, who is sympathetic to science, is sure to be the new Pope. Virginia leaves to get her bridal veil to show Ludovico. Galileo begins to show interest in the sunspot book. Ludovico uneasily tells Galileo that a person from a prominent family must be careful about whom he marries; seeing that his fiancée's father is now committed to his heresy, he leaves. Galileo turns his telescope on the sun. Virginia runs in; when she sees her father looking through his telescope and realizes that Ludovico has left, she faints.

Scene 9. On April Fool's Day, 1632, a street singer in Florence and his partner sing about the new universe with its new order and freedoms from the old order. Passers-by in carnival costume are caught up in the singing and dancing. As the singer repeats his refrain, "It is nice, just for a little change, to do just as one pleases," the carnival revelers become frantic in their dancing. They begin to abuse a rich couple who have been watching. As the singer ends his song, the carnival procession enters. At its head is a float with a figure of Galileo shaking his head at a Bible with the pages crossed out.

Scene 10. Galileo and Virginia wait to see Prince Cosimo in his palace in Florence. The cardinal-inquisitor comes out of the prince's room, followed by the chamberlain. Galileo asks to be allowed to present his book to the prince. The chamberlain stalls him off and starts to leave but turns and tells Galileo that Florence can no longer oppose the request of the Inquisition to interrogate Galileo in Rome.

Scene 11. In his chamber in the Vatican, Pope Urban VIII, formerly

Cardinal Barberini, is being robed for a conclave. The cardinal-inquisitor tells him that he must confirm the truth of the Bible. Urban says that he cannot set himself up against the multiplication tables. The inquisitor answers that men are starting to put their faith in brass bowls called compasses, not God. Regretfully Urban relents but instructs that Galileo must not be tortured.

Scene 12. On June 22, 1633, in the Roman garden, Virginia, Federzoni, Andrea, and the monk are waiting for news of Galileo's trial before the Inquisition. His assistants are sure that Galileo will never relent, not even when threatened with death. A member of the tribunal enters to tell them that Galileo is expected to recant in one minute: at five o'clock. When he does, a bell will ring. At five o'clock no bell rings; they all exult. Then the bell is heard. Andrea says, "The mountain has turned to water." Galileo enters, somber and changed. They all ignore him, except Virginia.

Scene 13. In 1642, guarded by an official of the Inquisition, Galileo is working in his house near Florence. Nearly blind, he has to dictate his work to Virginia. Andrea, who deserted Galileo after his recantation, comes in on his way to Holland. Stiffly, they chat about each other's health. Andrea tells Galileo that since his recantation no new theories have been expounded in Italy. As Andrea is about to leave, Galileo tells him that at night he has rewritten the work he renounced at the Inquisition. He gives the manuscript to Andrea, who says that he cannot express the shame he feels. He states that Galileo has beaten the authorities by submitting to them in order to live and finish his work. Galileo tells Andrea that he is wrong; he was frightened of pain and betrayed science. Andrea leaves with the book.

Scene 14. In an Italian border town, customs inspectors look through Andrea's luggage. They ask if his books contain any dangerous material, such as religion or politics. Nothing but figures, says Andrea. No harm in figures, answers the chief inspector. Children nearby, seeing the shadow of a woman stirring her porridge, cry that they are going to break her windows, for they think she is a witch. Andrea lifts one boy up to a window to show him that she is only a woman cooking her supper, not a witch stirring a hellbroth. As Andrea is crossing the border, the boy shouts after him, "She *is* a witch! She *is* a witch!" This scene is sometimes omitted in performance.

BERTOLT BRECHT

The Good Woman of Setzuan

[*Der gute Mensch von Sezuan,* written 1939;

performed 1943]

Prologue. At the gates of Setzuan the water-seller Wong waits for the gods, expected to come in answer to the inhabitants' rising complaints of poverty. Three gods appear and ask him to find them a place to stay, but everyone Wong asks refuses. The gods comment that their mission to find good people has failed again. Their resolution reads: "The world can stay as it is if enough people are found living lives worthy of human beings." The first god says that if they fail in their search, the atheists will have a right to change the world and that, at the moment, just one good person is enough for the gods.

Wong, in desperation, asks Shen Te, a prostitute, whether the gods can spend the night in her house. She agrees. The gods rejoice to find a good person at last. The next morning they leave her house and pay her for allowing them to stay.

Scene 1. Shen Te has bought a tobacco shop with the gods' money. Mrs. Shin, the former owner, comes and demands food for herself and her children. An elderly couple and their nephew enter next and ask for a place to stay. Shen Te gives them a room in the back of the shop. A carpenter comes in; he threatens to remove the shelves he built because they have not been paid for. Mrs. Mi Tzu, the landlady, enters and demands character references from Shen Te before signing the lease, for she is critical of Shen Te's past profession. The rest of the elderly couple's family come in to live with Shen Te: a brother, pregnant sister-in-law, grandfather, niece, and a boy. Shen Te tells the landlady and carpenter that her cousin Shui Ta will pay all their bills. The family sings the "Song of the Smoke" to cheer up Shen Te.

Scene 1a. Wong is asleep in his house, a sewer pipe. The three gods appear to him in a dream. They ask him to watch Shen Te and to report her actions to them. Meanwhile, they will continue to search for good people.

Scene 2. Shui Ta, Shen Te's cousin, enters the shop and bargains with the carpenter, paying him a smaller amount than he asked from Shen Te. Shui Ta then chases the old couple and their family out and calls a policeman and turns in the boy for stealing. The landlady comes in and asks for six months' rent because of Shen Te's bad reputation. The cousin doesn't have the money. The policeman suggests placing an ad in the newspaper for a rich husband for Shen Te.

Scene 3. Yang Sun, an unemployed pilot, is about to hang himself in a park. Two prostitutes enter and proposition him, but when they discover he has no money, they leave. They return, followed by Shen Te, who is on her way to meet her prospective husband, a widower with three children. The prostitutes leave again. Shen Te talks to Yang Sun, who is bitter and despondent because he can't get a job as a pilot. Wong enters singing "The Song of the Water Seller in the Rain."

Scene 3a. The gods again appear to Wong in a dream. Wong happily reports that Shen Te is as good as ever and that she is in love with the pilot. He also tells the gods that she gives rice to the poor every morning. The gods are satisfied, although they wish they could find another good person on a more heroic scale.

Scene 4. The family of eight is back in Shen Te's shop. Shen Te, returning from Yang Sun's, decides she is in love and goes to buy herself a scarf in the carpet shop next to her store. The owners, an old couple, discover that Shen Te needs money for her rent. They lend her the money, and she pledges her shop. Yang Sun's mother comes in to see Shen Te with news that her son has been offered a job as a pilot if he can pay five hundred silver dollars. Shen Te gives her the two hundred dollars loaned for the rent and wonders how to get the other three hundred dollars.

Scene 4a. Shen Te enters carrying a mask of Shui Ta's face. She sings the "Song of Defenselessness," asking the gods why they don't protect the good and punish the bad.

Scene 5. Shen Te, disguised as Shui Ta, is in her tobacco shop. Yang Sun enters, unaware of Shui Ta's identity. He reveals that he is eager for Shen Te to sell her shop so he can get the three hundred dollars he needs. As soon as he gets it, he will leave for his job. He does not plan to take her along. He leaves, and Shen Te goes berserk with grief. Mrs. Shin, who was listening in the back room, tells Shui Ta that the rich barber next door is interested in Shen Te: he can help her if she cooperates. Mrs. Shin runs out and returns with the barber, Mr. Shu Fu. Shui Ta and the barber arrange for his possible engagement to Shen Te. Shui Ta tells him he must first confer with Shen Te in the back room. Yang Sun comes back and is told not to bother Shen Te, because she is promised to the barber. But when Shen Te enters from the back room, Yang Sun talks her into going back to him. He admits he planned to use her to get the money, but he stills needs her. They leave together.

Scene 5a. Shen Te is on the way to be married to Yang Sun. She tells the audience that the old couple want their loan back. She believes Yang Sun would give up his hopes for the pilot's job rather than rob the old couple.

Scene 6. The wedding is about to take place in the private dining room of a cheap restaurant. Yang Sun tells his mother that Shen Te won't sell her shop and give him the money because of her debt to the old couple. He has sent for Shui Ta, hoping the cousin will change her mind, and keeps delaying the wedding, waiting for Shui Ta's arrival. When Shui Ta does not appear, Yang Sun admits to Shen Te that he still wants her to sell her shop and give him the money for the job. She refuses. The priest and guests finally leave, and Yang Sun sings "The Song of St. Nevercome's Day."

Scene 6a. In Wong's den, the gods appear in a dream. Wong asks them to help Shen Te, who is about to lose her shop. The gods answer that her goodness is help enough.

Scene 7. Shen Te is in the back yard of her shop with Mrs. Shin, having decided to sell the shop to pay back her debt to the old couple. Shu Fu, the barber, comes in and begs her not to sell her shop; he gives her a blank check and tells her he will make no claims on her if she uses it. She does not want it at first, but after Shu Fu leaves she feels dizzy and realizes she is pregnant. Wong enters with the carpenter's son. He asks Shen Te to help the boy and his family, because the carpenter has lost his shop and is poor and homeless. She says they can all live in the cabins Shu Fu has offered her. The couple who lived in Shen

Te's shop come in with stolen sacks of tobacco and ask her to keep them. She agrees and leaves. Shui Ta enters and tells the people gathered in the shop that they will all have rooms if they work in Shen Te's new tobacco factory, which is opening in Shu Fu's cabins. They ask where the tobacco will come from. Shui Ta points to the stolen sacks. The couple who stole them are too scared to say anything. The landlady is paid the rent with Shu Fu's blank check.

Scene 7a. Wong is again visited by the gods. He pleads for help for Shen Te, but the gods say they can't change the rules.

Scene 8. Several families are working in Shen Te's tobacco factory. Mrs. Yang recalls to the audience how her son started working here three months ago. He was unable to get the pilot's job because he could not get the rest of the money and squandered what he had. He has worked hard in the factory and become a foreman. Yang Sun and the workers sing the "Song of the Eighth Elephant."

Scene 9. Shen Te's old shop is now the main office of the factory. Shui Ta, who has become very fat, is talking to the old couple. They want to thank Shen Te for the debt she paid back, even though it came too late to save their carpet shop. Yang Sun enters and announces that the authorities want to close down the tobacco factory, because it is too damp. Wong comes in looking for Shen Te. He says that there are rumors in Setzuan that Shen Te was pregnant before she disappeared and adds that it seems she has returned, because rice has been left for the poor again. Yang Sun is struck by the news and demands to see Shen Te, since he is the father of her child. Shui Ta goes to the back room, and Yang Sun thinks he hears Shen Te crying. Suspicious, he leaves to get the police to help him find Shen Te. Yang Sun and the police return and find only Shen Te's clothing in the back room. They assume Shui Ta has murdered his cousin and arrest him.

Scene 9a. The gods appear to Wong. They are tired and bruised. At the end of their long search, Shen Te is still the only good person they have found. They leave to find her again.

Scene 10. A crowd is gathered in a courtroom. The gods enter disguised as the judges. Shui Ta is accused of Shen Te's murder. Shui Ta's employees denounce him as the worst enemy Shen Te ever had. Shui Ta asks the judges to clear the courtroom; he has a confession to make. The judges comply. When they are alone, he tears off his mask, revealing himself as Shen Te. She explains that without her disguise she would have been destroyed by her goodness. She asks the gods to help her with her present problems: she needs her bad cousin. The gods tell her to remain good: they can't help her and they can't change the rules or the world; they must leave. As a rising cloud transports them out of the stage, they sing the "Valedictory Hymn." Shen Te is left alone. Her last word is "Help!"

BERTOLT BRECHT

Mother Courage and Her Children

[*Mutter Courage und ihre Kinder*, 1941]

Prologue. Mother Courage and her mute daughter Kattrin ride on a vivandière's wagon drawn by Eilif and Swiss Cheese, Mother Courage's two sons. They sing how soldiers must have food and drink if they are to fight.

Scene 1. On a road in Sweden in the spring of 1624, a recruiting officer complains to his sergeant that he can't find men. The sergeant explains that nothing goes right during peace. Mother Courage and her children enter on the wagon. The sergeant tries to recruit her sons, but Mother Courage resists him. The sergeant lures Mother Courage aside while buying a belt from her. While she is gone, Eilif is recruited by the officer.

Scene 2. In the camp of the Swedish army in Poland in 1626, Mother Courage tries to sell a capon to the commander's cook. The commander, the chaplain, and Eilif enter. The commander compliments Eilif on his bravery and tells him to stay for a meal. The commander asks whether Eilif's father was a soldier. Eilif says yes and sings the song he learned from his mother, "The Fishwife and the Soldier." Mother Courage sings the last stanza from inside the cook tent. Eilif recognizes her voice and runs to embrace her. She tells him that Swiss Cheese is in the army too; he is a paymaster.

Scene 3. Three years later, in the camp of the Protestant army, Mother Courage haggles over the price of a sack of bullets. After completing her deal she reminds Swiss Chesse not to forget his underwear when he leaves. Yvette, a camp follower, complains that her business is no good, singing "The Camp Follower's Song." The cook and the chaplain enter and discuss the war with Mother Courage. The chaplain says that a religious war pleases God; Mother Courage adds that there is profit to be made. As they drink to the Protestant flag, cannon are heard. The Catholics have attacked. The chaplain hides, but Yvette puts on her make-up. Swiss Cheese runs in with his cashbox; he wants to hide it in the wagon.

Three days later, Mother Courage, Kattrin, the chaplain, and Swiss Cheese are eating a meal by the wagon. Swiss Cheese is worried about his cashbox; the chaplain is worried about his life. Mother Courage and the chaplain leave to buy a Catholic flag. Two Catholic soldiers approach Kattrin while Swiss Cheese is behind the wagon getting his cashbox to take it to a safer place. Kattrin runs to Swiss Cheese and tries to warn him, but he cannot understand her. He leaves and the two soldiers follow him. Mother Courage and the chaplain come back and raise the new flag. The two soldiers re-enter with Swiss Cheese, whom they have captured. Mother Courage and the chaplain pretend they don't know him.

One soldier tells Swiss Cheese that if he doesn't tell where he hid the cashbox he will be killed. He says nothing, and they lead him off.

That evening, Mother Courage tells Kattrin and the chaplain that they can buy Swiss Cheese's freedom if they can raise some money. Yvette enters with an old colonel, her lover. She offers to buy the wagon; Mother Courage tells her that it is only for pawn. Yvette accepts: if Mother Courage can't repay 200 guilders after two weeks, she forfeits the wagon. The colonel leaves. Mother Courage sends Yvette to the Catholic camp and tells her to offer 150 guilders for Swiss Cheese. Mother Courage tells the chaplain that she is counting on the cashbox to repay the pawn. Yvette runs in; she says the Catholics want 200 guilders and that Swiss Cheese has thrown the cashbox into a river. Desperate to save something, Mother Courage sends Yvette back to offer 120 guilders. When she returns Yvette says that it's no deal even at 150 guilders. Mother Courage tells her to offer the whole 200. "I believe I haggled too long," she says. There is a drum roll off stage. The stage grows dark, then light again. Yvette enters; she says Swiss Cheese has eleven bullets in him.

Scene 4. Mother Courage is waiting in a tent to lodge a complaint with a Catholic officer; her wagon was vandalized by his troops. A young soldier rushes in; he has rescued the officer's horse but has not been given his reward. He threatens to kill the officer and says that he will not stand for injustice. Mother Courage asks him how long he won't stand for injustice: an hour, maybe two? An orderly says the officer will be right out; the young soldier begins to look cowed. Mother Courage sings "The Song of the Great Capitulation." The young soldier slinks out. The orderly tells Mother Courage that she can see the officer now. She answers that she has changed her mind and leaves.

Scene 5. Two years later, in a war-ruined village, Mother Courage and Kattrin are serving brandy to soldiers. The chaplain enters and tells Mother Courage that he must have linen to bandage a family of wounded peasants. She tells him that he can't have any without paying. Kattrin picks up a board and threatens her mother. A child is heard crying in the farmhouse; Kattrin runs in. The chaplain lifts Mother Courage from the wagon and takes four linen shirts. Kattrin comes in holding a baby. She is happy and sings a lullaby. One of the soldiers tries to steal a jug of brandy. Mother Courage grabs the coat off his back.

Scene 6. In 1632, inside their canteen tent, Mother Courage and Kattrin are taking inventory. The noises of General Till's funeral can be heard. After urging his men to fight to the death, he was returning to his headquarters behind the lines; unfortunately, he got lost in the fog and ended up in the thick of the fighting, where he was shot. Mother Courage wonders whether his death might bring the war to an end. The chaplain says the war will never end, although it might slow down for a while. Mother Courage says she doesn't want to start an argument; she's just wondering whether she should buy more supplies while they're cheap. The chaplain sings "The Army Chaplain's Song," explaining how war satisfies all needs. Mother Courage decides to buy supplies and sends Kattrin into town to get them. Mother Courage gets out a pipe; the chaplain observes that it once belonged to the cook. He warns her that the cook was a violent man. Approaching her, he asks whether the two of them might not have a closer relationship. Mother Courage tells him to get back to work. Kattrin enters, cut over one eye. Mother Courage bandages her and tells the chaplain that with a scar like the one Kattrin will have she'll never be able to get a husband. Seeing Kattrin, Mother Courage is reminded of her dead son and wonders where her other one is. "Curse the war!" she says.

Scene 7. On a highway, Mother Courage and Kattrin pull their wagon. Mother Courage vows not to let the war destroy her. She sings "The Song of Mother Courage."

Scene 8. On a summer morning in 1632, an old woman and her son are trying to sell some bedding to Mother Courage. Bells are heard ringing and an off-stage voice calls, "It's peace! The King of Sweden got killed!" Mother Courage laments that she has bought new supplies. The cook enters looking bedraggled. He says that Eilif is coming, too, and drinks to peace. Mother Courage says that peace has ruined her, because she bought new supplies on the chaplain's advice. The chaplain enters, wearing his pastor's coat again. Filled with righteousness, he calls Mother Courage a hyena of the battlefield. Yvette, older and fatter, enters with her valet. She recognizes the cook as the man who caused her downfall years before and reveals that now she is married to the older brother of the colonel who nearly bought Mother Courage's wagon. Mother Courage and Yvette go to town to try to sell their goods before prices fall. Eilif, escorted by two guards, enters in chains. He asks for his mother, for he is on his way to be executed, having stolen some cattle and killed a peasant. He tells the cook that when he did this before, he was a hero. "That was in war time," answers the cook. Eilif is led off; the chaplain follows. Mother Courage runs in with her goods and says that the peace is over. The cook tells her that Eilif was there but had to go away. Mother Courage says they'll see him later, the war will never get the boy. She invites the cook to go with them. As he and Kattrin pull the wagon off, Mother Courage sings "The Song of Mother Courage."

Scene 9. In the autumn of 1634, Mother Courage, the cook, and Kattrin are stopped in front of a parsonage. The cook tells Mother Courage that he has a letter informing him that his mother died, leaving him an inn in Utrecht. He asks Mother Courage to come with him and help him run it, but he says Kattrin can't come. Kattrin listens from inside the wagon. A light goes on in the parsonage, and Mother Courage and the cook sing "The Song of the Wise and Good." A voice asks them to come in for hot soup. The cook and Mother Courage go in. Kattrin gets out of the wagon with a bundle; she is about to leave when her mother comes back. Mother Courage sees the bundle and tells Kattrin that the cook can go to Utrecht if he wants to, but she will stay, not for Kattrin, but for the wagon. They pull the wagon off together.

Scene 10. Mother Courage and Kattrin pull the wagon past a farmhouse where voices are singing "The Song of Shelter." The two women listen to the words about warmth and shelter, then start out again.

Scene 11. In January 1636, the wagon is drawn up in front of a farmhouse. An officer and three soldiers knock at the farmhouse door. When an old woman answers, they grab her and drag out her husband and son. Kattrin peers out of the wagon and is seized. The old woman tells the soldiers that Kattrin's mother is in town buying supplies. The soldiers want a guide into town. The son says that he doesn't help Catholics. He does not relent even when the soldiers put a sword to his throat. When they threaten to kill the livestock, his parents force him to guide the soldiers into town. The soldiers leave with the son. The old man climbs onto the roof and reports that he sees hundreds of soldiers and cannon; they are grouped to attack the town. He says the watchman must have been killed, for he hasn't sounded the warning yet. The old woman falls on her knees and prays that her grandchildren in the town might be spared. As she prays for the townspeople to wake up, Kattrin creeps out of the wagon and up the ladder to the roof, a drum hidden under her skirt. She takes it out and starts to beat it. The peasant couple, frantic, beg her to stop before the soldiers come back, but she does not. The soldiers run in with the son. They threaten Kattrin, but she keeps on drumming. They offer to spare her mother when they attack the town, but she won't stop. A soldier orders the son to destroy the wagon; he beats it feebly with a board then throws it down and cheers for Kattrin. A soldier knocks him down and stabs him. Another soldier runs in with a gun and shoots Kattrin. The last beats of her drum are lost in the noise of the town's cannon. A soldier says, "She made it."

Scene 12. The next morning, Mother Courage is holding Kattrin's body. Marching soldiers are heard off stage. The old peasants look on. Mother Courage sings a lullaby to Kattrin. The old peasants urge Mother Courage to leave before all the soldiers are gone, saying that they'll bury Kattrin. "Have you no one left?" asks the old man. "Yes, my son Eilif," answers Mother Courage. She harnesses herself to the wagon. "I'll manage. There's not much in it now," she says. As she calls after the last regiment of passing soldiers, they are heard singing "The Song of Mother Courage."

BERTOLT BRECHT

The Threepenny Opera

[*Die Dreigroschenoper*, 1928]

ACT ONE

In the Prologue, a street singer sings to the rabble of Soho a ballad which tells of the grim exploits of a well-known underworld character named Mackie the Knife.

In his establishment for beggars, Mr. Peachum, after singing his cynical

"Morning Hymn," explains to the audience the difficulties that human nature presents to one whose business it is to soften the hearts of men with pity for beggars. A young man named Filch comes in, asking Mr. Peachum's help. They strike a bargain: Filch pays a fee for a license to beg in one of Mr. Peachum's districts and promises 50 percent of his takings, and Mr. Peachum gives him a beggar's outfit from among his five models. When Filch goes to try it on, Peachum questions Mrs. Peachum concerning their daughter Polly's new beau, known to them only as "the Captain," whom he has never seen but of whom he disapproves nonetheless. Through his wife's replies he ascertains that "the Captain" is Mackie the Knife. He runs upstairs to seek Polly and finds her gone. Together the Peachums sing a song of the illusion and disillusion of love.

In an empty stable in Soho, Polly and Macheath, or Mackie the Knife, celebrate their wedding. Just as Polly objects to the surroundings, five of Macheath's men enter with stolen furnishings and transform the place into an ornate living room. The men change into evening dress, and Matthew, on behalf of them all, offers formal congratulations to the couple, but is struck to the ground by Macheath for an obscene remark to Polly. Peace is restored and the gifts are presented. The company sits down to the elegant stolen wedding breakfast; Macheath demands a song to make the occasion more festive, but when Reverend Mr. Kimball arrives, requests instead a hymn. Three of the men sing "The Wedding Song for Poorer People," an obscene little ditty. Polly then sings "Jenny, the Pirate's Bride," telling of a barmaid who sees the entire town destroyed by pirates and sails triumphantly away on their ship. When Tiger Brown, chief of police and sheriff of London, enters, the gang retreats, but Macheath nonchalantly greets his old friend and introduces him to Polly. The gang comes warily back. Macheath and Brown sing "The Army Song," after which Macheath extols their friendship and the many ways in which they have helped each other professionally. After Brown leaves, the gang reveals its surprise gift, a bed. After they leave, Polly and Macheath sing of their love.

In Mr. Peachum's establishment, Polly sings to her parents "The Barbara Song," in which she explains why Macheath was the man to whom she could not say no. Both parents are furious, and Mrs. Peachum orders Polly to get a divorce. Mr. Peachum sends his daughter out of the room and tells his wife that they will get Macheath hanged by reporting him to the sheriff. They will discover his hiding place by bribing his women in Wapping. Polly, who has overheard, tells them of Macheath's friendship with Brown, but the plan stands. All three sing a song which teaches that "the world is rotten through and through."

ACT TWO

Polly rushes into the stable to warn Macheath of the plan to apprehend him. When Macheath hears that because of Peachum's influence Brown can no longer protect him, he explains his business to Polly and describes the various crooks in his employ, so that she can carry on in his absence. The gang arrives, bursting with plans to exploit the coronation of the queen, which is about to

take place in London. Macheath introduces their temporary leader, who immediately wins their respect with a most unwomanly speech. After the men depart,
Macheath takes leave of Polly, promising to be true to her. She feels that he
will not return.

In an Interlude, Mrs. Peachum offers the prostitute Jenny ten shillings to
report Macheath to the police if she sees him and explains that he will surely
visit the brothel, despite the dangers, because he is a slave to his desires.

At the brothel in Wapping, the girls are discussing Macheath when he arrives. Jenny reads his palm, foretells bad times, and disappears. As he sings of
the days when he lived with Jenny, she, Mrs. Peachum, and three constables
listen through the window. Jenny returns and joins him in the song, leading
him to one of the constables. He jumps out the window, only to be confronted
by Mrs. Peachum and the other two constables, who lead him away.

At the prison in the Old Bailey, Brown prays that Macheath will not be
caught. He is desolate when Macheath, led in by the constables, refuses to
speak to him. Left alone, Macheath sings "The Ballad of Comfort," in which
he repudiates poverty and sacrifice. Brown's daughter Lucy enters, furious at
the rumors about Polly and Macheath. Macheath denies being married to Polly
and promises to marry Lucy. When Polly arrives, Macheath postpones his decision between the two women. The two women sing the biting "Jealousy Duet."
At last he chooses Lucy. Polly protests tearfully and is dragged away by Mrs.
Peachum. Lucy agrees to help Macheath escape and brings him his hat and
walking stick. When she leaves, Constable Smith enters Macheath's cell and
chases him until the prisoner climbs over the bars and flees. Brown enters and is
relieved to find his prisoner gone. Peachum comes to claim the reward for
Macheath's capture, discovers the situation, and threatens Brown. If Brown
does not find Macheath, Peachum will instigate the lower classes to ruin the
coronation procession. Any trouble will, of course, be blamed on Brown.

Macheath and Jenny step before the curtain and sing "The Necessity of
Foul Misdeeds."

ACT THREE

In Peachum's establishment, Mr. and Mrs. Peachum and several clients are
preparing for the show of misery with which they hope to disrupt the coronation procession. Jenny and the girls arrive to demand the money promised them
in return for handing over Macheath. When Mrs. Peachum withholds the reward because of the prisoner's escape, Jenny tells how Macheath visited her
after his escape and says he is probably now with Suky Tawdry. Peachum sends
Filch to the police with this news. Suddenly Filch runs in, shouting that the
police are coming. Mrs. Peachum and the beggars hide as Brown and the three
constables enter. While Peachum repeats his threat, Brown confidently announces that he will foil Peachum's plan by arresting his beggars. But Peachum
sings "The Futility of All Human Endeavor" and reminds Brown that the
really poor number in the thousands; when they appear en masse, it will hardly

make a favorable impression if they are mistreated by the police. Trapped, Brown dispatches a constable to arrest Macheath at Suky Tawdry's. Peachum warns that Macheath must be hanged by six; he then changes his plans and sends the procession of beggars to the prison.

In an Interlude, Jenny sings "The Song of Solomon," describing the downfall of great personages, including Macheath.

In the Old Bailey, Polly comes to apologize to Lucy for her behavior of the previous day. Their exaggeratedly polite and friendly conversation continues until Lucy discovers that Polly has come only to find out Macheath's whereabouts. Just as Polly learns that Lucy does not know where he is, they see through the window Macheath's return to prison. Mrs. Peachum conveniently appears with Polly's widow's weeds.

It is four minutes past five. In the death cell, the constables discuss the hanging, to be held at six o'clock in the morning. After he tries to bribe a constable, Macheath begins to sing "The Epistle to His Friends," begging their aid. When two of his men come to visit, Macheath sends them out to raise money for him. It is five thirty-eight. The constable inquires how the money-raising is progressing. As Macheath continues singing his "Epistle," Polly arrives. She is composed as Macheath asks her for money, but at length she breaks down and is dragged away by the constable. Brown himself helps to carry in Macheath's last meal, a plate of asparagus. Macheath calls Brown a faithless friend, and Brown leaves in anger and sadness. Peachum, Mrs. Peachum, Polly, Lucy, Jenny, the girls, several of his men, and Reverend Mr. Kimball enter. After they file past the cell, the constable announces that it is six o'clock. Macheath sings a ballad asking forgiveness of God and men.

As Macheath stands on the gallows, Peachum announces that Macheath will not be hanged, for the opera is to end differently. A royal messenger appears on horseback, announcing that the queen, because of her coronation, has decreed that Macheath shall be released. He is to become a noble with a castle and a pension. Amid the rejoicing, Mr. and Mrs. Peachum observe that life never ends happily in this fashion. Thus one should not seek justice too eagerly. All sing the "Valedictory Hymn," reminding the audience that "the world's a vale of misery and woe."

KAREL ČAPEK

R.U.R. [1921]

ACT ONE

Helena Glory visits the island factory of Rossum's Universal Robots, manufacturers of mechanical people designed to perform man's menial tasks. Harry Domin, general manager of R.U.R., describes the mad physiologist Rossum's discovery of a substance behaving exactly like living matter that, together with the engineering accomplishments of Rossum's son, led to the invention of the robot. When Helena reveals that, as a representative of the Humanity League, her mission is to protect and ensure the good treatment of the robots, Domin explains that, although the robots have enormously developed intelligences, they have no souls and therefore have no interest in materially improving their condition. Except for Mr. Alquist, architect of R.U.R., who feels there is virtue in human toil and weariness, the managers of the works agree that the end of man's servitude to manual labor will eventually enable him to perfect himself. There are, however, some technical flaws in the robot's mechanism: Dr. Hallemeir, head of the Institute for the Psychological Training of Robots, tells of the occasional breakdowns that resemble defiance. Dr. Gall explains that it has become necessary to introduce suffering to the robots as an automatic protection against accidental damage. The head of the Physiological and Experimental Department, Dr. Gall is currently experimenting with pain-nerves for this purpose.

When the managers leave to prepare lunch for their guest, Domin unexpectedly proposes marriage to Helena, who hesitates, then accepts.

ACT TWO

On the tenth anniversary of Helena's arrival on the island, with news of an impending robot revolution spreading, Domin presents her with the "Ultimus," a gunboat intended as a means of escape should the rebellion reach the island. Newspaper accounts tell that countries have manned their armies with robots who assassinate the civilian populations of occupied territories. This, together with a steadily declining birth rate, threatens mankind with extinction.

Already, there have been incidents of insubordinate behavior at the factory, and Nana, a companion-maid to Helena, decries the conduct of the robot Radius. He has had an attack similar to an epileptic fit, and when Dr. Gall torments him with a pain test, Radius exhibits human emotions.

When the scheduled mail boat arrives on time, Domin, believing the crisis ended, plans the manufacture of a new kind of robot, with distinct national traits, which will despise foreign robots. Helena is pleading with him to abandon this project when Mr. Fabry, general technical manager, announces that the mail boat is controlled by the robots distributing leaflets calling for the destruction of all humanity; they have boarded the "Ultimus" and surrounded the house in preparation for attack.

ACT THREE

Domin, Helena, and the managers are barricaded in the apartment, and Mr. Fabry has contrived a device for running high-voltage current along the garden railing electrocuting any who touch it. When Dr. Gall confesses that over the last three years he has introduced physiological changes in the robots altering their character and, thus, is responsible for the uprising, Helena insists that she influenced Dr. Gall by encouraging him to give the robots souls.

Consul Busman, general business manager of R.U.R., suggests selling Rossum's secret of their manufacture to the robots, who cannot reproduce themselves, in return for the safety of the humans on the island. But Helena, distraught, has burned the manuscripts that morning in the empty hope that disaster could somehow be forestalled by the cessation of robot production.

Busman decides to negotiate, using the half-billion dollars in the company's safe, and runs out to the garden with bundles of money, but he inadvertently grasps the electrified railing and dies. A failure of the electricity signals the robots' march on the house. Except for Alquist, whose nonresistance puzzles the robots, all die at the hands of the mechanical insurgents.

EPILOGUE

A year has passed; Alquist, the sole survivor of humanity, is now working for the robots, fruitlessly experimenting with a robot reproductive process. Faced with extinction, the robots have pinned all their hopes on these experiments. They offer their finest specimens for dissection, but Alquist, considering such dissection murder, refuses. He despairs of ever discovering Rossum's secret, when two robots, Primus and Helena, appear. They exhibit a sense of humor, an appreciation of beauty, a kinship with nature, and an affection for each other. Alquist, sensing the presence of human qualities, tests the robots by ordering Primus to take Helena to the dissecting room for experimentation. Primus protests, offering to go in Helena's place, and she, in turn, threatens suicide if Primus is killed. Alquist, realizing that Dr. Gall's final experiments succeeded, bids Primus and Helena to go forth as the new Adam and Eve.

KAREL AND JOSEF ČAPEK

The Insect Comedy

[*Ze Zivota Hmyzu*,* 1921]

PROLOGUE

A Lepidopterist and a Tramp encounter each other in a wood. Two butterflies have just escaped the Professor's net, when he notices the Tramp. The Tramp protests that, despite appearances, he is not drunk: if he just fell down, he did so heroically, re-enacting the fall of man. He asks the Professor why he catches butterflies that are playing so happily. The Professor explains that he kills and preserves the butterflies out of a deep love of nature and that what appears to be playful and purposeless flitting is, in reality, the prologue to the "Great Act of Nature." In the butterfly world, the female constantly allures; the male pursues; the female flees—but only to be captured. The Professor, spotting another butterfly, resumes his chase. The Tramp watches the Professor leave and considers what he has said. Suddenly, everything in the world seems, to him, to come in pairs, and he mumbles about a girl he once knew. Deciding that he does not care if he *is* drunk, he lies down to meditate.

ACT ONE. The Butterflies

The Tramp looks about him, sees beautifully colored lights and soft cushions, and is aware of a pleasant odor. He decides to stay and watch the butterflies. Felix, a poet butterfly, enters, pursued by some young female butterflies whom he ignores, for he is trying to find a suitable rhyme for Iris, the object of his desire. Iris enters, followed by Victor. She flirts with Felix, who pretends indifference, declaring that women no longer interest him. Iris asks him to tell about his previous romances. Victor reads Felix's latest poem and makes fun of it until Iris sends him away. She then teases Felix, tempting him to kiss her. He is too shy and reveals that he has never had a woman: he desires the impossible, the beautiful Iris. She replies that she is attainable. Felix composes a poem to her on the spot.

Clytie, another female butterfly, arrives, pursued by Otto, as Victor returns. Clytie flirts with Felix, thus annoying Iris. The two females rival and insult each other. Suddenly, Iris dares Victor to catch her if he can and flies off with him. Clytie asks Felix how he could love a butterfly as old and unattractive as Iris. He replies that his love for Iris ended ages ago. Clytie admits that men bore her: she has had too many lovers. Now, she tells Felix, she yearns for

* This play is also known in English as *The World We Live In* and *And So Ad Infinitum.*

95

something new and pure. Felix suggests that he create a poem for her and announces that he loves her passionately. She is delighted. But Otto now insists that Clytie love him immediately; and the two start to go off together, leaving Felix without his audience.

Suddenly, Clytie notices the Tramp. She is attracted by the irresistible scent of garbage about him and commands him to love her. He calls her a hussy and tries to chase her away. Iris arrives, laughing because Victor has just been eaten up by a bird. The two females fly away, with Otto in hot pursuit. Felix tries to read his newest poem to the Tramp, who chases him away.

ACT TWO. Creepers and Crawlers

The Tramp, sitting on a sandy hill, hears a Chrysalis announce that all the world is bursting into bloom because it is about to be born. The "Great Adventure" will begin; the earth trembles. The Tramp is not impressed and turns to observe two beetles pushing a ball of dung. They are very excited because they have made a great fortune at last; their futures are secure, their dreams fulfilled. Husband Beetle informs his wife that he must now rush out and make a second fortune. But since she is afraid that the first will be stolen, Husband tells her to guard it while he searches for a hiding place. Then, he tells her, they will invest both fortunes and live off their capital. While he is gone, Mrs. Beetle notices a suitable hole and goes off to investigate it. A strange Beetle comes along and greedily steals the dung. When Mrs. Beetle returns, the Tramp points out the direction the strange Beetle took. She follows it, believing the stranger to be her husband. The Tramp reflects upon the hard-working nature of beetles.

The Chrysalis cries out to the universe to prepare for its arrival. The Tramp asks the Chrysalis what it will do upon birth. It replies that, though it does not yet know, it is certain to do something great and extraordinary that will astound the world.

An Ichneumon Fly arrives and enters its lair, bringing a cricket for its daughter Larva to devour. Noticing the Tramp, the Fly asks him if he is edible and expresses his parental pride in his daughter. Hearing the Chrysalis announce the rebirth of the world brought on by its own birth, the Tramp turns to examine it. Regretfully deciding that the Tramp is inedible and that the Chrysalis is unripe, the Fly goes off in search of more crickets.

The Larva emerges from her father's lair and expresses her desire to devour or destroy something. She and the Tramp exchange compliments, each deciding that the other is extremely ugly and rude. Mr. Beetle returns. The Tramp tells him that his wife left, following a male Beetle. Mr. Beetle leaves, lamenting the loss of his fortune and the infidelity of his wife. The Tramp laughs at the loss of all that Mr. and Mrs. Beetle labored for, comparing them to crickets who never work but only sing until death stops their song. Just then, a cricket arrives, tenderly leading his pregnant wife. They are moving to a new house, vacated by a cricket who was fed to Ichneumon Fly's daughter Larva. Mr. and Mrs. Cricket laugh at the fate of the deceased cricket and dream about their future family. Mr. Cricket puts up a sign reading "Mr. Cricket, Fiddler." Then he goes out to look for work, despite the protests of his wife, who is afraid of being alone.

Mrs. Cricket starts to cry and the Tramp tries to comfort her. Mrs. Beetle arrives and asks if her husband and their dung pile have been seen. The two women try to comfort each other but they soon start to argue. Mrs. Beetle insists that one must have a dung pile before having children, while Mrs. Cricket insists that without children a man will leave his wife and take the money too. Mrs. Beetle runs off as the Ichneumon Fly enters. The Fly stabs Mrs. Cricket and drags her off to his lair.

The Tramp is horrified. He screams, "Murder!" and looks around for someone to do something about the crime. A Parasite arrives and agrees with the Tramp that murder is an awful thing. After all, everyone is hungry and it is scandalous that some should have plenty while others starve. He himself is unfitted to kill, lacking sharp teeth or claws, and so he takes from his hosts only as much as he needs.

Ichneumon Fly returns, gloating over the way he killed Mrs. Cricket, and calls the Parasite a lazy thing. One must be ambitious, imaginative, enterprising, and courageous to get ahead and raise one's family, he lectures. While the two argue and the Tramp broods about Mrs. Cricket, Mr. Cricket returns. Before he can discover his wife's death, Ichneumon Fly kills him. The Fly and the Parasite go off together.

The Tramp cries out for an explanation for such killing. He tries to calm himself by reflecting that these events only took place in the insect world. The human world is different. Men work hard to save for the future—then he remembers the beetles. Men have idealism, dreams for the future, devotion to the family—then he remembers the crickets. Men have purpose, resolution, and ambition—then he recalls Ichneumon Fly.

The Parasite returns, hiccupping, and announces that he has eaten the Fly and Larva.

ACT THREE. The Ants

The Tramp reflects that insects are egotists. Each believes he is all-important. They have no fellow-feeling, no higher loyalties. Man, however, will follow a general plan and will sacrifice for his country. The existence of the nation gives man nobility. As the Tramp arrives at these conclusions, a colony of ants appears. Large numbers of them scurry back and forth, carrying goods and implements of labor. In their center sits a blind ant, continually beating the four-four time to which the others work.

The Chief Engineer Ant arrives and questions the Tramp. An inventor rushes in announcing a new time-saving discovery. The Chief Engineer asks in what part of the ant colony the Tramp originated; the Tramp replies that he is a human being. The Engineer asks the location of the "Human Ant Heap"; the Tramp replies that it is everywhere and that man is the "Lord of Creation."

This answer causes laughter among the ants who consider themselves the "Masters of the World," a great democracy, a world power, and the largest ant state in the universe. Each ant strives only for the ends of the state, which are the destruction of the state's enemies. They have destroyed the Black Ants, starved the Brown Ants, subjugated the Grey Ants—only the Yellows are left. The inventor returns, announcing his greatest discovery: a war machine. The ants now have the power to destroy the Yellows and they declare war. The Chief Engineer announces his appointment as dictator. A journalist-ant reports the battles. Whole armies are killed, yet the Dictator never doubts the certainty of victory. As he announces his elevation to emperor, the Yellows invade, killing all defenders. The Yellow leader proclaims himself ruler of the universe as the Tramp squashes him.

EPILOGUE. Life and Death

The Tramp talks to himself in a midnight-dark forest. All around him the voices of the ants, the crickets, the beetles, Ichneumon Fly, Larva, and the butterflies are heard. The Chrysalis announces that it shall live forever. Moths arrive, dancing and singing, and one by one they fall dead. Chrysalis leaps forth a moth, begins to sing the song of the moths, and falls dead.

The Tramp kneels by its side, sorrowing for it and its dreams of greatness. Suddenly a heavy weight oppresses him. He struggles to rise but can't and cries out, "I know you, you're Death." He pleads for one more day, one more hour, but falls dead. Two snails, passing by, observe the struggle and comment on its interest.

Dawn lights up the sky as a woodcutter and a woman with a baby pass by. She fears bad luck will come of seeing the body, but the woodcutter says death is everywhere, yet there are always enough people. They cover the body with leaves and the woman drops a flower, as school girls pass by.

PAUL CLAUDEL

Break of Noon   [*Partage de midi*, written 1905,

performed 1916; revised and performed 1948]

ACT ONE

The Indian Ocean is absolutely calm, and four passengers sun themselves
on the deck of a packet boat on its way from Europe to the Far East at the end
of the nineteenth century. When De Ciz and his wife Yse leave, Mesa admits to
Amalric that though he knows little about women, Yse seems to him an im-
pudent coquette. His friend assures him that, on the contrary, she is a noble and
spirited woman, needing either to conquer and tyrannize or to offer herself
completely. She ought, he says, to be a hero's wife with some great duty to con-
sume her energies, but De Ciz is merely an ordinary man and a mediocre lover
who has only known how to give her one child after another in their ten years
of marriage.

When the couple return, the four chat about the homeless state all are in
physically and spiritually. Amalric, a commercial adventurer of buoyant temperament, lost his fortune last year and is going to the Orient to seek it again. De
Ciz, although less self-confident, also hopes to find a new career in the new
frontiers opening to trade in China. Yse makes herself a comfortable temporary
home wherever the trunks, her hatbox, and her children happen to be. Mesa is
discontentedly fleeing his past and wondering pessimistically about his future,
despite the fact that in worldly matters he has done well. They note that just as
the sun is approaching high noon, they four are approaching the crucial "break
of noon" in their affairs.

De Ciz pulls Mesa aside to discuss business prospects, leaving Yse and
Amalric alone to reminisce about their brief period of love ten years ago when
Yse was twenty and about their mixed emotions upon unexpectedly recognizing
each other after the boat had sailed. She protests that she and De Ciz love each
other, after a fashion, although Amalric's strength and confidence obviously
tempt her again. Indeed, Amalric is *too* strong, she explains; she prefers to have
her lover have some need of her. She questions him about Mesa, who puzzles
her by not succumbing to her charm. Amalric tries to explain what he himself
cannot understand: this highly successful young administrative official, who advises the viceroy of southern China and is responsible for the railroad and
telegraph lines pushing their way into the interior, this Mesa has "other ideas
. . . religious mania," and intends on this trip to find other men to take over
all his worldly responsibilities.

Amalric tries once more to win Yse; shrugged off, he withdraws as Mesa

99

approaches. Although Mesa resents Yse's attempts to draw him out, he feels a mysterious compulsion to speak before her of his struggles with the devouring presence of God in his soul. He describes how at first he had tried to ignore the divine call, traveling the globe to find an activity energy-consuming enough to exclude it. Finally he had turned, overcome, and offered his soul to the service of God. But he had been refused. Or rather, there was the terrible absence of any answer whatsoever; now he is vainly flying from that silence. But his spiritual path is blocked by this woman who says, "Mesa, I am Yse, it is I"—only to wonder at herself for saying it a moment later. They are both rather frightened at the implications of their recognition of each other, each the necessary complement of the other's soul. They will admit for the moment only that Yse is the woman Mesa *would have* loved had circumstances been otherwise, but, unspoken, the tense awareness grows that inevitably they *will* love each other, despite Yse's marriage and Mesa's prior commitment of his soul to God.

They are trying to obviate this discovery by solemnly swearing not to love each other, when Amalric returns carrying a tray of drinks, already slightly intoxicated and very voluble. De Ciz joins them, and all drink to their coming adventures in the East as the ship's bell rings out noon.

ACT TWO

Mesa explores the Hong Kong cemetery, where Yse has asked him to meet her, but disappears just before Yse enters with De Ciz, who boasts to his wife about his current business affairs. When he says that in a few days he will have to leave her for a month or two, Yse begs him not to. He is surprised, for there is no apparent danger to either of them, and she has never before exhibited unreasonable nervous whims. He is rather pleased that the proud and independent Yse is actually begging him for something, but can see no reason for yielding, and finally persuades her to say she won't be angry if he goes. Then he mentions the career possibilities that Mesa has offered him: one of dull routine in the city, the other with the railroads in the interior, full of danger and exciting challenge and almost limitless opportunity for a capable man, its worst drawback being that he would have to go alone for a year or two before Yse could join him. For that reason, says Yse, he must not take it. He leaves for a business appointment, and Mesa reappears.

Yse tells him that he must not come to visit her when De Ciz is away; Mesa agrees. Nevertheless, he approaches closer to her, with trembling hands. "God has repulsed you," says Yse, "but I do not." They commit themselves deliberately and solemnly, each to give his soul freely and totally, not so much to the other as to that mysterious entity that results of their union. They acknowledge that their unlawful love cannot be a fertile love, bringing happiness, but a destructive love, bringing death; yet they consent to be condemned to each other. Yse's first request is that Mesa send De Ciz on the long and dangerous mission—where he wants to go anyway.

De Ciz returns, and Yse leaves the two men together. De Ciz announces his regretful intention to take the safe position in town, because Yse wants him to. Mesa congratulates him on his wisdom but manages to praise the security of the one job and deplore the difficulties of the other in such terms that De Ciz is overcome by a joyous determination to change his mind despite—as he thinks —the wishes of his wife and the earnest concern of his good friend Mesa.

ACT THREE

One evening about two years later, Yse sits knitting an infant's garment in a barricaded Confucian temple in a small Chinese port. Amalric enters, and they embrace at length, commenting calmly that the setting sun is the last they will see. The revolutionary fever of the natives has broken out in a wave of indiscriminate violence toward all white men; the rest of the community here was tortured and massacred last night, and since there is no hope of escape, Amalric buries a time bomb under the floor so that at least they will not be taken alive.

As they settle down for their last night together, they reminisce. Yse recollects that she loved Mesa for a year, De Ciz being off in the interior; but she began to feel that, despite his love for her, he really wanted her to leave him, that he could not help but reserve some part of his soul from her, and that this secret part resented her presence as an obstacle to some even greater love—the love of God. So when business forces them to separate for the first time, she deliberately yielded to Amalric, although pregnant with Mesa's child, who now is lying ill in the next room. And even though Amalric betrayed his promise to have her other children brought to her, she says she does not regret her decision; it was for Mesa's own good, despite the terrible accusing letters that he has written for a year and that she has not answered. She has come close, with Amalric, to finding a satisfying kind of ordinary domestic peaceful love.

Amalric goes out to make his final rounds; soon afterwards Mesa enters, demanding to know what he has done that she should leave him and not even answer his letters. At the same time he declares that the past doesn't matter, for he has found her; he has a pass that will take them through the rebel-held territory, and since De Ciz is dead, they can get married. Yse will not look at him or answer him. Accused by her silence, he alternately accuses and defends himself: no, he could never succeed in giving her that last important part of himself, but neither could she elicit it from him. It was neither's fault, and the fault of both. But he staunchly refuses to believe that she no longer loves him; they share something mysterious and profound, and he protests that she has not the right to abandon it.

Amalric enters, quickly grasps the situation, and tells Yse that she has only to speak if she wants to go with Mesa. As she continues silent, Mesa pulls a gun from his pocket; Amalric wrestles with him until Mesa falls unconscious, a leg and a shoulder obviously injured. Yse finally speaks the one word *assassin*. But soon she is answering Amalric matter-of-factly; they agree to take Mesa's pass and escape, leaving him to explode in their place, since he cannot move. Yse goes to get the infant, but it has died; they leave.

Mesa recovers consciousness. He addresses to God a long monologue of confession, self-explanation, and the beginning of an understanding of the pattern of his life. Yse returns, all urgency to talk, not to allocate blame, but to share it and pardon it in each other. She states that earthly happiness, like their infant, was doomed to a brief life, for they had demanded of their love an impossible totality of communion. Mesa recognizes what Yse has always known instinctively—that there is an analogy between his inability to dedicate his soul totally to God and his inability totally to share it with Yse. As he had glimpsed in his solitude, perhaps it was God who had deliberately used Yse to reveal to him his own egoism and the real significance of involvement with another. Mesa and Yse exult in the affirmation that they can never escape each other— and thus never lose each other. They share a strangely joyous mood as they anticipate the "break of midnight" and the explosion that will transmute their love into eternity.

PAUL   CLAUDEL

The Satin Slipper [*Le Soulier de satin,*

written 1919–1924; performed 1943]

NOTE: The original version of the play is a "Spanish action in four days," each "day" analogous to one play in a tetralogy. The revision for the stage (1943), little more than half the length of the original, combines the first two "days" as Part I, calls the third "day" Part II, and reduces the fourth "day" to an Epilogue.

PART I

The announcer informs the audience that the scene is the entire world, especially Spain, at the close of the sixteenth century, warning that the author has freely condensed countries and periods.

Somewhere in the middle of the Atlantic Ocean, a Jesuit father, bound to the mast of a stricken vessel that pirates have left to sink, joyfully accepts his fate as God's will and prays for his brother Rodrigo, who has left his novitiate in the holy order and mistakenly believes himself to have turned away from God. The Jesuit prays that Rodrigo's circuitous and turbulent path will still lead him to the Lord and that his unconsummated love for a woman will so wound his proud and independent concern with self that he learns what it means to long for, and be longed for, by another.

Standing before his prosperous home in Spain, the aging Don Pelagio explains to his knight Don Balthazar that, since he is called to attend to the affairs of a dying cousin, he must entrust his wife, Doña Prouheze, to the knight's care. He directs that Prouheze shall journey to an inn at the seashore to await his return and the ship that will carry them back to their governorship in Africa; he furthermore commands the reluctant Don Balthazar to serve as her knight-protector.

Elsewhere in the garden, Doña Prouheze converses with Don Camillo, keeping a hedge between them. Camillo declares his love and begs her to join him in responding to the mysterious and urgent call of pagan Africa. When she refuses, he pledges to make Mogador, the garrison on the Moroccan coast assigned him by the Spanish king, a dominion all his own, the site of such criminal deeds that Prouheze will be forced to come, to save his soul and the king's sovereignty.

From behind a barred window in a village near the sea, Doña Isabel whispers to her lover, Don Luis. She urges him to rescue her from her tyrannical brother tomorrow by ambushing the procession of Our Lady, in which she will be a maid of honor, as it goes ceremonially into the mountains to meet the procession of Santiago (Saint James), the patron saint of Spain.

As her caravan approaches to leave Don Pelagio's house, Doña Prouheze begs Don Balthazar to guard her well, confessing that she has written Rodrigo to meet her at the inn and that she will make every effort to escape with him. When Balthazar protests such ill conduct toward her noble husband, she retorts that the just but stern Don Pelagio has never spoken a tender word of love to her, whereas she constantly hears the voice of Rodrigo calling her, although she was acquainted with him only a few days. She knows she is pursuing a course toward sin but cannot stop of her own will: therefore she warns her protector to stop her by force, and as they pass the statue of Our Lady, she places one of her satin slippers in its hands, praying that when she tries to rush toward evil, it will be with a limping foot.

In the royal palace, the chancellor persuades the king of Spain that Don Rodrigo of Manacor, although young and hard to discipline, is the only man suitable for the post of viceroy of all the Spanish conquests in the Americas.

Rodrigo, hiding in the hills from the king's messengers, discusses his love for Prouheze with his Chinese servant. They watch the ceremonial meeting of the processions of Our Lady and Santiago. When they see an armed attack on the group, they assume that bandits are trying to steal the solid silver statue of Saint James and rush to the rescue.

At the seaside inn nearby, a rascally Neapolitan sergeant confides to the Negress Jobarbara, Prouheze's attendant, that the young girl he brought to the inn hidden in a cartload of rushes is Doña Musica, who detested the ugly peasant whom Don Pelagio was trying to make her marry. The sergeant enticed her to flee with him by telling her that the king of Naples had seen her in a dream and sent him to find her, a birthmark proving her identity.

In the garden of the inn, Prouheze and Musica sit chattering together. Charmed with one another, they discuss their loves: Musica's is all fantasy and joy, Prouheze's a suffering that she gladly accepts, stating that she will be to Rodrigo a sword through the heart.

After noises of battle, Rodrigo appears, badly wounded, near the corpse of Don Luis. Still ignorant of the true nature of the attack he thwarted, he borrows a carriage from Don Fernand, Isabel's brother. Fernand forces Isabel, aghast at her lover's death, to thank Rodrigo for saving the procession.

A day or so later, the Chinese servant finds Jobarbara dancing in the garden of the inn. He informs her that Rodrigo is at his mother's castle four leagues away, dying of his wounds and calling for Prouheze. Jobarbara asks how Prouheze is supposed to escape her guard, and the servant explains that he told a party searching for Doña Musica that they would find her held by pirates at this inn: an attack is planned for the next evening, and Prouheze is to slip out in the confusion.

The next evening, Prouheze scrambles with immense difficulty through the briary ravine. Her guardian angel observes and comments: she does not see him, although she occasionally hears his words, interpreting them to suit her own thoughts. The angel must officially condemn her action, but secretly he is sympathetic toward her and even proud of the fight she makes for her passion.

Meanwhile, Don Balthazar confesses indirectly to his lieutenant that he could not resist Doña Prouheze's appeals. Although still pretending to fortify the inn against both escape and attack, he ensures that her way is left unguarded; then, having betrayed both Don Pelagio and his own honor, he also ensures his own death when the search party attacks. In the background, a boat carries Doña Musica, Jobarbara, and the Neapolitan sergeant out to sea; their singing mixes with the noise of the muskets' firing.

Two weeks later Doña Honoria, Rodrigo's mother, receives Don Pelagio at her castle. She informs him that, although Rodrigo is close to death, Prouheze has not asked to go to his bedside but has remained silent in her room. Pelagio suggests that the women desire his death so that Prouheze, widowed and free, could inspire Rodrigo with the will to live. Honoria denies the suggestion but admits that she fears Pelagio's notions of what is good for his young wife. Pelagio retorts that he has been misunderstood: he brings neither reproaches nor a tender appeal, but rather "to replace one temptation, another temptation still greater."

Alone with her in her room, Pelagio pretends to believe that Prouheze very sensibly remembered their distant kinship with Honoria and fled to her after Balthazar died in the attack on the inn. Surprised, she lets him distract her with reminiscences of Africa and indignantly repudiates his accusation that she has lost interest in continuing their fierce struggle there. But how can she be of service any more, she cried, when she cannot even keep Rodrigo from dying? Pelagio convinces her that she can never help Rodrigo—except to damnation— with the gift of herself, because she has already given her soul, the most valuable part of her, into her husband's keeping and cannot reclaim it to give another. But she *can* do Rodrigo good, he proposes, simply by doing that which is good in itself. He excites her interest with news that the king is giving her a task the size of her soul, a castle tremendously difficult to hold, and that she must die rather than give up its keys. The castle is Mogador: the king distrusts

Don Camillo and wants Prouheze to replace him as governor. Prouheze states that she cannot accept the charge, but Pelagio replies that he knows she has already accepted it. She rises and goes to put on her traveling clothes.

In the palace, the king tells Pelagio that he has changed his mind about leaving Prouheze at Mogador, threatened by Moors from without and treason from within. Since Rodrigo has finally agreed to go to America on condition that Prouheze be recalled, the king is sending him to Mogador with the royal order. Pelagio asks the purpose of thus torturing the lovers. The king answers that he wants his viceroy's heart stuffed with enough fuel for a lifetime's consuming fire, so that he will be immune to the lesser passions of ambition, greed, or luxury. Pelagio agrees to attach his own letter of recall to the king's and Rodrigo's but predicts that Prouheze has come to grips with her destiny and will choose to remain.

Becalmed at sea within sight of Mogador, the impatient Rodrigo confesses to his ship's captain that it was hearing his rival Camillo's name in conjunction with Prouheze's that called him back from the shores of death when his mother's prayers had failed. He ruefully admires Pelagio's strategy: "His wife guarantees him against Don Camillo, and Don Camillo guarantees him against me."

Within the fortress, Camillo gloats over having Prouheze in his power. She reveals that she has already won the loyalty of all the soldiers and thus has him instead in her power. She points out that unless he wants to declare openly his piratical intentions against his king and confess his fear of a woman to boot, he cannot even send her away with Rodrigo.

In a moonlit forest near Sicily, Doña Musica entertains the viceroy of Naples, who found her cave accidentally after wandering away from his men. Although he has not identified himself, she knows him for the king of Naples promised her by the sergeant, who drowned when their boat sank a little way from this shore. Although at first puzzled, the young man responds to her gay chatter and soon is convinced that he has always known her as a singing in his heart, even when he wasn't aware that it was she. They delight in having found each other and anticipate further mysteries of joy when God unites them.

Rodrigo confronts Camillo in a room of the fortress. Camillo hints that Prouheze may be listening to their interview from behind a curtain; his language is formal and exaggeratedly polite, but he taunts Rodrigo scathingly with allusions to his own official intimacy with her excellency and the absurdity of Rodrigo's mission, which amounts to saying, "Come, Madam, prove you love me by returning to your husband while I go to America." Camillo returns Rodrigo's letter, on the back of which Prouheze has written, "I stay. You go." Although tempted to cry out an appeal that she could not resist, Rodrigo accepts her answer and retires.

The double shadow of a man with a woman appears and speaks. It accuses Prouheze and Rodrigo of having created it for a single instant when they met by accident and kissed on the watchman's walk at Mogador—and then of cruelly severing it, carrying its quivering halves to opposite ends of the globe. And yet, the shadow complains, what has once existed is forever "stamped on the page of eternity," so that its oneness still exists despite earthly separation of the bodies that created it.

The moon now looks down at Prouheze, sleeping at Mogador on one side of the stage, and at Rodrigo, sleeping at sea on the other. The moon speaks of kissing the heart of each. Prouheze stirs and murmurs that the Cross will be her marriage bed with Rodrigo, for he will suffer through her until he is stripped of his selfish ego and is prepared to meet her in the presence of God. Rodrigo stirs and groans that Prouheze's arms opened to his sight the Paradise that God never revealed to him—only to show him that he is excluded from it.

PART II

The announcer summarizes the developments of more than ten years later. At Mogador, Camillo watches over the sleeping Prouheze, now his wife. At Prague, Musica prays with gratitude for her husband's military victory and with hope for the unborn child she carries. In Panama, viceroy Rodrigo has become exceedingly powerful: all the world considers him with respect and some fear, but he is incorruptible and unfailing in guarding his king's interests. And all the world—except Rodrigo—has heard of the "letter to Rodrigo" that Prouheze started on its journey ten years ago, calling him to Mogador; it has passed through countless hands, usually bringing misfortune to those who touch it.

Prouheze awakens alone, hearing Rodrigo's voice in the sound of the ocean that both separates and unites them. Her guardian angel appears to her. Their dialogue demonstrates the guardian angel's role as spiritual fisherman: he has hooked her, but never tugs too hard, rather playing his line out and in as her writhings require. Furthermore, he explains, she is not the major prize he angles for, but the bait for Rodrigo. Surprised, Prouheze learns that God is not jealous of man's love for woman, and that although love outside the sacrament is a sin, even sin also serves God's purposes. Angling carefully, the angel persuades Prouheze that she can best serve Rodrigo and keep his love by becoming a guiding star for him. She eagerly consents. However, the angel tells her, she must first obtain Rodrigo's permission to die for him; moreover, she must receive death at his hands.

Doña Isabel, now wife of Rodrigo's chief subordinate and a favored attendant on the viceroy, obtains possession of the "letter to Rodrigo." Calculating that her husband's only hope of advancement lies in Rodrigo's departure, she puts the viceroy in a nostalgic mood by singing a plaintive love song before giving him the letter. The letter's request moves Rodrigo to depart for Mogador, and he entrusts his authority to Isabel's husband as he boards ship.

At Mogador, Camillo and Prouheze, both in Arab costume, engage in a duel of wits and wills. Camillo has vowed never to touch her again, since she is insultingly indifferent to his body, but asks curiously why she married him. She replies that when her husband died and the troops deserted her, it was the best way she could think of to retain some influence over him; and indeed she had been able to soften the effects of his piratical attacks on passing ships, now that he had openly declared the independence of his little domain from the king of Spain. He laughs at the power she thinks she has, pointing out that he has been able to have her whipped and indirectly threatening to have her killed. She retorts that she has already received notice of her death from another. Camillo furiously recognizes that Rodrigo's spirit has visited her nightly, to the extent that Prouheze's little daughter, whom Camillo physically fathered, resembled Rodrigo instead. Camillo also recognizes, perhaps even better than she does, that Prouheze is to Rodrigo, more than a body or even a soul, a bringer of God; he despairs at her refusal to be a bringer of God through love to him as well. He warns her that to be a true star for Rodrigo she must belong to God alone.

On board Rodrigo's ship, becalmed off Mogador for two weeks, the viceroy and the captain observe the Moors retreating after the day's attack on the fortress. They guess that the Moors interpret the ship's presence to mean that Spain is going to reclaim the fortress from Camillo; apparently the Moors, aided by mutineers among Camillo's troops, intend to plunder the castle before its defense is taken over again by Spain. The captain spots a boat approaching under the white flag of parley.

The envoy is Prouheze, leading her little girl. Rodrigo asks her to speak before all his assembled sailors. Her official message is that Rodrigo must leave and that Camillo will defend Mogador. Rodrigo replies that Mogador's fate is of no interest to him, for he came only in response to a letter. She declares that in the ten years since she sent out that appeal, she has decided no longer to cry for help. Her work is here, she says, doing as much as she can against Camillo's evil tendency; he sometimes has her whipped out of fury, she boasts, but he more or less obeys her. It was after the first whipping that she despairingly wrote the famous letter. Rodrigo, who had been deeply hurt by the knowledge that she had married Camillo, now rejoices to learn that only her body has been with the renegade, that her spirit has been true to him. He accepts responsibility for the daughter she says she is giving him to keep but asks whether she thereby implies that she herself means to return to Camillo. She answers that Camillo's proposition is that Rodrigo may take Prouheze with him if he will leave with his fleet immediately—and that she expects to hear him refuse the offer. Rodrigo and some of the ship's officers demand why. She answers that Camillo would be only too pleased to get rid of her and make Rodrigo obliged to him with one stroke. For her to come with him would be only a sordid adultery; the only way not to degrade their love is for him to let her die. If she returns, the castle will be blown up at midnight, so he need not be tortured by the thought of her in the hands of either Camillo or the Moors.

Addressing his men at length, Rodrigo complains that the humblest laborer receives his wages but that he who created a new world is being refused his. He then leads Prouheze to a great cross with no figure on it, confessing he knows that it is the nuptial couch awaiting them. As she prepares to leave the ship, emotion overpowers him again, and he threatens to keep her by force. "Say one word, then, and I stay," tempts Prouheze, repeating the offer over and over as she goes over the side. But Rodrigo cannot say the word; and the child begins to scream for her mother as Prouheze's boat is rowed away.

EPILOGUE

The announcer summarizes the events of the next dozen years or more. The king of Spain, fearing the power of his viceroy of the Indies, dispatched him to the Orient to make further conquests for Christendom, but was not too displeased when Rodrigo lost his leg as well as a battle and was imprisoned for several years. Rodrigo returned with a wooden leg and a Japanese servant, who executed on paper his master's grand conceptions of pictures of the saints and sold them to the fishermen. The king divined the defeat of the Spanish Armada while the rest of his court still believed the rumors of victory; he decided, for sport, to pretend to make Rodrigo viceroy of the supposedly conquered England. To the king's uneasy amusement, Rodrigo imperiously refused the mission because the king would not agree to his conditions as to the treatment of the conquered nation; the spectacle of mockery over, the king called Rodrigo a traitor and gave him as a salable slave to his chamberlain. After passing through several hands, Rodrigo is now in chains, being rowed by two soldiers to the slave market at Barcelona. In the meantime, Prouheze's daughter, Mary of the Seven Swords, met and fell in love with Don John of Austria, heroic son of Musica and the former viceroy of Naples; ignorant of Rodrigo's fate, she is now swimming out to join her beloved's ship and help him fight the Turks.

The two soldiers tease Rodrigo by refusing to give him a letter from his daughter, as he calls Doña Sevenswords. Finally they read it aloud, interrupting with insulting comments. The letter discloses her plan to join Don John, saying, "The king has given you England; you have no more need of me." A postscript adds that she will have the ship fire its cannon as a sign of her safe arrival. In the boat is the monk Brother Leon, who tries to stop the soldiers' rudeness. He proves to have been the captive monk who married Prouheze and Camillo; he tries to distract Rodrigo from his agonized reflections on his dead beloved, which finally culminate in a calmer sense of freedom and sorrowful joy. A nun boards their boat, looking for cast-off odds and ends to sell for the benefit of the convents of Mother Teresa. Rodrigo asks her to take him with her to be a servant of a convent. Brother Leon persuades the soldiers to give up their captive, on the ground that this queer old Rodrigo might yet prove to be a dangerous possession, and the nun consents to take him if they will also give her the iron cauldron she has her eye on.

As they go over the side into the nun's boat, trumpets and cannon are heard from the direction of John of Austria's ship. Rodrigo rejoices that his child is safe, and Brother Leon prays for deliverance of souls in prison.

PAUL CLAUDEL

The Tidings Brought to Mary

[*L'Annonce faite à Marie,* 1912; this version performed 1948]

PROLOGUE

At dawn on a prosperous medieval French farm, eighteen-year-old Violaine Vercors intercepts the architect-builder Pierre de Craon as he is about to steal quietly away. They allude to a previous meeting when Violaine rebuffed his attempt to make love to her. He states that he still loves her but knows his life has been destined, not for domesticity, but for the raising of beautiful churches to the glory of God. Furthermore, he has discovered on his body the first signs of leprosy, which must enforce his withdrawal from the comforts of human contact. Violaine, in contrast, anticipates a future of the simplest human happiness; for she is pledged to the man she loves.

Having heard that the women of Rheims are donating their jewels toward the construction of Pierre's next cathedral, she asks Pierre to take the antique golden ring that Jacques gave her as a love token. Pierre asks whether a ring, not her entire soul, is all she will contribute to the glory of God; but she makes him admit that God commands most people to His service through ordinary life, and only a few through the saintly self-sacrifice of total dedication, such as that of Pierre or of the nuns immured in the convent supported by the Vercors farm. She exclaims, "How beautiful the world is, and how happy I am!" To which he replies, "How beautiful the world is, and how unhappy I am!" She bids him be worthy of the difficult life to which his creative gift compels him, then, unaware that her younger sister Mara is now watching, cries, "Poor Pierre," and kisses him on the mouth before he leaves.

ACT ONE

Anne Vercors, a vigorous man of sixty, tells his wife Elizabeth that since they have no son, he intends to marry their eldest daughter Violaine to Jacques Hury, whom they have raised from childhood; Anne is confident he is a good man and a well-trained manager to take over the farm. Elizabeth suggests that perhaps the young people have other preferences: Violaine has obviously been admiring their guest Pierre all winter, and Mara has confided to her mother her violent love for Jacques. Anne is angry, and wants to settle the matter immediately. Elizabeth asks why he is in such a hurry; Anne announces that he is leaving that day on a pilgrimage to Jerusalem, and thus anxious to put a man at the head of his farm and family before departing. Elizabeth tries to restrain him with pleas that the family might need him; but Anne's soul is disturbed by the social and spiritual turmoil in the world—there is no real king of France, and there are three rival Popes instead of one—and he wins Elizabeth's release to reaffirm his sense of order and purpose by touching himself the geographical center of the world's moral order, the hole on Calvary wherein stood the Cross.

As Anne leaves in search of Jacques, Mara reveals herself, insisting that her mother tell Violaine that Mara will hang herself if her sister marries Jacques. Anne enters with Jacques, followed by Violaine and all the servants and peasants who work the farm. He ceremonially turns his leadership over to the young man, joining Jacques's hand with Violaine's when the young people accept each other. Content, he breaks and blesses bread for the whole community, bids his family farewell, and departs.

ACT TWO

Elizabeth, sadly puzzled, reports to Mara that Violaine merely laughed strangely when her mother gave her Mara's ultimatum. Mara goes to meet Jacques, who returns today from two weeks of preparation for his wedding tomorrow. She had told him previously about seeing Violaine kiss Pierre, but now it is Jacques who brings up the subject of his fiancée's apparent perfidy, although declaring himself certain that Violaine will somehow explain everything.

Jacques and Violaine meet tenderly by a fountain. He notices the absence of his ring on her hand but has faith when she says she will shortly explain. She insists with peculiar urgency on reiterating her love for him and on hearing him repeat his love for her. Finally, when he is baffled and hurt because she cries, "Don't touch me!" at his proffered embrace, she gives her explanation. Requesting his knife, she slits her dress and shows him the leprous patch on her skin. His sympathy for her affliction is drowned in his agony that this must prove that Violaine has yielded her body to the leper Pierre. He demands point-blank to know whether Mara saw her kiss Pierre; she replies that Mara never lies. He asks whether she denies that Pierre has possessed her. She says, "I deny nothing," and announces her intention to obey the law that evening by showing her contagion to the priest and seeking seclusion in the leper's hovel near Geyn. To avoid scandal, he helps her disguise her departure as a visit to Jacques's mother, but they actually fool neither Mara nor Elizabeth.

ACT THREE

On Christmas Eve seven years later, workmen are preparing the road by which Joan of Arc will lead King Charles the next day to be consecrated at Rheims Cathedral, the spire of which is just being finished tonight by Pierre de Craon. Mara approaches, carrying a parcel under her cloak, and inquires the whereabouts of the leper woman of Geyn. As they tell her, cursing the object of their grudging charity, Violaine comes begging for her meager dole; Mara follows her back to the hovel in the forest.

Violaine at first mistakes her sister's voice for her mother's, and Mara learns that the disease has made her blind. Violaine inquires after the farm, which has prospered and grown. She learns that her mother is dead, that her father has not yet returned, and that Mara and Jacques are lovingly married and have a daughter Aubaine. Mara cannot comprehend Violaine's loving devotion to God, since God has obviously made her suffer terribly. Nor can she comprehend her sister's behavior when she learns that Violaine had not been Pierre's lover, but had deliberately let Jacques think so to free him of his love for her so that he could marry Mara. Mara protests that she would never willingly have relinquished anything she wanted. Violaine replies that she was not *willing* to relinquish Jacques but that God forced her with the touch of leprosy.

Suddenly Mara takes her dead infant Aubaine from under her cloak, thrusts it into Violaine's arms, and demands that she return it to life. Violaine protests that she is no saint to perform miracles but can only suffer and supplicate. Mara cries angrily that if she had Violaine's access to God, she wouldn't let Him snatch her baby so easily.

Violaine snuggles the tiny corpse under her robe, and as the church bells begin to ring for midnight Mass and trumpets announce the king's approach to Rheims, she gives Mara a prayer book and asks her to read the Office for Christmas. Mara reads haltingly, feeling herself unworthy of the words; angels, heard only by Violaine, chant the responses. At last Violaine repeats with double significance, "For unto us a child is born"; and Mara bursts into tears. But when she is calm enough to receive her living daughter, she sees that the infant's eyes, formerly dark like hers, are now blue like Violaine's, and there are traces of milk on the child's lips.

ACT FOUR [stage version]

The next spring, shortly before dawn, Jacques and Mara are talking of Anne when he unexpectedly walks in carrying the body of the dying Violaine, whom he has found almost buried in a nearby sand pit. Anne tells the still-jealous Jacques that he met Pierre—cured of his leprosy—in Jerusalem and learned the innocence of that single kiss. As the father interprets it, the same call that drew him to Jerusalem came to Violaine, like the angel's call to Mary when she conceived of the Holy Ghost. At the time of her most serene happiness, Violaine conceived of the great sadness in the world and kissed Pierre in compassionate homage to the suffering in human life. Jacques now learns that he owes his daughter's life to Violaine, but Mara fiercely argues that it was God's deed, and that she herself had compelled God by her passionate need and faith, and was thus most responsible for the miracle. She was also responsible, she admits, for silently leading Violaine to the edge of the sand pit a few hours before, when she found her sister wandering blindly in the neighborhood. But Anne mitigates her guilt and says that the same fierce instinct that recovered Aubaine's life compelled her to protect Jacques from a painful distraction and her child from the dichotomy of having two mothers. Violaine recovers consciousness long enough to be reconciled with Jacques and Mara, to breathe a wistful praise of the living world she has little known and now leaves, and to sigh her relief as she slips into the comforting obscurity of death. As the angelus of dawn rings out, Jacques and Mara turn toward each other in profound acceptance both of their new understanding and of each other.

In the much longer reading version of this act, Pierre has returned; the various confrontations after all these years begin acrimoniously and develop gradually into a much fuller exposition of the characters' reconciliations with each other, with life, and with God.

J E A N   C O C T E A U

The Infernal Machine

[*La Machine infernale*, 1934]

A Voice reviews the story of Oedipus. To defeat Apollo's oracle that her infant will kill his father and marry his mother, Queen Jocasta of Thebes pierces and binds the baby's ankles and abandons him on a mountain. When a shepherd finds him and carries him to the childless rulers of Corinth, they adopt him and raise him as their own. To defeat Apollo's oracle that he will kill his father and marry his mother, young Oedipus flees Corinth. In a stupid quarrel at a crossroads he accidentally kills an old man, ignorant that it is his real father Laius.

He learns that Thebes is suffering under the scourge of a Sphinx that reportedly poses riddles to the young men who go out to slay the monster and kills them when they cannot answer. Queen Jocasta has vowed to wed whoever conquers the Sphinx. Oedipus goes, he conquers, he marries; and four children are born of the incest. Then the plague attacks Thebes, and the priests say the gods are punishing the city for harboring a terrible criminal who must be cast out. As Oedipus investigates, the truth of his own history is revealed. Jocasta hangs herself; then Oedipus stabs out his eyes with her brooch and wanders off as the unhappiest of mortals. The Voice invites the spectator to watch the tightly coiled spring unwind slowly throughout a human life, "one of the most perfect machines constructed by the infernal gods for the mathematical annihilation of a mortal."

ACT ONE

Two soldiers on the watchtower of Thebes recount to their chief how they have been visited on several occasions by the ghost of Laius. The phantom seemed to have some urgent warning for them to convey to Jocasta, but could never muster the strength to stay visible and audible at the same time and to fight off the invisible forces which apparently were restraining him. The soldiers passed the incomplete message on to Jocasta via palace servants, and the chief is incensed that they did not first report directly to him. He commands them not to let anyone approach without the password, ghost or no ghost, and leaves them to realize that he no more believes in the phantom than he does in the Sphinx. The cynical view prevalent among many is that both are tricks played by a politically ambitious Tiresias and his priests to disguise their usurpation of power from a weak and credulous queen.

Youthful-looking Jocasta begins to climb the stairs to the platform with the almost blind Tiresias. Nervous, querulous, and fanciful, she is determined to speak with the soldiers who saw the ghost of Laius, despite the opposition of Tiresias and the chief. She is captivated by the younger soldier, who is just the age her son would have been, and willingly believes his story.

The ghost of Laius materializes during the interview, calling pitifully to his wife, but neither she nor the soldiers can see or hear him. Only when the two soldiers are left alone again can they perceive him, but the phantom is forced to disappear just as he is saying, "Tell the Queen that a young man approaches Thebes and that he must not under any pretext . . ."

ACT TWO

Out in the desert, the Sphinx, in the form of a young girl dressed in white, complains that she is tired of killing. Her companion Anubis, a god of the dead in the shape of a jackal, laughs at her for developing such human sensibilities and reminds her that they must obey their orders, just as the gods whom they obey must obey theirs. He slips away as a matron with two small children mistakes the Sphinx for a late traveler like herself; the woman chatters about the different opinions held in Thebes concerning the Sphinx and about her own sorrow in losing a son to the monster, then leaves with her children.

Anubis reappears to talk to the Sphinx. More than ever the Sphinx would like to die herself in order to stop killing. But this can only happen when a young man comes with whom she falls in love and who can answer her riddle fearlessly and as an equal.

Anubis leaves as Oedipus comes. After questioning him as a young girl, the Sphinx mounts her pedestal and reveals her true self, binding him with invisible ties so that he cannot move. It is clear from her words that she wants to show him the full extent of her power so that he will realize how great is her favor when she refrains from killing him, hoping that he will love her in return. She tells him the riddle, laughs that he cannot answer it despite his earlier boasting, then tells him the solution. Thus, when Anubis appears and forces her to pose the riddle, Oedipus boldly gives the answer and is free. The Sphinx's love turns to spiteful wrath, however, when Oedipus runs off toward Thebes without so much as a grateful glance for her. Anubis reminds her that vengeance will be hers, since she is actually Nemesis, goddess of retributive justice.

Oedipus returns, having remembered that he needs a slain body to prove his conquest. The Sphinx amiably goes behind a ruin to strip off her body, even substituting the jackal's head for her own, since the Thebans expect a monster. Oedipus carts the corpse off boastfully, while Anubis and Nemesis, veiled, take pity on "poor, poor, poor men."

ACT THREE

Jocasta and Oedipus are exhausted from a full day of coronation and wedding festivities, but while Jocasta leaves the bedchamber to make herself beautiful for her wedding night, tradition demands that Oedipus receive a visit from Tiresias. The seer warns him that the sacrificial omens have not been favorable. Oedipus, hostile, interprets that to mean that while Jocasta enjoys the romance of marrying an unknown, fallen from the skies, her brother Creon and Tiresias find the union with a common adventurer degrading. Tiresias cynically asks whether Oedipus can really love a woman old enough to be his mother and asserts that he loves only her title, power, and wealth. Oedipus replies that of course her queenliness is part of the reason for his love, but he feels absolutely right at her side and refuses to be threatened away.

Tiresias accuses him of outrageous pride, until Oedipus reaches out to throttle the old man. But looking into the blind eyes, he sees his future unrolling through years of children and successful reign, until suddenly his own eyes burn terribly. Tiresias scolds that thus his impudence is punished. Oedipus apologizes for his violence, making a peace offering of the fact that he is a true prince of Corinth and thus worthy of a queen's bed.

Jocasta and Oedipus laugh together over the old man. Jocasta begs to hear Oedipus' story but then dozes off. They decide to nap briefly, the better then to enjoy their bridal night, but Oedipus awakes screaming from a nightmare of Anubis. Jocasta maternally starts to undress him but cries out when she sees the scars on his ankles, for which he gives her the false explanation that he was given. To cover her confusion, she tells the story of abandoning her child, but pretends that it is the story of her laundress. She cringes when he violently denounces such an unnatural mother. She calms him to sleep again, and as a drunkard sings outside the window, she examines her face in the mirror and tries to rub a bloom into it.

ACT FOUR

After seventeen happy years the plague has come to Thebes, but Oedipus is momentarily gladdened; for a messenger has brought news that the king of Corinth has died of old age, and not by the hand of Oedipus, so that the oracle seems to have been disproven. But the messenger continues that on his deathbed the king wanted Oedipus told of his adoption. One by one the facts now come out: that Laius was killed at the crossroads where Oedipus killed a nameless old man, that the laundress was an invention and Oedipus the abandoned infant, that the oracle has been fulfilled and the blasphemous cause of the plague been found. Tiresias restrains Creon in the courtyard, telling him not to interfere while a "chef d'oeuvre of horror is completed" by destiny. Oedipus rushes up to find that Jocasta has hanged herself, and their daughter Antigone comes out, crying that her father is putting out his eyes. She leads her disfigured father forth, and he accepts the offer of Tiresias' cane. The ghost of Jocasta appears, but only to the sight of the two blind men; she shadows and echoes her daughter as the child guides her father toward their future.

JEAN COCTEAU

Orpheus [*Orphée*, 1926]

PROLOGUE

The actor playing Orpheus appears before the curtain and announces that the lines he now speaks are not part of the script. Since the actors are performing at a great height and without a safety net, any noise would be severely distracting; therefore, he requests the audience not to express any reactions until the end.

THE PLAY

Orpheus and Eurydice, his wife, are at their villa in the Greek city of Thrace on a beautiful April morning. Despite the clear day, the room has the appearance of a magician's chamber. There are several French doors, a large mirror, and two niches. In one niche, there is a white horse's head upon the body of a man in ballet attire; in the other stands an empty pedestal framed with laurel branches. Orpheus, holding a spiritualist alphabet tablet, requests that the horse continue to dictate. Eurydice reproaches him for his fascination with the horse and his loss of interest in her. As they argue, the horse taps his foot, spelling out the word "hello." Orpheus is delighted at this friendly greeting. Eurydice denies the validity of the horse as a source of poetic inspiration. Orpheus replies that his life of art began in earnest only after the arrival of the horse. Now there is neither sun nor moon, only the night of the self, the uncharted universe into which the horse leads him. He then recites the sentence dictated by the horse: "Orpheus hunts Eurydice's lost life." Eurydice finds the sentence meaningless. Orpheus declares it full of mystery and beauty, "a poem of vision, a flower deep-rooted in death." With that sentence, he will win the poetry contest and defeat Aglaonice, the leader of the Bacchantes, his mortal enemy and from whom he won Eurydice.

He prepares to depart, but Eurydice begs him to stay and to beware of the Bacchantes. He laughs: let them throw stones; he will use their pebbles to make a bust of himself to place upon the empty pedestal in the niche. He dares Eurydice to break a window in his presence, as she does daily after he has gone. She admits that she does break them on purpose but refuses to do so now. Orpheus smashes one instead. Heurtebise, the glazier, appears immediately, and Orpheus departs.

Heurtebise and Eurydice lament Orpheus' absorption with the horse. Fearing that the horse will overhear and report their conversation, they move to another part of the room. Heurtebise gives Eurydice the poison he has secured from Aglaonice and an envelope for communication with her. The poison is concealed in a piece of sugar; they are about to give it to the horse when Orpheus returns. Heurtebise dashes to the window and climbs on a chair to pretend that he was repairing a pane. Orpheus, requiring a chair to reach the papers he forgot, takes the chair Heurtebise is standing on. Heurtebise remains suspended in mid-air, seemingly unaware of a lack of support. Eurydice suppresses a shriek. Orpheus then replaces the chair beneath Heurtebise's feet and leaves. Eurydice demands an explanation for this marvelous feat, stating that it is one thing to live with a horse but that when one's only friend floats on air, he becomes an object of suspicion. She now realizes that he is of the race of the horse, a part of the mystery that she has sworn to combat. Heurtebise protests that he noticed nothing and tries unsuccessfully to regain her confidence. She writes a letter to Aglaonice and seals the envelope, commenting on its peculiar taste, and orders Heurtebise to deliver it immediately. Suddenly she feels faint and paralyzed. Recognizing the peculiar poison of the Bacchantes, she urges Heurtebise to fetch Orpheus: she is dying and must tell him once more that she loves him. Apologizing to Heurtebise for insulting him, she retires to her room, crying out for Orpheus.

Death, a beautiful woman attired in a magnificent pink evening gown and fur cloak, enters through the mirror, accompanied by two assistants in surgeons' uniforms and masks. Death feeds the poisoned sugar to the horse: it dies and disappears. Azrael, the experienced assistant, instructs Raphael, the novice, in the complex procedure. Death laughs at Raphael's naïveté. Naturally, if she were a skeleton with a scythe, people would recognize her; whereas she must enter unperceived. Azrael notices that they forgot the chronometer and politely turns to the audience to borrow one. A gentleman volunteers his own and is thanked. All is now ready. Death puts on a surgeon's robe, mask, and rubber gloves. Azrael turns on a loud electric machine which, he explains, helps Death to deform and displace living things. Death slowly waves her arms, then rushes into the bedroom and returns with a dove, which she releases at the door. Their task completed, Death instructs her assistants to pack their equipment, being certain to take everything. The watch is returned to the gentleman in the audience. Death and her assistants depart through the mirror. Death's red rubber gloves, however, have been left accidentally behind.

Orpheus and Heurtebise return. Orpheus says that Eurydice is merely playing a trick, for he can see her through the window. When she disappears, Heurtebise explains that Eurydice is dead and now lives in the abode of Death. Orpheus notices the absence of the horse but declares it of no consequence. It is Eurydice he desires. For her, he would brave the Underworld. Heurtebise notices that Death has forgotten her gloves and tells Orpheus that he knows a way: if Orpheus were to return the gloves, Death would be so pleased and startled at his audacity that she would offer to reward him. Orpheus declares his readiness, but is troubled when Heurtebise entrusts him with the "secret of secrets. Mirrors are the doors through which Death comes and goes." Heurtebise evades revealing the source of his occult knowledge. Orpheus has trepidations about his capacity to enter a mirror, but Heurtebise tells him that the gloves will facilitate this. Orpheus departs through the mirror.

Heurtebise, alone, answers a knock at the door. It is a postman, and Heurtebise instructs him to slip the letter beneath the door.

Orpheus returns with Eurydice via the mirror. They declare their happiness, protest their love, and promise never to mention either the horse or the Bacchantes again. Orpheus relates that it was all very simple. There is only one terrifying detail, but they are already quite adjusted to it: if he looks at Eurydice, she must return to Death's realm. The three sit down to lunch, but Eurydice and Orpheus recommence their arguments. Heurtebise tries to keep Orpheus from facing Eurydice and to end the fighting. Suddenly, Orpheus looks at Eurydice, who immediately disappears into the mirror. Heurtebise begins to comfort Orpheus. But Orpheus announces that he did it on purpose: Eurydice irritated him; besides, she is just angry and will return momentarily. Heurtebise gives Orpheus five minutes to realize his misfortune and to comprehend the irreparable deed he has committed: to have killed the dead Eurydice who now can never return.

Orpheus, beginning to despair, notices the letter left by the postman. It is anonymous and warns Orpheus of the approaching vengeance of the Bacchantes because the initial letters of his poem, "O hell," form a word offensive to them. Heurtebise urges Orpheus to flee; Orpheus refuses. If he is hacked to pieces, he can rejoin Eurydice. He declares, "Life is shaping me, making a masterpiece," as stones fly through the window, shattering the mirror. Heurtebise is transfigured with joy. Orpheus rushes to the balcony; darkness falls and drums beat.

Orpheus' head rolls into the room, screaming in pain, crying for his body, and calling to Eurydice and Heurtebise for aid. Eurydice enters through the mirror and comforts Orpheus. She grasps his invisible hand and leads the invisible Orpheus through the mirror. The disembodied head of Orpheus remains on the floor.

A knock is heard. Heurtebise picks up the head of Orpheus and places it upon the pedestal. Then he admits the police commissioner and a scribe. The commissioner accuses Heurtebise of murdering Orpheus and relates that the Bacchantes, five hundred screaming women, came to defame Orpheus. A bleeding and torn Orpheus appeared on the balcony, and the sun went into eclipse at the outrage done to his worshiper. The women fled in terror. He states that these strange events have brought about a change of heart among the population: they now wish to honor Orpheus. Therefore, the commissioner requires a bust of Orpheus and Heurtebise points out the head of Orpheus in the niche. The commissioner is satisfied and begins an interrogation of Heurtebise. Heurtebise has difficulty answering and is without papers. Eurydice appears halfway through the mirror and calls to Heurtebise. She says she now knows his true identity. The head of Orpheus urges Heurtebise to follow Eurydice. Heurtebise plunges into the mirror. The head supplies answers to the commissioner's questions. To the question: "What is your name?" the head replies,

"Jean Cocteau." Suddenly, the commissioner perceives that though all the exits are barred, Heurtebise has vanished. He and the scribe depart, with the head of Orpheus, in search of Heurtebise.

Eurydice, Orpheus, and Heurtebise re-enter through the mirror; but the location is now heaven. They exude joy and peace as they prepare to dine. Orpheus sends up a prayer of thanksgiving for being assigned paradise as a dwelling place; for having been sent Heurtebise as a guardian angel; for the salvation of Eurydice—who died because she killed the devil in the guise of a horse and thereby served love; for the salvation of Orpheus because he worshiped poetry—for God is poetry.

Orpheus and Eurydice sit down. Heurtebise offers to serve them, but Orpheus, respectfully, requests that Eurydice pour the wine.

N O E L   C O W A R D

Blithe Spirit [1941]

ACT ONE

On a summer evening in the living room of Charles Condomine's house in Kent, Ruth gives her new maid, Edith, instructions for dinner and asks her to walk, not run, about the house. She tells her husband Charles that she is afraid the evening will be awful: they have invited Madame Arcati, a spiritualist, and Dr. and Mrs. Bradman, who are certain to be skeptical of spiritualism, and she is afraid that she will burst out laughing. Charles proposes a toast to *The Unseen*, the title of his projected book. Ruth asks whether Charles's first wife, Elvira, was a help to him in thinking out his books; Charles replies that she was helpful now and then.

The Bradmans arrive, and Dr. Bradman asks Charles what he is hoping to get from Madame Arcati. Charles explains that he needs the jargon and a few tricks of the spiritualist's trade in order to draw a character in his book; the character will be a complete impostor, as—he suspects—is Madame Arcati. The doorbell rings and Madame Arcati comes in, apologizing for being late: she had a premonition that her bicycle tire would blow and had to go back for a pump. The maid announces dinner; hoping that there will be no red meat, Madame Arcati joins the others.

After dinner, taking their coffee in the living room, the women discuss the mechanics of communication with the spirit world. Edith brings drinks, and Ruth instructs her that they do not wish under any circumstances to be disturbed during the next hour. Charles and Dr. Bradman come in, still smoking their cigars, and Madame Arcati prepares the séance by seating the Bradmans and the Condomines at the table, telling them to touch fingertips. Charles cannot repress an exclamation when she selects a phonograph record—Irving Berlin's "Always"—that she says is congenial to her favorite spirit. She starts the music, switches off the light, and sits at the table with the others.

Madame Arcati asks whether there is someone "there" who wants to speak to someone "here." The table raps once, and by a series of eliminating questions she establishes that someone wishes to speak to Charles. She asks him whether he knows anyone who died recently, but he cannot think of anybody. She announces that the only solution is for her to go into a trance: she starts the phonograph again and falls on the floor unconscious. The table tips over, and a voice says, "Good evening, Charles." Charles accuses the others of playing a trick; they in turn accuse him of trying to frighten them, since they have heard nobody. The voice announces itself as Elvira, Charles's first wife. Charles quickly revives Madame Arcati with brandy. She says that if the séance has released anything, they will know in a day or two. She thanks her host and brushes aside Dr. Bradman's ironic congratulations, and Charles escorts her out.

While Ruth and the Bradmans chat, a very gray Elvira enters unseen through the closed French windows. Charles returns; the Bradmans refuse a last brandy and leave. As Charles makes himself a drink, he sees Elvira and drops his glass. Ruth asks him what has happened. He attempts to introduce her to Elvira, and Ruth calls him mad. Elvira tells Charles he could at least act pleased to see her, since he conjured her up. Charles insists that he did nothing of the sort, and Ruth tells him the joke has gone far enough and pours him some brandy. Elvira keeps interrupting, and as Charles replies to her, Ruth takes his replies as aimed at her and becomes thoroughly insulted. She accuses him of trying to create a situation for his novel and protests that she will not be a guinea pig. Charles tells Elvira that she is acting like a guttersnipe, and Ruth, believing the remark is directed at her, leaves the room furious.

Elvira accuses Charles of not loving her any more; he says that he loves her memory. Feeling strangely peaceful, he sits down and lets Elvira stroke his hair, though all he can feel of her hand is a breeze. He supposes that he will be put in an asylum if he is out of his mind. "Poor Ruth," he says, and Elvira gently replies, "To hell with Ruth."

ACT TWO

The next morning, Ruth accuses Charles of behaving abominably the night before. Charles tells her she is jealous because his hallucination concerned his dead wife. Ruth replies that simply because he has been dominated by women all his life he doesn't need to pretend to understand them. She suggests that he see a nerve specialist or a psychoanalyst, and he rejects both suggestions.

Elvira enters from the garden with an armful of gray roses and criticizes the condition of the flower beds. Charles's reply touches off another furious outburst from Ruth. Charles tries to persuade Elvira to talk to him only when he is alone, and Ruth stares at her husband in horror, then pleads with him to come upstairs and rest and wait for the doctor.

Charles asks her to give him five minutes to prove Elvira's existence. Ruth sits while Charles instructs Elvira to move flowers from the piano to the mantelpiece and back again. Elvira obeys. Ruth, almost hysterical, accuses him of playing tricks. Elvira waltzes around the room with a chair and shuts the windows in Ruth's face when she tries to run from the room. Ruth collapses into hysterics as Elvira smashes a vase against the grate.

Over tea the following afternoon, Ruth asks Madame Arcati to send Elvira back to wherever she came from. Madame Arcati produces a notebook to jot down notes for a report to the Psychical Research Society. Learning that Elvira died seven years ago, she remarks that Elvira could never have gotten back if there had not been a strong influence at work. Ruth asks whether this means that Charles was anxious to have her back; Madame Arcati replies that either that or Elvira's own determination was the cause. She admits that she hasn't the slightest idea how to get rid of Elvira and reminds Ruth that she had no inkling of Charles's desire to get in touch with his dead wife when she agreed to the séance. Ruth corrects Madame Arcati and tells her that the whole thing was planned in order to get background for a mystery story. Incensed, Madame Arcati tells Ruth that she can stew in her own juice and leaves in a rage.

Charles comes in with Elvira. Ruth asks how long Elvira intends to stay: Elvira, replying through Charles, says she doesn't know, and Charles suggests that there's no reason they couldn't all have some fun out of the arrangement: he himself is beginning to enjoy it. Ruth breaks into tears and threatens to go in the morning to the Psychical Research Society and, if they cannot help, straight to the Archbishop of Canterbury. She leaves, saying she will take dinner in her room.

Charles asks Elvira what she wants of him. She answers that she wants to be alone with him—that's only natural after seven years. Charles goes to comfort Ruth, and Elvira puts the recording of "Always," her favorite song, on the phonograph and dances about the room. Edith comes in and turns off the phonograph. When Elvira turns it on again, Edith shrieks, drops her tray, and rushes from the room.

Several days later, in the evening, Ruth stands at the window staring into the rain while Mrs. Bradman tries to console her on the long string of accidents that have been plaguing the household. Dr. Bradman assures Ruth that there is nothing wrong with Charles's arm except a slight sprain, even though Charles does stare into space and occasionally shout irrelevancies; the doctor recommends rest and a change and adds that Edith will recover from her concussion in a few days. Charles comes in, followed by Elvira, and tells the doctor that his sling is inconvenient, since he must drive down to Folkestone. The doctor allows him to remove the sling provided he drives slowly and uses his left hand as little as possible.

After the Bradmans have gone, Ruth tells Elvira that she surely could wait another night to go to Folkestone for her movie. Elvira throws a rose at Ruth and leaves the room. Ruth warns Charles that Elvira is dangerous; she came for one reason only: she wants to get Charles to herself—by killing him. She reminds Charles of the mysterious grease at the top of the stairs and the sabotaged ladder and decides to go to Madame Arcati immediately to find some way of rendering Elvira harmless.

Elvira returns and asks Charles if he is ready to drive to Folkestone. When she learns that Ruth has taken the car, she cries that Charles must stop her at once. At that moment the telephone rings, and Charles receives word that there has been an auto accident at the bridge at the bottom of the hill. The door bursts open, and Elvira, shrieking at Ruth, retreats under the blows of an invisible assailant. She runs from the room, slamming the door; the door opens and slams behind her. Charles stares, aghast.

ACT THREE

A few days later, Charles, dressed in deep mourning, is drinking his after-dinner coffee when Madame Arcati comes in, apologizing for the intrusion: she has bicycled down in the grip of a tremendous urge. She produces a formula which will get rid of Elvira without hurting her in the least. Elvira enters, and Charles introduces her to Madame Arcati, who, though she cannot see Elvira, is thrilled to meet a spirit. Charles asks Madame Arcati to leave the room a moment so that Elvira can speak to him.

Elvira complains that her high hopes in returning have all ended in failure. She reproaches Charles for having married Ruth and for having changed: his books have become worse, too. They trade insults, and finally Elvira proclaims that he is a monumental bore and a pompous ass and that she allowed a Captain Bracegirdle to make love to her on her and Charles's honeymoon. Charles remarks that he is well rid of her; Elvira reminds him that since he called her back, he can never be rid of her. Charles assures her that he did not call her. She tells him she can take no more of the situation.

Charles calls Madame Arcati and explains that, after serious discussion, Elvira has decided that she wants to go home as soon as possible. Since there is not enough time to organize the ingredients of the ritual, Madame Arcati performs it with salt and pepper, snapdragons, and the recording of "Always." The table thumps and falls over with a crash. When Charles turns on the lights, Elvira is still in the room. Just as Madame Arcati says that something went wrong, a completely gray Ruth walks into the room and asks Charles what the hell this means.

Several hours later, while Madame Arcati lies with her eyes shut on the sofa, Charles walks the room unhappily, and Ruth and Elvira snap at each other. He asks them to leave the house and go stay in the guest cottage, and Elvira upbraids him for his ingratitude toward two wives who have served him, whom he has called back after their deaths, and whom he is now trying to get rid of.

Charles reawakens Madame Arcati and tells her that his wives are utterly convinced he called them back, while he is utterly convinced that he did not. Madame Arcati states that neither could have appeared unless there had been somebody—a psychic subject—in the house who wanted them. Charles says firmly that it wasn't he. Madame Arcati looks into her crystal ball and begins to understand. She waves a birch branch and intones a verse summoning the psychic subject.

The door opens, and Edith, the maid, comes into the room in her dressing gown and asks if Charles rang. Madame Arcati asks her whom she sees in the room: Edith replies that she sees Charles and Madame Arcati. Madame Arcati demands sharply where the spirits are, and Edith lets slip that they are by the fireplace. Charles asks whether she can see them, and Madame Arcati explains that Edith is a "natural" who can probably see them indistinctly. Ruth remarks that if it was Edith who summoned them back, she'll give her a week's notice.

Madame Arcati puts Edith into a trance and asks Charles to have his wives stand close together. Madame Arcati switches off the light, and while Edith sings "Always" in a high, cockney voice, Elvira taunts Charles with confessions of two more deceptions, while Ruth tells him that he has behaved atrociously and will not get rid of them easily. Their voices fade, and when Madame Arcati turns on the lights, they have gone.

Charles sends Edith back to bed with a pound note. Madame Arcati advises him to leave immediately, since the spirits may still be in the house. She collects her paraphernalia and goes. Alone, Charles announces that he has been hag-ridden all his life but that now he is free and enjoys his freedom immensely. A vase crashes into the fireplace. He taunts Elvira that he not only knew about Captain Bracegirdle, but was very much attached to another woman at the same time. The clock strikes sixteen. He says that he was reasonably faithful to Ruth, but it would not have lasted long, as she was becoming more and more domineering. A picture falls from the wall. Charles bids Ruth and Elvira farewell, saying that he plans to enjoy himself as never before. As he leaves, the mantel falls and the curtain pole crashes down.

E . E . C U M M I N G S

him [1927]

ACT ONE

Scene 1. The three weirds sit with their backs to the audience, rocking and knitting. They face a board painted with the figures of a doctor anesthetizing a woman. The live heads of a man and a woman protrude through holes cut in the board where the heads of the painted figures are supposed to be. In a nonsense parody of women's chit-chat over their knitting, the weirds chatter about pets, their husbands, etc. The doctor withdraws his head from the board, then comes on-stage with Him and introduces Him to the three weirds. As they turn around, the weirds are seen to be wearing identical masks. Him and the doctor leave, and the three weirds resume their knitting and talk.

Scene 2. Me primps in a mirror as she talks to Him. Me is edgy, complaining that Him doesn't care about her because she doesn't understand him; she asks to see the play Him is working on and finally asks Him to go and investigate what she thinks is a parade outside.

Scene 3. The painted picture is as in scene 1, with both heads protruding; the woman's eyes are closed. The three weirds rock and knit with their backs to the audience as before. Him enters. He tries to shake hands with the weirds, but they take turns reading his palm rapidly and incomprehensibly. Him leaves. The three weirds resume their knitting and rocking.

Scene 4. Me is still in front of the mirror when Him returns. The resume their talk, with Me as nervous as before. She goes to rest on the sofa. Him stands before the mirror, takes out a pistol, and puts it to his temple. Me wakes and screams. Him pretends his actions are part of the play he is writing. He talks to her about his two selves, his real self and the one that Me sees, the one he can see in the mirror, whom he calls O. Him. Me, as she had complained before, doesn't understand him.

Scene 5. The painted picture remains as in scene 3, with both heads protruding. The three weirds rock, knit, and continue their chatter.

ACT TWO

Scene 1. The curtain rises on an empty stage, stays up one minute, and descends. The voices of Him and Me are heard. She asks what the raising and lowering of the curtain meant. He tells her it is the other play—the popular play she hoped he would write—written by O. Him. He describes the next scene: the lawn of a bungalow in the wee small hours of the morning.

Scene 2. Three middle-aged men, all drunk, stagger in, followed soon by Virgo, in black pajamas and carrying a candle. Me is fascinated and scandalized by their behavior.

Scene 3. On a streetcorner, a soap box salesman is hawking miraculous Radioleum, a wonder cure, to the passing crowds, who stop in increasing numbers, then drift away.

Scene 4. Will and Bill are partners in business who through long association have "become each other." An intruder enters their office, and is held at gun point by Will. Bill comes in but sees no intruder; Will fires the gun and himself falls lifeless. The intruder tells Bill to turn himself in for murdering Will. Confused, Bill knocks off the mask Will is wearing, revealing a face identical to the mask Bill is wearing.

Scene 5. Black figures dance and sing "Frankie and Johnnie" until they are interrupted by a personage in the audience who claims to represent the Society for the Contraception of Vice. He accuses the singers of being about to utter obscenities and administers an oath and tries to collect a dollar fee. Frankie herself frightens him away by waving a bloody napkin containing the "best part of the man who done me wrong."

Scene 6. At midnight on Fifth Avenue a plainclothesman encounters an Englishman carrying a large trunk marked "Fragile." The plainclothesman is suspicious and forces the Englishman to drop the trunk, which the latter claims is his unconscious. The plainclothesman peeks in the trunk, recoils in horror, and falls lifeless. A cop hurries in, does the same thing.

Scene 7. Aboard a transatlantic steamer, two passengers, each holding a balloon, are strolling the decks. They pass one another six times, hold six brief pointless conversations, and each time explode the balloon that the other holds.

Scene 8. The scene is Fascist Italy, set in ancient Roman times, with Mussolini as Caesar. He brags to four adoring fairies about his burning of Communists, then orders prayers to the gods when he hears that Rome is burning.

Scene 9. On an empty stage, a Gentleman (played by the doctor), apparently a rich American in Europe, cannot understand the poverty of the post–World War I Continent. A face-to-face meeting with a grotesque, starving mob gives him a severe shock. He is discovered by a policeman as he strips off his clothing, claiming he has just been born.

ACT THREE

Scene 1. Him and Me are seated at opposite ends of the sofa in Me's room. They talk about their life together and the point they are now at in their relationship. Him is about to leave her and go to Paris. Me claims that they have never really been in love, that she is not the sort of person he thinks, that he has been loving someone he invented. Him tells her that she has made him realize that in his life he has been several different people, but never himself.

Scene 2. The three weirds, rocking and knitting, sit facing the picture, from which both heads protrude. Two of the weirds continue their old wives' chatter, while the third utters advertising slogans.

Scene 3. In a dive in Paris, whores are asleep at the tables, musicians asleep at the bandstand. At a corner table sit the Blond Gonzesse and the Gentleman of Act II, scene 9. The headwaiter rushes in and rouses the sleeping whores and the musicians, who try to make the place seem lively. Two American females enter, take a seat, and order *Hommes* (one stewed and one boiled). Will and Bill enter with two women, one old and one fairly young, and order a dinner in atrocious French. Him enters, carrying a cabbage in his left hand, and takes a seat at the table of the Gentleman and the Blond Gonzesse. The headwaiter informs the women who ordered *Hommes* that they (Will and Bill) will be ready soon. The woman with Will ogles the Gentleman. The Blond Gonzesse gazes amorously at Him. The Gentleman pays the bill, passes out, and his wallet is lifted by the Blond Gonzesse. Him is left with the Gonzesse. The woman with Bill vomits into his lap.

Scene 4. The three knitting weirds face the picture, from which the doctor's head has disappeared. The weirds continue their chatter as before, interrupted at the end by the doctor poking his head through the hole in the picture and telling them, "If you wore your garters around your neck you'd change them oftener."

Scene 5. Him and Me sit on the sofa in Me's room, facing away from audience. They talk about his return from Paris and his failure to recognize Me at first. Him tells her that he is no longer troubled by the split within himself into his real self and O. Him, the other man. Him has drawn closer to reality because he now knows that the beauty he once wanted is not the same as the truth he now wants; in fact, that beauty he had created in his imagination had shut him away from the truth about himself and Me. To himself, Him still doubts, however, that what is desirable would shut him away from what is.

Scene 6. Him, the three weirds, and the other characters from Act II are at a freak show. Nine platforms stand in a semicircle. On eight of them are the freaks. On the middle platform is a small booth with a curtain. The barker, played by the doctor, goes from one platform to the other, describing the freaks. At the fifth platform he announces Princess Anankay and pulls aside the curtain. A woman's figure, draped in white, stands motionless, holding a newborn babe in her arms. The crowd recoils; the weirds exclaim with disgust, "It's all done with mirrors!" The woman lifts her head, revealing the face of Me. Him cries out in terror.

Scene 7. Him and Me are standing in Me's room. Me tells Him she is thinking something about the room—that it has only three walls. He points to the three walls, then to the invisible wall toward the audience, and asks what she sees there. People, she answers, who are "pretending that this room and you and I are real." Me walks toward the door. Him, standing in the middle of the room, says he wishes he could believe it. Me tells him he can't, because it is true.

FRIEDRICH DÜRRENMATT

The Physicists [*Die Physiker*, 1961]

ACT ONE

In the drawing room of a private sanatorium that was once a villa, police-men are busying themselves around the corpse of Nurse Irene. Inspector Voss asks Head Nurse Boll whether he may smoke, but she discourages him; he asks for brandy and is refused. From her he learns that Irene was strangled in this room by a patient who thinks he is Einstein. Objecting to the employment of female attendants, he reminds Nurse Boll that this is the second murder—accident—at Les Cerisiers within three months: on August 12, a patient who calls himself Newton strangled Nurse Dorothea in this very room.

Asking to see the murderer—assailant—the inspector is again refused. Ein-stein is playing the fiddle and must not be disturbed, Nurse Boll says firmly, and the Fräulein Doktor cannot be called because she is accompanying him on the piano. Voss roars that he will wait and sinks into an easy chair. Nurse Boll escorts the body from the room.

Dressed in eighteenth-century costume, Newton comes out of Room 3. He lights a cigarette, explaining to the inspector that patients are allowed to smoke, and from behind the fireguard he takes a bottle of brandy and a glass. Wonder-ing aloud how Einstein could have brought himself to strangle a nurse, he is re-minded by Voss that he himself strangled one. They loved one another, Newton replies, and this dilemma could only be resolved with a curtain cord. Presently he hides the brandy bottle and disappears into his room.

Determinedly taking out a cigar, the inspector puffs out clouds of smoke. Dr. Zahnd comes from Room 2, wearing a white surgical coat; she is about fifty-five and is hunchbacked. Seeing Voss examining a portrait on the wall, she ex-plains that it is of her father, who once lived in this villa. She lights a cigarette and, noticing Newton's brandy glass, hides it. Medically speaking, the doctor says, there is no explanation for the two accidents: it is interesting, however, that the three patients left in the villa (the others having been transferred to a new wing) are nuclear physicists. Möbius, who has been there for fifteen years, is harmless, she maintains. Voss, nevertheless, insists that male nurses must re-place the female nurses. He takes his leave.

Nurse Boll enters and sniffs, and Dr. Zahnd stubs her cigarette. The head nurse is asked to send in Frau Möbius, who enters, followed by her three teen-age sons and a man. Frau Möbius explains that she has just married Herr Rose, widower and missionary; and that since Rose has a new post in the Marianas, they have come to bid Möbius goodby. Weeping, she confesses that she can no longer support Möbius, since her husband has six sons of his own to care for.

Dr. Zahnd tells her kindly that she will keep him in the sanatorium anyway.

Coming from Room 1, Möbius doesn't at first recognize his ex-wife and boys. When Frau Rose introduces her husband, Möbius informs Rose that he has met Solomon face to face. Dashing into his room, he overturns a table, sits inside it, and recites a new Song of Solomon for cosmonauts. When Sister Boll arrives with Nurse Monika, he dismisses his family threateningly. They are led out, horrified.

Accused by Monika of having purposely put on a show, Möbius admits that he did it so that his family could forget him with a clear conscience. Now she must say goodby too, Monika tells him, for she is to be transferred to the main building. Möbius is dejected; through her, he says, he has found the courage to accept a madman's fate. Monika replies that she doesn't consider him mad and confesses her love. Leaping up, Möbius commands her to leave: because he loves her too, she is in danger.

Einstein enters and, perceiving the situation, remarks thoughtfully that he and Nurse Irene were in love. After advising Monika to run away, he returns to his room. Möbius urgently warns Monika to escape, but she tells him that she has arranged for his freedom so that they can marry; and she has asked his former teacher to read his manuscripts, for he must make known Solomon's scientific proclamations. With tears in his eyes Möbius strangles her.

ACT TWO

An hour later, Dr. Zahnd, sitting on the sofa, offers the inspector a cigar and brandy, which he refuses. Asked whether he would like to see the murderer, he answers no. Presently three huge male attendants arrive with the patients' sumptuous dinner, and as Nurse Monika's body is carried out, Möbius rushes in crying for her. Dr. Zahnd excuses herself. Lighting a gigantic cigar, Voss tells Möbius where to find the brandy and downs several glassfuls. The patient asks to be arrested, but the inspector replies jovially that Justice is on holiday and leaves.

Newton enters and, helping himself to soup, reveals to Möbius that he is a spy and had to kill Nurse Dorothea when she no longer considered him mad. His real name is Kilton. He explains that, on reading Möbius' dissertation on a new concept of physics, he had realized that its author was the greatest physicist of all time and had informed his country's intelligence service. They sent Kilton into the sanatorium to abduct him.

Einstein, having entered during the conversation, discloses that he is in the intelligence service of another country and is here for the same purpose as Kilton; his real name is Eisler. He was forced to kill Nurse Irene because she too was becoming suspicious. Having taken each other for madmen, both spies now realize that their plans have gone awry.

As the patients eat, attendants fasten a new grille on the window. Eisler suggests that they must act together to get away, but Möbius doesn't wish to escape. Kilton tries to persuade him to come to his country, for a genius is common property, he declares, and it is Möbius' duty to publicize his knowledge. Eisler also tries persuasion: physicists must become power politicians, he says, and must decide in whose favor they will apply their knowledge. He recommends his chosen country. The two agents rise to do battle, but Möbius informs them that he burned his manuscripts before the police arrived. Telling of his decision, fifteen years ago, to play the fool, he convinces them that they must stay with him in the madhouse, for if he is found sane, the world will destroy itself with his discoveries. In the madhouse they are free to think and not to act.

The three drink to their dead nurses and return to their rooms, but are soon called back by Dr. Zahnd. She informs them that their conversation was overheard on secret radio transmitters, and to their stupefaction she announces earnestly that Solomon appeared to her when Möbius betrayed him by trying to hide things that should be known. So, all these years, she has been making photocopies of his revelations to Möbius, and with the knowledge gained, she has built factories and created a giant cartel, which will dictate to the universe. Because she was the last sane member of her family, King Solomon took pity and chose her to be his handmaiden, she says. The physicists are her prisoners, for, because they murdered the nurses whom she drove into their arms precisely for that purpose, they are officially mad. Dr. Zahnd leaves for a board meeting.

"What was once thought can never be unthought," says Möbius. The three resume their roles as madmen.

FRIEDRICH DÜRRENMATT

The Visit [*Der Besuch der Alten Dame*, 1955;

this adaptation by Maurice Valency, 1958]

ACT ONE

At the railway station, the impoverished townspeople of Gullen await the homecoming of a local girl—Claire Wascher, now the world-famous multimillionairess Claire Zachanassian. The people have prepared a welcoming reception for Claire, with the town band, the choir, and the children's chorus. They hope that Claire will give money to revive the town's industries—the wagon-works, the foundry, and the Golden Eagle Pencil Company, all of which have long been shut down. Hopes are high because Claire is renowned for her philanthropy and because one of the townsfolk, Anton Schill, was Claire's lover years ago. Schill is really the only person who remembers Claire; his position with regard to her has made him popular with the town leaders, and he is told he will be elected the next burgomaster.

Claire is expected on the 12:40 P.M. local from Kalberstadt. Express trains no longer stop at Gullen, but the "Flying Dutchman" express unexpectedly screeches to a stop at the station. Claire, who has pulled the emergency cord, gets off and calmly bribes the indignant conductor. The townsfolk are in a panic. The reception was not planned for another hour. The burgomaster hurriedly sends for the band and the singers and makes a welcoming speech that is drowned out by the noise of the departing express. With Claire are her new fiancé Pedro, a rich Brazilian playboy; her seventy-year-old butler Bobby; two blind men called Kobby and Lobby; and two ex-convicts named Mike and Max. There are also a black panther in a cage and an empty coffin.

Claire sets off in a sedan chair, carried by Mike and Max, to see the town and nearby forest with Schill. In the forest, where they used to meet, Schill and Claire recall their early days together. Schill's recollections are vague, but Claire's memory is sharp. She remembers their love affair, Schill's marriage to Mathilde Blumhard, daughter of a well-to-do merchant, and her own departure from Gullen.

The scene changes to a luncheon in Claire's honor at the Golden Apostle Inn. Claire announces her intention to give the town one billion marks—500 million marks to the town and 500 million to be divided among the citizens. Her offer has one condition, which is explained by her butler Bobby. He is actually the former Magistrate Hofer of Gullen. Years ago, Claire charged Schill with being the father of her unborn child. Schill denied the charge and bribed two men to swear falsely that they also slept with Claire. The two men are identified as Kobby and Lobby. Claire left town in disgrace, bore the baby, who lived a year, and became a prostitute. In a Hamburg brothel she met the wealthy old Zachanassian and married him. Her condition for giving Gullen the billion marks is that she be given justice for the wrong done her. For the money she wants Schill's life. The burgomaster refuses the proposal as the townsfolk applaud him. Claire says that she can wait.

ACT TWO

In the shop of Anton Schill, the once-frugal townsfolk are on a reckless spree of credit buying. Schill realizes the implications of this and appeals for help to the policeman, the burgomaster, and the pastor. Each one offers him no help at all. They too are indulging in the credit buying. The burgomaster tells Schill that his moral lapse with Claire makes him unfit to be the town's next burgomaster. The pastor implores Schill to leave town and not tempt the people any further. In the meantime, Claire's panther escapes from its cage. The townsfolk set out with rifles to hunt for it. Schill takes a rifle and goes to the inn. He attempts to threaten Claire, but she seems not to notice the danger; as she once again recalls their young love, Schill's resolution wavers and disappears.

The scene changes to the railway station. Schill, with his suitcase, is waiting for the local to Kalberstadt. The townspeople enter, claiming they have come to see him off. They accuse him of not trusting them by running away, but their tone and the way they crowd around him frighten Schill. He fears they intend to push him under the train wheels and falls to the ground in terror. The train leaves and the people disperse as Schill slowly rises. A truck driver offers him a ride to Kalberstadt, but he declines, saying he has decided to stay.

ACT THREE

Claire's wedding to Pedro, her ninth husband, has taken place that day in the town cathedral. Pedro has left for the honeymoon in Brazil, alone. The town is full of reporters who have come from all over the world to cover the event. Claire is implored by the doctor and the teacher to help the townsfolk, who are deeper in debt than ever because of their credit buying. She is asked to buy the closed factories and to reopen them. Claire replies that she already owns the factories and everything else in Gullen. She has bought everything bit by bit and has deliberately reduced the town to poverty. This is not enough revenge for her, however. She wants Schill's life.

In Schill's shop, the townsfolk are worried that the reporters will learn of the condition attached to Claire's offer to the town. Schill, who has been in isolation for days, assures them that he will not say anything, and the people leave. The burgomaster arrives to tell Schill that the town council meets that night to decide about Claire's offer. He offers Schill a pistol as an easy way out for everyone. Schill is determined, however, that the town must judge him and carry out the sentence itself.

Even his wife and children have abandoned him now, and Schill resigns himself to his fate. He walks to the forest, meets Claire, and tells her that her demands are about to be met. She tells him that she will take his body in the coffin to Capri and bury it near her villa overlooking the Mediterranean.

The scene changes to the town meeting. To conceal Claire's demands from the press, the council discusses only whether to accept the money, without mentioning the specific condition attached. The teacher is the only one in opposition, but his speech is vague and confused and is taken for approval rather than rejection of the offer. The vote is taken and all vote to accept Claire's offer. The teacher is the last to slowly raise his hand in approval.

The meeting ends, the press leaves, and the execution proceeds. Schill smokes a last cigarette, sinks to his knees, and the townsmen close in around him. When they move back, the doctor is bending over Schill's body with a stethoscope. Death, he announces, was caused by heart failure. "Died of joy," says the burgomaster, and the others echo his statement. Claire enters, looks at the body, and her butler hands a check to the burgomaster.

The scene changes to the railway station, now gleaming newly like the rest of the town. The townsfolk, in brand-new clothes, are gathered to see Claire depart on the new Gullen-Rome express. Kobby and Lobby, and Mike and Max with the coffin, board the train. Then Claire, all in black, gets aboard. The train pulls out, watched by the silent crowd.

T . S . E L I O T

Murder in the Cathedral [1935]

PART I

The scene is the archbishop's hall in Canterbury, December 2, 1170. A chorus of women tells of the archbishop's seven-year exile from England and of their own sufferings. It is better, they say, that the archbishop, Thomas à Becket, not return. His struggles with the king have repercussions on all the people, and the poor suffer the most. Now at least they are left alone. Three priests talk about Thomas' absence and about the intrigues of the king. A messenger enters and announces that Thomas is back in England and is on his way to Canterbury. The struggle with the king is not over, he says, but an uncertain truce has been called. The chorus laments Thomas' return, fearful of what a new struggle might mean for the people. A priest rebukes them for their attitude as Thomas enters. He tells the priest that some of the king's supporters have already threatened him and reveals that he expects to be martyred in the struggle against the king.

The first tempter enters. He reminds Thomas of the good times he and the king had had in their youth, before Thomas became the archbishop. He advises Thomas to turn again to pleasure-seeking and to give up the struggle with the king. Thomas tells him that he has come twenty years too late. The second tempter reminds Thomas of the power he had as chancellor, before he gave up the office to become archbishop. Thomas says that his power now, as the representative of the Church and of God, is even greater than that he had as chancellor. The third tempter tries to persuade Thomas to align himself with the English barons, the richest segment of the society, who are also opposed to the king. The fourth tempter is a surprise to Thomas, who had expected the first three. Quoting Thomas' own arguments against pleasure, power, and wealth, the fourth tempter tries to entice Thomas into desiring martyrdom, thus falling into the sin of pride. Thomas rejects martyrdom motivated by spiritual pride, for only martyrdom humbly undergone is acceptable to God.

The chorus, the tempters, and the priests try to persuade the archbishop not to persist in his opposition to the king. The chorus of women say that if he does persist, he will be killed and they will be without a spiritual leader. Thomas says that this plea is the last temptation—"To do the right deed for the wrong reason."

INTERLUDE

The archbishop preaches in the cathedral on Christmas morning, 1170. The theme of the sermon is martyrdom, which Thomas says is the design of

God to warn men and lead them back to His ways. He hints that he will be the next martyr.

PART II

The scene is the archbishop's hall, December 29, 1170. The chorus tells of the dying of the old year in the winter, which is necessary before new life can begin in the spring. The three priests enter, carrying the banners of St. Stephen, St. John the Apostle, and the Holy Innocents. They are awaiting the fulfillment of Thomas' expectation of martyrdom.

Four knights enter, saying they have come from the king to see Thomas on urgent business. Thomas is called in and is left alone with the knights. They abuse Thomas for revolting against the king, who put him in his position as archbishop. Thomas replies that if they have charges to make, they should make them in public where he will refute them. The knights are about to attack Thomas, but the priests and attendants come in and stand between the knights and the archbishop. The knights accuse Thomas of betraying the pact of peace between himself and the king. Thomas has suspended the bishops who took part in an illegal coronation of the king's heir apparent while Thomas was still in France. The knights tell Thomas that the king has ordered him to leave England. He refuses to leave his congregation again after his seven-year exile. The knights leave, threatening to return with force.

The chorus expresses its support of Thomas and asks his forgiveness for its former faintheartedness. The priests urge Thomas to go into the cathedral where he would be safe from attack. He refuses, but they drag him off forcibly.

As the chorus speaks of the nearness of death, the scene changes to the cathedral. The priests bar the door of the church but Thomas demands that it be opened. He will not conquer by fighting, he says, but by suffering. The priests open the door, and the four knights, slightly tipsy, come in. They demand that Thomas absolve those he has excommunicated and subject himself to the king's authority. He refuses and the knights kill him. As the murder takes place, the chorus says that the house, the city, and the world are defiled. The chorus calls for clearing the air, cleaning the sky, "washing the wind and the stones."

After completing the murder, the knights come to the front of the stage and face the audience. In prose, the knights try to convince the audience of the necessity for killing Thomas. Their speeches resemble those made at political meetings. They say that they were completely disinterested in the murder of Thomas; none of them has anything to gain from it personally. They point out that Thomas had himself caused the division between the state and the Church by refusing to hold the offices of chancellor and archbishop simultaneously, as King Henry had wanted him to do. The fourth knight, making the final speech, claims that Thomas actually sought martyrdom by refusing to submit to the king, deliberately exasperating the knights, and by ordering the priests to unlock the cathedral doors. A verdict of "suicide while of unsound mind" should be rendered, the knight says. This is "the only charitable verdict you can give, upon one who was, after all, a great man," the knight concludes. After advising the audience to disperse quietly to their homes, not to loiter in groups, and to do nothing that might provoke any public outbreak, the knights exit.

The three priests discuss the consequences of the murder. They say that the Church is stronger for the incident, that it is supreme so long as men will die for it. They pray to Thomas, now "conjoined with all the saints and martyrs gone before," to remember them. While a Te Deum is sung in Latin by a choir, the chorus praises God, thanks Him for His redemption by the blood of the martyrs and saints. They ask that the Lord have mercy on them and end with "Blessed Thomas, pray for us."

CHRISTOPHER FRY

The Lady's Not for Burning   [1948]

ACT ONE

In the house of Hebbel Tyson, mayor of the medieval town of Cool Clary, Richard, the young clerk, is busily performing his duties. Thomas Mendip appears at the window and requests to see the mayor; with great vehemence he expresses his aversion to the world and tells Richard that he has come to request his own hanging. The startled Richard is diverted when seventeen-year-old Alizon Eliot comes into the room; she is betrothed to Humphrey Devize, the mayor's nephew. Nicholas, Humphrey's brother, appears and informs Alizon that according to the stars, she is meant to marry him instead of Humphrey. He is about to carry her off when his mother, Margaret Devize, enters and orders him to fetch Humphrey; Nicholas extravagantly claims that he has killed his brother in order to gain Alizon. He and Richard then go off to retrieve Humphrey, who has been lying out in the rain where Nicholas struck him and who refuses to pick himself up since he did not knock himself down.

As Humphrey is carried into the mayor's house by Richard and Nicholas, he and Nicholas argue over Alizon. When the mayor appears, Thomas, still at the window, insists again that he be sent to the gallows. The mayor, incredulous in the face of such a request, suspects that Thomas is making fun of him. Thomas confesses to the murder of Skipps, the rag-and-bone merchant, as well as of another man, and reiterates that he must be hanged; the mayor, however, refuses to be bothered with him.

Nicholas interrupts to announce that there is a beautiful young witch to see the mayor. The mayor protests, still fearful that he is being made fun of. Jennet Jourdemayne appears. She says that she hopes to find refuge in the mayor's reason, for the populace is up in arms against her; they accuse her of having turned Skipps into a dog. She is certain that the mayor will be amused and will find the accusation ludicrous, but he can think of nothing to do but arrest her. Thomas, meantime, is still at the window and in a fury at being ignored. News comes of a riot in the street; the bodies of the two men Thomas claims to have killed cannot be found, and it is rumored among the populace that Thomas is the devil and has Jennet in his clutches. As proof that he is the devil, Thomas announces that that night the world will come to an end. Jennet continues to appeal to the mayor's reason. When the mayor arrests them both, Thomas pleads to be hanged before he falls in love with Jennet.

136

ACT TWO

At the mayor's house an hour later, the mayor advises the town's justice, Edward Tappercoom, to handle Thomas carefully in case he turns out to be the devil; Tappercoom reports that, in spite of his efforts, Jennet has confessed to nothing. When Nicholas and Humphrey appear, the mayor explains his plan to eavesdrop on Jennet and Thomas in the hope of getting conclusive evidence; he hopes that Jennet is guilty, for she is propertied and her property would go to the town; he is less interested in Thomas, who is poor.

When Jennet and Thomas are left alone, Jennet confesses her fears to Thomas, telling of her deceased father, an alchemist, and of her own preference, in reaction, for the world of the actual, of facts and reason. Thomas, still claiming to be the devil, chides her for her rejection of the world of imagination and fancy. Jennet confesses that she has begun to be drawn to him; Thomas, distressed, expresses his bitter hatred of the world. Jennet says that if he is the devil, then hell shall be her home. Interpreting these words the way he wants to, the mayor bursts in and pronounces her statement a confession of guilt; she will be burned next day. Realizing that Thomas wants to be hanged simply because he hates life, the mayor sentences him to spend the evening in joy and revelry at the party to be given in honor of the betrothal of Humphrey and Alizon. Thomas insists that Jennet be allowed to share in his punishment.

ACT THREE

Escaping the boring festivities, Thomas and Jennet encounter Humphrey and Nicholas; both brothers confess that they have fallen out of love with Alizon and that they are intoxicated by Jennet's beauty. Thomas is impressed more by her words, which indicate that she has loosened up and reached new heights of imagination. She explains that she has much living to compress into this one last night. As the three men vie for the honor of leading Jennet back to the fete, the mayor appears, chastising his nephews for leaving the guests. After the two brothers lead Jennet off, Thomas accuses the mayor of sentencing Jennet in order to hide the weaknesses in his own soul. After Thomas disappears, Tappercoom finds the mayor crying and insisting, in his confusion, that they must kill Jennet before she destroys the orderly nature of things.

Out in the garden, Alizon and Richard discover each other. Alizon says that she cannot bear those who would send Jennet to her death and that she has come to be with Richard, for she loves him. They agree to run away together; Richard sends her to wait for him at the gate.

In the house, Jennet appears, followed by Humphrey and Nicholas; she is looking for Thomas, who, she fears, is seeking death. While Nicholas goes off to the cellar to find something to drink, Humphrey tries to convince Jennet to spend her last hours in bed with him, telling her that as a member of the council he can have her execution postponed. Thomas climbs in through the window, disgusted and angry, and when Jennet tells him that her conversation with Humphrey doesn't concern him, he admits that, much to his distress, he loves her. Jennet is cynical about Thomas' love, since he is so determined to die. He urges her to save herself by accepting Humphrey's offer.

Margaret appears, looking for Alizon; Humphrey admits to his mother that he doesn't want to marry Alizon. Richard and Alizon appear and lead in the drunken Skipps; Thomas and the two brothers convince Skipps that he is dead, and he is escorted home. Margaret discovers that in the confusion Richard and Alizon have run off together. Tappercoom enters and tells Jennet that since, despite the accusation against her, Skipps does not appear to be changed into a dog, she might find this a good night for sneaking out of town. She and Thomas, who still proclaims his loathing for the world but is willing to live in it if Jennet is with him, set out together for home, "though neither of us / Knows where on earth it is."

JOHN GALSWORTHY

Justice [1910]

ACT ONE

In the law office of James and Walter How, the managing clerk, Cokeson, is sitting at a desk, adding up figures in a passbook. An office boy brings in a young woman, Ruth Honeywill, who wants to see Falder, a junior clerk. Cokeson says that Falder is out and asks to know her business; his sense of decorum is much disturbed when she replies that it is a personal matter. Falder returns and Cokeson agrees to make an exception to the rules and to let her speak to him. Ruth whispers to Falder that her husband is hitting the bottle again, that he tried to cut her throat last night, and that she took the children and ran off before he woke this morning. Falder replies that everything is set for tonight and arranges to meet her later.

After Ruth's departure, Cokeson chides Falder for having personal callers at the office and sends him off with a warning not to let his private life interfere with his work. Walter How comes in and is soon joined by his father, James How. A discrepancy in the firm's bank balance is discovered; James, checking the counterfoils in the checkbook, finds one for ninety pounds that Walter insists he drew for nine. It is apparent that whoever cashed the check altered the amount. The bank cashier is brought in, and he identifies Falder as the person who cashed the check. James presents Falder with the check and the evidence against him. Falder finally confesses. He pleads to be allowed to pay the money back, but James is determined to prosecute him, despite Walter's and Cokeson's intercession on Falder's behalf. A detective arrives and takes Falder away.

ACT TWO

At Falder's trial the counsel for the defense argues that Falder committed his crime in a moment of temporary insanity due to great emotional stress. The defense points out that Falder is only twenty-three and that he had fallen in love with a married woman whose husband brutally maltreated her; Falder wanted to rescue her from her plight by running away with her to another country, but he was unable to do so because he had no money.

Falder himself testifies that the forgery was the impulse of a moment and that he cannot actually remember adding the "ty" and the "O" to the check. But he admits trying to cover up his act later by altering the counterfoil in the checkbook. His counsel does not deny the seriousness of the crime but stresses the mitigating circumstances and urges leniency, saying that Falder will be destroyed by imprisonment. However, the jury find him guilty, and the judge, in handing down the sentence, says that he cannot overlook the fact that the crime was committed to further an immoral design—the elopement with a married woman—and that therefore the defendant's appeal for mercy must be denied. He sentences Falder to three years' penal servitude.

ACT THREE

Scene 1. At the prison on Christmas Eve, the governor and the chief warder, Wooder, are examining the homemade saw found in the prisoner Moaney's mattress. The chaplain enters, and soon a visitor is shown in— Cokeson, who has been to see Falder. He says that Falder seems lonely and asks whether he might be allowed to take exercise with the others. The governor replies that the convicts must be kept in separate confinement. Cokeson goes on to say that Falder is depressed, having learned that Ruth, unable to earn her living alone, was forced to go back to her husband. Eliciting little sympathy for Falder's plight, Cokeson remarks that the chaplain would not shut a dog up by itself month after month even if the animal had bitten him all over. The chaplain replies that the prison authorities are the best judges of how to handle the prisoners. When the doctor comes in, the governor explains that Cokeson thinks separate confinement is too hard on Falder. The doctor replies that the prisoner has lost no weight and that therefore it isn't doing him any harm. Cokeson, somewhat mollified and apologetic, leaves.

Scene 2. In the prison, the warder instructor is making the rounds of the prisoners. The cells have solid walls, not bars, and a covered peephole on the outside of each door. Wooder and the governor enter and go down to the cell occupied by Moaney, who made the saw. The governor offers to let Moaney off his punishment if the prisoner will not try to make another saw, but Moaney replies that he must have something to interest him and therefore can promise nothing. The governor says that he will get two days of bread and water and moves on to the next cell.

The occupant complains of another prisoner who bangs on his door. The governor speaks to O'Cleary, the banger, who protests that making the noise is a kind of substitute for conversation. The governor goes into Falder's cell and advises him to take hold of himself. The doctor arrives to examine Falder and says he is not suffering from confinement any more than many of the other prisoners. The governor replies that Falder must put up with it like the others. As they leave, there is a sound of banging.

Scene 3. In his cell, Falder stands by the door, trying to hear any little thing going on outside. He begins to pace like an animal in a cage, then stops and puts his forehead to the door and listens. He moves away as with a sharp click the cell lights come on. From far away the sound of beating on metal is faintly heard. It grows closer and swells in volume, and suddenly Falder, his fists clenched, throws himself at his door and beats on it.

ACT FOUR

Some two years later, Ruth Honeywill comes into Cokeson's office. In response to his questions, she says that she is not living with her husband any more; she couldn't bear it when he began to mistreat the children. Cokeson hopes, without too much conviction, that she hasn't done anything "rash" in order to support herself. She says she ran into Falder yesterday and that he cannot get a job and is in a dreadful state. Cokeson is dubious that the Hows would take him on again, but says he will speak to them in Falder's behalf. Ruth pleads that it would be the saving of him. She leaves before Falder arrives.

Falder tells Cokeson that the prison authorities got him a job, but the other clerks, learning that he was an ex-convict, made life unbearable for him; he had a job after that but forged a reference to get it, and the forgery made him so afraid that he left that job as well. James and Walter How enter, and Cokeson asks Falder to step into an adjoining room. Alone with the partners, Cokeson presents Falder's case to them. James is opposed to the idea of having a jailbird in the office, though Walter thinks they owe him another start in life. James says that Falder can have his job back only if he promises to live a completely respectable life and to have nothing to do with the woman for whom he had committed his crime.

Cokeson brings Falder in, and James tells him of his decision. Falder replies that returning to Ruth was the one thing he looked forward to all the time he was in prison and that he found her only yesterday. He refuses to give her up and pleads that there is a chance that evidence could be found against her husband so that she could get a divorce and they could be married. Encouraged by Walter, James agrees and asks that she come up. But Cokeson whispers to the partners that the woman was not "quite what she ought to ha' been" while Falder was in prison and therefore is legally not entitled to a divorce. Falder sees the change in the others' expressions and assures them that there has never been anything in his relationship with Ruth to prevent her getting a divorce.

Ruth comes in, and James tells her that he has promised to take Falder back if he will make a fresh start and points out that she will not want to stand in his way. Falder interjects that she can get a divorce and finally, when Ruth seems to have agreed to give him up, cries that he doesn't understand, for he thought the Hows were going to help them. Ruth is silent, and the truth begins to dawn on him that she has supported herself and her children by immoral earnings while he was in prison. There is a noise of someone entering the outer office, and Cokeson sends Ruth into an adjoining room; Falder follows her. A detective comes looking for Falder, since he failed to report to his probation officer and obtained employment with a forged reference. The Hows claim they know nothing about Falder. The detective accidentally goes to the door of the adjoining room instead of the outer office and discovers Falder and drags him out. There are sounds of footsteps descending the stone stairs and then a thud.

The detective returns, carrying Falder's body; he says that Falder jumped down the stairs in an attempt to escape. James shouts for someone to run for a doctor, and Ruth, dropping on her knees beside the body, cries that Falder is dead. Cokeson, holding out his hand to her as one would to a lost dog, attempts to comfort her.

FEDERICO GARCÍA LORCA

Blood Wedding [*Bodas de Sangre,* 1933]

ACT ONE

In a yellow room, the bridegroom, setting out for his newly bought vineyard, asks his mother for the knife so that he may cut grapes. She reminds him of his father and brother, both dead, and asks how it is that a small thing like a knife or pistol can finish a man; she asks how it is that the killers can sit carefree in the jail, eating, smoking, making music, while her husband and eldest son lie buried. She wishes that her son were a woman so that he would stay at home.

Her son tells her that he wants soon to be married. He tells her she will live with him and his wife, but she refuses to leave his father and brother for fear that one of the Felix family, the killers, might die and be buried next to their graves. She agrees to go and ask for the girl's hand on Sunday. Her son promises her that she will have grandchildren and says that she will love his bride.

After the son sets out, the mother asks a neighbor woman whether her son's sweetheart had another suitor at one time. The neighbor says that she had a suitor when she was fifteen, but he has been married for two years to a cousin of hers. The mother asks who the suitor was and is startled to learn that he was Leonardo Felix. Even though he was only a boy of eight when the Felixes killed her husband and eldest son, she feels a repulsion for the name. The neighbor urges her not to get in the way of her son's happiness.

In a pink room of his house, Leonardo returns from the blacksmith's, saying that for two months he has had to keep putting new shoes on the horse. His wife asks him whether it isn't because he rides the horse so much: yesterday the neighbors said they saw him on the far side of the plains. His mother-in-law asks who has been racing the horse so hard, and he replies that he has been.

His wife mentions that her cousin is to be married but begins to cry when her mother reminds her that Leonardo once courted her cousin. A girl appears from the store with news of the expensive stuff that the bridegroom and his mother have bought for the wedding. Leonardo silences the girl. His mother-in-law asks what is the matter with him; his wife asks where he is going. He tells them to be quiet and leaves.

In the cave where the bride lives, the bridegroom and his mother, dressed in black, arrive to meet the bride's father. The mother asks his opinion on the marriage; he says that he agrees to it. Each parent praises his child's good name and ability, and a servant brings drinks and sweets. The father summons the bride. She appears, head bowed, and when asked by the mother whether she is happy, replies that she is. The mother asks whether she knows what it is to be married: the bride replies that she does. The mother gives her the presents they have bought, kisses her, and leaves with her son, escorted by the father.

The servant begs the bride to let her look at the presents, but the bride refuses to open them. The servant asks if she heard a horse last night at three. The bride says that it must have been a riderless horse. The servant says that she saw the rider standing by the bride's window: Leonardo. The bride calls the servant a liar, but at that moment a horse is heard. The servant and the bride look out the window and see Leonardo ride by.

ACT TWO

Combing the bride's hair, the servant tells her that she is beautiful and lucky to be going to be married. The bride asks her to be quiet. The servant tries to put a bridal wreath of orange blossoms on the bride's head, but the bride throws the wreath on the floor. The first guest knocks; the servant opens the door and is astonished to see Leonardo, who says ironically that the bride must be happy today. Despite the servant's warning not to come out, the bride appears in her petticoats and asks what Leonardo wants. He taunts her that she despised him because he had nothing but two oxen and an ugly little hut; he says that he has burned for her all the time that he has not seen her, that time heals no wounds. The servant warns Leonardo to stay away from the bride.

The guests enter, singing a wedding song, and the bride greets them in a black wedding dress. She tells the bridegroom that she wants to be his bride this instant so that she may hear no voice and see no eyes but his. The party sets out for the church, only Leonardo and his wife remaining behind. Leonardo refuses to ride in the cart, and his wife refuses to go to the wedding without him. She says that she knows he has cast her off. Voices are heard singing outside, and Leonardo gruffly tells his wife to start moving.

Outside the bride's cave home, the servant sings as she arranges the glasses and trays on the table. The mother of the bridegroom and the father of the bride arrive; the servant tells them that Leonardo and his wife arrived before them, driving like demons. The father says that Leonardo is looking for trouble: he is not of good blood. The mother answers that his bad blood began with his great grandfather, who killed, and continues through the whole line of knife-wielders. Leonardo and his wife enter. The wife offers good wishes to the mother, and Leonardo asks if there will be a celebration. The father replies that the celebration will be short. Leonardo leaves as the guests enter in gay groups.

The bridegroom observes to the bride that there has never been such a wedding, and she sullenly agrees. The mother asks the bride why her blessings weigh so heavily, when today she ought to be happy as a dove. The bride leaves to take out her pins, saying she will be right back. Two youths enter and try to pull the groom away to drink with them; he says that he is waiting for his bride, but they tell him he will have her at dawn and take him away. The bride returns, and two girls beg her to say which one she gave her first pin to. She says she doesn't remember. The groom creeps up behind her and embraces her.

Frightened, she screams at him to let her go. He asks who she thought he was: her father? She will not let him hug her, complaining that there are people. He asks what of it, they are married. She says they will hug later.

Leonardo's wife returns and says that his horse is missing from the stable. The bride goes to lie down. The groom's mother appears and asks where the bride is: when he says she has gone to rest, the mother comments that today ought to be the bride's one happy day. The father enters, looking for his daughter: she is not in the bedroom. Leonardo's wife cries that Leonardo and the bride have gone off on the horse, their arms around each other. The bridegroom calls for a horse to pursue them, and the mother urges the guests to join in the pursuit.

ACT THREE

In a forest at night, three woodcutters wonder whether the lovers have yet been found. One describes the ashen face of the groom as he set out in pursuit and says that he will catch them, for they are trapped in a ten-league circle of knives and guns. The moon appears through the branches and sings of being cold and of wanting a warm heart to spurt over it. Death, an old beggar woman, announces that the lovers will not get past this spot. She calls the moon back and tells him to light up the victims for the knives. The moon asks Death to let them be a long time dying so that he may be warmed by their blood.

The bridegroom and a youth enter. Though the youth says that they will never find the lovers, the groom insists that they will, for his arm has the strength of all the dead men in his family. He asks the beggar woman whether she has seen a man and a woman running away on a horse. She answers that they are coming from the hill and offers to show him the road; they set out together.

Leonardo and the bride come through the woods. She begs him to run away so that he will not be punished for taking her; he replies that he wants to carry her to a hidden corner where he can love her forever. As the sound of pursuers draws closer, she urges him to run. He embraces her and says that if they are separated, it will only be because he is dead. They leave in each other's arms. There are two shrieks, and Death comes and spreads her cape.

In a white dwelling with arches and thick walls, two girls chant of the tragic wedding. Leonardo's mother-in-law instructs his widow to shut herself in her house and grow old weeping, with a cross of ashes on the pillow where her husband lay. The beggar woman appears at the door, begging bread, and the girls ask whether she saw the tragedy. She says that she saw it and that the bodies of the two men will soon be brought, covered with sheets, and that the bride will come with blood on her skirt and hair.

The mother tells the neighbors to stop crying: she wants to be alone with her grief and these four walls. The bride enters in a black shawl: the mother sets upon her, beating her till she drops. The neighbor tries to separate them, but the bride says that she wants the mother to kill her, so that she can be buried with the dead men, a virgin. She cries that she burned with desire: Leonardo was a dark river that she could not resist, who would have dragged her along even had she been an old married woman.

The mother condemns the bride for her act, then blesses the wheat that covers her sons, the rain that wets them, and God, who stretches the dead out to rest. She tells the bride to weep at the door. Leonardo's wife enters, and the women chant a lament for the dead, a bitter song of the knife that brings death.

FEDERICO GARCÍA LORCA

The House of Bernarda Alba

[*La Casa de Bernarda Alba*, 1936]

ACT ONE

In the white, scrubbed house of Bernarda Alba, Poncia and another servant prepare to receive the people now at the funeral of Bernarda's husband. For thirty years Poncia has been Bernarda's confidante, but now she curses her employer as a tyrannical, gossiping, ungenerous old shrew. As the bells toll, the other servant apostrophizes the dead man, "Take what's coming to you! You'll never again lift my skirts behind the corral door!" But as the black-dressed women come in, she breaks into a suitable mourning wail.

The guests stay only briefly, saying a last prayer for the departed and filing out, but they have managed to provoke Bernarda's piously sheathed ire and to denounce her among themselves as a "sanctimonious old snake"! Bernarda is glad to see them go, for she despises this village. She informs her five daughters that they will observe strictly the eight years of mourning, as was done in her father's and her grandfather's houses. They are never to leave the house, but will remain inside embroidering hopechest linens. Magdelena, age thirty, rebelliously declares that she knows she's not going to marry and would rather carry sacks to the mill than stay cooped up with a needle. When Bernarda says, "That's what a woman is for," Magdelena retorts, "Cursed be all women."

Eighty-year-old Maria Josefa, Bernarda's mother, has been locked up, for they do not want the neighbors to see her craziness; now she can be heard yelling to be let out; the servants say she has put on her rings and earrings and has announced that she wants to get married.

Adela, at twenty the youngest and prettiest of the daughters, comes tattling to Bernarda that Angustias, at thirty-nine the eldest and ugliest, has been peeking through the back door and listening to the men's talk. Bernarda is furious at Angustias and hits her, then dismisses all but Poncia. She asks Poncia what the men were talking about and learns the gossip about the local "bad woman" who was carried off to the olive grove by a group of men the night before. Bernarda bemoans the fact that a daughter of hers cares to listen to such talk, and Poncia points out that all her daughters are in need of husbands —indeed, they have never even had beaux. Bernarda snaps that her daughters have no need of any beaux to be found in this village, for there's no one good enough to come near them. Poncia suggests that they could have moved to another town, although then they wouldn't have been the highest-ranking family; Bernarda furiously shuts her up, and goes out.

Amelia, twenty-seven, and Martirio, twenty-four, gossip about a neighbor's troubles and agree that it must be terrible to belong to a man. Once, indeed, Martirio had thought she was being courted by Enrique Humanas, but he didn't come when he said he would, and now she says she no longer wants a man. Magdelena comes in, and they discuss the fact that Pepe el Romano, handsome and twenty-five and the only eligible bachelor in their mother's eyes, is expected to ask Angustias to marry him, for she is the daughter of Bernarda's first marriage and possesses a far greater fortune than her half-sisters. Adela enters in a bright new dress she had hoped to wear to a party and rebelliously sobs that she can't bear to be locked up in mourning until her lovely skin looks sickly like her sisters'.

At the word that Pepe el Romano is approaching, the daughters all run off to peek out at him. Bernarda discovers that Angustias has powdered her face and, violently denouncing her as a painted hussy, wipes off the powder. Maria Josefa comes in decked with flowers, declaring she has escaped from her room because she wants to "get married to a beautiful manly man from the shore of the sea . . . . I don't want to see these single women, longing for marriage, turning their hearts to dust."

ACT TWO

All the daughters except Adela sit sewing with Poncia in another white room, sweetly exchanging catty insults. While Angustias triumphantly admits talking at her window until one in the morning with Pepe el Romano and agreeing to marry him, Poncia and the others are sure they heard him leave about four. Just as Adela comes in, the other daughters are called out to see about some laces. Poncia knows Adela was talking to Pepe after he left Angustias' window. She advises the girl not to "go against God's law" in her desire for Pepe, but simply to wait for the sickly Angustias to die with her first child and then to marry him openly. Adela warns her not to snoop, but Poncia says she will snoop and tell, for she doesn't want to live in a dirtied house. Adela is defiant: "No one can stop what has to happen."

The others come back and return to yearning over the marvelous freedom enjoyed by men. Suddenly Angustias bursts in, furiously demanding to know who has stolen the picture of Pepe she had under her pillow. Bernarda, hearing the fray, sends Poncia to search all the beds; the picture is found in Martirio's. She tries to pass the theft off as a practical joke, but Adela jealously insists that

it was a much more meaningful gesture. All the daughters fall to spitting spite-
fully until Bernarda silences them and vows to chain them all up so no one will
know of their disgraceful hates.

Bernarda confides to Poncia that she wants to get Angustias married as
soon as possible so as to get Pepe away from the house. Poncia forces her to
admit that she secretly prevented Enrique Humanas from coming to court Martirio only because his father was a shepherd. "And you see now what's happening to you with these airs!" But Bernarda refuses to recognize that anything
very grave is brewing in her house—and if it should, "you can be sure it won't
go beyond these walls." Again Poncia emphasizes that Pepe has been leaving at
four, while Angustias swears he leaves her at one, but Bernarda insists that her
own eyes are watchful enough to run her house alone.

In a moment alone together, Martirio taunts Adela, having seen her in
Pepe's embrace; Adela taunts back that Martirio just wishes it had been herself.
Martirio cries, "None of us will have him! . . . I'll see you dead first!"

Scandal has erupted in the street: an unmarried neighbor girl has killed her
illegitimate baby to try to conceal her shame, and now she is being dragged
through the town. Bernarda is foremost in screaming for her death, "Hot
coals in the place where she sinned!" This makes Adela clutch her own belly
and cry, "No! No!"

ACT THREE

Prudencia has been visiting; she admires Angustias' engagement ring and
new furniture, then leaves. Bernarda tells Angustias that she must make up
with Martirio over the picture incident, for she wants to put up a good front
and have family harmony. Pepe has said he couldn't come this evening, so
Bernarda chases her girls off to an early bedtime, then boasts that the "very
grave thing" Poncia has been prophesying doesn't seem to be happening.

Adela passes through in her petticoats as the servants notice the dogs barking at something outside and go off to bed. Maria Josefa enters singing with a
lamb in her arms that she says is a baby. When Martirio comes and tries to
send her back to bed, the old woman chatters crazily but perceptively about the
manless, joyless condition of the house. Martirio finally locks her grandmother
in her room, then calls out into the yard to Adela, who comes in with her
clothes in disarray. When Martirio warns her to stay away from Pepe, Adela
vaunts their love and says she'll even be proud to be his mistress when he has
married Angustias. Martirio vows to thwart her. As Bernarda and the others
enter, Martirio denounces Adela as a fallen woman, which Adela boastfully
confirms. Bernarda runs out looking for a gun, followed by Martirio. A shot is
hard, and Martirio returns announcing, "That does away with Pepe el Romano," whereupon Adela rushes out. It then turns out that Bernarda missed
her aim and Pepe merely raced away on his mare; but Martirio's spiteful trick
of words has worked—investigation of a thud reveals that Adela has already
hanged herself.

Bernarda starts giving orders, emphasizing that they must dress Adela "as though she were a virgin" and "drown ourselves in a sea of mourning" to avoid scandal. Martirio weeps, "A thousand times happy she, who had him." To which Bernarda storms, "Silence! She, the youngest daughter of Bernarda Alba, died a virgin . . . . Silence!"

F E D E R I C O   G A R C Í A   L O R C A

The Shoemaker's Prodigious Wife

[*La Zapatera Prodigiosa*, written 1926; performed 1934]

PROLOGUE

The Author comes on stage to tell the audience that his poetry is dramatized by an ordinary little shoemaker's wife. She is heard demanding to come out, and soon the Author wishes his hearers good evening. He takes off his hat, and a green light glows inside it; then water gushes out. He apologizes and retreats.

ACT ONE

The play proper takes place in a Spanish village. The eighteen-year-old Shoemaker's Wife enters the shop from a rear door and slams it. Indignant with the village gossips and angry with herself for having married an old man, she weeps. There is a knock on the door, and a Boy comes in with a pair of patent-leather shoes to be fixed. He repeats his mother's instructions that they should be treated with care. When the Wife answers rudely, his face puckers. Immediately, she kisses him and offers him a doll. He accepts it, telling her that his mother said the other day that the Shoemaker's Wife wouldn't have any children. On the Shoemaker's arrival, the Boy flees.

The Wife continues to lament her marriage and talks of the handsome young suitors that she refused. Hammering furiously, the Shoemaker, who is fifty-three, reminds her that she was without dress and home when he took her. As she rages, two neighbors pass the window smiling, and he begs her to be quieter. Looking into a mirror and counting his wrinkles, he curses his sister for having frightened him into marrying so as not to be left alone.

A neighbor, accompanied by her two daughters, appears at the window and commiserates with the Shoemaker while his Wife watches, unnoticed. When the woman tries to cheat him, the Wife flies at her, and the woman goes resentfully away. Controlling himself, the Shoemaker tells his Wife that he has always avoided scenes. They have been married three months, he says, and, while he has loved her, she has mocked him; now he is fed up. She doesn't care three whistles for him, answers the Wife, storming out.

149

The Mayor stops in. Having tamed four wives of his own, he advises that women should be squeezed at the waist and stepped on. Hearing the Shoemaker confess that he intends to fly the coop, the Mayor decries his weakness of character. Presently the Wife enters, powdering her face. Complimenting her on her pretty figure, the Mayor takes his leave.

She spins a chair, and the superstitious Shoemaker is compelled to spin another one in the opposite direction. A flute is heard in the street, and she stops spinning to nod in rhythm. Her husband goes out, and Don Blackbird appears at the window in a swallow-tail coat. He addresses her passionately, but, irritated, she sends him packing. A sad-looking youth wearing a sash looks in. He makes romantic speeches to the Shoemaker's Wife, but her response is sour. When he tries to embrace her, she closes the window violently.

It is growing dark as the Shoemaker enters, wearing a cape and carrying a bundle. "Better alone than pointed at by everybody!" he says, going out again rapidly. Coming from another room, his Wife calls him to supper and, finding the shop empty, concludes that he has gone to the café. Presently the Boy returns, and she holds him on her lap. He has come to tell her something, but his attention is caught by a butterfly, which he pursues through the door. The Wife stops him, demanding to know his message, and he tells her that her husband has left, never to return. Stamping, she cries, "What is going to happen to me all alone in life?" She blames her troubles on the gossiping neighbors, who enter in mock sympathy, carrying large glasses of cooling drinks. The Shoemaker's Wife wails at the top of her lungs.

ACT TWO

The Shoemaker's Wife has converted the room into a tavern. While she washes cups behind the counter, Don Blackbird and a youth with a hat pulled down over his face sit at separate tables. Standing at the door, the Sash Youth gazes sadly at the Wife, who invites him in roughly. He is dying, he moans: "Ay!" The other youths echo him. At this, the Wife threatens to throw them all out, but the Hat Youth defies her. She answers fiercely that her husband has been gone four months, but she will not give in to anybody. One by one the suitors leave.

The Boy enters, and he and the Wife kiss. He shows her the bruise on his knee where someone hit him with a rock for defending her. She takes him in her arms and talks of how the Shoemaker came courting her on a white mare. Presently a song is heard in the distance, and the Boy interprets for her the taunting couplets addressed to Mistress Cobbler. Running to the door, she encounters the Mayor, who offers her a fine house if she will be his. She refuses him insultingly.

At the sound of a trumpet call, she grows wide-eyed with expectance. Soon, surrounded by villagers, the Shoemaker appears in the street, disguised as a puppeteer. The throng enters the tavern. Asked where he is from, the puppeteer answers, "From the Philippine Islands." The Wife is ecstatic. Unrolling a scroll, he begins a ballad about a delicious little tanner's wife and her patient old husband. Halfway through the story, the Wife bursts into tears.

During the final verse a scuffle is heard in the street, and the villagers go out quickly, giving the Wife looks of hatred. The puppeteer asks where her husband is, and, sobbing, she answers that he has left her. She adored him, she adds. Expressing sympathy, the Shoemaker says that he was abandoned by his wife; she was flighty and domineering, but he is searching for her to offer forgiveness.

The Boy runs in to report that several young men have wounded each other with knives and that they are blaming the Shoemaker's Wife. The plaza is full of people talking against her, he says. Hurrying in, the neighbor women advise the puppeteer to leave the house of this hyena, but he calls them harpies. Courageously the Wife waits for the crowd. She bids the departing puppeteer to tell her husband, if he should meet him, that she finds the Shoemaker more slender and graceful than all the men in the world, and would receive him as if he were the king and queen together. Trembling with joy, the puppeteer removes his disguise and embraces her.

From the street the taunting couplets are heard, and the Wife, recovering, calls her husband a scoundrel. She tells him how happy she is that he has returned, for the life she is going to lead him will be worse than the inquisition. But the Shoemaker, sitting happily again at his bench, is unheeding. The noise outside grows louder, and neighbors are seen at the window. But the Shoemaker's Wife insults and defies them. As the sound of the couplets fills the stage, a distant bell rings wildly.

JEAN GENÊT

The Blacks [*Les Nègres*, 1958]

Four Negroes, three in white tie and tails and one in sweater and bare feet, are dancing a Mozart minuet with four Negresses in vulgar evening gowns around the flower-laden catafalque of a white woman whom they have murdered. Members of the court watch them. Archibald, one of the dancers, introduces the others to the judges; he names them as Village, Newport News, Diouf, Miss Bobo, Mrs. Snow, Mrs. Felicity Pardon, and Miss Virtue Diop. Archibald tells Newport News that he is superfluous and sends him off.

Village then describes how he and a man named Herod Adventure found the woman, a tramp, in the docks area; Adventure held her hands while Village strangled her; they then brought her to the courtroom in a crate. The Negroes seat themselves round the catafalque and ceremoniously light cigarettes, puffing smoke to overcome the smell of the dead woman. The court grows agitated, and the Queen weeps; all kneel as her valet wipes her eyes. The Missionary, one of the judges, assures the other judges—all of whom are Negroes wearing white masks—that "God is white." Village, continuing the tale, says they had no trouble bringing the body up to the court, adding that he carried his revolver just in case; Village puts the gun on the shoeshine box at the foot of the catafalque.

Newport News returns with the news that "he" has arrived and is in handcuffs; News takes the revolver and leaves to question the man, ignoring Diouf's timid attempt to persuade him to leave the gun behind. Diouf, a clergyman, proposes a compromise with the white judges; as he speaks, his fellows close their eyes and stop up their ears. The Governor intervenes, ordering Village and Virtue to start the story. Village tells of the near love he felt for Virtue on first seeing her walking in the rain and waiting for customers—white customers. He says that he loves Virtue and that they want to marry; Archibald tells him that in that case he and Virtue should go and join the audience—if the people will allow Negroes among them; the others, Archibald says, will be saved by the woman on the catafalque. The court shrinks in horror when Bobo tells them that they have murdered many kinds of white people; the valet asks whether they would kill a little boy, and Bobo replies yes, or anything else they could get their hands on. Village tries to take Virtue off into the audience, but instead, Archibald, Bobo, Diouf, Snow, and Felicity move back and turn away, leaving the pair alone. As Village tells Virtue he loves her, the Queen falls asleep and starts snoring; the Judge and the Governor try to wake her. The whole court listens attentively as Virtue speaks a poem describing the Queen's whiteness. Awakened but apparently dazed, she begins reciting the poem with Virtue, who moves to Village and, together with the Queen, tells him she loves him. The Queen suddenly awakens, and her fellow judges comfort her.

Archibald and the others turn back to Village and tell him to get on with the story; they accuse him of having loved the dead woman. Snow says Village had to force himself to kill her. As Village denies their charges, Felicity moves to the catafalque and slips a few grains of corn inside. Village continues his story: the white woman was standing behind her counter . . . . The Negroes then decide that they need someone to take the part of the dead woman in a reconstruction of the murder; Diouf is nominated, much against his will, and is dressed in a blonde wig and a crude mask representing a laughing white woman.

Diouf stands in front of the catafalque as the others walk slowly backwards waving handkerchiefs in farewell; Diouf acknowledges their salute with bows. Before Village can continue, Bobo cries that he is too pale; she blackens him with polish from the shoeshine box. Village says he entered the room where the woman was sitting knitting and accepted a glass of rum; he asks for Diouf to wear a skirt; Felicity takes hers off, and Diouf puts it on. Village says the woman's mother called for her medicine from the adjoining room; Felicity imitates the mother calling. Diouf moves toward the voice, but is stopped by Village, who imitates a woman's voice and says the medicine will be brought in soon. The mother calls again, reminding her daughter that the baker's wife will be calling. Bobo, acting the part of the baker's wife, comes in, sees that the woman has a visitor, and says she will strain her eyes working in the dark, then leaves. Felicity, as the mother, calls that Susan, the woman's sister, should be told to come in; Village, in a woman's voice, calls for Susan. Snow, as Susan, calls that she is playing alone in the garden, and Village tells her to watch for prowlers.

Virtue rushes to Village, imploring him to stop; Village declares that he loves her and can bear it no longer. Snow tells Virtue that Village is addressing the white woman, not Virtue. Village uses some of the words he spoke to Virtue earlier in telling the white woman he loves her; he describes how she began moving toward her bedroom, but as Diouf, in his mask, starts moving, Village stops him and says first he wants the court to see some of the things the white woman could do. He orders her to play, and she plays an invisible piano; he orders her to pray, and she falls on her knees. The Queen exits weeping with her valet when Village says that one day the woman was put in prison and later burned at the stake. Bobo becomes a midwife and delivers the woman of a two-foot-long doll representing the Governor, then another, representing the valet, another—the Judge, then the Missionary and the Queen, who returns in time to witness her birth and exits again, followed by the Governor.

The white woman, played by Diouf, begins re-enacting the walk to the bedroom; Village follows. The Governor returns and reports that the Queen is weeping; the valet goes off to comfort her, while the Negroes encourage Village, who finally disappears behind a screen with the white woman, while the others sing to the tune of "Dies Irae." Newport News returns, and Archibald asks whether it's all over, then screams at the judges that they must keep their masks on as they raise their hands to shed them. News says it's not quite finished but that "he" will certainly be executed. The valet returns and says that the Queen is still weeping. Village finally reappears, his collar awry, and says that everything went off as usual. Newport News reports that Village and Diouf sat on a bench off stage and smiled at each other in amusement. A solemn march is heard, and the Queen enters leading Diouf, still in his mask; she announces that they must avenge this white woman. The Judge tells the Queen that the Negroes are angry and dumfounded; there might be a crime being judged elsewhere, he says.

The entire court of judges leaves, apparently for a long journey; the Negroes gather together, anxiously waiting. There is a sound of tramping feet, and the valet appears, followed by the members of the court, all walking backwards and all drunk. While the Negroes imitate animal and bird calls of the forest, they tell of the strangeness of their journey into the bush. The Negroes advance on the members of the court, who fall back; the Governor declares they must make a stand. The Judge tells the Negroes to prepare for judgment and orders them to tremble, which they do, huddled together. The Judge declares that there was no body in the packing case, and Archibald says there was no packing case either; they are all actors, Archibald says, and wanted merely to entertain. The Queen and Felicity then engage in a verbal duel, the one representing white imperialism, the other Africa. The Judge calls on the culprit to own up, and suddenly a firecracker explodes off stage, followed by others. The members of the court remove their masks and Newport News announces that "he" has paid the price and that they will have to get used to executing traitors. While the court was sentencing the man who just died, Newport News says, a congress was acclaiming another who is already on his way to organize and continue the fight against the whites. Archibald says that they have to finish the performance; the judges mask themselves again, and the Governor makes a heroic speech, after which Village draws a pistol and pretends to shoot him. Archibald indicates a point at the center of the stage and tells the Governor to die there; he sets off a small cap with his heel, and the Governor falls.

Village and Virtue move away from the group and flirt during a speech by the Judge, who then falls on the Governor. The Missionary falls in his turn, followed by the valet. The Queen orders the members of the court to stand up and go with her to hell, but before they leave Archibald thanks them for their good performance; they remove their masks and bow, then leave. The play ends with all the Negroes grouped round the catafalque as the Mozart minuet is played.

MICHEL DE GHELDERODE

Chronicles of Hell [*Fastes d'enfer*, 1929]

Carnibos, the chaplain, is greedily feeding at laden tables in an episcopal palace in ancient Flanders while Krakenbus, the vicar-general, spies through a keyhole at the back of the room. Turning to Carnibos, Krakenbus berates him for his gluttony, then leads him to the back, where Carnibas peers through the keyhole and says he sees a dead man in the other room. Dom Pikkendoncker, the plebian, enters, and the three priests discuss the dead man, the episcopal bishop, in cynical terms.

Duvelhond, the guardian of the holy relics, comes in, and is prevented by Krakenbus from revealing the bishop's last words. The archdeacon, Real-Tremblor, arrives with reports that the people are saying that the bishop was a saint and that his death was not a natural one; the storm clouds that blotted out the sun when the bishop died are taken by the people as an evil portent. In the heavy atmosphere and the gathering storm, the people grouping outside the palace are now in a dangerous mood. Simon Laquedeem, the auxiliary bishop, arrives in time to break up the struggling priests, who have resolved to make Real-Tremblor lick the bishop's nose for having told his tale badly. Laquedeem tells the priests to assume masks of sorrow; speaking to himself, he vows to purge the palace of these debauched men and of the shadow of the bishop.

As Real-Tremblor leaves on Laquedeem's orders to see if the expected nuncio is coming, Veneranda, the bishop's ninety-year-old servant, is spotted leaving the room in which the dead man lies. Laquedeem tells the others to let her go, and Duvelhond says this is imprudent—she knows too much. Laquedeem hints that they can get rid of her later by an "accident."

Real-Tremblor returns with Sodomati, a young priest who is secretary to the nuncio; the crowd, Sodomati complains, threatened him as he passed in his carriage. Sodomati is disgusted by the sight of the bishop's collection of pagan idols, witches' masks, and totems that line the walls, and declares that the bad influence of the false gods has affected both the palace staff and the population; they must burn the idols, he says. The supercilious secretary and Laquedeem quarrel and nearly come to blows after Laquedeem mocks Sodomati's effeminacy and Sodomati retorts with a thrust at Laquedeem's Jewish origins.

Lightning flashes outside, recalling the priests to the main problem: the angry people collecting outside the palace. The priests decide to make an appearance on the balcony, but a roar of boos and jeers greets them and they hurriedly withdraw. Four Swiss guards appear and are taken into the death chamber to guard the funeral couch. The priests decide that it would be proper to enter and gaze upon the mortal remains of John of Eremo, bishop of Lapideopolis.

The bishop, an enormous man, is lying on the funeral couch in a room brightly lit by a hundred candles; the priests kneel and Laquedeem speaks a perfunctory prayer to which the others confusedly respond. They return to the other room and begin eating. At Sodomati's prompting, Laquedeem describes the life of John of Eremo—John of the desert—so-called because he had been found as a child by monks in the dunes. Of unknown parentage, John grew up in the monastery and was considered slightly mad by the monks. One day he put to sea in a leaky boat, and when he failed to return, the monks believed him dead.

Years later he returned in an equally worm-eaten boat, which, as he beached it, disintegrated and disgorged a load of idols. It was a time of plague and famine; John performed an apparent miracle when he marched into the town bearing a cross made from the planks of his wrecked boat and threw the cross into the huge fire that was incinerating the corpses of plague victims in the market place: a great flame arose and lifted the thick yellow mist shrouding the town, and suddenly the plague disappeared. John found stores laid by in case of siege and distributed them to the starving people; amid great rejoicing, life returned to normal. When the bishop and his servants, who had fled the plague, returned, they found John ensconced in the palace, a self-declared bishop. John drove them away, and was later consecrated in his position by Rome.

Laquedeem describes the bishop's death, but grows nervous on being pressed for details by Sodomati; he finally bursts out that he had nothing to do with the bishop's death: may a thunderbolt fall if he was responsible, he protests. As he utters the oath, a thunderbolt does indeed fall close to the palace, causing uproar and panic in the room. The Swiss guards suddenly flee from the death chamber. Laquedeem runs to the room and, throwing open the doors, reveals Bishop John standing by the funeral couch. The bishop slowly and stiffly walks toward the cowering priests, who fall back and finally flee, locking the doors behind them. Bishop John, moving jerkily, like an automaton, crosses from the death chamber into the room, poking in his mouth and spitting out the wax that had been sealing the aperture. A door opens in the wall on his left and John goes through it. The priests return through the rear of the death chamber, and Laquedeem runs to lock the door through which John has just passed.

They hold a council of war, but the priests are confused and frightened, and only Laquedeem is master of himself. Real-Tremblor, who has been sent to report on the crowd outside, returns with bad news: the people are charging the militia and stacking up gunpowder barrels to blow up the palace. The priests crowd round Laquedeem with urgent questions: Is the bishop threatening them or imploring them? What is stuck in his throat? Laquedeem says that the bishop failed to swallow the last sacrament, and now it is burning his throat; both heaven and hell have rejected his soul because the communion has not been received.

Duvelhond brings a guard who carries an arquebus. On Laquedeem's orders he sets it up pointing at the locked door; Laquedeem sends everyone away, then fires the gun, shattering part of the door behind which the bishop stands. John, unhurt, shows his face in the hole torn in the door, and Laquedeem thrusts the gun through the aperture; the bishop grabs it and, after a struggle, pulls it from Laquedeem. An explosion shakes the palace, and people are heard cheering; Laquedeem rushes out. John manages to unlock the door and steps into the room. Laquedeem rushes back after a second explosion has rocked the palace, carrying an ax. John throws himself at Laquedeem, and a death struggle begins. The others arrive just as John is advancing on the fallen Laquedeem with up-raised ax. The old servant Veneranda runs in as the priests stand frozen in hor-ror; John lowers the ax at her command and falls to his knees. Veneranda thrusts a finger into John's throat to dislodge the obstruction; John spits it out and stares at it in amazement.

Veneranda leads the bishop back to the couch "to die." Before doing so, the bishop makes a threatening gesture at the priests; his servant tries to re-strain him, imploring him to forgive them, but John raises a clenched fist at the priests. Again Veneranda implores him to absolve them, then, slapping him in the face, says: "Your mother is ordering you to do it." John's fist slowly be-comes an open hand, blessing the bowed heads of the priests. His mother leads him to the couch and lays him to rest. Sodomati retrieves the thing spat out by John and hands it to Laquedeem: it is the host given by Laquedeem to John at the last communion.

Laquedeem asks, "Who wants the communion?" and Real-Tremblor an-swers, "She does," pointing to Veneranda, who is trying to slip away. La-quedeem strides to the old servant and thrusts the poisoned host into her mouth; Veneranda takes two steps toward the door, then slowly falls and dies. Suddenly the people thrust their way into the room, demanding John's body; they bear it away in mourning.

Laquedeem, who has bowel trouble, shakes with an awful convulsion and, after losing his balance in a tremendous shudder, stands erect, declaring "deliv-erance." A stink pervades the room, and Carnibos rushes out, returning swing-ing a censer and stating majestically, "I'm censing!"

Pikkendoncker shouts "Dung!" and amid great laughter the priests run round sniffing each other like dogs. The pitch of hilarity rises. The priests, in frantic joy, jump around comically in clouds of incense, shouting, "Dung! Dung!" The curtain falls on these chronicles of hell with Laquedeem crouch-ing, cassock raised, face in demonic bliss, thundering: "The pigs! They've filled their cassocks with dung!"

JEAN GIRAUDOUX

Electra [*Electre*, 1937]

ACT ONE

Orestes, a handsome twenty-year-old stranger, comes with three little girls, the Eumenides, to the front of Agamemnon's palace in Argos. He does not identify himself as Agamemnon's son to the gardener who, dressed in wedding clothes, comes up to him, accompanied by wedding guests. The little girls recount some of the horrible things that have happened in the palace: Atreus slew his brother's sons and cooked their hearts; Cassandra was strangled; Agamemnon slipped and killed himself by falling on his sword; and Orestes was banished when he was two years old.

The gardener tries to shoo away the little girls, who say their job is to lie, slander, and insult. He tells Orestes that in a "terrifying" way, they grow before your eyes. Before they leave, the girls tell Orestes that Electra, Orestes' sister, will marry the gardener tomorrow.

The judge, middle-aged and fatuous, arrives with his frivolous young wife Agatha Theocathocles. He warns the gardener not to marry Electra. Though she is beautiful and intelligent, he says, she will never let well enough alone; because she pursues justice in an implacable way, she interferes with the ordinary course of life, which gradually covers and obscures the past. The gardener protests that Electra is devout and that the dead are her advocates, but the judge disagrees. He says that the dead, sleeping peacefully—murderers, murdered, robbed, robbers—must exclaim with dismay when they see Electra coming, for she will not let them be at peace.

Agatha and Orestes leave as Aegisthus, Agamemnon's cousin and the regent, enters and sits on a throne which his servants install. They also set up a stool for a beggar who is wandering through town, since they suspect he may be a god and want to treat him well. The beggar enters and sits on his stool. Aegisthus, discussing the gods, states his belief that they are not eternally watching us, but are, rather, in a state of lethargy from which we shouldn't rouse them. He says Argos is prospering mainly because he, as regent, has waged war against those who signal to the gods. In Argos now, he notes, no one signals the gods except Electra. The beggar comments that he would like to see her before she is killed. Aegisthus protests that no one wants to kill her, but the beggar says that Aegisthus does want to and must kill her before she, as a wolf cub turns into a wolf, becomes truly herself.

Aegisthus tells the beggar he plans to make her invisible to the gods by marrying her to the gardener. He sends for Clytemnestra, Agamemnon's widow, and Electra, her twenty-one-year-old daughter. Electra says she knows of the plot to marry her to the gardener. Clytemnestra calls it no plot, for at Electra's age, she already carried two babies in her arms. Electra spits at her that she didn't carry them safely, for she dropped Orestes. Clytemnestra accuses Electra of pushing Orestes, and they argue bitterly about the long-past incident. Electra consents to marrying the gardener, but Clytemnestra suddenly changes her mind. The beggar asks her to let herself be persuaded, for by the marriage Electra's life may be saved. Aegisthus summons the gardener and Electra to step forward for the marriage, but Clytemnestra and Electra start their terrible quarrel over Orestes' fall again. Aegisthus finally decides that Clytemnestra is right about the marriage, and he and Clytemnestra leave.

Agatha and Orestes return. Agatha gives Electra's hand in marriage to Orestes, then leaves with the gardener. Electra and Orestes struggle with each other until Orestes tells her who he is. She greets him with joy. Clytemnestra enters, and Electra introduces her "husband"; Clytemnestra does not recognize her son. When Clytemnestra goes, Orestes and Electra speak of Electra's hatred for her mother and Aegisthus. Orestes asks her to leave hatred until tomorrow and to lie in his arms tasting sweetness tonight.

Aegisthus appears on a balcony of the palace. He announces that he has had word that Orestes is alive and is returning to take over his father's throne.

Clytemnestra returns and recognizes Orestes. They speak, but Orestes fears to go too near his mother. She leaves, and Orestes and Electra go to sleep.

The beggar steps forward to clear up the mystery of Orestes' fall. The queen, he says, could have saved Orestes; Electra remembered correctly. He says Electra is truth itself and, because she is, she will kill all peace and happiness; she has become truly herself in Orestes' arms.

ACT TWO

Electra is still seated before the palace, holding the sleeping Orestes. She asks the beggar whether she should awaken her brother, but he tells her to give Orestes five minutes more. He says that Orestes was meant to laugh, to love, to wear fine clothes. She agrees with him but says that because he will awaken to a life of horror without end, she will give him five minutes more.

Electra wakes Orestes. The Eumenides, now fifteen years old, enter and try to coax Orestes to flee from Electra and live a happy life. Orestes listens to them and tries to get Electra to leave with him for happiness in Thessaly, but she insists on giving him her fateful information: their mother has a lover, and their father was murdered. Clytemnestra enters; accused of having a lover, she inadvertently reveals to Electra that her lover is Aegisthus.

Aegisthus enters. A bird hovers high above him, and his appearance is majestic and serene. On learning that the Corinthians are invading Argos, he decides to give the city the king it needs by marrying Clytemnestra. He says that today he was given the city by God and that he will save it. Electra forbids the marriage and, sensing that her mother hated her father, suddenly realizes who killed Agamemnon. She threatens Clytemnestra if she moves one step toward marriage to Aegisthus; when Clytemnestra moves, Electra screams, "Orestes!"

Aegisthus begs Electra to understand; he wants her to help him save Argos. She says no, she will not compromise, for the whole world was given to her this morning—a country called Tenderness and Justice; she wants justice and doesn't trust the gods. Aegisthus asks her whether she knows what a nation is; she says it is a pure spirit that looks at you directly. He denies this and says a nation is a tremendous organism that must be ruled and sustained. He wants to save his nation, she to save the look in their eyes, no matter how many die. The city starts to fall. Aegisthus, in desperation, promises to restore the throne to Orestes tomorrow if Electra will agree to let him save the city today; Electra will not, but instead pursues the regent and Clytemnestra with accusations of murder. They leave.

Narses' wife, a friend of the beggar, and a crowd of beggars come to save Orestes and Electra. The beggar reveals to all how Agamemnon died. He first slipped on soaped steps, then died under Aegisthus' sword while Clytemnestra held him pinned to the floor. Then the beggar tells of two more deaths—those of Aegisthus and Clytemnestra by the hand of Orestes.

The Eumenides enter, now of the age and height of Electra. While the palace flames, they tell Electra that she is the guilty one now, but she says that she has justice, she has everything. The Eumenides leave, promising to pursue Orestes with Electra's appearance until he goes mad and kills himself, cursing her. Narses' wife, bewildered, wants to know what is happening. What is the name, she asks, of this time when the city is in ruins, when the innocent are killing each other and the guilty are dying, yet when there is a freshness in the air and morning is coming?

The beggar tells her that the name of this time is very beautiful. It is called the dawn.

JEAN GIRAUDOUX

The Enchanted [*Intermezzo,* 1933;

this adaptation by Maurice Valency, 1950]

ACT ONE

The Mayor and the Doctor of a provincial French town meet by appointment at a lovely clearing in the woods near a lake, the very spot said to be haunted by a young and handsome Ghost. Eight excited little ten-year-old girls troop through looking for mandrake, followed by their temporary teacher Isabel, who has taught them to consider the spring their classroom.

When the Inspector and the Supervisor of Weights and Measures arrive for the appointment, the Inspector confidently asserts the nonexistence of the spirit world. The other three men explain the nature of the recent "haunting" of the town: dogs no longer cringe when beaten—they bite; mistreated women don't just cry—they quietly run off with more attractive men; at the civic lottery the motorcycle was won by the captain of the football team, and not, as usual, by the mother superior of the convent, and the cash prize went to the neediest couple in town—not, as usual, to the millionaire. In short, "in this community it is no longer respectable to be unhappy," and the Inspector is scandalized at this "nullification of human liberty."

The elderly, spinster Mangebois sisters arrive to give evidence, since they know everything being done and discussed in town. They believe the Ghost is that of the pale young stranger who came to town, shot his wife with her lover, and disappeared, leaving only his hat at the edge of the lake. The Inspector doubts the suicide, suggesting that murderers as well as ghosts are said to return to the scene of the crime. But in any case, the sisters don't hold the Ghost responsible for the scandalous behavior of the townfolk; that they lay to the pernicious influence of young Isabel and present her diary as proof. In her latest entry Isabel has written that she believes the Ghost is trying to help her make the town perfect, and will speak to her shortly. The Inspector is convinced that contact and collusion between these two evil forces must be prevented.

When Isabel and her class return, the Inspector examines them to see just what Isabel is really teaching them. Dissatisfied with the first child's answer, he gives her a zero, only to discover that "in our class, zero is the highest mark—it's closest to infinity." Another girl pleases him by announcing that "the flower is one of the most beautiful aspects of nature," but then shocks him by continuing, "it is a practical demonstration of the beauty of the sexual process." He discovers that each girl's neck bears a red mark, which Isabel puts on with lipstick each morning so that the spirits may recognize their friends. At last he dismisses Isabel from her teaching post and makes the Supervisor the temporary substitute.

Alone at twilight, Isabel is shy when the Ghost first appears, but soon is enthusiastically asking his help in waking up his fellow spirits of the dead and bringing them back to help the living with their wisdom—to "save the world from itself, and make life as sensible and happy as a fairy tale." He at first wants only to know her name but finally starts to answer her questions about death—and vanishes.

ACT TWO

A few weeks later the Doctor finds the Supervisor in the same clearing teaching the little girls astronomy. The two discuss the increasing enchantment of the town, where "every dream comes true and every wish is granted," and connect this condition with Isabel's increasing fraternization with the Ghost. The Inspector and the Mayor arrive with a mandate from the government to liquidate the alleged phantom as a subversive element that has drawn the entire town into a "conspiracy against constituted authority." The Inspector, convinced that the phantom is still quite mortal, intends to have him shot when he appears to meet Isabel that evening.

The Supervisor, long the gallant defender of feminine honor in general, and now obviously enamored of Isabel, is to be allowed a private word with her before such drastic measures are taken. He tries to persuade her that the Ghost is trying for his own dark purposes to cut her off from humanity; she will not, as she believes, be able to divide her life between such ghostly acquaintances and the living man who will one day ask her to be his wife. In that case, she replies, she will reject the man, who wants to shut her eyes and lips with kisses, in favor of the spirit, who will open them to the new world behind the darkness of what we now know about life and death. He finally warns her of the Inspector's trap, but she laughingly dismisses him.

Two executioners and the Inspector agree that the signal to shoot will be the first time the supposed Ghost speaks the word "alive." The phantom, in time, appears to Isabel, reporting that all their schemes have failed, that he cannot penetrate the sleep of the dead. She is not convinced, for has she not succeeded in entrancing *him* so that he does not sleep but comes to talk to her? He begins to confess that he has been deceiving her, that he is not a ghost, but very much "alive"—and at the word two shots strike him dead. The Doctor mourns that "in this world the Inspector is always right, and the spectre is false," whereupon a genuine phantom arises from the corpse and promises to meet Isabel at her home at six the next evening, bringing a number of fellow spirits with him.

ACT THREE

Half an hour before six the Inspector enters Isabel's room with the Mayor and the class of girls, whom he posts as lookouts. He explains that he has written an official adjuration to exorcize the Ghost, for if the inhabitants of the other world were permitted to colonize France, they would soon take over the government. The Mayor is even more concerned by the realization that ghosts would violate those "safeguards of human dignity," the door latch and the window shade, and that his secret passion for stamp-collecting would no longer be private.

As the girls warn of the approach of Isabel and the Doctor, the Inspector retreats with his company to another room. When they enter, Isabel is suddenly reluctant to meet the Ghost alone, and asks the Doctor to stay; but he leaves when a knock at the door announces the arrival of the Supervisor, who formally requests Isabel's hand in marriage. Before the Ghost comes, the Supervisor wants her to know that she has a choice of roads to the other world. He represents the road of life with a government employee, which moves smoothly from post to post to retirement to death, easily and pleasantly and perhaps even more surely than the way the young phantom has to offer. Furthermore, there is even the poetry of suspense and surprise in the Bureau of Weights and Measures: at the beginning of each three-year post, he learns that his next post will be in one of two places, but he doesn't know which one until the week he is to leave.

She is won, but a moment's regretful pity for "my poor ghost" invites the latter's appearance. He promises to give her the key to the riddle of death if she will ask the Supervisor to leave. The official retorts that an answered riddle is no longer a riddle and has no dignity whatsoever; besides, the dead probably don't know any more about death than the living do about life. The Ghost is growing noticeably more transparent, and the Supervisor taunts triumphantly that he'd better make a good exit while he can, or suffer the indignity of disintegrating before Isabel's very eyes. The Ghost derides him as the "lump of concrete out of which destiny is forced to make spirits," but the Supervisor is confident that he will make as adequate and reliable a spirit as he is now a dependable man, devoted to his job and to his loved one. He lets slip some of the things he has already done for Isabel without her knowledge, and she exclaims "dear Robert!" which the Ghost takes to be the sign of his own defeat and betrayal. He expounds scathingly on the nature of young girls, who appear to have "souls through which the infinite could flow into the finite," and who are invariably distracted by some worthless beast of a man. He derides the pleasures of life until Isabel rushes into his arms begging him to save her. He kisses her, then pushes her away and disappears, whereupon she falls senseless.

All the others, entering, flutter worriedly around her, but the Doctor takes over calmly. To call her back to the world of the living, he organizes a symphony of the sounds of life: he sets the children to reciting lessons, the Mangebois sisters to chattering, the Supervisor to saying "I love you," and a group of citizens to playing cards. Out of all the mélange, the words which seem to recall Isabel are the Mangebois sisters' censorious discussion of black lace petticoats with crimson satin linings; but once awake, the girl is content to listen only to the Supervisor's professions of love.

The Mayor dashes in to report the results of the new lottery: the motorcycle goes to the mother superior and the grand cash prize to the millionaire. The Inspector concludes that "enlightened democracy is working as usual," and the Doctor announces that "the interlude is over."

JEAN GIRAUDOUX

The Madwoman of Chaillot [*La Folle de Chaillot*, 1945; this adaptation by Maurice Valency, 1949]

ACT ONE

At a sidewalk café, the President and the Baron are celebrating the stock market success of half a million shares in a corporation still lacking both a name and a function. The Broker comes to report that financial manipulation this morning has gained them three and a half million francs already, whereupon an eavesdropper rushes up to dump on their table a sack full of his life's savings.

The Prospector, sipping water at another table, and the President have recognized a source of profit in each other's faces. The President needs a name for his corporation; the Prospector, fifty thousand francs for his mistress. So "International Substrate of Paris, Inc." is exchanged for the eavesdropper's money. But the Prospector has more to offer; he reveals himself as an expert who can taste oil in water that has flowed through pipes passing through earth containing a trace of it, and he declares that this café lies directly above an immense pool of oil. The City Architect, however, has refused to give him a permit to drill for oil within the city limits; so he has employed a man to plant a bomb in the Architect's office building across the river, confident that the next Architect will be more cooperative. As a matter of fact, the bomb is set to explode at noon, only a few minutes away.

All this time the President has been interrupted in turn by a street singer, a Flower Girl, a Ragpicker, a deaf-mute, a shoe-lace peddler, a Juggler, and a specialist in the extraction of bunions and corns. All are trying to earn a few sous, all enliven the scene with their by-play, and all greatly irritate the President by their presence. But most annoying, right in the middle of the Prospector's exposition, has been Countess Aurelia, the Madwoman of Chaillot, an apparition wearing the remnants of what had been the grand fashion in dress in 1885. During the conversation between the President and the Prospector, she asks the waitress Irma for chicken giblets for the tomcat that lives under the bridge, then takes her stance before the President and surveys him with undisguised disapproval. When he demands that the waiter make her move on, he learns that she owns the café. She finally dons a scarf with a grand gesture that upsets a glass of water into the President's lap and stalks off.

When the clock strikes noon, there is no explosion; instead a policeman carries in an unconscious man whom he had dutifully slugged to prevent his jumping into the river. It is Pierre, who had been blackmailed into being the Prospector's bomb-setter but who could not bring himself to do it. Irma falls in love with him at first sight, and he with her upon regaining consciousness. The Countess demands that a police-sergeant convince the would-be suicide of the value of life, but he makes even the so-called pleasures sound dull; so the Countess chatters of the details that fill her own life—feeding cats, watering plants, keeping an eye on the evil ones in her district and circumventing their plots, and being a little nostalgic for Adolphe Bertaut, whom she had loved and lost in the days when her dress was new.

Pierre is totally won by the freshness of the Countess's approach to life. She gets rid of the Prospector, who has been trying to drag his ex-agent away, and Pierre tells her about the evil plot to destroy Paris and cover it with derricks and drills. The Ragpicker, as spokesman for all the vagabonds who are the Countess's friends, chimes in to convince her that this wickedness is connected to all that is wrong with the modern world. These presidents and trustees and brokers, he says, are the "pimps" who take a percentage of all that is bought and sold, so that where there used to be shopkeepers who owned what they sold and smiled at their customers, both shopkeepers and customers are being replaced by inhuman faces with gelatine eyes. The Flower Girl complains that flowers wilt overnight these days; the Juggler, that pigeons never fly any more and that even the air has changed, for if he throws his torches too high, they go out.

The Countess refuses to be convinced that the evil ones are too many and too well organized to be destroyed. She dictates a letter to the President, purporting to come from the Prospector and inviting him to see a spontaneous outcrop of oil in the cellar of her house at three that afternoon. Since the evil ones are said to be connected like the works of a machine, she is confident that they will all come to her trap together.

ACT TWO

A sewerman she once helped is keeping his promise to show the Countess the secret of the moving stone in her cellar. Properly pushed, it pivots to disclose a circular staircase winding down into the bowels of the earth; those who start down it never return. As he closes the stone and leaves, Constance and Gabrielle, the Madwomen of Passy and St. Sulpice, arrive in their most extravagant 1880's dress. Constance brings her imaginary dog Dickie, but the Countess begs her to put the dog away, just this once. Gabrielle offers to take Dickie on her lap, but Constance accuses her of hypocritically pretending the dog is there even when he has actually been left at home. In the ensuing argument, Constance reprimands Gabrielle for inviting total strangers to the Countess's teas, people who exist only in her imagination.

The Countess begs her guests to put imaginary subjects aside for a moment and discuss the fate of humanity. She warns that mankind—particularly the male sex—is reverting to beasts. Constance begs her not to talk sex in front of Gabrielle, a virgin, but the Countess remarks that Gabrielle could not be *that* innocent; after all she keeps canaries. Gabrielle defends men as sweet creatures, but the Countess retorts that her guests are merely living in a dream, as she did until waking up to the danger facing humanity. When Constance persists in reminiscing about her husband, the Countess disparages memories and make-believe, begging that they stick to reality and, just this once, tell the truth. Defending her memories, Constance asks what the Countess would think if someone called her pearls false. The Countess replies that, as everyone knows, pearls become more real the longer you wear them. Exactly the same with memories, Constance retorts.

The Countess pulls the conversation back to the subject: humanity is doomed, *unless* . . . She asks the ladies what they propose. They have no workable suggestions. The Countess then explains the nature of the evil destroying the world and asks her friends' opinions on a moral problem: if she can gather all the wicked men here in her cellar, does she have the right to exterminate them like rats for the good of the world?

They welcome the arrival of Josephine, the Madwoman of La Concorde, for her sister's husband was a lawyer. She affirms that getting all your enemies together and killing them at once is a basic military principle and therefore legal. She does introduce the necessity of giving them a fair trial but adds that the court may designate an attorney to represent them *in absentia*.

The vagabond friends are called in to fill out the jury, and the Ragpicker is chosen attorney for the defense. He speaks directly in the character of the accused, making a brilliant speech in defense of his rich man's respectability and innocence. He does not worship money, he explains; money worships him. It won't let him alone. In order to get rid of it, he buys things—railroads, refineries, stores, expensive clothes, and so on. Accused of refusing money to the peddler and the other vagabonds, he proves that he simply cannot afford to waste time giving them a few sous when he is so conscientiously busy spending large sums to get rid of the wealth that afflicts him. The impressionable Constance is almost sympathetic until the defendant announces that he intends to use the oil to make war and conquer the world. When the trial is over, the verdict is a unanimous "guilty," and the Countess is fully authorized to exterminate the wicked men.

After everyone leaves, Pierre finds the Countess resting and, touched, helps her pretend that he is Adolphe Bertaut, come to tell her that he has always loved her, despite his infidelities. Alone again, she pushes the secret stone, and then the crowd of men, and the women who influence them, begins to arrive. The presidents and prospectors and press agents give the Countess contracts to sign, ostensibly to allow her a share of the profits, actually to obtain a waiver of her rights; but since she pretends to be deaf, they freely chatter and reveal their soulless deceitfulness. All rush eagerly to the circular stairway, which the Countess closes after the last of them.

The stage is immediately suffused with a glowing radiance, reflected in the faces of all the vagabonds crowding in again to marvel gratefully that the pigeons are flying, strangers are stopping each other on the street to share almond bars, the air is pure, and grass is sprouting on the pavements; disembodied voices and music also thank the Countess. A group called the Adolphe Bertauts of the world appear, declaring that henceforth they can and will be stronger of character and that they are finally proposing marriage to her. But for them it is too late, says the Countess, who immediately remembers to make Pierre and Irma kiss each other, so that it will not be too late for them as well.

She scolds everyone for waiting so long to tell her about these wicked men, announces that "nothing is ever so wrong in this world that a sensible woman can't set it right in the course of an afternoon," and goes off to feed her cats.

J E A N G I R A U D O U X

Ondine [1939; this adaptation by Maurice Valency, 1954]

ACT ONE

Two old people, Auguste and Eugenie, sit in the living room of a fisherman's hut as a storm rages outside. The time is the Middle Ages. Auguste discusses crossly with Eugenie, his wife, the doings of Ondine, a sixteen-year-old; he says she is a strange creature who is not wet by the rain, dives down waterfalls, and says her prayers under water.

The windows spring open. Hoping Ondine will not start her tricks again, Auguste closes them, but they spring open again, first to show an old man's head, then a naiad with a pearl necklace. Auguste becomes angry at Ondine— not visible—and threatens to bolt her out of the house if she doesn't come in by the count of three. At three, he bolts the door, but it bursts open to reveal a knight in full armor.

He announces himself as Ritter Hans von Wittenstein zu Wittenstein, a knight-errant who has spent a month in the forest; he is very hungry. The old people offer him a trout. He insists it be poached, that is, thrown into boiling water alive, and Eugenie, after attempts to change his mind about the method of cooking, goes into the kitchen to comply with his request. Hans tells Auguste he is there because his betrothed, Bertha, told him she would marry him only if he came back alive after spending a month in the "enchanted forest."

Ondine comes in and admires Hans. After praising his beautiful ears and beautiful name in unspoiled candor, she asks him to take her away with him. The admiration ceases abruptly when Eugenie brings in the poached trout.

Ondine is outraged that anyone should kill her "poor darling trout," and throws it out the window. She says she is going out to listen to the Old One, who will tell her about men. She says ". . . I already know that I hate them." Hans says, "They already know that they love you." She runs out into the night.

Hans is still hungry, and Eugenie goes out to get him some ham. Auguste joins her. Ondine returns and tells Hans that the Old One, the King of the Sea, said Hans will deceive her. The two old people return with the ham. Hans eats it placidly, while Ondine woos him with tender words.

Auguste proposes a toast to the Princess Bertha, Hans's betrothed. Ondine wildly accuses Hans of deceiving her, but Hans says he thinks there is no longer any Bertha. After Ondine runs out, Auguste and Eugenie confess she is not their daughter, but a creature they found at the edge of the lake after their own child had been stolen. Hans asks them for her hand. Auguste says Ondine is strange and belongs to the lake.

The two older people retire; Hans sits by the fire, and the walls of the hut becomes transparent. In the background comes a figure of an Ondine, blonde and naked; then, a dark, dressed Ondine. One begs him to take her; the other warns him not to touch her.

Ondine herself comes to Hans and tells him to ignore the other two, but they persist in distracting him with words and songs. Finally, Ondine says yes to them, agreeing to a pact that they apparently propose. As the Ondines disappear, the walls of the hut become solid. Hans says he is caught, body and soul. Ondine observes that it takes longer to catch a bass.

They plan to leave in the morning to see the world. Ondine asks him whether lovers in the world are always together. When he says no, she tells him there are fish in the sea, dogfish, which, once they mate, are never more than two fingers apart.

ACT TWO

In the ornate hall of honor in the king's palace, the lord chamberlain and the superintendent of the royal theaters, two officials of the king's court, try to decide on entertainment for the occasion when Hans will present his bride, Ondine, at court. Near them stands the Illusionist, actually the Old One, the King of the Sea. The Illusionist performs supernatural tricks as samples of his entertainment and even offers to produce an illusion of Hans and Bertha brought together.

All hide as the illusory Hans and Bertha meet. Bertha queries him bitterly about his honeymoon with Ondine. He says that Bertha should not have sent him off if she loved him but should have declared her love before all the world. She kisses him, and he holds her by the hands. She cries out that he has killed a bird she had in one hand. He begs her forgiveness and they part.

The Illusionist causes them to meet again, but it is eight months hence, and this time they discuss Ondine's shortcomings as a wife, such as not being able to read or write, to dance, or to listen without interruption. Bertha mentions her own talents and knowledge of the terms of jousting and of the Wittenstein family traditions.

The Illusionist stops his tricks as Ondine enters with the chamberlain. She finds Bertram, a poet, hiding and discusses his poems with him, while revealing to the chamberlain that she knows he has damp hands, a source of "infinite embarrassment" to him. The chamberlain begs her not to be so frank with his majesty, who has a wart on his nose.

Suddenly, with a flourish of trumpets, the reception begins. Hans comes in and the Illusionist approaches Ondine, who tells him to go away. When introduced to the king, she answers him distractedly, for she cannot take her eyes from Bertha. She finally cries out her fear that Bertha wants Hans. Bertha protests the attack. Ondine accuses her of killing the bird to get Hans's sympathy.

She says Bertha is a hypocrite and blurts out that Bertha would never mention the wart on the king's nose. This remark causes general consternation and the king orders everyone out except Ondine.

The king, who admits he is fascinated by the voice of truth, questions her and finds out she is an Ondine who belongs to the water. She reveals the pact made with the King of the Sea, her uncle, that if Hans deceives her, he will die. She plans to save him by stopping her attacks on Bertha. Instead, she will praise Bertha and keep them together, until Hans tires of Bertha.

When the reception continues, Ondine asks Bertha's forgiveness but gets embroiled in another crisis by saying Bertha is no princess, but the daughter of a fisherman. The Illusionist presents a scene depicting the theft of Eugenie's baby, who was wrapped in silk and left to be taken to the king's palace. The baby was marked with the imprint of her father's hook and line on her shoulder. Ondine tears the dress from Bertha's shoulders, revealing the mark.

Weeping, Bertha refuses to speak to Auguste and Eugenie when they are brought in to confront her. All leave. Then the Illusionist returns. He says he will show the spectators, who are all now hidden, the rest of the plot.

ACT THREE

The magician's illusion is of events five years in the future. In the courtyard of the castle of the Wittensteins, Hans sits, head in hands, splendidly dressed for his wedding to Bertha. Bertha enters in bridal array. Hans says he is upset, explaining that he fears that the flowery speech of his servants is a portent of misfortune, for should the servants speak in rhyme, death is at hand for him. He says he is thinking of Ondine, of her leaving him, of the words reminding him of her deception which come to him constantly from water. Bertha reminds him how they two first deceived Ondine.

A fisherman who has netted an Ondine enters. A second fisherman, actually the Old One, the King of the Sea, announces the judges are coming to try the creature. Despite Bertha's protests, they prepare to hold the trial immediately.

Hans states his complaint to the judges: he wishes to be allowed to live in peace without trespass by the creatures from another world. Ondine is brought in, clothed only in the net that caught her. The fisherman who trapped her gives a wandering testimony about catching her. The judges dismiss him.

The second fisherman declares her no longer an Ondine at all, but a human. The judges again try to find out what Hans's complaint is, and at first it seems to be that Ondine was too loving, then that she deceived him with Bertram. The second fisherman asks that she prove her love by kissing Bertram. Bertram takes her in his arms, but at his kiss, she cries, "Hans, Hans!" The judges decide she did transgress the boundaries of nature but did so with kindness and love. Their sentence, therefore, is that she be killed privately, rather than publicly.

The kitchenmaid approaches Hans, speaking in verse. The wedding bell tolls as if for a funeral, and Hans and the judges go off. The second fisherman reminds Ondine that Hans must die and that at the third call of her sisters, she will forget everything.

Ondine begs him to save Hans, but the second fisherman says Hans's heart is broken. He goes off, and Hans returns and reminisces with Ondine about their life together. He speaks of parting, each to different worlds, never to meet again. She says she will mourn for him always, for she trained herself to remember the motions and steps of their life together and will relive them in the water.

The voices begin to call her; Ondine and Hans kiss, and he dies. At the third call Ondine forgets everything. The second fisherman appears and begins to lead her away. She asks him: who is the handsome young man lying on the steps? When told that he is dead and cannot be brought back to life, she says, "What a pity! How I should have loved him!"

JEAN GIRAUDOUX

Tiger at the Gates [*La Guerre de Troie n'aura pas lieu*, 1935; translation by Christopher Fry performed 1955]

ACT ONE

Andromache, pregnant wife of the Trojan hero Hector, awaits his return from what he has sworn to be the last war Troy will have to fight with her neighbors. She is disturbed by her brother-in-law Paris' abduction of the Grecian Helen and by the imminent arrival of the envoys from Greece, ready to declare war if Helen is not returned to her husband Menelaus; but it seems clear to her that Troy will simply send Helen back and settle down to domestic joys. Her sister-in-law, the prophetess Cassandra, is willing to wager otherwise. Destiny, she says, is like a sleeping tiger that is now being roused by Andromache's own affirmations that things have never gone so well for Troy.

Hector learns of the trouble over Helen and sets out confidently to arrange her return. First he interrogates Paris, and learns that Helen was taken from the sea while she was bathing in the nude; since he did not trespass on Greek land, steal Greek clothes, or have to speak to the husband, Paris has not irremediably insulted Greece, and therefore Hector feels sure it will be easy to smooth everything over. Paris grumbles a bit—he says making love to Helen is like making love to all the women in the world at once—but he agrees to Hector's offer to abide by the decision of their father Priam. Cassandra warns Hector that this is unwise, for Priam has gone mad over Helen, along with all the men of the city. Indeed, worshiping cries are heard outside as Helen strolls along.

Priam enters with his wife Hecuba and the poet Demokos, and all debate Helen's significance in Troy. Priam and Demokos declare her a symbol of beauty and her coupling with Paris the symbol of ideal love. Her actual worth or their actual love—or lack of it—is irrelevant to the important imaginative stimulus of her coming. But Andromache and Hector insist stubbornly that she is still only one woman and not worth the bloody cost of a war. Priam finally agrees that if Helen is willing to return, he won't stop her, and he gives the order to prepare for the ceremonial closing of the gates of war.

Paris later presents Helen to Hector. At her lover's demand she absent-mindedly repeats that she loves him, hates Menelaus, and will never return to Greece; but as soon as he leaves, she admits to Hector that she has no reason to hate Menelaus and no objection to returning to Greece. But then she has never really *seen* Menelaus, she says. As Hector is puzzled, she explains that all objects, events, and people are to her eyes divided into two groups: some few she sees clearly and in color, others remain indistinct and shadowy. Menelaus she never saw in color; Paris, at the beginning of their romance, was quite vivid. But now she realizes, as Hector points to Paris waiting for her, that he too is becoming dim. Hector takes this as an admission that she no longer loves Paris and jubilantly calls Cassandra to say that Helen is leaving this evening. But Helen says, not that she *won't* leave, but that she can't *see* herself leaving, no matter how vividly Hector describes the scene. What she *can* see, when asked, are scenes of battle and Troy burning; she reluctantly admits that she can discern the corpses of Paris and Hector.

A messenger comes to call Hector to his father, for the priests claim that the gods have rejected their sacrifices and do not want the gates of war closed; another messenger reports the arrival of the Greek fleet, flying their flags in a manner interpreted as an insult by the Trojans. Hector leaves angrily, beginning to realize that although Paris, Priam, and Helen have all yielded to him in theory, he seems to be "fighting an inflexible something which is no more than the reflection on a woman's retina."

ACT TWO

Hector has stubbornly ordered preparations for the closing of the gates of war, but Helen flirts with the young Troilus, another of Priam's sons; Demokos airs his plans for a new song of battle personifying War as having Helen's face; and Hecuba, although profoundly sympathetic to Hector's purposes, regularly interjects caustic comments, expressing her pessimistic conviction that men cannot do anything very well—she even out-curses Paris as a practical demonstration. Demokos brings the legal expert Busiris to explain that the Greeks' conduct in approaching Troy constitutes a deliberate breach of international etiquette on three counts and that Troy must retaliate or lose honor among nations. Hector then forces Busiris to reinterpret the same behavior as highly complimentary, thus justifying the cordial reception Hector is determined to offer the Greek envoys.

At the closing of the gates of war, Demokos demands that Hector make the usual address of homage to the dead soldiers who helped him achieve victory and thus end the war, but Hector shocks everyone present with a bitter speech exposing the hypocritical and self-justifying sentimentality of the conventional clichés mouthed by the living about the dead.

Alone with Helen, Andromache pleads with her to love Paris, saying that if the war that seems to be coming were at least to be fought over a true love, she could be reconciled to it. Helen mocks her reasoning with fair plausibility and defends her own approach to life, unsentimental but highly perceptive of human reality.

The Greek Ajax enters, drunken and belligerent, but Hector refuses to recognize insult, even when Ajax slaps him. When Demokos arrives just in time to discover the slap and wants to use it as an excuse for declaring honorable war, Hector himself slaps Demokos to keep him quiet. Demokos vows revenge, but Ajax admires Hector's slapping technique so heartily that he is all friendliness by the time his leader Ulysses arrives. Ulysses and the Trojans thronging around are equally taken aback to discover that Hector plans to exchange Helen quietly for a guarantee of peace, making everything the same as before. Ulysses temporizes with the question of whether Helen *is* the same as before. The crowd shouts that she isn't, but Helen and Paris both dutifully assert that the three days' sail back to Troy was completely innocent. Paris' sailors, however, refuse to permit this shameful slur against their leader's virility and describe in vivid detail the lovemaking they witnessed.

At this point the goddess Iris, messenger of the gods, appears with three divine commands: Aphrodite, goddess of love, warns that there will be war if Hector and Ulysses separate Paris from Helen; Pallas Athena, goddess of reason, warns that there will be war if the two are *not* separated. And the master Zeus orders the throng to leave the two negotiators alone so that they may arrange to separate Paris and Helen without separating them; if they don't thus avert war, he swears, there will be war.

The youthful Hector and the more mature Ulysses find themselves on the invisible scales of destiny, and even Hector soon concedes that the weight of the future seems to be on Ulysses' side. At first he accuses the other of deceit and shrewd malevolence, but Ulysses explains that he has no personal animosity toward Hector or toward Troy. He simply has learned to recognize the designs of fate as nations unconsciously are prepared to fight each other. Nevertheless, he agrees to try to trick destiny, to receive Helen and depart speedily, although he fears that destiny will somehow outtrick the tricker as he walks from here to the ships.

He leaves, and Hector calls Andromache and Cassandra to hear the good news. Ajax, very drunk now, begins to creep amorously toward Andromache; he does not see Hector raising his javelin, but decides on his own to leave her untouched and exits precipitately. Demokos simultaneously enters, shouting that this return of Helen is cowardly treason and trying to present his new song of war. Hector hurls the raised javelin at him, and the curtain begins to fall on his declaration that "the war will not take place, Andromache!" But others enter and see the stricken Demokos, and the curtain rises again. The newcomers demand to know who has killed Demokos, and the dying poet replies, "Ajax—kill him!" Hector tries to claim his deed, but in vain; Demokos dies insisting on the guilt of Ajax, successfully inciting the others to violence. "The war will take place," admits Hector, and the gates of war open—to discover Helen kissing Troilus. Cassandra declares, "The Trojan poet is dead . . . . Now the word is with the Greek poet."

MAKSIM GORKI

The Lower Depths [*Na dne*, 1902]

ACT ONE

In the dismal basement of Kostylyov's lodging house in a Volga town, various lodgers are busy quarreling and calling names, as is their custom. They awaken the locksmith's wife, Anna Klestch, whose coughing is a constant reminder that she has not long to live. As they are arguing over who is to sweep the floor, an Actor among them proudly informs the others that alcohol has poisoned his system. Several reminisce about happier times when they had a place in life, before they came to live among the down-and-out inhabitants of this cellar.

Klestch, who has earlier tried clumsily to comfort his wife, becomes annoyed at her complaints and leaves the Actor to assist her into the hall to seek fresh air. Kostylyov, the landlord, who is always alert to ways of augmenting his income, comes seeking his wife. As he approaches Vassily Peppel's door, Satin hints that he will find his wife in Peppel's room. Peppel drives Kostylyov out of the room, and Satin teases Peppel about Vassilissa, Kostylyov's wife. Satin and the Actor go off to drink with some money that Peppel gives them. Peppel, trying to convince Klestch that the latter is no better than the other tenants merely because he believes in working for a living, argues that conscience is a useless commodity among the poor.

Natasha, Vassilissa's sister, leads in Luka, a friendly, elderly pilgrim, who is to be a new lodger. After she leaves, Peppel expresses interest in Natasha, but is soon complaining of boredom. Luka, however, seems able to amuse him. As the Baron mentions his former days, Luka reflects that all men are living in the hope of something better.

Peppel and the Baron leave to have a drink, and Alyoshka, a young cobbler, comes drunkenly in and raves defiantly against the world until Vassilissa sends him roughly away. After delivering a tirade concerning the unswept floor, she storms out. Luka offers to sweep the floor, and Bubnov, a capmaker, reveals that Vassilissa's ire is due to the rumor, spread by Alyoshka, that Peppel's interest has turned from her to her sister Natasha. Medvedev, a policeman and uncle of Vassilissa and Natasha, arrives and tries to convince Kvashnya to marry him, but she refuses, citing the horrors of her first marriage. Luka leads Anna in, scolds the others for their carelessness toward her, and asserts that every human life is valuable. When Kostylyov bursts in shouting that Vassilissa is killing Natasha, all rush out except Luka and Anna, who is touched by Luka's gentleness.

174

ACT TWO

In the basement, the lodgers are playing cards and checkers in their usual noisy manner, as Luka tries to comfort Anna, who is nearing the end of her miserable life. The card game ends when the Tartar, who has caught the Baron cheating, refuses to continue. When the Actor describes to Luka his former successes and his decline through alcohol, Luka tells him of a hospital in another town, whose name he cannot recall, where drunkards are cured free of charge. The Actor goes off, happy at the thought of a new start in life.

Luka comforts Anna, assuring her that death will bring her rest. Peppel, slightly drunk, accuses him of telling pleasant lies, then asks Medvedev whether Natasha was hurt by her sister. Receiving no reply, he threatens to reveal to the authorities that it was Vassilissa and her husband who introduced him to thievery. Luka tries to convince Peppel to go to Siberia to begin a new life, but Peppel once again accuses him of telling lies. Luka retorts that the truth can be too much to bear. In answer to a question of Peppel's, Luka asserts that God exists if one believes in him. Peppel tells Vassilissa that he has never loved her; she accepts this fact but asks his aid, offering to help him marry Natasha if he will rid her of her husband. As Peppel voices his suspicions concerning the proposal, Kostylyov sneaks in and screams furiously at Vassilissa when he finds her alone with Peppel. Peppel grabs him, but at a noise from the top of the stove releases him. Luka, who made the noise in order to prevent Peppel from killing Kostylyov, appears and advises Peppel to flee from Vassilissa and to take Natasha with him. When Luka goes to see how Anna is, he discovers that she is dead, whereupon the two men leave to find Klestch.

The Actor returns seeking Luka. Natasha appears, and he reveals that he is going away to be cured and to begin life anew. When Natasha discovers that Anna is dead, the Actor leaves to seek Klestch, who arrives in a few minutes with several others. Natasha is shocked by their callous attitude toward Anna. When Satin and the Actor enter, Satin assures the Actor that Luka has lied to him about the cure.

ACT THREE

In a vacant plot outside the lodging house, Nastya, the young prostitute, relates to some of the lodgers the romantic story of a young man who once loved her. While Bubnov and the Baron tease her and accuse her of lying, Luka and Natasha encourage her to continue. After Luka gently leads Nastya away, the others discuss the lies that are told to brighten up drab lives. Bubnov persists in demanding the solid truth. Luka returns and reflects that truth is not always the best cure for the soul, illustrating with a story about a man who killed himself because a scientist told him that the true and just land, in whose existence the man believed, does not exist. He tells Natasha and Peppel that he will soon depart to continue his pilgrimage. Peppel asks Natasha to go to Siberia with him to begin a new life, as Luka earlier suggested, promising her that he will give up thieving. Natasha replies she does not love him, but he declares his love for her anyway. Vassilissa appears and listens, unnoticed. When Peppel describes his hopeless life and his optimism concerning himself and Natasha, Luka urges Natasha to go with Peppel.

As Natasha finally agrees, Vassilissa makes her presence known, frightening Natasha. Kostylyov appears and scolds Natasha for neglecting her tasks. After Natasha goes, Peppel declares she is his. Threatening Kostylyov and Vassilissa, he leaves. Kostylyov, who has heard of Luka's planned departure, tells Luka that a true pilgrim should not interfere in the lives of men. When Luka tries to explain himself, he inadvertently insults Kostylyov, who orders him to leave. After the irate Kostylyov and his wife leave, Bubnov, Satin, and the Actor appear, Satin assuring the Actor that his proposed trip is a pipe dream. The Actor relates that he has earned some money that day and saved it for the trip rather than spending it on drink; Satin becomes scornful and tells Luka how the success and happiness of his younger days were completely destroyed by his four and a half years in prison. As Luka questions him about his life, from within come sounds of Kostylyov and Vassilissa beating Natasha. The others run to investigate. Nastya and Kvashnya help Natasha outdoors, as Vassilissa still tries to strike her sister. In the midst of the confusion, Peppel races in and knocks Kostylyov to the ground. As Medvedev tries to restore order, Vassilissa discovers that her husband is dead and accuses Peppel of killing him. Peppel, in order to involve Vassilissa, announces that it was she who wanted him to kill her husband. Natasha interprets this to mean that Vassilissa and Peppel plotted everything, including his earlier speech to her. Peppel is crushed at her bitter accusations.

ACT FOUR

That evening in the basement, several lodgers discuss the disappearance of Luka. Satin and the Baron chide Nastya and the Actor for their dreams of escaping the wretched world of the basement. Satin takes it upon himself to explain to the Baron why Luka was not a faker, but a man who told lies in order to ease the burden of life for those who could not bear it. Waxing eloquent, Satin expounds Luka's belief that men live in the hope of something better to come. When the Baron reminisces about his glorious ancestors, Nastya expresses her doubts as to the truth of his tales, and an argument ensues. Satin calms them and inquires after the vanished Natasha, whose fate is unknown to any of them, though Vassilissa and Peppel are known to be still trying to ruin each other. Satin again tries to calm Nastya and the Baron and is amused at his new role as humanitarian in the style of Luka. He delivers a panegyric on the subject of man and the respect due him, to which the Baron responds with a sad account of his own unexamined life.

The Actor asks the Tartar, who is quietly praying, to pray for him and runs out. Medvedev, now Kvashnya's husband, and Bubnov come in drunk and invite all to drink with them. Others wander in and take their places for the night on the plank beds scattered over the basement. Kvashnya enters, sends Medvedev to bed, and complains to Satin that her new husband has taken to drink. As Satin and the others prepare to drink and sing, the Baron bursts in and announces that the Actor has hanged himself. Satin is the only one who can speak: "Ah, spoiled the song—the fool!"

NORDAHL GRIEG

The Defeat [*Nederlaget,* 1937]

ACT ONE

The Franco-Prussian war has just ended with disastrous results for the French economy. Food and money are scarce. In order to get money to survive, workmen have had to sell their tools, which are useless in any case since no work is available. Mothers are selling their daughters into brothels, children are starving to death in the streets and are trying to catch sewer rats for food. Only the rich can afford to eat the latest delicacies offered by expensive restaurants—the animals from the Paris zoo that have been slaughtered for food.

In the Montmartre section of Paris in March, 1871, the poor are in a revolutionary temper, which is expressed by the bookbinder Varlin and the mechanic Beslay. They urge the people not to let the president of France, Thiers, disarm the people's militia. If the militia stays armed, they see an opportunity to prevent the re-establishment of Thiers' regime. This period of chaos at the end of the war is their best chance, they say, to set up a people's government, a commune, the best hope for eventual peace and freedom. Rigault, a medical student, expresses another aspect of the revolutionary outlook, the terroristic. He is eager for a chance to begin the wholesale destruction of the old society and all its leaders and supporters.

The police commission arrives with an announcement that Thiers has ordered the army to occupy the city and to disarm the militia. As Varlin, Rigault, Beslay, and others protest and are arrested, Delescluze, a journalist who has spent half his life in prison for revolutionary activity, incites the crowd to resist the police. The soldiers who have come to occupy the city refuse to fire on the crowd. The cry of "long live the commune" goes up.

In the library of his house, Thiers gloats over his success in the rapid re-establishment of governmental authority in the city. An officer brings news that the people have revolted. Thiers prepares to leave for Versailles, whence he intends to direct the quelling of the revolution.

ACT TWO

Two weeks later, the commune is in complete control of Paris, with Varlin, Beslay, and Delescluze among the leaders. At a café in a public square, Varlin talks excitedly about building a peaceful and free world where everyone can work and enjoy the results of his labor. Delescluze brings sobering news—the Versailles troops directed by Thiers are preparing to attack Paris; these troops, released from Prussian prison camps by arrangement with Bismarck, are not in sympathy with the commune: they have been away too long and have lived too well to sympathize with the poor classes. The idealist Varlin is against fighting his brothers, but Delescluze convinces him that they must fight to preserve the commune.

In the streets, wounded communards return from a battle with the Versailles troops on the outskirts of Paris; they bring word that Thiers' army has a terrible new weapon, the machine gun, and that the communards were unable to throw the enemy back.

In a sidewalk café near the Place Vendôme, Gustave Courbet, the painter, tells Beslay of his dislike for the Vendôme column that Napoleon built with a statue of himself on top: an ever-present reminder of a militaristic tyrant, it should be removed. Colonel Rossel, a former French army officer who is now leading the commune troops, complains about the lack of discipline of the communards, who obey orders only when they choose to. He claims that if discipline is not established among the troops, the commune cannot win the fight with Thiers' army.

In the private rooms of a restaurant where he has set up headquarters, Rigault, head of the commune secret service, ruthlessly orders the execution of members of the upper class and keeps himself well supplied with wine and women. Varlin complains to him about his behavior, but Rigault insists that he must act in the way he does: the revolution will never be safe if its enemies are left alive, and he needs his occasional debauches to relax from his rigorous duties. While Varlin states his belief that "the commune is against terror and bloodshed," Rigault claims that all new life is born in blood and that annihilating violence creates peace.

Some days later, Rigault's militancy shows itself in the arrest of the archbishop of Paris. The revolution is also beginning to destroy its own: Colonel Rossel is arrested for complaining about the commune troops.

In the offices of the Bank of France, the bank governor tells a secret Versailles emissary that he is preventing the communards from getting their hands on most of the bank's funds. Since the governor deals with the commune through Beslay, who has a petit-bourgeois respect for money, he is able to keep Beslay from demanding or simply seizing the money that could buy the commune the weapons it needs to defend itself by acting shocked at requests for a large sum; Beslay always settles for a much smaller amount.

ACT THREE

Since the Versailles troops are gradually fighting their way into Paris, the communards have built barricades in the streets. On one barricade Lucien and Pauline, young lovers, wait for the enemy with other commune fighters. They have one machine gun, insignificant compared to the arms possessed by Thiers' soldiers.

The Place Vendôme barricade is overrun and the Versailles troops move toward Lucien, Pauline, and their comrades. To prevent snipers from using a nearby house, Lucien and Pauline daringly make their way to it and burn it down. This does little good, however: the Versailles troops attack and take the barricade.

ACT FOUR

In Thiers' headquarters, the president tells his generals how he wants the occupation of Paris to proceed: each rebel district is to be thoroughly subdued before the army moves on to the next one, so that commune troops do not slip behind the army and attack. He orders wholesale executions of all communards —men, women, and children.

In Paris, where the Versailles troops are steadily advancing, Rigault orders all hostages shot, including the archbishop. Courbet, who has had Napoleon's Vendôme column torn down and who is terrified by the prospect of being shot by Thiers' army, hears that someone else has been mistaken for him and shot. Overjoyed at this news, he sets off to make his escape.

Most of the remaining communards flee to the cemetery, where they are trapped by the oncoming army, but Varlin and Rigault, who remain behind, are caught and shot together. In the graveyard and Delescluze, Lucien and Pauline, the teacher Gabrielle Langevin, three children, and other communards calmly await the arrival of the execution squads. Delescluze expresses hope that in the future the lower classes will become tough enough eventually to win their struggle with their oppressors. Gabrielle answers that toughness and brutality are not the solution: there is only one defense against terror, and that is the refusal of human thought to compromise with injustice. As the troops enter the cemetery, the communards line up against the wall to be shot. Gabrielle urges the children to smile to show the enemy soldiers that the communards' hope is not defeated.

GERHART HAUPTMANN

The Rats [*Die Ratten*, 1911]

ACT ONE

On a Sunday in May, Mrs. John, a cleaning woman, brings a young servant girl, Pauline, to the attic of a former cavalry barracks in Berlin, currently used by Mrs. John's employer as a storeroom for theatrical properties. Pauline is pregnant and alternately vows to commit suicide and infanticide or to avenge herself upon her faithless lover. Mrs. John offers Pauline money for her baby, explaining that she and her husband yearn for a child to replace their own dead infant and assuring her that they will cherish her baby as their own. Mrs. John's stupid and brutal brother Bruno enters, frightening Pauline. Mrs. John sends Pauline and Bruno to the loft as Walburga Hassenreuter, the daughter of the theatrical manager, enters.

Walburga is sixteen and very pretty, and unwittingly reveals that she has come for a secret rendezvous with her tutor, a divinity student, Mr. Spitta. She asks Mrs. John to tell Spitta that she came and left immediately. Mrs. John begins to make insinuations as a key is heard in the lock. She hurries Walburga into the loft with the others and greets Hassenreuter, the manager.

Hassenreuter reveals that he has come to have a secret rendezvous with an attractive actress, Alice. While the two reminisce about their romance and their careers, Spitta arrives. He asks for Walburga, expresses disappointment over her absence, and announces his intention to leave the priesthood and go on the stage. He asks to be taken on as a pupil; Hassenreuter, eager to return to Alice, accepts him scornfully and escorts him out.

The trap door opens and Walburga appears, crying. Mrs. John tries to placate her, but Walburga, frightened by Bruno and Pauline and shocked by her father and Alice, departs before Hassenreuter returns on his way to rejoin Alice.

ACT TWO

In his apartment on another floor of the same building a few weeks later, Mr. John decides to refrain from smoking, since it might irritate the new baby. A mason, Mr. John frequently works in another city; as a result, Mrs. John is able to deceive him, claiming Pauline's child as their own. Mr. John describes his unsuccessful trip to the registry office to report the birth of the baby: he became confused by the registrar's questions and did not present the information exactly as Mrs. John had instructed. Mrs. John severely reprimands him for this failure and for working in another city. She admits her fear that, without a baby to bind them together, he would run off to America.

181

While they argue, Selma Knobbe, the twelve-year-old daughter of a prostitute, enters with her baby brother, a tiny, dirty, ragged, and sick baby about the
same age as Pauline's child. Mrs. John orders Selma out of the house. Mr. John
voices his surprise, for Mrs. John has always welcomed the girl and cared for the
infant. But Mrs. John explains that it is dangerous for their infant to be exposed to Mrs. Knobbe's sick brat. Mr. John is distressed by her reference to
their second son by the name—Adelbert—of their dead first-born. Mrs. John
suggests the name "Bruno" after her brother. Mr. John refuses, expressing his
antipathy for Bruno, who is under surveillance by the police. Mrs. John continues to call the child Adelbert.

The Hassenreuters arrive, bearing gifts, and congratulate Mrs. John.
Though proud and pleased, the Johns continue bickering, each attempting to
enlist the guests on his side. Two students of Hassenreuter arrive, laughing at
the tender heart and missionary zeal of Spitta, who is downstairs defending
Mrs. Knobbe against the abuses of the people. Spitta enters, and he and
Walburga remain with the Johns after the others depart. Mrs. John shows them
a lock of the first Adelbert's hair, insisting that they declare it identical to that
of the second. The Johns leave the room with the baby. Walburga and Spitta
discuss their love and sufferings, but are interrupted by the arrival of Pauline.
Mrs. John sends everyone but Pauline away.

Pauline says she had to see "it." Mrs. John pretends bafflement. Finally,
Pauline mentions the word "child." Mrs. John demands, "What child?" Pauline
replies, "My child!" and Mrs. John slaps her. Pauline begins to cry and shout
for help. Mrs. John repents, guiltily offering her own cheek to be slapped.
When Pauline refuses, Mrs. John slaps herself. Pauline places the money Mrs.
John gave her on the table and again demands to see the child. Mrs. John tries
ignorance as a tactic again, but sees that it is ineffective. Expressing her hatred
for Pauline, Mrs. John denies the girl's right to the child she would have killed.
Pauline recalls how she was followed by Mrs. John and Bruno until she agreed
to give them the child; she insists that it is hers, nevertheless. Mrs. John asserts
that Pauline's child is drowned in the canal and that the child inside is now
hers alone. Pauline attempts to find the child, but Mrs. John bars the way, declaring that before Pauline will see the child it will be dead. Pauline replies that
she *will* see her child tomorrow when she will return with the registrar and her
landlady. Furious at the discovery that Pauline registered the child as her own
in violation of their agreement, Mrs. John pushes Pauline out of the house and
broods silently, obviously hatching a plot keep the baby without Pauline's interference. Selma enters, asks for bread, and expresses fear at the sight of Mrs.
John's face.

ACT THREE

At Hassenreuter's office, his two students and Spitta are receiving a dramatic lesson, while Walburga watches silently. A debate on theatrical styles develops between Hassenreuter and Spitta. Spitta defends realism and naturalism,

announcing that a scrubwoman and Lear can both have tragic stature and in-sisting that all men are equal before the law and before art. Hassenreuter up-holds the classic and romantic theater. The argument ends when Hassenreuter turns his attention to Quaquaro, the building superintendent, who resembles a sinister circus athlete. Quaquaro is ordered to investigate the disorder in the attic: the absence of some costumes and a singular and bloody mess. Hassen-reuter adds that a very distracted Mrs. John is already in the attic. Quaquaro goes to investigate and returns brandishing a baby bottle. Mrs. John quickly ex-plains that she fed Adelbert there and merely forgot the bottle. She is very ex-cited and raves, and Hassenreuter and Quaquaro agree that she hasn't been herself since the birth of the child.

The doorbell rings, and Hassenreuter sends everyone out before admitting Spitta's father. An argument between Hassenreuter and Spitta, Senior, arises, in the course of which Spitta, Senior, unwittingly reveals the romance between Spitta and Walburga. Hassenreuter, enraged, throws the father out, calls down the son, sends him after the father, and rebukes his daughter.

The younger Spitta returns almost immediately with Pauline, who holds Mrs. Knobbe's starving baby in her arms, believing it to be hers. She says that her landlady is searching the building for Mrs. John and that they and the registrar found the baby alone in the John flat. A policeman arrives to reclaim Mrs. Knobbe's baby, and Mrs. Knobbe enters, frantically weeping. A prostitute, ravaged by alcohol and morphine, she tells of her terrible past and of the child's noble father. Mrs. Knobbe and Pauline struggle over the child, each swearing it is hers. Hassenreuter announces that he will settle the dispute, when Walburga notices that the unfortunate child has died in the course of the argu-ment. The policeman leads the two women out. Pauline still clings to the baby, unable to believe that it is dead.

ACT FOUR

Mr. John has just returned to his flat from a business trip and is in high spirits. Quaquaro enters, suspiciously questioning John about his whereabouts and those of his wife, child, and Bruno. Quaquaro alludes mysteriously to the strange events at the Hassenreuter flat when, about a week ago, a strange serv-ant girl appeared, claiming that Mrs. Knobbe's baby—which she found in the John flat—was her own. John admits ignorance of these events but insists that they cannot concern his family. Quaquaro leaves as Selma and Spitta enter, soon followed by Walburga. John begins questioning a frightened and contra-dictory Selma. Walburga and Spitta have a lovers' conference, comparing their sufferings at the hands of intolerant parents.

A frightened and suspicious Mrs. John enters with Pauline's living baby. Deranged, she raves about a secret that restores dead babies to life. Walburga and Spitta depart. John, startled by his wife's behavior, questions her about her absence and supposed visit to his sister. She ignores his questions, asking that he take her and the child to America immediately. When he refuses, she accuses him of betraying her and the child. Bruno arrives, threatens John, and forces him to leave. Bruno relates his obedience to Mrs. John's orders: he followed Pauline and frightened her to make her stay away. But in the course of this duty, he became aroused by her and killed her. Mrs. John is horrified, but gives Bruno the money she promised him. He leaves, and Mrs. John declares that while Pauline deserved to die, she is no murderer.

ACT FIVE

On her flat, Mrs. John lies asleep, crying out incoherently. Walburga and Spitta enter, prevented from leaving the building by a police guard searching for Bruno. Mrs. Hassenreuter enters, joyously greeting her daughter and promising support for the lovers. The reunion is interrupted by Mrs. John; awakened, but not come to her senses, she speaks of the dead and the living Adelberts as one and the same and addresses the absent Bruno. Hassenreuter enters, exultant over a professional triumph and enraged about newspaper notice of the mess in his attic. He explains that the funeral procession for Mrs. Knobbe's baby is being halted by the police. Roused, Mrs. John tries to dispel the Hassenreuters' notion that Pauline was Bruno's mistress, inadvertently revealing that she is not the physical mother of the baby in the room. When John announces that he will take his child to his sister's, Mrs. John replies that it is not his. Confusion rages while everyone tries to guess the facts. Finally Selma, frightened of being sent to an orphanage, reveals that she assisted at the birth of Pauline's baby in the Hassenreuter attic, that she carried the newborn infant to the John flat, that on the day of Mrs. John's disappearance to the country she put her own brother in the John flat, where it was discovered by Pauline. Mr. John, disgusted and disappointed, leaves. A policeman arrives to take Pauline's baby to the orphanage. Mrs. John grabs it, trying to flee with it, but she is overcome, and the baby is taken from her. She rushes outside. The Hassenreuters debate who now will care for the child. Quaquaro denies the possibility that John himself might still care for it. Hassenreuter applauds the fierce motherly courage and desperation of Mrs. John, agreeing that tragedy is not confined to any class of society. Selma rushes in to announce that Mrs. John has killed herself.

GERHART HAUPTMANN

The Weavers [*Die Weber*, 1893]

ACT ONE

One day in the 1840's, in a German city at the foot of a mountain, the room at the cloth manufacturer's is full of weavers who have come to deliver their finished webs of cotton cloth. Pfeifer, the clerk, examines and weighs the cloth and decides upon the payment due to each weaver. The weavers crowd the large room; larger groups of waiting weavers can be seen outside. They stand about as though awaiting judgment, fearful, cowering, and humiliated. Their sickly bodies and ragged clothes testify to their poverty and hunger, and there is a strange nervousness and tension in the air as they voice their grumblings over the low rate of pay.

Pfeifer is busily finding flaws in the work while rejecting pleas for advances or higher wages. He and his assistant discuss the bad habits of the weavers, their drinking, their large families, their general dissatisfaction with their lot, and the poor quality of their work.

Two men stand out in the crowd: old Baumert, dignified despite his poverty, and young Baecker, an unusually well-built specimen with a ready wit and jaunty air. Baumert confides that he has just had a beloved dog killed—he could not bear to do it himself—to provide his family with some food. Baecker scoffs at the pay allotted to him, declaring it "a handout for a beggar, not pay," and curses Pfeifer. Pfeifer, exasperated and fearful, calls for the owner, Dreissiger.

Dreissiger recognizes Baecker as an acknowledged troublemaker and accuses him of being one of the band that serenaded his house the night before. Baecker replies that the song "Bloody Justice" is beautiful! Insults are hurled back and forth, but Baecker wins a victory: though his pay was thrown at him by Dreissiger, an apprentice picks it up and hands it to him. The skirmish ends when an eight-year-old boy faints in the line. Dreissiger and his assistants carry the child into the house, loudly proclaiming their humanitarian instincts and ranting against the cruelty of the parents who sent a sick child on such an errand. The crowd replies that the child's disease, like that of his parents, is starvation. Dreissiger addresses the crowd on the trials of being a rich manufacturer: to be given the blame for everyone's troubles but never given the credit for having his own worries. To prove his Christian and humanitarian nature, he declares that he is more than fulfilling his responsibility to the weavers because he will accept the work of two hundred more weavers, thereby cutting the general rate of pay. He wishes to aid the unemployed, though he is sure that they will merely drink up the money. He exhorts the stunned weavers to be glad that they are not linen weavers: the linen weavers, starving in the hills, are dying like flies.

ACT TWO

In the Baumerts' flat, Mother Baumert, crippled with age and labor, attempts to spin thread, while her two daughters weave. The two sons, one an idiot, are also weaving. They are all worried because Baumert has not yet returned and because there is neither food nor firewood in the house. A neighbor woman enters, weeping and unwilling to go home because she must return empty-handed to her famished children.

Baumert arrives announcing a surprise: Moritz Jaeger is back. Jaeger, a neighborhood boy who became a hussar, salutes the company. Young, red-cheeked, well-fed, well-dressed, pleasant, and cheerful, he has acquired good manners and speech and has money in his pockets. In short, as he says, he was a success as a soldier because he knew how to polish his sergeant's boots and was as keen for the battle as a hunting dog. A discussion on the current state of dire poverty among the weavers begins. Baumert and Ansorge, a neighboring weaver, complain, murmuring platitudes about praying and hoping for the best, and dreaming of the aid the king would provide if he but knew. Jaeger spikes the conversation with touches of gallows humor. The tone becomes increasingly bitter until Jaeger announces that it was he and Baecker who led the group to Dreissiger's house to sing the weavers' song "Bloody Justice." As Jaeger recites the words, the truth of every line touches old Baumert to the core—at last he has found expression for his pain and resentment. The Dreissigers are indeed hangmen, coolly observing the torture to death of the weavers. Weeping and enraged, Baumert and Ansorge—two gentle, weary, aged men—declare that, come what may, they will accept the status quo no longer.

ACT THREE

In the quiet tavern, the innkeeper's daughter irons while a traveling salesman tries tentatively to seduce her. The local carpenter and the innkeeper discuss the weavers' restlessness and growing anger, and the salesman mouths the usual clichés about the moral worthlessness of the weavers as the root to their supposed misery. A fight ensues between the carpenter and a peddler, Hornig, who accuses the carpenter of rejoicing at the suffering of the weavers because each dead child or parent provides him with the profit from the coffins. Hornig ridicules the government inspectors and the journalists who come to investigate conditions among the weavers. He states that they merely walk through the more profitable sections of the towns and then report that the rumors of hunger and disease are false: let them come with him and he will show them a misery they have never dreamt of. The gathering voices anticlerical sentiments.

Gradually the tavern fills up with weavers and other local people, Baumert and Ansorge among them. Tempers rise. A band of young weavers enter, led by Baecker and Jaeger. They declare that the time for vengeance has come and that blood has already begun to flow, revealing their bleeding tattooed arms. The blacksmith appears, a huge, swarthy man and a fiery revolutionary, whose constant theme is the French Revolution. Lines from "Bloody Justice" are shouted out, as the innkeeper tries to quiet the crowd. An old weaver, maddened by pain and hunger, begins to "speak with tongues," crying out that judgment day is approaching. A policeman enters, his presence only inciting the crowd still further. The insults become more vehement, and the demand for action more irresistible. Finally the crowd surges on to Dreissiger's to demand higher wages. Even old Baumert joins the screaming mob, quietly stating that "a young man may [chose to join], and an old man must." Hornig, the peddler, follows, adding, "Every man must have his dream."

ACT FOUR

The party at Dreissiger's isn't going too well. Dinner was disturbed because the children's tutor started a violent argument defending the weavers. The pastor attributes this attitude to the tutor's youth and laments because the good poor people of God are not behaving like the mild lambs they should be. Mrs. Dreissiger, an ex-innkeeper's daughter, wonders whether it was worth climbing so high to be rewarded, not by comfort, but by such violence.

Though angered by the constant singing of "Bloody Justice" before his house, Mr. Dreissiger strives to end the discussion and begin the game of whist. The tutor, however, announces his resignation and prepares to leave. Pfeifer bursts in, declaring that the situation is becoming more serious moment by moment. The chief of police arrives to assure everyone that all will be well in a few moments, for a ringleader has been captured. Jaeger is led in, roundly and proudly insulting the assembled company. Outside, the crowd, incensed at his capture, demand his return and succeed in overwhelming the police chief and officers and in regaining Jaeger. They chant for Pfeifer, the butt of their hatred.

The drawing room is quiet again and the game of whist about to begin, when the tutor returns to announce that he plans to escape from the mob with the children, he advises the family to join him. Dreissiger demands, "Am I really a slave driver?" Mrs. Dreissiger cries, "Is it a sin to be rich?" But the pastor has a moment of courage and announces that he will go out to appease the crowd. He disappears in the crowd, whether beaten or dead, no one knows. The Dreissiger family flees. The mob invades the house, destroying everything in its wake.

ACT FIVE

Old Hilse's family sit by their looms, weaving at their house. Hilse, an ex-soldier, one-armed and bent, aids his blind wife. The family speak of their suffering. Hornig, the peddler, arrives with news of the events at Dreissiger's: the mob has not yet dispersed, but are marching onward, looting everything in their path, to Hilse's town. The family react with shock to the news. Hilse prays that God will lead the weavers back to their old moral paths. The son wavers between his wife's excitement and his father's dismay. His wife Luise is exalted, however, and announces that she will join the bands of fighting weavers: she has laid too many of her own children in the grave from hunger and cold; now let the rich suffer and know her anger.

A doctor arrives and describes the mad violence of the mob, whose approach is now audible. The weavers' song rings in the air. Baecker, Baumert, Jaeger, the blacksmith, and others arrive at Hilse's hovel and urge him to rejoice and join them; they are going onward, from town to town, to sack and destroy. Hilse replies with maxims and prayer. Luise applauds and joins, but her husband, intimidated, stays behind.

The soldiers arrive in the town and the shooting begins. From their windows Hilse and his son watch the massacre of the weavers and see Luise dancing like a madwoman before the guns and bayonets, taunting the soldiers. A stray shot strikes Hilse. His son, shouting that he will not let his wife be shot, rushes out to join the weavers. Blind old Mother Hilse and her little grandchild cry out to Hilse to tell them what is going on, but the old man lies dead on the floor.

L I L L I A N   H E L L M A N

The Children's Hour [1934]

ACT ONE

In the living room of a farmhouse, now converted into the Wright-Dobie School for Girls, Mrs. Lillie Mortar, a plump, overdressed woman, coaches an apathetic student in the reading of Shakespeare, while other girls indifferently sew and study Latin. Mary Tilford, a sullen girl of fourteen, arrives tardily; Mrs. Mortar reprimands her but changes her tone when the girl claims to have been picking wildflowers for her. Karen Wright, an attractive, pleasant, dignified woman of twenty-eight, enters and identifies the flowers as the same that were in the garbage can that morning. When the girls depart for class, Karen detains Mary and inquires why she is not happy and why she persists in lying. Mary refuses to admit the lie and responds with defensive tears to Karen's sympathetic attempts to understand her; Karen takes away some of Mary's privileges. Complaining of pains in her heart, Mary faints. Strongly suspecting a ruse, Karen carries Mary away and asks that Joe, the doctor, be called.

Upon her return, Karen encounters Martha Dobie, a nervous woman of her own age, her friend since college and her partner in the school. Their discussion turns from Mary, whose grandmother has been helpful to them in establishing the school, to Martha's aunt Mrs. Mortar, a former actress, whose influence on the students they find negative. When Karen mentions her forthcoming marriage to Joe, Martha bitterly conjectures that Karen will lose interest in the school and in her partner. As Karen protests that this will not happen, Joe arrives and takes her to examine Mary. When Mrs. Mortar returns, Martha urges her to leave the school and offers to pay her passage to London. In her indignation, Mrs. Mortar insinuates that Martha resents the marriage because of an unnatural attachment to Karen. Martha reacts violently, and noises are heard outside the door. She opens it to discover two students, Evelyn and Peggy, obviously eavesdropping. She tells them to go upstairs, promising to deal with them later, and Joe returns to inform her that there is nothing wrong with Mary.

Karen confronts Mary, Evelyn, and Peggy. Disturbed at the bad influence of Mary upon the other two, Karen informs them that they are no longer to share a room. Mary throws a tantrum, but Karen and Joe do not take it seriously. After the adults leave, Mary blackmails Rosalie, another student, into moving her belongings into her new room. She then forces her former roommates to repeat to her what they overheard a short while before. Smiling mysteriously, she announces that she is going home to her grandmother. Jerking Peggy's arm, Mary extorts some of her painfully saved money to pay for the escape.

ACT TWO

Mary's unexpected arrival in Mrs. Tilford's living room surprises the maid. When her grandmother appears, Mary embraces her tearfully and begs not to be sent back to school, where, she insists, she will be killed. In an attempt to cajole her grandmother into letting her stay, Mary relates tales of the hostility with which she is treated at school. When this elicits no reaction from Mrs. Tilford, Mary insinuates that there is something curious going on at school. She recounts the conversation between Mrs. Mortar and Martha, as well as strange things the girls have overheard concerning Karen and Martha. Mrs. Tilford becomes more and more shocked as Mary elaborates, and at length argues that Mary should not go back to school. She sends Mary upstairs, telephones Joe, and asks him to come over. She then calls Emily's mother and repeats Mary's story to her.

A few hours later, after Mrs. Tilford has made a long-distance telephone call to Rosalie's mother and explained the situation, Rosalie comes to spend the night at Mrs. Tilford's house. When Mary threatens to reveal that Rosalie stole a schoolmate's bracelet, Rosalie tearfully agrees to swear an oath to do and say whatever Mary orders. When Mrs. Tilford enters and Joe arrives, the two girls are sent to bed.

After some small talk, Mrs. Tilford tells Joe that he must not marry Karen because there is something wrong with her. At this moment, Karen and Martha arrive, dazed and angry; they explain to Joe that their students were taken home because Mrs. Tilford told the parents that they were in love with each other. The two young women and Joe try to make Mrs. Tilford understand the terrible thing she is doing, but she refuses to believe that the story is anything but true. Martha decides that the best revenge would be to take Mrs. Tilford to court on a libel charge. Mrs. Tilford insists that Mary is telling the truth and orders the teachers to leave, but Joe demands to see Mary, who approaches shyly and refuses to change her story. When Mary describes a scene she witnessed through the keyhole of Karen's door, Karen states that there is no keyhole in her door. In her confusion, Mary tells them that it was Rosalie who actually witnessed the scene. Rosalie is summoned and denies any knowledge of what they are talking about, until Mary reminds her of her oath by mentioning the disappearance of Helen Burton's bracelet; Rosalie tearfully says that Mary has spoken the truth.

ACT THREE

In the neglected living room of the school, the curtains drawn, Karen and Martha sit listlessly, and silently, as they have been doing for eight days. They consider taking a walk but balk at the thought of encountering the hostility of the townspeople. When the grocery boy comes, he stares at them and giggles, reminding them of the nightmarish quality of the situation. When Mrs. Mortar appears unexpectedly, Martha angrily tells her that her refusal to appear at the libel suit against Mrs. Tilford was an important factor in their losing the case. Just as Martha orders her to leave, Joe arrives with the news that he has severed his professional ties in order to marry Karen immediately and take both her and Martha to Vienna, where he can earn enough for them to live. Martha protests that she cannot come with them, and Karen insists that he must not give up his practice; but Joe explains that there is no choice.

Alone with Karen, Joe speaks of a new beginning. Karen, however, believes that there will always be a subtle barrier between them, for he will never be entirely certain that she has told the truth about herself and Martha. At her coaxing, he voices his uncertainty, and she replies that she and Martha have never touched each other. He suggests that they forget the past and build a future, but she explains that it will be impossible and sends him away, under protest, to reflect. When Karen tells Martha that Joe will not be back, Martha begs her to return to him. They speak of the fact that there is now no place for them to go, and Martha slowly admits to Karen, as if realizing it for the first time herself, that she loves Karen in the way in which the others think they love one another. Karen listens, horrified and incredulous, as Martha confesses her feeling of guilt at having ruined both their lives. Martha leaves the room, and a few minutes later Karen is stunned to hear a shot. Mrs. Mortar comes running, learns that Martha has killed herself, and breaks down in nervous chatter. When the doorbell rings, Mrs. Mortar admits Mrs. Tilford's maid, who tells Karen that Mrs. Tilford wants to see her. Karen consents, and Mrs. Tilford, who seems older and more feeble than before, enters and announces that she now knows that none of the accusations are true; Mary's blackmailing of Rosalie has come to light, and a public apology is to take place. Karen informs Mrs. Tilford that Martha is dead and accuses her of offering aid only to relieve her own aching conscience. Mrs. Tilford tries to convince Karen to make something of her future. At length, Karen feels compassion for Mrs. Tilford and admits the possibility of someday going back to Joe and agrees to accept Mrs. Tilford's aid. As the older woman is leaving, Karen opens the window to breathe the air. She promises to write to Mrs. Tilford if she ever has anything to say.

LILLIAN HELLMAN

The Little Foxes [1939]

ACT ONE

In a small town in the Deep South in 1900, Birdie Hubbard, a pretty, nervous woman, runs gaily out of the dining room of the Giddens' home, followed by her husband Oscar, who scolds her as though she were a child for chattering at and boring the guest of honor, Mr. Marshall from Chicago. Their twenty-year-old son Leo comes in, followed by Regina Giddens, Mr. Marshall, Regina's seventeen-year-old daughter Alexandra, and Benjamin Hubbard, Oscar's older brother. During the ensuing polite conversation, Marshall learns that Ben and Oscar are partners in Hubbard Sons, and that Horace Giddens, the banker husband of their sister Regina, is now being treated for a heart ailment in Baltimore. They explain that Birdie is the only one of them to come from an aristocratic background and that while her family was ruined by the Civil War, the Hubbard family firm was able to adapt to changes and to prosper. A toast is drunk to the business deal by which Marshall and the Hubbard brothers will establish a cotton mill.

After Marshall, escorted to the carriage by the brothers, leaves for the station with Alexandra and Leo, Regina tells Birdie her hope of achieving social success with the money that this deal seems to promise. When Ben and Oscar return, they discuss with Regina the business success of the evening. When each describes what he would most like to do with the money that is hopefully forthcoming, Birdie dreamily speaks of restoring her family plantation, now owned by the Hubbard brothers. Oscar and Ben remind Regina that Horace has not yet produced his third of the money with which the family will purchase the controlling interest in the mill. Regina suggests that perhaps Horace is holding out because he wants more than a third of the share in return for his third of the money and hints that he might be given part of Oscar's share. She decides to send Alexandra to Baltimore to persuade Horace to come home. Ben agrees to give Horace 40 percent, pointing out that since he himself is a bachelor, he will leave his money to Alexandra and Leo, who perhaps might marry. Oscar, who is against giving Horace 40 percent, is somewhat placated by the idea of this marriage, though Regina disapproves of it because of Leo's wildness and irresponsibility. She agrees, however, to consider it.

When Alexandra and Leo return from the station, Regina informs Alexandra that she is to go to Baltimore. The girl is delighted at the thought of bringing her father home but is surprised that she is to go alone, without Addie, the faithful Negro woman who has always taken care of her. When Alexandra and Birdie are left alone, Birdie warns Alexandra, whom she loves more than anyone else, that the others will try to make her marry Leo. As Alexandra makes her way upstairs, Oscar, who has overheard, slaps Birdie hard across the face.

ACT TWO

One morning a week later, Oscar visits Regina's house to find her awaiting Alexandra and Horace. When Oscar is alone, Leo, who works at Horace's bank, arrives and discusses the business deal with his father. He describes the contents of Horace's safe-deposit box, and Oscar forces him to admit that he opened the box. Oscar suggests that perhaps Leo could borrow the valuable bonds in the box, have a share in the deal, and put them back before Horace even becomes aware of their absence. Ben arrives, and the three men sit down to breakfast in the other room with Regina.

Horace arrives with Alexandra, who explains to Addie that her father is not feeling well and must rest. Addie sends Alexandra upstairs and tells Horace that she has heard that everyone is going to be rich and that Alexandra is going to marry Leo. At the last item of news, Horace becomes angry and asks that his return be announced. As Regina, Ben, and Oscar greet him perfunctorily, Birdie rushes in and kisses him excitedly. Oscar scolds her for going out dressed in a kimono and sends her home before she can greet her beloved Alexandra.

Regina and Horace are left alone, but are not able to talk without arguing. He tells her that he has done much thinking in the five months he has been away and that he has been told that he will not live long. Regina agrees with him that they should try to get along. Though he is tired, she asks that he remain downstairs long enough to talk to Ben. As Ben explains the deal, Horace begins to understand the situation and the reason for the rumors of a marriage between Alexandra and Leo. He calmly refuses to put up the money. Regina becomes furious, unintentionally revealing that this is the reason she wanted him home. Despite his weakened condition she follows him upstairs, demanding an explanation for his decision.

Oscar suggests to Ben that if Horace refuses to put up the money, they can still keep the controlling interest within the family if Leo borrows Horace's bonds surreptitiously. Ben agrees to the idea. After Oscar and Leo leave, the voices upstairs grow louder. Regina appears, asking Ben to wait to settle the deal until Horace changes his mind. She is furious to learn that everything has been settled without her and cannot understand where the money for the third share is to come from. After Ben leaves, Alexandra watches in horror as Regina tells Horace that she hopes he will die soon. Horace tells her that he will not give her money for her and her brothers to use to exploit the Negroes and become rich.

ACT THREE

Two weeks later, Birdie and Alexandra are playing the piano as Horace, preoccupied, sits near the window with a safe-deposit box nearby. Birdie reminisces happily, and Alexandra comments on what a happy group they are. Birdie drinks more and more wine and recalls how kind Horace has been to her, in contrast to her husband. Horace sends Cal, the Negro servant, to the bank to thank one of the officers for bringing the safe-deposit box and to fetch his lawyer. Birdie becomes drunker and says that Oscar married her for her family's cotton fields, a fact that everyone but she knew at the time; she has been unhappy ever since. She warns Alexandra that she will suffer a similar fate at the hands of the Hubbards.

Alexandra leaves to walk Birdie home, and Horace confides to Addie that he is glad that Alexandra heard Birdie's bitter speech, for it is important that she learn to hate and fear the evil in the midst of which she lives, so that she can escape from it. He asks Addie to go away with her after he is gone and says that he will arrange for her to have money. Cal returns, relating how Leo reacted with intense surprise to his message. Hearing Regina, Horace asks to be left alone with her. He tells her that he has discovered that Leo used his bonds without his permission. Regina wants to confront Ben and Oscar with the fact, but Horace informs her that he will claim he has loaned them the bonds; he will allow them to keep all the profits and thus ruin her glorious and selfish plans. Furthermore, he will change his will, leaving the bonds to her and everything else to Alexandra. Horace feels an attack coming and reaches for his medicine, but drops and breaks the bottle. He asks Regina to have Addie fetch the other bottle, but Regina does not move. Terrified, Horace leaps out of his wheel chair and reaches the first landing of the staircase before he collapses. Only then does Regina call to Addie and Cal for aid, and they take him upstairs. Alexandra arrives and runs to help.

Oscar and Ben arrive. Leo tells them that Horace knows about the bonds. Regina descends the stairs, announcing that Horace has had a bad heart attack. She repeats what Horace told her about the bonds, and they are happy and relieved to learn of Horace's plan to foil Regina. The tables are turned, however, when Regina tells them that the plan will backfire if Horace dies, for then she can demand 75 percent of the family's interest or else send them all to prison. Alexandra comes slowly in, revealing by her silent expression that Horace is dead. Regina asks her to go, but Alexandra insists on talking to her. Regina finishes outlining her plan for ruining her brothers if they do not bow to her wishes. They leave her in her triumph, hinting that an investigation of Horace's death might someday prove interesting.

Regina tells Alexandra that she will take her away, but Alexandra announces that she is going away from Regina, as her father would wish her to do. Alexandra has understood what her father so desperately wanted her to understand. Regina agrees to let Alexandra live as she chooses, and Alexandra says that she will not stand and watch her mother devour the earth, but will fight her. Shaken, Regina asks Alexandra to be friends, to come talk to her and sleep in her room. Alexandra refuses and asks, "Are you afraid, Mother?"

EUGÈNE IONESCO

Amédée or How to Get Rid of It

[*Amédée ou Comment s'en débarrasser*, 1954]

ACT ONE

Amédée Buccinioni, a balding, middle-aged playwright, is nervously walking around the living room of his small Paris apartment trying to get ideas for dialogue, when to his annoyance he discovers a mushroom growing behind a chair. He calls his wife, Madeleine, and impatiently tells her not to spend so much time cleaning the other room as a pretext for staring at the man in there. Madeleine says that Amédée ought to get on with his writing, and when he complains that he has no inspiration, she retorts that it is fifteen years since he wrote anything.

Suddenly Madeleine notices the mushroom and says she has just pulled up fifty from the other room; Amédée desperately cries that the mushrooms are spreading. Madeleine says that it is all the fault of the dead man in the other room; then she realizes that it is nine o'clock, says she is late for work, and crosses to a switchboard, where she busily puts through calls for the President of the Republic, Charles Chaplin, the grocer, and others. Amédée tries to work on his play and add to the eleven words he has written during the past fifteen years.

Noticing that his wife is very busy with the switchboard, Amédée abandons the hopeless task of writing and softly crosses to the room where the man is. Madeleine realizes where he has gone and goes after him to drag him back to work. Amédée hesitantly tells her he hoped the man might have disappeared. He notes that the man has grown and is already too big for the divan, and Madeleine replies that the dead grow faster than the living. She tells Amédée that he has again forgotten to close the man's eyes, which are lighting up the room. Back at her switchboard, Madeleine tells Amédée to do the shopping; he takes a basket and drops it at the end of a rope into the street, shouting his order to someone below.

Over lunch, Amédée wonders whether the man has forgiven them; his wife points out that if the man had forgiven them he would have stopped growing. They are thrown into a fit of panic when they hear their name being called outside and someone knocking at the door. Amédée, after much hesitation, opens the door when he realizes that it is the postman; Madeleine, who has thrown herself in front of the bedroom door, assures the postman that they have nothing to hide. The couple, who have not left the apartment in all the fifteen years that the dead man has been with them, are terrified at the unex-

195

pected visit; they tell the postman that the letter can't possibly be for them, since they have no friends. They get rid of the postman by persuading him that they are not the Buccinionis to whom the letter is addressed.

Just as the couple sigh with relief at avoiding this crisis, they hear a crash from the bedroom and are horrified to discover that the body has grown still more and its head has burst through the window. They try to avoid scandal by calling through the window that the postman was to blame for the noise. But then they are almost struck dumb with terror when they see that the body is visibly growing: two enormous feet slide slowly through the open bedroom door and advance about eighteen inches into the living room. Just as Amédée attempts to console his wife by telling her that "everyone has problems," the body grows another twelve inches. A sudden buzz from the switchboard reminds Madeleine that it is time to get back to work; but she collapses in tears, sobbing that it is more than she can bear.

ACT TWO

Two hours later the dead man is growing at a rate of six inches every twenty minutes; furniture from the bedroom is now piled up on the right-hand side of the living room to make space for the body's growth. The mushrooms are also sprouting rapidly, and Amédée bitterly notes that they are poisonous. The couple wrangle acrimoniously over the situation: Madeleine tells her husband that he is lazy, a useless idler, merely procrastinating when he promises to get rid of the body tomorrow; Amédée declares that he is tired and drained of will power. Madeleine says that it is all Amédée's fault—he should have reported the man's death at the time it occurred; instead he has let fifteen years slip by. He retorts that if they had gone to the police then, they would have been executed or put in prison.

Madeleine states that if he had told the police that he murdered the man in a fit of jealousy if would have been accounted a crime of passion and the police would have let him go free. As she tries to persuade her husband to do something, Amédée prevaricates, saying he doesn't remember having killed the man; at that moment the body's jerky movements convince him he must at last act. He promises to try to get rid of the body that night. The couple sit, waiting for night to fall; Madeleine is knitting and Amédée drifts off into a revery, saying he sees figures and images. Sitting quite motionless, he seemingly wills the images to materialize: Amédée II and Madeleine II appear in wedding clothes. The second Madeleine is frightened and horrified, seeing a hell of darkness and swamps and massacres and feeling needle-like flames; the second Amédée is happy and joyful, seeing a heaven of sunshine, green valleys and flowers, and singing and dancing: "We are at the gates of the world," he declares. He says he has found an "insubstantial universe . . . ethereal power." Madeleine II rushes out screaming, followed by Amédée II.

As though nothing had happened, Madeleine, still knitting, asks her husband whether it is time. Amédée says not yet; he pleadingly tells his wife that through love they could get over the problem of the growing body, but Madeleine brusquely declares that feelings won't get rid of the body. Suddenly, strange music is heard from the man's room; Amédée says that the body is singing; a green light illuminates the room, and Amédée says that it is coming from the body's eyes. The body has grown and now stretches across the living room and almost to the landing door; it is midnight, and the time has come for Amédée to get rid of the body.

Declaring that he has grown used to the body and will miss it, he throws open the shutters and allows moonlight to stream into the room, contrasting strangely with the lurid green light from the man's eyes. Amédée is now very calm, regretting having to dispose of the body; Madeleine is very excited and agitated; they begin dragging the body's enormous feet toward the window.

Amédée heaves the great feet through the window and begins pulling at the legs, threading them through; they are incredibly long, and the whole operation takes several minutes. Finally the feet hit the pavement below, and Amédée goes off to tug at the body from outside. At last he pulls the whole body through the window and begins dragging it toward the river.

ACT THREE

A drunken American soldier has just been heaved out of a bar near the river when Amédée appears, dragging the body feet-first. The American begins helping Amédée, then has an idea: he spins Amédée round, causing the body to wind about him like a rope. In the meantime the noise has set dogs barking, trains shunting, stars shooting; the owner of the bar appears with several American soldiers. Whistles are heard, and two policemen arrive: Amédée flees toward his home, the policemen chasing him. He hides behind a low wall, the body still dragging behind him; as the police search, the body seems to open out like a huge parachute and draws Amédée upward; he flies out of reach of the policemen. The soldiers and people watching from the windows cheer as Amédée makes his escape into the sky. Madeleine appears and attempts to cajole her husband into coming back to earth.

Amédée calls that he is going unwillingly and slowly disappears from sight into the sky. Madeleine, lamenting the fact that her husband hasn't finished his play, goes into the bar with the others for a drink.

EUGÈNE IONESCO

The Chairs [*Les Chaises*, 1952]

In a semicircular room with a blackboard, seven doors, and two windows, the Old Woman lights the gas lamp; she cautions the Old Man against leaning too far out the window, lest he fall into the stagnant water that surrounds the house and stretches to the horizon. Observing that it is dark earlier this evening than yesterday, the Old Man ponders why things change. The Old Woman compliments him on his intellect and says that with a little ambition he could have been a head president in life; but the Old Man is content to be general factotum of the house.

The Old Woman begs him to imitate the months of the year, a game they have played every night for all seventy-five years of their marriage. Telling her several times to drink her tea, which is invisible, he unwillingly imitates the month of February. She pleads with him to tell the story he has told every night for seventy-five years, the story of their arrival at the city Paris, which has been extinguished for 400,000 years. They break into laughter, and he is unable to finish.

She tells him he could have been anything in life, and he weeps over his spoiled, spilled career, sobbing that he is an orphan. She caresses him and tells him she is his mother now, but he refuses to be comforted and wants his real mother. She tells him that his mother is in heaven and that he must dry his tears, for tonight he must reveal his message to mankind. The Old Man explains that, since he has difficulty expressing himself, he has hired an Orator to speak for him; he has invited everybody to hear the message, all the intellectuals and all the proprietors. The Old Woman worries that the evening may be too tiring for them; they consider calling it off, but the doorbell rings.

They welcome their first guest, an invisible lady, and bring a chair for her. The invisible lady tells them an inaudible story, to which they listen attentively, then explain their retired life: a modest existence but a full one. The bell rings again: the Old Man welcomes an invisible colonel, and the Old Woman brings another chair. The Old Man and Woman are scandalized by the colonel's conversation and behavior with the lady. The Old Man cautions that the lady's husband may arrive at any moment and tries to impress the colonel with his own war experiences; the Old Woman tells the colonel he must stop: after all, she and her husband have their dignity.

The doorbell rings, and the Old Man welcomes two more invisible guests: La Belle, an old flame whose nose has grown a good deal longer and whose ears have become more pointed since he last saw her, and her husband. The Old Woman gets another chair. La Belle's husband has brought the Old Woman a present: an invisible painting. The Old Woman complains to him of various physical ailments, but the Old Man informs her that the husband is a photoengraver, not a doctor. While the Old Man is declaring to La Belle that he has loved her for a hundred years, the Old Woman flirts with the photoengraver, pulling up her skirt, laughing, and encouraging him to pinch and tickle her. The Old Man invites La Belle to play Tristan and Isolde with him; the Old Woman gives the invisible lady a recipe for Crêpes de Chine and abruptly repulses the photoengraver, explaining that she has never deceived her husband. The Old Man tells La Belle that only his inner life, his investigations, and his message have saved him.

While the Old Woman explains to the photoengraver that their seven-year-old son abandoned his parents, accusing them of killing birds, the Old Man explains to La Belle that he and his wife wanted a son but never had one, adding that perhaps it is just as well, since he himself was an ungrateful son who abandoned his mother to die in a ditch. The Old Woman tells the photoengraver not to mention their son to the Old Man, for he is too sensitive and loved his own parents too much: they died in his arms calling him a perfect son. Conversation bogs down and stops. The doorbell breaks the silence.

The Old Man welcomes the invisible newsmen who have come to hear his message. He tries to keep the guests entertained and comfortable and to answer their questions and tells the Woman to hurry up and bring more chairs. The bell rings, and more invisible guests arrive with children. The Old Woman attempts to make introductions but does not know the people's names. There are sounds of boat after boat drawing up outside, and the invisible guests keep pouring in till finally the Old Man skips introductions and greetings and simply points them to their places. When the room is packed, the Old Woman peddles invisible programs, ice cream sandwiches, and candies, and the Old Man asks the standees to move to the walls, assuring them that they'll still be able to see and hear everything.

The pushing crowd separates the Old Man and Woman to different windows. They cannot see each other through the people, and are frightened to be separated at their age. While the Old Woman attempts small talk with the guests near her, the Old Man speaks to those near him of ethics, economics, and philosophy but stops short of revealing his message, which must await the Orator.

Suddenly the main door opens, and the invisible emperor arrives in a blinding light. The Old Man and Woman protest that they are the emperor's loyal servants, slaves, dogs, and begin barking, but the emperor does not notice them. The Old Man cries that the emperor is his last recourse: while life and humanity have mistreated him cruelly, he could have saved humanity and spared it the horrors of the last twenty-five years if only he had had the opportunity of communicating his message; he begs the emperor to take his message into consideration and to forgive the Orator for making his majesty wait. To keep him from being bored, the Old Man explains that he had his revelation when he was a child of forty on his father's knee. The Old Man and Woman assure the emperor that the Orator will come, that he is coming, that he is here.

The Orator appears, flamboyantly dressed, mustached, and goateed. The Old Man and Woman are astonished that he exists in flesh and blood and is not a dream, and the invisible crowd besieges him for autographs, which he grants automatically and without speaking. Thanking the guests, the emperor, and everyone who has given financial or moral support toward the success of this gathering, the Old Man announces that his mission is done, that his message will be revealed to the ladies and gentlemen gathered here, who are all that is left of humanity. He entrusts to the Orator the dissemination of his philosophy and all the details of his life and work: he and his wife, after their years of humble service on behalf of human progress, must now withdraw, making the ultimate sacrifice. The woman sobs in agreement: they will die in glory, become a legend, and have a street named after them. The Old Man bids the Orator one last time to communicate his message: he and his wife bid farewell to all, to each other, and shouting, "Long live the Emperor!" throw themselves to their deaths out their separate windows.

At last the Orator faces the crowd: but he is a deaf mute and cannot speak. He goes to the blackboard and writes: ANGELFOOD NNAA NNM NW NW V, and then, dissatisfied, erases it and writes: ADIEU DIEU P.* At first satisfied and solemn, but then disconcerted by the lack of reaction to his message, he bows brusquely and leaves the room. The invisible audience breaks into noise, laughter, and coughs that diminish into silence.

EUGÈNE IONESCO

The Lesson [*La Leçon*, 1951]

The doorbell's ringing summons forth the Maid, a sturdy middle-aged peasant woman, who arrives in a great hurry, wiping her hands on her apron. She ushers a girl into the study, confirms that she is the new Student come for a lesson, and calls the Professor.

The Student appears to be a poised, confident, lively young lady of about eighteen, but she wears the sober uniform and carries the satchel appropriate to a much younger schoolgirl. When the white-bearded, timid-voiced old Professor comes in, they begin a long exchange of politenesses. He tentatively begins to test her knowledge and compliments her profusely when she can answer that France is the country of which Paris is the capital. When she names the four seasons, he has to give her a hint about "autumn" but concludes, nevertheless, that with a little effort she should do very well. She is relieved, for in three weeks she hopes to pass the examination, not merely for a normal college degree in either science or the liberal arts, but for a "total doctorate."

They settle down to serious business. The Professor's eyes light up, and his voice becomes stronger, as well as more authoritative, as he introduces the subject of arithmetic. The Maid enters, ostensibly to look for a plate, and he is visibly annoyed when she interrupts his lesson to say, "Excuse me, sir, but listen: I recommend that you keep calm." He seems to understand this apparently unprovoked warning, and replies huffily that there is no basis for insinuations. She insists that he had better not begin with arithmetic. He dismisses her imperiously, and she leaves with a parting shot that he won't be able to say she didn't warn him.

The Student passes the addition test brilliantly by successfully adding one to every number from one to seven but fails in several awkward attempts to

---

* Goodby God P.

subtract three from four. The Professor tries to explain subtraction, oddly combining practical examples with abstruse explanations of mathematical concepts. The Student, hopelessly lost, stubbornly insists on the verities she thinks she's sure of, such as the fact that she has ten fingers, none of which he can possibly "take away," subtraction or no subtraction. More and more impatiently angry, the Professor threatens that she will never pass any degree at all, for if she cannot understand these principles, how will she ever be able to multiply in her head—the simplest of things for even a mediocre engineer, he says—3,755,998,251 times 5,162,303,508! She immediately spits out the correct answer. He is astounded. She explains that, since she knew already that she couldn't trust her powers of reason, she has simply learned by heart all the results of all possible multiplications. He is not at all pleased, for he maintains that true mathematics must achieve its results solely by reason and understanding, and he is thus the passionate enemy of memorization. She is thoroughly discouraged at having failed to please, even when she had the right answer.

The Professor suggests that although she clearly must not hope to pass her "total doctorate," they may still work toward a "partial doctorate." The Maid enters and begins tugging at his sleeve as he enthusiastically announces that he will deliver his prepared lecture on comparative philology. The Maid cries out that he must not, that philology above all else leads to the worst; but once again she is sent off muttering prophetically that he won't be able to say she didn't warn him.

The Professor begins his lecture with its basic proposition that Spanish is the mother language from which were born all the neo-Spanish languages, such as Spanish, Latin, Italian, French, Portuguese, and Sardanapalian. He continues in similar style, scrambling the technical terminology of linguistics and of philological history to produce an air of thoroughgoing scholarship and a content of thoroughgoing absurdity. The Student occasionally supplies a word to show that she is comprehending, but he is by now too interested in his subject to care for her responses and brusquely tells her to listen quietly. Suddenly she seems to be in pain. He learns that she has a toothache but dismisses it as unimportant. The Student now punctuates every pause in the lecture with the refrain, "I have a toothache." The Professor is expounding the fact that although the neo-Spanish languages are exactly identical in vocabulary, grammar, pronunciation, and intonation, there are very obvious differences between them to the experienced ear. He repeats exactly the same sentence several times, presumably in a different language each time, and demands that the student learn to recognize and pronounce the distinctions. She dutifully tries, but in vain, accompanying every response with a complaint about her teeth.

He gets more and more impatient; she gets more and more fidgety. When he grabs and twists her wrists to make her pay attention, she begins to whimper. He interpolates his lecture with reprimands in angry volubility and finally yells in exasperation for the Maid. When she enters, he complains how bad a listener the Student is, and the girl complains how bad her toothache is. The Maid warns the Professor that this is the final symptom and that he must beware. He brushes off her pleas and demands that she find his Spanish, neo-Spanish, French, Oriental, Sardanapalian, and Latin knives, for he is going to teach all the translations of the word "knife." The Maid refuses and leaves.

The Professor finds a single knife, brandishes it under the Student's eyes, and starts making her repeat the word "knife." She complies but retreats toward the window. Suddenly his voice changes, and with a grand gesture he stabs the Student, who falls into a chair. He kills her with a second stroke, then shudders convulsively, which seems to leave him out of breath, and murmurs, "Ah, that did me good . . . but oh, I'm tired . . . ."

He collapses into another chair, then suddenly becomes remorsefully panicky and yells for the Maid. She scolds him sternly: "That's the fortieth time today, and every day the same thing! Aren't you ashamed, at your age! But you're going to make yourself sick! And there won't be any more students for you!" He protests feebly that it isn't his fault, that the girl was a bad student. She calls him a liar, and he sneaks up on her with the knife behind his back to try to stab her. She disarms him, slaps him angrily, and again scolds him like a child, "And I warned you, too—arithmetic leads to philology, and philology leads to crime." The Professor is sobbing and helpless now, and she efficiently begins to discuss arrangements for the discreet funeral of all forty corpses. She puts an armband on him, an armband with "an insignia, perhaps the Nazi swastika." She makes him help her carry out the body, and when the stage is empty, the doorbell rings.

The Maid returns in a great hurry, wiping her hands on her apron. She ushers a girl into the study, confirms that she is the new student come for a lesson . . . .

EUGÈNE IONESCO

Rhinoceros [Le Rhinocéros, 1960]

ACT ONE

A housewife crosses the square of a small French town, carrying a cat and a basket of provisions. Watching her pass, the grocer's wife remarks irritably that the woman is too stuck-up to buy from them nowadays. Jean and Berenger enter from opposite directions to meet at an outside café table. Fastidiously dressed himself, Jean chides his embarrassed friend for his disheveled appearance and recurrent Sunday-morning hangovers.

Just as the waitress comes to take orders, a heavy animal is heard galloping at high speed, panting and trumpeting. The noise grows intense as the animal passes close by. "Oh, a rhinoceros!" exclaims Jean, echoed by the waitress, the grocer's wife, her husband, and a logician who has just entered the square. Running back excitedly, the housewife drops her basket; its contents scatter and a bottle breaks. An elegant old gentleman rushes into the grocery store for protection; but Berenger sits listlessly. Soon the noise fades into the distance. "Well, of all things!" says the café proprietor. Several people repeat his words. Emerging from the store, the old gentleman gallantly helps the housewife pick up her things, while the logician holds her cat. The grocer sells her a bottle of wine.

Now the waitress brings drinks for Jean and Berenger, and the others leave the square, conversing amicably. The two friends argue about where the rhinoceros might have come from. Presently the logician and the old gentleman return and sit at another table. Daisy, a young blonde typist, crosses the square, and Berenger, not wishing her to see him looking so unkempt, hides till she passes. Jean lectures him on the evils of alcoholism, while the logician lectures the old gentleman on syllogism. "All cats die," states the logician: "Socrates is dead. Therefore Socrates is a cat." Both pupils listen attentively and promise to cultivate their minds.

A deafening roar drowns out the talkers as a rhinoceros passes in the opposite direction. Everyone exclaims as before, and Daisy, returning, repeats, "Oh, a rhinoceros!" A piteous mewing is heard, and the housewife appears. Wailing, she carries the corpse of her cat, which has been trampled. "Poor little thing!" chorus the onlookers. Jean and Berenger dispute whether it was the same rhinoceros, whether it had one or two horns, and whether it was Asiatic or African; Jean walks off, furious. Presently the waitress and Daisy lead away the inconsolable housewife, while the others continue the dispute. After a long discourse from the logician, Berenger mentions that the question is still unanswered. No, but it has been correctly posed, answers the logician, raising his hat and departing.

In deep mourning, the housewife comes from the café carrying a box, followed by the waitress and Daisy; Berenger, remorseful for having insulted his friend, drinks a double brandy to console himself.

ACT TWO

The next morning inside a printing office, the workers stand around a table as Papillon, the chief, points to the newspaper. It is all nonsense, snorts Botard, an old schoolteacher; but Daisy insists that she herself saw the rhinoceros. She is defended by Dudard, a young man on the way up. Papillon reads aloud that, the day before, a cat was trampled to death by a pachyderm. A heated argument follows. Entering cautiously, Berenger hurries to sign the time sheet. However, he has been noticed by Papillon, who asks whether he saw the rhinoceros. Yes, Berenger answers. Botard is still scornfully disbelieving. At last Papillon orders them all to start working and leaves the room.

Suddenly Papillon reappears to inquire where Boeuf is. Mrs. Boeuf bursts in breathlessly, explaining that she was chased all the way from home by a rhinoceros and that it tried to follow her up to the office. There is a rumble as the staircase collapses. Rushing to look, the workers see the animal turning round and round in anguished search. Mrs. Boeuf recognizes it as her husband and almost faints. Then she rises, saying that she can't desert him, and jumps off the landing onto his back. Tender trumpeting is heard as they gallop off.

Daisy, who has phoned the fire brigade for help, reports that she had difficulty reaching them, since they have been called out for rhinoceroses all over town. Presently, however, the fire engine clangs, a ladder is placed against the window, and one by one the workers climb out and disappear below.

That afternoon Jean lies in bed in his flat, as Berenger knocks repeatedly on his door. Another door opens into the hall; an old man looks out and is called back by his wife. At last Jean answers in a hoarse voice and lets his friend in. Berenger apologizes for getting angry the previous day. They were both right, he says: there are some rhinoceroses in town with two horns and others with one.

Jean complains that his forehead hurts, and on examining it, Berenger finds a small bump. Jean goes to look in the bathroom mirror. On his return, Berenger sees that his friend is breathing heavily and that his skin is green; while taking Jean's pulse he is alarmed to find that the skin is hardening. He tries to phone the doctor, but Jean pushes him away angrily. Pacing the room, Jean growls that his pajamas irritate him and takes off the jacket.

They discuss Boeuf's transformation. Jean considers Boeuf the better for it: he himself would like to get back to the integrity of Nature, he declares. But man's mentality and moral values raise him far above the animals, Berenger rejoins. Jean trumpets mockingly. Dropping his pajama trousers, he lunges, head down, for Berenger, who jumps aside. He darts into the bathroom, and Berenger, his coat pierced by a horn, locks him in.

Calling for help, Berenger discovers that the porter and the old couple have turned into rhinoceroses. He starts to climb out of Jean's window but is deterred by the spectacle of the animals swarming up the street. While the bathroom door shakes with Jean's efforts to get out, Berenger rushes from exit to exit, each time confronted by rhinoceroses. Finally he crashes through the back wall and flees.

ACT THREE

Berenger is sleeping, fully dressed, on his divan, his head bandaged. Fighting something in a bad dream, he falls to the floor and wakes. He goes to the mirror, lifts the bandage, and sighs with relief to see a smooth forehead. Then he coughs, and the sound worries him. At Dudard's arrival, he questions his associate anxiously, but Dudard assures him that he looks and sounds perfectly normal.

Berenger is unnerved by Jean's transformation, but Dudard scolds him for taking things so seriously, for one must accept the *fait accompli*. He discloses that Papillon too has turned into a rhinoceros. Shocked, Berenger deplores Papillon's lack of will power. Berenger is too intolerant, Dudard says. Excessive tolerance is only blindness, Berenger replies, adding that he wishes he could find

the logician to argue for him. Moving to the window, he shakes his fist at the
herd of rhinoceroses surging below, and is appalled to glimpse the logician
among them. The logician must have weighed all the evidence before deciding
to change, Dudard says thoughtfully.

Now Daisy appears with a basket of food, bringing news that Botard is a
rhinoceros. His last human words were: "We must move with the times."
Berenger is disgusted, but Dudard sees the triumph of community spirit. There
is a crumbling sound outside, and Berenger announces that the fire station has
been demolished and that all the firemen, a regiment of rhinoceroses, are pouring up the street. When Daisy calls the men to lunch, Dudard says that he
would prefer to eat on the grass. Berenger tries to persuade him not to go, but,
after circling the table several times, Dudard dashes out.

Daisy should have influenced him to stay, Berenger tells her, but she says
she doesn't believe in interfering with other people's lives. Berenger caresses her
tenderly, and they talk of their future life together. Reproaching himself for
failing to save his friends, he says that he should have been kinder to them.
Daisy advises him to forget those bad memories: guilt shows a lack of purity,
she declares. The telephone rings, and answering it, Berenger hears only trumpeting; he turns on the radio, and there is more trumpeting. He and Daisy realize that they are the only humans left.

They will have children and regenerate the human race, Berenger proposes.
Daisy suggests that they two are the abnormal ones. The rhinoceroses are the
real people, she says: love is a weakness and can't compare with the ardent
energy emanating from the animals. Berenger slaps her, then is repentant. She
promises to help him resist the rhinoceroses but suddenly observes that they are
singing. No, they are roaring, Berenger replies. They are like gods and he is
jealous, Daisy says. When he turns to the mirror, she goes quietly out. Finding
himself alone, he calls despairingly, but she does not return.

Berenger looks in the mirror again and sees that he is ugly. He tries to imitate the song of the rhinoceroses, but it is too late for him to change. So defiantly he vows that he will fight them to the end.

ALFRED JARRY

Ubu Roi [1896]

ACT ONE

In his house in Poland, Père Ubu, ex-king of Aragon and now an officer of the Polish dragoons, talks with his wife Mère Ubu. She urges Père Ubu to kill King Venceslas of Poland and take the throne himself. Père Ubu is reluctant to do this until he is told that as king he could have an umbrella and a great big cloak.

Captain Bordure and his men come to the Ubus' for dinner, which includes a lavatory brush tossed on the table by Père Ubu. Ubu promises to make Bordure the Duke of Lithuania if he will help overthrow King Venceslas. Bordure accepts.

Later, a messenger summons Ubu to the palace. Thinking the plot is discovered, Ubu rushes to the king, blaming everything on Mère Ubu and Bordure. Bordure is present and covers up Ubu's raving. The king, unsuspicious, tells Ubu that he has decided to make him the Count of Sandomir and orders him to be present at the review of troops the next day.

In Ubu's house, Père and Mère Ubu, Bordure, and other conspirators plan the assassination of the king. Père Ubu suggests using poison, but the others scoff at this cowardly method. Bordure says he will kill the king with his sword. Ubu, who is always careful about his own safety, is hesitant, but finally agrees to give the signal for the attack. The signal word will be "merde" (Ubu pronounces it "merdre"), one of his favorite expressions.

ACT TWO

At the palace, the king forbids his son Bougrelas to attend the review, since Bougrelas was rude to Ubu the day before. Queen Rosemonde is worried about Venceslas going to the review, for in a dream she has seen Ubu killing her husband. Venceslas scoffs and goes to the review with his other sons, Ladislas and Boleslas.

At the review ground, Ubu gives the signal, and the king is cut down. Ladislas and Boleslas are pursued to the palace and killed. Bougrelas fights off the attackers. He and Queen Rosemonde escape to the mountains where the queen dies of grief and exhaustion. The spirit of an ancestor brings a sword to Bougrelas, who swears vengeance on Père Ubu.

The new king is traditionally supposed to distribute gold and food to the people, but Père Ubu is tight-fisted and does not want to part with any money.

Bordure and Mère Ubu persuade him by saying that unless he distributes gold, the people will not pay taxes to him.

ACT THREE

At home, Ubu tells Mère Ubu that he no longer needs Bordure and that he will not keep his promise to make him Duke of Lithuania. He also refuses to concern himself about Bougrelas, despite Mère Ubu's insistence that Bougrelas has the right on his side and will eventually triumph. Ubu claims it might be just as good to have the wrong on his side.

Having put the nobles to death so that he can seize their property, Ubu tells the magistrates that they will no longer be paid but instead can have the fines they impose and the property of people they condemn to death. The magistrates refuse this plan and are killed. Ubu tells the financiers that he intends to take half of all the tax money for himself. There will be new taxes on property, commerce, marriages, and deaths. The financiers oppose the idea and are also put to death. Ubu says he will collect the taxes himself.

Bordure revolts against Ubu and is imprisoned. He escapes to Russia and obtains the promise of Tsar Alexis to help in deposing Ubu and reestablishing Bougrelas on the throne. Ubu, frightened when he hears the news, asks the saints for protection, promising them money, which he calls "phynance," for their help.

Ubu decides to make war against the Russians but refuses to give out any money for the undertaking. Because of Ubu's miserliness, even his horse is too underfed and weak to carry him in his battle armor. Before he goes off to war, he tells Mère Ubu that he leaves the regency in her hands but is taking the cash book with him. Left alone, Mère Ubu schemes to kill Bougrelas, their most dangerous rival, and to take the king's treasure for herself.

ACT FOUR

Bougrelas and his supporters attack and capture Warsaw. Mère Ubu flees the city.

In the Ukraine, Ubu and the Polish army encounter the Russians. During the battle, Ubu is alternately cowardly and ferocious, especially against helpless foes. He meets Bordure and kills him. Tsar Alexis is too much for Ubu, who is able to escape only when Alexis topples into a ditch. Seeing that the Russians are winning, Ubu leaves his troops and runs away.

Ubu hides in a cave in Lithuania with two of his men, Pile and Cotice. He boasts that he has displayed the greatest valor and without exposing himself has killed four of the enemy, "without counting all those who were already dead and whom we finished off."

A bear enters the cave. While Pile and Cotice desperately fight it off, Ubu clambers onto a rock and says a paternoster. The bear is finally killed, and Ubu comes down, claiming that Pile and Cotice are alive only because he strained himself to the uttermost, broke his back, and bawled himself hoarse to churn out paternosters for their salvation. He orders his men to build a fire and cook the bear, then falls asleep.

Pile and Cotice take the opportunity to desert Ubu.

ACT FIVE

Mère Ubu, still fleeing from Bougrelas, enters the cave. Ubu is half-awake and Mère Ubu, pretending to be an apparition, tries to convince him to forgive her for stealing money. Ubu wakes up and sees that the apparition is really Mère Ubu. Ubu loses his temper and threatens her with torture—"twisting of the nose, pulling out of the hair, shoving of the little bit of wood into the earens [Ubu's pronunciation of ears], extraction of the brain by the heels." Before Ubu can carry out his threats, Bougrelas and his soldiers rush into the cave. Ubu fends them off by swinging the dead bear at them. Pile and Cotice rush in to the aid of the Ubus, and the four fight their way out and escape.

Bougrelas eventually gives up the pursuit and instead goes to Warsaw to be crowned king. Ubu says that he doesn't envy Bougrelas the crown.

Ubu and his followers take a ship on the Baltic Sea to return to France, where Ubu plans to get himself appointed master of finances.

Passing by Elsinore castle on the North Sea, Mère Ubu remarks on the beauty of the country there. Père Ubu says it is beautiful but it can't equal Poland because, "If there weren't any Poland, there wouldn't be any Poles."

GEORG KAISER

From Morn to Midnight [*Von Morgen bis*

Mitternachts, written 1912; performed 1917]

Scene 1. To the counter of a provincial bank comes the Lady, dressed in furs, to request three thousand marks on a letter of credit. The Cashier sends for the Manager, who informs the Lady that since her bank in Florence has not sent duplicate signatures, the bank cannot comply with her request. Despite her protests that she needs the money, the Manager can only advise her to remain in town until the letter arrives. After she leaves, the Manager assures the Cashier that the elegant Lady is one of the glamorous swindlers who inhabit the Riviera, warning him against such involvements.

After the Manager has left, the Lady returns to implore the Cashier to accept her diamonds as security. As her attention is momentarily diverted, her hand comes to rest upon that of the Cashier, who regards the hand and its owner intently. After asking the nearly hypnotized Cashier to fasten her bracelet, she leaves. When a serving maid asks to cash a check, the flustered Cashier gives her too much money. After she leaves, he sends the clerk and the porter separately to fetch water for him. Left alone, he stuffs his pockets with money and leaves.

Scene 2. In the writing room of a hotel, the son unveils to his mother, the Lady, a painting of great value that he has just arranged to purchase. A learned art historian, he is delighted in the successful termination of his quest, which was the express purpose of their trip. When he asks, however, for the three thousand marks to pay for it, his mother informs him that she does not have it. As the Cashier arrives, the son leaves. A misunderstanding mushrooms between the Lady, who assumes that he has come officially with her three thousand marks, and the Cashier, who, having stolen the money believing that she, a swindler herself, encouraged him, now expects her to flee with him. After he confesses to the robbery, he gradually comes to believe the story of her son and the painting. The crushing realization that he has committed his crime in vain and is now and evermore a criminal drives him to flee. After the son returns, a telephone call brings the news that the letter has arrived and the money is available. The Lady and the son prepare to leave town after their visit to the bank.

Scene 3. In a field deep in snow, the Cashier, in the course of his escape, muses aloud upon his cirumstances; though he feels humiliated by the Lady, he is grateful to her for having set him free. He determines to find something worth the embezzled money. He revels in a sudden storm, identifying it with the chaos created by his own deed. When the tree changes into a skeleton, he speaks to it as a symbol of the emptiness that is perhaps the answer to his quest. At length he bids farewell to the skeleton, preferring the complications of continued existence to a visit to the skeleton's domain, though the confrontation has given him the strength to face the future. As the skeleton reverts to the tree, the sun comes out again.

Scene 4. In the Cashier's house, the mother, the wife, and the two daughters are engaged in their customary activities when the Cashier returns home, ranting that he has come from the grave. He speaks mysteriously of the deed that has proved to be his escape from his prison-like existence. He looks around his snug domicile as if seeing it for the first time, realizing that it is not the goal of his search. At the realization that he is going out before the meal, the mother dies. Unwilling to grieve, the Cashier leaves them some bank notes and departs. The Manager comes seeking him, explaining to the family what has happened. The wife becomes hysterical when she realizes that her husband has left her.

Scene 5. In the steward's box at a bicycle race, several gentlemen, all of whom look alike, are watching the races and announcing the prizes. The Cashier, elegantly attired in evening clothes, enters the box with one of the gentlemen. At the news that he is offering a prize of a thousand marks, he is made welcome. The crowd approves the announcement of the prize and the race is begun. The Cashier admits that his interest is not in the sport itself but in the mélange of audience reactions, which he sees becoming pure passion. This is the magic that he seeks to purchase with his offer. When the race has ended, the Cashier demands another to follow immediately, despite the exhaustion of the competitors, in order to keep the audience aflame. To this end he offers a prize of fifty thousand marks, which the amazed and happy gentlemen leave to discuss. A Salvation Lass enters but is driven away by the Cashier. The gentlemen return to announce the Cashier's offer to the audience, which attains a state of pandemonium. Suddenly there is silence, as everyone reverently arises. The Cashier, irritated to learn that the sudden calm is caused by the arrival of his royal highness, angrily withdraws the money, disappointed to find such a groveling attitude governing the formerly raging crowd. He leaves in a huff.

Scene 6. In a private supper room in a cabaret, the elegantly dressed Cashier orders a dinner for two. He disappears and returns with a woman in a silken mask and harlequin's costume. He orders her to drink, then approaches her, only to find her drunk. When she falls asleep, he throws a glass of wine in her face, and she angrily leaves. Again he disappears and returns, this time with two black Masks. After he gives them food, he tries to remove their masks. They elude him and then lift their dominoes. Furious, he drives them away. He fetches yet another Mask, this one wearing a long cloak. He orders her to dance but she does not. The Salvation Lass appears again but is driven away. The Mask admits to the Cashier that she cannot dance because she has a wooden leg. At his show of anger, she leaves. Putting a bank note on the table, he too leaves.

Guests enter, seeking the man who has lured their girls away and pocketing the money lying on the table. The waiter returns, finds no money, and despairs that he will be held responsible. The guests knock him down and leave him locked in the room, as he shouts that he will go into the river.

Scene 7. In a Salvation Army hall, a woman officer invites the members of the audience to come forward to sit on the bench of the penitent form. The Cashier, still in evening dress, is led into the hall by the Salvation Lass. A soldier of the Salvation Army tells the audience how he was moved to sit on the penitent bench after a successful career in bicycle racing. At the urging of the officer, a penitent comes forward to confess his sins, also as a bicycle racer, and to sit on the penitent bench. A female soldier tells of her life as a lost woman. In response to the further urging of the officer, an old prostitute comes forward to tell her story and to sit on the penitent bench. Another soldier tells how he awakened from the spiritual lethargy of a contented family life to the life of the soul. Another penitent, describing his cozy home with its spiritual emptiness, stumbles to the penitent bench. Yet another soldier narrates how he stole money entrusted to him and went to jail, where he discovered the voice of his soul.

The Salvation Lass, who has remained by the Cashier, leads him to the platform and remains with him. He tells of his day's journey, of the search for something worth the separation from his old life, of his failure to find it until he found this hall, where fulfillment of the spirit is desired and imminent. He tells the story of his crime and of his discovery of the meanness of money and its corruption of men. Caught up in the spirit of his speech, he throws rolls of bank notes into the audience, confident that they will be trampled by his listeners, who know that money cannot buy anything worthwhile. The crowd, however, fights fiercely over the money and rolls in a tangled mass out the door. Only the Salvation Lass remains with the Cashier. He regards her as the only remaining worthwhile thing, until she delivers him into the hands of the police in order to obtain the reward. To a skeleton, which appears in the tangle of wires that support and provide current for the huge hanging lamps, he admits that he should not have taken to the road that morning, but should have accepted the silent invitation of the skeleton in the tree. He shoots himself, his dying gasp sounding like the words "Ecce Homo." All the lamps explode, and in the darkness a policeman says, "There must be a short circuit."

GEORGE S. KAUFMAN AND

MOSS HART

You Can't Take It with You [1936]

ACT ONE

The living room in the home of Martin Vanderhof, just around the corner from Columbia University in New York City, also serves as a dining room, as well as a center for numerous hobbies and projects. It is here that Penny Vanderhof Sycamore, Martin's daughter, writes her plays. She is at work on her love play now, having underway a war play, a religious play, a sex play, and a labor play. We meet the other inhabitants of the house, including Penny's older daughter Essie, who studies ballet with Boris Kolenkhov, a Russian émigré. Essie makes her living by making and selling candy. Her husband, Ed Carmichael, delivers the candy to customers. Ed's hobby is printing. He sets up type for anything and prints it—the family menu or slogans from revolutionary and anarchist writers. The slogans he usually inserts, as "descriptive literature," in Essie's candy boxes. Ed also is an avid xylophone player. He plays Essie's dance music when she takes her lessons from Kolenkhov.

Penny's husband, Paul Sycamore, makes fireworks in the basement and sells them for the Fourth of July each year. His helper in contriving new and more spectacular rockets and firecrackers is Mr. De Pinna, who came to deliver ice eight years ago and just stayed on.

Martin Vanderhof, who is called Grandpa by everyone, has several hobbies. He collects stamps, keeps snakes, which live in a goldfish aquarium in the living room, and goes to commencement exercises, especially to those around the corner at Columbia. He has just returned from one this evening.

Other members of the household are Rheba, the Negro cook, her boy friend Donald, and Alice Sycamore, the younger daughter of Penny and Paul. Alice is the only member of the family who has a regular job. She is a secretary at Kirby & Co. She announces this evening that she will not be home for dinner: a young man is calling for her. He is Tony Kirby, the boss's son. Alice is plainly apprehensive about the impression her odd family will make on Tony.

Before Tony arrives, Mr. Henderson of the Internal Revenue Service stops in. Grandpa has not paid income tax for twenty-two years. Infuriated and baffled by Grandpa's calm dismissal of the whole affair, Henderson finally leaves, badly shaken by an impromptu fireworks display set off by Paul and Mr. De Pinna in the hallway.

Tony arrives and is introduced to the family. Alice hurries downstairs to meet him as quickly as she can, but not before Penny has time to make several references to marriage. Before Alice and Tony leave, Kolenkhov makes his customary loud entrance. Alice manages to get Tony out of the house just as Kolenkhov, hearing they are going to the Monte Carlo ballet, flies into a rage and shouts that the Monte Carlo ballet stinks.

Later that night, Tony brings Alice home. The house is quiet except for an occasional bang from the fireworks shop in the cellar. Though Tony and Alice like each other very much, Alice believes that romance between them is impossible, for Tony's parents would never accept her odd family as relatives. Tony convinces her that all that is important is that they love one another.

ACT TWO

A week later, after the family has finished dinner, everyone takes up his favorite pursuit: Grandpa begins throwing darts at his target; Penny gets into her smock and beret and starts work on a painting of a discus thrower, for which Mr. De Pinna poses in a Roman toga; Essie takes her dancing lesson from Kolenkhov, to Ed's xylophone accompaniment; Miss Gay Wellington, a drunken actress who is Penny's dinner guest, passes out on the sofa. At this point the doorbell rings and Tony comes in with his parents: he has brought them for dinner one night too soon.

The Kirbys are obviously taken aback by the strange household, but the family tries to make the best of the situation. Penny sends Donald out for food—frankfurters, canned corn, Campbell's soup, and beer; Miss Wellington wakes up, playfully rumples Mr. Kirby's hair, and staggers upstairs. Kolenkhov insists on demonstrating wrestling holds to Kirby, throws the staid businessman to the floor, and breaks his glasses. Penny attempts to relieve the strain by beginning a word association game. This does not help matters, and the Kirbys excuse themselves and prepare to leave.

Before they can depart, three Justice Department men come to investigate the source of the revolutionary slogans in Essie's candy boxes. When the investigators discover the fireworks powder in the basement, they are convinced they have caught a gang of terrorists and arrest everyone. At this point the fireworks in the basement, set off by Mr. De Pinna's smoldering pipe, explode noisily.

ACT THREE

The following day, Donald reads the newspaper story of the arrest, in which Mr. Kirby's name figures prominently, and discusses with Rheba the night in jail. Packing to leave, Alice wanders in and out of the room; she realizes that the adventure has borne out her fears, for apparently the Kirbys will have nothing to do with her family now; she is therefore preparing to go away alone to get over her sorrow. Tony declares that he still wants to marry her despite his family's attitude, but is unable to talk her out of going away. Alice's family is saddened by their part in the debacle and by Alice's departure.

Kolenkhov brings the Grand Duchess Olga Katrina to the house for dinner.

The Grand Duchess, a cousin of the late tsar, is now a waitress at Childs restaurant. Her charm and courage in the face of her misfortunes help revive the family's spirits a little. She goes into the kitchen to make some Russian blintzes.

Mr. Kirby arrives to ask Tony to come home. Grandpa advises Kirby to give up his business on Wall Street and to start getting some fun out of life. Grandpa tells of his own decision thirty-five years ago to quit business and enjoy himself by doing what he wants. Tony supports Grandpa's argument. He reminds his father that Kirby had never really wanted to go into business, but had wanted to be a saxophone player until his own father forced him into the business. Tony says that he will not be forced in the same way and that he is quitting Kirby & Co.

Kirby finally sees the truth in what Grandpa and Tony say. Disregarding his indigestion troubles, he agrees to stay for dinner to eat some of Grand Duchess Olga's blintzes. Alice gratefully kisses Grandpa for his efforts and sends away the cab that has come to take her to the station. Everyone sits down to dinner and Grandpa makes his customary casual and friendly prayer of thanks to God.

SOMERSET MAUGHAM

The Circle [1921]

ACT ONE

Arnold Champion-Cheney and his young wife Elizabeth are having a talk in the drawing room of Arnold's house, Aston-Ardly, in Dorset. Unwillingly but at the insistence of Elizabeth, who thinks it a shame that he has not seen his mother since he was five, Arnold has invited Lady Kitty Champion-Cheney and Lord Porteous, for whom she thirty years ago abandoned his father, to come for a visit at his country house. Two friends, Mrs. Anna Shenstone, a woman of forty, and Teddie Luton, a young man, are present as shock absorbers. Arnold is distressed to learn that his father, Clive Champion-Cheney, has arrived and spent the night in the cottage. He frets that Elizabeth insisted on Kitty's visit, and Elizabeth replies that he could at least try to be friends with his mother.

Arnold explains that his mother's running off with another man cast a shadow of scandal over him at school, at Oxford, and in London; forced his father to withdraw from politics; and ruined the career of Lord Porteous, who had been expected to become prime minister. Though his father divorced his mother, Lord Porteous' wife refused to divorce, and consequently Lady Kitty and Lord Porteous were forced to live in Italy, in the only society that would accept them. Arnold describes their flight from England: neither of them came down to dinner, and Lady Kitty left a note on her pincushion. His father has never lived in the house since, and will probably never forgive Arnold for inviting the adulterers back. Elizabeth promises to take all the blame on herself.

When Clive Champion-Cheney appears, Arnold and the guest make embarrassed excuses and depart, and Elizabeth breaks the news to him that his ex-wife and her lover are arriving before lunch. Clive's unruffled reaction and willingness to have lunch by himself encourage Elizabeth to ask him about Kitty. Clive describes her beauty as something like Elizabeth's and speculates that she probably has white hair by now. Elizabeth protests that a person who has loved as Lady Kitty has grows old beautifully. Clive accuses her of romanticism.

As soon as Clive is gone, Teddie steps through the French window and asks how it went. Elizabeth says that Clive has promised to keep out of the way. They discuss Malaya, where Teddie lives, and she asks whether he has a woman out there. He explains that it takes a very special kind of girl to get along in Malaya, a woman of courage, endurance, and sincerity—the kind who helped make the Empire. They exchange a long look, and he asks whether she knows that he loves her. She replies that she had wondered.

Arnold and Anna, greatly perturbed, interrupt with the announcement that

Lady Kitty and Lord Porteous are arriving. Lady Kitty appears with dyed red hair, outrageous clothes, and the manner of a twenty-five-year-old; Lord Porteous is bald, eccentrically dressed, and gruff. Kitty embraces the startled Elizabeth and is about to mistake Teddie for Arnold when Elizabeth points out the mistake. Kitty says that she would have known her son anywhere and compliments his taste in refurnishing the house. Arnold asks whether she likes his latest chair, but Porteous bluntly calls it a fake.

Kitty invites Elizabeth to have a long talk about religion one of these days, having recently been received into the Catholic church. Porteous complains that his false teeth hurt, and Kitty observes that while men complain at the slightest pain, women—whose entire waking life is pain—never complain. Luncheon is announced, and Kitty fumbles in her bag for her lipstick. At that moment Clive appears at the window, holding the lipstick: he found it in the drive. Porteous recognizes him, but Kitty has to be told who he is; she remarks that his hair has gone white and says that he may kiss her cheek. Clive ironically asks Porteous' permission before doing so. He explains that his servants are too busy to prepare his lunch, and Elizabeth says that he may lunch with them.

ACT TWO

It is two days later and Porteous and Kitty are quarreling over a card game; Porteous loses his temper, speaks harshly to Kitty, and follows her out of the room when she leaves weeping. Clive remarks that they act like married people. Elizabeth asks why Clive has not kept his promise to stay away. He replies that he has come out of curiosity and points out that Kitty has turned into a silly, worthless woman because she has led a silly, worthless life. Elizabeth professes pity and affection for Kitty, who at least dared to love greatly. Clive points out that Kitty has ruined Porteous, who has been getting tight after dinner and has probably been doing the same for thirty years. He asks Teddie when he will be going back to Malaya, and leaves to go to look at the goldfish.

Teddie tells Elizabeth that he is leaving the next day and announces that he not only loves her, but likes her and wants to be with her. In tears, Elizabeth says that she loves him and will go wherever he takes her. They plan that Teddie will wait for her in London, and she will tell Arnold to his face rather than leave a note as Kitty did. At the sound of a car driving up, Elizabeth goes to bathe her eyes and Teddie goes into the garden.

Arnold comes to take his tea, followed by Kitty, who has decided that they ought to chat and get acquainted. Clive enters and joins in a conversation on interior decoration. When Porteous arrives, Arnold goes to fetch a book on chairs and clears up the question of the fake. Porteous upbraids Clive for hanging around; Clive asks why bygones can't be bygones—after all he, not Porteous, is the injured party. Porteous asks how the devil Clive can consider himself the injured party and states that he has never liked Clive. Clive replies that he has always liked Porteous. Kitty remarks that Clive has always been nice, and Porteous asks her why, in that case, she left him. Clive tells them not to quarrel, and Porteous asks him to mind his business.

Kitty details the sacrifices she has made for Porteous: thirty years of living in a marble palace with no bath; Porteous counters that he sacrificed the prime ministry for her. At the height of their disagreement Porteous' teeth start to come out and he rushes from the room. Alone with Clive, Kitty declares that she is finished with Porteous, adding that in the eyes of the church she is still married to Clive and that she has sown her wild oats. Clive replies that he has not sown his. Kitty calls him a wicked man; but a happy one, Clive adds.

As Kitty leaves to dress for dinner, Elizabeth enters, looking for Arnold. Clive leaves her alone with him. She says that she cannot beat about the bush and asks Arnold to let her go. Arnold replies that he loves her and that in her interest and his he will not allow her to leave him. She says that she loves Teddie and intends to join him as soon as possible. Arnold sends for Teddie and asks him to leave the house, warning that he will never divorce Elizabeth.

ACT THREE

That evening, as Arnold paces the room, Clive tries to persuade him to follow his advice in handling Elizabeth. Porteous and Kitty, who are not on speaking terms, enter and sit at opposite ends of the room. When Elizabeth enters, Clive gives her a photograph album so that she can see what pretty women looked like thirty-five years ago. She comes across a picture of Kitty and rushes to show it to her. Kitty bursts into tears. Perplexed and embarrassed, Elizabeth takes Clive's arm and walks with him to the terrace, asking whether he intended the incident.

Porteous apologizes to Kitty for his earlier rudeness, and she apologizes for hers. He tells her that she has improved with maturity, as all women do. The flattery restores her spirits, and she reciprocates, telling him that Clive always lacked Porteous' style and presence; moreover, Clive has degenerated terribly. Porteous suggests that they return to San Michele, where they ran off together; Kitty does not dare, lest it be filled with ghosts of their past happiness.

Clive returns and breaks the news that Elizabeth wants to run off with Teddie; he asks Kitty to speak to her. When Elizabeth returns from the garden, Kitty sends the others away and tries to convince her that, though the tie between married people can be broken by separation, only death can break the tie between two people who are not married; women are economically dependent on men, and it is folly to suppose that love can be pursued in violation of economic necessities and habits—only an economically independent woman can love whom she will and renounce whom she will. Kitty confesses a secret: she dyes her hair; she has to resort to tricks to keep Porteous' love because his love is the only security she has. She describes her heartbreak when Porteous was attracted to other women and then, to Elizabeth's shock, describes her own occasional affairs with other men. Kitty warns Elizabeth: one sacrifices one's life for love and finds that love turns to indifference.

Arnold returns and asks to speak to Elizabeth alone. He tells her that he will put no obstacles in her way, but will give her complete freedom, even if it should ruin his career; moreover, he will put two thousand pounds annually into a bank account for her so that she need never go without the luxury to which she is used. Elizabeth asks him only to divorce her as soon as possible. He refuses: instead, he will let her divorce him. He kisses her on the forehead and goes.

Elizabeth stands shattered as Kitty and Porteous return. She asks Porteous to go fetch Teddie, who is waiting in the summer house for her. Porteous brings him, and Elizabeth announces that she cannot run off: Arnold has been so good to her, and is willing to sacrifice so much for her that her hands are tied. Teddie tells her she is an idiot if she sacrifices her life to a slushy sentiment. Elizabeth asks whether he would be as good as Arnold: if she wanted to leave him for another man, would he be as noble? Teddie replies that if she did that he would black both her eyes; he states that he has never offered her happiness—he has offered a life of unrest, anxiety, and love. Elizabeth embraces him and declares that she adores him. They decide to bolt at once.

Porteous offers his car and says he will wire to San Michele for their reservations. He gives Elizabeth Kitty's cloak, and Kitty offers to pin a note on the pincushion for her. Elizabeth kisses them goodnight and leaves with Teddie. Kitty wonders whether they will suffer; Porteous replies that he and Kitty made a hash of things because they were trivial, but that one can do anything in life if one has the character to take the consequences.

Clive, unaware that Elizabeth has run off, enters rubbing his hands, gloating that he has taken care of Teddie Luton: he states that he advised his son to offer to sacrifice himself completely, for once the obstacles to marriage with Teddie were gone, half the allure would vanish: in order to keep the prisoner from wanting to escape, one has only to remove the prison bars. Clive is willing to bet five hundred pounds to a penny that Elizabeth won't bolt. As he laughs over his fine plan, Porteous and Kitty join in his laughter.

VLADIMIR VLADIMIROVICH MAYAKOVSKY

Mystery-Bouffe [*Misteriya-buff*, 1918; second version, 1921]

PROLOGUE

One of the Unclean briefly summarizes the action of the play.

ACT ONE

An Eskimo hunter sticks his finger into the globe, which rests on two walruses, and shouts to an Eskimo fisherman that there is a hole in the earth. The fisherman runs off, but is stopped by a German, who describes how a sudden flood engulfed Berlin and carried him, the sole vestige of Europe, to this polar spot. As the fisherman starts to leave again, he meets two Australians, who weep over the loss of their possessions in the flood. Lloyd George and Clemenceau appear, plant their respective flags, and begin to argue over which of them possesses this colony. A fat Russian merchant drops on the fisherman's head and describes how the flood came to his town.

Voices are heard; a procession enters, consisting of the Negus of Abyssinia, a Chinese, a Persian, a Turkish pasha, a rajah, a Russian priest, a Compromiser, a diplomat and an Intelligent, followed by seven pairs of the Unclean. Several of them describe the effects of the flood on their own countries. A lady with many bandboxes, one of the Clean, describes how she fled before the Bolshevik revolution. The Compromiser begs to be allowed to go home to his books. A fight begins to brew; the Unclean chide Clemenceau, and the Clean become frightened. When the Compromiser begs for peace, he is attacked and retreats.

The Clean try to discover the meaning of the flood. When the merchant shoves the Eskimo hunter away, water streams from the hole in the earth, striking the Clean. The merchant suggests they build an ark. All agree, and Clemenceau stipulates that none of the Unclean may come along, until the carpenter points out that only the Unclean can build the ark. An American arrives on a motorcycle and contributes a huge sum of money. The Unclean start to work.

ACT TWO

On the deck of the ark, the Unclean descend into the hold to eat walrus. The Clean discuss their problem: they have money, but there is no food to be bought. Lloyd George and Clemenceau, now reconciled, propose that the Clean make the Unclean work for them, taking the profit for themselves. They will choose for the Unclean a tsar, who will decree that all belongs to him; he will then share everything with the Clean. The Negus is chosen tsar, and the decree drawn up. The Unclean emerge from the hold, and the others tie them up in a rope. The priest reads the decree appropriating all the foodstuffs of the Unclean, who descend, guarded by the Clean, into the hold and return with food, which they pile in front of the Negus. While the priest chases the Unclean back into the hold, the Negus eats all the food. The Clean return and become furious with the Negus. They settle down for the night, which passes swiftly.

In the morning, the Clean decide to replace autocracy with democracy. The Unclean join them, and they all throw the Negus overboard. Clemenceau sets the Unclean to work, while the Clean busy themselves with papers. The Clean record the food that the Unclean bring in, then devour it after the Unclean leave. The Unclean protest and finally throw the Clean overboard, except for the merchant, the lady, and the Intelligent, who hide.

When the Unclean begin to celebrate their victory, they become sober at the realization that they have no food. They steel themselves to survive until they reach Mount Ararat. The lady and the Intelligent emerge and pledge allegiance to the Soviet authority.

Someone sights a speck. When they see it is a man approaching, they think it is Christ and turn away. The man steps onto the deck and calls himself the Man of the Future. He invites them to his paradise, not Christ's heavenly paradise, but a flourishing earthly paradise, complete with electricity. When they ask him to lead them to it, he replies that it lies beneath their hands, for they will build it. When he disappears, several feel that he has entered into them.

The Unclean take up their tools and decide that the only course of action is to ascend the shrouds. With a rousing battle song, they climb and disappear, followed by the lady and the Intelligent. The Compromiser, after hesitating, follows them. The merchant does not follow, for he hopes to sell the ark they have abandoned. As it begins to break up, he calls for help.

ACT THREE

In hell, two devil couriers discuss the hunger existent in hell since the Clean took over. The Clean enter and order the devils to find them some food. Beelzebub, the leader of the devils, enters and announces that food supplies have arrived in the form of fifteen sinners. From below come the sounds of the Unclean ascending the masts. When they storm in, the devils rush at them. The Unclean laugh and hiss at the devils, who become quiet. As Beelzebub threatens the Unclean with various devilish tortures, the Unclean describe comparable earthly hardships, which are much worse. Soon the devils are aghast at the stories of earthly suffering.

The Compromiser tries to establish concord, but receives blows from both the devils and the Unclean for his trouble. Singing, the Unclean begin to ascend to purgatory. Back in hell, the lady begs Beelzebub to allow her to enter his hall. He agrees, and two devils drag her away to become part of dinner.

ACT FOUR

In paradise, the inhabitants prepare to welcome the Unclean, who rush in, ignore the welcome and look around for food. When Methuselah, leader of the inhabitants of paradise, offers cloud milk and cloud bread, the Unclean fling it away and demand something more substantial, voicing their disappointment in heaven and chiding the angels for their easy, unproductive, boring life. When the Unclean decide to destroy paradise, the Compromiser tries to restore peace, but is attacked by both sides.

The Unclean decide to seek the promised land. When Methuselah sees how they have destroyed paradise, he calls for the Lord to destroy them. The Lord appears with thunderbolts in hand, but cannot throw them for fear of striking his angels. The Unclean seize the thunderbolts, which will be useful for electric power, and proceed upward over the fragments of paradise. The Compromiser remains with the angels.

ACT FIVE

In the land of fragments, the Unclean stop to discuss the different ways they could organize to clear away the rubble that stands in their way. Soon they decide that such discussion is useless and start to work. When the Compromiser appears and counsels them to stop working, they chase him away.

As they dig, they find a Locomotive and a Steamboat, who claim to be hungry. The Unclean immediately begin digging to find coal and oil for them.

Suddenly Confusion appears with her host and orders the Unclean to cease working and worship her unassailable power. The Unclean drive Confusion's host away and slay Confusion herself.

The triumphant Unclean descend into a mine shaft and begin bringing up coal and oil for the Locomotive and the Steamboat, who quickly revive. The Unclean emerge from the mine and see a vision of the future, which is at hand. Climbing onto the Locomotive and the Steamboat, the Unclean head for the joyful land, which they can reach only "on the wings of the machines."

ACT SIX

At the gate to the promised land, the Unclean are told by the lamplighter, mounted on a ladder, of the beautiful, well-supplied, and productive city they are about to enter. When he tells them that the machines stand unused, the Unclean decide to enter the city.

The gates open, revealing the beautiful industrial city. Goods leave store windows and proceed to the city gate, led by the Sickle and the Hammer, to offer food to the newcomers, who cannot believe that food is being freely offered to them. When they also voice suspicion of the Machines, who formerly injured them, the Machines beg forgiveness, pleading that the fat men usurped and drove them. The Machines and the Things (tools of the trades) claim that they are now free and anxious to serve the workmen. The Edibles urge the Unclean to eat freely. The Unclean advance and form a ring with the Things and the Machines. The Locomotive engineer praises the new world they will create and invites the audience to mount the stage. All sing together a hymn to the commune and their new freedom.

ARTHUR MILLER

The Crucible [1953]

ACT ONE

On a spring morning in Salem, Massachusetts, in 1692, the Reverend Samuel Parris prays and weeps at the bedside of his daughter Betty, who lies inert. His Barbados slave woman Tituba comes in to ask after the child, but he roughly sends her away. His handsome niece Abigail enters with a messenger from the doctor, who reports he can find no natural cause for Betty's condition. Anxiously Parris questions his niece, for last night he surprised her and Betty dancing in the forest; he saw Tituba swaying and gibbering over a fire, and someone running naked. He adds that Abigail's virtue is suspect, for since Goody Proctor dismissed her from service no one has hired her. Abigail vehemently defends her innocence.

With eyes gleaming, Goody Putnam runs in to inquire how high Betty flew; she reveals that her daughter Ruth is in a trance too, having gone to Tituba to communicate with her dead sisters. Presently the Putnams' servant, Mercy Lewis, appears to announce that Ruth has sneezed.

Fearful that these events may damage his position, Parris leaves to lead the waiting crowd in a psalm. Alone with mercy, Abigail reveals that Mercy was seen naked; Mercy is panic-stricken. The Proctors' servant, Mary Warren, arrives in alarm; she suggests that they admit the truth, for witchery is a hanging crime while dancing is only a whipping one. Betty rouses from her bed, calls her dead mother, and tries to fly out the window. She accuses her cousin Abigail of drinking blood to charm Goody Proctor dead, then collapses again. With dire threats Abigail charges the girls not to reveal anything more.

John Proctor, a strong young farmer, comes in and sternly orders Mary home. Mercy sidles out. He asks Abigail what mischief is going on, but she only smiles wickedly and says that Betty is just silly from fright at her father's sudden appearance. As she tries to entice him again, it is clear that Abigail has had intimate relations with Proctor; he resolutely resists her advances.

As the psalm words "going up to Jesus" rise from the parlor, Betty wails. Parris rushes upstairs, followed by several others who interpret the child's apparent pain at the Lord's name as a clear sign of witchcraft. Rebecca Nurse, mother of eleven and grandmother of twenty-six, quiets Betty.

Parris has sent for Reverend Hale of Beverly, a man skilled in demonology. Proctor questions this act, but since he seldom attends church now, his words carry little weight. He declares that he grew tired of hearing hellfire and damnation; Rebecca agrees that many fear to bring their children to Parris' sermons. Parris complains that there is a faction against him, but old Giles Corey—

himself well known as a plaintiff—thinks the whole town is at fault, for everybody sues everybody else.

On Hale's arrival Proctor leaves. Hale, after hearing all the symptoms of witchcraft in the village, eagerly consults his heavy tomes to discover which disguise the devil might be wearing. In disapproval Rebecca goes out. When Tituba is called up, Abigail accuses the slave of trying to corrupt her with sorcery, and Hale demands that Tituba confess her compact with the devil. Putnam, a rich landowner, calls for her hanging. The terrified woman confesses and, on the promise of pardon, names several women she has seen with the devil. Now Abigail, as though inspired, declares that she wants to open herself to the Lord. She cries out more names, and Betty, rising, follows suit hysterically. Parris embraces her, Hale praises God, and Putnam goes to call the marshal.

ACT TWO

Eight days later in the Proctor farmhouse near Salem, Elizabeth Proctor tells her husband that Mary Warren defied him and spent the day in court, over which four judges from Boston and the deputy governor of the province now preside. Elizabeth urges John to go and disclose what Abigail told him; his temporizing suggests that he is still attracted to the girl. Proctor is angered by his wife's suspicions.

Mary returns and gives Elizabeth a small rag doll, which she made in court to pass the time. She says thirty-nine are arrested and one condemned, adding that the beggar woman Sarah Good saved herself by confessing. There is weighty work to be done, Mary declares, and she will go to court every day. As Proctor approaches her with a whip, she cries that she saved Elizabeth's life that day by testifying in her favor. Refusing to give the name of Elizabeth's accuser, she goes to bed.

Hale arrives unexpectedly to question the Proctors about their Christian practices and is dissatisfied with their answers, and when John, pressed by his wife, tells what he knows about Abigail, Hale is dubious. Corey and Francis Nurse come in, exclaiming that their wives have been jailed—one for bewitching pigs and the other for murdering Goody Putnam's seven babies. Ezekiel Cheever, the court clerk, arrives with Marshal Herrick. Spying Mary's rag doll, Cheever lifts up its dress and, shocked, draws out a needle. He explains that Abigail Williams fell screaming to the floor at dinner and that when Parris pulled a needle from her belly, she claimed that Goody Proctor's familiar spirit had pushed it in. Elizabeth fetches Mary, who admits that she herself stuck the needle in the doll for safekeeping and recalls that Abigail sat next to her in court. Elizabeth exclaims that Abigail should be ripped out of the world; at this Herrick, despite Proctor's strong opposition, carries her off in chains.

Perplexed, Hale counsels Proctor, Corey, and Nurse to find the real root of Salem's trouble: it could not be caused merely by the vengefulness of a young girl. Alone with Mary Warren, Proctor tells her she must inform the court of the truth. She cannot, Mary squeaks, for Abigail will kill her and charge him with lechery. Proctor grabs her by the throat and throws her sobbing to the floor.

ACT THREE

In the vestry room of the meeting house, now the anteroom of the court, Martha Corey's voice is heard denying witchcraft and Giles Corey is heard accusing Putnam of grabbing land. Corey is propelled into the vestry, where Francis Nurse waits to protest Rebecca's sentence.

Proctor arrives with Mary Warren, who has signed a statement admitting that her testimony was a fraud. Parris declares the statement a lie, and Deputy Governor Danforth accuses Proctor of undermining the court. Proctor is informed that Elizabeth is pregnant and cannot be sentenced for a year. When Danforth asks him to drop his charge of fraud, Proctor refuses and gives him a sheet of ninety-one signatures declaring the good reputation of Rebecca, Elizabeth, and Martha. Danforth orders the arrest of all those who have signed. Corey submits a statement to Danforth that Putnam prompted his daughter to cry witchery on George Jacobs so that he could take Jacobs' land. Refusing to disclose his informant, Corey is arrested.

Abigail enters with several of her friends, denies fraud, charges Mary with lying, and pretends to be bewitched by her. Proctor jerks her up by the hair, confesses to adultery with her, and adds that Abigail hopes to dance with him on his wife's grave. When Abigail denies the charge, Elizabeth is brought in and asked whether her husband is a lecher. She answers that he is not.

Realizing that Elizabeth is protecting her husband, Hale pleads with Danforth, who believes Proctor a liar. With a weird cry Abigail points to the rafters, where she seems to see a great bird: she begs Mary not to hurt her. Trembling, Mary implores her to stop, but Abigail, transfixed, mimics her words, the other girls joining in chorus. Defeated, Mary screams at Proctor's approach and accuses him of forcing her to sign the devil's book to keep his wife from hanging. Proctor and Corey are ordered to jail. Hale denounces the proceedings and quits the court.

ACT FOUR

Early one morning that autumn, Herrick enters the village jail and awakens Sarah Good and Tituba, who call on the devil to take them home as they are led away. Danforth enters, followed by Cheever with his writing materials. Herrick is sent to fetch Parris who, with Hale, has spent the night praying with the condemned. Parris enters, weeping, with the news that Abigail and Mercy Lewis have robbed his strongbox and fled, leaving him penniless. He states that there are rumors of rebellion and that hardly thirty of his congregation came to hear John Proctor's excommunication; he fears for his life.

Hale appears, exhausted from sorrow. Since none of the accused has confessed, they must be pardoned, he says. Danforth replies that they cannot be pardoned, since twelve have already been hanged. However, he is eager for Proctor to confess, and suggests that Elizabeth might persuade him. Hale reflects bitterly that he, a minister, has come to do the devil's work, to urge Christians to lie to save themselves.

Elizabeth and Proctor are led in and left by themselves. Wishing to save himself but ashamed, John asks whether many have confessed. Elizabeth tells him that many have, that Rebecca still denies and that, in order to die Christian under the law and leave his farm to his sons, Giles refused to say aye or nay; and so huge stones were laid on his chest to make him speak. He said, "More weight," and died. John asks Elizabeth whether he should confess, but she can only tell him that whatever he does, a good man does it. It takes a cold wife to prompt lechery, she adds.

When the other men come back, Proctor announces his decision to confess. They rejoice, and Rebecca is brought in to witness his good example. Though humiliated, he acknowledges consorting with the devil, but will not name others. He signs his confession, but on learning that it is to be nailed to the church for the instruction of the village, he tears it up with a terrible anger and cries that he cannot live without his good name.

Denouncing the prisoners, Danforth strides from the room. The prisoners are taken away, and a drumroll is heard. Anguished for his own fate, Parris rushes after them, but Hale drops to his knees, pleading with Elizabeth to intercede with Proctor while there is still time. Almost collapsing, she cries: "He have his goodness now. God forbid I take it from him!" Hale weeps in frantic prayer.

ARTHUR MILLER

Death of a Salesman [1949]

ACT ONE

Willy Loman, a salesman past sixty, returns dejectedly to his small house, which stands overshadowed by large apartment buildings. His wife Linda hears him and asks why he is returning early from his sales trip. He says he was on his way to New England but couldn't drive any farther than Yonkers, because he kept losing control of the car. She persuades him to ask his boss for a job in New York. He agrees and goes into the kitchen, talking to himself about his glorious hopes for his boy Biff. He talks so loud that he wakes Biff and his brother Happy. They listen amazed as their father rambles on.

In a scene from Willy's memory, Biff and Happy as teen-agers do their father's bidding with enthusiasm. He tells them he's going to own his own business someday, like Uncle Charley, but bigger, for Charley is liked but not "well-liked." Being "well-liked" is Willy's criterion of success. Biff's scholarly friend

Bernard, who Willy says is not "well-liked," runs in and makes a futile attempt to get Biff to study for his math exam; he leaves, crestfallen. Willy, still in the past, tells Linda he's not doing too well but says he loves her dearly. The lighting shifts to show Willy on the road as a salesman, amorously playing with a woman friend.

In the present again, Happy comes down and offers to retire his father, but Willy scorns the offer; he similarly scorns a job offer from Uncle Charley, a large kindly man, who comes in from next door, having been awakened by Willy's wandering speech. From the past, Uncle Ben, a heavy-set, obviously successful man in his sixties, drifts in, unseen to Charley; Willy talks to him while playing cards with Charley, who cannot understand why he is talking to himself; Willy insults Charley and Charley leaves. Completely in the past again, Willy sends the boys off to steal sand from a building site where they have been stealing lumber; Charley comes in to warn that they'll end up in jail.

The scene drifts back into the present as Linda, Biff, and Happy discuss Willy's wandering mind. The trouble, Linda tells the boys, is that he is exhausted: the firm has taken his salary away and he is working on commission alone; he borrows fifty dollars a week from Charley and pretends to Linda it's his salary—at sixty-three Willy is unknown and unwanted. She tells the boys she thinks he is trying to kill himself by crashing the car or perhaps by inhaling gas.

As Willy wanders in, Happy tells him that Biff is going to see Bill Oliver, a former employer; Willy is interested. When Biff says he's going to ask Oliver to set him up in business, Willy enthusiastically joins in with a plan to open a sporting goods store, called The Loman Brothers. Everyone retires for the night, voicing their happiness in the dream of tomorrow.

ACT TWO

At breakfast, Linda tells Willy to ask Howard, his boss, for a New York job and also for an advance: they need two hundred dollars, which will include the last payment on their house mortgage. Linda tells Willy the boys want him to be their guest at a celebration dinner that night.

Willy goes to his office, where Howard Wagner, his thirty-six-year-old boss, is playing a tape recording of his family. Willy listens and comments politely on the banal tape. When he finally gets Howard's full attention, Howard asks why he isn't in Boston. Willy says he would like to work in the office instead; Howard says there is no room for him. Willy begs him for fifty a week, then forty, but Howard walks out on him. Willy switches on the tape recorder by accident; unable to control it, he shouts to Howard for help. Howard runs in, finds Willy terrified, and fires him. Howard leaves the office, and Ben enters from the past again. He offers Willy a chance to make a fortune in Alaska. Linda enters and persuades Willy to turn down the offer.

The light comes up on Charley's office, in the present. Willy comes in and meets Bernard, now a poised and earnest young man, who reveals he's on his way to Washington to try a case. Willy tries to accept Bernard's success calmly, but breaks down and begs Bernard to tell him where he went wrong with his boys. Bernard said Biff could have gone to summer school to make up his math course and thus be eligible for college, but that after going to New England to see Willy, he gave up all his ambitions. Bernard asks Willy what happened in Boston, but Willy won't answer the question. Charley comes in, gives Willy fifty dollars, and offers him a job again, but Willy turns him down and leaves.

Happy and Biff meet in a restaurant for the dinner party. Biff says that Oliver kept him waiting all day, then didn't recognize him. Alone in the office, Biff stole Oliver's fountain pen and ran. Willy joins them, and Biff tries desperately to tell him the truth, despite Willy's enthusiastic notions of what happened in Oliver's office. Biff finally gets through to Willy, and Willy is crushed. The scene shifts to long ago when Willy, in Boston with a woman friend, hears knocks on his hotel room door. He tells the woman to get in the bathroom, and opens the door to see young Biff. He tries to send Biff downstairs, but the woman appears, and Biff is horror-stricken. Broken and weeping, Biff calls Willy a fake and a phony and leaves.

During Willy's revery, the boys go off with two girls; alone in the restaurant, Willy talks to the waiter a while and then goes home. When Biff and Happy return, Willy is planting seeds out in his back yard. Linda, bitter at them for deserting their father in the restaurant, tells them both to get out. In the garden, Willy dreamily tells Uncle Ben about a new proposition—to give Biff twenty thousand dollars insurance money by killing himself.

Biff comes out to say goodby, but they get into an argument, and Biff tells Willy to see that his whole life and teaching to the boys has been false. "We never told the truth for ten minutes in this house!" he says, and blames Willy for blowing him full of hot air. He says he is nothing and breaks down into sobs. Willy is touched and overjoyed to find what he considers proof that Biff loves him. Ben returns again as Willy dreams of giving Biff a real push with the twenty thousand dollars.

Linda, frightened, begs Willy to come up to bed. He refuses, and when everyone else is upstairs, he leaves the house and speeds off in his car to his death. Happy, Biff, Linda, Charley, and Bernard walk slowly forward. Linda carries a bunch of roses, which she lays at a grave, then sits back on her heels.

REQUIEM

The mourners talk about Willy. Biff thinks he was all wrong, but Charley says ". . . Willy was a salesman." Biff says, "I know who I am," and asks Happy to come West with him, but Happy wants to prove Willy was right by trying himself to become top man. All move away except Linda, who stays to say goodby to Willy. She says she can't cry, for she still expects him home from a trip. She tells him she made the last payment on the house today and there'll be nobody home. "We're free and clear," she sobs at last. "We're free . . . . We're free . . . ." Biff lifts her to her feet. Everyone slowly leaves.

A R T H U R   M I L L E R

A View from the Bridge   [1955]

ACT ONE

Mr. Alfieri, a lawyer, strolls down a street near Brooklyn Bridge, exchanges nods with two longshoremen, Louis and Mike, and enters a tenement. From his law office inside, he tells the audience about the neighborhood and about another longshoreman: Eddie Carbone. The stage lights fade as Alfieri's office becomes the Carbone apartment.

Eddie enters and is greeted by his niece Catherine. He admires her new skirt and hairdo but chides her for walking "wavy" in the street and attracting attention; he reminds her that he promised Catherine's mother on her deathbed that he would be responsible for the girl. Eddie has news for his wife Beatrice: her cousins' ship has docked. Beatrice worries that her cousins won't be allowed off, since they are entering the country illegally, but Eddie assures her that they will just walk off with the crew. Catherine has news, too. She has been offered a stenography job with a big plumbing company. Eddie is dismayed, for he had wanted her to finish secretarial school and work in a respectable place. But Beatrice pleads that Catherine isn't a baby any more and that he can't always keep her at home. Eddie gives in, and Catherine rewards him with a hug; he smiles so as not to cry. The women are apprehensive at the prospect of keeping illegal immigrants. Eddie warns them not to mention the matter to anyone and explains that the ship's captain has been paid off and that the Syndicate will find jobs for the men. The apartment fades, and Alfieri appears momentarily to say that Eddie was a good man and worked hard.

That night Marco and his brother Rodolpho arrive; they and the Carbones sit down for coffee. Catherine can't take her eyes off Rodolpho's blond hair. The brothers tell of their life in Italy and how difficult it was to find work. Marco says that he must send money to his wife and children; they are so poor, he says, that they eat sunshine. With tears in his eyes he thanks Eddie for his hospitality. Asked if he is married too, Rodolpho laughs that he is not. He states that he is a singer and wants to become an American. Encouraged by Catherine, he croons "Paper Doll" in a high tenor. Eddie halts him, saying he is advertising his presence in the house.

The lights dim to brighten again on Alfieri, who expresses wonder that Eddie Carbone, a man who had expected merely to work and grow old, should have a destiny. A moment later Eddie is seen at his doorway, waiting for Catherine and Rodolpho to come home from the movies. Beatrice walks up the street and smiles, but Eddie looks away. She asks what he has against Rodolpho. The boy sings songs—with all the motions—on the ships, he answers, and with that wacky hair he's like a chorus girl. He didn't bring up his niece for a character like that, Eddie says. But Beatrice has other worries. It is three months, she tells him, since he was a husband to her. She goes inside.

Louis and Mike stroll by and invite Eddie to go bowling, but he says he is too tired. They remark on Rodolpho's sense of humor and laugh as they see him enter the street. Alone with his niece, Eddie tells her that Rodolpho plans to marry her just so he can become a citizen, the oldest racket in the country. Vehemently Catherine denies this, retorting that Rodolpho loves her; she rushes sobbing into the house. Beatrice admonishes Catherine for walking around in her slip and talking to Eddie while he is shaving in his underwear as though she were still a baby: she is a grown woman in a house with a grown man and must act differently. Shaken, Catherine promises to try.

At his desk, Alfieri listens to Eddie, who complains that Rodolpho is weird, for he's platinum blond, he sings, and he even designed a dress for Catherine. The law cannot prevent their marriage, Alfieri states. He advises Eddie to let his niece grow up and leave.

After dinner in the Carbone apartment, the conversation turns to fidelity. Eddie suggests that immigrant husbands usually find a couple of extra kids when they get home to Italy, but Marco assures him that the women are faithful. His brother adds that their town is strict. It isn't so free here either, Eddie tells Rodolpho meaningfully. In rebellion, Catherine puts on a record and invites Rodolpho to dance, and though hesitant, he rises. Marco mentions that his brother is an excellent cook, and Eddie replies tensely that if he could do all the things Rodolpho is good at, he'd be in a dress store, not on the waterfront. Rodolpho stops the phonograph, and Eddie, getting up, insists that he should learn to box. He staggers the young man with a blow. Determinedly now, Rodolpho takes Catherine in his arms, and they dance again. Placing a chair in front of Eddie, Marco challenges him to raise it with one hand. When Eddie fails, Marco grasps it by a leg and slowly raises it over Eddie's head. His glare turns into a triumphant smile.

ACT TWO

Alfieri tells the audience that on December 23rd Rodolpho was alone with Catherine in the apartment for the first time. The lights rise on them. Rodolpho announces that he has saved nearly three hundred dollars, but Catherine is preoccupied. Could they live in Italy, she asks. No, he replies, astonished, because she would starve there. Realizing that she is testing him, he furiously accuses Eddie of planting mistrust. Catherine weeps that Eddie has always been so good to her that she can't suddenly turn against him. Rodolpho leads her gently into the bedroom.

Slightly drunk, Eddie enters the apartment. Catherine comes from the bedroom adjusting her dress, and Rodolpho appears behind her. In shock Eddie orders him to pack. Trembling, Catherine tells Eddie that she is going too, that she is not going to be a baby any more. Suddenly he draws her close, kissing her on the mouth. Rodolpho flies to her defense, but Eddie pins the boy's arms, laughs at him, and kisses him derisively.

On December 27th Eddie tells Alfieri that Rodolpho refuses to get out. The lawyer brusquely warns Eddie that a river will drown him if he bucks nature. In desperation Eddie finds a telephone booth and calls the Immigration Bureau; as he leaves, Louis and Mike pass him on the street.

Entering his apartment, Eddie asks Beatrice where everybody is. She says wearily that she moved the brothers upstairs with Mrs. Dondero and that Catherine went up with pillowcases. Disliking his wife's tone, Eddie complains that she isn't respecting him. She's sick of the whole business, Beatrice tells him; the young people are getting married next week, and she advises Eddie to wish Catherine good luck.

When his niece returns for more pillowcases, Eddie learns that Mrs. Dondero is boarding two other illegal immigrants, relatives of Lipari the butcher; he exclaims in alarm at the news. There is a repeated knocking on the door; Eddie opens it at last. Two immigration officers enter, look around, then go upstairs; they return with the four immigrants. Marco breaks away and spits in Eddie's face. As the men are led off, neighbors gather around the stoop. Again freeing himself momentarily, Marco points at Eddie. "That one killed my children!" he yells. Eddie turns to Lipari, Louis, and Mike to defend himself, but they walk away.

The lights rise on a prison reception room where Alfieri, Rodolpho, and Catherine plead with Marco to promise that he won't kill Eddie. The lawyer has offered to bail him out until the hearing, after which he will be deported. To Marco a promise not to kill is dishonorable, but he grudgingly assents.

In the apartment Beatrice and Catherine are dressed for the wedding, but Eddie is waiting for Marco's apology. Rodolpho enters with the warning that his brother is coming for Eddie. He reaches for Eddie's hand, saying that everything is his fault, but Eddie jerks it away. Marco must give him back his name in front of the neighborhood, he replies, starting out the door. Despairingly, Beatrice tries to bar his way.

From the street Marco calls to Eddie, who emerges from the house. Addressing the gathered crowd, Eddie accuses Marco of monstrous ingratitude. He moves toward Marco with arms spread, then lunges with a knife in his hand. Marco grabs his arm and, turning the blade inward, presses it home. Eddie dies in Beatrice's arms. From the crowd Alfieri turns to the audience to say that he loved Eddie better than his sensible clients, because Eddie let himself be wholly known.

FERENC MOLNÁR

Liliom [1909]

Prologue. In a park on the outskirts of Budapest, the barker Liliom stands at the entrance of Mrs. Muskat's carousel, coaxing customers to buy tickets. Girls screech with pleasure when he pushes them, and their escorts swallow their protests at a glance from him. As he mounts the barker's stand and harangues the crowd, people desert the other booths and flock to the carousel.

Scene 1. Later that same evening, in a deserted park, Marie and Julie, two young servant girls, flee the enraged Mrs. Muskat, who accuses Julie of having let Liliom fool with her on the carousel. Liliom enters, and Mrs. Muskat instructs him never to allow Julie on the carousel again. Liliom asks what she has done, and Julie explains that Mrs. Muskat claims he put his arm around her waist. Liliom asks whether he needs Mrs. Muskat's permission to touch girls and tells Julie that she can come and ride as often as she wants: if she hasn't any money, he'll pay for her. Mrs. Muskat tells Liliom that he is discharged. Julie begs Liliom not to get fired on her account. Liliom tells Mrs. Muskat to apologize to Julie; she refuses, tells him he can go to the devil, and leaves in a fury.

Liliom tells the girls not to pity him and invites them to a beer garden. While he is gone to collect his things, Marie says that Liliom has fallen in love with Julie. Julie denies that she has anything to do with Liliom. When Liliom returns and says that he expected only one girl to wait, Julie tells Marie that she can go. Alone with Julie, Liliom asks whether she has a sweetheart; she replies that she has never had one. He asks why she stayed with him: she says that she stayed because he has been good to her.

Two policemen, searching the park for vagabonds, ask Liliom what he is doing and warn Julie that he is only after her money. Liliom asks her whether she is afraid of him, and she replies that if she had any money she would give it to him. He asks whether she wants to dance; she refuses, for she must be careful of her reputation, since she doesn't intend to marry. Liliom asks her whether she would dare marry anyone like him. She says that if she loved someone it wouldn't make any difference what he was like. They sit silently on the bench smelling the white acacia blossoms.

Scene 2. Two months have elapsed, and Liliom and Julie have set up house in the photography studio run by Julie's aunt. Julie sits telling Marie how Liliom has twice beaten up Mrs. Muskat's new barker and how the police have twice let him go. Mother Hollunder, Julie's aunt, passes through the studio complaining that Liliom just lies around and never works, that he ought to be in jail, out of the way of hard-working people. Julie explains that since Liliom never learned a trade and since he refuses to be a day laborer, there is nothing for him to do but sit around; he refuses to go back to work for Mrs. Muskat. She remarks that he has not come home since the night before and adds that he has struck her.

Mother Hollunder says that the carpenter, a respectable widower with a good business, has been around looking for Julie and suggests that he would be a good husband. Marie urges Julie to marry the carpenter and says that Liliom is a bad man. Julie replies that though he is sometimes wild, he is gentle too, and he only hit her because he does not have a job; anyway, the blow did not hurt.

Mrs. Muskat enters haughtily and asks if Liliom is home, explaining to Julie that she has come to offer him his old job. Marie tells Mrs. Muskat that Liliom doesn't depend on her for his bread, says goodby to Julie, and goes. Liliom returns home with his friend Ficsur and tells Julie to keep her mouth shut and not to nag him about being out late, out of work, and living off her relations. Mrs. Muskat warns him that Ficsur will get him mixed up in a robbery and says that there is work for him at the carousel. Liliom sends Julie for a cup of coffee.

Mrs. Muskat tells Liliom he ought to sleep home nights, he looks a sight; he ought not to beat his wife—it is plain that he is sick of marriage after two months; that he is an artist, not a husband; that his wife will be better off without him; and that he is a fool to give up the excitement and money of working at the carousel, where he could have pretty girls, beer, cigars, and music. Liliom admits that he is unhappy.

Julie returns with the coffee and says she has something to tell Liliom. He orders her out, but she refuses to go. He rises to strike her, but Mrs. Muskat tells them not to start fighting and leaves the room. Julie tells him that she has found out why she has been having headaches: she is going to have a baby. As Julie leaves the room, Mrs. Muskat returns with ten crowns' advance. Liliom tells her to let him finish his coffee in peace and sends her away. He calls Ficsur to ask him about his scheme involving the cashier of the leather factory. Ficsur says that there is a lot of money involved, but that the job will take two people. Liliom asks him to come back later, then shouts with joy that he is going to be a father.

Scene 3. Later the same afternoon, as Ficsur explains to Liliom his plan for the robbery, Julie keeps coming back into the room, plainly worried, and tries to catch a bit of the conversation. As soon as she goes, Ficsur explains that they will bury the money for six months and then go to America, taking Liliom's baby. Over Liliom's protests that a weapon will not be necessary, Ficsur persuades him to dart into the kitchen to steal a knife. Liliom returns, buttoning his coat, and Julie asks where he is going with Ficsur, pleading with him to stay home. Trying to act gruff in order to hide the fact that he cannot bear her suffering, Liliom clenches his fist at her and orders her out of his way. Julie asks what he is hiding under his coat. He says he has cards, showing her a pack, ignores her pleas, and leaves with Ficsur.

Mother Hollunder comes into the room saying that she cannot find the kitchen knife, which she left on the table. Julie, horrified, says that she has not seen it and assures her that Liliom has not taken it. Marie arrives, happy and beaming, to introduce her fiancé Wolf to Julie: she tells how he has gotten a good job, how they have rented two rooms for themselves and, if things go well, hope to buy a place in the country so that their children can enjoy healthy surroundings. Julie wishes them luck, kisses them, and begins crying. Marie and Wolf, thinking she is crying because she has a good heart, become tearful too. Mother Hollunder bustles in again with her son to photograph the fiancés. As young Hollunder snaps the picture, Liliom and Ficsur can faintly be heard in the distance, singing.

Scene 4. Shortly afterwards on a railway embankment, Liliom and Ficsur sit and play cards, waiting for the cashier to pass by. Liliom loses, and Ficsur offers to let him play on credit, deducting his losses from his share of the crime. An inexperienced gambler, Liliom loses his entire half of the sixteen thousand crowns and is about to accuse Ficsur of cheating when the cashier comes along the embankment, carrying a leather bag over his shoulder.

Trembling, Liliom asks the cashier for the time. Ficsur springs at him with a knife in his hand, but the cashier catches his hand, forces him to his knees, and draws a revolver on Liliom, advising him not to run before the police arrive. He chides the would-be thieves for not realizing that he was not going to the factory, but coming from it, with an empty bag. Ficsur wrenches himself loose, and both he and Liliom run. Liliom climbs the embankment, shouts that he will not be taken, and crying Julie's name, plunges the kitchen knife into his breast and falls.

Scene 5. Half an hour later, two workmen bring Liliom on a stretcher to the studio to await the police surgeon. Raising himself with difficulty, Liliom tells Julie that he beat her, not because he was mad at her, but because he could not bear to see her crying; he tells her to marry the carpenter, asks her to hold his hand tight, and sinks back and dies. Marie, Wolf, and Mother Hollunder draw near to comfort Julie, telling her that she is better off without Liliom and will have forgotten him in a year. Mrs. Muskat comes to see the body: she asks Julie to make up with her, saying that they were the only people who loved Liliom. Julie refuses coldly. The carpenter comes and asks whether he can be of any help; she asks him to go. Ficsur enters, looks at the body and shakes his head, and tells Julie to come for coffee.

Two men in black stride into the empty room and tell Liliom that they are God's police and that he is under arrest. Liliom rises and leaves with them.

Scene 6. The guards bring Liliom into the courtroom in the Beyond for suicide cases and seat him on a bench next to a richly dressed man and a poorly dressed man. As the magistrate enters, all except Liliom rise. The magistrate hears the rich man's case first, then Liliom's. Liliom rises, and when asked whether he left anything unfinished on earth, replies that he would like to break Ficsur's head. The magistrate reminds him that he left a wife three months pregnant and asks him whether he is not ashamed to have been a bad husband

and to have deserted his family. Is he not ashamed to have beaten Julie? Liliom says that he is sorry for nothing. The magistrate says that it will be hard to help him and sends him back to his seat.

The magistrate hears next the case of the poor man, who after thirteen years of purification by fire returned to earth and repaired the roof on the cottage where his widow and orphans were sleeping; the poor man is admitted to the eternal light. The magistrate informs Liliom that he will remain for sixteen years in the crimson fire, until his pride and stubbornness have been burnt out of him. When his daughter has reached the age of sixteen, he will be sent back to earth for a day to do something good for his child, and on his deed depends which door shall be opened to him in heaven. The guards throw open the door into the fire, and, covering his eyes, Liliom steps through it.

Scene 7. It is a spring day sixteen years later, and Julie and her daughter Louise are talking to Marie and Wolf, who have visited them in their small, tumble-down house. Marie and Wolf, very prosperously dressed, bid goodby to Julie and Louise and apologize that they are too busy to stay to lunch. Julie tells Louise to bring the soup from the kitchen, and they sit at an outdoor table. They are eating as the heavenly policemen bring Liliom to the gate. Julie takes Liliom for a beggar and offers him soup. Liliom comments that her daughter is a fine, healthy girl. As Louise gives him his plate, he touches her. She tells her mother that the stranger tried to take her arm; Julie replies that she is imagining.

When Liliom asks Julie about her husband, she says that she is a widow. Louise explains that her father died in a hospital in America, that he was a very handsome man, and that he juggled so well that people advised him to go on the stage. Liliom says that he knew her father, a barker in a carousel who told funny jokes and sang funny songs: he was a bully, and he hit his wife. Julie orders him to leave and tells Louise not to speak to him.

As Louise puts him out the gate, Liliom takes a handkerchief from his pocket, making sure that the policemen are not watching, and unwraps a star, pointing to the sky to indicate where it came from. He begs her to accept it, for he must do a good deed. When she refuses, he slaps her hand, then bows his head in dismay. Louise runs to her mother and says that when he slapped her, she heard the sound but felt nothing except a caress. Julie sends Louise into the house and asks Liliom who he is.

Liliom says that he is a poor beggar and asks whether she is angry. She replies that, though she cannot understand it, she is not at all angry. Liliom goes, followed by the two policemen, who shake their heads deploringly. Julie calls her daughter from the house, and they sit to finish their soup. Julie says that the beggar reminded her of Liliom. Louise asks her mother whether anyone ever hit her without in the least hurting her. Julie replies that it has happened to her too: that it is possible for someone to beat you and beat you and never hurt you at all.

HENRY DE MONTHERLANT

Queen after Death [*La Reine morte*, 1942]

ACT ONE

The imperiously proud Infanta of Navarre has been invited to the medieval court of King Ferrante of Portugal so that she and the king's son Pedro may become engaged, thus assuring political union of the two kingdoms. Unfortunately, Ferrante has not consulted his son first, and now the Infanta is complaining violently to Ferrante and his court of the humiliation she has received; for Pedro has informed her of his undying love for Ines de Castro, vowing that the union his father wishes is impossible. Ferrante is shocked at both the news and the insult, and goes to interview Pedro.

Their talk reveals that although father and son once loved each other, for the last thirteen of Pedro's twenty-six years the two have been unhappily estranged by their inability to understand each other's totally disparate temperament and interests. Ferrante now explains to his son that he does not wish to be harsh: he considers Ines a charming lady of high birth, although illegitimate; let her continue to be Pedro's mistress, but the royal heir must marry the Infanta for the good of the kingdom. Pedro protests that he does not understand his royal duties but that he does feel the importance of the duties of personal life, such as making a woman and a child happy. To Ferrante, Pedro's lack of aptitude for ruling is all the more reason for marrying the Infanta, since she has more than her share, and Pedro will soon be king, prepared or not, for Ferrante feels he will not live much longer. He threatens to use force to make Pedro comply.

Returning to Ines, Pedro confesses that his father's anger prevented him from admitting their secret marriage. Ines urges that he do so immediately. After all, Ferrante is currently in very bad favor with the Pope, who will thus indubitably refuse to annul their marriage; when Ferrante realizes that marriage to the Infanta is out of the question, perhaps he will resign himself to the situation—especially if Pedro will start taking a responsible interest in state affairs, which she begs him to do. Their exchange of tendernesses is interrupted by the arrival of Ferrante, who demands to see Ines alone.

The king is gentle and polite to Ines, almost tender. He asks her to speak of his son, and is amusedly pleased at her impassioned declaration of love and admiration for Pedro. In that case, he says, she will want what is best for Pedro and his kingly position and will nobly use her own influence to make him marry the Infanta. Again he emphasizes that the liaison may continue. But Ines informs him that their liaison is marriage. The king explodes furiously, first assuming that Pedro was too cowardly to tell him, and then that perhaps his son has been planning his death so that Ines could reign. He tells Ines to return home but has Pedro arrested.

ACT TWO

The king's counselors assist him in his study with various official documents, jesting that the art of diplomacy consists of being able to lie effectively and elegantly. The king encourages them to speak of the present crisis, the imprisonment of Pedro and the bishop who married him. The counselors, led with particular insistence by Egas Coelho, argue for executing Ines. Putting her in a convent or exiling her would merely incite Pedro to a seditious plot to bring her back, but once she were irrevocably dead, Pedro could eventually be brought around. Ferrante protests that she is only guilty of returning love for love, whereas Pedro and the bishop are guilty of betraying their responsibilities, but they accuse him of weakness toward a woman. He says he "will reflect," and dismisses all but Coelho. He demands to know why Coelho is so personally eager for Ines' blood, certain that this urgency conceals some private or political secret. The counselor fawns, but remains impenetrable. Ferrante shouts that if Coelho is so anxious for an execution, he can have the bishop, but Ines will remain free.

Having sent for Ines, Ferrante soliloquizes bitterly in her presence on the ignobleness of his counselors and of the work of governing in general, although he has tried to rule responsibly according to the highest principles. Ines is so full of the joy of life, and he feels so empty and tired; everything he does seems only an inferior repetition of something he has done before and ceased to care for. He tells her that despite his counselors he does not want to punish either her or Pedro. Instead, he is sending her to visit Pedro in prison, so that she may obtain his promise to marry the Infanta if Ferrante is successful in negotiating with the Pope for the annulment of Ines' marriage.

At the prison, Ines and Pedro embrace joyously after their separation. She delivers the king's message, but neither wastes an instant in considering it. Then she tells Pedro how freely his father had conversed with her, saying that she finds him sympathetic, essentially benevolent although he forces himself to be severe. When the Infanta approaches unexpectedly, Ines assumes she is coming from the king to demand an engagement and hastens jealously to bar the way. But the Infanta has come to see Ines, not Pedro, on her way home to Navarre. She explains that the youngest of Ferrante's pages has reported to her the meeting with the counselors; she is certain that the king will shortly decide to execute Ines, although he doesn't yet know it himself. She has heard so much good of Ines that she wants to take her to safety in Navarre, for she has never cared for Pedro, and therefore is not jealous of his wife. Indeed, she has never loved any man, for she finds all men weak and cowardly, and love would be an insult to her own majestic strength of character. Ines defends the sublimity of love and, though sincerely touched by the other's offer, declares herself incapable of deserting her beloved, even if it means dying with or for him. The

Infanta is at first irritated by this opposition to her will, but then, although totally incapable of understanding the cause for such steadfastness, comes to respect Ines for the steadfastness itself.

ACT THREE

Once again Ferrante is confiding the bitterness of his soul to Ines in a palace reception room. He is interrupted by a counselor, who reports the Pope's indignation and advises the release of the imprisoned bishop; he adds that it is nevertheless certain that the Pope will refuse the annulment. Ferrante has Pedro released from prison and confined to quarters in the palace. There seems nothing the king can do to achieve the marriage he wishes, and he voices the depth of his discouragement. More counselors burst in to announce an African massacre of a port momentarily left unguarded by the fleet under Lourenco Payva. They demand Payva's execution, for the government needs a scapegoat on whom to blame all its current embarrassments, and they have been robbed of the bishop. Ferrante agrees to make Payva the recipient of his "justice." Satisfied, the group appears to leave, but Coelho and others remain in the shadows to eavesdrop, for they are greatly disturbed by the frequency of Ines' interviews with the king.

As the king vents at length his impatience that life, like war, is conducted by men who don't deserve to live, in the name of ideas that don't deserve that men die for them, the counselors take fright at the cascade of mad truths and slip away. Ines is emboldened by his confidences to confide her own great secret that she carries an infant of Ferrante's blood. Saddened that another beginning will thus continue the cycle of ever-degenerating life, he harshly tries to destroy her maternal illusions about the joys of having children, then dismisses her abruptly.

Painfully divided in his own mind, he finally commands one of his soldiers to overtake and kill Ines, then calls his court around him to announce that he has had her executed because her child would spoil the purity of the royal succession and cause trouble in the state. Suddenly he sinks weakly and knows he is dying. He enjoys making Coelho cringe with terror at the realization that he will probably die for his malicious instigation of Ines' murder as soon as Pedro becomes king. Aware that he has been "much better and much worse" than the world has known him, Ferrante begs God to give him one moment's knowledge of the self underlying the knot of contradictions he has been. As he dies, the corpse of Ines is brought in on a litter; and Pedro, released from confinement to be the new king, kneels sobbing at her side. All the crowd who had been kneeling by Ferrante desert him and regroup around Ines' body, on which is placed the royal crown.

SEAN O'CASEY

Cock-a-Doodle Dandy [1949]

SCENE ONE

In the garden in front of Michael Marthraun's house in Nyadnanave, a brilliant cock dances in and disappears around the house. As Michael and Sailor Mahan emerge from the house, Michael explains that since pretty young Loreleen, Michael's daughter by his first wife, arrived from England for a holiday, her mysterious sinful attraction, shared by Michael's young wife Lorna, has been upsetting the holy objects. Michael goes to get a bottle of whiskey and returns immediately to say that Loreleen approaches. He advises that they ignore her. The appearance of Loreleen, lovely and gay, is accompanied by a cock's crow. Both men attempt to ignore her, arguing about the price to be paid to Mahan for hauling the turf from Michael's bog. When Loreleen leaves, two rough fellows appear, demanding higher wages from Mahan, whose lorries they drive. They are about to follow Loreleen but are astonished to see her change into a cock. As they flee, Michael reminds the skeptical Mahan that a good Christian should be disturbed by such goings-on.

As the two men resume their argument over business, Shanaar, reputed to be a wise old man, arrives. He instructs them with stories of evil spirits that appear as animals or women. Suddenly a great commotion is heard from the house. Marion, the pretty young maid, rushes out to say that a wild goose is flying around the house, upsetting the holy objects. The frightened men send her to fetch the priest, Father Domineer. On her way out the gate, she meets the messenger, who kisses her warmly. He presents a telegram to Michael, who puts it in his pocket. When the messenger hears of the wild goose, he rushes into the house and after much commotion emerges, leading the cock by a green ribbon. Shanaar advises everyone to take no notice of it. Michael is furious that the cock has ruined his new silk tall-hat, in which he was to greet the President of Eire. The messenger leads the cock away, and Marion returns to the house.

After Shanaar leaves, Marion brings a bottle of whiskey. Mahan and Michael tease her amorously until, terrified, they notice that the ornament on her head has become two branching horns. Lorna calls Marion to come in, for Lorna's sister Julia is about to depart for Lourdes. The two rough fellows enter, bearing Julia on a stretcher. Lorna and Marion join the procession, as Julia airs her hopes of being cured by the Virgin at Lourdes. Father Domineer enters and leads them all away.

SCENE TWO

Later in the garden, Michael and Mahan are frightened when their chairs mysteriously collapse under them. The messenger comes to see them, but when

Marion, her ornament back to normal, comes out of the house, he seizes and kisses her. He tells the two men that he has come to ask whether they have seen the cock. A cock's crow is heard, and the messenger sets off to follow it. Marion returns to the house; the two frightened men decide to have a drink but find that the bottle is bewitched and has turned to glowing red.

A porter appears, seeking someone to claim a package bearing no name, which he is to deliver. Michael claims to have ordered the tall-hat which the package contains. The porter admits that it is damaged, for someone shot a bullet through it. Just then another bullet is shot through it. Refusing to take the hat back, the porter leaves. The sergeant appears with a rifle, explaining that he shot three times at the cock, but the third time the cock turned into a tall-hat. As he raises his rifle to show how he shot at it, the garden suddenly becomes dark. A flash of lightning reveals the cock standing where the hat lay. When the garden becomes light again, both cock and hat are gone. The bellman appears, ringing his bell and ordering everyone indoors, for the cock is coming in the shape of woman. After he disappears, the three men sit on the ground and sing to keep calm.

Loreleen appears and calls to Lorna and Marion to join the company. The two young women are dressed in gay costumes for that evening's fancy-dress ball. The sergeant and Mahan react to Lorna and Loreleen as if enchanted. Marion produces an unharmed tall-hat, and Lorna, a normal bottle of whiskey. The women persuade the men to drink with them. As the men become animated, Michael and Mahan each offer to settle their deal to the other's advantage. They all begin to dance until, at the height of the dance, Father Domineer appears and reprimands them for dancing. He orders Mahan to dismiss one of his lorry drivers, who is living with a woman in sin, but Mahan refuses. The driver himself appears and informs Mahan that the turf-workers have stopped working, having received no answer to the telegram that they sent to Michael. Father Domineer interrupts to order the driver either to leave the woman or to go away himself. The driver refuses to do either. Father Domineer savagely strikes him, and he falls to the ground. The priest assures everyone that he did not intend to hurt the man.

SCENE THREE

That evening at dusk, Mahan, Lorna, and Marion are in the garden when the cock glides through and disappears around the house, startling all of them. Michael, Father Domineer, and One-eyed Larry, who wears a cassock, arrive to purge the house of evil spirits and disappear inside.

Loreleen runs in, explaining that men and women have been throwing stones at her, for they associate her with the evil spirits. Lorna and Marion go to scold the people, leaving Loreleen alone with Mahan, who offers to help her flee if she will meet him that night to receive the money she will need. As he puts his arm around her, a terrible commotion comes from the house. Marion and Lorna return as One-eyed Larry rushes out of the house to describe the fearful struggle Father Domineer and Michael are waging against the evil spirits. The terrible noises suddenly cease. Father Domineer and Michael, bedraggled and tired, emerge from the house. Father Domineer announces that the house is safe and free of evil spirits. He sends Marion and Lorna into the house and reprimands Loreleen for reading books. When he tells her he will destroy the books, she grabs them and flees. When the men go to chase her, their legs will not move. The cock appears and dances around. The sergeant appears with a rifle and all remain transfixed as the garden grows dark and two shots are heard. When the light returns, the priest is gone, Michael and Mahan are lying on the ground, and One-eyed Larry is half over the wall. Michael and Mahan each think they are shot, until Lorna and Marion run out and assure them that they are unharmed. One-eyed Larry disappears.

The two men reopen their business argument and Mahan leaves. A sudden blast of wind, unnoticed by the women, pushes Michael toward the gate. One-eyed Larry runs in and shouts that Father Domineer was carried home safely on the back of a white duck. He explains that the cock, angry that the priest escaped his clutches, has raised a tremendous wind by beating his wings. The bellman appears, shouting to everyone to go inside and describing how the priest was carried home on the back of a speckled duck. An argument develops over the color of the duck and is further complicated by the arrival of the sergeant, who claims it was a barnacle goose. As the messenger appears, a strong wind arises, but it affects only Michael, the bellman, One-eyed Larry, and the sergeant. Father Domineer arrives, and the rough fellows, accompanied by Shanaar, drag Loreleen before him. She explains that they found her with Sailor Mahan because he was to give her money to go away. At the messenger's insistence, the rough fellows release Loreleen. Father Domineer orders Loreleen to leave. As she starts to go, Lorna runs from the house and joins her. Father Domineer assures Michael that all is safe now and departs with the sergeant. Marion follows the path taken by Lorna and Loreleen.

Just then Julia returns from Lourdes, and Shanaar sneaks away. Julia, obviously not cured, asks for Lorna and is told by the messenger that she has gone "to a place where life resembles life more than it does here." Julia is carried out on her stretcher as Michael sadly ponders his loneliness without Lorna. Leaving Michael alone, the messenger goes off to follow the women, singing a song about Marion.

S E A N   O ' C A S E Y

Juno and the Paycock [1924]

ACT ONE

Johnny and Mary Boyle are in the living room of a two-room apartment in a working-class tenement in post-World War One Dublin when their mother Juno enters from a shopping expedition. Juno asks whether her husband "Captain" Jack Boyle has got back, and her grown-up children say that he has not. Mary reads aloud a newspaper account of a shooting; her brother impatiently springs up; he is thin and delicate and rather younger than his sister and has a limp; the left sleeve of his coat is empty. He goes into the other room. Juno and Mary discuss the workers' strike, of which Mary is part, and Juno bitterly observes that striking over a principle might be very fine but the family has no money left to buy food. Juno says she doesn't know what will become of Johnny: the bullet he got in his hip some time back was bad enough, but the bomb that shattered his arm has put the finishing touch to him. Jerry Devine, an earnest young labor man, enters and breathlessly asks for the captain; he says he has heard of a job for him. Juno sends him off, saying her husband will be in one of two taverns.

"Captain" Boyle is heard outside singing with his drinking-companion Joxer Daly; he enters the room, calling to Joxer to come up; for it's all right, Juno is out. The captain, a sixty-year-old, graying man who wears a seaman's cap and walks with a strut, tells Joxer it's a terrible thing to be married to a nagging wife. Both men are stupefied to discover that Juno is there after all.

To placate his wife, the captain pretends that he has a job lined up. Juno, a tired, resigned woman, tells her husband that she isn't fooled; she has to slave to provide the little food there is in the home, while he struts around the town like a peacock. Jerry returns and tells the captain about the job. Juno goes off to work as Mary appears; Jerry tells Mary he has a chance of being elected secretary of the trade union and that he could marry her on the salary he would get. Mary is evasive and goes out, followed by the amorous Jerry.

Juno is heard outside and Joxer dives for the window; she enters excitedly, and tells her husband to put on a tie, because Mary will be back in a moment with a visitor. Mary enters with Charlie Bentham, a tall, good-looking, and well-dressed young man. Juno rushes round trying to make Bentham comfortable; he is obviously out of place in the poor home.

The captain and Johnny meet Bentham, who tells the family that a relative has died leaving them half his property. The captain swears that their life is going to change and he will have no more to do with Joxer. Joxer, who has been hiding on the roof, enters and says he is disgusted that the captain should let old friends drop so quickly. Clasping his wife's hand, Boyle sings emotionally, "Oh, me darlin' Juno, I will be thrue to thee."

ACT TWO

The captain is lazing in his now over-decorated living room when he hears Joxer outside; he pretends to busy himself with papers and tells Joxer to come in. They talk a while about the captain's new state of wealth. After Joxer leaves, Juno enters with Mary, who carries a gramophone. Bentham arrives shortly after, and as they sit drinking tea, Bentham talks about his religion, Theosophy. When the talk turns to ghosts and murder, Johnny grows pale and leaves the room. Suddenly he is heard screaming, and rushes back, telling the group that he has just seen the ghost of Robbie Tancred, the man shot down a few days ago. Joxer enters with Mrs. Madigan, a middle-aged, ignorant woman; they sit drinking, and the women sing a couple of songs.

They are interrupted by a noise on the staircase, and the captain says it must be Mrs. Tancred going to the hospital. They open the door to give her light, and Mrs. Tancred enters with several neighbors; she is obviously shaken by the death of her son. The family tries to comfort her, and when she leaves Juno explains to Bentham that Robbie Tancred was a Republican fighter found riddled with bullets one day; he had been a close friend of Johnny, she adds, but Johnny immediately denies this, saying Tancred was simply in the same battalion as himself.

Mary and Bentham, who is now her fiancé, leave, and the others are listening to records when "Needle" Nugent, a tailor, enters and tells them they should have more respect for the dead. Singing is heard in the street outside, and from the window the family sees the Tancred funeral procession; all except Johnny go down to watch from the street. A young man comes in and tells Johnny that they are to go to a meeting at which Johnny might be able to explain some of the circumstances of Tancred's death. Johnny says he won't go and asks, "Haven't I done enough for Ireland?" The young man replies that "no man can do enough for Ireland."

ACT THREE

Mary is sitting dejectedly by the fire two months later, telling her mother that she has not heard from Bentham for a whole month. Juno tells the captain, who is in bed, that he ought to do something about getting the money that is coming to them under the will but of which they haven't yet seen a penny, for they are up to their ears in debt. Juno goes out with Mary to see a doctor, and Joxer comes in with Nugent, who says that he has been to the lawyer and has learnt that the Boyles are not going to get any of the money after all. Nugent goes into the bedroom, grabs the suit that he made for the captain, and rushes out with it; since it has not been paid for, he has a right to take it back. He goes out with Joxer, who quickly returns to talk to the captain.

Mrs. Madigan enters and demands her loan back; when the captain tells her she will have to wait, she snatches up the gramophone and announces she is going to pawn it to get her money that way. When she has gone, Joxer hints that perhaps she has heard that the captain isn't going to get the legacy after all. Joxer goes out as Johnny enters, followed by Juno. Juno declares that she has bad news about Mary: the girl is pregnant. The captain, furious, tells Juno he has bad news too: they won't be getting any money from the will; Bentham made out the will incorrectly, and the Boyles won't get a penny.

The captain angrily goes out to drink with Joxer, telling Juno he doesn't want to set eyes on Mary again.

Two men arrive and announce they have come to take back the furniture, which hasn't been paid for. Juno runs to find the captain, and Mary comes in;

Jerry arrives and tells her that Juno has explained everything and he still wants to marry her. But when Mary reveals that she is pregnant, Jerry sadly leaves. Two underground soldiers enter and at pistol point force the furniture men to face the wall; they tell Johnny they are taking him away. Johnny pleads to be left alone, but the soldiers tell him they know that he betrayed Tancred and drag him out.

An hour later Juno and Mary are sitting in their empty room, fearfully awaiting news of Johnny. Mrs. Madigan enters and tells Juno two policemen are waiting to see her. Mrs. Madigan says the police have found a dead man and think it is Johnny. Juno sadly goes off to identify her son, accompanied by Mary; Juno tells her they will leave the captain and go to live with Juno's sister and work for Mary's child.

Boyle enters with Joxer, both very drunk, and the play ends on their maudlin, drunken talk. "I'm telling you . . . Joxer," mumbles "Captain" Boyle, "th' whole worl's . . . in a terr . . . ible state o' . . . chassis!"

SEAN O'CASEY

The Plough and the Stars [1926]

NOTE: During the First World War, when England was fighting Germany in the trenches of France and Belgium, the Irish nationalists took advantage of the situation to raise a rebellion in hopes of securing independence for Ireland. Fighting broke out in Dublin and elsewhere on April 24, 1916 (the Easter Rebellion), but after a week of bloodshed, the English troops suppressed the insurrection. The plough and the stars were the insignia on the flag of the Irish Citizen Army.

ACT ONE

In November of 1915, in the living room of the Clitheroe flat in a Dublin tenement, Fluther Good, a carpenter, is repairing a lock, and Peter Flynn, Nora Clitheroe's uncle, is airing a shirt. Mrs. Gogan, a charwoman, arrives, and she and Fluther gossip about the demonstrative affection between the young couple Jack and Nora Clitheroe; Mrs. Gogan complains about Nora's superior airs. They discuss the meeting to be held that night, at which the oath of fealty to the Irish Republic is to be sworn, speculating about the fact that Jack Clitheroe has severed his ties with the Citizen Army, much to the relief of Nora, since he failed to be appointed a captain. The young Covey, Jack Clitheroe's cousin, joins them. An ardent socialist, he is disgusted by the patriotic fervor sweeping Dublin and enters readily into a vehement argument with Fluther, matching his revolutionary doctrines against Fluther's traditional religious and patriotic loyalties. The Covey then antagonizes old Peter, their more personal skirmish being interrupted by the entrance of Nora Clitheroe, an attractive, lively young woman of twenty-two. She attempts to halt the quarrel, threatening to evict them both from her household. As she is testing the new lock, Mrs. Bessie Burgess, a vigorous, hardened woman of forty, appears at the door, and, accusing Nora of being proud, she shakes her vigorously in retaliation for Nora's complaints against her as a noisy neighbor. After Nora is rescued by Fluther, Jack Clitheroe, her husband, returns home, driving Bessie away and comforting Nora. Jack, Nora, Peter, and the Covey sit down to tea. Jack suggests that he and Nora attend the meeting that evening, and Peter and the Covey antagonize one another as is their wont.

When Nora and Jack are at last alone, Nora charges that his devotion to her is waning. Angry words turn to tender ones, however, and Jack sings an old love song to her. When a knock at the door interrupts, Nora begs Jack to ignore it. Captain Brennan, in the uniform of the Irish Citizen Army, has come to relay the message that Commandant Clitheroe is to take command of a battalion at the meeting that night, after which they are to depart for an attack. Astonished at being called commandant, Jack learns that the appointment was announced in a letter that Nora burned. With Nora screaming that he cares only for the Citizen Army and not for her, Jack angrily gathers his equipment and leaves with Captain Brennan. Mollser, Mrs. Gogan's consumptive daughter, comes to ask Nora whether she might spend the evening with her. As the singing of the passing regiment is heard, Bessie Burgess appears, prophesying times of danger for all, even for the proud Nora.

ACT TWO

An hour later in a public house, outside of which the meeting is being held, Rosie Redmond, a well-shaped young girl, is complaining to the bartender of the dearth of clients for her on a night when men's thoughts are lofty, patriotic ones. From the platform outside the window comes a rousing patriotic speech. Peter and Fluther, enveloped in the emotional fervor of the occasion, come storming in, ordering drinks, and discussing their zealous involvement in the patriotic cause. The resumption of the speech outside lures them out again as the Covey comes in. Approached by Rosie, the Covey replies to her attempts at conversation with socialist doctrine; when she becomes bolder, he flees. Peter and Fluther return with Mrs. Gogan. As they are drinking, the Covey and Bessie Burgess station themselves at the other end of the bar and begin to drink. As Peter and the Covey throw antagonistic remarks at one another, Mrs. Gogan and Bessie Burgess do the same, beginning with politics and mounting, with personal accusations of unrespectable behavior, toward a furious battle, which neither the intermittent speeches from outside nor the peacemaking efforts of those inside can prevent, until the bartender comes between them and pushes them both out the door. Left in relative peace, Fluther orders drinks for himself, the Covey, and Rosie. An argument ensues between the two men, Fluther trying to present himself as a sympathizer of the labor movement and the Covey disdaining his ignorant attitudes. As their argument blossoms into yet another battle, the Covey is thrown out by the bartender. Rosie's praise for Fluther arouses his amorous feelings, and the two disappear into a corner. Clitheroe, Captain Brennan, and Lieutenant Langon appear, nearly hypnotized by the emotion of the occasion. Their fervor fed by the speech from outside, they pledge their lives for Ireland. After they leave, Rosie and Fluther depart somewhat drunkenly for her house, Rosie singing a bawdy song as Jack's voice is heard ordering his battalion to march.

ACT THREE

During Easter Week, 1916, Mrs. Gogan is helping Mollser to a chair outside the tenement house; she expresses concern for Fluther, who has ventured into the battle-torn city streets to find Nora, who has tried to follow her husband, fearing for his life. The Covey and Peter appear with news of the declaration of an Irish Republic. Fluther returns, half-carrying Nora, who could not find Jack and was accused of cowardice in seeking him. Her hysteria evokes bitter words and dark prophecies from Bessie Burgess. When Fluther and Mrs. Gogan try to comfort Nora, she confesses that she cares only about Jack and attributes similar selfish feelings to all women. Admitting that she feels as if she is going mad, she is led indoors by Mrs. Gogan.

Bessie emerges from the tenement, and, before disappearing, expresses contempt for the battle itself, yet also for the men gathered there, who are not fighting. She returns in a few minutes with the news that people are plundering the stores, she herself laden down with the merchandise that she has taken. Despite the danger, Fluther and the Covey set out to obtain what they can. As Mrs. Gogan emerges with an old pram that has been standing in the hall, Bessie Burgess stops her and challenges her right to the pram. They depart reluctantly together, still squabbling, to join in the plundering. The Covey returns, happily burdened with goods, as do Bessie and Mrs. Gogan. A rifle shot drives them all inside, as Captain Brennan, supporting the wounded Lieutenant Langon, comes in, followed by Jack Clitheroe. Nora races out of the house and throws her arms around her husband, who welcomes her with kisses and tender words. As Bessie taunts them, Jack tries to release himself from Nora's embrace so that he can obtain help for the wounded man. Nora, however, clings to him frantically. Embarrassed by the scene and the accusations of desertion that it provokes, Jack angrily pushes Nora away and departs with his comrades-in-arms. Bessie carries Nora inside. As screams of pain are heard from Nora, Bessie decides to risk going to seek a doctor for Nora, who is about to have a miscarriage.

ACT FOUR

A few days later in the attic living room of Bessie Burgess, Peter and the Covey are playing cards as Fluther peeps out the window at the burning city. They discuss the deaths of Mollser and of Nora's child, who lie together in the nearby coffin. As they ponder Nora's wandering mind, Bessie comes in, cautioning them to be quiet for Nora's sake and sinking wearily into an armchair. Captain Brennan, dressed in civilian clothes, brings the news that Jack Clitheroe has been killed. Nora, to whom this news is never told, wanders vacantly in, dressed in a nightgown, pale, unkempt, walking in a dream of Jack and speaking to him. She screams for her baby and her husband, clinging to Bessie, who sings to her as she leads her back to bed. Captain Brennan stays, it being too dangerous to leave. Corporal Stoddart, a British soldier, comes to take the coffin away, delivering the opinion that the British victory is close at hand. The four cardplayers carry out the coffin, followed by Mrs. Gogan. Corporal Stoddart informs them upon their return that all men in the area are to be rounded up and confined until the fighting is over, for fear they are aiding the snipers. Sergeant Tinley arrives and helps the corporal escort Peter, Brennan, the Covey, and Fluther away.

As Bessie sleeps, Nora wanders in and arranges tea for Jack, singing the song he used to sing to her. Frightened by rifle fire, she begins to scream and runs to the window. Bessie awakens; realizing the danger, she tries to pull Nora away from the window, and is herself shot. She screams for help, but Nora, crying to Jack for help, cannot move. Singing a hymn, Bessie dies. Mrs. Gogan returns, to find Bessie dead. The two British soldiers also return, and, as Mrs. Gogan gently leads the terrified Nora away, they drink tea and join the distant soldiers' voices singing, "Keep the 'owme fires burning."

S E A N   O ' C A S E Y

Purple Dust   [1945; published 1942]

ACT ONE

In the gloomy living room of an old Tudor mansion in Clune na Geera, three Irish workmen discuss the two wealthy Englishmen who have hired them to restore the house and who are living there with their Irish mistresses. The four in question, as well as Cloyne, the maidservant, and Barney, the manservant, appear, dance what they think to be a country dance, and sing a song about the joys of rural life. The Englishmen, Cyril Poges and Basil Stoke, are sixty-five and thirty, respectively. Souhaun, Poges' mistress, is thirty-two, and Avril, Basil's mistress, is about twenty-one. After they disappear singing, the wondering workmen comment on Avril's interest in O'Killigain, the handsome young foreman, who comes in at that moment. He explains that Souhaun claims to be a descendant of the Ormand family, the intention of the four being to revive the old aristocratic way of life in the family mansion.

Avril trips in and greets the workmen. As she begins to dance and sing, O'Killigain whirls her around the room, finishing with a solid whack on the behind. The other workmen defend O'Killigain, and Avril indignantly sends them away. With suspiciously little protest, she succumbs to the foreman's eloquence and to his embrace and agrees to meet him under the rowan tree. Souhaun, Poges, Basil, and Cloyne file in, busy about the tasks of decorating the house. When the two men leave, O'Killigain makes small, surreptitious advances to Cloyne and then to Souhaun, singing a song about the pleasures of courting women. When Poges and Basil return, a dispute develops between Poges, who values the glory and excitement of the past, and O'Killigain, who is a man of the living present. After O'Killigain leaves, Poges and Basil discuss their plans for learning about nature by living in the country and keeping hens as well as a Cow.

After Basil leaves, Poges is accosted by Barney, Cloyne, and a workman, each announcing the arrival of someone with hens, roosters, or a cow to sell; he sends them all away. When Poges needs the telephone and finds it not working, he calls the second workman, who, indignant at Poges' rude impatience, informs him that Ireland has always been far ahead of England in the development of civilization, after which he storms out. Cloyne announces the arrival of the horses ordered by Basil and Avril. O'Killigain warns that the horses are dangerous, but Basil and Avril depart confidently. Cloyne announces the arrival of Canon Creehewel, setting off an anticlerical tirade from Poges. Suddenly Basil, frightened and dazed, is helped into the room. He has fallen off his horse, and Avril has ridden away with O'Killigain. After the others lead Basil away, the workmen discuss Avril and O'Killigain.

ACT TWO

On a cold morning in the same living room, Poges and Basil, wrapped in blankets, toss about on two mattresses. Basil rues his helplessness in the face of Avril's disloyal behavior, for he has settled five hundred a year on her for life. Poges has done the same for Souhaun. They bravely rise from their warm beds and summon Barney to light a fire. When the men leave, the two servants discuss the unbearable conditions in the old house. Poges returns briskly, dressed in shorts. Cloyne, sent on an errand, runs back into the room screaming, insisting that there is a wild bull in the entrance hall. General panic ensues until a workman drives the animal, in reality a cow, out of the house. Poges pretends to the workman that he remained calm throughout the crisis, as the workman lights the fire and praises, with tongue in cheek, the house and its elegant past. Souhaun appears, alarmed that Basil is carrying a gun, which he does not know how to use, to protect himself in case of unexpected dangers. Poges instructs her to get Avril to take it from him. Cloyne announces that the garden tools and roller have been delivered and left in front of the hall door, obstructing the passage.

Before Poges leaves to clear the way, the second workman appears. Poges, who has heard that he knows all the stories and legends of Ireland, questions him about them. The workman dreamily speaks of the days of the mighty Finn

MacCoole and of his own visions of Ireland's past. O'Killigain has wandered in and softly encourages him to continue. The workman mourns the fact that only a few like O'Killigain understand and believe in and perhaps even embody the glorious aliveness that used to be. After the workman leaves, O'Killigain expresses scorn for Poges' worthless project, whereupon Poges defends himself and all England with inflated boasting. Souhaun sends him out to move the roller and stays to drop a reference to O'Killigain concerning his interest in Avril. O'Killigain retorts with a reference to the second workman's interest in Souhaun. As O'Killigain leaves, the workman in question appears. He assures Souhaun that she is as attractive as her younger friend Avril, whereupon Souhaun admits that Poges is too old for her. He sings to her; as she is about to reply tenderly, Poges arrives pulling a huge, brightly painted roller nearly as tall as he is, followed by a workman and a laughing O'Killigain.

Everyone agrees that Poges has been taken in by the man who sold him such a monstrosity to roll his lawn. Poges refuses aid in pushing the roller but loses control of it; it rolls out of sight down a declivity and right through a wall of the house. As Poges returns sadly, O'Killigain orders that someone take the gun from Basil. After Poges sends Souhaun to take care of it, he tells O'Killigain to stay away from Avril. The young man is not cowed. When a shot rings out, a voice shouts, "He's shot her." Poges assumes that Basil has shot Avril. A workman tells him, however, that Basil has shot the cow, taking it for a dangerous bull. Recalling all the recent fiascos, Poges asserts that they are living in a terrible country.

ACT THREE

On a rainy, windy day, Poges dashes into the living room and telephones London about the purchase of a certain stock. Canon Creehewel arrives to welcome Poges to the district, expressing approval of Poges' project, for he believes that in the past lived the virtue that is so shockingly absent from the present. He asks Poges to help in the campaign to restore virtue, warning him that O'Killigain is the worst enemy of such a campaign. Avril and Souhaun, both dressed in a racy manner, enter and are hesitantly introduced by Poges. After Basil makes a pedantic entrance, the canon leaves.

When Avril leaves to go walking in the rain, refusing his company, Basil knows she is going with O'Killigain. After the two men depart, Souhaun summons a workman. The second workman appears and tells her that she doesn't belong in this old house with the foolish Poges, but rather out in the hills with a real man like himself. After looking at him for a moment, she goes slowly out. The second workman goes to help the other two, who, under the nervous supervision of Poges, are trying to bring an antique gilded dresser through the rather narrow entrance to the living room. When Poges leaves to get some protective cushions, the workmen decide to try their own less delicate method, but Poges stops them in time. Despite his care, they manage to damage both the entrance and the dresser. After the workmen leave, the second workman wheels a wheelbarrow over the new rug. Poges is furious, claiming, along with Basil, superiority over the workman, who is defended by O'Killigain.

Observing that it is raining hard, O'Killigain permits the men to stop working. The second workman poetically invites Souhaun to ride over the waters with him, promising her joy upon their return. Ignoring the mocking of Poges, Souhaun becomes more and more entranced. O'Killigain invites Avril, who has come in, to come away with him to find life and love. Souhaun and the second workman urge her to go, but the confused girl runs to Souhaun. As the two Irishmen urge them to come away, Souhaun and Avril leave to think out an answer. Announcing that they will come for them when the river rises, O'Killigain and the workman leave. Basil and Poges mock the scene they have just witnessed, though admitting that they feel uneasy. After Basil leaves, Poges is interrupted by a strange little man bearing a message from the postmaster. He gets Poges to admit that the postmaster should have his share of sleep. Then he announces that now he won't have to keep watch for late calls. Ascertaining that the man is the postmaster, Poges is furious at the idea of having his use of the telephone limited. The postmaster reprimands him, referring in a sinister way to the rising river.

Suddenly in the darkened room appears a figure in oilskins and a blue mask, looking like the spirit of the rising waters. Basil, Barney, and Cloyne appear, as frightened as are Poges and the postmaster. The figure states that the waters will tear out the "trees of an ancient heritage," but that there is safety in the hills. After the figure disappears, panic spreads. Avril comes in and says that Souhaun has gone away with the second workman. O'Killigain arrives, and she leaves with him; as they row away, O'Killigain can be heard singing. Faced with disaster, Basil flees to the roof; as the waters surge around, Poges climbs into his precious dresser, his ark, and implores it to take him back to England.

CLIFFORD ODETS

Awake and Sing! [1935]

ACT ONE

In the Berger apartment in the Bronx, the family is at the dinner table. Ralph Berger complains about his dull stock clerk's job and about having to contribute money to the family. He angers his mother Bessie, who is calmed by her husband Myron, a haberdashery clerk. Myron wishes they could be as lucky as the butcher on Beck Street who won the Irish sweepstakes. At this, Jacob, Bessie's father, asks, "If it rained pearls, who would work?" Jacob lives with the family and has hung pictures of Sacco and Vanzetti in his room, which is visible from the parlor. His main duty in the household is to feed the family dog Tootsie and to walk her on the roof.

Hennie, Ralph's sister, in an excited mood, invites her parents to a vaudeville show. Myron tells her that Moe Axelrod has said he would call that evening for her. Hennie says that she has refused to go out with Moe any more but that he won't accept her refusal.

Bessie, Myron, and Hennie leave. Ralph talks about his girl friend Blanche, an orphan whose guardians are not friendly to him. Jacob advises him to think about more important problems. Fix it so that life isn't printed on dollar bills, Jacob says; girls can wait.

Moe Axelrod, a war veteran with a wooden leg, arrives and learns that Hennie has gone out; he shrugs and settles down to a game of cards with Jacob. Shortly afterward, Hennie and her parents return, for she has become ill on the way to the theater. Moe leaves.

Bessie suspects that Hennie is pregnant; Hennie finally admits that this is true, saying that the father is a man from out of town and that the company he claimed to work for had never heard of him. Bessie tells Myron to invite Sam Feinschreiber home from work the next evening. Sam is a young man at Myron's shop who has shown an interest in Hennie. Bessie says Hennie and Sam will be engaged by Saturday. Hennie refuses to have anything to do with the scheme. Jacob is indignant at Bessie and argues with her.

ACT TWO

A year later the family are gathered for Sunday dinner. Bessie's brother Morty, a wealthy garment manufacturer, is visiting. Also present are Hennie, her husband Sam, the baby, and Moe Axelrod, now a boarder in the Bergers' apartment.

Bessie complains to Morty about Ralph's romance with Blanche. Ralph once brought Blanche to dinner, but Bessie was not friendly to her. Bessie says she is only a poor girl who is not a fit match for her son: she wants Ralph to make a good marriage and to be successful like Morty. Jacob scoffs, "Don't live, make a success." Citing Marx as an authority, Jacob says that life in which money is all-important is not a real life. Bessie becomes angry, and Morty simply laughs at Jacob.

Ralph calls Blanche on the telephone and learns that her guardians are sending her away to Cleveland. He leaves immediately to go to see her. Alone with Hennie, Moe reminds her of her former interest in him. He confidently tells her that someday she will realize she is wasting herself on Sam and will come to him.

Late that night, Jacob is up reading when Ralph comes home. Ralph says that he has asked Blanche to marry him, but he thinks she lacks the courage to do it.

Sam comes in, excited and disheveled after an argument with Hennie in which she has told him that the baby is not his. Awakened, Bessie and Myron come in. Bessie orders Jacob to go into his room. Jacob goes and puts on one of his beloved Caruso phonograph records. Bessie gives Sam a glass of tea, calms him down, and sends him home to Hennie. Ralph is shocked when Myron reveals that what Hennie has told Sam is true. He turns to Jacob, who confirms it, then turns angrily on his mother and father. In a fury at Jacob, Bessie runs into his room and breaks the Caruso records.

Jacob quietly takes Tootsie up to the roof. Shortly afterward, Schlosser, the superintendent, rings the bell and says that Jacob has fallen from the roof and been killed.

ACT THREE

In the dining room a week later, Morty, Bessie, and Myron are eating. Morty announces that the insurance man is due to arrive that day and that, though Jacob made Ralph the beneficiary of his three-thousand-dollar policy, Ralph is not yet aware of the legacy. Morty says that he will get Ralph to sign the money over to Bessie and Myron.

In the parlor Moe tells Ralph about Jacob's insurance policy. Moe says that Jacob left Ralph the money so that he could build a life for himself. Hennie and Sam come in from the kitchen. Sam wants to go home to their child, but Hennie coldly refuses to go with him.

Ralph asks about the insurance money. Morty tells him that Jacob left it in his name but meant the money for the whole family. Moe breaks in to say that Jacob left a suicide note. He threatens to show the note to the insurance company if they try to take the money from Ralph. Morty leaves, accompanied by Sam.

Bessie continues trying to persuade Ralph to give the money to the family. She talks about the hard time she has had taking care of the family. Ralph says that if life has made Bessie the way she is, then life is wrong. Bessie suggests that he change life if he doesn't like it the way it is. Reminded of Jacob's speeches, Ralph says that he will give up the money and will study Jacob's books and try to learn how to change life.

After Bessie goes to bed, Moe tells Ralph that there was no suicide note. Ralph, too excited by his plans to be affected by the news, says that eventually he will fix it so that life won't be printed on dollar bills; he remembers the passage Jacob quoted from the Bible, "Awake and sing, ye that dwell in dust."

While Ralph looks over the books Jacob has left him, Moe talks to Hennie and persuades her to leave Sam and the baby and go away with him. Moe and Hennie leave together, as Ralph happily bids them farewell.

CLIFFORD ODETS

The Flowering Peach [1954]

Near dawn, Noah stumbles into the room and drinks deeply from a jug. His wife Esther comes in, and he tells her of a terrible dream he has had: the world is going to be destroyed by a flood. Esther scoffs at the old man.

Their son Japheth enters, and Noah orders him to summon the other sons, Shem and Ham. They must build an ark before the rains bring the flood, Noah says. Esther reminds him that he knows nothing about boats, but Noah tells her that God has given him the details of how to build the craft.

The family gathers to discuss the dream. Noah relates what he has heard from God about the flood and the ark, including instructions to take pairs of animals of every kind on board the ark with them. Ham asks how they can catch even one pair of animals. Only Japheth seems ready to believe the dream, but he is troubled by the impending destruction of the world. That is the act of a vengeful God, he says.

Japheth goes out to tend the sheep and returns excited. He tells the others to look out the window. They see that the yard is full of animals of all kinds and that more are arriving continually.

Noah and his sons set to work on the ark on a high hill. Japheth does most of the work, but Noah is displeased with his son's attitude: the boy is still brooding over the world's destruction and insists that the ark should be fitted with a rudder. Noah refuses, for God did not tell them to put on a rudder.

Japheth goes away, saying he will not work for a vengeful God who would destroy the world. He changes his mind and returns with Goldie, a woman who helped save him from a drunken mob that regarded Noah's family with suspicion because of their strange project. Goldie is more to Ham's taste than his more demure wife Rachel, and he begins to woo her, at first with some success.

Noah, despondent because he is too old to work, tells God that he cannot carry out the task. He falls asleep and awakens to find himself changed into a vigorous man of fifty. He takes up his share of the work with energy, and the ark soon nears completion.

Japheth tells the family he will not go with them on the ark; he will stay and let himself be destroyed in protest against God's act. Esther tries to persuade him to go, without success; Rachel also tries. Japheth tells her that things would be too difficult on the ark anyway, because he is in love with her and they would be in close contact.

Before the rains begin the ark is visited by three old men who ask that at least one of them be taken. They know the old laws, they say, and this knowledge should be preserved. Noah refuses. God has told him to take only his family and the animals.

When the rains begin, the family prepares to enter the ark. Japheth still says he will not go. Noah knocks him unconscious and has Shem carry him aboard. Goldie is allowed to go because Noah has decided Japheth should marry her. Noah is the only person ignorant of the connection between Ham and Goldie.

On the ark Japheth and Noah still argue about the rudder and about Japheth's refusal to marry Goldie. Esther, who feels too old for Noah now that he is fifty again, refuses to let him sleep with her.

Japheth reveals that the ark has been tilting to one side because Shem and Leah are hoarding animal dung in their room; with their usual eye for good business, they plan to have a monopoly on fuel when they land. At Esther's prompting Shem says he really was saving the dung for everyone to use.

Noah tries to force the marriage of Japheth and Goldie. Japheth says he wants to marry Rachel, and Ham announces his intention to marry Goldie. Noah is against this, but even Esther opposes him.

Noah goes on a drinking binge, and Esther is taken seriously ill. Japheth fits a rudder to the ark while Noah is drunk. When Noah sobers up, he orders Japheth to take off the rudder. While they are arguing, the ark springs a bad leak. Only Japheth knows how to repair it, but he refuses unless Noah agrees to leave the rudder on. Noah gives in reluctantly.

As the waters recede, Noah sends out two doves to look for land. Weak with illness, Esther tries to persuade Noah to marry the young people as they request, but he still refuses. One of the doves returns with an olive leaf. The joy this causes is dampened when it is discovered that Esther has died. Noah, grief-stricken, agrees to marry the couples as Esther wanted.

The ark comes to rest, and the family disembarks, having been afloat for a year. Rachel, Goldie, and Leah are pregnant. On the ground near the gangplank grows a young peach tree, newly blossoming.

The sons wonder which couple Noah will go with. He says he will go with Shem and Leah and bids the others farewell. "Go now, children, and be fruitful and multiply," he says. As the others set off down the hill, Noah, Japheth, and Rachel linger by the peach tree for a moment. Japheth breaks off a small branch and gives it to Rachel, who hands it to Noah. Japheth asks what is ahead for them. Noah holds up the branch and says, "This is ahead—a fruitful world."

After Japheth and Rachel take their leave, Noah asks God for a sign that He will not destroy the world again. Noah turns and sees a rainbow in the sky. "Yes, I hear You, God," Noah says. "Now it's in man's hands to make or destroy the world."

C L I F F O R D   O D E T S

Golden Boy [1937]

ACT ONE

In his office, Tom Moody, a fight manager, argues with his girl friend Lorna Moon, who is impatient for him to divorce his wife and marry her. Moody says that divorces cost money and that he does not make enough with the kind of fighters he manages now: Kaplan, his top fighter, who has a bout that night, is only a bum and not a big earner.

A young man enters with the news that Kaplan has just broken his hand while training in the gym and tells Moody that he will take Kaplan's place. He identifies himself as Joe Bonaparte. Tokio, the trainer for Moody's fighters, comes in and tells Moody that it was Joe who broke Kaplan's hand while sparring with him. Moody is angered but at the same time attracted by Joe's confidence. He agrees to let Joe replace Kaplan in the bout.

In the Bonaparte home, Joe's father is talking with his neighbor Mr. Carp. Since tomorrow is Joe's twenty-first birthday, Mrs. Bonaparte has bought him an expensive violin, for he is a talented violinist. Frank, Joe's older brother, notices Joe's picture on the fight page of the late edition of the newspaper. Joe comes in and admits that he has been in a prize fight. Over his father's disapproval he staunchly defends his boxing: he wants good things from life, and the money he can make in boxing will get them for him.

In Moody's office two months later, Moody and his partner, Roxy Gottlieb, discuss their new fighter. Joe shows skill, but he always seems to hold back in the ring. This puzzles the men until Joe's father drops in to talk with them about Joe's new career. Learning that Joe has studied the violin for years, they now understand why he is so careful of his hands in the ring. Moody worries that Joe might decide to give up fighting and go back to music. Lorna assures Moody that she can persuade Joe to continue fighting.

A few nights later, Joe and Lorna are sitting together on a park bench. Joe tells her of his lonely boyhood and the refuge music offered him. Realizing that Joe still is inclined toward a music career, Lorna tries to convince him that boxing can give him anything he wants and accuses him of being afraid to reach out for what he wants. Stirred, Joe says that he will go on fighting. With his first large sum of money, he will buy something he has always wanted—a fast car.

The next week, in the Bonaparte home, Joe is packing for a boxing tour.

Mr. Bonaparte gives him the violin and asks him to take it with him and practice. Joe takes the instrument, plays it, then hands it back to his father and tells him to return it to the store. Ready to leave, Joe asks his father to give his approval of his boxing career, but Mr. Bonaparte refuses.

ACT TWO

Six months later, after a successful tour of the Middle West, Joe is training in the gym. Tokio tells Moody and Roxy that Joe is now ready for bigger fights. Eddie Fuseli, a notorious gunman, approaches Moody with an offer to buy a share in Joe's management. Moody refuses, saying that they have enough trouble with Joe now: he has recently bought a Dusenberg and drives wildly at high speeds. Joe, who has become tougher than before, says he does not care if Fuseli helps manage him. All he wants are higher-paying fights. Moody asks Lorna to use her wiles to keep Joe out of trouble.

A few nights later, Joe and Lorna are sitting together again on a park bench. Joe tells Lorna that he loves her, but she resists romance with him: love has always given her nothing but pain. She prefers the safety of her relationship with Moody, although she does not love him. Joe finally gets her to admit that she is in love with him, and they go home together.

The next day in Moody's office, Moody and Joe argue about Fuseli's taking part in the management. Moody says he will sell out and settle down with Lorna. Joe announces that Lorna is in love with him; but to spare Moody pain, Lorna denies that she loves Joe.

Six weeks later, just before an important bout, Mr. Bonaparte talks with Joe in his dressing room. He realizes that Joe has given up music for good and sadly gives his approval to Joe's boxing career. He tells Joe that he is sorry for him, because he has let himself become brutal and insensitive. Hurt by his father's words and bitter about Lorna's betrayal, Joe grimly goes out to the ring. He returns a few minutes later, having knocked out his opponent in two rounds. He has broken one of his hands, but this no longer concerns him: he has committed himself to becoming a fighter.

ACT THREE

In Moody's office six months later, two newsmen interview Joe, now a prosperous, conceited boxer. Annoyed with his flippancy, they leave as Lorna enters. Having heard that she is going to marry Moody the next week, Joe exchanges bitter words with her. She leaves as Fuseli, who now arranges everything for Joe, comes in to chat. Despite his fine clothes and dinners at expensive restaurants, Joe clearly is no longer interested in the luxuries about which he had once dreamed.

The next night at the arena, Joe is fighting the Baltimore Chocolate Drop for a chance at a championship bout but is taking a beating in the early rounds. In Joe's dressing room, Fuseli blames Lorna for upsetting Joe and threatens her unless she gets out of Joe's life.

Word comes that Joe has won the bout by knocking out the Chocolate Drop in the eighth round. As his managers rejoice, the news comes in that the Chocolate Drop has died as a result of the knockout. Joe is stunned; everyone leaves except Lorna, who tries to comfort him, assuring him that she does love him. They go off for a ride in his car.

Later that night, Fuseli, Moody, and Roxy wait at the Bonaparte home for word of Joe and Lorna, who have disappeared. Fuseli announces that he intends to take over Joe's management completely. Moody and Roxy argue with him as a phone call comes from the police. Joe and Lorna have been killed in an automobile crash.

CLIFFORD ODETS

Waiting for Lefty [1935]

The curtain rises on a bare stage, at the rear of which six or seven men—members of a strike committee elected by the taxi drivers' union—are seated in a semicircle. Harry Fatt, the union head, stands facing the audience and addresses the union members, trying to persuade them not to go on strike. The time is not right for a strike, he claims, even though wages are low and conditions bad. He is interrupted by shouts of disagreement and is asked where Lefty Costello is. Fatt suggests that Lefty, one of the union's militant members, has run out on them.

The members demand to hear from the committeemen. One of the committee members, Joe Mitchell, comes forward and tells why he decided in favor of a strike. As he speaks, the lights fade. A spotlight turns on Edna, Joe's wife, in their home. Joe arrives home from work to find all their furniture repossessed by the finance company. Edna is angry and tells Joe that if he does not do something to improve their situation she will leave him. Joe tries to explain that the union bosses would have him killed if he agitated for a strike. Edna suggests that he get together with the other members and force a strike.

The spotlight picks out Miller, another of the committeemen, working as a laboratory assistant. His employer, Fayette, tells him that henceforth he is to work under Dr. Brenner, a well-known chemist, and will receive a salary increase; the project, research in poison gas, is to be ready for the next war. In addition, Fayette tells Miller to submit a confidential report to him each week on Dr. Brenner. Miller refuses and strikes Fayette as the lights fade.

The spotlight next picks out Sid, another committeeman, with his girl friend Florence; they discuss the fact that, because Sid cannot make enough money as a taxi driver to support her, Florence's mother and brother oppose their marriage. Sid and Florence both recognize the hopelessness of their situation and sadly decide to stop seeing one another.

The stage lights come back on, and Fatt calls on Tom Clayton to tell the union members what happens when a strike is called. Fatt explains that Clayton was a Philadelphia taxi driver until the strike took place there. Clayton begins to speak, but is interrupted by a member from the audience who forces his way to the stage and says that Clayton is actually a labor spy named Clancy; he says, furthermore, that Clayton-Clancy is his own brother and has worked in other industries as a spy for management. Some of Fatt's men try to silence the man, but several of the committeemen protect him.

The lights fade out, and the spotlight picks out another committee member, Benjamin, an intern in a hospital. He complains to his supervisor, Dr. Barnes, that a hysterectomy operation has been taken from him and assigned to Leeds, who is not competent. Dr. Barnes agrees but points out that Leeds is the nephew of Senator Leeds. Barnes says that Ward C, the charity ward, is being closed by order of the hospital trustees and reveals that Benjamin is to be fired. Benjamin, realizing he is being discharged because he is a Jew, expresses his indignation at the action but says he is too old now to fight the corruption and prejudice any longer. Word comes that the hysterectomy patient has died on the operating table. Benjamin angrily vows to keep fighting until he has changed the society that lets such things happen.

The stage lights come on again, and Agate Keller, another committeeman, addresses the meeting. He bluntly condemns the union leadership and urges the members to call a strike. He calls on Edna, Sid and Florence, Dr. Barnes, and others to help fight for a better society. As Agate speaks, news comes that Lefty Costello has been found in back of the car barns with a bullet in his head. Agate asks the members what they intend to do now. The answer is a loud, unanimous call for a strike.

E U G E N E   O ' N E I L L

Desire Under the Elms [1924]

PART I

At sundown on an evening in 1850, Eben Cabot appears on the porch of the Cabot farmhouse in New England ringing a great bell, summoning his half brothers Simeon and Peter up from their work in the fields to supper. The conversation at the kitchen table turns to speculation about the disappearance of their father, who rode off in the wagon two months ago; he hasn't been off the farm, except to go to the village, since he married Eben's mother, now dead, thirty years before. It is evident that all three men hate and fear their father Ephraim, apparently an iron-willed, greedy hypocrite; they discuss the fact that when he dies, each can take his share in the farm. Eben, however, contends that his father stole the farm from his mother and worked her to death on it and that he himself is the only one who truly has a claim to it. He tries to disassociate himself from their father, insisting that he is entirely like his mother and does not resemble his father in any way. He then goes off to town to the local prostitute, Minnie, whose customers include Peter and Simeon—and old Ephraim, who was first.

Just before dawn the next day, Eben, feeling his way through the dark, enters the house and goes upstairs to his and his brothers' room, which becomes visible as he enters with a candle. He wakens Simeon and Peter and tells them that he has heard in town that their father has remarried. All three seize on what for them is the only implication of this news: the new wife will get the farm. Eben then offers Simeon and Peter six hundred dollars if they will sign their claims to the farm over to him; the six hundred dollars is money that their father has hoarded away, and Eben's mother told him where it was hidden just before she died. With the money Simeon and Peter can realize their dream of going to California to prospect for gold.

Feeling rebellious and free, Peter and Simeon loll over breakfast in the kitchen, intoxicated with the novelty of not working. They sign Eben's paper and he gives them the money. Hearing their father arrive outside, they go out, insult his new wife Abbie and announce to the stunned old man their intentions; they go off down the road singing while their father shouts after them that California gold is sinful. Abbie, it is immediately apparent, married the old man for his home, and at once she evinces a possessive attitude toward the place. She goes into the kitchen where she meets Eben. In spite of his surly rudeness—he unceremoniously expresses his opinion of her motives and swears that the farm is his and that she'll never get it—there is immediately a strong sense of physical attraction between them.

PART II

On a very hot Sunday afternoon two months later, Abbie sits on the porch as Eben comes out dressed in his Sunday best. She taunts him and alludes, with a trace of jealousy, to the fact that he is going to see Minnie. Her unequivocal efforts to seduce him evidently stir him, but he meets them with a rebuff; he stings her by comparing her to Minnie and goes off down the road. When Ephraim comes up from the fields, it is obvious that he has become mellower. He even speaks affectionately of Eben, and Abbie accuses him of planning to leave the farm to Eben. Ephraim retorts that he hasn't left it to anyone yet and that what he'd like to do would be to burn it in his dying hour. He then says a son is more part of him than a wife. Abbie panics at the thought of losing all that she has struggled to possess—enduring even her manifest repugnance for Ephraim. In an extravagant attempt to set Ephraim against Eben, she accuses Eben of lusting after her; when Ephraim threatens to kill Eben, Abbie, frightened, backtracks, calling it boy's fun. She then shrewdly suggests that the best way for Ephraim to revenge himself on Eben would be for them to have a son. Flattered, Ephraim promises her anything if she will bear him a son.

It is later the same evening, and the two bedrooms upstairs are visible. Abbie, in bed, stares intently at the wall, on the other side of which is Eben, moving restlessly about in his room. Ephraim, trying to make Abbie understand him, delivers a monologue about his life. He identifies himself with his farm and ends in saying, "Me and the farm has got t' beget a son!" He then tells Abbie that he feels uneasy and cold in the house and goes off to sleep in the barn with the cows, where he feels warm and at home. Abbie immediately gets up and goes to Eben's room, throwing herself in his arms; he succumbs for a moment, kissing her, and then repulses her. Stung, she tells him that she wants him for purposes of her own, not because she loves him. She then tells him that she is going down to light up the parlor and that she expects him to follow. Eben begs her not to; the parlor hasn't been used since his mother was laid out in it. Abbie leaves and Eben, in a trancelike state, begins to follow and then, as if remembering something, puts on his white shirt, a tie, and his coat, and calls softly for his mother.

In the parlor, Eben tells Abbie that he feels his mother's presence, and he is puzzled because he feels that she is not hostile to Abbie. Abbie says that she will be kind to him, that she will love him like a mother. Following his own thoughts, Eben tries to divine his mother's wishes, and suddenly feels he understands; his loving his father's wife will be his mother's vengeance. At this point he gives himself completely to Abbie. The next morning, as Eben gets ready for work, he offers to make up with his father and even starts to order old Ephraim around. "I'm the prize rooster o' this roost," he says laughingly.

PART III

On an evening a year later, a party is underway in the Cabot farmhouse. A fiddler is playing and the guests from neighboring farms are laughing noisily.

Abbie, pale and tired-looking, sits quietly in a chair. Ephraim is strutting about, bragging about the birth of his son. The guests, scandalized and enjoying it, make obvious references to their conviction that the baby is Eben's, but the remarks are lost on Abbie and Ephraim. Upstairs, Eben leaves his room and stands over the little cradle in his father's room. Abbie excuses herself from the party below and joins Eben at the cradle. He complains about the pretense; he is proud and wants to claim his son. Abbie, apparently truly in love with him now, says they will have to wait.

Eben is standing out in front of the house when his father comes out from the party; he derisively tells Eben to get married. They fall into dispute, Eben accusing his father of stealing his mother's farm. Ephraim hotly tells Eben that he'll never get a piece of the farm, that Abbie planned having a baby to cut Eben off from the farm. Stunned, Eben grapples with his father, who proves too strong for him. As Abbie appears, Ephraim leaves Eben sprawling. When Abbie tries to comfort him, Eben repulses her violently, accusing her of using him to have a baby so that she could get the farm away from him. Abbie protests that she felt that way in the beginning, but that she truly loves him. Eben remains implacable, and Abbie, with desperation, promises to prove her love.

In the early morning, Abbie gets out of bed, leaving Ephraim sound asleep, and goes over to the cradle where she smothers the baby with a pillow. She goes down to the kitchen, sobbing, to tell Eben of her proof of love. When the sense of what she has done finally penetrates, Eben shrinks back from her in horror. As Abbie explains that she did it because the baby came between them and that she loves Eben more than anything else, Eben rushes wildly off to get the sheriff.

Ephraim appears in the kitchen and Abbie tells him everything. As always, he braces himself against God's ways. He expresses contempt for Eben when he discovers that he has gone off to turn Abbie in. His contempt transforms into a grudging admiration when Eben reappears and insists on sharing the crime with Abbie. He tells her that he loves her and that he always will. The sheriff comes to take them away, and Ephraim goes down to the barn to work. As he leaves, the sheriff remarks, "It's a jim-dandy farm, no denyin'. Wished I owned it!"

E U G E N E   O ' N E I L L

The Great God Brown [1926]

PROLOGUE

During the commencement dance, handsome Billy Brown and his well-dressed parents stroll on the pier of the casino, discussing Billy's friend Dion Anthony, who is the son of Mr. Brown's partner in the building business and for whom they have high hopes as an architect. After the Browns return to the dance, Mr. and Mrs. Anthony, shabbily dressed, walk along the pier, followed by their son Dion, who wears a mocking, scornful mask over his own spiritual, painfully sensitive face. The father refuses to send Dion to college but orders Dion to become a better architect than Billy. Unable to understand their son's weird, mocking behavior, Mr. and Mrs. Anthony follow him out. Pretty young Margaret, wearing a mask nearly like her own face, wanders along the pier, followed by a worshipful Billy. While he tries stumblingly to propose to her, she, with her mask removed, drifts in a romantic reverie of Dion. Billy admits defeat and leaves her to wander off in her trance.

Dion appears and, finding himself alone, unmasks himself to mourn the fears that keep him from life and love. He masks himself when Billy comes to announce that Margaret loves Dion. After Billy leaves, Dion rejoices in his requited love and in the disappearance both of his fear and of his need for his mask. When he beholds Margaret, however, his real face frightens her, and, not recognizing him, she masks herself. Brokenhearted, Dion puts on his mask and ironically declares his love in the most theatrical manner; she responds passionately. When once again he tries to tell her of his love without his mask, she reaches for hers. Vowing never to let her see his face again, he leads her back to the dance, speaking of their future marriage.

ACT ONE

Seven years later, Dion, his face grown more tortured, his mask more mocking, sits alone, when the arrival of his wife Margaret causes him to mask himself. As he mocks their lack of communication, she reprimands him for his drinking and gambling, which began, during their comparatively happy years abroad, when he realized that he could not be an artist. Because of their dwindling bank account, she begs him to ask Billy Brown, now a successful architect, for a job. Eventually Dion, mocking himself, agrees.

Margaret arrives at Billy Brown's elegant office, wearing the mask of a hopeful young matron; trying to be gay and confident, she defends Dion. Knowing the truth of the situation, Billy offers Dion a job, much to Margaret's relief.

That same evening, Dion awakens in the parlor of Cybel, a large, calm young blonde, on whose doorstep he fell asleep. When he masks himself, she puts on the harsh mask of a prostitute. He apologizes and unmasks, Cybel following suit. Recognizing that she too is lost, though strong, he asks for her friendship. When the doorbell sounds, they both mask themselves. Billy comes in and is disgusted to find Dion there, having searched the town for him. When Dion responds mockingly to Billy's offer of a job, Billy lectures him upon his irresponsible behavior toward Margaret. Dion bitterly accepts the job, declaring that he will abandon his quest for God and dedicate himself to the "Great God Mr. Brown."

ACT TWO

In Cybel's parlor seven years later, Cybel and Dion, both unmasked, are playing cards and discussing Billy Brown, who has been supporting Cybel for years. The understanding and love that Cybel and Dion share is evident. When Dion tells her that drinking has ruined his heart, she comforts his fears of death like an Earth Mother. He mocks Billy Brown for taking credit for architectural designs that are mostly his own; he also mocks the fact that, because Cybel loves Dion, Billy Brown wants exclusive possession of her. As he leaves, Cybel has a premonition that she will not see him again. Brown enters and surprises Cybel without her mask. Since he does not recognize her, she tells him she is Cybel's sister. When he learns that Dion comes to see her, he offers to support her if she will never see Dion again.

In the drafting room of Brown's office, Dion reads to his mask, as if instructing it in the spiritual preparation for death. When Margaret appears, her mask of bravery hidden behind her, Dion puts his mask on. She reprimands him for not coming home for two days. Suddenly Dion frantically confesses his loneliness and his love for her; he tells her that he is going away, tears off his mask, and begs her forgiveness. Unable to bear the sight of his face, she faints. When their sons arrive, he quickly puts his mask on and announces to the boys that he is going to pay a farewell call on Billy Brown.

Later that night, Dion appears at the library of Brown's home in wild disarray. He angers and frightens Brown as he contrasts Brown's successful, loveless life with his own unsuccessful but deeply lived one. When Brown brokenly admits his love for Margaret, Dion mockingly announces that in his will he is leaving Brown himself and his position as husband to Margaret and father to his sons. He has taken a drink, knowing full well it will kill him; his mask drops off and, asking Brown's forgiveness, he dies. Brown's shock turns to triumph as he views Dion's real face for the first time and realizes that Margaret never loved the real Dion. There is a knock at the door, and he removes the body. When Margaret appears, looking for her husband, Brown tells her that Dion has sworn off alcohol for her sake, and is now asleep. He disappears and returns in Dion's mask and clothing. Margaret, delighted by her husband's healthy appearance and romantic behavior, jubilantly throws her mask away.

ACT THREE

In Brown's drafting room, two draftsmen discuss Brown's recent strange behavior and his firing of Dion and all his servants. Margaret appears, youthful and happy, and asks for Dion. She is unable to understand the confusion of the draftsmen, who have not seen Dion. Brown, wearing the mask of the successful man, escorts her hastily into his office and explains that Dion is busy on a project and cannot be disturbed. As Margaret expresses her joy at the change in Dion, Brown suddenly tears off his mask, revealing a face ravaged by Dion's demon, and declares his love for her. When she reacts with shock and fright, he masks himself and asks forgiveness. After she leaves, Brown cynically tells his mask that it is *Dion* who has killed *him*.

That night in his library, Brown tells Dion's mask of the plan by which Brown will supposedly go to Europe and die there, leaving the way clear for Brown, as Dion, to live happily with Margaret. Someday, he asserts, she will love him as Brown. Drawing strength from Dion's mask, he goes boldly home to Margaret.

Later that same night, when Brown, as Dion, comes home to an eagerly expectant Margaret, she tells him how happy she has been since the great change in him. When she describes her disgust at Brown's outburst in his office earlier in the day, his cynical and tortured reaction frightens her.

ACT FOUR

A month later in Brown's office, Brown, as Dion, is finishing up the plans for the capitol, laughing contemptuously over the mockery hidden beneath their thin veneer of respectability. Without Dion's mask, he loathes the plans. When Margaret arrives to see Brown, he puts on the Brown mask. She asks that Dion not be overworked. Brown's strange mocking behavior repels her. When she asks to see Dion, he disappears and returns in Dion's mask; his behavior as Dion also alarms her. He leaves, and she receives the committee that has come to look over the plans for the capitol. She is proud when they react enthusiastically but is appalled to realize that they do not know the plans are Dion's. Brown returns and explains that the work is Dion's, but terms it an insulting joke and tears up the plans. He leaves and returns as Dion to assure the committee that the damage can be repaired. Laughing strangely, he tells the draftsmen that Brown is dead and leaves. Certain that Dion has killed Brown, the draftsmen and the committee carry out Brown's mask as though it were a body.

In his library, Brown prays for mercy, but seems to lack the answer he seeks. Cybel runs in and, looking from Brown's to Dion's mask, understands. She warns him to flee, as a murderer is being sought, but he is too tired to run. Shots come from the crowd in his garden, and one hits him. The police enter, triumphant over having shot Dion, and Margaret grieves over Dion's mask. Left alone with Brown, Cybel, as Mother Earth, presides over his death, feeling the agony of the cycle of life and death. Margaret sadly but triumphantly tells Dion's mask that he is not dead, but will always live in her heart.

EPILOGUE

Four years later on the pier of the casino, Margaret bids a strangely sudden goodby to her three fine sons. Sending them indoors to dance, she removes her mask of the proud mother. Taking Dion's mask from under her cloak, she tells Dion that he will always live in her heart.

E U G E N E   O ' N E I L L

The Iceman Cometh

[written 1939; performed 1946]

ACT ONE

The usual gang sits in drunken stupors or hangover-induced dozes around the tables of the back room of Harry Hope's Hotel and Bar on New York's lower West Side. It is early morning, in 1912, the day before Harry's birthday. Of the group, only Larry Slade, a filthy, bitter Irishman, is awake. His tolerantly pitying stare surveys the room. Rocky, the night bartender, enters, sneaking a drink to Larry. Larry asserts his detachment from all desires, dreams, and delusions: he intends to be a grandstand spectator observing the boring game of life and to wait with patient eagerness for death's long sleep.

Rocky and Larry laugh at the dreams of the assembled drunks. Harry, in a periodic miserly fit, makes his regular decree that the freeloading roomers must pay their back rent and liquor debts or get out; Rocky and Harry reflect that, despite Harry's generosity, the bar comes out even. As usual, Harry has sworn that tomorrow, on his birthday, he will walk around the block. Since the day of his wife Bessie's death, Harry has not emerged from the bar; that was twenty years ago. At that time, he was a minor Tammany Hall pawn, set up for a local election by the political machine. But he lost heart and ambition when his beloved Bessie died and has stayed indoors since—always meaning to take a walk.

Occasionally, one of the men stirs or cries out in his sleep, while Rocky and Larry discuss them. Beside Harry, his two permanent boarders, McGloin and Mosher, snore. McGloin is an ex-police lieutenant who was involved in a graft scandal and released from the police force in disgrace. One day, he intends to force his crooked superiors to reinstate him. Mosher was a small time circus con man. Since he was the brother of Bessie, Harry keeps him for sentimental reasons. Occasionally, Mosher misses the old circus world and its special breed of people and declares his intention of returning to it. At another table, Cecil Lewis, an ex-captain in the British army, and Piet Wetjoen, an ex-Boer soldier, sleep: they met when participating in a display on the Boer War at the World's Fair; though they constantly state regret at not having killed each other, they are inseparable. Each dreams of returning to his native land. Beside them sleeps Joe Mott, a light-skinned Negro, one-time owner of a Negro gambling house: Mott intends to make another fortune and reopen the house. Jimmy Cameron, nicknamed "Jimmy Tomorrow," snores beside Joe: he was a newspaper correspondent and retains a Victorian and prim air.

The worst-dressed of the crew is Willie Oban; in his thirties, twenty to thirty years younger than the rest, Willie graduated from Harvard Law School with brilliant grades, but has never practiced. At the time of his graduation, his father was tried, found guilty, and imprisoned for illegal business practices. Willie intends to practice law, however, by getting a position from the D.A., a bribed agent of his father's. At Harry's table, Hugo Kalmar sleeps in his habitual position: his head resting on his arms. An anarchist, nearsighted, dark, immaculately clothed, and with a thick accent, he might have posed for the newspaper cartoons of his type. Occasionally his head flies up as he shouts insults at capitalism and predicts the revolution. Then he subsides, pleading for a drink and reassuming his position. Larry himself was an anarchist. But he has long since left the movement, disillusioned with humanity and troubled by a disconcerting inclination to view both sides of every argument.

The men have chosen to pass out at the tables rather than go up to their rooms, because they await the belated arrival of Hickey, a hardware salesman, who comes on his yearly binge to celebrate Harry's birthday festivities, buying drinks for all.

Larry admits that he has the blues: he can't get drunk enough to pass out. Rocky assures him that Hickey will soon arrive with his tricks, jokes, and money. He will make them laugh and forget themselves, providing all the liquor desired. Best of all, Hickey will tell his favorite joke, in which he sobs over a picture of his wife, then suddenly declares that he found her in the hay with the iceman. Willie has an attack of the DT's, and his screams rouse Harry, who orders a drink for Willie, thus ending the ban on free drinks. This wakes the others, who demand drinks and voice concern over Hickey's lateness.

Don Parritt, a young, unappealing newcomer in flashy clothes, enters. He was given lodgings by claiming to be a friend of Larry's. Larry claims that the boy is nothing to him: years ago, he knew the boy's mother, Rosa Parritt, a leading woman anarchist; a recent bombing on the West Coast led to her arrest. Larry greets Parritt coldly. The others hint that he should treat them. Parritt claims he's broke, buys a few drinks, inadvertently reveals a lot of money, and antagonizes everyone. He expresses disdain for the place and those present and curiosity about Hickey. But he quickly returns to the subject of his own troubles: his escape from the police manhunt for anarchists on the Coast, his pain over his mother's imprisonment, his penniless retreat across the country in search of Larry. Larry was the only person he could turn to, the only man among his mother's lovers who noticed him, the only deserter from the movement whom his mother ever forgave. He asks whether Larry quit the movement because of Rosa's promiscuous nature, and is incredulous when Larry denies this. Suddenly, Parritt changes his tone, denouncing the movement, expressing hatred for his mother, and affirming the rumor that the arrests were arranged by an inside informer. This change arouses a rebuke from Larry, who immediately reassumes his detachment. He warns that Parritt will be disappointed if he expects anything from him: he has nothing to give and wants only to die.

The men stir, each voicing his refrain of complaint, his pipe dream, or his favorite memory. Rocky's prostitutes, Margie and Pearl, arrive laughing over their night's work. Still young and pretty, they insist that they are respectable tarts, not prostitutes or whores, while Rocky denies being a pimp, since he is a bartender. The three laugh at Cora, another prostitute, and her pimp Chuck, who dream of marriage and a farm while Cora waits for Chuck to give up drinking and forget her past. Cora and Chuck enter fighting and announce that they have seen Hickey outside. He promised to come in, but first has to think some more about "saving" various people.

The group expresses mystification as Hickey enters singing. Theodore Hickman, fat and twinkling, exudes confidence, generosity, humor, and ability. His infectious mirth rouses choruses of welcome. Drinks are poured all around. They toast happily, then notice with astonishment that Hickey did not drink. He explains that he freed himself of the need for liquor by facing the truth about himself. He promises to help them rid themselves of guilt and fear by his simple method of dispelling self-delusion.

Larry agrees that Harry's Bar can be called the "Palace of Pipe Dreams." But Hickey declares that Larry, too, has his pipe dream. He is the "Old Foolosopher" and "Old Graveyard," posing as a detached observer and pretending to desire death. In reality, he fears both the involvements of life and the mysteries of death. Stung, Larry turns away. Hickey notices Parritt and declares that he has an intuition of kinship: Parritt has some trouble with himself. While the group stares in disappointment and disbelief, Hickey falls asleep at the table. But soon, under the influence of alcohol, their spirits revive.

ACT TWO

It is almost midnight, and in the back room, the preparations for Harry's birthday party are under way. But Hickey has been at work truth-spreading all day, with the result that tempers are high. Lewis and Wetjoen are fighting. Cora and Chuck, in sober but horrified earnest, are planning marriage. Margie and Pearl are acknowledging their profession, and insulting Rocky by calling him a pimp. Joe feels discriminated against. Only by reminding each other of Harry's birthday do they calm down.

A beaming Hickey returns with presents and continues preaching. Other members of the group arrive, all scared of Hickey, all shakily sober, fighting desperately against the truth and accusing others of deceit.

Parritt flies to Larry's side, pleading for help, then begging for punishment, and finally revealing that he betrayed his mother and her associates to the police. Larry strives to remain impassive despite his disgust for Parritt and Hickey's taunting. Suddenly, it occurs to Larry that Hickey's madness may be due to the discovery of infidelity on his wife's part.

Harry appears, and "Happy Birthday" is sung. But he, too, is touchy and sober. Hickey taunts him that the truth is that he is afraid of going outside, that he hated the nagging, ambitious Bessie, that her death was a relief, since it permitted him to drink and loaf. Harry loses his temper, then apologizes, and festivities resume.

Hickey announces that he owes an explanation for the pain he's causing the others; he says that he always had the capacity to understand people, to discover each person's particular self-illusion. Finally, he unmasked himself and found freedom and happiness. It is the freedom from guilt-producing pipe dreams and the happiness of self-acceptance that he endeavors to bring to them, his dearest and only friends.

Larry interrupts, asking whether Hickey's conversion was due to Mrs. Hickman's infidelity. Did the Iceman joke come true? Everyone joins in mocking laughter. Hickey replies that his wife is dead. Everyone apologizes and expresses regret. Hickey thanks them but insists that regrets are unnecessary. Poor Evelyn suffered throughout her marriage to him—a drunk, a drifter, and a cheater. All she wanted was her own peace and Hickey's happiness. Now she has both.

ACT THREE

The next morning, Rocky complains about having to take Chuck's day shift while that fool marries Cora. Larry agrees that Harry's party turned into a wake: everyone left early and locked their doors to keep the insistent Hickey out, yet all night Hickey's preaching could be heard.

Parritt comes down, begging Larry for punishment. Larry retains his detachment with a struggle and continues puzzling over the cause of Hickey's conversion and Evelyn's death.

Hugo worries about Hickey's accusations that he has a lust for power and aristocratic tastes and that he is forgotten by the movement. Joe goes to gamble, renouncing the white world. Willie goes to the D.A. Wetjoen and Lewis dare each other to go to their respective embassies. McGloin and Mosher dare each other to go to their ex-bosses. A drunken Cora drags the sober Chuck to the license bureau. Jimmy goes to his newspaper office. Margie and Pearl go to Coney Island to spend their money. They all curse Hickey as the devil incarnate. Larry surveys the proceedings with pity.

Hickey leads Harry downstairs and pushes him out the door. Harry protests that he is too blind and deaf to cross a street crowded with speeding automobiles, but goes. Rocky cheers and Larry pities as they watch, reporting Harry's journey. Harry gets halfway across the empty street, then staggers and runs back, claiming that he was almost killed by a recklessly driven automobile and swearing never to go out again. Rocky is bitterly disappointed. Hickey explains that *that* is precisely the point. They will *all* be back—but unburdened by guilt-producing dreams of tomorrow and tormenting vows of reform. He assures Harry that in a few moments the pain and shock will wear off and he will be a free and happy man. Larry says Hickey speaks of the peace of death and accuses him of driving Evelyn to suicide. Hickey accuses Larry of yielding to the easy but wrong kind of pity that makes people sink deeper into the morass of guilt and self-deceit. He adds that Evelyn would never have committed suicide, for fear of hurting him: she was murdered. Meanwhile, Hickey begins to be worried by the delay of Harry's joyous rebirth.

ACT FOUR

Having spent the day in neighborhood bars or on park benches, most of the group except Hickey are back by one in the morning, sunk in numb stupors. Rocky warns each late arrival to avoid Hickey, should he return, and to deny any knowledge of him or his wife. Larry says Hickey must return, because he has to keep on selling his brand of salvation to save his confidence in it.

Hickey appears, denying any loss of confidence. Grinning broadly, he explains he left only to make a phone call. While Hickey talks, two men, obviously detectives, enter, bar the exits, and wait silently. Hickey explains that they should be exultant and free, having licked the evil game of dreaming to reform. He, too, once despised himself and hated anyone less depraved than he. He describes his wild and restless youth: he learned the art of salesmanship from his preacher father, and picked up the rest from hotels, bars, and whorehouses; meanwhile, he loved and married Evelyn, his childhood sweetheart. He describes the vicious cycle of his marriage to the ever-loving, ever-believing, and ever-forgiving Evelyn: temptation, women, and liquor would overcome him; he would beg to be forgiven and vow to repent and reform. Then, he would sin again. He began to hate himself, and when his self-loathing became unendurable, he began to hate Evelyn. Yet he always loved her. He could not commit suicide or leave her, for then she would have doubted his love. Meanwhile, Harry's birthday was approaching. He knew he could not bear to disappoint her and be forgiven again, but he also knew he had to come to the bar. He swore he would not go; she believed him. The night before arrived, and Evelyn, trusting him, went to sleep. There was only one way to free her from the misery of loving him and to give her peace, and to free himself from hatred and to go to Harry's: Evelyn must die in her sleep. He shot her, then laughed. Realizing that he laughed, Hickey now decides he must have been insane.

Relieved, the others take up the idea of Hickey's insanity as an excuse for his behavior and their torment. The detectives lead Hickey away. After he is gone, the liquor finally begins to take effect and taste good again: everyone resumes his old delusion freely and gets drunk happily. Larry advises Parritt to commit suicide from an upstairs window. While the rest celebrate, he listens for the sound of Parritt's fall to death. Hearing it, he expresses a longing for his own release by death, realizing that he means it for the first time. The others sing drunkenly, then pass out.

EUGENE O'NEILL

Long Day's Journey into Night

[written 1940; performed 1956]

ACT ONE

On an August morning in 1912, James Tyrone, an aged but still imposing actor, leads his wife Mary, a very nervous but still pretty woman, into the parlor of their New England summer home. He compliments her on her improved appearance but rebukes her for not breakfasting heartily. They dispute about Tyrone's real estate speculations and the poor health and appetite of Edmund, their younger son. Agreeing that Edmund is merely suffering from a bad summer cold, Tyrone returns to the subject of Mary's health. She expresses annoyance at his watchfulness, and her hands, crippled with rheumatism, flutter to her hair. She admits she had an uncomfortable night and expresses relief at the disappearance of the fog and silence of the foghorn.

The laughter of their sons is heard, and Tyrone complains about the wastrel habits of Jamie, the elder. The boys enter: James, Junior, thirty-four, robust yet obviously decadent; Edmund, twenty-three, thin, obviously feverish and sick. Both sons praise and compliment Mary. But tempers flare and Edmund departs. Mary defends him: his irritability is due to his cold. Jamie declares Edmund seriously ill. Mary agitatedly denies this. Jamie and Tyrone hurriedly agree with her, stating that Dr. Hardy will surely take care of Edmund. Mary denounces Hardy vehemently: like all doctors, he is a fool, concerned only to keep his patients constantly returning. Aware of the scrutiny of Jamie and Tyrone, she stops suddenly, asking whether her hair is mussed. Appeased by a flood of compliments and chattering about the servants, she departs.

Jamie and Tyrone express their anxiety about the probability of Edmund's suffering from consumption and about Mary's state. They speculate that the strain of worrying over Edmund may be too much for her to bear, only two months out of a sanitarium. Tyrone calls Jamie a bun and a parasite and he accuses him of instructing Edmund in the cynical and evil ways of Times Square because he jealously feared Edmund would surpass him. Jamie calls Tyrone a miser with a fortune in land and Hardy a cheap but incompetent physician. He blames Mary's tragedy on Tyrone's greed, claiming that had Tyrone, when Mary was ill after Edmund's birth, brought her to a good physician—not a cheap hotel quack—her morphine addiction would have been averted. He bases his suspicion that she has yielded anew to her addiction on the fact that she used the spare room the previous night.

Mary's reappearance silences the argument. She predicts the return of the fog and laments her once-beautiful hands. The two men calm her with compliments, then depart. Edmund enters and Mary fusses over him, insisting that he is not really ill. She complains about her loneliness: Tyrone has never given her a proper home, only hotel rooms and this hateful summer place; Tyrone and Jamie prefer bars and Edmund went to sea. The constant spying and suspicion of the three men depress her: it would serve them right if *it* was true. Edmund denies this, assuring her of their trust. At this, Mary says she wishes to take a nap. Edmund regards her with doubt but lets her go alone.

ACT TWO

Edmund is alone in the parlor when the maid, Cathleen, announces lunch. Jamie arrives; the brothers have a drink and refill the bottle with water. Jamie becomes infuriated when he learns that Mary has been alone upstairs all morning. A less nervous, rather distant and bright-eyed Mary appears, carefully avoiding her sons' probing stares.

Tyrone enters, appraises his wife, and takes a stiff drink. Mary begs him not to believe *that*, she tried so hard. He cries out that she should have had more strength but adds that it is not hopeless. The family leaves to eat, then reappears.

Mary complains absently. Tyrone reminds Edmund of his appointment with Dr. Hardy. Mary, suddenly intense, expresses her contempt for the humiliating Dr. Hardy and his sermons on will power when she would sell her soul for some medicine. Just as suddenly resuming an uncanny detachment, she announces that her hair needs fixing and invites Tyrone to accompany her upstairs to allay his suspicions. He refuses, stating that he is not her jailer and that she would only postpone her activity. She leaves. The men argue, each accusing the other of undue suspicion or unfounded hope. Edmund departs to dress for his appointment. Jamie requests that Edmund be sent to a good sanitarium, then departs to accompany him.

Mary returns, her detachment increased, her eyes still brighter. She predicts the return of the fog but declares her indifference to it now. She asks Tyrone to stay, for she dreads being alone and has no friends. He begs her to stop. She first pretends ignorance of his meaning: then asks him to forget what life has done to them, remembering only that they love each other. She recalls her girlhood in a convent school and the early years of their marriage. She confesses to a sense of guilt over the death of their second son and her conviction that her illness after Edmund's birth and his current illness are retribution for her sins. Tyrone asks: if she is so far in the past by midday, where will she be by nightfall? But Mary, in the calm present, announces that she has errands at the drugstore.

Edmund returns and asks for carfare. Startled at receiving a ten-dollar bill, he asks whether his father's generosity signifies that he is indeed dying. Tyrone leaves, embarrassed. Edmund begs Mary to exert will and faith. She says that effort is impossible since she has neither will nor faith now, but one day the Virgin will help her and it will be very simple. Edmund leaves in despair.

Alone, Mary says she is lonely, admits that she wants to be alone, and cries to the Mother of God that she is so lonely.

ACT THREE

In the early evening, Mary appears younger and more detached as she sits chattering with the maid in the parlor. Cathleen, giddy from drinking, relates the impertinence of the druggist when he examined Mrs. Tyrone's prescription. Mary explains the medicine is for her rheumatism and contemplates her disfigured hands. She recalls her days at the convent when she wanted to be a pianist or a nun and relates her courtship with Tyrone. Mary sends Cathleen out and murmurs plans to take another dose. Tyrone and Edmund return; both have been drinking heavily. Mary greets them warmly, alternately chattering happily and complaining bitterly, but oblivious to their sullen disappointment. Her manner touches Tyrone, however, and he agrees with her that above and in spite of everything they love each other. His words recall her wedding day, and Mary describes her beautiful dress, on which no expense was spared by her adoring father, and wonders where it is now. But she and Tyrone quickly argue again. Edmund tries to interrupt to tell her that Hardy diagnosed his illness as consumption. She ignores this information, insisting that he exaggerates and that Hardy is a quack, until Edmund calls her a dope fiend. Shattered, Mary regards the advancing fog, praying that one day—accidentally, or the Virgin would never forgive her—she will take an overdose. Edmund leaves the house hurriedly. Tyrone returns and comforts Mary, insisting that Edmund does respect her great suffering. The maid announces dinner. Mary grows abstracted again and declines dinner, stating that she wishes to rest. Tyrone begs her not to take more poison, lest she soon be a mad ghost. But Mary is deaf to his pleas and goes off.

ACT FOUR

About midnight, the foghorn sounds constantly, and a drunken Tyrone plays solitaire as Edmund, also drunk, stumbles in. They argue about the electricity bill and agree that, since Edmund gave him money, Jamie is probably in the whorehouse. Edmund recites passages from the decadent romantic poets, especially Baudelaire. Tyrone, scornful of Edmund's literary tastes, replies with Shakespearean passages. They begin a card game. Hearing Mary wandering about upstairs, both hope that she will not come down. Tyrone explains that Mary's memory glorifies the past; he presents his unglorified version while they play cards intermittently. They talk of Edmund's illness and argue about the sanitarium Tyrone has chosen for him. After a battle, Edmund succeeds in obtaining permission to go to another, slightly more expensive, institution. Tyrone admits to cherishing money perhaps over-much, but attributes this to his impoverished childhood; he admits that he traded artistic success for financial security. Edmund relates some of his adventures as a sailor, his feeling of estrangement and his love for death.

Jamie is heard stumbling outside, and, to avoid him, Tyrone goes to another room. A very drunken Jamie enters, singing and quoting Oscar Wilde. He relates his adventures at the whorehouse with Fat Violet, ridicules his father for being a miser, and expresses self-contempt. He begs Edmund to regain his health. He admits to great jealousy of Edmund, hence his cynicism toward the young man. But he insists that Edmund is all he possesses. He advises Edmund to forget his brother Jamie, to get well, and to succeed. He then appears to doze off. Tyrone returns, regarding Jamie with disgust and disappointment. They argue briefly but lapse into half-dozing.

Suddenly, the chandelier in another room blazes with light, and a Chopin waltz is played brokenly on the piano. The Tyrone men watch with sober dread as Mary appears, trailing her faded wedding gown. She is extremely pale, her eyes enormous and shining, and her face completely youthful. Jamie announces, "The Mad Scene. Enter Ophelia"; and Tyrone swears he will disown him. But Mary is oblivious to her surroundings and is deep in the past. She complains that she cannot play well because her fingers are strangely warped. Sister Theresa will scold. She must see Sister Martha at the infirmary. Tyrone interrupts, offering to hold the gown to prevent her from tripping over it. She thanks him, explaining that she is to be a nun. Jamie quotes Swinburne's "A Leave-Taking," and Edmund cries, "Mama, I've got consumption." Mary responds momentarily but quickly summons up the past again: Mother Elizabeth is wonderful, but she was not understanding when Mary declared her intention of being a nun; Mother Elizabeth said she must wait a year or two. Yet nothing could change her inclination. But something did happen. Ah yes, she married James Tyrone "and was so happy for a time."

Mary stares at her dream; the men stir but remain seated.

E U G E N E   O ' N E I L L

Mourning Becomes Electra [1931]

1. HOMECOMING

ACT ONE

The setting sun of an afternoon in 1865, shortly after the end of the Civil War, shines brightly on the Grecian temple portico of the Mannon residence on the outskirts of a New England town, while from the distance the town band can be heard celebrating the Northern victory. Singing "Shenandoah," Seth, the Mannon handyman, arrives with some drunken cronies. They peer at the Mannon mansion with curious masklike expressions and gossip about the family's secrets. The Mannon wealth has been accrued over generations, but the Mannons' haughty reserve implies mysterious doings. Ezra Mannon, one of the town's most prominent citizens, has been a hero of the Mexican War, a judge, and currently is a general in the Union army. His wife, Christine, is much admired for her beauty but is distrusted for her foreign air.

Christine emerges from the house; the hidden observers praise her extraordinary beauty, grace, and sensuality, but the cold mask of her face intimidates them. She goes to the greenhouse as Lavinia, her daughter, appears. Seth's friends note the striking resemblance and shared beauty of the two women and the severity of Lavinia's clothes and the awkwardness of her body. Seth leads the gaping onlookers off as Hazel and Peter Niles, friends of the Mannons, arrive. Lavinia pretends cordiality to Hazel, who asks for news of Orin, Lavinia's brother, also with the Union army. Hazel leaves, disappointed. Peter asks Lavinia about a Captain Brant who is reputedly courting her. She denies this; Peter proposes but is refused. Christine returns laden with flowers as Peter departs. Christine and Lavinia argue about Ezra's approaching return and Captain Brant's forthcoming visit. Lavinia inquires about Christine's recent visit to New York to see her ailing father. Lavinia issues a warning that certain matters shall be discussed shortly. Christine enters the house, calling its façade a pagan mask hiding Puritan ugliness.

Seth returns and Lavinia admits to him that she too has returned from a mysterious visit to New York. Seth reveals the suspicion that Captain Brant may be Marie Brantôme's son. Marie, he explains, was the governess of the Mannon children and the mistress of David Mannon; when Abe Mannon, Ezra's father, discovered the liaison, he disowned his brother David and tore down the old residence, replacing it with the present mansion. Rumor has it that David died an alcoholic and that Marie died in poverty, but that a son survived, and the striking resemblance between Captain Brant and the Mannon men gave birth to this speculation. Captain Brant approaches, so Seth leaves. Lavinia greets Brant's flirtatious approaches coldly. He tries to win her over by relating his adventures as captain of a clipper ship and on South Sea islands. When he attempts to touch Lavinia, she accuses him of being Marie's son. Accusing her of insulting his mother, Brant admits the truth, declares his renunciation of the Mannon blood, and vows to avenge his mother. Lavinia calls him a coward and threatens to inform her father unless Brant obeys her orders.

ACT TWO

Mother and daughter stand beneath family portraits in Ezra's study as Lavinia reveals her knowledge of the affair between Christine and Brant and of Brant's parentage. The two women express mutual hatred. Lavinia calls Christine a wanton harlot and unloving mother. Christine admits to despising Ezra and his daughter but affirms her love for Orin. She insists that her affair with Brant would not have occurred if Orin were home. Lavinia, she declares, loves

Brant and seeks a jealous revenge, just as she always tried to usurp Christine's place in the hearts of Ezra and Orin. Christine refuses to renounce Brant but is forced to agree to when Lavinia reveals that she has aroused Ezra's suspicions by letter and will, if necessary, tell him everything. Lavinia leaves.

Christine calls Brant into the study to inform him of Lavinia's actions. After Brant assures her of his passionate devotion, she reveals a plan utilizing Ezra's weak heart and information in her father's medical books. Appealing to Brant's greed for a ship and his lust for her, she succeeds in overcoming his objections to this cowardly trick. As he departs, Christine whispers that now he will never be able to leave her, despite her age or his island maidens.

ACT THREE

A week later, Lavinia walks in the moonlight as Seth passes singing "Shenandoah." When questioned, Lavinia denies any connection between Brant and Marie. Seth describes Marie as beautiful and appealing, the darling of everyone, including Abe and the young Ezra, adding that she shared the rare and beautiful red-brown hair of Lavinia and Christine. Lavinia sends Seth away as Christine appears. Christine derides Lavinia for awaiting Ezra as though he were a favorite beau. Ezra appears; Lavinia greets him with joy, Christine coldly and formally. Ezra explains that Orin is recuperating slowly from a head injury. Both women try to get Ezra alone, but he expresses his desire for Christine and sends Lavinia inside. He questions Christine about Brant. She states that Brant was seeking preferment in the shipping industry under the pretense of courting Lavinia and that she therefore barred his visits. Reassured, Ezra relates his experiences: war is a nightmare that degrades both life and death; yet, for him, war was a liberator, allowing him to return to Christine, life, and love. No more will he follow the Mannon way of life and contemplate and glorify death above life. He asks Christine to go with him to a South Sea island.

Christine tries to silence him and to hide her revulsion, but when Lavinia appears, she rushes Ezra inside. Lavinia, alone, decides that the revelation of Christine's sinfulness is her duty. She calls Ezra for that purpose, but when he appears, she merely says goodnight.

ACT FOUR

In his bedroom, Ezra dozes as Christine rises from his bed. He asks her to return, to be patient with his attempts to demonstrate love. He explains that he feels usurped, a stranger in his own house, and asks whether Christine wishes him to die. Christine, declaring her refusal to forget or forgive the evil years of their marriage, reveals the truth about Brant and herself. Ezra screams in pain and calls for his medicine. Christine gives him the poison procured by Brant. Lavinia bursts in. Ezra points to Christine, cries "She's guilty," and dies. Christine faints, dropping the false medicine. Lavinia picks it up and vows revenge.

2. THE HUNTED

ACT ONE

Two nights after the murder of Ezra, the minister and the physician walk away from the Mannon mansion with their wives, discussing the funeral, commenting upon Chistine's aged and devastated appearance and Lavinia's unemotional poise. After they leave, Christine, followed by Hazel, emerges. Christine is waiting impatiently for Lavinia and Peter to return from the station with Orin, and expresses her desire to see Orin and Hazel married. Hazel conveys her willingness as they return to the house.

Lavinia, Peter, and Orin arrive. Orin's masklike expression greatly resembles those of Brant and Ezra. Lavinia, sending Peter inside, admonishes Orin to mourn properly for his father, to be deaf to Christine's charms, and to be prepared for strange revelations. Christine appears, rushes into Orin's arms, and then sends him inside. She asks Lavinia for the medicine she dropped after Ezra's death, explaining that it was her sleeping potion. Lavinia remains silent. Christine, accusing her of plotting against her to win Orin, returns inside.

ACT TWO

In the Mannon drawing room, Peter and Hazel discuss Orin's haggard and haunted appearance, abandoning the subject when Orin and Christine enter. Orin is so full of admiration for his mother's appearance that he ignores Peter and Hazel, who soon depart. Christine suggests that Orin marry Hazel. Stung, Orin replies that Christine has forgotten him for Brant. He describes Christine as a beautiful South Sea island that he dreamt of while delirious in the hospital, an island inhabited only by himself. Christine extracts a promise that Orin will not permit Lavinia to influence him against her, convincing him that Lavinia is maddened by grief.

Lavinia enters to demand that Orin pay his respects to Ezra's body. After he leaves, Christine announces that Orin is hers, that he believes Lavinia insane, and that he rejoices at the death of a father he hated. Then she begs Lavinia not to reveal the truth about Brant. Orin would kill him, and, without Brant, she would die. Lavinia departs silently, and Christine determines to warn Brant.

ACT THREE

Orin addresses Ezra's body, which lies beneath his portrait in his study, with a familiarity and disrespect that shock Lavinia. Orin explains that his attitude is a result of the war: war, he says, is a dirty joke; Ezra was nicknamed "Old Stick"; and he himself was a coward. He describes a recurrent dream in which he repeatedly kills the same man while the man's face changes, becoming ultimately Ezra's face, then his own. Lavinia begins her story, while Orin tries to stop her, insisting that he is fully informed and that she is insane. But

Lavinia persuades him to place the false medicine on Ezra's heart and observe Christine's reaction. Orin swears to kill both Christine and Brant if they are lovers.

Christine enters and is about to regain Orin's confidence when her eyes note the medicine. She shrinks in guilty horror as Lavinia leads Orin out. Christine appeals to the dead Ezra's body to protect Brant.

ACT FOUR

A few days later on a dark night in Boston harbor, a drunken sailor sings "Shenandoah," and Brant orders him off his ship. The moment the sailor is gone, Christine appears. Brant leads her to his quarters. Unseen, Lavinia and Orin steal on board and crouch beside a transom to eavesdrop.

Christine relates the events of the preceding days to Brant, warning him against Orin; they agree to sail for China in a few days. Brant expresses misgivings at leaving his command but assures Christine of his love and describes the beauties of the South Seas. Hearing this, Orin must be restrained by Lavinia from bursting out of hiding and killing Brant immediately. Brant soon leads Christine back to shore as Lavinia and Orin steal into his cabin. When he returns, Orin shoots him. Lavinia, looking at Brant's dead body, wonders why so young and handsome a man loved her vile old mother. Orin, noticing Brant's resemblance to himself and Ezra, declares that his dream has been fulfilled. He cries out that Christine is a worthy prize for any action, however evil, and that life is a dirty joke. Lavinia and Orin ransack the cabin, to give the appearance of robbery, and depart.

ACT FIVE

The next night, Christine sits alone on the portico. Hazel arrives, summoned, Christine says, because in the absence of Lavinia and Orin the house is oppressive. As Lavinia and Orin are seen approaching, Hazel departs. Orin announces that they followed Christine and murdered Brant. He begs her forgiveness, vows to replace Brant's love, and asks her to go to the South Seas with him. Christine laughs hysterically and goes inside. Lavinia rebukes Orin for his weakness and orders him inside.

Seth strolls by, singing "Shenandoah." A shot is heard, and Orin emerges to announce that Christine has killed herself. He weeps and calls for Christine's forgiveness. Lavinia sends Seth for the doctor and announces that justice has been done.

3. THE HAUNTED

ACT ONE

A year later, about sunset, Seth and some drunken cronies stand before the Mannon mansion. Seth has wagered that Abner Small does not have the courage to spend a night in the house for fear of ghosts. The others have come to witness the bet and are drinking and joking. Hazel and Peter Niles arrive, explaining that, since Lavinia and Orin will arrive tomorrow, they wished to see that all was in order. Small runs out of the house, screaming that he has seen Ezra's ghost. The men depart, laughing but frightened. Peter and Hazel, discussing the improbability of ghosts, enter the house.

Lavinia and Orin arrive, staring with cold, masklike expressions at the house. Orin is wooden, awkward, and childlike. Lavinia, having adopted Christine's style in clothes and hairdo, appears as sensual and striking as her mother once did. She orders Orin into the house, but he stops in horror before the spot where he last saw Christine alive.

ACT TWO

Lavinia and Orin enter the drawing room; Lavinia assures Orin that there are no ghosts in the house. Orin identifies Lavinia with Christine: he explains that her appearance and ideas are as daring, striking, and sensual as Christine's, citing especially her behavior on a South Sea island they stopped at. He alludes to a sailor and a native, insinuating affairs. Lavinia asks for more compliments, denies having been promiscuous, and calls Orin morbid and ill. She catechizes Orin on the facts of their mother's sins and death. Peter enters, expressing his admiration for Lavinia's new beauty. Lavinia, warm and flirtatious, declares her joy at their reunion. Orin begins to relate Lavinia's lascivious behavior during their journey, but she sends him off to Hazel. She explains to Peter that Orin is still grieving and is going insane with false guilt; she suggests that Hazel be warned. She asks Peter whether he still loves her and accepts his proposal immediately. She describes the beauty of the South Seas, the freedom of the natives, and the liberation she underwent there. She kisses Peter as Hazel and Orin appear in the doorway. Orin, enraged and shocked, stammers congratulations ironically.

ACT THREE

A month later, Orin is writing in Ezra's study. Lavinia demands an explanation of his activity. He replies that he is writing the chronicle of the Mannon family, revealing all their sins from the time of their arrival in the New World to a description of Lavinia's deeds and lusts. Lavinia confesses her sexual activities, but when Orin taunts her with the resemblance of her two lovers to Brant and calls her a whore, she denies everything. Orin offers to help her plan his suicide as they planned Brant's murder, so that she can be free to marry Peter. But, he warns, he will show Peter his manuscript and thereby prevent the marriage, dead or alive. Lavinia departs in tears, and Orin continues writing.

ACT FOUR

A few moments later, Lavinia is pacing in the drawing room and contemplating the idea of Orin's death. Seth enters and requests that she calm the maid, who is seeing ghosts. They depart, and Hazel and Peter arrive. Orin enters to greet them, and Peter leaves quickly. Orin gives Hazel his manuscript, instructing her to guard it carefully and to give it to Peter only in the event of his death or of a marriage between Lavinia and Peter. Explaining that love is forbidden to both Lavinia and himself, Orin asks Hazel to leave immediately and to forget the Mannons. When Lavinia enters, Hazel announces that Orin is to spend a week at her home. Lavinia forbids this, notices the manuscript, and bars the door. She urges Orin not to betray the Mannons and to retrieve the manuscript. Only after Lavinia has promised to do anything and everything that he asks does he order Hazel to return the manuscript. Hazel leaves in tears.

Orin declares that he will never set Lavinia free: they share the guilt of their mother's suicide, and he loves her with a lust born of that guilt; now Lavinia appears to be neither beautiful mother nor older sister, but an attractive stranger whom he will possess. Perhaps she is Marie Brantôme. Lavinia refuses in horror, declaring Orin too cowardly to commit suicide. Orin asks whether, were he driven to suicide by Lavinia as he drove his mother to that act, justice would again be done. He suddenly decides, however, that only by suicide can Christine's forgiveness be obtained.

Peter returns suddenly; Orin announces that he will clean his gun and departs to the study. Lavinia rushes into Peter's arms and prevents his following Orin by describing the home and the life that they will share. A shot rings out. Peter goes to the study. Lavinia, alone, addresses the portraits that line the walls, announcing that she has renounced the Mannons and henceforth is Christine's daughter only.

ACT FIVE

About sunset a few days later, Seth strolls by, singing "Shenandoah." Lavinia appears, dressed in black, again wooden, thin, and awkward. She calls the house a temple of hate and death, which she will leave to rot after she has gone away with Peter to a new life.

Hazel arrives to state that Peter has fought with their mother and left their home. She swears that she will stop a marriage between Peter and Lavinia. Lavinia threatens to kill Hazel. Peter approaches, so Hazel leaves quickly. Lavinia begs Peter to marry her immediately. Stunned by the suggestion, he hesitates. Lavinia asks him to take her immediately, so that love and joy can dispel death and disapproval from the Mannon house. Crying out that he must want her enough to murder for her, she calls him by Brant's name. Deciding then that the dead are too strong and that love is forbidden to her, she sends Peter away. Shocked, Peter asks whether Orin's insinuations about the South Sea islander were true. Lavinia proudly asserts that they were. Peter calls her immoral and rushes away.

Seth passes, singing "Shenandoah." Lavinia informs him of her intention to endure her punishment by living out her life in the Mannon house. She orders him to nail the shutters over the windows and to throw away the flowers. She enters the house alone.

EUGENE O'NEILL

Strange Interlude [1928]

NOTE: Throughout this play, the characters voice their secret thoughts to the audience. These thoughts are inaudible to the other characters.

PART I

ACT ONE

The novelist Charles Marsden enters the empty study of Professor Leeds in a New England college town. An old student of the professor's, Marsden reminisces and reflects aloud. He eagerly anticipates his reunion with the professor. He wonders that he never fell in love with Nina, the professor's lovely daughter. Leeds enters, greeting Marsden warmly and confiding in him. He describes Nina's recovery from the nervous breakdown that followed the shock of her fiancé's death. He admits that he prevented Nina's hasty marriage by explaining to Gordon, the fiancé, that it was dishonorable to marry on the eve of going to war as a pilot. He now fears that Nina has guessed this interference and hates him for it. He tries to justify this action to Marsden, but in his thoughts he admits that he hated Gordon and wished for his death. Marsden's thoughts are full of excitement at the prospect of seeing Nina. But he reminds himself that sex disgusts him and that the difference in their ages is considerable.

Nina enters, a striking girl with a beautiful body, and greets Marsden casually. She announces her intention of leaving immediately to work at a veterans' hospital under a friend of Gordon's, a Dr. Darrell. Leeds, frightened at the prospect of loneliness, tries to dissuade her. Marsden aids him, his mind revolted at the thought of Nina's beautiful body exposed to the eyes and lusts of wounded men. Nina, intently thinking of her debt to her lost lover, determines to be deaf to their arguments. Having made her announcement, Nina invites Marsden to help her pack. He leaves thinking that Nina has become a basely sensual woman and envying Gordon, the hero of the sports arena, the battlefield, and Nina's heart. He is anxious to be home where his mother will be waiting with tea. Leeds, alone, thinks of his new freedom to devote all his energies to his studies and contemplates the prospect of his death with a repentant Nina returning to mourn—but too late.

ACT TWO

Over a year later, Marsden, dressed in mourning and alone in the professor's study, awaits Nina's arrival. He considers the professor's lonely death and speculates about Nina's year as a nurse, the nature of her sexual activities and mental attitudes. He anticipates her tears and hopes to comfort her, but the direction of his thoughts begins to disgust him.

Nina arrives, accompanied by Dr. Darrell and the boyish, collegiate Sam Evans. The study evokes her father's memory, and she addresses him in her thoughts, remembering her childhood love for him and attempting to rouse some sort of emotion at his death. Nina and Darrell go upstairs to see the professor's body. Evans and Marsden appraise each other. Marsden thinks Evans is a fool, and the thought of Nina and Darrell together fills him with jealousy. He wants Nina to stay at home so that he could visit her daily: it would be wonderful for his work. Evans declares his unbounded admiration for Gordon and his selfless love for Nina. Looking upon Marsden as her guardian, he asks for Nina's hand in marriage. Marsden, not flattered by this estimate of his age and prowess, dismisses the subject.

Darrell enters and sends Evans on an errand. He appraises Marsden as an old-maidenish writer, afraid of reality and sexuality. He decides that Marsden's aid can better be enlisted by merely alluding to the possibility of promiscuity rather than by giving any facts about Nina's behavior. Meanwhile, Marsden's thoughts try to outguess Darrell; he is piqued at his "Uncle Charlie" role. He concludes that Darrell is Nina's lover. Darrell presents his professional advice that Nina should be persuaded to marry Evans.

Nina returns, and Darrell leaves her alone with the frightened and disturbed Marsden. Nina crawls on Marsden's lap and kisses his cheek. He is delighted, sure of his love for her, and satisfied to the full extent of his desire. Nina states that God is a Mother; Marsden agrees. She asks Marsden to portray her father so that she may confess, be punished, and receive absolution for her sins. She confesses to casual affairs with several veterans in expiation of her debt to Gordon. Marsden is revolted. Deciding that Nina is a whore, he wants to rush home to mother and tea. The only solution seems to be Darrell's advice. Nina must marry Evans. When Marsden suggests this, Nina replies that it is a mild punishment and will provide her with the children she desires. She calls Marsden "Father," and dozes off. Evans returns. Marsden encourages him and hands him the sleeping Nina, then departs.

ACT THREE

About seven months later, Nina, healthy, robust, and cheerful, sits in the dining room of the Evans upper New York State homestead. She is rereading her letter to Darrell. It tells that she and Evans are on a belated honeymoon and, with Marsden and his car, are visiting Evans' mother. Mrs. Evans' letters begged with such desperation for a visit that Nina was touched and urged Sam to go, though he had never mentioned his mother. The house, she describes, is very ugly and strange, as though it were once haunted by ghosts that since have fled. Nina breaks off reading to wonder whether she should tell Darrell her precious and beautiful secret. She decides to cherish it privately—to keep the baby all her own—a bit longer.

Marsden enters, his thoughts bitterly appraising Nina's improved health, noting that she hides a letter, estimating the probability that she is pregnant, and working out a description of Sam's enigmatic mother. Seeing the Evanses approach, Marsden leaves to permit them a private family conference.

Evans enters looking boyishly and self-consciously happy, boasting gaily of his successes to his mother. Mrs. Evans asks whether Nina is pregnant. Sam's negative reply pleases her, but his thoughts reveal great disappointment and guilt. Sam leaves and Nina joins Mrs. Evans.

The two women make gestures of friendliness while appraising each other in their thoughts. Mrs. Evans asks whether Nina is pregnant and whether she loves Sam. Nina replies yes to both questions, thinking that, since Sam is the father of her child, she does now, or shortly will, love him. Mrs. Evans then reveals a family history of insanity. She advises Nina to have an abortion and subsequently a child by another man, always keeping the truth from Sam. If Sam were to know of the insanity or to fear its development in his child, he would surely succumb to it. She insists that Nina and Sam leave immediately, never return and never write. She relates her own life of self-sacrificing care for the insane Evanses, declaring that happiness is the closest we come to God or the Good. She agrees with Nina that God the Father is cruel and selfish, while God the Mother is loving and suffering, and comforts the sobbing Nina.

ACT FOUR

About seven months later, a disheveled Sam tries to bang out advertising copy in the professor's study. His thoughts hover about Nina's physical rejection of him, her unexplained internal sickness, and their childlessness. He cannot comprehend the difference between Nina—cheerful and plump—at his mother's house and Nina—bitter and emaciated—since then. His job is in danger, and he knows that without Nina's love and a child he must fail. Suddenly, he remembers that he has secretly invited Ned Darrell, the only person he trusts, to look at Nina.

Nina enters, her thoughts expressing disgust for Sam, hatred of being burdened by him, and a longing for his death. Remorsefully remembering his mother's words and her own dead baby, she decides that she must pretend to love him and desire his embraces. But she also remembers Gordon and the abortion and cringes with pain. Sam tells of Darrell's imminent visit, and Nina joyfully rushes up to change. Marsden arrives with his suggestions on Nina's biography of Gordon. He reflects on his intuition that Nina has had an abortion, seeks the motive for it, and recalls her activities in the hospital. Darrell's arrival is announced. Marsden wonders whether Darrell was either the father or the abortionist. Disgusted with himself, he decides to consult Darrell on his mother's condition. The antagonism between Darrell and Marsden has not diminished, and each insults the other in his thoughts. Darrell decides to upset Marsden and declares that his mother probably has cancer. A frightened Marsden and a hopeful Evans leave together on an errand.

Nina reappears, dressed and beautiful. She and Darrell exchange news while each notes the attractiveness of the other in his thoughts. Darrell is eager for Nina to confess her problems. She does so, relating Mrs. Evans' revelation, the abortion, and finally, Mrs. Evans' advice. Still addressing him coolly as "Doctor," Nina asks Darrell whether he would oblige and act as the impregnating male. Darrell strives desperately to be rational and to prescribe accurately for the patient, but Nina's beauty excites him. He fears to betray his professional demeanor and lose his complete absorption in his career. But Nina's beauty and urgency overcome his objections. Deciding that he will view the parents and child as merely three guinea pigs, he agrees. Nina is exultant: she shall be happy, Sam shall be happy, and she will have her child.

ACT FIVE

A few months later, in their new but very modest suburban New York home, Nina sits alone reading. Suddenly, she feels the stirrings of an infant within her womb and reflects joyfully on her love for Ned Darrell. She remembers the first afternoon of cold, scientific detachment and purposefulness, then the succession of afternoons of passion. She exults in her triumph over Darrell: she remained cool and calculating while he fell ever more in love. Sam wavers on the threshold, trying to screw up his courage to tell Nina that he is setting her free because of his failure as a businessman and his seeming incapacity to be a father. Nina sees him and her thoughts fill with disgust for him and with her determination to get a divorce and live with Darrell.

Darrell arrives, and Nina runs to him. He has brought the unemployed Evans a letter of introduction with which Evans quickly departs. Nina and Darrell talk calmly, each thinking excitedly of the other's attractions and estimating the degree of the other's devotion. Both remember Evans with guilt, but are overcome with desire and love. Nina brings Darrell to state his love.

They are interrupted by the arrival of Marsden, distracted with grief over his mother's death from cancer. While Nina pauses to welcome and comfort Marsden, Darrell recovers from her spell. Nina sends Marsden upstairs and informs Darrell of the intention to reveal the truth and then live with him. Darrell, having resumed his professional manner, refuses and lectures Nina on the absurdity of her romantic notions. His thoughts vow defiance of Nina and fidelity to his career. Nina's passion and beauty are about to overwhelm him again, when Sam returns. Both Nina and Sam urge Darrell to stay for lunch.

Darrell, fearful that he will succumb to Nina's temptations, waits until she leaves the room before congratulating Evans on being about to become a father. Evans is deliriously happy. Darrell explains that Nina consulted him and intended to surprise Evans with the good news at lunch, but that he is leaving for Europe immediately and had to see Evans' reaction. He departs quickly.

Evans kneels to offer thanks to God as Nina returns. He joyfully reveals his knowledge to the shocked and hurt Nina. She mentally swears revenge on Darrell, but is touched by Evans' emotion and determines to let him be happy.

PART II

ACT SIX

Over a year later, the Evanses' house looks more prosperous, and Nina appears content as she wonders whether the baby is asleep. She reflects on the events of the preceding year: Sam's business success and excellence as a father; the resemblance of her baby to his namesake, Gordon, her old fiancé; and the absence of any word from Darrell. Marsden, sitting in the room, tries to guess Nina's thoughts. His curiosity over the relationship between Nina and Darrell has increased. He mentions that he encountered Darrell with a beautiful woman while in Europe. This is successful in arousing Nina's jealousy. She recalls the long afternoons in Darrell's arms and desires his return. A self-confident Evans, having heard Darrell's name, rushes in to hear of his old friend. Marsden, pleased at this success, tries to probe further. But Nina grows wary and determines never to reveal to Marsden the facts surrounding Gordon's birth. She also considers that Marsden loves her after his fashion and is her most faithful servant.

While Marsden thinks of his platonic desire for Nina and his hatred of her complacent acceptance of him as "Uncle Charlie," Evans thinks out a business problem and decides to approach Marsden with a request for financial backing. He does so with great aplomb. Marsden refuses, but the proposition begins to appeal to him. Evans and Nina go upstairs to see the baby.

The doorbell rings, and Darrell enters. His thoughts reveal that he has inherited a fortune at his father's death and has returned to reclaim Nina and his child. While he waits for the return of Nina and Evans, he is interrogated by the suspicious and jealous Marsden. Nina enters, expressing her pleasure at his return. Darrell is pained to learn that his child was named Gordon by its hero-worshiping parents and that Evans is proving an excellent husband, provider, and father. Nina pushes Charlie out of the room and embraces Darrell while thinking that for Gordon and herself, all three men—Marsden, Evans, and Darrell—are necessary for satisfaction and security. She refuses Darrell's request to be his wife and give him his child, but offers to be his mistress again. Darrell is enraged and threatens to tell Evans the truth.

Evans enters, and Nina dares Darrell to speak up. He tries, but finds it impossible to destroy Sam. He realizes that this failure implies that he has accepted Nina's terms. Evans thinks of Darrell with compassion, a lonely man without a Nina and a Gordon in his life. He decides to ask Darrell for financial backing. Marsden realizes that Nina has tapped some deep resource of Darrell's personality and that jealousy of Darrell is no longer necessary, for he can never take Nina away again. Nina reflects with pride and triumph on her four men—father, husband, lover, and son—all in one room, all in her power. Saying that she is fatigued and wishes to retire, she exits, kissing each man on the cheek.

ACT SEVEN

Nearly eleven years later, Nina and Darrell sit, impatient with each other, thinking their own thoughts in the Evanses' exquisite Park Avenue apartment. Gordon, their son, plays, jealously hoping that Darrell will leave. Nina regards with pride her handsome son and with pity her bitter lover. She thinks of the long years of her affair with Darrell: the brief intervals of passion and the sustained periods of hatred and recrimination; his attempted escapes through other women or travel. She absolves herself from the guilt of making Darrell weak, for it was she who encouraged him to start a biological station at Antigua; she wishes he would return to it.

Darrell reflects on the sanity of Evans, the preservation of which demanded the sacrifice of the sanity and happiness of Nina and himself. Nina asks Darrell whether he will return to Antigua soon, to the delight of Gordon. Darrell does not answer directly but speaks slightingly of Evans. Gordon, passionately devoted to his supposed father, is enraged and insults Darrell. Nina orders Gordon out of the room and threatens to cancel his eleventh birthday party. Darrell advises Nina that if she does not give him up, Gordon will turn to Evans as the favorite parent. Nina decides to accept this advice. Yet she and Darrell agree that they still love each other. They kiss, observed by the unseen Gordon.

Marsden arrives, joyously greeted by Gordon. Nina informs both Marsden and Gordon that Darrell is leaving for two years. Darrell and Marsden, whose backing of Evans has greatly increased their fortunes, discuss the business situation while thinking hostile thoughts about each other. Gordon discovers Darrell's birthday present: a beautiful model of a ship, which Darrell had hidden so that he would not have to see his son destroy it. Gordon, torn with hostility and desire for the wonderful present, destroys it thoroughly. Darrell and Gordon have a little talk, after which both mentally admit to mutual liking despite all desire and pretense to the contrary.

Evans arrives, a prosperous and confident businessman, and Darrell leaves for Antigua. Evans tells Gordon the boy's favorite stories of his namesake, the great athlete and warrior Gordon Shaw. Nina sees the solidarity between Evans and Gordon with great jealousy. She woos Gordon back, thinking that one day she will reveal the truth to Evans.

ACT EIGHT

Ten years later, aboard the Evanses' luxurious yacht, Darrell, Marsden, and Nina recline in chairs while Evans and Gordon's fiancée, Madeline Arnold, stand by the rail waiting for a sight of Gordon and the crew race. Nina observes Madeline with hatred, determined to prevent the marriage. Evans is delighted with Gordon, the great athlete, who has surpassed his predecessor's records. He is also fond of Madeline and irritated by Nina's rudeness. Marsden is in mourning for his sister, who kept house for him after the death of his mother. He is maudlin and tearful, yet his curiosity about the relationship between Darrell and Nina and about the paternity of Gordon is ever alert. Darrell is once again the brilliant and attractive scientist. He hopes Gordon will come in last or drown in the race. He is fully aware that he has transferred his affections from Nina and Gordon to his work and his assistant, Preston.

Evans, Madeline, and Marsden alternately go below and return in their effort to get either radio reports or a view of the race. Nina, thinking that her love for Darrell is utterly dead, declares she loves him, trying to enlist his aid against Madeline and Gordon's marriage. He refuses, reminding her of his vow never again to meddle in human lives. She considers telling Madeline what Mrs. Evans once told her about hereditary insanity—omitting to mention that Gordon is not Evans' son. But Darrell foils this plan by telling Madeline to disregard Nina's speeches. Next, Nina tries to get Darrell to reveal the truth to Evans. Darrell admits the temptation to claim the great athlete from the adoring assumed father but refuses. He says that Gordon is neither his nor Evans' son, but that of Nina and Gordon Shaw, her dead fiancé.

Marsden, very drunk, babbles about the great novel he will write after his marriage to Nina. But observing the strange triangle of Madeline and Darrell and Nina, he decides to investigate. He invites Nina to confide in him. In a trance of despair, she does so, telling him all the truth and calling him "Father." He is horrified, but tells her that he forgives her everything.

Gordon wins the race at the last second, then faints. Madeline and Evans are ecstatic. Evans has a heart attack. Nina thinks fearfully that Darrell's and her wishes have lead to this. Darrell assures her that Evans is alive, but requires great care. Both vow to care for Evans constantly and never to disturb his happiness. Nina promises to let Madeline marry Gordon.

ACT NINE

Several months later, Gordon and Madeline sit in mourning on a bench on the Evans estate and think about Evans' funeral. Gordon confides his doubts of his mother to Madeline, but is indignant at the thought of an affair between Darrell and Nina. Marsden passes them, noting with disgust that they embrace on the day of a funeral. But he reflects that they are young and passionate, while he and Nina are old and serene. He gives Madeline a rose and offers to fetch Nina so Gordon can say goodby before returning to school.

Nina arrives to say goodby with Darrell. Gordon regards Darrell with distaste, thinking that Nina is now free to marry him. Nina realizes that she is not showing sufficient grief to please Gordon. But she cannot feel guilt now: Sam was happy and sane to the end. She will live a quiet life in her father's old house, which Sam bought back for her. Darrell is disturbed by the complacency and insensitivity of his muscular son; he considers the temptation of revealing the truth and shaking Gordon up.

Gordon begins to inform Nina and Darrell of Evans' will. It leaves Darrell a vast sum for his experimental biological station. Darrell is enraged by Evans' last gesture of ownership. Gordon and Darrell begin to argue. Gordon slaps Darrell. Nina screams that Gordon has hit his father. Gordon apologizes, agreeing that to hit one's father's best friend is to hit one's father. While Nina and Darrell stand amazed at Gordon's lack of comprehension, Gordon continues to say that he has known that Nina and Darrell have loved each other for years and wishes them marriage and happiness. He bids them goodby and goes to Madeline and his private plane.

Darrell proposes. When Nina refuses, he asks her to marry Charlie Marsden so that he can know she will be cared for. Marsden appears, and Nina informs him that she has refused Darrell's proposal but would accept his. He promises to let her have peace and tells her that he has already planned their wedding ceremony for the late afternoon.

Gordon passes overhead, circling in his plane, while Darrell, Marsden, and Nina wave. Darrell leaves for Antigua, never to return. Nina, in a stupor, calls Marsden "Father," and says that she has just received a telegram stating that Gordon Shaw was killed in battle. Marsden quiets her, adding that all that has happened since her first meeting with Gordon Shaw was a strange interlude of passion and torment. Nina agrees that our lives are strange dark interludes in the electrical display of God the Father and falls asleep.

JOHN OSBORNE

Look Back in Anger [1956]

ACT ONE

One evening in April in a one-room flat in an English Midlands town, Jimmy Porter and Cliff Lewis are reading the Sunday newspapers. Jimmy's wife Alison, wearing one of his old shirts, is ironing. Jimmy complains of boredom, banters with Cliff, and tries to start an argument with Alison, calling her brother Nigel "the Platitude from Outer Space" and referring to her as "the Lady Pusillanimous"; she does not react. Cliff and Jimmy grapple playfully on the floor, and Jimmy pushes Cliff into the ironing board. All of them fall on the floor, and Alison's arm is burned by the iron. Seeing her anger, Jimmy retires across the hall to Cliff's room. While Cliff tends to the burn, Alison tells him she is pregnant but has not yet told Jimmy, afraid of how he will react to the news.

Jimmy returns to make his peace with Alison. They play an old game of theirs—pretending he is a bear and she is a squirrel. Alison receives a phone call from Helena Charles, a friend of hers who has arrived in town for a week with an acting troupe, and invites her to stay upstairs in a spare room. Jimmy, who cannot stand Helena, lashes out at Alison for inviting her over. He tells Alison he hopes she will one day have to face something that will turn her into a human being, such as having a child of hers die; but he doubts that even that would affect Alison.

ACT TWO

Two weeks later, Alison and Helena, who has prolonged her stay because of Alison's illness, are preparing Sunday tea. Jimmy is playing his trumpet loudly across the hall in Cliff's room, and Helena says that the noise must be for her benefit, for she knows Jimmy detests her: she can see the hatred in his eyes and finds it both frightening and fascinating.

Alison tells Helena about her meeting Jimmy three years ago and about their marriage. Her parents strongly disapproved, and when Jimmy learned this, he seemed more determined than ever to have her; they lived at first with Hugh Tanner, a friend of Jimmy's who was even more deliberately antagonistic to Alison's upper-class family and friends than Jimmy. Jimmy and Hugh used Alison to help them gate-crash parties and dinners given by her parents' friends; they had looked upon themselves as barbarian invaders, Alison says. Pointing to the stuffed toy animals on the chest of drawers, Alison tells Helena about the bear-and-squirrel game she and Jimmy created together—"a silly symphony for people who couldn't bear the pain of being human beings any longer."

288

Cliff and Jimmy come in for tea. Jimmy does his best to insult Helena and becomes more vehement when he learns that Alison is going to church with Helena that evening. When Helena threatens to slap his face, he warns her not to mistake him for a gentleman. Helena remarks on Jimmy's sense of self-pity. Alison tells her not to take his suffering from him; he would be lost without it.

Jimmy asks Helena whether she has ever seen a person die. Anyone who hasn't, he says, is suffering from a bad case of virginity. He tells how he watched his father take twelve months to die after coming home wounded from the war in Spain; he was only ten years old, Jimmy says, but when his father finally died, he knew more about love and betrayal and death than Helena would know all her life. A phone call from London informs Jimmy that Mrs. Tanner, Hugh's mother, has had a stroke and is dying. While he is taking the call, Helena tells Alison she has sent for Alison's father to come and take his daughter home. Preparing to go to London to be at Mrs. Tanner's bedside, Jimmy asks Alison to come with him, but she leaves for church with Helena. He throws the stuffed teddy bear across the room and falls face down on the bed.

The next evening Alison is packing to leave. Her father, Colonel Redfern, waits for her, puzzled by the situation. For one thing, he says he cannot understand why an educated young man like Jimmy runs a candy shop. He talks about the trouble Alison's mother caused when Jimmy was about to marry Alison. Things have generally been unsettled, he says, since they returned to England after thirty years in India. The colonel accepts the term Jimmy once used for him—"an old plant left over from the Edwardian Wilderness."

Helena comes in and tells Alison she will remain there that night, since she has a job interview nearby the next day. Alison says goodby to Cliff, gives him a note for Jimmy, and leaves with her father. Cliff tells Helena he does not want to be there when Jimmy returns from London, gives Helena the note, and goes. Helena picks up the stuffed bear and lies on the bed holding it.

Jimmy arrives and reads the note from Alison. Helena tells him that Alison is pregnant. The news surprises him, but he says he does not care: he has sat for eleven hours with Mrs. Tanner while she died. Alison didn't care about the old woman, he says, and he is not going to be overcome with awe on hearing that "that cruel stupid girl" is going to have a baby. He leans over Helena, calls her an evil-minded virgin, and orders her to leave. She slaps his face, then kisses him passionately, and pulls him down onto the bed.

ACT THREE

Sunday evening several months later, Jimmy and Cliff are reading the papers while Helena, wearing one of Jimmy's old shirts, irons. Jimmy and Cliff banter and tussle with one another as usual. When Helena leaves the room, Cliff tells Jimmy that he is going to leave; he is tired of working with Jimmy in the candy shop, and things are not the same as when Alison was there. Cliff goes to his room when Helena returns. Jimmy suggests they all go for a drink and starts out to call Cliff as Alison comes in, looking haggard and ill. Jimmy tells Helena, "friend of yours to see you," and walks out.

A few minutes later, Alison and Helena are having tea and talking. The sound of Jimmy's trumpet is heard from Cliff's room. Alison apologizes for coming back. She says she had stopped herself many times from returning. She assures Helena she does not want to interfere. Helena tells her that everything was over between her and Jimmy the moment she saw Alison in the doorway. She knew by looking at her that Alison had lost the baby, Helena says, and that seems like a judgment upon them.

Helena calls Jimmy in and tells him she is going away. After she has gone, Jimmy talks to Alison about their past. He says that when he first met her he thought she had a wonderful relaxation of spirit but later realized he was wrong about that. To be relaxed, he says, you first have to sweat your guts out, and Alison had never had a hair out of place. Weeping, Alison tells him of the pain of losing the baby; she has known pain now, as he wanted her to, she says. She collapses at his feet, and Jimmy bends down to embrace her. He tells her it's all right now: they will be together like bears and squirrels and will be careful because there are cruel steel traps all around, waiting for slightly mad, satanic, and timid little animals such as squirrels. "Poor squirrels," Jimmy says, and, laughing a little, Alison replies, "Oh, poor, poor bears," and puts her arms around him.

JOHN OSBORNE

Luther [1961]

ACT ONE

At the Augustinian monastery in Erfurt in 1506, Martin Luther is received into the order. His father Hans, who witnesses the ceremony, is not pleased: Martin could have been a man of stature—a lawyer—Hans tells a friend; he admits that he pinned his hopes on Martin after losing his other two sons in the plague.

In the monastery, Martin serves the meals to the other monks, then takes part in a communal confession. He castigates himself for chafing at the lowly duties assigned to him. Prayers are about to begin when Martin is seized with a convulsive fit and is carried off.

Martin walks downstage through a large brilliant cone of light, haggard and sweating. He says that he lost the body of a child and tried to find it again but could not; he complains of his fears of the darkness and of the chronic constipation from which he suffers.

In his cell, Martin prepares to say his first Mass. He has been in the monastery one year. Brother Weinand tells Martin that he abuses himself with too-rigorous mortifications and advises him to trust in God's mercy. The lights dim, and Martin is again seen walking downstage through the cone, carrying a naked child in his arms. "And so the praising ended," Martin says, "and the blasphemy began."

Two hours after the Mass, Hans is still waiting to see Martin in the monastery's refectory. Martin, having been taken ill after the Mass, comes in and talks with his father, who still is not accustomed to his son being a monk. Hans says he thinks men murder themselves in a monastery. He remembers Martin's vision of St. Anne, which induced him to join the monks. It was no vision, Hans claims, but only a flash of lightning during the storm. Martin insists it was a vision. After Hans leaves, Martin asks himself, "But what if it isn't true?"

ACT TWO

In the market place at Jüterbog in 1517, John Tetzel, a Dominican monk and a famed vendor of indulgences from the Church, hawks his wares to the crowd. Even sins not yet committed can be taken care of by indulgences, Tetzel says. Money pours into the coffers.

In the monastery at Wittenberg, Martin talks with Johann von Staupitz, vicar-general of the Augustinian order. Staupitz is pleased with the reputation Martin now has as a scholar, but warns him about his mortifications of the flesh. He says Martin is demanding an impossible perfection from himself. Martin admits that he is under great strain; he says that he is like a ripe stool in the world's straining anus. Staupitz also cautions Martin to be prudent about criticizing the sale of indulgences. The duke, who has the concession for them in the area, has complained. Staupitz finally advises Martin to do something about his bowels, from which he obviously suffers. Martin says he will. "Who knows?" he says. "If I break wind in Wittenberg they might smell it in Rome."

At the church in Wittenberg, on October 31, 1517, Martin preaches against the sale of indulgences. He then nails his ninety-five theses against indulgences to the church door.

A year later in Augsburg, Thomas de Vio (known as Cajetan), the papal legate to Germany, has an interview with Martin and demands that he retract his statements about indulgences. Martin says that he will if he is shown in the Scriptures that he is wrong. Cajetan says that the Pope does not engage in disputations on matters of faith: the faithful must accept and obey. Martin refuses.

At a hunting lodge in northern Italy in 1519, Pope Leo X receives a letter from Martin. He cannot come to Rome as ordered, Martin writes, because of his health; he says he is willing to have his statements about the indulgences judged by any impartial university in Germany and will accept the verdict. Leo orders that Martin be seized and brought to Rome; if that is not possible, then Martin and his followers are to be excommunicated if they persist in disobedience.

A year later in Wittenberg, Martin's followers are burning the books of canon law and papal decrees. Martin enters with a papal bull from Leo excommunicating him. He refers to Leo as "that over-indulged jakes' attendant to Satan, that glittering worm in excrement." Martin scornfully tosses the papal decree into the fire.

ACT THREE

Martin is called before the Diet of Worms, on April 18, 1521, and asked to retract his antichurch statements. Having requested and been granted a day to think over his answer, he answers that the church at Rome is the enemy of his religion and that he will not retract unless shown in the Scriptures that he is wrong. "Here I stand," he says. "God help me; I can do no more."

In Wittenberg in 1525, the uprising of the Bundschuh, the peasants' movement, has taken place and been quelled. A knight, bloodstained and weary, accosts Martin and accuses him of being responsible for the carnage; he calls Martin a canting pig and says he is killing the spirit with the letter. Martin says the peasants had to be put down, for they rebelled against the Word. Slumped in the pulpit, Martin talks about the story of Abraham and Isaac. "In the teeth of life we seem to die," Martin says, "but God says no—in the teeth of death we live. If He butchers us, He makes us live."

Martin's new bride, Katherine von Bora, a former nun, enters. They kneel together. The knight, who has picked up a banner of the Bundschuh, throws it onto the altar.

Five years later, Martin and Katherine are living with their small son Hans in the vacated Eremite cloister in Wittenberg, where they are visited by Staupitz. Martin feels that Staupitz disapproves of him. Staupitz admits that he disagrees with Martin's stand against the peasants. They were a mob, Martin says: a mob is always against Christ, he claims, because each man tries to live and die for others and each man can only do that for himself.

Staupitz assures Martin of his approval: Martin has created Germany and her language, he says, and he has taken God away from the soft lights and mumblings and jeweled gowns and put Him back where He belongs—in the soul of each man.

One thing puzzles Staupitz. Why did Martin take the extra day at Worms to think over his answer? Martin says he was not certain his stand was right. Was he certain afterwards? asks Staupitz. No, says Martin. Staupitz goes off to bed. Martin sits and mutters, "Oh, Lord, I believe, I believe . . . . Only help my unbelief."

Katherine comes in carrying little Hans, who had awakened with a bad dream and is now asleep again. Martin takes the boy and Katherine goes to bed. Martin talks to the sleeping child, telling him of the hard lesson he had to learn—that a human being is a helpless little animal and that he's not created by his father, but by God. Martin says that at Worms he was just like little Hans, just like a child who's learned to play again, naked out in the world. He says that at Worms he told them, "I have come to set a man against his father," and they listened to him. Martin carries Hans off to bed.

LUIGI PIRANDELLO

Henry IV   [*Enrico IV*, 1922]

ACT ONE

In the modern Italian villa of the young Marquis Charles di Nolli is a replica of the throne room of the eleventh-century German emperor Henry IV. Three young men dressed as knights of that time are enlightening a fourth as to their life and duties; the marquis pays them to support his uncle's delusion of being Henry IV, so they pretend to be that emperor's "secret counselors" and gay companions. Berthold, the newcomer, rightly identifies one of the two full-length portraits in the room as Henry IV, but mistakes the second for his wife, Bertha of Susa. The others correct him: the emperor is tired of Bertha and wants to put her away, and the portrait represents the Marchioness Matilda of Tuscany, who is Henry IV's enemy, since she gave hospitality at Canossa to Pope Gregory VII, his bitterest foe.

John, the old waiter, announces the arrival of visitors, including a modern Marchioness Matilda. The young men go out to see to their charge. The newcomers' talk reveals that almost twenty years ago, this Matilda refused the intense love offered by di Nolli's uncle. When their aristocratic club decided to stage a masked pageant, she lightly announced she would dress as her eleventh-century namesake of Tuscany, whereupon her admirer replied that he would come as Henry IV so that he could be at her feet, just as the emperor himself had to kneel to Matilda at Canossa. The carnival was a great success, and Henry IV the best actor present—until his horse reared and threw him off, so that he fell on his head. When he regained consciousness, his companions began to sense that he was no longer *playing* the part of Henry IV, but had entered the role in profound earnestness. His sister, di Nolli's mother, established this suite of rooms as a setting for his madness, but just before her death a month ago she told her son that she detected signs of returning sanity and begged him to call in a doctor once more to see what might be done. At his suggestion, a party has been arranged to cure her brother, consisting of Matilda, her lover Baron Tito Belcredi, her daughter Frida, engaged to marry di Nolli, and the doctor Dionysius Genoni. The throne room portraits are those painted of the young people in their disguises for the fateful masquerade, and it is obvious that nineteen-year-old Frida now is the living image of what her mother looked like all those years ago.

Berthold bursts in, followed by the other young men. He has been unable to adapt himself to the madness lived in Henry IV's suite, and has consequently enraged the emperor. The young men suggest that the visitors adopt some easy disguise and request an audience with the madman, so as to distract him.

Matilda decides to play Adelaide, mother of the Empress Bertha, and the doctor will be Abbot Hugh of Cluny; these two historically helped to intercede for Henry with Gregory at Canossa, and thus will be welcome. Belcredi will dress as a monk attending the abbot.

Henry IV enters for the interview; he is fifty and graying, but grotesquely daubed with make-up to appear young and garbed in the penitent's sack appropriate to the incident at Canossa. He speaks sometimes as the young Henry at Canossa, sometimes as an older Henry remembering those events, sometimes as an older Henry who knows that he is wearing the mask of a younger Henry and hates it, wishing to be freed into the older man he has become: "A man can't always be twenty-six, my Lady."

ACT TWO

The visitors are in an adjoining room trying to analyze the strange interview, especially some of Henry's ambiguous remarks about masks and disguises. The doctor prefers a technical explanation of the childlike psychological make-up which, recognizing a disguise yet choosing to believe in it, can play quite seriously a role it knows is a make-believe act. The Marchioness Matilda insists that her admirer has recognized her and betrayed his still fervent love through his double meanings. This would account also for the way he had instinctively considered the disguised Belcredi an enemy.

All agree, however, that the madman no longer seems quite consistent, nor quite comfortable, in his delusion, that recollections of the modern world have begun to intrude upon his fantasy, and that therefore the time is indeed ripe to help wrench him into the present. He must traverse at once the eight centuries since Canossa and the almost two decades since he last lived in the modern world; all except Belcredi minimize the risk involved.

The doctor's plan is to shock the patient into reality by confronting him with two examples of Matilda of Tuscany. Frida is to wear the robe her mother wore when the portrait was painted, and Charles will dress as young Henry. At the same time Matilda will appear in a duplicate costume, so that she and the present Henry will make an age-worn shadow of the young couple.

One of the "secret counselors" comes to tell them that Henry IV wishes another interview to make certain they will help him win Pope Gregory's pardon. Historical legend hints that Henry IV nursed a secret love for his political enemy Matilda of Tuscany; and the modern Henry, says the young man, seems afraid that she knows and resents his passion and thus will influence Gregory against him. The modern Matilda takes this as another sign that he has recognized her. She and the doctor resume their earlier disguises, and Matilda, as Adelaide, tries to persuade Henry IV that the Marchioness of Tuscany feels more kindly toward him than he realizes. He sarcastically rebukes her as a mother for speaking more of another woman when she should be speaking of her daughter Bertha, his rambling speech again full of ambiguous allusions that interweave his actual and imaginary lives.

As soon as he has dismissed his visitors, Henry IV derides them to the young men as "miserable, frightened clowns," with whom he has been playing, tearing "off their ridiculous masks now, just as if it wasn't I who had made them mask themselves to satisfy this taste of mine for playing the madman!" As he talks coherently about his fall from the horse, about Matilda's effrontery in bringing her lover to see him while dressing up as his mother-in-law, and about other things of which he is supposed to be ignorant, the young men stare dumfounded; he castigates them contemptuously as a pack of sheep without the imagination to appreciate the esthetic beauty of the life they've been leading, of living history over again with full knowledge of the future consequences of every action, admiring the precise logic of cause and effect—for which ordinary life cannot give sufficient perspective.

ACT THREE

In the darkened throne room, the canvas portraits have been removed; and Frida and di Nolli, costumed as their living images, pose within the frames. As Henry IV enters, Frida is obviously frightened, but she fulfills her part, calling his name softly. He turns, startled, and she leans toward him. He cowers and cries out with fear, while she begins to scream hysterically. All the others rush in, and during the ensuing confusion Matilda reveals what the young men have just told her, that Henry IV has been cured for some time. They try to reproach him with the cruelty of the jest of pretending to be mad when he wasn't, but he retorts that their little "jest" of making the portraits come alive as a "shock cure" was almost enough to drive him mad in earnest.

He explains his unique case for the doctor's benefit. For about twelve years after the fall from the horse, he really was insane. But when he gradually recovered, he realized that his hair was graying and that he was "all gray inside"; his beloved and his companions had lived out their youth during his twelve years of absence, and if he returned to the normal world, he would "arrive, hungry as a wolf, at a banquet which had already been cleared away." Besides, he knew that Matilda would not love him, that one of his companions had treacherously pricked his horse to make it rear, and that the others were also variously hypocritical phantoms in an eternal masquerade of thoughts and emotions. So he deliberately chose to remain mad, to create a world of historical fantasy in fully lucid consciousness of the masquerade rather than to live in the "normal" world where people do not even realize they wear masks.

Growing more and more excited, he cries that Matilda has been *living* all these years, while he has remained caught at one instant of time, so that he can no longer recognize her. No, Frida is the marchioness he knows, an image in his fantasy whom they've made come to life. He grabs hold of her, laughing madly that she's "mine, mine, mine in my own right!" They try to tear Frida away, Belcredi shouting, "Leave her alone! You're no madman!" Henry IV jeers, "I'm not mad, eh!" and thrusts a sword into Belcredi, who is carried out fatally wounded.

Henry IV remains, "terrified by the life of his own masquerade which has driven him to crime," calling his counselors around him, "inevitably . . . here together . . . for ever . . . for ever."

LUIGI PIRANDELLO

Naked [*Vestire gli ignudi,* 1922]

ACT ONE

Ersilia Drei, a pale beautiful girl of twenty-five, comes to the rooms of Ludovico Nota, a novelist; she has just been released from a hospital; the story of her "desperate attempt" has been published in the newspaper; of the offers made to her, she has accepted Nota's. He is stirred by the novelistic possibilities of her story, and she, in turn, is excited by this prospect. She is not interested in his advances toward her and rejects them. Fragments of her story emerge: she was a governess at a Mediterranean villa; the baby fell from the roof, and she was sent away. She returned to Rome penniless and in her extremity tried to prostitute herself in the street and failed. When Nota's talk suggests various identities for her—the woman he imagined for his novel, the woman she is now, and the woman she will be with him—she is greatly disturbed about whether she has ever been anybody at all.

The sounds of an auto accident in the street outside interrupt them; a man is dead. Ersilia, shaken, speaks of the suicide attempt that put her in the hospital. Trying to find an identity, she fiercely questions Nota on the newspaper accounts about her. Her story continues to unfold fragmentarily: at Smyrna she cared for the little girl of the Italian consul and his wife. There she became engaged to a sailor, to whom she gave herself. The sailor jilted her, and thereafter the consul's wife, who had been like a mother, became increasingly cruel to her. When the baby was killed, she was blamed for the accident and sent away with no money. In Rome she learned that her sailor was engaged to marry another girl. Crushed by this betrayal, she poisoned herself.

Ersilia is distressed by certain exaggerations in the paper and by the fact that the other people involved were identified by their real names. After telling the story, she entreats Nota to let her be the woman he imagined for his novel.

Signoria Onoria, the landlady, announces a visitor—a reporter. Ersilia's anxiety becomes physically painful. The reporter, Cantavalle, tells them that the dead child's father, the consul at Smyrna, is in Rome and that he demands a retraction of the story, claiming it is a lie. Ersilia faints and is taken into the bedroom.

Cantavalle warns Nota of Laspiga, the sailor who jilted Ersilia; he was about to be married, but when the article appeared, the wedding was canceled. Laspiga rushes in, agitated, and asks for Ersilia, who he has learned tried to kill herself on his account; he is determined to undo his wrong. But Ersilia has heard everything from the other room; she refuses to see him and wants him to marry the other girl. Finally she agrees to see him tomorrow, and the three men go out.

Left alone with Signoria Onoria, Ersilia insists that she is going away—she must "disappear . . . in the street." The landlady convinces her to stay, despite Ersilia's protests that she has no baggage and is "naked."

ACT TWO

The following morning, Nota returns with Laspiga. The landlady describes with concern Ersilia's actions of the night before. Laspiga is agitated, and he and Nota rhapsodize on the freedom of possibility of the soul soaring above the commonplace, though Nota warns of the inevitable pull back to solid earth. Ersilia enters and recoils from Laspiga's advances, stating that all is over between them, for she is no longer the woman who tried to kill herself for his sake. His protests are to no avail.

When Signor Grotti, the consul at Smyrna, arrives, Ersilia is eager to see him privately. Nota and Laspiga leave. Alone with Grotti, Ersilia loses her composure. In the course of their argument it is revealed that she did not try to kill herself on Laspiga's account: when Laspiga left her, she and Grotti had an affair; he seduced her on the roof, while the child, neglected, fell to its death. Now Grotti insists that she tell Laspiga the truth and free him to marry his fiancée. He embraces Ersilia and pleads with her to go away with him and live out the guilt they share. She rejects him with finality.

ACT THREE

Ersilia and Nota have gone out to try to recover her baggage. Signoria Onoria laments Ersilia's plight. It is late in the day, toward evening, and Nota comes back alone. Laspiga arrives and reveals that he has just learned that Ersilia was Grotti's mistress, for Grotti's wife, on discovering that Grotti had been to see Ersilia, went to Laspiga's fiancée's family and told them everything, including her discovery of the seduction and the cause of the baby's death. All of them, except Nota, now denounce Ersilia as a monstrous fraud. Calmly, Nota states that, now that the truth has been told, he is interested in the motive for the lie—particularly the lie that she tried to kill herself on Laspiga's account. The other lies can be explained by the newspaper's exaggerations and by the need to cover up her affair with Grotti, but this one strikes him as useless, especially for a person intending to die. Laspiga points out that, because she lived, the lie proved useful: it enabled her to secure Nota's interest, "to see her lie picked up from the gutter and glorified in the realm of art." Nota adds that the story is made more beautiful by the uncovered lie. Grotti arrives and denies the truth of the story.

A maid runs in and tells them that Ersilia has fainted in the doorway.

When Ersilia appears, pale and calm, the others realize that she has poisoned herself a second time and is dying. Amid the general panic of calling for doctors and an ambulance, Ersilia explains her lie—now that she feels she has earned the right to be believed. "The worse we are, the uglier we are—the more anxious we are to appear good and beautiful . . . . But I was naked! I had nothing beautiful to put on!" She wanted only "something beautiful to be buried in . . . the dress of a bride." Her final words are: "I am dead . . . and . . . I died naked."

LUIGI PIRANDELLO

Right You Are, If You Think You Are [*Così è, se vi pare,* 1917]

ACT ONE

In Mrs. Agazzi's drawing room, Amalia and Dina, the wife and daughter of Commendatore Agazzi, an important official in a small provincial Italian town, indignantly explain to Lamberto Laudisi, Amalia's brother, the inexcusable social snub they have received from the woman recently moved into the apartment next door.

As the whole town knows, Signora Frola is the mother-in-law of Ponza, one of Agazzi's subordinates. Ponza has installed her in a fashionable apartment while he seems to keep his wife imprisoned on the fifth floor of a walk-up tenement on the outskirts of town. Although the wife never leaves her rooms, her mother is frequently seen going to the tenement. But their only conversation consists of the mother's shouting from the courtyard up to the daughter on her balcony. Disguising their curiosity as the desire to welcome a neighbor who is new to the town, Amalia and Dina have twice tried in vain to call on Signora Frola; once they received no answer at all, although they were sure she was home, and the second time Ponza appeared and curtly told them his mother-in-law could not receive visitors. Agazzi has gone to the Prefect to demand that Ponza be made to apologize for discourtesy to his superior's family.

Three visitors arrive to explore the whole scandalous mystery with the Agazzi family. Laudisi derides them all for a bunch of impertinent gossips, but they argue that they have a right to know the truth about the new civil servant, since all they know is that he, his wife, and his mother-in-law have come from a small village recently destroyed by an earthquake. Laudisi tries to prove that no one ever knows the "truth" about another—indeed, that everyone is actually a different person in the eyes of the different people who think they know him, including himself. But the others, although temporarily swayed, finally refuse categorically to listen to him. There is an absolute truth behind all relative truths, they are sure; facts are facts and can be found out.

Agazzi returns from his talk with the Prefect and announces that Signora Frola is soon to call on them. When she arrives, they very graciously accept her apology: she did not receive them before because she was still so upset about the tragedy of the earthquake. When they ask why she and her daughter visit at such a distance, Signora Frola hesitates. She explains that Ponza does not forbid her to visit her daughter, but is a good man who so passionately adores his wife that he wants to occupy her whole heart. Since he wants even her love for her mother to be filtered through him, mother and daughter have voluntarily decided to sacrifice their yearnings and remain at a distance, exchanging letters through a basket pulled up and down between the balcony and the courtyard, while Ponza visits his mother-in-law daily in her apartment.

The gossips are dissatisfied; after Signora Frola leaves they agree that Ponza must really be a cruel monster whose reputation the mother is protecting for the daughter's sake. Ponza appears and asks to be received; obviously upset, he confesses that his mother-in-law is insane. He states that her daughter's death four years ago drove her mad, so that she was institutionalized. Two years ago he married a second wife; and when the mother chanced to see them together, she conceived the delusion that her daughter was alive, but had been secreted away because Ponza had such a jealous passion for her. Thus the mother recovered from all her madness and despondency, and now appears totally sane—except for this single delusion, which keeps her resignedly happy. His second wife cooperates by appearing at the balcony and writing the letters, but he really cannot ask her to accept the actual embraces of his first wife's mother.

The group are reasonably satisfied and sympathetic when Ponza leaves, but then Signora Frola returns. Now that Ponza has spoken to them, she must confess that she had not told the entire sad truth before. According to her, the daughter had fallen seriously ill with a contagious disease and had been hospitalized for a long time. Ponza had suffered a nervous breakdown and had been put in a sanatorium; he was convinced that his beloved wife had died in the hospital, probably murdered. When she recovered and came to him, he refused to recognize her. Eventually, to get him to take her back, the girl pretended to be a second woman, and the family and officials cooperated in arranging a fake "second" marriage. Her daughter is now very happy, but of course Signora Frola is not supposed to be her mother, so they let Ponza keep his delusion by pretending that Signora Frola is the one with a delusion about a reincarnated daughter and get along as best they can.

"So you want the truth, eh?" laughs Laudisi. "The truth! . . . Hah! hah! hah!"

ACT TWO

Agazzi has instigated a police investigation of the earthquake-stricken village in hopes that public documents—of marriage, death, or hospitalization—

might confirm one story or the other. But all the public records were destroyed by the quake and the fire that followed. All but Laudisi have summed up the mystery as "either he is crazy, or she is." Agazzi and the Prefect, having spoken more to Ponza, believe that Signora Frola is the deluded one; the others have seen more of Signora Frola, and thus are fairly certain that Ponza is crazy. Laudisi heckles them all, suggesting that the various public documents, even if found, could be used to prove either case. He claims that each person is as right as he thinks he is, since different "truths" can exist simultaneously, and that even if "facts" could be determined, they would be less interesting than the minds of the people involved, which can be penetrated only through what they say.

Agazzi arranges with the others to bring Ponza and Signora Frola together by subterfuge, certain that in direct confrontation the truth should become obvious. Ponza hears the mother in another room playing on the piano a tune she says her daughter Lena "plays." He rushes at her, furious at her use of the present tense, and stormily forces her to admit that Lena plays no more, being dead, and that the woman he now lives with is named Julia. He accuses her of trying to ruin his reputation with these people, and she finally leaves in apparently penitent tears. He has been so emotional and uncontrollable, she so quiet and dignified, that opinion has been shifting to consider him the lunatic; but he now immediately becomes cool and composed, apologizing for having had to act out such a violent role in front of them, but explaining that it was necessary to keep Signora Frola in her happy delusion that he is the deluded one.

As he leaves, Laudisi laughs, "And there, ladies and gentlemen, you have the truth!"

ACT THREE

The police commissioner enters with the first evidence—gathered after great trouble in finding a few people who had actually lived in the now deserted village. Everyone is greatly excited until the report proves to contain nothing more conclusive than the vague recollection of an old man that "the Frola woman" was in an institution of some sort. Exactly which Frola woman, mother or daughter, is unclear.

Laudisi ingeniously suggests that the Prefect use his authority to interview the third person involved, the hitherto invisible young wife. The Prefect agrees, but at this point Ponza enters to announce his resignation, so that he won't have to endure any more invasions of his family's privacy. The Prefect, however, convinces Ponza that he absolutely believes in him and persuades him to bring his wife to be interviewed so that the others will also be convinced once and for all. As Ponza leaves, Signora Frola comes to beg them to call off the investigation, since they are so upsetting poor Ponza that she will have to leave town and never see her daughter at all, for fear of irritating him any further.

When Ponza and his veiled wife enter, the meeting of the three is emotional but ambiguous. Signora Ponza sends husband and mother out and tells the others that something in their lives "must remain concealed. Otherwise the remedy which our love for each other has found cannot avail." Still pressed for the "truth," she replies, "I am the daughter of Signora Frola, and I am the second wife of Signor Ponza . . . for myself, I am nobody." They insist that she must be one or the other, but she persists, "No, for myself I am . . . whoever you choose to have me."

She leaves them in a profound silence, finally broken by Laudisi's laugh, "You have the truth! But are you satisfied?"

LUIGI PIRANDELLO

Six Characters in Search of an Author

[*Sei personaggi in cerca d'autore,* 1921]

ACT ONE

The Manager and cast are preparing a rehearsal of a play by Pirandello when a strange family—a Father, a Mother in mourning, the elder Son, a Stepdaughter, and three children—interrupt them, looking for an author. The Father explains that they are characters but that the author who called them into being was unable to put them into a finished work of art; their play is still within them, and they are anxious to play it. The Stepdaughter offers to show her skill and does a little song and dance. The actors and actresses applaud, but the Manager silences her and asks the Father whether she is mad.

The Stepdaughter replies that when the moment in the drama comes, when God takes the little girl from the Mother, when the little boy commits his folly, then she will run away worse than mad. She winks horribly at the Father and says that because of what has happened between him and her, she cannot stay with the family; she cannot bear to watch her Mother's anguished love for the elder Son, the only legitimate child in the family, who despises his bastard half-brethren and his bastard-bearing Mother. The Mother implores the Manager, in the name of her two little children, to keep the Father from acting out the drama; she falls in a faint. The Father calls for a chair, and the actors excitedly ask whether she has really fainted or is only pretending.

The Manager, utterly confused, asks why the Mother wears mourning. The Father explains that his wife had a lover, who died and whom she mourns, and that her drama lies in the four children she had by two men. The Mother insists that she did not abandon her home and her Son through any fault or passion of her own. The Father admits that the fault was his. A clerk in his employ and his wife developed a strong sympathetic bond; though of course there was nothing evil between them, the bond so irritated the Father that he dismissed the clerk, whereupon his wife began wilting. At about the same time he sent his

Son to a wet nurse in the country, that he might grow up strong. The Mother interrupts to accuse him of having taken her Son away from her. The Father protests that all his life he has aspired to moral sanity; that—out of pity—he released his wife and sent her, well provided for, to live with the clerk. The Mother adds that, in freeing her, he also freed himself. He insists that he had the tenderest regard for his wife's new family, for her children by the clerk; the Stepdaughter tells how he used to watch her and follow her when she came out of school; she did not know who he was, but he would wave and smile at her and give her flowers. The Manager allows that this may be life, passion, or literature, but it will not act.

The Father explains that this part of the story is not to be staged; the drama begins when the clerk died, leaving his family in utter misery, and the Mother—too stupid to realize that her husband would gladly have assisted her and her illegitimate family—returned with her children and took a job with her daughter in the shop of Madame Pace. The Stepdaughter says that Madame Pace's dress shop was a false front for a house of assignation, but the Mother insists that she did not know this when she took the job. The Stepdaughter tells how, one day at the shop, a client came to her: her Stepfather. The Stepfather cries that the Mother interrupted them just in time; the Stepdaughter corrects him treacherously, "Almost in time."

The Father continues his story: he took the family to live with him at his house, and from this point the drama takes on tremendous interest: there is, for example, the elder Son's position. The Son exclaims that he does not want to be dragged into this. The Stepdaughter protests that she owes her present state to the Son, whose attitude of superiority and contempt forced her to take the very role he accused her of: that of his Father's mistress. The Son begs the Manager to let him out of this company. The Father chides the Son for his cold aloofness and insists that he is the hinge of the entire affair: It is the Son's attitude that made the little children feel that they were in a house of charity.

The Manager says that child actors are impossible and cannot be used. The Father replies that there is no problem, since the children die in the drama and the Stepdaughter flees; the remaining three find themselves living together as unhappy strangers. The Manager reflects that this could make a good drama and confesses that he is tempted. He gives the company a twenty-minute break and leaves with the characters. The actors speculate whether this is madness or a joke: what has the stage come to?

ACT TWO

Twenty minutes later, the Stepdaughter brings the little children back to the stage; seeing a revolver in the boy's pocket, she calls him an idiot and says that in his place she would have killed the Father and the Son, not herself. The Manager returns with the other characters and calls to the stagehands to set up a parlor, assuring the actors that they will not be called upon to improvise but will get their parts written out after having watched the rehearsal. The Father asks the Manager what he means by "rehearsal": since actors only interpret characters, and since in this case the real characters are present, why can't the characters be themselves? The Manager scoffs at the idea of characters acting and begins casting the parts. The Stepdaughter bursts out laughing upon seeing the woman who is to play her and objects that the scene is not right: there must be another prop, an envelope to hold the money her Father offered her.

The Manager calls for the scene to begin, but there is no Madame Pace. Over the actresses' objections the Father takes their hats and hangs them on pegs, explaining that Madame Pace will certainly be attracted by the articles of her trade. Madame Pace appears at the back of the stage. The Manager and actors are astonished, but the Father silences their protests of trickery: the reality of the theater, the characters of drama have a greater right to the stage than do actors and actresses, for they are truer.

The Stepdaughter wants to get on with the main business of the scene, but the Manager insists on the opening conversation between her and Madame Pace, who begins speaking in a ridiculous dialect. The actors laugh at her, but the Manager is delighted: the comic touch is perfect, it relieves the crudity of the situation. Madame Pace assures the Stepdaughter that the customer is not so very old, and that if she doesn't like him, he won't make any scandal. The Mother attempts to interrupt the scene, but the Father and Stepdaughter restrain her. Madame Pace refuses to continue with the Mother present and leaves in a fury. The others carry on without her.

The Father comes forward, says good day to the Stepdaughter, and asks whether he may remove her hat. She lifts it off. The Mother, her two little children clinging to her, covers her face and sobs. The Father comments that such a dear head deserves a prettier hat and offers to buy the girl one; she refuses, for—as her dress indicates—she is in mourning.

The Manager interrupts and tells the prompter not to take down what the father just said. He tells the actors to go through the same scene and invents a line for the Father. The Stepdaughter protests that the Father really said, "Lets take off this little frock." The Manager says that the line is impossible: it would cause a riot. The girl cries out that the Father is getting his remorses and torments acted, while her story is silenced; tomorrow the Manager may have the drama performed as he wishes, but if he would like to know what really happened at Madame Pace's, he must let the scene be played.

The Mother begs the Manager not to permit it. The Manager observes that, since it has already happened, it could make no difference. But the Mother replies that it is happening now, that her tortures are constantly renewed. The Manager says that the scene will form the nucleus of the first act, right up to the Mother's discovery of the couple. The Stepdaughter and Father enact the scene, the Stepdaughter laying her head on her Father's breast. The Mother comes forward to separate them, shrieking at the Father that the girl is her daughter. The Manager, pleased, steps backward and says that the curtain will fall at that moment. The stagehand, misunderstanding, lets the curtain fall.

ACT THREE

The stagehands have shifted the scenery and rigged up a drop representing trees and a portion of a fountain basin. The Manager attempts to begin the second act, begging characters and actors to leave everything to him, but the Stepdaughter tells him that the set is wrong: the Son must be shut up in his room and the little boy's part takes place indoors. The Manager protests that the scene cannot be changed three or four times in an act, though the actors remind him that in the old days scenery was frequently changed and that such changes greatly helped the illusion. The Father begs them not to use the word "illusion": for while the illusion of reality is the actors' game, illusion is the characters' only reality. He begs the actors and the Manager to picture the misfortune of such characters as himself and his family, born of an author's fantasy and still denied life by him. The Mother and the Stepdaughter describe the strategies by which they tried to induce the author to put them into a finished work—strategies all doomed to failure.

The Manager protests that drama is action, not philosophy, and begs the characters to hurry up and get to the scene. He explains that all the facts must be grouped into close-knit action: it is impossible to have the little brother wandering from room to room, contemplating the project that consumes him, while the little girl plays in the garden. He decides that the action will all take place in the garden and arranges the set, asking whether the little boy couldn't be given a few words to say. The Stepdaughter says that it is useless to try to get him to speak so long as the Son is present. The Son jumps up and says he will be delighted to go, and though he insists that when his mother came to his room to empty her heart to him, he simply walked away, the Manager states that a scene between the Mother and Son is indispensable.

The Mother says she is ready and begs for a chance to tell her Son what is in her heart; the Father, in a rage, orders the Son to do the scene. The Son refuses: he asks why his family must parade their shame and claims that he stands for the will of their author in refusing to put them on the stage. The Manager, furious, demands to know what happened after the Son walked away from his Mother.

The Son tells how he went walking in the garden and discovered the little girl in the fountain and the little boy standing, watching his drowned sister without moving. And then . . . . At that moment a revolver shot rings out from behind the trees where the boy is hidden. The Mother runs to the trees and calls for help. The Manager asks whether the boy is wounded: some of the actors cry that he is dead, others that it is only make-believe. The Father cries that it is not make-believe, but reality. The Manager says, "To hell with it all!" Never in his life has such a thing happened to him: he has lost a whole day on these people!

L U I G I   P I R A N D E L L O

Tonight We Improvise   [*Questa sera si recita*

a soggetto, 1930]

PROLOGUE

The audience has been sitting in the darkened auditorium for several minutes, and is becoming rather impatient for the play to begin; actors seated among the audience begin making joking comments. As a bell at last signals the start of the performance, Dr. Hinkfuss, the manager, bursts in through a door at the rear of the auditorium and runs angrily down the center aisle and up onto the stage. After a tart exchange with the people who were shouting comments, Hinkfuss delivers a long speech about the relation of the artist to his art. He then announces that this evening the actors are improvising a play set in a Sicilian village and calls on the actors to introduce themselves to the audience.

ACT ONE

The Leading Man, who is waiting behind the curtain, is unwilling to come on at Hinkfuss' call, but finally appears, made up as a Sicilian, Rico Verri, dressed in an air force uniform. He is angry over the way Hinkfuss is managing the performance; their argument is interrupted by the appearance of the Old Character Actor and the Character Woman, dressed for their parts as Signor Palmiro and Signora Ignazia, a married couple. Hinkfuss tells all his actors to remember the audience and to stop arguing. The Character Woman says she is now in her role and introduces her daughters Mommina, Totina, Dorina, and Nene; she then calls on the rest of the cast, five young flying officers. When the Leading Lady, playing Mommina, becomes difficult and starts arguing, Hinkfuss shoos them all off stage and tells the audience the play will begin in a few seconds.

The curtain rises on a village street scene; a religious procession, followed by villagers, passes down the center aisle of the auditorium to the stage and enters the church depicted on the set. As the sound of organ music fades, loud jazz music is heard, and the interior of a cheap cabaret is lighted up. The weak, henpecked Palmiro is sitting with other clients, watching a dance routine. One of the clients surreptitiously puts a pair of cardboard horns on Palmiro's head, and Palmiro, unaware of this, joins in the laughter directed at himself. The aging and half-crazy Chanteuse steps from the cabaret stage to defend Palmiro, who is ridiculously obsessed with the woman. Palmiro leaves the cabaret with some of the clients; as they stand in the street, his wife Ignazia appears with their four girls. Escorted by the flying officers, Ignazia and her daughters are on their way to an opera performance. They are horrified to see the head of the family wearing horns, and the officers challenge the cabaret clients, whom they accuse of mocking Palmiro. Finally Ignazia orders her husband home and leaves with the girls and the officers.

Hinkfuss, who has just sat down in the front row of the stalls, now gives stage directions, and the stage is set for the opera; the high-spirited girls, their mother, and their young escorts are noisily arriving late for the first act. Hinkfuss intervenes with more directions, then announces that the first act of the opera is over and that they can go out for drinks during the interval. The actors leave and Hinkfuss jumps onto the stage and tells the real audience that they too have an interlude and may either stay in the auditorium or go out into the lobby. During the interlude, the actors, in their parts, mix with the real audience in the lobby, while Hinkfuss directs stage operations for the benefit of the members of the audience who remain in the auditorium.

ACT TWO

During the real-life intermission, Nene and Totina and their two officer friends are mixing with the real audience in the lobby, the girls trying to persuade the men to take them for a flight. Dorina and her officer are strolling, the officer telling Dorina that her father is enamored of the singer at the cabaret. Rico Verri, the quick-tempered, hypersensitive Sicilian, is with Mommina; he is angry about the disturbance they caused when they arrived late for the opera; Ignazia, with the two remaining officers, is unfavorably comparing her dull life in Sicily with the gay life of the mainland cities, where they all come from.

Hinkfuss is meanwhile entertaining those of the real audience who have remained in the auditorium by staging a representation of an airfield under a starry sky. The curtain drops and the house lights go up as the audience returns from the lobby. Hinkfuss asks what happened in the lobby, and two people in the audience briefly explain for the benefit of those who stayed in the auditorium.

ACT THREE

The operagoers have returned to Ignazia's home after the opera; Ignazia is suffering from toothache, and Nene suggests that she say an Ave Maria, since Ignazia achieved a "miracle" cure that way once before. As Ignazia recites the prayer, Totina erupts into the room dressed up as an officer, followed by her officer friend Manzini, who wears a dressing gown belonging to Palmiro. To try to forget her pain, Ignazia orders them all to sing and dance; they dress up the protesting Mommina and begin singing the chorus from the beginning of the second act of *Il Trovatore*.

Verri, who has been to fetch medicine for Ignazia, returns and furiously stops the singing; he is frenzied with anger because his girl, Mommina, is dressed up like an actress. Nene, sent to fetch her father Palmiro to eject the raging Verri, excitedly returns with the news that Palmiro is not in. The officers prepare to go and search for him at the cabaret, but confusion ensues when the Leading Man steps out of his role, and an argument develops between the actors, some in role and some out.

Suddenly the Character Actor appears, hands clutching his bloodied stomach, and says he is waiting to die but can't come on because of the argument. Hinkfuss arranges everything and the actors recommence. Palmiro appears, helped by the Chanteuse and a cabaret client; Ignazia and the girls scream as they see he is bleeding. The client says Palmiro was stabbed as he tried to protect the Chanteuse from a drunk. The officer Sarelli goes for a doctor, and the others crowd round Palmiro, imploring him to speak and not just lie there smiling. Palmiro finally speaks, but he is out of role; he says he is grinning because the whole thing is ridiculous. The Character Actor works himself into a fury as he denounces the others for holding up the action of the play; he says he was supposed to die saying that his wife, daughters, and friends were wicked and that he was not the simpleton they all supposed—he was the only good one among them; the Character Actor slowly moves back into his role and chokes and dies. Hinkfuss rises, calling, "Splendid!" as the curtain falls. He tells the audience that Palmiro's death scene was not very good but will be better the next time; he chatters on about the development of the play and tells how Verri will ruin Mommina by marrying her.

Growing impatient, Hinkfuss shouts to the actors to hurry up for the next act. The cast come out, headed by the Character Woman, who is taking off her wig, and tell him they are quitting because they are sick of his ideas about theater and dislike his management; they want proper scripts, they say. Finally they throw Hinkfuss out and say they will continue the performance themselves. The Leading Lady and the Leading Man are going to act out the tragedy of Mommina and Verri; the actors grab make-up and begin aging the Leading Lady, who is then left alone.

Verri, now married to Mommina, is driving her crazy by constantly taunting her and jealously goading her; she is careworn and aged and living in a prisonlike atmosphere. As Verri torments his wife, their children, frightened by the shouting, run in to their mother. Outside the house, Ignazia and her daughters protest Verri's treatment of Mommina. Verri rushes from the house, screaming that he is going mad, and Mommina's family appear to her as in a dream and tell her to look in the pocket of Verri's coat. Mommina finds a theater program announcing that Totina, who has become a well-known singer, is playing the part of Leonora in *Il Trovatore* that evening. Not having seen her sisters for years, she is very excited; clutching her two children to her, she begins describing the opera; she grows more and more excited and finds herself struggling for breath. She starts singing one of the songs from the opera, then suddenly collapses and falls dead.

Ignazia and her daughters come to the house with Verri. Totina has tri-

umphed, and Verri has agreed to their seeing Mommina again. They are horrified to find Mommina lying dead, and as they stand in tableau, Dr. Hinkfuss
rushes down the auditorium aisle crying, "Splendid!" The Character Actor
comes on stage and tells the others that Hinkfuss has been working the lighting
effects.

Hinkfuss bows to the audience and the curtain falls.

E L M E R   R I C E

Street Scene [1929]

ACT ONE

Mrs. Fiorentino, leaning from a window on the ground floor of a run-down apartment house in New York, is discussing the hot weather with Mrs. Jones. Twelve-year-old Willie Maurrant skates in, yells up to his mother for a dime, which she throws out the window, and skates off. The women discuss Sankey, the man who comes to visit Mrs. Maurrant, until Mrs. Maurrant joins them on the stoop. Mr. Buchanan, unseen, chats with them out of a third-story window about his wife, who is about to have a baby. Mr. Maurrant comes home, angry to find that their daughter Rose is not yet home. He goes inside as Mr. Jones comes out.

Steve Sankey, the collector for the milk company, joins the company, trying to hide his interest in Mrs. Maurrant. After he leaves, Mrs. Maurrant leaves, supposedly to look for Willie. Knowing she has really gone to meet Sankey, the others discuss the scandalous situation. Old Miss Cushing, another tenant, rushes in to report that she just saw Mrs. Maurrant and Sankey together. The excited talk ceases as Maurrant comes out to look for his wife. Mrs. Jones tells him his wife has gone to look for Willie.

Mrs. Fiorentino's husband Filippo enters carrying, along with a violin, five ice cream cones, which he distributes. After he sits down, Miss Simpson, a social worker, comes to look for Mrs. Hildebrand, who, Mrs. Jones tells her, has taken her children to the movies. When Mrs. Hildebrand and her two children appear, Miss Simpson scolds them for wasting charity money; since Mr. Hildebrand has left them, they are to be dispossessed. Mr. Kaplan, who has been sitting at his ground-floor window, expresses his disgust at this sort of charity, and Mr. Fiorentino forces some coins on Mrs. Hildebrand, who is sternly led inside by Miss Simpson. As all make fun of Miss Simpson, Mrs. Maurrant returns and seats herself. After Miss Simpson emerges from the house and departs, Mr. Kaplan delivers a lecture to the others on communism, but they all assert that they want no revolution.

Young Samuel Kaplan walks slowly in, reading a book, and sits down. During a general discussion about music, Mr. Jones heads for the pool hall, and Mr. Fiorentino begins to dance gaily with Mrs. Maurrant. Sankey appears, and the dance ceases. After he has left, Maurrant asks his wife who Sankey is. Willie appears, his clothes torn and his face scratched, and confesses that he was fighting because of a remark another boy made to him. Maurrant sends Willie upstairs and goes off to a bar, and Mrs. Maurrant follows her son. Sam defends

Mrs. Maurrant against the cruel words of the neighbors, but they accuse him of being in love with the Maurrants' daughter.

As all the neighbors gradually disappear into the house, Rose Maurrant appears with Harry Easter, the manager of the office where she works. She tries to go inside quickly, but Easter detains her. When he tries to kiss her, she reminds him that he is married. He offers to get her an apartment and a job on the stage, but is interrupted by a cry from Mrs. Buchanan. At Maurrant's approach, Rose quickly sends Easter away. Meeting her on the steps, Maurrant asks her about Easter. Buchanan rushes out to call the doctor for his wife, who is about to give birth. Rose offers to telephone the doctor, and Maurrant follows Buchanan into the house.

Mae Jones and Dick McGann come in drunk, sit on the stoop, and drink from a flask. Mae agrees to go with him to his friend's empty apartment, and they stumble out. Rose returns and meets Mae's brother Vincent Jones, a taxi driver, who handles her roughly. Sam climbs out the window of the Kaplan apartment and orders Vincent to release Rose. Vincent easily pushes Sam to the ground and goes inside. Sam's fury subsides under the kind words of Rose, who expresses faith in his intelligence and his future. She asks whether the stories about her mother are true, explaining how her strict father stifles the joy and love that are part of her mother's nature. When Sam voices despair, Rose tries to comfort him, asking him to recite a poem to her. The doctor arrives, and Maurrant calls Rose to come inside. After Sam kisses her, she goes inside and in a few moments calls another good night to him from her window.

ACT TWO

At daybreak the next morning, Jones reels home from the speak-easy as the doctor emerges from the apartment house. Mae and Dick return and part company hostilely. As the neighborhood begins to awaken, Sam comes out and sits down to read. Rose appears at the window and promises to come down. When Sam's sister Shirley calls him to breakfast, he goes in. Buchanan emerges and spreads word of his new daughter to the Fiorentinos and the mailman.

Rose comes out onto the stoop. When Willie emerges on his way to school, Rose tries to improve his disheveled appearance, but he runs off. Mrs. Jones returns from walking her dog and meets Mrs. Maurrant, who has spent the night attending Mrs. Buchanan. After Mrs. Jones enters the house, Rose suggests to her mother that they move out of the city. Maurrant appears and inquires angrily of Mrs. Maurrant where she has been and where she is going, reacting suspiciously when she asks when he will return from the trip he is to make that day. After Mrs. Maurrant leaves, Rose defends her mother to her father, but he only reprimands Rose for her own behavior. When Rose suggests that they move out of the city, he curtly replies that he is content and leaves.

Mr. Kaplan emerges and inquires why Rose is sad. When the Hildebrand children, on their way to school, announce that they are to be dispossessed that day, Kaplan begins a communistic tirade. He leaves as Mrs. Maurrant returns to learn from Rose that Maurrant departed with a flask. Rose sympathizes when her mother explains that she has tried to be a good wife to her strict and unresponsive husband. Rose only suggests that Sankey not come around so often. As Mrs. Maurrant returns to the house, Shirley, who is a schoolteacher, emerges on her way to school. She asks Rose not to distract Sam from his work, for with Shirley's dedicated help he must study to become a lawyer. Shirley leaves when Sam appears at the window.

To counteract Sam's total despair, Rose tells him of things that she enjoys. When she mentions Easter's offer, which, she suggests, might enable her to improve her family's situation, Sam is horrified. Vincent Jones comes out, teases them both, and seizes Sam's hand in a painful grip. When Vincent leaves, Rose voices a despairing wish to escape. Sam suggests they go away together, but Rose does not want him to give up his studies. Easter appears, claiming to have had business in the neighborhood, and offers to accompany Rose to the funeral of their employer. Reluctantly, she leaves with him, and Sam jealously enters the house.

Mrs. Maurrant sits expectantly at her window. When Sankey appears, she tells him to come up. He goes into the house, passing Sam coming out. As Sam sits reading on the stoop, a city marshal and his assistant arrive to dispossess Mrs. Hildebrand and begin carrying out furniture. Suddenly Maurrant appears, looks up at the drawn shades of his apartment, and heads for the front door. Sam tries unsuccessfully to block his way, then shouts a warning to Mrs. Maurrant. Two shots are heard, and Sankey appears at the window. Maurrant is seen pulling him back, and another shot rings out. The marshal sends Sam to get an ambulance, as a crowd gathers. Maurrant emerges from the house, threatens the crowd with a revolver, and runs into the cellar. Policemen arrive, and Sam returns. After the ambulance arrives, a policeman reports that Sankey is dead. Suddenly Sam spies Rose and runs to her, urging her to go away, but she sees her mother being carried out on a stretcher. Mrs. Maurrant feebly recognizes Rose, who follows the stretcher out.

ACT THREE

That afternoon, two young nursemaids stop their carriages in front of the apartment house to discuss the murder they have read about in the paper. As a policeman sends them away, Easter appears, looking for Rose, and learns that Maurrant has not yet been caught. When Rose appears, she expresses the hope that her father got away, as he could not have been in his right mind. Easter offers his help, which she refuses. Shirley runs in and sympathetically embraces Rose, who politely sends Easter away. Shirley accompanies Rose upstairs.

Sam rushes in to ask whether Maurrant has been caught. Shots are heard, and heads peer out of the apartment house. Buchanan returns to say that Maurrant has been caught. When Maurrant himself, dirty and bloody, is brought in by the police, Rose rushes to him. He tells her sadly that he lost his senses when he shot his wife and her lover. She embraces him and remains with Sam as the police lead her father away, followed by the crowd.

When Rose announces that she plans to go away with her brother, now that her mother is dead, Sam begs to go with her so that they can build a better life together. Rose, however, foreseeing the problems they would face, refuses. She does not feel that they should belong to each other, as Sam desires, but that each should first belong to himself and that Sam should acquire faith in himself. Crushed, Sam goes into the house when Shirley comes out to say goodby to Rose. After Rose leaves, Kaplan settles down to read his newspaper, a couple stops to look at the apartment for rent, and several of the neighbor women resume their usual gossip.

ARMAND SALACROU

The Unknown of Arras

[*L'Inconnue d'Arras*, 1935]

ACT ONE

The thirty-five-year-old Ulysse has just shot himself after learning that his wife had been unfaithful to him. His servant Nicolas rushes into the street, calling for help, and his wife Yolande runs into the room. Nicolas cries that Ulysse killed himself because his wife was a bad woman who committed adultery with her husband's lifelong friend Maxime. As Yolande protests, Nicolas tells her to mind what she is saying—her husband's spirit might be listening. Yoland cries that her husband is moving, and Ulysse stands and declares he is feeling very well. Nicolas tells him that in the time between the revolver shot and his death he must watch his life pass before his eyes.

A cloud appears. It represents, Nicolas says, all the words used by Ulysse during his life. Another cloud of words appears—all the words Ulysse has heard in his life. Yolande is angry to learn that she never spoke the words "I love you," and angrier still when Ulysse says that he has had many mistresses, even during their marriage. Yolande says that in that case it was absurd of Ulysse to commit suicide over her affair; Ulysse replies that his memory is filled with many women in ridiculous postures and that he couldn't bear the thought that another man had a similar memory of his wife.

A noise is heard in the street, and Nicolas says that all the things and people from Ulysse's life are crowding to get in. Mother Venot, heading the crowd of memories, enters the room as Yolande leads Ulysse out. The people from Ulysse's past talk to one another. Among them are Yette, a girl who nearly died in a suicide attempt after an unhappy affair with Ulysse, and the Unknown, a girl who says she doesn't know her name. Yolande returns and is shocked to find herself among so many women from her husband's past. Two men arrive, Maxime-20, Ulysse's best friend, and a young man dressed in a soldier's uniform of 1870, who says he is Ulysse's revered grandfather, killed in the war at the age of twenty.

Ulysse enters with his father and greets his younger-looking grandfather with great emotion. Ulysse's father and grandfather are shocked and sad that Ulysse has committed suicide and ask why he killed himself when he was so young and happy. Ulysse promises to show them that he was right to kill himself and tells them to watch his life; he orders Nicolas to let his memories in.

ACT TWO

Mother Venot, Ulysse's old nurse, tells Yolande and Maxime-37 (the age of Maxime at the time Ulysse died) of the Ulysse she knew when he was a child. Alone, Yolande and Maxime-37 discuss the affair that led to Ulysse's suicide. Yolande says she no longer loves Maxime and never really loved him. Maxime-20 enters, furious with the older Maxime for having betrayed all his youthful ideals and for having become a paunchy bourgeois and a traitor to Ulysse. The younger Maxime recalls that he and Ulysse grew up together, swam nude together, and told each other of their love affairs; he speculates that the elder Maxime may have seduced Yolande simply because he was no longer Ulysse's confidant: it was a form of keyhole spying. Maxime-37 leaves, and Yette enters with Madeleine, Mother Venot, and the grandfather. Yette says she tried to commit suicide because she deeply loved Ulysse; she later married and had four children, but she doesn't love her husband and feels unattached to the children. The memories leave as Ulysse enters with Nicolas; Ulysse asks whether he can see again a person whose name he never knew, and the unknown woman comes in. Ulysse tells Nicolas of how they met at Arras during the war; the woman seemed confused, and, assuming her to be a prostitute, Ulysse led her to an abandoned house; the woman told him she was alone and hungry, that she had come to the village to search for her sister and found all the people evacuated. Ulysse went to buy food for her and returned intending to rape her, partly to discover whether she was the virgin she claimed to be. The girl was asleep when he got to the house, so he left the food with a note saying he would return the next day; although he kept his promise, he never saw the girl again. Ulysse asks the girl her name, but she says she doesn't know, she doesn't know anything.

The young and beautiful Madeleine enters and talks of her love affair with Ulysse: they were in love for two years and were very happy, but the affair ended when Madeleine began seeing a wealthier man and taking money from him. As Madeleine leaves to rejoin her rich lover, Ulysse sends Maxime-20 to bring her back; Maxime misunderstands the situation and returns with Yolande instead of Madeleine. Ulysse sends her away. Ulysse complains that no woman has ever loved him, not even his wife; but when Yette appears, he realizes that *she* really loved him. He says he wants to spend the rest of the time available to him with Yette, but Yolande bursts in clamoring for attention.

ACT THREE

The grandfather tells the father that Ulysse will fail to prove that his life was intolerable and that he was right to kill himself, but Nicolas tells them to wait—the unhappy part is coming. Ulysse enters with Yette, Madeleine, and the Unknown. Yolande angrily appears and says she wants to explain her letter to her lover, which Ulysse found. Ulysse says he has read the letter to the other women and asks why Yolande betrayed him. She replies she doesn't know.

Furious at not taking precedence in her husband's memory, she tells him she is in the memory of Maxime; Ulysse, raging, throws himself at her; she calls Maxime, who tells his friend he loves Yolande.

Ulysse is in agony until Madeleine reminds him that he suffered in the same way after his affair with her, then got over it; in the same way he will get over Yolande. But Ulysse says that there is no tomorrow for him. Nicolas brings in a table with the suicide revolver in the drawer. Ulysse asks Yolande why she began singing when he confronted her with her unfaithfulness. Yolande says she was afraid and wanted to throw herself in his arms and ask for forgiveness, but instead stupidly began singing.

Now the time has come for her to sing again—"Parlez-moi-d'amour . . . ," the signal for Ulysse to shoot himself.

Ulysse takes the revolver and fires. Nicolas shouts for help and Yolande arrives. Nicolas says Ulysse is dead and adds: "And to think my master has just killed himself for this woman!"

WILLIAM SAROYAN

My Heart's in the Highlands [1939]

The action takes place inside, and in front of, a broken-down house on San Benito Avenue and in Mr. Kosak's grocery store, in Fresno, California, in August and November, 1914.

Nine-year-old Johnny sits on the porch steps, listening to the sounds of the world, while inside the house his Father composes poetry aloud. An old man, Jasper MacGregor, plays "My Heart's in the Highlands" on a bugle, stops in front of the house, and asks whether Johnny could find a glass of water for a man whose heart is grieving in the Scottish Highlands. Johnny's Father comes angrily out of the house and tells Johnny to get the old man some water before he dies.

MacGregor accepts the Father's invitation to dinner, introduces himself as an actor, and empties the water pitcher in one swig. He asks for a little bread and cheese to keep body and spirit together. Johnny's Father tells Johnny to run to the grocer for bread and cheese. Johnny predicts that the grocer won't give them any more credit, but runs to the store.

In the grocery store, Mr. Kosak says that he cannot let Johnny have any more food on credit. Johnny asks how Mr. Kosak's family is and says that he only came to chat, adding that he needs a loaf of French bread and some cheese. Mr. Kosak tells him he must pay cash, and Johnny immediately asks how his daughter Esther is. Mr. Kosak says that Esther is fine and lets Johnny have the bread and cheese but tells him that this is his last credit. Johnny asks Mr. Kosak to tell Esther that he loves her.

After dinner, MacGregor plays "Drink to Me Only with Thine Eyes" on his bugle. Eighteen neighbors gather in front of the house and cheer. Johnny's Father introduces MacGregor as one of the greatest Shakespearean actors of the day. When a carpenter asks for another song, MacGregor asks him for an egg, then asks all the others to go home and return with a morsel of food. The people return with food, and Esther Kosak brings an eggplant. MacGregor plays "My Heart's in the Highlands." The people weep, kneel, sing the chorus, and go away. MacGregor asks Johnny's Father whether he can live with them. Johnny's Father says the house is his.

Eighteen days later, a young man knocks at the door and asks for Jasper MacGregor, the actor, who is needed to play King Lear in the annual show at the old folks' home. MacGregor bids his hosts goodby, saying that he has never communed with purer, loftier, or more delightful souls. After MacGregor's departure, Johnny's Father tells Johnny to go down to Kosak's for food. Johnny runs off to do his best.

316

One morning in November, Johnny sits on the steps before daybreak; there is a *for rent* sign on the house. A newsboy walks by, whistling. Johnny says hello to him; they talk; the newsboy tries to teach him to whistle and gives him a free paper with news of the war in Europe. The boys discuss money and food and what they want to do when they grow up. The newsboy is uncertain, but Johnny wants to be a poet like his Father. The newsboy leaves, whistling.

Johnny's Grandmother comes out to sweep, asking him in Armenian how his Father is. Johnny calls into the house, wakes his Father, and ascertains that he is fine. Johnny's Father comes onto the porch and says that he wrote great poetry yesterday and is sending it to the *Atlantic Monthly*. Johnny's Grandmother says that the old folks' home is a prison and furiously demands why MacGregor doesn't come back where he belongs. Johnny asks whether Mac-Gregor's heart is really in the Highlands and whether he will ever get home. His Father answers that MacGregor's heart is not really in the Highlands and that he'll get home when he dies. Johnny asks if that is the only way a man gets home, and his Father says it is.

Mr. Wiley, the mailman, arrives on his bicycle with a letter from New York. Johnny's Father opens the returned manuscript of his poems and inveighs against maniacs whose greatness is measured by their destructiveness. He tells them to fire their guns: they won't kill anything, for there will always be poets in the world.

Several hours later, the real estate man arrives with a man and wife who are looking for a place. Johnny's Father offers to leave the furniture to make up for the eighteen dollars' back rent he owes for three months. The man and woman are reluctant to take his furniture, but say they will be back in the afternoon or the next day.

Johnny brings a plate of grapes, and he and his Father eat together. Johnny asks whether it is stealing to have taken the grapes off the vines, and his Father says that it is not: stealing is unnecessary damage or cruelty to an innocent one. Johnny says that, in that case, he'll get some more grapes. He goes, and his Father reflects how lucky he is to have such a son.

Johnny's Father goes to Mr. Kosak's store and offers his poems in place of money to pay his debts. When Esther hears that Johnny's family is moving, she runs, in tears, from the store. Johnny's Father leaves the poems; the grocer takes out his glasses and reads them, first to himself, then aloud. His daughter returns tearfully, and he comforts her.

Johnny's Father is looking over a stack of manuscripts when Johnny bursts into the house with apples, figs, and pomegranates, and bolts the door behind him: he explains that a farmer's huge dog is chasing him. His Father goes to the window and sees a tiny dog, asleep, but jumps back when he hears someone coming. They push furniture against the door, and Johnny's Father says that he will take the blame for stealing the fruit. There is a knock, then a silence that is broken by a solo bugle playing "My Heart's in the Highlands."

Johnny and his Father open the door and welcome MacGregor and a little dog. MacGregor asks whether he may spend his last days with Johnny's family and begs them not to let him be taken back to the old folks' home. The carpenter knocks at the door, carrying bread, a sausage, and two eggs, which he brought when he heard the song. There is another knock, and a lineman appears with cheese, tomatoes, and radishes. MacGregor, saying that he is not long for the world, but would like to become a part of those who live after him, plays for the gathered crowd.

Esther Kosak steps out of the crowd and tells Johnny that her father read her the poems; she gives him the coins she has been saving up for Christmas and runs out of the house. MacGregor returns into the house and says that if they try to take him back to the old folks' home, he will play the death scene from *King Lear*.

The young man from the old folks' home arrives to take MacGregor away, but the old man does not answer when Johnny's Father calls him: he is dead. Johnny insists that he must be acting, but the guards from the home carry his body away. There is another knock, and the young couple, with their baby, arrive to claim the house.

Johnny and his Grandmother go with his Father into the street. Johnny asks where they are going, and his Father tells him simply to follow. Johnny says that he is not mentioning any names, but something is wrong somewhere.

JEAN-PAUL SARTRE

The Devil and the Good Lord

[*Le Diable et le Bon Dieu,* 1951]

ACT ONE

In a hall of his palace during the Peasants' Revolt period of the Renaissance, the archbishop of the German city of Worms anxiously awaits news of a battle outside the town. A servant tries to announce the banker Foucre, but is brusquely dismissed by the archbishop, who sees ruin and poverty ahead if the battle goes against him. The servant returns shouting, "Victory!" as he ushers in Colonel Linehart, who confirms that the enemy has been routed.

Lights reveal the right-hand side of the stage and the ramparts of the besieged city. Heinz, Schmidt, and Nasti, townspeople of Worms, discuss the new situation created by the archbishop's defeat of Conrad and realize that the archbishop's army can now join forces with the army of Goetz, who is besieging the town. They also learn that the town council is meeting, probably to discuss surrender terms. The lights dim on the ramparts as a man is sent to discover the council's decision.

In his palace, the archbishop is receiving the banker, who has come to warn the archbishop against sacking the town and thus robbing the banker of loan repayments and the archbishop of most of his taxes. The archbishop says he loves the town and would readily spare it; the trouble, he says, is Goetz. He explains that the brothers Goetz and Conrad invaded his territories but that he split them by promising Goetz his brother's lands if he would double-cross Conrad and join with the archbishop. Everything went well until the strong-willed Goetz decided to lay siege to the city, which had revolted, without seeking the archbishop's agreement; and, the archbishop confesses, he is now unable to get Goetz to obey him.

The ramparts are again revealed, and conversation between the archbishop and the banker on the one hand and the townspeople on the other shows that Goetz is an evil genius intent on razing the city and killing all the people and that the town council has decided to send a deputation to Goetz. Lights dim on the archbishop's palace; on the ramparts Nasti says he will slip out of Worms in the night and try to raise an army, but his companions object that it will take too long: the other citizens might open the city to Goetz that very night. Nasti says that they must compromise the citizens by a massacre and make them fear for their lives; then the city will never be opened.

A scene below the ramparts lights up: a woman in rags calls after a priest, Heinrich, beloved of the poor people because he lives as they do; for this reason

319

he is the only priest not to have been imprisoned by the townspeople. The woman asks Heinrich to explain why her little child died of hunger; Heinrich replies that he cannot explain: it was God's will. When the woman asks whether he understands, he says no; they must have faith and believe. The woman turns to Nasti, who has come down from the ramparts; he says that the child died because the rich burghers of Worms revolted against the archbishop and that when "the rich fight the rich, it is the poor who die." Nasti says it is man's wickedness that causes evil, not God's will. The priest is silent, but after the woman has gone, asserts that all is Good, and that he believes precisely "because it is absurd" to believe.

The whole stage lights up, showing citizens gathered around the bishop's palace, where the bishop is now imprisoned. They call for him to appear; finally he does so, dressed in full regalia, and tells the people that they are alone, abandoned by friends and by God. Heinrich appeals to him to encourage the people, not to discourage them. The bishop angrily tells him to keep quiet, reminding him that he owes everything to the Church; if the people persist in their rebellion, the bishop commands, Heinrich must stop giving them comfort and join his brother priests in imprisonment. The poor people remain standing as Heinrich and the rich burghers kneel before the bishop, who says he will go to Goetz and plead for their lives.

Nasti intervenes to tell the people that Goetz won't listen, for he has already betrayed his brother and is in league with the devil; furthermore, the bishop, the council, and the burghers are in a conspiracy against the poor. When Nasti says that the bishop has grain stored away in his palace, the men attack the doors, knocking Heinrich to the ground. Heinrich pleads for the life of the bishop, but as the doors give way, the bishop curses Heinrich as an apostate, and the men strike the bishop down. Nasti is satisfied that with this act the people won't dare surrender the city and says he will go to seek aid that night. The crowd, failing to find grain, rushes off to the monastery.

The dying bishop tries to prevent Heinrich from entering the palace, and Heinrich realizes that both the people and the Church consider him a traitor. The bishop, almost unable to speak, drops a key; Heinrich asks whether it fits the door in the crypt that is always locked, and is horrified to learn that the door leads to an underground passage running from the palace to outside the town. The bishop tells Heinrich that the lives of two hundred priests are in his hands, and Heinrich understands his terrible responsibility: he must either let the poor massacre the priests or let Goetz and his troops massacre the poor. The bishop dies. Taking the key, Heinrich says God has decreed that he should be a traitor and that God's will must be done.

On the outskirts of Goetz's camp, struck by cholera, officers discuss the epidemic; the men are dying and will soon revolt, they say. Hermann, another officer, enters and suggests that the brutal Goetz should be murdered to end the whole problem. Goetz comes in with his mistress Catherine: they bitterly goad each other and Goetz declares that what he likes in Catherine is the horror she feels for him. Goetz tells the officers that they are to attack Worms that night: a priest will show them the way into the city. Heinrich is brought in, but says he has decided against revealing the secret entrance, having seen the faces of Goetz's soldiers. A long conversation between the two men ends with Goetz convincing Heinrich that the priest is as evil as Goetz is; Heinrich hands over the key to the tunnel.

In Goetz's tent later, Catherine surprises Hermann as he tries to hide himself under the bed. They agree that Catherine will find out whether Goetz intends to keep her after the siege is ended; if not, she will give Hermann a signal, and he will stab Goetz. Goetz enters; his conversation with Catherine is interrupted by the appearance of the banker, come to plead for the town. Goetz tells him that by morning all the townspeople will be dead. The banker notes that the archbishop can give or confiscate the land of Goetz's dead brother Conrad; Goetz is unimpressed. The banker offers Goetz money if he will abandon his intention to destroy the city; Goetz refuses. Asked why he should want to raze the city, Goetz tells the banker: "Because everyone wants me to spare it." Goetz orders the banker to be taken away and bound hand and foot.

Catherine discusses her future with Goetz, who, beginning to suspect that she loves him, tells her she should go to a brothel. He orders her from his tent, and at this point Catherine gives the hidden Hermann the signal to kill Goetz; but as Hermann dives, dagger in hand, Catherine calls a warning, and Goetz disarms Hermann and has him led away. As Goetz plans to give Catherine to the soldiers, Nasti enters and strikes him. Nasti says that he surrendered because as he crossed the camp he heard that a traitor had betrayed the town; then he felt impelled to visit Goetz. Nasti tells Goetz that by destroying Worms he is helping established power, because disorder is its servant. He proposes a new alliance between the army of Goetz and the people; with the rich and the priests massacred, the whole country would march behind Goetz: they would raze palaces and cathedrals and begin building a society of equality and love.

Goetz replies that he loves the nobles and that his real fight is with God, the only enemy worthy of his talents. Catherine wittily suggests that before being put to death Nasti, the humanist, should confess and be given absolution. Heinrich is brought in, and an argument between the priest and Nasti develops, Nasti accusing the priest of being a traitor and Heinrich accusing Nasti of responsibility because Nasti killed the bishop. An officer enters and announces that all is ready for the assault on the town. Goetz orders Nasti and Heinrich to pass the night together; Nasti shall be under torture until he agrees to confess to the priest and then shall be hanged. Goetz also orders that the stableboys be assembled: they may do whatever they wish to Catherine, short of killing her. Goetz declares that God is working through him by sending the key to help the operation, but at the same time God declines responsibility for what is actually done with the key. Heinrich laughs that it is ludicrous that Goetz should believe that hell is like an empty desert waiting for Goetz alone: he is in fact just a soldier doing his duty, not the devil incarnate. Heinrich then declares that man can *only* do evil, since love and justice are impossible on earth; the world itself is iniquity.

Heinrich suddenly makes the decisive argument that if God were so to choose, He could forgive even Goetz and raise him to heaven, despite all the evil Goetz tries to do; further, Heinrich tells Goetz, everyone is doing evil. Goetz, contrary as ever, is delighted: in this case, Goetz will be the only one to do good. Goetz says that the dice will decide the issue: if he wins, he will do evil; if he loses, good. Catherine throws with Goetz and wins. Goetz gives his mistress money, telling her to go where she pleases; he tells an officer to send the soldiers back to their tents. He sends Nasti back to the town, telling him that the siege will be lifted at noon if the gates are opened and the priests allowed to leave; Heinrich is to judge whether Goetz does good, and will give his decision one year and one day later. As Goetz goes out Catherine begins laughing: "He cheated! I saw it! He cheated in order to lose!"

ACT TWO

Two months later in Goetz's property at Heidenstamm, formerly belonging to his dead brother Conrad, Goetz's servants mock the new Goetz who treats the peasants as equals. Karl, one of the servants, sends others away to the estates of Barons Nossak and Schulheim to stir up trouble among the peasants there by telling them that Goetz is giving his lands to his peasants. Nasti appears, summoned by Goetz, who arrives with three angry barons: Nossak, Schulheim, and Rietschel; they shout that by giving away his lands, Goetz will cause peasant revolts elsewhere. Goetz refuses to change his mind and turns the other cheek when struck by Schulheim; finally the barons go off disappointed. Goetz describes his plan to Nasti to give the peasants his estate and establish an egalitarian society at Heidenstamm. Nasti urges Goetz to abandon the plan, because the peasants are not yet ready: they need seven years to prepare their revolt; if it occurs now they will be suppressed within days. Goetz rejects Nasti's argument; as the instrument of God, he must do good—now.

Later, in one of Goetz's villages, Goetz tries to persuade a crowd of peasants to accept his gift of land, but as he talks to them, monks arrive selling indulgences. The peasants desert Goetz to buy their way into heaven. Goetz furiously challenges the monks; as one of them is saying that the Church loves everybody, a leper appears, and the people and monks draw back in horror. Goetz challenges the monk Tetzel to embrace the leper; Tetzel refuses with disgust, and Goetz moves forward to kiss the leper, who has been through this before and is angry that martyrs should seek their salvation by kissing lepers. Tetzel tells the leper to choose between an indulgence and a kiss; the leper selects the indulgence and goes away happily. The peasants cheer Tetzel for having given an indulgence *gratis pro Deo*. The monks and peasants go into a church, and Goetz laments his inability to communicate with the peasants. Heinrich appears and says that Catherine is in miserable circumstances, dying because Goetz deserted her.

Goetz goes off to find Catherine, and Heinrich and Nasti discuss the impending peasants' revolt. Heinrich says that it must be stopped to prevent a massacre and proposes a clever plan: the peasants stand in awe of the Church;

therefore, if provocateurs stage an apparent murder of a priest and later the priests leave their churches and assemble in Markstein castle, the peasants will be terrified of the lengths to which the revolt seems to be going and frightened because they no longer have church rites. Fear, Heinrich says, will stifle the revolt.

The peasants are huddling in the church two weeks later, the incipient revolt over; Nasti and Heinrich regard the crowd, Nasti both glad and unhappy that the revolt has not taken place. Goetz enters as they leave; he has just discovered that Catherine has all the time been in the church. He meets Hilda, daughter of the richest man in the village, who had been going to take the veil but then decided to live with and help the peasants. Hilda has just spent five days with Catherine, who finally died in torment. As she talks with Goetz, the supposedly dead Catherine is carried in, screaming that the devil is waiting for her and she cannot die without confessing. Heinrich is in disgrace with the Church and cannot give extreme unction; no other priest is present. Goetz sends everyone away and tells Catherine that he will save her soul by taking her sins on himself; praying, he asks God for a sign that Catherine's sins are now his. With no divine signal forthcoming and Catherine's cries growing more urgent, Goetz impetuously seizes a dagger from his belt and stabs his hands and side; he smears blood on the Christ above the altar, then calls the people back. Goetz claims that the Christ has bled and that God has allowed Goetz to carry the stigmata; Catherine dies in peace, and the peasants obey Goetz's order to return to their homes and rejoice that this day marks the start of Goetz's plans for building heaven on earth. "They are mine at last," Goetz weakly declares as the people leave the church.

ACT THREE

In a village, the peasants, now happy and with complete faith in Goetz, are learning to read and write; they also learn a catechism to the effect that their natures were evil before they knew Goetz and that they must learn a second nature by learning to love. They are interrupted by the appearance of Hilda, who disapproves of the new state of things, and by Karl, the former servant of Goetz who earlier tried to stir up trouble among the peasants; Karl is blindfolded and led by a girl. In an argument with the peasants, Karl declares that they have found happiness at the expense of their brothers, who are now trying to rise up against their overlords. If the peasants lose, Karl says, the barons will destroy the City of the Sun, as Goetz calls his new society; if the peasants win, they themselves will destroy the society, because Goetz's people refused to fight with them. Hilda agrees with Karl, because "all joy is obscene" until universal happiness is established. Goetz enters as Karl is unmasked and orders that he be given food and be sent on his way. Karl leaves, forecasting that "everything will end in a massacre."

Alone with Goetz, Hilda says she must leave, since there is nothing left for her to do: Goetz's peasants have found happiness but it is a "sheep-like happiness," she says. As Goetz pleads with her to stay and laments the fact that he cannnot love the people as she does, Nasti enters and announces that the revolt has broken out. It is all Goetz's fault, Nasti declares, because the peasants have been held back only by their fear of the Church, and now Goetz has proved that the peasants have no need of the priests. Nasti states that the peasants, who lack arms and discipline, will be massacred—unless they win one pitched battle against the barons, in which case the nobles will sue for peace; and Goetz is the only man who can lead the peasants. Goetz, appalled, objects that to take command of undisciplined peasants will mean hanging people to create discipline and wasting thousands of lives on the battlefield; he will have to become a butcher again. Goetz asks Hilda's advice; she replies that he must refuse, there must be no more bloodshed. Goetz decides that there is one chance: he has gained the confidence of the peasants, now he must use his credit and tell them that they stand no chance in revolting against the barons.

In a camp, Goetz tries to convince the peasants that they are bound to fail; they accuse him of being a traitor. As Goetz tells them that they are weak and untrained, a giant peasant steps forward; in a stick fight, Goetz uses tactics against brute force and fells the giant. Goetz then simulates a vision and tells the men that he sees them all marked for death; God is against the revolt. He shows the stigmata as proof of his powers of prophecy; but just as he has the men convinced, Karl steps forward. He performs juggling tricks, claiming to be as much a prophet as Goetz; claiming that God speaks through him, he declares that Goetz's proclaimed reason for giving away his lands is false; the peasants were unable to refuse the gift and, since they were poor, were unable to equal it; thus Goetz has further enslaved the people and further humiliated them. Seeing that he is losing the argument, Goetz appeals for help to Nasti, but Nasti astonishes him by deciding that Karl is right.

Goetz passes the night alone; at dawn he returns to his City of the Sun—to find it in ruins. All have been killed save Hilda, who tells him that the other peasants did it because Goetz's people refused to fight. Hilda says that she and Goetz are responsible; Goetz says they are not: "Man dreams he can act, but it is God who leads him." Goetz says he will spend the rest of his life in penitence, meditating on dissolution; he tries to send Hilda away, but she refuses.

Six months later Heinrich reaches the ruined village and finds Hilda; it is one year and a day since Worms. Heinrich, who is accompanied by the devil, seeks Goetz; but Hilda asks him to spare Goetz and tells Heinrich that he is not there. As Heinrich goes off to search the forest, Goetz enters, apparently exhausted; he carries a whip and a pitcher of water: it is three days since he drank and he must hold out another day before drinking. Hilda tells him he is being childish in setting himself tasks he cannot fulfill; Goetz pours the water on flowers, then falls. Hilda laughs, tells him he knows very well that she has reserves, fetches them, and makes Goetz drink. "Another defeat!" Goetz sighs. He goes on to torture himself further by exciting his desire of Hilda, then denying himself that pleasure—which Hilda, who has admitted her love for him, would give. Heinrich returns and tells Goetz that the peasants have just lost twenty-five thousand men in a battle; they blame Goetz for the defeat, which, they say, would not have happened if Goetz had led them; now they want to kill him.

Hilda fails to persuade Goetz to leave while there is still time; she withdraws at his command so that the two men can begin judging whether Goetz has won against Heinrich by doing good. Heinrich begins by showing that Goetz didn't really give away his lands—he only donated them; and the peasants didn't really receive them, since the barons are going to seize them. Goetz agrees but asks about the good intention. Heinrich says that it was all pretense: since Goetz couldn't enjoy his lands, he sought to exalt himself by pretending to abandon his wealth. Heinrich, with Goetz's enthusiastic approval, accuses him of giving only to destroy; Goetz is responsible for the thousands of dead peasants and always detested the poor. Goetz masochistically confesses he has tried to betray even evil but only achieved worse evil; he says that Heinrich has won his case. But Heinrich finds victory hollow; all men, he says, are unimportant to God; all the time Goetz has been pretending, giving himself orders, as is proved by the fact that he tricked the dice throw that sent him out to do good.

Goetz declares that "if God exists, man is nothing . . . ." Before he can finish, Heinrich begins running away, but Goetz cries out, "I'm going to tell you a colossal joke: God doesn't exist." Heinrich throws himself on Goetz, lashing him with blows; he prefers to be damned a thousand times rather than have God not exist, he says. There is no heaven, no hell, Goetz says, only mankind. At this Heinrich seizes Goetz in a stranglehold; in desperation Goetz draws a dagger and fatally stabs him. Goetz joyfully shouts for Hilda, declaring that God is dead. As he takes Hilda in his arms, peasants approach, and Goetz prepares to meet them.

In a peasants' camp later, Nasti tries to prevent a witch from making the men "invulnerable"; Karl intervenes, telling Nasti that the men are deserting in hundreds and better superstition than loss of men; as Nasti wearily agrees, Goetz and Hilda are brought in by armed men. Goetz admits he has been foolish to believe in pure love and good; good and evil are inseparable "on this earth at present." Goetz asks to be allowed to serve under Nasti, who refuses but says Goetz can take command. Goetz refuses this, saying he wants to be one of the men among the men; he has had enough of loneliness. The pleas of Nasti and Hilda fail to weaken him, but then the witch reappears with some peasants who say they will believe the potency of her magic only if Nasti lets himself be made "invulnerable." Nasti has to agree to the witch touching himself and Goetz, who is shocked. A soldier announces that the captains want to speak to Nasti, who tells Goetz they have come to say they have no more authority over the men. Seeing Nasti's suffering, Goetz declares that if Nasti suffers, "the last candle goes out; darkness will fall." Goetz promises to take command.

The captains enter, and Nasti tells them that Goetz is taking command. In the general amazement one captain says that Goetz is a traitor and is probably leading them into a trap. Goetz asks him whether he will obey orders; the man replies, "I'd rather die." Goetz then stabs him: "Then die, brother!" Goetz issues concise orders, starting with the command that a man trying to desert will be hanged. They can be sure of victory, Goetz tells them, when the men are more afraid of him than of the enemy.

The captains go out; and Goetz, in a moment of weakness, turns to Nasti, saying, "I told you I would be a hangman and butcher." But the play ends with Goetz vowing to make the men hate him, because he knows no other way of loving them: "There is this war to fight, and I will fight it."

JEAN-PAUL SARTRE

Dirty Hands [*Les Mains sales*, 1948]

ACT ONE

In a little cottage in the small mid-European country of Illyria, early in 1945, Olga suspiciously admits Hugo Barine, unexpectedly released after serving two years of a prison term to which he was sentenced when, in a fit of jealousy over his wife Jessica, he murdered another man. Since Olga and Hugo were once intimate friends, as well as comrades in the Proletarian Party, she lets him hide in the bedroom when two Party gunmen come looking for him. She demands to speak to their leader, Louis, who contends that Hugo is an "undisciplined anarchistic individualist," and a dangerous chatterbox who knows too much. Olga pleads that he is a desperate man who may still be fit for good use by the Party. Louis finally agrees to let Olga examine Hugo's motives and state of mind for three hours. She will then let Louis know whether he is "salvageable" and ready for another assignment or "unsalvageable," in which case she will allow the gunmen to shoot him.

When the others leave, Hugo begins to tell his story . . . .

ACT TWO

In Olga's place in 1943, twenty-one-year-old Hugo frets that he has been given no more active and dangerous an assignment than working on the Party newspaper. Olga forces him to admit that he has no aptitude for direct action, being the physically delicate son of an upper-class family, an intellectual whose college degree is of no use in sabotaging railroad tracks. He is all the more eager, however, to prove his renunciation of his family and class, the oppressors of society. Louis returns from a conference in which the vote favored Hoederer, leader of the opposing Party faction. Olga and Hugo take Louis' word that Hoederer's intention to compromise with the fascist government of the regent and the bourgeois party of the Pentagon is "objectively" treasonable to the aims of the Party, even if it might help Illyria's present defense needs.

Olga persuades Louis to give the boy his big chance: since Hoederer has asked the Party for a married male secretary at his isolated country place, Hugo can take the position and find an opportunity to kill him.

ACT THREE

Hugo returns to his quarters after his first interview with Hoederer to find his wife Jessica unpacking. She teases him with her discovery that his suitcase contains a revolver and twelve pictures of himself at various stages of childhood. He tries to impress her by revealing his resolve to shoot Hoederer, but she refuses to take him seriously. They have spent most of their marriage in "playing," and now, when they try, neither can say "I love you" convincingly, nor can Hugo believe that Jessica believes he really intends to kill, and his belief in himself is shaken.

Two of Hoederer's three tough bodyguards enter "to help unpack," and reveal a malicious contempt for Hugo's aristocratic mien and intellectual background. Hugo refuses to let them search his belongings, and they finally call their employer. Hoederer diplomatically convinces the toughs that it's unfair to hold Hugo's upbringing against him, since he has committed himself to the cause of the common people. He then convinces Hugo that the room must be searched. Finding no weapons, the toughs leave. Hoederer finds the pictures in the suitcase and amusedly asks why Hugo lugs his past around with him if, as he claims, he is in the Party to forget himself.

When Hoederer leaves, Jessica withdraws the revolver from inside her dress and falls to teasing Hugo again.

ACT FOUR

Over a week later, Jessica finds Hugo alone in Hoederer's office and makes him accept the gun she teasingly says he "forgot" to bring. She asks why she caught him brooding over the coffee pot, and Hugo confesses that he's fascinated at the way everything Hoederer touches seems so "real," while he feels himself living "in a stage set." Hoederer enters, evicts Jessica, and chats sympathetically with Hugo, offering to help him outgrow the youthful sensitivities he finds so awkward.

Visitors arrive: Prince Paul, the regent's son, and Karsky, secretary of the Pentagon. Their parties are both stronger than the Proletarian Party, and they offer a union disadvantageous to the latter. Hoederer counters with a proposition sharply reducing their power. Karsky tries to walk out, but the Prince convinces him that they simply must come to terms with Hoederer, since his party alone has maintained friendly contact with the advancing Soviet armies. Just as they are about to come to an agreement, Hugo, unable to control himself, bursts out in angry protest, his hand on the gun in his pocket. A bomb explodes outside the window.

Shattered glass injures Karsky, and the three negotiators go upstairs to talk while he is being bandaged. Jessica comes in, and Hugo begins drinking. He is so furious with Louis for sending the bomb-thrower instead of trusting him to complete his assignment that he all but gives himself away to the bodyguards before passing out drunk.

ACT FIVE

Olga slips into the room where Jessica is tending to Hugo; she explains that she threw the bomb on her own in hopes of saving Hugo's reputation. Since it missed, Hugo must finish the job before tomorrow night, for the Party is impatient. When she leaves, Hugo tries unsuccessfully to convince Jessica that it is right to kill Hoederer, for she keeps voicing his own growing secret conviction that Hoederer is sincerely and plausibly working for the good of the Party.

When Hoederer enters, Jessica challenges the two men to debate. Hugo argues that the Party's ideals will be debased by lying compromise with its enemies. Hoederer claims that the Party needs power to realize its ideals, and that all means are good that help acquire that power. He sneers that idealists like Hugo are afraid to get their hands dirty in the work of building the new society. Hugo retorts that he isn't afraid of blood. Hoederer counters that "red gloves" seem elegant and pure, but "dirty hands" do not; Hugo might make an assassin, a destroyer, but never a true revolutionary.

Jessica has previously suggested that if Hugo had met Hoederer before Louis, he would have been on Hoederer's side, but Hugo, unable to question his total faith in Louis, now says Hoederer's very persuasiveness is a reason for silencing him.

ACT SIX

The next day Jessica finds Hoederer making coffee in his office. She explains that Hugo will try to kill him but that he doesn't really want to, and asks Hoederer simply to have him disarmed.

When Hugo enters, she hides behind the curtains. Hoederer talks paternally to him, again offering help. He indirectly dares Hugo to shoot him, then casually turns his back to pour coffee. Hugo struggles, but cannot shoot; he lets Hoederer give him coffee and take away his gun, then goes off miserably to think things over. Jessica comes out from behind the curtains and states that for the first time she has found a man she can admire seriously. She entices him to kiss her; unlike Hugo's touch, Hoederer's embrace doesn't make her "feel like laughing."

Hugo enters and catches them. He says he isn't jealous of Jessica, since their love had only been a game, but is furious that Hoederer had fooled him with his sympathetic offers of help when the only one he really cared for was Jessica. Seizing the gun from the table, he shoots Hoederer, and the dying man lies to the entering bodyguards, "I've been sleeping with his wife."

. . . And so, Hugo tells Olga now, he does not believe he shot Hoederer either over politics or over Jessica. Perhaps he was jealous of Hoederer's regard, for he loved the man he killed. Olga merely says it's a good thing he is not proud of his crime, for now he can return to work for the Party again. Just recently the Party has switched over to Hoederer's policies, finding them now expedient. Hoederer will have a statue in his honor, and the Party is deliberately forgetting that it was concerned in his death.

Hugo laughs hysterically that Olga, who had taught him idealistic purity, is echoing Hoederer's words about expediency. Hoederer's death now has no public significance, just as the act of killing had no private meaning for him. But he, still idealistic, cannot bear for the man he loved to have died for nothing through an insignificant accident. To justify Hoederer's death, Hugo will now claim his crime properly. When the gunmen return for Olga's decision, Hugo rushes toward them crying, "Not salvageable!"

JEAN-PAUL SARTRE

No Exit [*Huis-clos,* 1944]

The valet ushers Garcin into a drawing room furnished in Second Empire style. Puzzled, Garcin asks the valet about the absence of instruments of torture—racks, red-hot pincers, etc. The amused valet responds that this place has been totally misrepresented by the people "down there." Garcin notices the absence of windows, mirrors, breakable objects—and beds. One never sleeps here, he learns: the eyelids are paralyzed, and the electric light can never be turned off. No blinking, no dreaming, no refreshing little respites of darkness in this "life without a break" that appears to be his eternal future. There is a call-bell, which seems to work, but the valet warns him it is "capricious" and leaves. Garcin immediately tries the door, which remains locked, and the call-bell, which remains silent.

The valet returns with Inez, then leaves again. Inez mistakes Garcin for "the torturer"; Garcin introduces himself and suggests that as they seem to be locked in together, they "should make a point of being extremely courteous to each other" so as to make the best of the situation. "I'm not polite," replies Inez, and soon reproaches him for impolitely allowing his mouth to twitch with unconscious fear. He buries his face in his hands just before the valet ushers in Estelle, who cries out, "No! Don't look up . . . . I know you've no face left." When he exposes his face, she is surprised that she doesn't know him, and asks the valet if anyone else is coming. He replies in the negative and leaves for the last time.

Estelle says she became an "absentee"—she considers the word "dead" in terribly bad taste—through pneumonia; even now she can watch her own funeral in progress and can see her "bosom friend" Olga trying unsuccessfully to cry. Garcin is an absentee from Rio; he can see his wife: in her big, tragic eyes is the martyred look that always got on his nerves. The heat in the drawing room makes him start to take off his jacket, but he refrains when Estelle says she loathes men in their shirtsleeves. Asked for an opinion, Inez remarks that she doesn't "care much for men any way."

They begin to wonder why the three of them, strangers, have been put together, and Inez derides any suggestion that it was either chance or a mistake on the part of some underling. She suggests that if each had the guts to tell why he is here, they might begin to interpret their situation. Estelle explains, too glibly, that her only "sin" was to marry a rich man three times her age whom she did not love, because she was a poor orphan with a brother in need of medical attention. After six years of marriage she fell in love with a young man but refused to run away with him, then was finished off by pneumonia. Garcin assures her she had not sinned and says that he likewise had only committed the "crime" of standing by his principles. He had run a pacifist newspaper; and when the war broke out, he refused to enlist, so they shot him.

Inez caustically chides them for play-acting, saying, "They never make mistakes, and people aren't damned for nothing . . . . There have been people who burned their lives out for our sakes—and we chuckled over it. So now we have to pay the reckoning." Garcin angrily tells her to shut up, but she now understands why there is no official torturer with them: the authorities have arranged it so that each of them will act as torturer of the other two. Garcin says he has no wish to hurt them and suggests they foil the plot by each staying silent and alone on his own sofa.

Estelle applies make-up to her face, then can't resist asking for a mirror: "When I can't see myself I begin to wonder if I really and truly exist." Garcin won't answer, but Inez does. In the absence of any glass, she offers to be a mirror, guiding Estelle in adjusting her lipstick, and proves Estelle to be at her mercy by giving her conflicting reports of her appearance. Inez says she wants to be great friends with Estelle and to exclude the unsociable Garcin, but Estelle is obviously trying to flirt with him because he is a man. Inez becomes contemptuous of Estelle and furiously resentful of Garcin for "winning" the girl just because he is male.

Garcin has been trying to hear what his journalist friends "down there" are saying about him, but the women's chatter interferes. He returns to the notion that they should bare their souls to each other—but for real, this time. He confesses that his pacifist "desertion" is a side issue; the real reason he's here is that he miserably mistreated his wife. She was a "born martyr . . . a victim by vocation," and never reproached him, which irritated him to grosser and grosser insults, even to making her bring breakfast to him and his mistress in bed.

Inez confesses that she had always been a "damned bitch," so cruel that she "can't get on without making people suffer . . . . A live coal in others' hearts. When I'm alone I flicker out." She had been living with her cousin and his wife Florence. Gradually sickening of the man, she crept into Florence's soul and made her hate him too, until the two of them left and took an apartment of their own. When the man was run over by a tram, she kept reminding Florence that "we killed him between us"—until one night Florence turned on the gas stove and killed them both.

Estelle is forced to admit that she did take Roger as her lover after all. But he wanted to have a baby by her, although she didn't want it, and they had to go to Switzerland for its birth—still managing to keep her husband ignorant. She dropped the infant, weighted with a stone, into the lake. Roger saw her and blew his brains out.

Now that they are spiritually nude, Garcin suggests they begin helping each other, but Inez says she is incapable of it. Estelle watches a scene "down there": her friend Olga destroys the young man Peter's illusions that Estelle had been as pure and transparent as a "glancing stream." As the tender memory of her dies in him, she desperately begins to seduce Garcin, since she *must* have someone watching her or thinking of her, responding to her, to assure herself of her own existence. Despite Inez' protests that she will always be watching them, Garcin decides to accommodate Estelle, chiefly to distract himself from the scenes "down there" where his journalist friends are deriding him as a coward. But the scenes and the question of his guilt distract him from his lovemaking. He confesses to the women that he didn't exactly stand up to the authorities, but was caught after he boarded a train for Mexico. His motive for saving his skin was ostensibly to carry on his work by starting another pacifist newspaper, but he's never been able fully to decide whether or not he was primarily afraid to die. Now he feels that his only hope for salvation is through the trust and love of someone else. If Estelle could believe that he wasn't a coward, then he would be brave and decent in his own eyes. She tries to answer as he wishes, but Inez proves that all Estelle cares about is getting a man's arm around her waist, and he repulses the girl as being "soft and slimy . . . like a quagmire." He bangs at the door, pleading to be let out and given any amount of physical torture instead of this agony of mind.

Suddenly the door flies open, but Garcin is suspicious as to why it opened, and will not go out. Neither will Estelle. "It's a scream!" laughs Inez. "We're —inseparables!" Estelle reacts by trying to push Inez out. Garcin unexpectedly helps Inez to remain within and declares that he is staying because of Inez; it is she, not Estelle, who knows what wickedness and shame and fear are, and thus can understand him. He cannot be saved until he destroys the thought in her mind that he is a coward; and since he cannot force her, but must convince her, he is at her mercy. He pleads that he died too soon to complete the deeds that would prove him a heroic man; she retorts that dreams do not count in the summing up of a life, that a life is always complete at the moment of death.

Estelle suggests that he can revenge himself on Inez for her cruelty simply by kissing Estelle—"then you'll hear her squeal." Garcin bends over Estelle, and Inez squeals indeed, but recovers her powers of cruelty and constantly reminds him that *she* is the one he must convince. Garcin finally gives up Estelle and returns obediently to Inez, fully comprehending at last that "there's no need for red-hot pokers. Hell is—other people!" Frustrated, Estelle tries to stab Inez with a convenient paper knife, and they all laugh hysterically at its impotence, for they are already dead and obviously together forever, and ever, and ever.

GEORGES SCHÉHADÉ

Vasco   [*Histoire de Vasco*, 1956]

Prologue. Cavalry lieutenant Septembre, on duty during a war in the middle of the last century, has just arrived in a forest clearing, breathless after pushing through the underbrush. Pausing to catch his breath, he sees rows of crows in the trees and draws his pistol and fires. A bird falls dead; the others do not move. César, a merchant, pokes his head out of the tarpaulin covering his home, an old cart, and emerges. Septembre tells him he is searching for the house of Vasco. They are joined by the beautiful daughter of César, Marguerite, who also lives in the cart. César declares himself a philosopher and indicates that the crows are in fact monks; his fantastic talk annoys Septembre, who moves off, then returns at Marguerite's call. She tells Septembre that Vasco probably lives in the village beyond the river; for a while the two stand close, and it seems that they are going to kiss, but they part, and Septembre leaves.

Marguerite, back in the cart, tells her father she is dreaming she is in a church; as she recounts the dream, Septembre returns and listens with César. Marguerite says she sees herself united with a young hairdresser whose scissors become flames. She then falls into a deep sleep. César brings out a strange collection of stuffed dogs, which he tries to sell to the lieutenant. The sky reddens as a distant village burns in a battle; César goes to his cart and sleeps, leaving Septembre in the darkness.

Scene 1. Two old peasants appear in a village square carrying pails; gay music is heard, and the old men perform a shaky, hopping dance as they approach the well. They draw water and go off. Emerita, sister of Vasco, comes from a house marked "Vasco, Hairdresser," but scampers back when Mother Hilboom appears, wandering toward the well calling, "Jerome!" The two peasants return and tell Mother Hilboom for the hundredth time that all the boys have gone off to the war. The first peasant pats her shoulder gently, and she moves off. Talking together, the two peasants note that the village has been drained of all its young men except one, Vasco, who, they say, is too scared to fight. Emerita reappears, and the old men hurry off; left alone, she calls up to Vasco's room that she is so ashamed of him for not going to the war that she intends to enter a convent and take the veil.

When she goes, Vasco sighs with relief behind his window, then begins a pantomime of lovingly trimming the hair of an imaginary client. The two peasants return and watch him. Mayor Corfan comes into the square with Septembre and shoos off the peasants. Septembre calls to Vasco that he carries a message from General Mirador. Vasco remains hidden despite all Septembre's blandishments and reveals himself only after Corfan has said that the message

333

concerns hairdressing. Septembre reads the order to the young, slim, and charming Vasco, who is trembling with nervousness: Septembre has been ordered to come to the village of Sosso, find Vasco, and enroll him for a secret assignment. Vasco seems uninterested until the mayor says he has been chosen to dress the most beautiful head of hair in the country, that of Armando the Third. Septembre, furious with the mayor, tells him he is contemptible, but Vasco is delighted and agrees to go.

The lieutenant leaves, innocently followed by Vasco; the two peasants return and sadly watch him go. César and Marguerite come into the square; they are chicken-rustling but so far haven't managed to steal a bird. They see Vasco's sign and, encountering the peasants, ask for Vasco. The old men say he has just left, and when they go on to describe Vasco, Marguerite recognizes him as the figure in her dream. Mother Hilboom enters and draws water; she utters a cry as she looks into her pail and says she has seen a face, a sword, and scissors. César says he also saw the face—Marguerite's. Emerita appears and is overjoyed to learn that her brother has gone off with an army lieutenant. A chorus of five widows enter, singing sadly of their lost husbands and brothers.

Scene 2. Septembre is shown into General Mirador's office at his camp and tells the aristocratic general in cold hard terms that Vasco is ready for his mission. Vasco thinks, Septembre adds, that he is off to dress the hair of Armando the Third and that en route he will deliver a letter to a Mr. Bertrand, who is trout fishing. Mirador laughs, then perceives Septembre's pent-up indignation and explains gently that war is a rough game and that he has been forced to send the simple-minded barber on the deadly mission behind the enemy lines because Vasco has one big advantage: his timidity and fear. Vasco will succeed where military heroes would fail. Septembre insists, however, that Vasco is being sent to his death.

César and Marguerite appear and say they are looking for the girl's fiancé, Vasco. Mirador says Vasco is a "great military figure" and tells them to go home and wait for his return.

Scene 3. Vasco has reached a hut on a small hill in the country, post number one; three soldiers—Major Brounst and lieutenants Latour and Hans—have hidden at his approach and come forth when he blows his pass whistle; the men are very clumsily dressed as women. Brounst, who wears a big black mustache, introduces the group as field intelligence officers, and they code-name Vasco Joachin the Idiot, mistaking his naive and simple-minded talk for perfected intelligence technique. Brounst and Latour go off to reconnoiter Vasco's route, which will take him to "Mr." Bertrand; while they are away, Vasco trims Hans's wig. Brounst and Latour return and tell Vasco his road is clear but behind his back make gestures to Hans that the position is terrible, hopeless.

Just as Vasco is about to set off, people are heard approaching; all hide. César and Marguerite appear and fall just short of getting killed when César, despite desperate efforts, fails to sound his pass whistle: he is blowing the wrong end. They hand Brounst a letter from one of General Mirador's captains stating they are on a mission to find Marguerite's fiancé. From the confused description given of the fiancé, the soldiers say he must be a new recruit and at a training camp ten leagues away. The men take César off to eat apples and drink wine, and Vasco comes out of hiding and talks to Marguerite, each unaware that Vasco is the man Marguerite is looking for. The men return and Vasco sets out. After he has gone, Marguerite notices a pair of scissors that he dropped and realizes that he is the man of her dreams; she calls after him and tries to follow him, but the others restrain her.

Scene 4. Vasco, walking across a plain, stops by some bushes to eat an apple; an enemy soldier takes aim at him from behind the bushes, then ducks, waiting for an explosion, as Vasco throws the bad apple into the bushes. The hairdresser escapes death a second time when the soldier stands transfixed while he takes out a second pair of scissors and rapidly transforms a ragged bush into a beautifully curled and pompadoured piece of coiffure. Vasco accidentally hypnotizes a soldier who is creeping up on him when he takes out his mirror to inspect his face, and the reflected sunlight puts the soldier into a trance.

In another part of the plain, Vasco is shadowed by enemy sergeants Paraz, Alexander, and Caquot, disguised as trees. He mentions "Mr." Bertrand as he talks to himself, and the trees correct him: "*General* Bertrand!" The sergeants finally reveal themselves to the bewildered Vasco. Caquot goes off to report the capture of a spy, returns, and takes Vasco away for interrogation by Lieutenant Barberis.

Under questioning Vasco gives his name as Joachin the Idiot; his innocently confused replies exasperate the lieutenant, who threatens to beat information out of him, and at this Vasco gives a detailed description of the three "women" he met at post one and describes his meeting with Marguerite, mentioning that she was searching for her fiancé. This greatly interests Barberis; pressed for details, Vasco, using Marguerite's idealized description of her dream man, says the fiancé is a terror, a man to be feared, whose movements are unknown to anyone else. Barberis reveals for the first time the name of the spy he seeks: Vasco the hairdresser. Vasco almost dies of surprise and sudden fear. Barberis has a whispered conversation with Caquot, then goes out; Caquot brings out wine and tries to make Vasco drunk so that he will give more information.

During the talk, Vasco becomes ecstatically aware that *he* is the man being sought by Marguerite. Having fallen in love with her at their meeting, he begins to wonder how he can measure up to the bravery of the man she visualizes. Caquot tells Vasco that they need as much information as they can get; Vasco cleverly finds out the sort of information wanted and learns that Septembre has been made a colonel. When Barberis returns, Vasco says he is ready to divulge everything; Barberis leaves, warning that if his information is not accurate and true, Vasco will be riddled with bullets and his body sent to post one. While waiting for a committee of enemy officers to arrive, Vasco fluctuates between panic and false bravery induced by frequent gulps of wine; his agitation changes to resolute calm as he decides what he is going to say: his false information will help Septembre win, and Marguerite will know that it is thanks to Vasco. The colonels come in, and Vasco gives his statement.

Epilogue. In the forest clearing of the Prologue, Marguerite kneels beside a body shrouded in a white cloth; César watches, and the crows are lined up in the trees. Two soldiers appear and tell César they belong to Colonel Septembre's regiment and are on their way to order a victory parade in Sosso; their victory, they say, was thanks to Vasco. The crows croak mournfully; César sends the soldiers on their way and tries to comfort Marguerite. A drum major appears with his assistant and tells César they are off to play a victory march called "A Hymn to a Hero—The Barber of Sosso."

Septembre appears, and César asks him whether he is looking for the house of Vasco. Septembre tells César to go with Marguerite and wait for him in Sosso while he stays with the body of Vasco. César and the girl move slowly off; Septembre calls after them fiercely, bitterly: "Don't forget, César and Marguerite! The victory parade at Sosso!" Marguerite looks round as though awaking from sleep; they regard each other, and Septembre repeats: "Victory Marguerite . . . victory at Sosso." Marguerite turns and goes off with her father.

GEORGE BERNARD SHAW

Back to Methuselah [1922]

A Metabiological Pentateuch

PART I. IN THE BEGINNING

ACT ONE

In the garden of Eden in the year 4004 B.C., Adam and Eve discover a fawn with its neck broken and realize the fact of death. Though there is theoretically no limit to their lives, they recognize that sooner or later they will trip and fall and become dead like the fawn. Adam despairs at the knowledge that they— and therefore their kind—shall cease to be, though almost simultaneously he complains of the horror of living forever. He carries the body of the fawn away, and the serpent, who has been lying unseen on a bed of Johns-wort, raises her head and speaks to Eve. The serpent, who is very wise, says that it is she who whispered the word "death" to Eve and tells her that death can be conquered through birth. She says that she remembers Lilith, who came before Adam and Eve and who, when she discovered death, willed to renew herself; her pangs were terrible, and finding them too much to be borne by one, she created two new beings, Adam and Eve, to share the labor. Adam returns, and Eve tells him that they need not live forever, since they can make new Adams and Eves to replace themselves. Adam vows to live a thousand years and no longer, and he and Eve promise to love one another until death, thus binding the future by their vows and eliminating what Adam feels is the dreadful uncertainty that life has now taken on. He leaves, and the serpent whispers to Eve the secret of birth.

ACT TWO

A few centuries later in an oasis in Mesopotamia, Adam is digging in the garden, and Eve is spinning flax. Cain enters, swaggering and chiding Adam for his perpetual digging and lack of progress. Cain glorifies the excitement and danger of killing and boasts of his mastery of his wife, making Adam a little sullen at the tameness of his own lot. Eve interrupts impatiently, points out Cain's distortion of the truth, and taxes him for his inability to taste life "without making it bitter and boiling hot." Cain suggests that they bring up men and women from childhood to be their slaves; Adam is impressed with the idea, but Eve contemptuously refuses to have such unnatural monsters around the house. Cain, who is bored when not killing and facing danger, suggests that death is really the gateway to a life of the soul, free from the bondage of earth;

he longs to be something purer and nobler than an Adam grubbing in the dirt. Since his parents invented death in the first place, he points out, they should hardly blame him for acting as its minister. He leaves, and Eve remarks that because of Cain and those like him death is gaining on life and that most of their grandchildren die before they have lived long enough to attain wisdom.

PART II. THE GOSPEL OF
THE BROTHERS BARNABAS

In about 1920 in the study of a house near London, the brothers Conrad and Franklyn Barnabas are visited by Mr. Haslam, the young rector, Franklyn's daughter, nicknamed Savvy (short for Savage), Mr. Joyce Burge, a leader of the Liberal Opposition in parliament, and Mr. Lubin, a former Liberal prime minister. Burge is aggressive and platitudinous, Lubin wryly charming, as they try to secure the support of the brothers Barnabas in a forthcoming election. The brothers think that the other men's politics are beside the point and suggest their own program—that the term of human life shall be extended to three hundred years. They point out that the rulers of Europe have been immature individuals who, with the best of intentions, have almost succeeded in wrecking European civilization and that the social and political problems of the present cannot be solved by men who die when they are just beginning to have a glimmer of wisdom.

Franklyn expresses his theories of how Adam and Eve invented death and birth to take the burden of immortality off any one individual and how wars and corruption quickly shortened their originally long life-span. The politicians are completely let down when they realize that the Barnabas brothers have not invented an elixir but are merely stating something that can happen if men will it; the brothers believe that men will come to live three hundred years, not simply because they would like to, but because deep down they know that they must if the world is to be saved. Burge and Lubin leave, convinced that the brothers have been pulling their legs.

PART III. THE THING HAPPENS

The scene takes place in the official parlor of the president of the British Islands in the year A.D. 2170 The president, who resembles a composite of Burge and Lubin, calls up on a kind of telescreen the accountant general, a man who somewhat resembles Conrad Barnabas. The accountant complains about being sent to receive an American who has invented a method of breathing under water and who argues its importance in view of the large number of first-rate persons who have died by drowning during the past two centuries. Burge-Lubin then receives a visit from Confucius, a Chinese sage and his chief secretary; in the course of their conversation they are interrupted by the accountant general, who has just come from a film that showed pictures of all the eminent Englishmen who have died by drowning since the cinema was invented. In great distress he tells the others that the present Archbishop Haslam is the same man as two previous archbishops, a president, and a general, all shown in the film.

The archbishop is summoned, and Barnabas accuses him of being a thief, since he has robbed the exchequer by drawing five or six incomes when he is entitled to only one. Confucius points out that if the archbishop is really 283 years old the government is then in his debt: the average man works only 30 years and is supported by the government during his following 35 years of superannuation, while Haslam has worked 260 years and has had no super-annuation. Haslam readily admits that he was born in 1887 and is the same man as the two previous archbishops, the president, and the general, pointing out that he periodically had to dispose of himself by a simulated drowning in order to maintain the fiction that he died at the same age as everyone else.

The domestic minister enters, a handsome, dynamic woman named Mrs. Lutestring. She and the archbishop find one another vaguely familiar, and she finally admits that she was the parlormaid in the household of the brothers Barnabas over two hundred years before. Mrs. Lutestring and the archbishop believe that the English have the possibility of becoming a great nation but that like all higher creatures they take a long time to mature, and their present short lifetimes make them a nonadult race. As a result, they have had to bring in Chinese and African advisors, who have become the actual, if unacknowledged, rulers of the country; and as the English are beginning to show a decided pref-erence for the colored peoples, a famous biologist has suggested that the future of the world belongs to the mulatto. Mrs. Lutestring and the archbishop thus feel that it is their destiny to save the white race by marrying and producing long-lived children.

PART IV. TRAGEDY OF
AN ELDERLY GENTLEMAN

ACT ONE

In A.D. 3000 on the Burrin pier on the south shore of Galway Bay in Ire-land, an elderly gentleman sits on a stone and sobs, but is interrupted by a woman wearing a silk tunic and sandals. He tells her that he comes from Bagh-dad, the capital of the British Commonwealth, on a pious pilgrimage to the land of his fathers. She, being in her second century, does not understand many of his commonplace expressions, and he becomes discouraged at their lack of communication. She reminds him that he was warned that it is dangerous for short-lived people to come to this country, for they are apt to succumb to a deadly disease called discouragement. She asks him how he obtained permis-sion to come, and he relates that he is with the party of his son-in-law, the prime minister, who has come to consult the oracle; also with them is the em-peror of Turania, traveling incognito.

The elderly gentleman is turned over to a young woman named Zoo, since talking to the older inhabitants discourages him so severely. In the course of their lengthy conversation he becomes irritated with her and tries to put her in her place as his inferior in age and dignity. This treatment raises wrath in Zoo, who feels for the first time an urge to kill or be killed, and she is forced to reconsider her political position; formerly she had been a Conservative and had believed that the long-lived people should keep to themselves and live as a race apart. Now she begins to agree with the Colonization Party that they should increase their numbers and colonize, eventually wiping out the short-lived people. More conversation follows, after which Zoo takes the elderly gentleman to the temple to hear the oracle.

ACT TWO

In a courtyard before the portico of a temple, a veiled and robed woman, coming toward the entrance, is met by the emperor of Turania, a man who very much resembles Napoleon I. He greets her by proclaiming that he is the man of destiny. She is unimpressed. He announces that he wants to speak to the oracle directly, without the hocus-pocus usually gone through to impress foreign visitors. She replies that she is the oracle and that he may consult her now. He demands to see the wise old man he imagines to be the real dispenser of knowledge, but the woman tells him that no really old person would bother with him in the first place and, furthermore, that the magnetic field of people in their second and third centuries is deadly to short-livers.

When the emperor is skeptical, she throws back her insulating veil, and her force makes him shriek and beg for mercy. He then describes, at great length, the problem that has brought him to seek the advice of the oracle: he is a military genius and is famous and powerful because he is victorious, but he knows that in the end the cost of victory is the ruin and demoralization of the victors as well as the vanquished. The oracle suggests that he die before the tide of glory turns and, producing the pistol she has previously taken from him, shoots him. He falls with a shriek and scrambles up, unhurt, vigorously cursing the oracle as an inhuman wretch with no respect for the sanctity of human life. She, meanwhile, has gone into the temple, and he is met by the elderly gentleman and his party. They go into the temple to hear the oracle.

ACT THREE

Inside the temple, where a gallery overhangs an abyss, the elderly gentleman and his party kneel, and the pythoness, seated on her tripod, seems to emerge out of the vapor of the abyss. The visitors are terrified and fall on their faces; finally the prime minister, fortified by a flask of brandy, presents his case at great length, at last demanding to be given the same favorable answer as that which won the election for his predecessor, Sir Fuller Eastwind. He is told, "Go home, poor fool." This, Zoo informs them, is the same answer given Eastwind fifteen years before; and the visitors realize that Eastwind faked the magnificent answer with which he won the election.

The prime minister, undaunted, announces that he is going to tell the electorate that the oracle repeated to him, word for word, what it said to Sir Fuller Eastwind and demands that the others support him. All leave except the elderly gentleman, who feels unable to connive at this lie. The oracle comes in, and he implores her to let him stay here, telling her that he cannot go back to live among people to whom nothing is real. She warns him that he will die of discouragement if he stays here, but he replies that he prefers that to dying of despair. She gives him permission to stay, and as he takes her hands to raise himself, she gazes at him steadily, and he falls dead.

PART V. AS FAR AS
THOUGHT CAN REACH

It is a summer afternoon in the year A.D. 31,920. In a glade at the foot of a hill, to one side a little classic temple, to the other a grove, youths and maidens are dancing, but when an ancient wanders through they break off in irritation. All leave except Chloe and her lover Strephon; Chloe is pensive because their amusements—dancing and playing and sweethearting—no longer seem very important to her, and she is beginning to be fascinated with the properties of numbers. Strephon accuses her of getting old, and she confesses that she is four, just twice his age, and getting ready to go out into the woods and live in solitude and contemplation like the ancients. She goes away, leaving Strephon heartbroken.

An ancient appears and a procession, bearing a huge egg, comes out of the temple. The ancient supervises the cracking of the egg, and a pretty girl, who looks about seventeen, emerges. She is told, among other things, that she has been growing for two years in the egg, will complete her period of immaturity in another four years, and then will live any number of centuries until, sooner or later, a fatal accident overtakes her. The ancient departs, and the youths prepare to celebrate their Festival Day, during which two sculptors are to exhibit their latest masterpieces. A crowd of youths emerges from the temple in a furor, dismayed because the sculptor Arjillax has unveiled twelve busts of ancients instead of idealistic studies of nymphs and youths.

Martellus, the master sculptor, discusses the inevitable disillusion of the artist with images because he cannot give them life, and life alone is true. He then produces Pygmalion, a scientist who, with the help of Martellus, has succeeded in making artificial human beings. These creations, says Martellus, are the highest achievements of which any artist has yet been capable; and they are so disgusting that they should cure everyone of caring about art forever. After a lengthy discussion of the difficulties involved in his work, Pygmalion brings out the two synthetic creatures, a noble-looking man and woman.

Vain, vulgar, and pompous, the man and woman proclaim that they are Ozymandias and Cleopatra-Semiranis. Almost immediately they begin to quarrel, and the woman attacks her consort. Pygmalion tries to stop her and she bites his hand, inflicting what is to his kind a fatal wound. A he-ancient appears to settle the problem of what to do with the creatures; the woman, frightened, blames Pygmalion's death on her husband, who promptly calls her a liar. A she-ancient appears, having sensed that she is needed. Each of the synthetic creatures pleads to have his own life spared at the expense of the other's. The he-ancient comments that they cannot help shrinking from death, since they are mere automata at the mercy of their own reflexes. He proposes to put a little more life in them and, taking the male figure by the hand, asks whether he or the woman should be destroyed. The man asks that the woman be spared; the woman, given the same choice, replies that they should both be killed, since neither could live without the other. They sink to the ground and die of discouragement.

The ancients remain to talk with some of the youths; in the course of their talk the Ancients confess to having one trouble: they are still tied to their bodies and subject to its death, and therefore their destiny to be immortal is not achieved. The day will come, they say, when there will be no people, but only thought, and that will be life eternal. The ancients finally depart, leaving the youths relieved to have them go. It grows dark, and the young people gradually drift away. A vague radiance appears near the temple and shapes itself into the ghost of Adam. The ghosts of Eve, Cain, the serpent, and finally Lilith appear. Each speaks his speech and departs, leaving Lilith, who sums up the achievements of her offspring and, in giving the final word, that of life only is there no end, suggests that ultimately life will overcome matter completely and make the universe into a vortex of pure mind.

GEORGE BERNARD SHAW

Candida [copyright performance 1895;

first public performance 1897]

ACT ONE

The Reverend James Morell, a Church of England clergyman, is working on his mail with his secretary, Miss Proserpine Garnett, at his home in a London East End district one autumn morning in the year 1894. When Morell's curate, the Reverend Alexander Mill, arrives, Morell tells him that Mrs. Morell is returning that morning with their two children from a three-week absence. Mill, in turn, states that he has just met Mr. Burgess, Morell's father-in-law, on his way to visit. Morell expresses surprise, having had no calls from Burgess for the last three years.

Alone with his father-in-law, a general contractor, Morell quickly makes it apparent that he disapproves of Burgess' practice of underpaying his employees. He is pleased to learn that Burgess is now paying higher wages but is again discouraged when he discovers that this is only because the county council would otherwise refuse Burgess contracts. Angry when Burgess pretends to be visiting out of pure friendliness, Morell tells him to be his true self, a scoundrel. Burgess admits that he hopes for eventual favors as Morell rises in the church. The two men are just shaking hands, the quarrel over, when Morell's wife Candida appears.

Morell apologizes for having forgotten the time and for failing to meet her at the station. Candida says that she has had no trouble, since she was accompanied by Eugene Marchbanks, an impecunious young poet whom Morell has been helping. Morell goes out to pay for the cab, and Candida whets her father's social appetite by telling him that Marchbanks is a nobleman, the nephew of an earl. When Morell returns with Marchbanks, Burgess departs to catch a train for the city.

Alone with Marchbanks, Morell asks him to stay for lunch. The young poet refuses and naively confesses that Candida told him not to stay. Morell explains that Candida doubtless assumed that he would prefer not to have Marchbanks present during their reunion, but that as an old friend the boy would not be in the way. Morell adds that he would like his protégé to see how happy his marriage with Candida is. Marchbanks incredulously repeats the word *happy* and, with wild lack of control, tells Morell that there is something to be settled between them. Marchbanks staggers the clergyman by proclaiming that he loves Candida. Morell tries to brush aside the declaration by calling it calf love, but Marchbanks refuses to be put off and dismisses Morell's appeals for reasonableness as more of the minister's sermonizing pomposity. Morell orders him to leave the house, almost striking him, while the youth cowers, terrified of the older man's physical strength. Marchbanks insists that Candida learn the details of their dispute, threatening that if Morell refuses to tell her, he will have to live with the knowledge that his wife really belongs to Marchbanks. Before the poet can leave, Candida reappears and, unaware of what has just passed between the two men, decides that Marchbanks should stay for lunch after all. Both men agree.

ACT TWO

In the same room later in the afternoon, Marchbanks discusses love with Miss Garnett. He is in despair when he asks whether it is possible for a woman to love a man like Morell and Miss Garnett replies warmly in the affirmative. Burgess comes back, intent on getting to know the young aristocrat better. A spurt of petty class warfare ensues between Burgess and Miss Garnett, each of whom clearly considers himself the social superior of the other, ending with Miss Garnett's departure from the room. When Morell returns, Burgess complains to him of Miss Garnett's conduct and, intimating that he will stay for dinner, retires to the fireside to read.

Morell says that Candida will be along when she is finished filling the oil lamps; Marchbanks is horrified that she should be doing menial work, and the rivals for her affection bicker. When Candida enters, Marchbanks declaims poetically on her purity and insists that she should not soil her hands. Miss Garnett interrupts to bring a cable that has just arrived, and Candida leaves to prepare dinner, Marchbanks rushing after her to help. Morell writes a reply to the cable and goes to give it to the telegraph boy. As he returns, Burgess goes out into the garden to smoke, and Morell playfully mentions the quarrel between his father-in-law and Miss Garnett, who bursts into tears and runs out of the room.

Candida returns, apparently unaware of what has passed between Marchbanks and her husband, and agonizes Morell with her unconsciously meaningful remarks about the youth. Burgess and Marchbanks suddenly reappear, and Morell controls himself with difficulty. Mill bursts in with word that the organizers of a socialist meeting at which Morell was to have spoken that evening are in a panic because he has cabled them saying he cannot speak. Morell reiterates his refusal to address the group, but Candida persuades him to change his mind, saying that they will all go to listen to him speak. Morell orders Miss Garnett to send a cable that he has changed his mind but declares that Candida and Marchbanks will remain behind together at the house while he, Miss Garnett, Mill, and Burgess attend the meeting; he tells the admiring Marchbanks that this will show how little afraid of the poet he is.

ACT THREE

Marchbanks is reading poetry to Candida as they sit by the fire in the late evening. Discovering that Candida is not listening, the young poet breaks off, and they begin chatting. Receiving permission to say anything he truly feels, Marchbanks for the first time pronounces Mrs. Morell's given name. Morell appears quietly, startling them, and when he says that the others are out having supper, Candida goes to dismiss the maidservant.

Morell, anxious to know what has passed between his wife and Marchbanks, for a time misinterprets Marchbanks' flowery phrases and fears the worst. Becoming more prosaic, Marchbanks reveals that he has made no declaration to Candida: he loves her so "exquisitely" that he wants nothing more than the happiness of that love. The argument between the two men breaks out afresh, and Candida returns just as Marchbanks excitedly demands of Morell that he let his wife choose between them.

As Candida scolds Marchbanks for upsetting her husband, the doorbell rings, and she goes off to let in Miss Garnett, Mill, and Burgess, who are exhilarated by Morell's address and by a champagne supper. Miss Garnett leaves tipsily for home; Mill rushes after her to make sure she arrives safely, and Burgess asks Marchbanks for the pleasure of his company on the way home. Candida orders Marchbanks to stay and goes out to see her father off. She returns, takes command of the situation, and asks her husband what the matter is. Morell finally blurts out that Marchbanks has said that Candida loves the youth.

Marchbanks excitedly objects that he said he was in love with Candida, and not the reverse, and that moreover he made the remark that morning, before he had a chance to be alone with Candida. After Marchbanks reveals that Morell that morning laid hands on him in anger, Morell says that he and Marchbanks have agreed that Candida shall choose between them. Candida coldly asks what each is bidding for her.

Morell offers his strength, honesty, ability, and authority; Marchbanks, his weakness and his "heart's need." Candida declares that she gives herself to "the weaker of the two." Morell, understanding by this that she means Marchbanks, is devastated, but the perceptive poet sees that she means her husband. Candida explains that Marchbanks' unhappy, lonely childhood was in great contrast to Morell's; her husband always had his mother and three sisters to wait upon him as a child, and now she must fulfill the role of mother, sisters, and wife for him. She notes ironically that she protects her husband from everyday worldly worries, and yet he tries to keep her by offering his strength, ability, and industry. Morell, overcome, admits his need of her.

Candida asks Marchbanks whether she is a mother and sister to him, to which he replies, "Never!" He declares that he does not need happiness: "Life is nobler than that." Candida kisses the poet's forehead, and he walks out into the night. She and her husband embrace, "but," Shaw's final stage direction states, "they do not know the secret in the poet's heart."

GEORGE BERNARD SHAW

Heartbreak House: A fantasia in the Russian manner on English themes [1920]

ACT ONE

In Captain Shotover's house, the interior of which is designed to resemble that of an old-fashioned ship, a visitor, Ellie Dunn, sits and waits, as she obviously has been doing for some time. Finally she falls asleep, but soon is awakened by Nurse Guinness, who seems not at all surprised that Ellie's hostess, Mrs. Hushabye, abandoned her. Nurse Guinness remarks that the house is full of surprises for people who aren't used to the occupants' ways. Captain Shotover appears, an ancient but vigorous man with an immense white beard; formerly a munitions manufacturer, he is one of the last of England's great men. On learning Ellie's name, he persists in thinking that she is the daughter of a former thieving boatswain of his named Billy Dunn. Nurse Guinness brings tea and reminds him that his second daughter, Ariadne, is arriving home for the first time in twenty-three years; Captain Shotover expresses annoyance and claims that he is extremely old and has totally forgotten the girl. He peremptorily throws out the tea Nurse Guinness has made for Ellie and insists on brewing her some of his own.

While he is in the pantry, Ariadne, now Lady Utterword, arrives with much fluster; she is highly disappointed at the state of the house and the casual way in which she is received. Captain Shotover, returning with his tea, does not recognize her and is not at all moved by her protestations that she is his daughter. Mrs. Hesione Hushabye, Captain Shotover's eldest daughter, enters, embraces Ellie, and makes a considerable fuss over her but fails to recognize Ariadne. After she is finally convinced that Ariadne is her sister, Mrs. Hushabye tells her that Ellie is going to marry a millionaire to help her poor father, and begs Ariadne to help her stop Ellie from taking such a step.

Mazzini Dunn, Ellie's father, arrives; Captain Shotover snorts that he is not a bit like the boatswain Billy Dunn and goes out to the garden. Ariadne follows him to convince him that she is really his daughter. While Mazzini Dunn is out of the room hanging up his overcoat, Mrs. Hushabye tells Ellie that he is a selfish brute to try to make her marry for money. Mazzini returns to announce that Mr. Mangan has come and is in the garden talking to Captain Shotover; summoned by the captain, Mazzini goes out. Ellie tells Mrs. Hushabye that her father was set up in business by Mr. Mangan, soon went bankrupt, and was rescued by Mangan, who bought the business and made Mazzini his manager. Ellie, who later met Mangan, came to a kind of understanding with him and feels bound to marry him out of gratitude. Mrs. Hushabye pries out of her the fact that Ellie is really in love with another man, a most romantic individual named Marcus Darnley.

A handsome man of fifty enters; Ellie, with glad surprise, introduces him as Mr. Darnley. Mrs. Hushabye replies that he is her husband Hector. Seeing that Ellie is very upset, Mrs. Hushabye tells her husband to leave them; Ellie curses herself for being taken in by his stories and observes thoughtfully that her heart is probably broken. Mangan and the captain enter, the captain still confusing Mazzini with his former boatswain, and Mrs. Hushabye takes Ellie to her room. Captain Shotover bluntly tells Mangan that he is too old to marry Ellie. A stranger enters, a very well-dressed man of about fifty, and introduces himself as Randall Utterword, Ariadne's brother-in-law. Mrs. Hushabye takes Randall out to see the garden, commenting that the only things in it to see are the observatory and the gravel pit where Captain Shotover keeps his dynamite; the dynamite, she explains, is to blow up the human race if it goes too far. All the others go out except Hector and Lady Utterword, who exercise their considerable powers of attraction on one another. As Lady Utterword leaves, Mrs. Hushabye comes in and remarks that she found being in love with Hector such an enchanting dream that she has never been able to grudge it to him or anyone else since, and thus is always inviting pretty women to the house to give him the chance of falling in love with them. She goes off to fascinate Mangan and thus sidetrack him from Ellie.

ACT TWO

In the same room after dinner, Mangan tries to talk to Ellie about their understanding, but she gives every sign of being quite satisfied with the idea of marrying him. He tells her that he deliberately ruined her father as part of a complex business scheme from which he profited. Ellie is unperturbed, and when he goes on to say that he is in love with another woman, Mrs. Hushabye, she calmly tells him that she is in love with Hector Hushabye. At this Mangan becomes quite beside himself and asks her to squeeze his temples to keep his head from splitting open. She strokes his head and chants to him, and he promptly falls into a hypnotic trance. Ellie turns out the light and leaves.

Nurse Guinness, walking through the room in the dark, stumbles over Mangan and, when he doesn't awaken, thinks that she has killed him. Mrs. Hushabye and Mazzini come in, discover Mangan to be breathing, and conclude that he has been hypnotized. Mrs. Hushabye accuses Mazzini of forcing Ellie to marry the brutish Mangan, but Mazzini defends poor Mangan, saying he is terribly afraid of being poor and is therefore wholly concerned with making money. Ellie comes in; Mrs. Hushabye announces that she has persuaded Mazzini that Ellie doesn't want to marry Mangan, but Ellie, annoyed, insists that she does and asks her father to leave her alone to talk with Mrs. Hushabye. Ellie declares that, since her heart has been broken, she is determined to be hard as nails henceforth; inasmuch as she can't have love, she might as well have money. After voicing several unflattering thoughts about Mr. Mangan, Ellie wakes him from his trance. He leaps up, claiming that he has heard everything; Mrs. Hushabye soothes him, and during their conversation discovers that he has a given name—Alfred—and a heart. Beside himself at being so adroitly gotten around, Mangan attempts to leave, but before he can get out, a shot and a yell are heard from upstairs.

Mazzini, very shaken, appears with an old and villainous-looking burglar and announces that he very nearly killed the man. The burglar complains that he will be sentenced to ten years, which he will never live out, and bemoans the unfairness of it all. Moved by this, and thinking of the inconvenience of having the burglary and all their family affairs in all the papers, the others agree to send the burglar on his way; but he refuses to go and demands his right to be punished so he can work out his salvation. He nearly succeeds in convincing them to take up a collection of twenty pounds to set him up in the locksmith business when Lady Utterword becomes tired of his impertinence and suggests that they should prosecute him after all.

At that moment Captain Shotover arrives and discovers the burglar to be none other than his former boatswain, Billy Dunn. Billy confesses that he only pretends to be a burglar; he lets himself be caught and usually collects a donation. Captain Shotover throws him out of the room. Mangan, meanwhile, is sulking because no one has paid him any attention since the burglar arrived;

Mrs. Hushabye entices him out for a walk in the garden. The others also go out, leaving Captain Shotover alone with Ellie. They carry on an epigrammatic conversation, in the course of which Ellie remarks that she would like to marry a very rich and very old man. Shotover rebukes her for seeking riches: at her age, he looked for "hardship, danger, horror, and death," that he might feel the life in him more intensely. Though the captain says he has no money, she decides that she would still rather marry him than Mangan. Hector and Randall come in as Ellie and the captain leave. Randall criticizes Hector's flirtation with Lady Utterword; Hector calls Lady Utterword, who says Randall is jealous, idle, and worthless, and finally reduces him to tears. That, she points out to Hector, is the way to manage him—like a child who is naughty and nervy and needs a spanking and a good cry. She sends Randall off to bed, and, with only a faint show of rebellion, he goes.

ACT THREE

Lady Utterword and Hector join Ellie and Captain Shotover in the garden. Mrs. Hushabye is strolling about with Mangan, who complains of a presentiment that he is going to die. Mrs. Hushabye asks Ariadne whether she thinks that Ellie ought to marry Mangan for his money. Though Mangan is distressed at having his affairs discussed before everyone, his protests are ignored. Lady Utterword wants to know how much money Mangan has and finally baits him into admitting that he has none and never had any, that he lives on traveling expenses and a small commission, that his industries are actually owned by syndicates and shareholders, and that he has no property of his own. He boasts, however, that he was given a high position in government because of his business abilities and that, when the other government men would not let him save the country and win a title, he threw a monkey wrench in their plans for saving the country and winning titles.

The men discuss which of them would be best fit to run the country, and Mrs. Hushabye interrupts that it matters very little as long as they—the lovely women—rule the men. Mangan wildly begins to tear off his clothes, crying that they have all been stripped morally naked and they might as well be physically naked. Lady Utterword dissuades him, and he then threatens to go back to the city, where he is respected and made much of. Told to think of the various wonderful things of the Shotover household that he will miss, he gives in, agrees to marry Ellie, and says he will do anything for a quiet life. Ellie placidly replies that she never intended to make him marry her but only wanted to know her strength; and in any event, she is already married, having become Captain Shotover's wife an hour before.

Mazzini appears in a dressing gown. Mangan complains that ever since he has been in the house he has been made to look like a fool; Ellie agrees that the house is strange and fascinating and names it Heartbreak House. Hector remarks that it is inhabited by a group of heartbroken imbeciles of one description or another, but Mazzini claims that they all exemplify what is best in English culture. Talk turns to the power of destruction wielded by Mangan and people like him and the necessity of controlling it. Mazzini reflects that it is amazing how well things go along, all things considered, and speculates that perhaps it is due to Providence. Captain Shotover interjects that every drunken skipper trusts to Providence, and Providence has a way of running them on the rocks.

The dull explosion of a bomb dropped by a German Zeppelin is heard in the distance. The lights go out, and Nurse Guinness comes out to say that the police have telephoned with an order to put out the lights; she adds that the rectory is rumored to be nothing but a heap of bricks. Mangan and the burglar hide in the cave in the gravel pit, thinking it safer than the cellar. There is another and louder explosion. Hector, in the house, turns on all the lights and throws open the curtains. A tremendous explosion shakes the earth; the bomb has struck the gravel pit. Everyone expects to be blown up, but after a time only a distant explosion is heard. They are disappointed, for life has become safe again. Mrs. Hushabye, echoed by Ellie, hopes that the danger will come again tomorrow night.

GEORGE BERNARD SHAW

Major Barbara [1905]

ACT ONE

In the library of her house, Lady Britomart and her son Stephen discuss family affairs—particularly the necessity of arranging a financial settlement for her daughters, who are both engaged to marry men with inadequate incomes. The source of money proposed by Lady Britomart is her estranged husband, Andrew Undershaft, who has made a fortune in manufacturing cannons and armaments. She reveals to Stephen that she left her husband because he insisted on carrying on a tradition whereby the Undershaft cannon business was always left to a foundling rather than to the legitimate heir of the owner; she also disliked Undershaft's manner of calling a spade a spade and his disconcern for her ideas of propriety. Shocked at this information about his father, Stephen is even more appalled when his mother tells him that they are living on Undershaft money; nevertheless, she gets him to agree that she must ask for more money for settlements for her daughters; she announces that Undershaft is due to arrive at any minute to discuss the matter.

The daughters, Sarah and Barbara, the latter a major in the Salvation Army, enter with their respective suitors, Charles Lomax and Adolphus Cusins. Lomax is a rather callow young man about town, Cusins a professor of Greek who has attached himself to the Salvation Army Band for the purpose of winning Barbara. The elder Undershaft arrives, and in the course of conversation agrees to go with Barbara to see her Salvation Army shelter if she will come to see his cannon works.

ACT TWO

In the yard of the Salvation Army shelter on a cold January morning, a man and a woman, both obviously down on their luck, are finishing a meal of bread and milk. The man is Snobby Price, an out-of-work house painter who excuses his laziness and petty pilfering with intellectual pretensions; the woman, Rummy Mitchens, is an old bundle of poverty who has pretended to be wicked in order to be rescued—and fed—by the Salvation Army. They are joined by Jenny Hill, a Salvation Army girl, who brings in Peter Shirley, a half-starved man of forty-six who has been dismissed from his job for being too old. Bill Walker, a young tough, appears and demands to see his ex-girl friend, threatening to beat her up for jilting him when she was rescued by the Army. Recognizing Jenny as the one who set his girl friend against him, he knocks her down. Rummy Mitchens mounts a verbal attack on him, but Bill hits her and sends her sprawling. Jenny runs to Rummy's assistance; Bill drags her by the hair and hits her in the mouth before she manages to get away from him. Peter Shirley, with a considerable show of spirit, taunts Bill for hitting a defenseless woman; he says Bill wouldn't dare hit someone like Todger Fairmile, Shirley's kinsman and a famous wrestler.

Barbara comes out to the yard, questions Shirley, notices Bill, and tells him that his girl has gone to another shelter and has a new boy friend, the brawny Todger Fairmile, also a Salvation Army convert. Barbara sends for Rummy to help clear away the dishes; the old woman is afraid of Bill and stays as far away from him as possible. Jenny, however, shows no fear or resentment of him, and Bill experiences considerable discomfort at her kind words toward him.

Mr. Undershaft arrives and watches Barbara go about her work, most of which consists in drawing out Bill's newly developed sense of remorse for having hit Jenny. Just as Bill is on the verge of conversion, Cusins enters beating his drum, and the spell is broken. Bill immediately heads off to the other shelter to spit in Todger Fairmile's eye and get his own face bashed, and thus expiate having hit Jenny. Barbara goes inside the shelter, leaving Undershaft and Cusins alone in the yard to talk. Undershaft says that in his religion there are two things necessary to salvation: money and gunpowder. He adds that the usual virtues of honor, justice, truth, and so forth are really luxuries of a rich and safe life.

The rest of the troupe return from a meeting, a few shillings richer. Undershaft offers to contribute a trifling amount, but Barbara refuses his money on the ground that he has made it with weapons of destruction; he cannot buy his salvation, she says, but must work it out. She adds that the shelter must close unless they can get more money and that their supervisor is praying that the shelter will be saved.

Bill Walker returns, having spat in the face of Todger Fairmile, who knelt

on him and prayed for him. Bill offers Jenny a sovereign as recompense for having hit her, pleading with her to accept it and to stop forgiving him and praying for him. Jenny refuses, and Barbara says that the Army wants his soul, not
his money. Undershaft offers to give an additional ninety-nine pounds if Barbara will accept Bill's pound; Barbara still refuses, and Bill flings his sovereign
on the drum and sits morosely on the horse trough. Snobby Price eyes the coin
and plans to filch it at the earliest opportunity.

Mrs. Baines, the supervisor, appears and announces that Sir Horace Bodger,
the whiskey distiller, has offered five thousand pounds to the Army if they can
find other contributors to give an equal amount. Undershaft offers the second
five thousand. Bill cynically mutters, "What price salvation?" Barbara reminds
them all of their spiritual campaign against Bodger and his whiskey; by sending
them money, she says, he is trying to buy salvation without changing his wicked
ways. The others protest that the money will do good and prepare to march off
in music and triumph to the meeting. Before he goes, she takes the silver pin
from her collar and pins it on her father. Seeing that the Army can be bought,
after all, Bill announces that he is no longer a candidate for salvation and feels
cheerfully free to go. Barbara, broken, leaves the yard with Shirley.

ACT THREE

Scene 1. Sarah and Barbara are with their mother in Lady Britomart's library. Charles enters and expresses surprise at seeing Barbara not in uniform;
Cusins arrives in poor condition, having spent the previous night drinking in
the company of Undershaft. Lady Britomart sends them out on various errands just as Undershaft arrives; he agrees to settle money on his daughters, and
as they are arguing what to do about Stephen, the young man comes in. He
disdainfully refuses, much to his mother's surprise and distress, to have anything to do with the cannon business even if it were offered to him. Questioned
about what career he is prepared to enter, he acknowledges that he is ignorant
of philosophy, law, literature, and business but proudly asserts that he knows
the difference between right and wrong. The others return, and all depart for
the cannon foundry.

Scene 2. The foundry town is white, beautiful, peaceful, and altogether an
ideal community. Stephen is vastly impressed by its organization, and Lady
Britomart takes an intense and proprietary interest in its homes and gardens.
Undershaft regrets that Cusins is not a foundling, since he is the ideal type of
man to inherit the business; but Cusins confesses that he is, in a manner of
speaking, a foundling, since his parents, though legally married in Australia, are
of a degree of kinship not permitted to marry in England. However, he is not
sure—because of the moral question involved in manufacturing weapons and
making a profit from war—whether or not to accept; and he also knows that
Barbara will not accept him unless he makes the right choice. Undershaft appeals to Barbara to explain to Cusins the realities of power, of being within the
grip of something beyond oneself; but Barbara complains that her father's buy-

ing of the Salvation Army has destroyed her religion and her belief that she was in the power of God. Undershaft compares the necessity of scrapping obsolete and inadequate religions and moralities to the necessity of scrapping obsolete or imperfect weapons; and when Barbara demands that he offer her a better religion than the one he destroyed for her, he points out the excellent working conditions, happy workmen, and model homes of his industrial community and compares it with the poverty, misery, and hunger of those he saw in the Army shelter. Poverty, says Undershaft, is the worst of all crimes.

Cusins, after some deliberation, accepts the inheritance in order to "make power for the world," acknowledging that power for good necessarily implies power for evil as well. Agreeing with him wholeheartedly, Barbara says that in order to be saved, she must have this place, with all its healthy, vigorous human souls. She admits that her converts in the Army were all weak souls bribed with bread and promises never to use the bribe of heaven again but to do the work of God for its own sake.

GEORGE BERNARD SHAW

Man and Superman [copyright performance 1903; first public performance 1905]

ACT ONE

Roebuck Ramsden, a middle-aged Englishman, is at work in his study as Octavius Robinson, a young man dressed in mourning, enters. They discuss the recent death of Mr. Whitefield, a close friend of Ramsden and the guardian of Octavius and his sister Violet. Ramsden says Octavius has turned out well but warns him against associating with Jack Tanner, the author of a book that Ramsden thinks is a scandalous attack on moral values.

Assuming he will be appointed guardian of Ann Whitefield, his friend's daughter, Ramsden says he will see to it that she stops seeing Tanner and urges Octavius to propose to Ann.

Tanner comes in with the news that he, with Ramsden, is to be joint guardian of Ann, whom he characterizes as a scheming, wily woman. Ramsden and Octavius disagree, and Ramsden angrily says he will not serve as co-guardian with Tanner.

Ann and her mother enter. Ann calms the men down and convinces Ramsden she would be lost without his guidance. She teases Tanner, calling him Don Juan and saying she will think of him as her guardian whether he accepts the job or not. After Ann, her mother, and Ramsden go out, Tanner tells Octavius to be careful. Ann has marked Octavius as her prey, Tanner says, calling her a boa constrictor.

Ann and Ramsden return with the news that Violet, Octavius' sister, is pregnant and refuses to name the father. Octavius is shocked, but Tanner says Violet should be praised for her bravery. Ramsden and Octavius go out to discuss the situation. Ann flirts with Tanner, reminding him of their childhood pact to tell each other all their secrets. Tanner says that he stopped confiding in Ann because he discovered something he wanted to keep to himself—his soul.

Ramsden and Octavius return, and Violet comes in. Tanner congratulates her on her flaunting of convention. Angry, Violet says that she is actually married but cannot yet reveal the name of her husband.

ACT TWO

At the Whitefields' house, Tanner meets Octavius, who says he has proposed to Ann but that he must first talk over the proposal with Tanner, her guardian. Tanner warns Octavius that if he marries Ann he will cease to idealize her.

Octavius gives Tanner a note from Ann's sister Rhoda, who writes that she cannot take a drive with Tanner as they had planned, because Ann has forbidden it. Ann comes in and says that Rhoda is too ill to go out. Tanner shows her the note and Ann says that their mother ordered Rhoda to write it.

Tanner launches into a tirade against mothers who interfere in their daughters' lives. He challenges Ann to prove her independence by coming away with him to Marseilles. To his surprise, she accepts immediately.

Ramsden and Mrs. Whitefield come in. Mrs. Whitefield approves of the proposed trip and suggests that Tanner take Rhoda out for a drive. Tanner realizes that Ann has lied about the note, but before he can make an issue of it, Hector Malone, an American, comes calling on Violet. Told that she is secretly married to some unknown person, Malone expresses shock.

Left alone together, Malone and Violet kiss. He says he wants everyone to know that he is her husband. Violet insists that they wait until Hector can get his father's permission to marry.

Preparing for the trip, Tanner tells his chauffeur Straker that Ann and Octavius are coming with them and he orders that the couple be left alone as much as possible. Straker says that Tanner is Ann's prey, not Octavius. Frightened at this prospect, Tanner leaves for Marseilles alone.

ACT THREE

Tanner has driven into the Sierra Nevada mountains to avoid pursuit by Ann. His car is stopped by a gang of bandits whose leader, Mendoza, says he was once a waiter and turned to banditry after an unsuccessful love affair. Tanner scoffs at Mendoza's romanticism. They all go to sleep.

Don Juan, who looks like Tanner, is seen sitting on a rock in hell. An old woman appears, shocked that she, a pillar of the church when alive, is in this place. Don Juan consoles her by saying that some of the best people are there and that she may now assume any age she wants. She goes out and reappears as a 27-year-old woman, resembling Ann. Don Juan realizes she is Doña Ana, a woman he had pursued years ago and whose father he had killed in a duel. He tells her that her father often comes down from heaven to visit him. Her father, in the guise of a statue and looking like Ramsden, soon appears. He says he is abandoning heaven for hell because it is boring up there: most of the people left in heaven are Englishmen who behave in a strictly proper manner, doing what they believe is expected of them. The devil, who looks like Mendoza, agrees and says he could go back to heaven if he wanted but he would rather stay where he is.

Don Juan tells Ana that hell is the last retreat of the romantics; it is in heaven that one can find reality and the Life Force. He says that man's intelligence was created to direct this Life Force. The devil says that all man's intelligence has ever created is war and machines of destruction. Don Juan insists that man is not evil, only cowardly: if men are given a cause, they will fight bravely and nobly. Ana says that men can indeed act bravely, but they leave all the responsible tasks to women. Don Juan retorts that women invented men to help them create children and to provide food, but men outwitted women and created civilization as well. He says he became disillusioned with doctors who wanted to save his body, philosophers who wanted to save his soul, and politicians who wanted to save the world. In romantics, he says, he found a new understanding of beauty, which in turn led him to women; in spite of his intellectual disdain for them, the Life Force made him continually seek them out. A new world is coming, he says, when men and women will recognize the Life Force for what it is and will not mask it in sentimentality and false promises. His main purpose in life, Don Juan claims, was to believe in and create something better than himself. Women distracted him but he never lost his sense of purpose. In hell, he says, the devil has no purpose except to lead people into the trap of meaningless pleasure.

Don Juan says he is going to go to heaven to develop his brain so that he can give direction to the Life Force. The devil says Juan is only exchanging one illusion for another. When Juan asks the statue the way to heaven, the statue replies that the difference between heaven and hell is only a matter of viewpoint and that the way is now open to Juan. The devil sadly says that all life worshipers—Rembrandt and Nietzsche, who invented the Superman—leave eventually for heaven. Juan leaves for heaven. Before the devil and the statue depart, Ana asks where the Superman is. They tell her he is not yet created. She says that in that case her work is not yet done and calls for a father for the Superman.

Tanner awakes to find that a rescue party composed of Ann, Octavius, Violet, Hector, Ramsden, and the police has come to his aid. They are appalled to find that the notorious bandit is an ex-waiter who served some of them in the past.

ACT FOUR

At a villa in Granada, Hector Malone's father calls on Violet, having intercepted a note she sent to Hector. Mr. Malone, a self-made millionaire, is against Hector's marrying someone from the middle class. Violet coolly begins to persuade him that Hector needs her. Hector enters and argues with his father. Tanner, Ann, Octavius, and Ramsden come in and join the heated discussion. Hector blurts out that he and Violet are already married. His father angrily says that he will cut him off with no money and Hector stalks out. Mr. Malone relents and sends Violet after him.

Alone with Ann, Octavius proposes again. She tells him that her mother insists she marry Tanner. When Tanner returns and hears this, he shouts that he will not marry her. Ann tells him that cynical men, such as he is, always marry and that romantics such as Octavius never do. Tanner admits that he loves her. She faints in his arms, accepting his proposal. Tanner's protests are to no avail as the others come in to congratulate him on his engagement. He says that both he and Ann have lost their freedom and peace of mind. Ann placidly tells him to keep talking.

GEORGE BERNARD SHAW

Pygmalion [1914]

ACT ONE

A heavy rain has sent pedestrians scattering for shelter under the portico of St. Paul's Church in Covent Garden. Among them, a young girl, Clara Eynsford-Hill, and her mother are waiting for Clara's brother Freddy, who is off hunting for a cab. Freddy appears, explaining he hasn't yet found a cab, then rushes off, knocking a flower girl's basket from her hand.

The flower girl, Eliza Doolittle, about eighteen, dirty and unkempt, with an almost unintelligible Cockney dialect, sits down to sort her flowers. A military man, Colonel Pickering, hurries into the shelter. Eliza tries to sell him flowers, but he wants none. As he gives her three ha'pence to keep her quiet, a stranger points out that a man is writing down her words and warns her to give the colonel some flowers for the money. Eliza bursts out in fright that she is "a respectable girl" and creates a hubbub.

The note-taker, Henry Higgins, professor of the science of speech and student of languages, a bachelor in his forties, comes over to her to find out why she's so upset. He shows her his notebook. The bystanders think he is a police informer or busybody, whereupon Higgins proceeds to show off his knowledge of dialect by identifying the home district of each of the crowd.

The rain stops, and Clara and her mother go off to catch a bus, leaving Higgins, the colonel, and Eliza. Eliza is still fussing, but listens as Higgins explains his profession to the colonel: he teaches those who wish to better themselves. Higgins boasts he could take Eliza and in three months pass her off as a duchess at a garden party or get her a job as a lady's maid or shop assistant.

Colonel Pickering reveals that he, too, is a dialect student; the two trade names and find they have long wanted to meet each other. They go off together, but not before Eliza manages to wangle another handful of change, this time from Higgins. When Freddy finally arrives with the cab only to find his mother and sister gone, Eliza takes it and rides home in style.

ACT TWO

Higgins and Pickering, enjoying a morning of listening to sounds in Higgins' Wimpole Street laboratory, receive Eliza, who has cleaned herself up a bit for the occasion. Eliza wishes to take lessons for a shilling an hour. Colonel Pickering offers to pay for the lessons and expenses if Higgins can make good on his boast to pass her off as a duchess. Higgins sends her off with Mrs. Pearce, his housekeeper, for a bath and new clothes. After she leaves, the Colonel asks Higgins whether he will respect Eliza. When the Colonel is reassured, Mrs. Pearce returns to warn Higgins to watch his language and personal habits.

Eliza's father, a dustman, appears and proclaims that he wants his daughter. Higgins tells him to take her away at once, but Doolittle backs down and confesses that he came just for some money to "let her go." He explains he's one of the "undeserving poor" who need just as much as the deserving, but never get anything because of the disapproval of middle-class morality. Higgins gives him a five-pound note, and Doolittle promises to spend it wildly.

Doolittle discusses the fact that his "missus" won't marry him. "I'm a slave to that woman, Governor," he says, "just because I'm not her lawful husband." Eliza returns and greets her father. He then goes off to spend his fiver and she to don her new clothes.

ACT THREE

"It is my at-home day; you promised not to come," is the greeting Henry Higgins receives from his pleasant, well-bred, sixty-year-old mother, as he appears in her drawing room. He tells her about Eliza and his bet with the Colonel; he announces that Eliza is coming today, prepared to speak properly.

Mrs. Eynsford-Hill and Clara enter, followed by Colonel Pickering and Freddy. They engage in small-talk until Eliza comes, speaking and acting like a lady. As her conversation, however, soon drifts into a lurid account of her aunt's death, Higgins signals her to leave. She goes, leaving Freddy quite enraptured and Clara adopting Eliza's new small-talk sprinkled with profanity.

After the Eynsford-Hills leave, Higgins asks his mother how his experiment is coming. She tries to get him and Colonel Pickering to consider the problem of what will become of the girl after their experiment is ended, but they pass it off, enthralled with the fun of what they are doing.

ACT FOUR

Higgins, Pickering, and Eliza return to the laboratory in Wimpole Street at midnight. All are in evening clothes and Eliza is dazzling. Higgins looks for his slippers and Eliza fetches them. The two men congratulate each other, for Higgins' experiment has worked: they have passed off Eliza as a duchess at a garden party, a dinner, and the opera. They take no note of Eliza's growing anger at their indifference and at remarks like Higgins' "However, it's over and done with."

Pickering retires and Higgins leaves. Eliza falls to the floor in a rage. Higgins returns to find her there. She throws his slippers at him. He pulls her up and tries to find out what's wrong. She asks despairingly, "What's to become of me?" He coolly suggests a job or a fashionable marriage or getting set up in a shop by Pickering. Eliza finally asks him whether the clothes she wears are hers, or his for the next experiment. He storms at her for being ungrateful and stalks out of the room.

ACT FIVE

Higgins and Pickering burst into Mrs. Higgins' drawing room, looking for Eliza, who has run off during the night, leaving Higgins distraught; he admits he has come to depend on her. His mother says the girl has a right to leave. Mr. Doolittle comes in—a gentleman now—and blames his prosperity on Higgins. Higgins had mentioned Doolittle to a philanthropist as an original moralist, and the man left Doolittle three thousand a year. He complains that he is now in the clutches of "middle-class morality" and is suffering the loss of his former free and easy life.

Mrs. Higgins suggests he can now support Eliza, but the professor objects, saying Eliza is his. His mother reveals Eliza is upstairs, but won't go back to Wimpole Street because of the indifference with which she was treated.

Eliza enters and greets them civilly, then praises Pickering for his gentlemanly ways toward her. Her father surprises her in his splendid clothes and announces he's off to be married, a concession to his new life of middle-class morality. Eliza and Higgins stay behind as the others leave.

The professor tries to get Eliza to change her mind. He explains that his seeming rudeness is his way with everyone—it is his nature. She says she can do without him, and he says he can do without her, but "I shall miss you, Eliza . . . I have grown accustomed to your voice and appearance . . . ." He asks her to come back "for the fun of it."

She discusses her possible future—as Freddy's wife or, possibly, as a phonetics teacher. Both suggestions dismay him, but he sees that she is now a woman of strength and suggests that she and Pickering and he be three old bachelors together. The carriage comes for Doolittle's wedding party; disdaining Higgins' parting remark, which takes the form of a few orders, Eliza leaves.

GEORGE BERNARD SHAW

Saint Joan [1923]

NOTE: The play is divided into scenes rather than acts.

On a spring morning in 1429, at the castle of Vaucouleurs on the river Meuse, Captain Robert de Baudricourt berates his steward for not producing any eggs, and the steward protests that there will be none so long as the girl from Lorraine persists in staying to see the master. Robert calls for her. A saucy wench of about seventeen, she appears, curtseying, and demands a horse, armor, and an escort to the dauphin, in accordance, she claims, with her orders from her Lord the King of Heaven.

Stupefied, Robert dismisses the girl and sends for Squire Bertrand de Poulengey, who has promised to take her to Chinon. Robert explains that if Poulengey makes off with her on the pretext of escorting her to the dauphin, he himself will be blamed. His interest is not sensual, the squire says: this girl is France's last card to play against the English, who hold half the country, for the dauphin refuses to fight them.

Robert recalls her, and Joan tells him of the voices she hears from God bidding her raise the siege of Orléans, crown the dauphin in Rheims Cathedral, and drive the English from France: God gave men their own countries and languages, and He meant them to keep it that way. Warned of the devilish English soldiers, Joan is unafraid. Robert reluctantly yields to her demands.

Alone, he is wondering whether he hasn't been made a fool of when the steward runs in with a basket of eggs, exclaiming that the hens have laid five dozen. Recognizing a miracle, Robert crosses himself.

In the throne room at Chinon, Touraine, on the afternoon of March 8, the archbishop of Rheims and the lord chamberlain, Msgr. de la Trémouille, await the dauphin. They discuss the large amount of money he owes them both. A page announces Gilles de Rais, a smart young man nicknamed Bluebeard. He brings the news that Foul Mouthed Frank, upon being told by a soldier that he shouldn't swear when about to die, promptly fell into a well and drowned. Captain La Hire, entering, declares that the soldier is an angel in disguise who has miraculously traveled unharmed from Champagne. The others laugh.

The Dauphin Charles comes in excitedly, holding a paper. Although his father is dead, the queen's denial of his legitimacy has prevented his coronation. An ill-favored young man of twenty-six, he is treated by his courtiers with the utmost disrespect. Snatching the paper, La Trémouille tries unsuccessfully to read it, then hands it to the Archbishop, who, reading, informs the group that

De Baudricourt is sending a crazy country girl to Chinon. The Archbishop refuses to let the dauphin see her. La Hire recognizes her by her description as the angel who struck Foul Mouthed Frank dead, and Bluebeard suggests they try her. He will pretend to be the dauphin: if she is an angel, she will find him out.

Left by themselves again, La Trémouille and the Archbishop discuss miracles. They go out, and presently curtains are drawn back to show the assembled court. The chatter stops when Joan, dressed as a soldier, is led in. She walks to the dais where Bluebeard is sitting, recognizes him, and, grinning, plunges into the crowd to capture the true dauphin. When she tells him her mission, Charles bids her talk to the Archbishop about his coronation. Joan kneels and asks the prelate's blessing. Touched, he blesses her but warns of danger. Joan replies that he has given her courage.

The courtiers dismissed, Charles confides to Joan that he doesn't want to be king or to fight, but she persuades him to pluck up his courage. He calls back the court and gives her the army, to the wrath of La Trémouille, who is commander. Joan waves her sword, and La Hire, followed by all the knights, rallies to her. She kneels in thanksgiving to God, and all kneel for the Archbishop's blessing, except La Trémouille, who collapses, cursing.

On the south bank of the river Loire at Orléans, on the evening of April 29, handsome young Jack Dunois is pacing; he glances at the streaming pennon stuck up on his lance and curses the west wind.

Joan arrives in a rage and says that her troops have brought her to the wrong side of the river and that they must cross over at once. Dunois points out two forts at the near end of the bridge, and Joan replies that she will take them. Admiring her courage, Dunois observes that she is in love with war. Joan muses that the Archbishop said she was in love with religion. Dunois asks: Does she want to be like a woman with two husbands? Joan says she will never take a husband: her dreams are of leading a charge. With the sword she found behind the altar in St. Catherine's Church, she may not strike a blow, but she will lead and the men will follow.

All in good time, agrees Dunois, but first his men must come upstream. His plan is to take the English in the rear, but until the wind changes, the boats can't sail. He starts for church with Joan so she can pray for a west wind. Rising to follow, Dunois's page sees the pennon streaming eastward. He calls them back and points to it. Dunois kneels and hands his baton to Joan. Now the boats are racing upstream, and Dunois, rising, dares her to lead him to battle. She bursts into tears and kisses him, and they go off, the page dancing after them.

Inside an English tent, a nobleman and a chaplain await the arrival of the Bishop of Beauvais. Since Orléans, defeat has been continuous, and the chaplain vows he will strangle the witch who has accomplished it. Presently the bishop, Msgr. Cauchon, arrives. The nobleman introduces himself as Richard de Beauchamp, Earl of Warwick, and the chaplain as Master John de Stogumber.

The chaplain tells how Joan, her throat pierced by an arrow, led the French soldiers to the Orléans fort; they fell on the paralyzed English and drove them onto the bridge, which burst into flames and collapsed, and they were drowned in heaps. To prevent more disasters Warwick is anxious to arrange with the bishop for the burning of the girl as a sorceress. Cauchon insists he must first try to save her soul, as she is not a witch but a heretic. Like Mahomet, she has ignored the Church and declared herself a messenger of God.

Inside Rheims Cathedral after the coronation, Dunois urges the kneeling Joan to greet the people outside. Joan says she would rather fight than have glory. She asks why the courtiers, knights, and churchmen hate her, and Dunois explains that they are envious.

King Charles comes from the vestry with Bluebeard and La Hire. He asks for the Maid, who has hidden behind a pillar. She steps out, saying that her work is done and she is going home. Seeing Charles's pleasure at this news, she is disappointed and tells Dunois they should first take Paris together. Terrified, Charles says he would prefer a treaty. Joan stamps with impatience.

Joining them, the Archbishop sternly reproves Joan for her pride. She learns that if she is captured none of them will rescue her: neither Dunois, who considers the time of miracles over, nor Charles, who pleads poverty, nor the Archbishop who disapproves of her presumption. Completely alone on earth, Joan goes out. The men reason that they can only leave her to her fate—except for La Hire, who admits he could follow her to hell.

In a castle hall at Rouen on May 30, 1431, an ecclesiastical court is assembling for a trial. Warwick, entering first, sends for Cauchon, who comes in with Brother John Lemaître, the inquisitor, and Canon John D'Estivet, the promoter.

Impatient at the long delay of this case, Warwick observes that more than nine months have passed since the Maid was taken at Compiègne by the Burgundians, four months since he bought her from them, and nearly three since he delivered her to the bishop. Cauchon replies that she has had fifteen examinations in that time. They dispute the necessity of her death.

Warwick leaves, and the assessors arrive, led by Chaplain de Stogumber and Canon de Courcelles, who have drawn up an indictment on sixty-four counts, most of them irrelevant. The inquisitor reduces the counts to twelve, stating that heresy is the chief question. Brother Martin Ladvenu, a young Dominican, suggests that the Maid's heresy is merely simplicity, but the inquisitor counters that the sincerest heresy results in monstrous wickedness.

Joan is brought in, chained by the ankles. Pale but unabashed, she retorts pertly to the foolish questions put by the promoter. Courcelles proposes torture, but Cauchon intervenes and asks Joan whether she will accept the judgment of the Church. She answers that she will not if the Church goes against her instructions from God. All are shocked. Cauchon and Ladvenu try in vain to make her retract.

At last Ladvenu points out that the stake is ready for her outside. Horrified and despairing, Joan signs the confession drawn up for her, but hearing her sentence of life imprisonment, she tears it up, saying that confinement is worse than burning. She is excommunicated, and De Stogumber rushes her out. Shaken, Ladvenu hurries to be at her side.

Alone, Cauchon and the inquisitor agree that, although the Maid should have been tried by the secular authorities, it is better to have the affair over now. On their way out they meet Warwick. Cauchon hints that the English, in their haste to burn Joan, have not fully observed the law. Warwick casts doubt on the bishop's authority in Rouen. They part with hostility.

Soon the chaplain staggers in, frantic with remorse. Sobbing, he tells Warwick of the burning, how the girl cried out to Jesus, how she asked for a cross and a soldier tied two sticks together for her. Then Ladvenu enters, carrying the bishop's cross, borrowed from a church, which he had held up until the flames crept too close. He predicts that it is not the end for Joan, but the beginning. Now the executioner arrives to inform Warwick that his orders have been carried out. The girl's heart wouldn't burn, he says, but all her remains are at the bottom of the river and Warwick has heard the last of her. Warwick wonders.

In an epilogue, King Charles, now fifty-one, in bed on a windy night in June, 1456, has a dream:

Ladvenu, twenty-five years older but still carrying the cross from Rouen, enters to announce that the Maid has been justified and her sentence annulled. Charles is overjoyed: now no one can challenge his coronation. Disgusted, Ladvenu leaves.

A gust of wind blows out the candles, and Joan appears. Charles tells her that he now leads his army into battle and is called Charles the Victorious. One by one, eight others arrive, some from the dead. Joan asks what luck they have had since burning her, and they tell her: Cauchon was excommunicated and his body dishonored; Dunois drove the English from France; the soldier who made a cross of sticks has one day off a year from hell for his good deed; John de Stogumber, slightly crazy but full of benevolence, is the well-loved rector of an English village. Warwick apologizes like a gentleman. The burning was purely political, he says, no personal feelings involved. The executioner, the Archbishop, and the inquisitor pay their respects.

A clerk, dressed in the fashion of 1920, announces the canonization of Joan of Arc and mentions politely that the numerous statues to her are obstructing traffic. Cauchon kneels to Joan, saying that the girls in the field praise her, for they now see nothing between themselves and heaven. The others kneel, one by one, giving reasons for praise. But when Joan asks whether she should come back to life, they jump up in consternation. Each gives an excuse for not wanting her back and sneaks out; Charles returns to bed. Joan is left with the soldier from hell, who hears the stroke of midnight and must go too. Alone, she says: "O God that madest this beautiful earth, when will it be ready to receive Thy saints? How long, O Lord, how long?"

GEORGE   BERNARD   SHAW

The Simpleton of the Unexpected Isles [1935]

PROLOGUE

Scene 1. In an office at a tropical port in the British Empire, the emigration officer and his clerk Wilks argue about admitting a girl who has neither papers nor passport and who is in excess of the quota. Wilks brings in the young woman, who is very sprightly and outspoken and who chides the emigration officer for drinking so early in the day. The officer has a fit of nerves, breaks down in tears, and gives the girl a landing ticket to get rid of her. She decides that if things are as bad here as the emigration officer says, she has no desire to stay; and having nothing to do until the next boat arrives, she asks him to show her around the town. Helpless against her directness, he feebly agrees. They go out, and Wilks is left alone to ponder his lot; he thinks himself an empire builder by nature, like Cecil Rhodes, except that Rhodes found his back yard full of diamonds to make him a millionaire. Having promised his mother to get in the papers, he writes an appropriate suicide note, ties it to his lapel, and singing "Rule, Britannia," blows his brains out.

Scene 2. The setting is a grassy cliff overhanging the sea. The emigration officer is telling the young woman how dreadful the climate is, how everyone here hates everyone else, and how he was planning to shoot Wilks and commit suicide himself if she hadn't turned up and taken him away. Insulted by the young woman's unsympathetic response, he begins to make for the cliff to jump over; but a handsome native priest comes up the path from the cliff and bars his way. The priest tells him that in this cliff is a temple to a great goddess of life and that he is not allowed to die here; but the priest offers to send him a guide to conduct him to the cliff of death. The emigration officer is offended at being told what to do by a native, and plants himself on the edge of the cliff and prepares to spring. When he cannot quite bring himself to do it, the priest assists by kicking him over the edge. There is a great splash. The young woman indignantly accuses the priest of being a murderer, but he assures her that there is a net below and that the shock will do the man good.

Scene 3. Halfway down the cliff is a shelf of rock; images of oriental gods are carved in shallow alcoves, and a feast of fruit is spread on the ground. The young woman, the priest, and a priestess are having lunch and talking. An English lady tourist wanders in and wants to know which of the carved figures is the principal god; the priest tells her that they are all different aspects of one god. The priestess, however, is rather sharp with her, and the lady tourist leaves. The emigration officer enters in a white robe. He remarks that what with being violently ill from the sea water he swallowed and from the beverage given him by the natives, he has been completely purified and regenerated. The lady tourist returns and gives the priest a tract entitled "Where will you spend eternity?" She has been haunted by his face, she says, and cannot bear to think of him spending eternity in torment. The priest politely promises to read the tract, but the priestess jibes at the lady tourist and accuses her of having fallen in love with the priest. The lady leaves indignantly. The priest, who is called Pra, discusses with Prola, the priestess, the devotion he inspires in women. The young woman makes a motion to leave but Prola stops her, saying that they can share Pra. The lady tourist returns again and asks to have a word alone with Pra. The lady's husband Sir Charles Farwaters appears asking for his wife. The priestess lures him off with her to look at the temple. The young woman, flabbergasted by these strange pairings, suggests to the emigration officer that they get out while they still can. The officer, however, replies blandly that he has been cleansed by his immersion and feels quite safe here; he then seizes her and pushes her over the edge to effect her purification.

ACT ONE

The scene is the lawn of a stately house on a tropical island. In the lawn is a flower garden in which are four shrines inhabited by two girls and two young men. A young English clergyman wanders into the garden and approaches the shrines apprehensively, with the air of one who is trespassing. At the same time Pra, about twenty years older than he was in the Prologue, comes down the stairs from the house. The Englishman apologizes for intruding on what he believes to be consecrated ground, thinking the four youths to be idols. He tells Pra that he was put on shore by pirates who had kidnaped him to serve as their chaplain and thus trick people into thinking them respectable. Prola arrives and they take the clergyman as an escapee from a lunatic asylum when he says that he was a nitrogen baby, for his chemist-father fed him a special diet containing nitrates. Pra suggests that they take him into the family, as a kind of experiment, and they go to tell the others.

The clergyman, left with the four figures, goes up to the blonde goddess and, overcome by her beauty, kisses her. He is astounded to discover that she is alive. The two youths warn him to beware, while the two girls greet him with poetic observations about him, themselves, and their brothers. The girls come toward him and put their arms around him. Lady Farwaters comes out of the house and shoos them away, telling the clergyman not to mind them. Prola and Pra come into the garden, followed by Sir Charles Farwaters and by Hugo Hyering (the former emigration officer) and his wife (the former emigrant girl). From the remarks of the six older people it is clear that the four youths are their children in common; the clergyman is extremely distressed at hearing this and cannot quite assimilate it. The others offer to make him a bishop if he will come to live with them; they explain their eugenic experiment of mixing east and west that produced the four young people. Now, the young people having grown up, the group needs to produce a second generation.

Pra explains that the youths have one deficiency: a total lack of moral conscience. Since the clergyman, a nitrogen baby, has an excessively active moral conscience, Pra suggests that there is a relationship between nitrogen and conscience and that, in any event, the clergyman is the perfect husband for the girls. The clergyman cannot at first take in the fact that he is expected to marry both girls and that, indeed, each girl would consider the rejection of her sister tantamount to the rejection of herself. The clergyman, in distress, asks the others to call him by his childish nickname, Iddy, short for idiot. Pra goes on to point out that not only the girls, but all the women, are included in the family group. Iddy misunderstands, thinking the older women mean to become his mothers. They decide to leave him alone to collect his thoughts. The girls, Maya and Vashti, creep up on him, speak to him seductively, and embrace him.

ACT TWO

Some years later, the harbor in the distance is crowded with ships. On the lawn is a writing table covered with papers and a telephone. Pra and Sir Charles are sitting at the table and writing. Hyering enters and says that the ships in the harbor are quarreling about everything imaginable and that he has received six ultimatums expiring at noon today from various admirals. The ultimatums concern Iddy, whose marital arrangements have brought conflicting protests from all over the Empire. Pra confesses that their attempt to found a millennial world culture by uniting east and west has gotten no further than their own little household and can go no further since Iddy is an impotent simpleton. In order to reform Iddy's morals, he adds, half the ships in the harbor are determined to destroy Iddy's household, while the other half are determined to sink them if they attempt it. However, he has sent a message asking them to wait another day, since there is a serious outbreak of smallpox near the harbor.

The garden and its occupants vanish; when they reappear, all the ships are gone from the harbor. In place of the writing table is a tea table. All are present except Iddy and the brothers. Sir Charles remarks to Pra that his message to get the ships to flee did the trick. Hyering adds that by the time the fleets realize that they have been fooled, the world will be tired of Iddy. This brings a chorus from the girls that *they* are tired of Iddy. Iddy enters to dead silence. He observes that it is terrible to be loved and that the love of the women in his family is just too much of a good thing. The girls reply that, if it is any consolation, they hate him intensely; this, he says, makes him happier than he has been for months but does not solve his problems.

The brothers enter with newspapers and announce that England has withdrawn from the Empire and gone back to being a tight little island. Sir Charles wonders what will happen to their jobs as government officials, and Hyering suggests that they proclaim themselves an independent republic. But the children want a monarchy with Prola as queen. Then they decide to make her empress of the world and announce that they will kill everyone who does not do as she tells them. Iddy excuses himself, saying he wants to get the field glasses to look at a strange bird in the sky, which he thinks is an albatross. The idiotic adulation of the young people provokes Prola into sending them away.

There is a trumpet call, and an angel—Iddy's "albatross"—flies into the middle of the garden. He announces that it is Judgment Day, and that the lives that are useless and meaningless shall disappear. He departs. The English people are slightly offended that they did not get more dramatic treatment and that the angel left without apparently judging them. Soon, however, newspaper reports come of people vanishing in England; Iddy, having gone off with Maya, comes back in shock to announce that she vanished out of his arms. Almost immediately the older people forget even the names of the youths, or how many of them there were. The telephone rings, bringing the news of a plot to destroy England's most valuable citizens, almost all the heads of commerce and state having disappeared. Hyering observes that the angels are weeding the garden and getting rid of the useless people; Prola remarks that henceforth they will all have to justify their existences or perish.

R . C . S H E R R I F F

Journey's End [1928]

Captain Hardy, a cheerful, red-faced man, sits drying a sock over a candle flame in a dugout in the British trenches before St. Quentin. The time is March 18, 1918; the dugout is fifty yards from the front line. Osborne, a forty-five-year-old lieutenant, who is among those relieving Hardy, comes down the steps. Hardy tells Osborne that the big German attack is expected in a few days and that Osborne, who is arriving for a six-day tour of duty, will probably be in the middle of it. Hardy asks how Stanhope, Osborne's commander, is, and is especially inquisitive about Stanhope's drinking. Osborne defends Captain Stanhope as a great company commander. He says Stanhope has been at the front for three years and the strain of the duty is the reason for his drinking. Hardy gets his gear together and leaves.

Raleigh, an eighteen-year-old second lieutenant, enters the dugout. He is obviously very new. He tells Osborne how thrilled he is to be at the front. He asked to be placed in Stanhope's company, for he knew Stanhope at school, and his sister is unofficially engaged to him. Osborne warns him Stanhope won't seem quite the same as before.

When Stanhope, a tall, thin, good-looking young man, comes in, accompanied by the fat, middle-aged Second Lieutenant Trotter, he is shocked to see Raleigh, his old school friend. When Raleigh and Trotter leave to go on duty, Stanhope tells Osborne what a blow it is to him to have Raleigh in the company, for the boy hero-worships him. Stanhope fears Raleigh will notice at once how heavily he drinks and report back to his sister about it. He then drinks himself into a stupor. Osborne puts him to bed while the rumble of distant guns echoes in the background.

ACT TWO

At breakfast in the dugout the next morning, Trotter and Osborne joke about the food. Trotter says he feels the big attack is coming soon, because the Germans are so quiet. Raleigh, breakfasting too, is quiet as Trotter discusses Stanhope's increasingly heavy drinking and strange conduct. When Stanhope enters, Raleigh leaves the room to write a letter home. Stanhope says the colonel expects the big attack to come in two days. He is himself concerned about Raleigh's letter, and when Raleigh brings it in for mailing, he takes it, insisting that he must censor it. After Raleigh, much upset, goes out, Osborne reads the letter aloud for Stanhope, who has lost stomach for the task, and finds it contains nothing but praise for the company commander.

In the afternoon of the same day, Stanhope explains to the burly sergeant-major that he intends to have his company stand firm against the attack. He wants wiring to be put down on both sides of their position and refuses even to discuss the possibility of withdrawal. The colonel comes in and says the general wants a raid made on the enemy lines to capture a German and secure information about the coming attack. The colonel decides that two officers and ten men should make the raid under a smoke screen cover. He suggests that Osborne and Raleigh be the two officers. When the colonel leaves, Hibbert, a second lieutenant in his early twenties, comes in complaining of his neuralgia. He says he is ill and must leave, but Stanhope won't let him go. When Hibbert gets his pack, Stanhope threatens to shoot him for desertion. At the confrontation, Hibbert breaks into sobs and finally agrees to stay. Stanhope confesses that he too fears the front lines but does his best to hide it. Osborne comes in, and Stanhope tells him the colonel wants him and Raleigh to raid the enemy lines. Osborne accepts the mission calmly, but Raleigh, coming in, finds it "frightfully exciting."

ACT THREE

The next day toward sunset, the colonel and Stanhope discuss the raid. Despite the fact that the Germans seem to expect it, it must go on, the colonel says. There has been a hole blown through the German wire, and the Germans have tied red cloths to it to show they know a raid will be made. After the colonel leaves, Osborne gives Stanhope his personal belongings, in case he doesn't return; Osborne and Raleigh drink coffee in the few minutes left before the raid. They should be back in three minutes, Osborne tells the young soldier. There will be a chicken and champagne to celebrate when they return, he adds. The two men leave and after a pause, the sound of machine guns and shells comes through the air. Finally everything is quiet. Stanhope and the colonel come down the steps. Stanhope tells him they have a German prisoner and leaves to see his men. The colonel questions the young German and, finding out what he wants to know, is elated. Stanhope returns and the colonel casually asks whether the raiding party is back. Stanhope, in restrained bitterness, says four men and Raleigh are back safely. The colonel expresses his sorrow that six men and Osborne were lost, but Stanhope tells him sarcastically, "Still it'll be awfully nice if the brigadier's pleased." The colonel stutters out embarrassed congratulations to Raleigh, who enters sleepily, and leaves.

Later that same day in the dugout, Stanhope, Trotter, and Hibbert gaily eat the celebration dinner. Stanhope inquires after Raleigh and is told he preferred to stay up with the men. When Raleigh comes in, Stanhope chides him for not joining the others. Raleigh makes various excuses, then blurts out that he couldn't eat the dinner with Osborne dead. Stanhope swears at him for thinking he's the only one who cares and says he himself acts the way he does only to forget. Raleigh apologizes.

As dawn of the next day approaches, the officers rise and ready themselves for the attack. Raleigh, Trotter, and Hibbert leave. While Stanhope gets ready, word comes that Raleigh is hit in the back. Stanhope directs that he be brought to the dugout. Raleigh is unconscious, but Stanhope bathes his face and he wakes. The boy tries to rise but can't move his legs. Raleigh asks for water, then for a light. Stanhope hurries for a light, but before he can get it, Raleigh gives a moan and dies. A messenger comes. Mr. Trotter wants Stanhope to come at once. After he leaves, a shell hits the dugout roof, and it collapses, extinguishing the solitary candle and leaving the dugout in darkness.

ROBERT SHERWOOD

The Petrified Forest [1935]

ACT ONE

Late one afternoon in 1934, in the lunchroom of the Black Mesa Filling Station and Bar-B-Q in the eastern Arizona desert, Gramp Maple listens to two telegraph linemen and Boze Herzlinger, the athletic young gas station attendant, as the first lineman voices approval of the Russian system and the other two assert that it is slavery. Jason Maple, the drab proprietor, enters and sends Boze out to a customer. The first lineman continues to praise the constructive pioneering spirit of the Russian system. As Gramp tells them about his youth in the pioneering days, pretty young Gabby Maple enters, sits down with a book, and begins to read. When she carries the empty plates to the kitchen, Jason, who sports an American Legion button, warns the first lineman against voicing radical opinions. After the linemen leave, Jason bitterly blames Gramp for Jason's dull existence, for Gramp refuses to sell the business and give Jason the chance to begin something better in Los Angeles.

Gabby enters to report that Paula, the Mexican cook, is frightened by reports that Duke Mantee, who is supposed to have massacred six people the previous day in Oklahoma City, is headed in their direction. When Jason leaves to dress for a legion meeting and Gramp goes to retrieve the mail, Gabby begins to read, indifferent to the approach of Boze. He examines her book, surprised to find it filled with erotic poems, which she defends as "great poetry." Proudly he recounts his success as a college football player and tells her that he is falling in love with her. As he kisses her, a shabby but vaguely elegant stranger appears in the doorway, carrying a rucksack. As he sits down, Boze leaves. The stranger, Alan Squier, tells Gabby that he has been hitchhiking. He orders a meal and goes out to the washroom as Jason enters in his uniform. When Gramp brings the news that Mantee is probably heading their way, Jason asserts that the Legion will act. Gabby returns with a bowl of soup, and Jason departs.

When Alan returns and sits down to eat, Gramp shows him the newspaper account of Duke Mantee. When Gramp leaves to eat his dinner, Gabby tells Alan, who has told them he was once a writer, that she was born in France, for her father married a Frenchwoman who couldn't stand the desert and returned to her own country. Though her father won't allow it, Gabby wants to visit her mother. She reads to Alan from the poems of François Villon, sent to her by her mother. After listening to her romantic idea of France, Alan, in warning her that she will be disappointed, tells how his wife, thinking he was a major writer, supported him for eight years on the Riviera, during which time he wrote nothing. After they parted, he returned to America and began to hitchhike, in the hope of finding something to live for.

Gabby admits to him that she paints and goes to fetch her paintings. He studies them in bewilderment. Gabby describes to Alan her distaste for the desert and the feelings in her that she attributes to her French blood. Alan describes himself as an intellectual, one of those useless, outmoded creatures. When Gabby mentions the nearby petrified forest, Alan calls it a proper place for such as he.

Suddenly Gabby announces that with her share of the money Gramp has in the bank, she would like to go to France with Alan and live with him in sin. Startled and moved, Alan explains that she would not be happy with a man who had nothing to do but to love her. As he kisses her goodby, Boze appears and orders him to pay and leave. When Alan confesses that he has no money, Boze starts to throw him out bodily. Just then, Mr. and Mrs. Chisholm and their chauffeur Joseph arrive. Mrs. Chisholm disappears into the ladies' room, and Gabby sends Boze back to his work. When Mr. Chisholm mentions that he and his wife are on their way west, Gabby asks whether they will give Alan a ride. Chisholm agrees. Gabby gives Alan a dollar, pretending that it is his change. Mrs. Chisholm returns and leaves with her husband. After a brief goodby Alan follows them.

Boze returns and tries to convince Gabby that his desire for her is strong and natural. As she agrees to a moonlight walk with him, a car is heard stopping. Jackie, a chubby little gangster with a submachine gun, enters, followed by Ruby and Duke Mantee. Jackie fetches the terrified Paula, along with Gramp, who is delighted to recognize Mantee. Duke orders food and sends Jackie out to the kitchen with Paula while she cooks. Alan bursts in and relates to Gabby how bandits stopped the Chisholm car and stole it. Suddenly he sees Duke and Ruby and sits down with a bottle of whiskey. As he drinks, he describes his feeling that destiny and his own demise are approaching.

ACT TWO

Half an hour later, Duke and Jackie are finishing their meal, Ruby is watching over everyone, and Gramp is talking about a great killer of whom he knows. Boze, trying to appear brave, insults the killers and is saved from Jackie's ire by Duke. Alan is slowly becoming drunker. A radio report of the manhunt for Mantee discloses that the other half of the gang, three men and a woman, are also still at large. Duke sends Ruby out to replace Pyles in keeping watch. Pyles enters and goes off to the kitchen with Paula to eat.

As Duke and Jackie study a map, Boze asks Alan how he expects to pay for his liquor. When Alan reveals that Gabby gave him a dollar, Boze starts to reveal what Gabby was about to bestow on him before the killers arrived. When Gabby becomes furious, Boze becomes contrite and reiterates his declaration of love. Gabby explains to Alan that she was about to give in to Boze. Jackie takes the map and goes into the kitchen. Alan, feeling that Duke, like himself, is an outmoded phenomenon, calls him "the last great apostle of rugged individualism."

Gabby tells Boze that she loves Alan, much to the surprise of Alan, who tells Gramp to use his saved-up money to help Gabby escape from the desert. Ruby appears and announces the approach of the Chisholms. As Duke turns to look out the window, Boze grabs Duke's shotgun. When Mr. and Mrs. Chisholm and Joseph appear, Mrs. Chisholm screams, and Boze turns to cover them. Duke whips out a revolver and fires, hitting Boze in the hand. Jackie disarms Boze, and Duke orders the Chisholms to sit down. Gabby goes to bandage Boze's hand; Jackie goes along to tie him up.

Alan, resentful of Boze's deed, takes out his life insurance policy and begins to write on it, explaining that he is making Gabby his beneficiary. He asks Duke to shoot him, for though he is of no use to Gabby alive, his death can provide her great opportunity. Duke agrees to kill Alan just before he leaves.

Pyles tells Duke they ought not to wait for the woman, who, with the three other men, is to meet them there. When Gramp doubts the wisdom of Alan's plan, Alan points to Duke as an example of a man who will risk his life for a woman. Gabby and Jackie return, and Jackie proceeds outside to visit Ruby. Gabby urges Gramp to sell the establishment, as the extraordinary publicity will boost the price, adding that she would use the money to help her father get established in Los Angeles. Alan and Mrs. Chisholm urge her to be more selfish, but she will not listen.

When Duke's departure nears, Alan announces to Gabby that he loves her, telling her mysteriously that the artist in him will live in her. When Gabby assures him that they would be happy together, he tells her that he has found what he was looking for. He then signals to Duke to carry out his promise.

At that moment, warning toots are heard from the car. Jason and two other legionnaires enter under the cover of the killers' guns. They reveal that the other four fugitives have been caught and that the woman has revealed to the police the rendezvous point. As the other outlaws press him to forget the woman and hasten their escape, Duke remains undecided, until Alan suggests that it is better to die for freedom than for revenge. As the gang is about to flee, another warning is heard. Duke sees that the sheriff has arrived with a posse. He begins to fire out the window, ordering the others to lie flat on the floor. Jackie goes to defend the kitchen door, while Pyles covers those on the floor. As the firing continues, Gabby asks Alan excitedly about France. As Alan kisses her, Duke announces that he is leaving. When Pyles goes to get Jackie, he reports that Jackie is dead. Duke selects the Chisholms, Joseph, and the two legionnaires to ride on the running board as shields. As Duke follows them out, Alan calls significantly to him. Duke shoots him and leaves.

As the car is heard driving away, the sheriff rushes in, followed by three deputies, and starts after the fugitives. Alan tells Gabby that he is dying but that he has found the reason in his life for which he was looking. After he dies, Gramp tells her about the insurance policy and Alan's wish that she go to France. Gabby announces that they will bury him in the petrified forest. She recites the lines from Villon about the seed that thrives in another's field, understanding now the purpose of her meeting with Alan.

REINHARD JOHANNES SORGE

The Beggar [*Der Bettler*, published 1912; performed 1917]

ACT ONE

The Poet is standing with an Older Friend in front of a curtain discussing a play, written by an acquaintance of the older man, which has just had a successful first night. The Older Friend tells the Poet to be tactful when he meets a possible patron later in the evening; the patron is unlikely to pay for a theater for the production of the Poet's avant-garde plays, but he might offer a stipend, the Older Friend indicates. The Poet speaks of the impossible situation at home, where he lives with his parents, as he moves slowly off with his friend.

The curtain parts to reveal the interior of a café where a group of people are idly waiting for news of the first night: the first editions of the newspapers arrive, and the group excitedly buy copies. As they skim through the news, the critics arrive and tell the waiting group that the play was a success but no good at all: it lacks inspiration and vision. They then leave for another café, and as they go one critic tells another that what they are searching for is the great dramatist of the time who can set down the destiny of his fellow men.

The curtain falls and the Older Friend, the Poet, and the Patron appear; the Poet sets the tone of the forthcoming discussion by saying that he fears he and the Patron might fail to agree. The three go off, and a group of prostitutes are revealed quarreling among themselves as they wait for their clients; the men arrive and go off with the girls. A young Girl enters with a Nurse; a waiter appears and draws back the curtain, and the two women sit at a table. Curtained from their view, the Poet, the Patron, and the Older Friend sit discussing the Poet's future. The Patron states that he will give the Poet an allowance; the Poet must travel and gain experience of the world, the Patron says. But the Poet answers that what he wants above all is his own theater in order to see his plays produced, learn from his mistakes, and gain further inspiration from seeing his work performed. The Poet makes a long romantic speech declaring that his dramatic verse will reveal to the masses transcendent beauty; as he speaks, the Girl moves to where she can see him. The Patron refuses to grant the Poet's request, and the Poet declares the meeting ended.

A group of fliers is revealed; like a Greek chorus, they speak of one of their group who flew too high and too confidently and fell to earth in his plane. Alone, the Poet and the Older Friend say goodby to each other; they shake hands, despite the friend's disappointment in the Poet's tactless behavior. As the Poet leaves, the Girl crosses to him and says she must speak to him.

ACT TWO

Before the curtain, the Poet's mad Father beats a drum wildly, driving off invisible demons and gods; he exits, driving the demons before him. The curtain parts, revealing the Poet sitting with his Mother, who is crushed by the burden of looking after the madman. She tells her son that she has received another letter from her husband's sister refusing to allow her to place the madman in an institution; the Poet says the aunt must have her way since she is giving them so much money. The Father reappears and dances crazily around the room. The Mother is at first terrified but then, as her husband calms, sits at the table with him and listens to his plans for getting back to work. She slips away as the Poet talks with his Father, who describes a dream in which he saw people and machines on the planet Mars. The Mother and her grown-up Daughter enter with food and drink, and the Poet proposes a toast. The two women leave for bed, and the Father continues the description of Mars: he wants to draw blueprints for the construction of the machines he saw there. At first ecstatic, the Father finishes in tears, imploring his son to give him poison and end his misery; the Poet leads him away to bed.

Three figures appear to the Poet and tell him that he must not fail his Father's request. The figures fade, and the young Girl enters and tells the Poet, who is now her lover, that an uncle has advised her to allow an illegitimate child she has had by another man to be adopted. The Poet tells her to wait and not to decide hastily.

ACT THREE

The Poet is with his Mother in the garden discussing a recent attack of madness suffered by his Father. The Mother leaves to prepare dinner; alone, the Poet says that his Friend has sent him poison and that the time has come to administer it to his Father, since his Mother is weakening daily under the strain of her husband's madness, and his Father's plans for the machines, which the Poet thought possibly workable, have been deemed crazy. The Girl arrives with the Poet's sister, who goes at once to help her Mother but quickly returns to say that their Father is coming into the garden with his attendant. The two girls leave and the Poet sends the attendant to fetch wine.

Alone with his Father, the Poet pours two glasses of wine for a toast; while the old man's attention is distracted, the Poet poisons his Father's wine. The madman has brought his blueprints with him; finding he lacks red ink, he seizes a fledgling fallen from a nest and stabs it with compasses to provide a substitute for ink. Just as he is about to drink the poisoned wine, the Father is interrupted by the appearance of the Mother and sends the Poet to fetch another glass.

The husband and wife raise the two glasses and drink together; the husband says that he is getting better and that soon they will have a second marriage feast. He takes the glass from which his wife drank and empties it; the woman takes the other glass, but it drops from her trembling hands and smashes. When the Poet returns, his Father tells him he must carry on the work with the machines; as he speaks, he falls back weakly and dies. The Poet's mother speaks lovingly of her husband and says wistfully how wonderful it would be if he could regain his sanity; her head falls back and she also dies.

ACT FOUR

The Poet stands before the curtain and laments that the world weighs heavy on him, that he can find no joy or peace in his art. He turns toward the spectators, calls for the thundering glass-factory, for the wan madhouse, that he may bless and burn them with the fire of his genius. He breaks down, only to say again that he will carry the world on his shoulders and go into the sun, since he is resolved to find work, to do work, to cast his circle to embrace eternity, to touch God.

He kneels; the curtain parts and a vision appears. The Figure of the Girl stands motionless and the Figure of the Poet moves, sowing seeds on a fresh grave. The Figure of the Poet says that springtime will flourish on this bed where love of children and love of parents sleeps, where his Father's fruit shall yet bear fruit.

The vision fades, the scene brightens to show a cottage on a fresh Thuringian hillside. The Poet yearns aloud for a love that has never yet been loved, for a song never wept, a sea not sailed, for the ecstasy of death. He rises and the Girl appears from the cottage doorway. The Poet tells her of his resolve to return to the city, to live life as well as to write about it, to cease creating alone, supported by the easy gifts of friends. The Girl tells him of her own decision to keep by her the illegitimate child and to be its mother. He replies that humility has raised both their eyes toward the sun.

ACT FIVE

The Poet stands to one side before the curtain, behind which are heard muted noises from a great city street. He laments that the city is a morass, too, that his path there is slime, beauty rots on his lips; he also rots, longing for death. Now he knows that he cannot work as a journalist and daily newspaperman because his day is made for the work which outlives the day. He draws the curtain somewhat aside. Marching and military music are heard, an occasional uniform glints, weapons. The Poet vows that somehow he will mold his life and work to an eternal crown cast from gold hopes and dreams. He enters the curtain and disappears.

When the curtain reopens, the scene is a poor attic; the Poet reappears, dressed in his Father's blue dressing gown. He leafs through a manuscript he has finished. He dreams of a new plot, of a Girl and a Youth and a falling star that sows light in her eyes and her eyes sow light in the Youth forever. Despairing, the Poet asks how he can preserve this burning moment of love's founding in mere words. He laments that he is only a mock-priest of the eternal, that art is a fraud. Suddenly he starts up, asking whether the poet is not a priest of the eternal through symbols. Yes, he answers, he sees his goal at last.

Exhausted, the Poet sinks back, when his Older Friend enters, telling him to stop writing or else to forfeit their friendship. The Poet replies that friendship cannot be broken except by falseness, that they will be friends although they never meet again, that he remains true to his art. The Older Friend leaves and the Girl enters, forswearing her first child, whom she loved only for the pain it caused her. Now she will give the Poet his own child, born of the spirit. The Poet is content. He closes his eyes, murmuring that it grows dark but that his star grows bright, since now they both live and work in the spirit of purity.

AUGUST STRINDBERG

Charles XII [*Karl XII*, 1902]

NOTE: The action of the play telescopes time from Charles's return to Sweden, after an absence of fifteen years at the wars, until his death in 1718. During Charles's reign Sweden lost almost all of the great territorial gains of the preceding 150 years, and the country suffered famine and plague during his lengthy and expensive wars against Russia and Poland.

ACT ONE

It is a cold December on the Scanian coast of Sweden; the year is 1715. At the center of the stage there is a dilapidated cottage, deserted in the plague of 1710, and a lone, leafless apple tree with one apple, which is being shaken in the wind. To the right of the cottage are the burned remains of a church and several houses. A man in rags, searching among the ruins, is met by a coast-guardsman who demands to know what he is doing. The man replies that this was his cottage and that he left it, and his wife and children, fifteen years ago to go to the wars. The guard tells him that Stralsund has fallen and that the King is fleeing by ship to Sweden, pursued by a Danish frigate. The man constantly refers to the King as "the villain." The guard points out a group of riders; they are, he says, a member of the National Council and the Speakers of the Four Estates (the lords, the clergy, the burghers, and the farmers); they are afraid for their heads, since they had summoned parliament in the King's absence and demanded his suspension.

The man and the guard leave, and the Councillor and the Speakers enter with a welcoming address to the King. The Speakers invoke pity on a country whose King is a madman and a villain. An Adjutant arrives to make way for the King. The Speakers agree among themselves not to kneel. The King enters and goes into the cottage with his attendants; the Speakers, in spite of themselves, fall to their knees. The Adjutant takes letters from the Councillor and the Speakers and gives them to the King, who opens them, glances through them, and throws them away. He takes counsel with the Adjutant and departs with some of his party, leaving two men, Hultman and Luxembourg, and a dwarf behind. The Adjutant returns and tells the Councillor and the Speakers to return to the capital and await the King's further decisions. He urges them to depart at once, for another traitor is to be executed here—the skipper of the brigantine that was supposed to meet the King after his defeat at Stralsund but which failed because of the ice to show up at the meeting place. The Adjutant tells Hultman that there are horses waiting for him in the next village; no provision is taken for the dwarf, who is left alone.

ACT TWO

While the King is temporarily quartered in a private house in Lund, the university city, two statesmen, Gyllenborg and Horn, are talking in the King's audience room; they are on opposite political sides, Horn in favor of curtailing the King's absolute power, Gyllenborg of continuing it. Feif, the King's secretary, enters and instructs the two men how to respond to the King. The King enters, sits down, and asks his questions through Feif; the latter asks Horn to characterize the notorious Baron Görtz. Horn, hesitantly, says that Görtz is an exceptional man with an exceptional desire for power, that he is brilliant and dangerous and not to be trusted. Gyllenborg and Horn are dismissed, and Baron Görtz announced. The King confronts him with a letter to the Czar, allegedly written by Görtz, containing a plan to depose the King and to marry the King's nephew Charles Fredrik to the Czar's daughter and put him on the Swedish throne. Görtz adroitly maneuvers himself out of this difficulty and, appealing to the King's desire for money to raise another army, says he could raise 60,000 soldiers in 60 days in order to take Norway as compensation for Sweden's loss of Finland. The King goes out briefly, and in his absence guards enter and arrest Görtz. The King returns, sends Feif to summon Emanuel Swedenborg, and gives an order that Görtz is to be set at liberty but told not to leave the city.

Alone, the King lies on his bed, the ragged man from the first act comes in, carrying a bludgeon. He and the King stare at one another, the King remaining silent and motionless while the man calls him a villain and accuses him of ruining Sweden. He says that his name is Svält (Hunger) and that he saved the King's life at a battle in 1709, a deed he regrets, since, had the King been killed, there would have been peace for six years now. He leaves, and the King rings; Hultman comes in and at the King's instruction looks up the cavalry lists for 1709, but the name Svält does not appear. The King remarks that he must have been dreaming. When questioned, Hultman says that there is no more money and that the recruiting is going badly. The King asks for Görtz to be sent to him immediately.

ACT THREE

Ruins of burned houses stand at one end of a square, Görtz's house at the other; at the tavern in the foreground the man and the dwarf sit at an outdoor table drinking beer. The man talks about his encounter with the King, and the dwarf remarks that Görtz has been put in charge of finances, that in spite of the fact that Görtz has been expelled from every country in Europe and has conspired to dethrone the King, he now has the King's total confidence and is the absolute minister of the whole country. A malcontent comes up to the table and complains about the dreadful things happening all around.

Upper-class women dressed in mourning go to the door of Görtz's house;

377

they are "widows" whose husbands have been taken prisoner in Russia and whom the King has refused to ransom: they are not admitted into the house. A procession of lords, headed by Horn, go to the door; they are also turned away. A poverty-stricken woman goes to the door, knocks, discovers a peephole, opens it, and places her petition in it. One of the noblewomen approaches her and asks her what she wants. The woman replies that she is trying to get mercy for her father, the skipper condemned to death when ice prevented him from meeting the King's boat. A courier arrives with a great deal of noise and goes into the house by the back way; a lackey comes out the front and lowers the flag to half-mast; a herald announces that Louis XIV of France is dead.* The people in the square mutter among themselves that this signals the end of absolute monarchy. The herald clears the square in order to have a salvo fired in mourning.

ACT FOUR

In a large garden adjoining the house where the King at present lives, Hultman talks with the Professor who owns the house. The Professor remarks that the King's sister, who is newly married, is in town to see him. They observe the approach of Dr. Swedenborg and his fiancée, Emerentia Polhem, whom Hultman terms a conceited girl, for she has sworn that she will have the King, a notorious woman-hater, at her feet. The two men leave, and Swedenborg and Emerentia enter; Emerentia complains because Swedenborg has to leave on business for the King, although he and Emerentia were supposed to celebrate their engagement tomorrow. She says that she wants to see the King, but Swedenborg tries to make her promise not to do so. They quarrel, she accuses him of never having loved her, and they leave in opposite directions.

The King enters, followed by Feif. The King worries because Görtz is away, complains that no one comes to see him any more, and finally sends Feif to send for his sister, Princess Ulrika Eleonora. Emerentia appears, carrying a bunch of roses. She flirts cagily with the King, not admitting who she is; when he mentions Swedenborg, she pretends that she scarcely knows him and calls him an ugly person. Asked whether she likes the King a little, she makes an evasive but provocative response; calling her by name, he tells her that she does not deserve Swedenborg and that he will see that she does not marry him. Ashamed, Emerentia leaves, and Feif enters to announce the Princess.

Ulrika Eleonora arrives and makes various insinuations about the King's plans and a comic quarrel breaks out over the question of the succession. The King states that Ulrika's husband, the Landgrave of Hesse, is a pig and that they do not want a pig on the throne; Ulrika counters that the King's nephew Charles Fredrik is a fool who is ruled by his valet. Though she despises her husband, Ulrika pleads with the King to name the Landgrave as his successor. The King finally admits that his position is desperate; he lies down on the cot, and Ulrika comforts him like a mother until he falls asleep. She then sends a

* This is an anachronism; Louis XIV died in September, 1715.

message to her husband that the situation is favorable for them. She leaves.

The King awakens as Swedenborg comes in. The King asks whether he is ready to go to Norway; Swedenborg hesitates and mentions his engagement; the King tells him of Emerentia's flirtation and ill words. Swedenborg weeps. Görtz enters hastily to report that everything is lost, for too many token coins have been issued and are ruining the economy; moreover, the Landgrave of Hesse is the most popular man in the country. The King pulls himself together to go out and find the Landgrave, whom he has just decided to make a general of the army. He says that he will leave this evening for Norway and the battlefield.

ACT FIVE

Before the Fredriksten Fortress in Norway, the King lies on his army bed staring into the fire. An occasional flare comes from the fortress. Swedenborg comments that it seems as if everyone is waiting for something; Feif replies that Görtz, sitting on the cannon, seems to be waiting to be blown sky high and that the Landgrave and the King's nephew are waiting for the throne. Horn and Gyllenborg come up and agree that they, too, sense something about to happen. Horn says that the King was once a man of destiny whom success attended as long as he walked the paths of justice, but who went his own way eighteen years ago when he determined to control the destinies of nations.

An Adjutant brings the despairing King a dispatch; he reads it, shows great distress, and gives it to Görtz, who also shows distress. The King says goodnight to Swedenborg and announces that he is going to start the assault. While the King is in the first trench, a flare lights up the sky and expires with a report. A cry comes that the King is shot. Feif says that the bullet came from the fortress, but Swedenborg points to heaven and says that it came from there. The stage is darkened, and a large lantern can be seen in the trench.

AUGUST STRINDBERG

The Dance of Death [*Dödsdansen*, published 1901; performed 1905]

PART I

In an old island prison fort made over into living quarters for the Captain in the Coast Artillery and his family.

Alice and Edgar sit in their house one autumn evening, bitterly discussing their twenty-five years of misery together. They bicker about lack of money; about their two children, who are away at school in the city; and about their isolation, which Alice ascribes to Edgar's contemptuous attitude toward everyone else on the island. Alice talks of having given up a great career on the stage for a living hell; on the walls of the room are laurels she received during her stage career. She then speaks with envy of a party going on that night at the doctor's, to which they are not invited. At that moment the telegraph receiver, which Edgar uses for communication because he is certain that telephone operators on the island listen in, clicks out a message from his daughter asking for money.

Curt enters, having arrived only that morning; he is Alice's cousin and has been appointed Quarantine Master on the island. Divorced from his wife and separated from his children, he has been traveling in America for fifteen years. Alice begs Curt to have dinner with them and forego his invitation to the doctor's that evening. Curt acquiesces. During the ensuing conversation, punctuated by sarcastic jibes between Edgar and Alice, Curt tries to learn something about the character of his new superior, the doctor, but receives only Edgar's prejudicial account of the officers on the island, whom he claims to be idiots, adding that he is on bad terms with all of them.

Edgar repeatedly criticizes Curt's "abandonment" of his children, even though Curt patiently explains that the court took his children from him. Curt also has to deny responsibility for having brought about the marriage of Alice and Edgar. He soon begins to feel infected and suffocated by the atmosphere of hatred in the house. Suddenly he is alarmed to see Edgar in an apathetic trance, apparently unable to see or hear. Alice, however, casually explains that Edgar is subject to these attacks, and she wishes he would die in one, for only death can free her from him. She complains that she has been for many years Edgar's prisoner; he has cut her off from family and friends; their life together is hell. Curt admits that he is puzzled by Edgar's insistence that he influenced their marriage, and that he is hurt by the suggestion that he has abandoned his children.

On recovering, Edgar asks Alice to play the piano; he begins a mad dance and falls down on the floor in another fit. Curt rushes to fetch the doctor, who knows Edgar's case. He returns with the report that Edgar has calcification of the heart and must stop smoking and drinking. Edgar recovers, but has felt death near and asks Curt to sit by his couch all night while Alice goes to bed. The two men talk of death and Edgar wishes he could believe in immortality.

The next morning, Curt and Alice talk while Edgar sleeps. Alice says that her husband tramples on anyone who lets him, but she speaks sympathetically of his hard and poverty-stricken childhood. Curt listens with neutral sympathy for both. When Edgar awakens, feeling better, he again attacks Curt as a father who has deserted his children, then goes out. Curt observes that when Edgar felt his own life slipping away, he seemed to grasp at Curt's life. Alice warns that Edgar is a vampire and reveals that he was responsible for dividing Curt from his children, for he showed their mother how to manage the separation legally. Curt is astonished and hurt, but still chides Alice when she admits that she, unlike him, loves revenge as a form of justice.

About two days later, while awaiting Edgar's return from the city, Alice and Curt remark on how quiet, considerate, and calm he has become since his illness. Alice finds him more dangerous this way and warns Curt not to be taken in. Edgar enters and informs them that a doctor in the city has predicted that he would probably live for another twenty years. Over Curt's pained protests, he announces that he has arranged with the mother to have Curt's son, a young cadet, transferred to the island. He then informs Alice of his intention to divorce her and bring a younger, more beautiful woman into his home. Alice retaliates with a secret she has long saved up: she tells Curt that Edgar once tried to murder her by pushing her into the water and that their daughter Judith was a witness. Edgar implies that he has seen Judith and made certain that she will never testify against him. Alone with Curt, Alice elaborates a plan to have Edgar convicted of embezzlement, claiming him actually guilty of the crime. Though horrified at Edgar, Curt still shrinks from such an idea and wins Alice's scorn. She begins to dance wildly around the room, imagining her coming freedom. Curt, fascinated and infected by Alice's madness, takes her in his arms and bites her throat. She shouts her plan to ruin her husband and sees Curt as her liberator.

That evening, having arranged for her husband to be imprisoned, Alice waits with Curt, who is now under control and coldly unresponsive, though nevertheless fascinated by her and her effect on him. Edgar enters and privately confesses to Curt that all his threats of the day before were false. Alice tries to arouse Edgar's jealousy by throwing herself into Curt's arms; Curt thrusts her from him and Edgar goes after her with his sabre. Curt refuses to escape with her, but both she and Edgar appeal to him not to leave them. When he rushes from the house, Alice complains to Edgar that Curt is a hypocrite. Edgar admits that he has lied; the doctor in the city has given him little time to live. Remorseful, Alice, without revealing that she has planned to have Edgar imprisoned, says she wishes she could undo what she has done—but Edgar reveals that he has known of the plan all along and foiled it; he now intends to have Alice nurse him. Resignedly, they are united, and speculate as to whether life is a joke and consider celebrating their silver wedding anniversary. The captain suggests that they cross out the past and move on.

PART II

As Judith enters the well-furnished, attractive drawing room of Curt's home on the island, Curt's son Allan, who has been studying at a desk, respectfully rises. She teases him about his studies and asks him to come play tennis with her. He begs her to leave him alone and accuses her of trifling with him and making him jealous of a young lieutenant who also seeks her attentions.

When she is gone, Curt enters. Although Allan tries to hide his unhappiness, his father divines his feelings and says that Judith is young and impetuous, but not cruel. He warns Allan about being too exacting of people. When Alice enters, Allan leaves. Reminding Curt that there was almost something between them once, though he prefers to forget it, she warns him again not to be deceived by Edgar's seeming transformation, for he is plotting some evil. Edgar arrives, and his cryptically sinister remarks seem to bear out Alice's suspicions. He claims credit for Curt's comfortable circumstances and even for his professional accomplishments. Privately, Alice confides that Edgar has been alienating Curt's friends among the officers. Edgar leaves to catch a boat to the city; Alice reveals to Curt that he plans to marry Judith to a sixty-year-old colonel, for he disapproves of her friendship with Allan.

A short while later, after embarrassing Allan with her banter, Judith warns him that trouble is coming to him soon. He leaves and Alice enters. She sends Judith to put up her hair, for she is now a young lady. Curt arrives and, shortly thereafter, Edgar. Edgar has long been quietly undermining Curt and has now achieved his ruin. By publishing articles on quarantine methods, he has claimed credit for Curt's work. A company in which he had advised Curt to buy stock has collapsed, and Curt will have to sell his house and furnishings. Claiming benevolence for sustaining Curt's position, Edgar suggests that Allan be sent to another regiment. Curt bears these outrages with a calm stoicism. When Edgar is gone, Alice and Curt realize that Allan must go because the colonel is soon to arrive, and that Edgar intends also to buy Curt's house himself.

A rainy day, some time later, Curt is visiting, on Edgar's invitation, in the house where he recently lived. Waiting for Edgar, Alice tells Curt that the colonel is expected today. Curt is now running for the national legislature, candidacy being the one plan to which he can see no obstructions. He and Alice go into the sitting room, and Allan and Edgar enter.

Edgar says that he will provide the finances for Allan's transfer to the north; Allan, ignorant of his motives, thanks him. Edgar leaves and Judith enters, exquisitely dressed and looking like a lady. She is as much altered in mood and feeling as in appearance; love finally has touched her, and she tells Allan how much it hurts. When she learns that he is leaving as a result of her father's machinations, she is in despair. She swears that she has no intention of marrying the colonel, regardless of her father's wishes. She begs Allan for a keepsake and promises to wait for him. They say a painful farewell, and Allan goes to pack up; Judith starts for the telegraph office, apparently with a plan in mind.

The others return, and Edgar reveals more of his villainies. Planning to run for the legislature himself, he has managed to discredit Curt with the voters by taking up a public subscription for Allan, thus making his father's financial embarrassments public. Edgar declares that, after fighting the world for fifty years, he at last has won the game. As a final triumph he produces a telegram from the colonel which, he supposes, will mention the coming engagement to Judith. Because of his dimming vision, however, Edgar asks Alice to read the telegram and waits smugly. Alice reads: "On account of Miss Judith's impertinent communication over the telephone, I consider the relationship ended—for ever!"

The strain of having his plans thwarted by his own daughter sends Edgar into an apoplectic stroke. As he lies mumbling unintelligibly, Alice leans over him and calls him a vampire. Edgar summons the strength to spit in her face. The lieutenant appears and Alice asks him to carry Edgar into the next room. Judith enters to say that Allan is gone, and for the first time Alice and Curt realize how serious is the feeling between the two young lovers. They agree that Judith should follow Allan. The lieutenant announces that Edgar is dead; his last words were, "Forgive them, for they know not what they do." Now that he is dead, Curt and Alice feel a strange inclination to speak well of him. Alice talks of how she loved and hated him; she wishes that he may find peace.

AUGUST STRINDBERG

A Dream Play [*Ett Drömspel,* published 1902; performed 1907]

PROLOGUE

There is an impression of clouds, crumbling cliffs, and ruined fortresses. The Daughter of Indra stands on the highest cloud peak, answering the call of her unseen father. He tells her that she has strayed into the dark and heavy atmosphere of Earth and asks her to descend to Earth and report to him whether the lamentations and complaints of human beings are justified.

ACT ONE

In front of a forest of giant hollyhocks is the Growing Castle, straw and manure piled below it and a giant chrysanthemum bud atop its highest tower. The Glazier and the Daughter enter. The Daughter remarks that she thinks there is a prisoner inside the Castle, waiting for her to set him free.

The background vanishes and discloses a bare room with a table at which a young Officer is sitting. A screen cuts the stage in two; the other half is unlit. The Officer says that he has been waiting for the daughter to set him free but isn't sure that he wants to be freed. Either way, he says, he will suffer, for every joy has to be paid for with twice as much sorrow. The Daughter replies that it is one's duty to seek freedom, but the Officer objects that life has not done its duty by him. The screen is drawn aside and the other half of the stage lit up, revealing the Mother, an invalid, sitting at a table on which a candle is burning. The Father brings her a silk shawl. She gives him some instructions about caring for the children after she dies and asks to see her son Alfred. The Officer moves forward to her. She tells him never to quarrel with God, never to feel he has been wronged by life. He objects that he has been treated unfairly, remembering the time he was punished for taking money that was afterwards found, and saying that this twisted his whole life. The Mother reminds him of a book that he had torn to pieces and for which his brother was punished. Lina, the maid, enters, saying she cannot go to the christening because she has nothing to wear. The Mother offers to lend Lina her shawl. The Father, however, is offended that his wife should offer to lend his present to the maid. The Mother laments that if one tries to do something good to one person, one invariably harms another. She snuffs out the candle and the room disappears in darkness. The Daughter reflects that human beings are to be pitied, for life is hard. But she adds that love conquers everything, telling the Officer to come and see.

The background disappears, revealing an old wall, which is broken by a gate opening on an alley, at the end of which is a plot of green with a giant blue monkshood growing in it. On one side of the gate is the Stage Doorkeeper's lodge. The Doorkeeper is sitting in the doorway, a gray shawl over her head and shoulders. A Billsticker is washing an announcement board. Nearby is a door with an air hole shaped like a four-leafed clover, and to one side is a small lime tree with a few green leaves. The Daughter talks to the Doorkeeper and the Billsticker, remarking that all people complain. The Billsticker says that he hasn't much to complain about now that he has gotten the green fishnet and green fish-box he dreamed of when he was a little boy. The Daughter asks the Doorkeeper for her shawl, so she can sit here and watch the children of men. The Officer comes down the alley, carrying a bouquet of roses. He calls for Miss Victoria, and a woman's voice answers from above. He begs to be allowed to go up and fetch her, but the Doorkeeper replies that nobody is allowed to go on stage. He remarks that in the seven years he has waited for Victoria he has never found where the door with the cloverleaf leads to. He asks whether he may step inside the Lodge and telephone to the Growing Castle. He goes in, and dusk falls quickly; when he comes out he looks shabbier, and the roses are withered. He asks whether Victoria has come down yet, but is told that she has not. The Doorkeeper tells the Daughter that there is no rest on this job, in which one has to listen to the tales of woe of all who pass. In her shawl, she says, are thirty years of torment; but when it gets too heavy for the Daughter, the Doorkeeper says that she will return and relieve her of it.

The stage is darkened; when it is lit again, the lime tree is bare, and the green plot has turned brown. The Officer enters, gray-haired and ragged. The petals have dropped from his bouquet of roses. He stops in front of the clover-leaf door and complains that he has no peace for not knowing what is behind it. The Billsticker enters with his net and equipment, saying that the fishing was not too bad, and that the net is all right but not quite what he had in mind. The Officer comments that nothing is ever as one imagined it, because one's mind goes further than the act. He asks the Billsticker whether he knows what is behind the cloverleaf door and says he is going to telephone a locksmith to come and open it. He goes into the lodge to make the call, and the stage is darkened. When the lights go up, the tree is in leaf and the plot green. The Officer returns from the Lodge; he is now old and white-haired, and his clothing is in tatters. A Ballet Girl comes out of the theater, and he asks her whether Miss Victoria has gone. The Girl replies that she has not, and is sure to come. He tells the Girl not to go, for the locksmith is coming to open the cloverleaf door. Others come from the theater, and he tells them the same thing. The

Glazier enters, saying the locksmith had company, so he came instead. All group themselves around the door. A Policeman comes through the gate and forbids the opening of the door. The Officer says they will go to the lawyer and see whether the law holds.

The gate becomes an office railing stretching across the stage. The Lawyer's face is hideous, mirroring all the crime and vice with which his profession has brought him in contact. He goes up to the Daughter and offers to burn her shawl and all its miseries. She refuses, saying she first wants it to gather up his sufferings. He replies that her shawl would not be big enough and goes on to talk of the evils that are brought to him; worst of all, he says, is husbands and wives in the process of separation. The Daughter repeats that human life is pitiable. The Officer asks whether Miss Victoria has gone, and the Lawyer replies that she has not. Church bells ring, and the Lawyer says that it is time for the Graduation, and that he himself is about to receive the degree of Doctor of Law.

The stage is darkened and becomes the interior of the church; the barrier is the chancel rail. In the background is a gigantic organ. Three Graduates enter, are crowned with laurel wreaths, and go out. The Lawyer goes up to receive his wreath, but the wreath-bearers refuse to crown him. He is left alone. The Daughter enters, wearing a white shawl. She says she has washed it and asks why the Lawyer was refused his laurels. She tells him that he shall have a wreath from her. She puts a crown of thorns on his head and then sits at the organ and plays a Kyrie. As she rises and approaches the Lawyer, the stage darkens and the organ is changed into the wall of a sea grotto. The Lawyer says he hears drops falling, which the Daughter identifies as the tears of mankind. When the Daughter asks whether there is no joy in life, the Lawyer says that the sweetest joy, love, is also the bitterest. The Daughter suggests that they, being intelligent and aware of the pitfalls, try to make a happy marriage.

ACT TWO

In a room adjoining the Lawyer's office, Kristin, the maid, is pasting strips of paper along the edges of the window. The Daughter complains that she is suffocating, for Kristin is shutting out the air. The Lawyer comes in and speaks to Kristin appreciatively, saying warmth is precious. The Daughter complains that their existence is worse than she ever imagined; they disagree on all sorts of matters, so that one suffers if the other is to be satisfied. But they say that they are enlightened and tolerant, and therefore can make allowances and forgive; and if nothing else, they must stay together for their child's sake. The Officer, now middle-aged, comes in and says that all paths are open to him now that he has his Doctor's degree. The Lawyer leaves, urging Kristin to paste until they cannot breathe. The Officer asks the Daughter whether she will come with him to Fairhaven, where the sun is shining and there is feasting and merrymaking.

In the background is a wooded shore, in the middle distance a strait, and in the foreground burnt hillsides and pigsties. To one side is a Quarantine Station of open sheds with furnaces and boilers. The Quarantine Master, dressed as a blackamoor, comes to meet the Officer and the Daughter. The Quarantine Master says that the sick live here, the healthy on the opposite shore. A Poet enters, carrying a pail of mud. The Quarantine Master says that the mud hardens the Poet's skin so he doesn't feel the gadflies stinging. A white boat glides into the strait. At the helm, their arms around one another, sit He and She. The Officer comments that here is the perfect happiness of young love. The young man salutes Fairhaven, but the Quarantine Master waves a yellow flag, and the Officer pulls a line that brings the boat in toward Foulstrand. The young lovers are horrified. The Quarantine Master tells them to go into a shed, from which sulphur fumes are issuing. They come out of the shed, their clothes bleached, their faces pale. The Officer cries that all of them are to be pitied, and all join in a cry of anguish.

The landscape changes to a winter scene with Foulstrand in the background and Fairhaven in the foreground. To the right is an Assembly Room, through the windows of which couples can be seen dancing. On the steps Ugly Edith is sitting before a piano. Three Maids are outside, watching the dancing. The Daughter and the Officer enter, saying that here is peace and happiness. The Daughter asks why the Maids are not dancing; the Officer objects that they are servants. The Daughter then asks why Edith is not dancing, and the Officer replies that she has been sitting there for hours without being asked to dance. Edith begins to play Bach on the piano; soon she drowns out the waltz music, and couples appear at the doorway, reverently listening. Then a Naval Officer takes a young girl by the waist and leads her away. Edith stops playing and looks after them in despair. The Daughter asks the Officer whether there is one happy person in this paradise. A newly wed couple enters, saying that their happiness is so complete they wish to die now, before it consumes itself. They go off toward the sea. The Lawyer enters and tells the Daughter that she has not yet experienced the worst thing of all: having to do one's duties over and over again. Duties are everything that one abominates, he says, and what one enjoys is a sin. The Daughter observes that it is not easy to be human. A distant lamentation is heard, which the Lawyer says is from those at Foulstrand, who suffer all the more because here the sun shines and there are music and dancing. The Daughter says that they must set the sufferers free, but the Lawyer replies that a deliverer came once and was hanged on a cross by all the righteous.

ACT THREE

In the grotto by the sea, where she has taken the Poet, the Daughter tells him that in this cave Indra listens to the lamentations of mortals carried in the singing of the wind and waves. The Daughter says that she means to leave the world, and the Poet gives her a petition he wants her to present to the ruler of the universe. She reads his poem, which asks why life, which should be joyous, is full of misery. The sea rises, threatening to trap them in the cave, and the

Poet sees a ship on the rocks. The sailors, singing a Kyrie, see a figure walking on the water. The Poet says it is He who was crucified by all righteous men. The Poet describes the crew screaming with horror because they have seen their Saviour; they are throwing themselves overboard in terror.

The light changes, and the scene becomes the alley of the Opera House in springtime. The Doorkeeper sits in her accustomed place. The Daughter says that the cloverleaf door, behind which the answer to the riddle of the universe is thought to be locked, is going to be opened. The Members of the Opera company enter, and the Officer, young again, comes carrying a bouquet and singing for his Victoria. Victoria's voice answers that she is coming. The Chancellor and the Deans of the Four Faculties at the University enter, followed by the Glazier and a group of Righteous People. The Glazier opens the door and the Deans look inside. There is nothing there. The Righteous cry that they have been swindled and that the Daughter is responsible. They threaten to stone her, though she says that the answer to the riddle is there and that they do not understand it. She tells the Poet to come with her and she will answer the riddle far out in the wilderness, where there is none to hear. The Lawyer interrupts, reminding her of her duties and her child, and she suffers the pangs of conscience that the Lawyer says come after every neglected duty. The Daughter, however, says that the higher duty comes first and tells the Lawyer to look after her child while she is away.

The scene changes to the Growing Castle. In the foreground is a fire. The Poet asks the Daughter whether Indra once sent his son to earth to hear man's complaint and then asks how he fulfilled his mission. The Daughter asks whether the state of mankind wasn't bettered by his visit. The Poet agrees that it was, a little, and asks the answer to the riddle of the universe. The Daughter replies that in the beginning Brahma, the divine primal force, was seduced by Maya, the World Mother; this union of the divine and the earthly was the fall from heaven. In order to be freed from the earthly element, the descendants of Brahma sought purification by suffering; but the desire for suffering and purification conflicts with the yearning for joy and love. In answer to the Poet's question, the Daughter says that in her sojourn on earth she suffered most from living, from having her perceptions dimmed by her human senses. She takes off her shoes and puts them in the fire, and one by one other characters come in and put their contributions in the fire: the Doorkeeper's shawl, the Officer's roses, Victoria's beauty, Edith's ugliness. The Dean of Theology, raging that God has disowned him and asking how he can have faith when no one else does, throws a Book of Martyrs in the fire. The Poet rescues it and, commenting on the lives of the martyrs, says that surely suffering must be redemption and death deliverance. The Daughter makes her farewell, saying that now she knows that to be a human being is to have one's heart split in two by conflict and discord. As she speaks, the fire grows higher until the Castle is aflame. She ends her speech and goes into the burning Castle, and the flower bud on the tower bursts into a giant chrysanthemum.

AUGUST STRINDBERG

The Father [*Fadren*, 1887]

ACT ONE

In the living room of his home in a remote country district in Sweden, just before Christmas in about 1886, the Captain is talking with his brother-in-law the Pastor about Nöjd, who has gotten one of the kitchen girls in trouble. Nöjd is summoned and asked whether he is the father of the girl's child; he admits to being with the girl but says he cannot be sure that he is the child's father and therefore refuses to accept sole responsibility for it. He is dismissed, and the conversation turns to the Captain's daughter Bertha and the Captain's problems with all the women in his house, each of whom wants to educate Bertha in a different way. Since the others oppose the Captain's attempts to guide Bertha, he wants to send her away where she will get the kind of education he thinks proper. Since he wants Bertha to be able to support herself if she doesn't marry, but does not want her to embark on a long training that would be entirely wasted if she did marry, his choice is that she become a school-teacher; his wife Laura, believing the girl has great talent, wants her to become an artist. The Captain is particularly disturbed because, as he observes to the Pastor, the women are deciding Bertha's future from motives of hate, trying to prove that women can do the same things as men. He remarks that he is expecting the new doctor and wonders whether the man will be his ally against the women.

The Pastor leaves, and the Captain begins to settle his accounts. Laura comes in to get her housekeeping money. The Captain asks her for her accounts and warns her that she must keep them; their financial position is precarious, due largely to the fact that Laura and the other women badgered the Captain to take on a worthless tenant farmer who does not pay his rent. The Captain informs Laura that he is going to send Bertha to live in town, at the house of Sävberg, a freethinker. He points out that according to the law children are to be brought up in their father's faith and that the mother has no rights in the matter. She asks about Nöjd, saying it is quite plain that he is the father of the expected child, but the Captain points out that one can never be sure who a child's father is. He leaves to go to his room, asking Laura to let him know as soon as the doctor comes.

Dr. Östermark arrives, and Laura tells him that her husband is out but will be back soon. She hints that things are not quite as they should be and finally says that her husband's mind is affected. The Doctor is astounded, for he has a high opinion of the Captain's learned treatise on mineralogy; but Laura gives instances of her husband's peculiar ideas and behavior and complains of the hardship she has suffered through their twenty years of marriage. She leaves to fetch the tea, and while she is out, the Captain enters. He asks whether the Doctor would prefer to live in a wing of the Captain's house or in the house of the previous doctor and displays considerable irritation when the Doctor repeatedly defers to him to make the choice. The Doctor finally chooses to live in the Captain's house, and the Captain sends for Margaret, the nurse of his childhood, to see whether the rooms are ready.

The Doctor leaves. When Margaret tries to persuade the Captain to come to some compromise with Laura in the matter of Bertha's education, the Captain accuses her, his only friend, of turning against him and going over to the "enemy." A scream is heard and Bertha runs in, crying to her father to save her from her grandmother, who is angry with her. She explains that her grandmother sometimes makes her sit in semidarkness and hold a pen over a piece of paper and let the spirits write: sometimes, the pen writes, but other times nothing happens and she has to do it herself, and this evening her grandmother caught on. Bertha does not know whether to believe her grandmother, who says there are spirits, or her father, who says there are not, but she is absolutely convinced that neither her grandmother nor mother would lie to her. The Captain asks her whether she wants to go to live in town; Bertha replies that she would love to go away from this miserable, gloomy house.

Laura enters and asks Bertha what she has to say regarding her future; since neither she nor her husband agree, Laura suggests that they give Bertha the deciding vote. The Captain, refusing to have anyone interfere with his rights to make the decision, sends Bertha out of the room. Laura charges that he was afraid to have Bertha's opinion because he knew the girl would agree with her; he counters that he knows she wants to leave home but also knows the power Laura has to make Bertha change her mind. He says that Bertha is to leave home in a fortnight, and Laura warns him that she will do her best to prevent it. She remarks that, since he maintains that no one can tell who is the father of a child, the education of Bertha shouldn't mean so much to him. He is at first incredulous at her suggestion, but Laura enlarges on the possibilities of her having been unfaithful and hints that she might even be able to prove it; deeply upset, the Captain orders her to stop. Laura stops, but threatens to take up the subject again if the Captain should cross her in the matter of Bertha's education. She remarks that because of her superior position he cannot fight her and goes on to say that she has never been able to look at a man without feeling herself his superior. Supper is announced, and Laura goes out; the Captain, refusing dinner, orders a sleigh and leaves, calling out to the women not to expect him home before midnight.

ACT TWO

Late the same evening, the Doctor and Laura are talking. The Doctor is somewhat skeptical of Laura's claims of her husband's insanity; he points out that one must be very accurate when making charges that might lead to a person's being certified, since the person declared insane loses all his civil and family rights. Laura remarks that she had not been aware of that. The Doctor asks what happened after he had seen the Captain earlier in the evening; Laura relates that he said the wildest and most fantastic things and even suggested that he wasn't Bertha's father. She says that he had a previous period of disturbance some six years before, at which time he actually admitted in a letter to his doctor that he feared for his reason. The Doctor proposes to stay until the Captain returns. Laura calls Margaret and tells her to wait here for the Captain; Laura and the Doctor go out. The Captain returns, and Margaret tells him that the Doctor is attending Laura's mother, who has a chill. The Doctor enters, remarking that his patient is only suffering from a slight sprain of the ankle. The Captain sends Margaret away and begins a conversation on fatherhood and the impossibility of knowing that a child is one's own. The Doctor warns against indulging a morbid turn of mind, but the Captain assures him that he is quite calm. He shows the Doctor out by the hall door, then crosses to the door opposite and opens it, discovering Laura eavesdropping. He tells her that he has been to the post office and discovered that she had been intercepting his mail and has thus prevented him from getting material to finish an important scientific article. He has also intercepted letters addressed to her, from which it appears that she has been spreading rumors to all his friends about his mental condition. Charging that she has filled him so full of suspicion that he is actually on the verge of insanity, he asks her to consider whether it is not more to her advantage to have him well than ill, since if he goes to pieces there will be no one to provide for her.

The Captain agrees to give up the fight over Bertha if Laura will let him preserve his reason and free him from doubt about Bertha's paternity. Since he can never be certain that he is Bertha's father, he demands to be told that he is *not* her father. Recalling some suspicious circumstances some months before her birth, he is further convinced that the child cannot be his. In his agony of uncertainty he weeps, renouncing every vestige of power and begging only for mercy. Laura states that the mother in her was his friend and that she loved the boy in him but that when he approached her as a lover she felt disgust, as if she had committed incest. In the fight between the sexes, she observes, the weaker must go under; she announces that she is the stronger, because tomorrow she will have the legal power to put him under restraint. She produces the letter he wrote six years before about his fears that he was mad. Now that he is no longer needed as a father and breadwinner, she says, he must go. The Captain picks up the lighted lamp and throws it at her.

ACT THREE

The following evening, the door to the Captain's room is locked and barricaded with a chair, and the sound of his pacing can be heard. The Pastor enters, and Laura tells him that her husband is raving; she says that the Doctor has sent to the hospital for a strait jacket. The Pastor tells Laura that he is quite aware how well it would suit her to have complete control of Bertha, but she ignores his insinuations and maintains that she is completely innocent of any blame for the Captain's condition.

The Doctor enters, sends for Margaret, and instructs her to slip the strait jacket on the Captain from behind when he gives her the signal. Margaret finally agrees and goes out, Laura following her. The Captain bursts through the door with a pile of books from which he cites examples of sons being uncertain of their paternity. He cries that he wants to die, having been robbed of his child and at the same stroke of his only concept of immortality. The Doctor and the Pastor whisper together, then leave. Bertha enters and asks him whether he realizes he threw a lamp at her mother; when he appears unconcerned about the possibility of having hurt her mother, Bertha retorts that he is not her father if he can talk like that. He takes down a revolver from the gun rack, and Bertha screams to her mother for help; Margaret hurries in and leads the Captain to a chair, and Bertha creeps out.

Margaret speaks to him as she did when he was a little boy, lulling him into docility; she takes the revolver from his hand, coaxes him into the strait jacket, and gets him to lie on the sofa. When he realizes what she has done to him, he becomes frantic. Laura enters and pleads that she didn't really mean for this to happen; the Captain weighed her down like a stone, she says, until finally she had to shake off her intolerable burden. She tells him that his suspicions about Bertha are totally unfounded, but he finds no consolation in that. If they had some foundation, he says, there would be something to catch hold of, something to cling to rather than mere shadows. He complains that he is terribly cold, and Laura takes off her shawl and spreads it over him. She asks whether he wants to see his child, but he replies that a man has no children; only women do. Lying with his head in Margaret's lap, he calls on her to put him to sleep; he raises himself, then with a cry falls back dead. Bertha comes in and runs to Laura, who cries, "My own child!"

A U G U S T   S T R I N D B E R G

The Ghost Sonata [*Spöksonaten,* 1908]

Scene 1. On the street in front of a handsome house, an Old Man sits in a wheelchair reading a paper. The windows in an upstairs room of the house are hung with white sheets, a sign of mourning. A Milkmaid approaches the fountain and, using the water as a mirror, arranges her hair. A Student goes up to the fountain and asks to use the cup; the Milkmaid looks at him in horror. The Old Man, who cannot see the Milkmaid, wonders to whom the Student is talking. The Milkmaid leaves and the Old Man addresses the Student, saying that it seems to him that the Student's voice is familiar. It appears that the Student's father once knew the Old Man, whom he blamed for his financial ruin. The Old Man tells the Student that in actuality he saved the youth's father from disaster and that the father hated his benefactor because he was obligated to him.

The Old Man asks the Student to wheel him to the advertising pillar so he can read the playbills. He wants to send the Student to the Opera that afternoon and proposes to buy him a seat next to the Colonel and his daughter so that he can make their acquaintance. He adds that he wants to see the Student happy, rich, and honored. He draws the Student's attention to the house, saying he knows all the inhabitants and takes an intense interest in human destiny. The blinds of the Round Room are opened, revealing the Colonel and a beautiful marble statue. The Old Man says that the statue is of the Colonel's wife, who now sits inside a cupboard, like a mummy, worshiping her own statue.

The Student asks about the Lady in Black who is on the front walk talking to the Caretaker's Wife. The Old Man claims to be connected to the Dead Man, a former Consul who—if the Student happens to be a Sunday child who can see what others can't—might soon be seen coming out to look at the Consulate flag flying at half-mast. When an old woman appears at a window, the Old Man says that sixty years ago she was his fiancée and that the Colonel took her away from him. The Caretaker's Wife comes out with fir branches with which to strew the ground for the funeral; the Old Man says that the Lady in Black is her daughter by the Dead Man, and that the daughter is now being courted by the Dead Man's son-in-law, an aristocrat in the process of getting a divorce.

The Old Man asks to be moved into the sun and tells the Student to take his hand to feel how cold it is. The Student, chilled, tries to free his hand, saying the Old Man is freezing him and sapping his strength. The Old Man tells him that their fates are entwined and says that if the Student will serve him, he will make him his heir. The Student is to go to the Opera as arranged, make the acquaintance of the Colonel and his daughter, and get himself invited to their house tonight. The Colonel's daughter appears at her window and waters her hyacinths. The Dead Man, wrapped in a winding sheet, comes out into the street to look at the flag. The Student sees him, though the Old Man does not. Johansson, the Old Man's servant, appears and at the Old Man's request pushes him around the corner. The Student remains watching the Girl. Johansson returns to remind the Student not to forget his instructions from the Old Man. In reply to the Student's questions, Johansson says that the Old Man wants power; he plays havoc with human destinies, metaphorically destroys houses, and is afraid of only one person in heaven and earth. The Student guesses that this person is the little Milkmaid.

Scene 2. Inside the Round Room, Johansson and Bengtsson, the Colonel's servant, are talking. Bengtsson says that the family is having what they call a ghost supper, during which no one says a word except the Colonel. They have kept up this custom for twenty years. The mistress of the house, Bengtsson goes on, is crazy; she looks like a mummy and lives in a cupboard because she can't stand the light. He opens the cupboard door to show Johansson; the Mummy squawks and talks like a parrot. Closing the cupboard door, Bengtsson remarks that the Mummy cannot bear cripples or sick people and therefore cannot stand the sight of her own ill daughter. He points to a screen, which he says is a death screen; when someone is dying, they put it around him as in a hospital.

The Old Man appears on crutches and demands to be announced to the Colonel. Both servants leave. Alone with the statue, the Old Man recognizes it as Amelia. The Mummy hears and talks to him in her parrot-like voice; he thinks the house is haunted. She comes unseen out of her cupboard and jerks his wig, making him jump with fright. In a natural voice she asks whether he is Jacob and indentifies herself as Amelia. He says that he has come for their child; the Mummy replies that the child is in the Hyacinth Room. She says that once she told her husband that the girl was not his, but he thought she was merely trying to be spiteful and refused to believe her. She asks what the Old Man wants, warning him on pain of death to spare the Girl and her putative father. They hear the Colonel coming, and the Mummy leaves.

The Colonel and the Old Man discuss the fact that the latter has bought all the Colonel's promissory notes, and thus has him in his power. The Old Man states that everything in the house now belongs to him and proceeds to give proofs that demolish even the Colonel's claims to nobility and military rank. The Student enters and the Colonel shows him into the Hyacinth Room. The Colonel says to the Old Man that the Student is a splendid youth, and if only he had blue blood and were of the same station, he would not object to a match between the Student and his daughter.

The Aristocrat, the Fiancée, and the Mummy enter, and the ghost supper begins. The Old Man makes a speech on the hiding and exposing of secrets. He announces that the Girl in the Hyacinth Room is his daughter and that she is withering away in this atmosphere of crime and deceit. For this reason, he says, he has brought her a noble friend so that, after all the others' crimes have been exposed, the young people might start life afresh in this house. He warns the others that when the clock strikes, their time will be up. The Mummy, however, goes up to the clock and stops it, saying that she can stop time, undo what has been done, and wipe out the past through suffering and repentance. She accuses the Old Man of being worse than all the rest of them, for he is the thief of human souls: he stole her with false promises, strangled the Consul with debts, and bound the Student to him with a false accusation of the young man's father.

The Milkmaid appears in the hallway, unseen by all but the Old Man, who is horrified by her. Bengtsson enters and says that the Old Man was once a sponger in his kitchen: he sucked the marrow out of the house like a vampire and was later charged with having lured a girl out on the ice in order to drown her, since she had seen him commit a crime. The Mummy demands that the Old Man give up the promissory notes and the will. The clock strikes, and she orders him to enter the cupboard in which she had lived for twenty years repenting their crime. The Old Man goes into the cupboard, and Bengtsson places the death screen before the door.

Scene 3. In the Hyacinth Room, the Girl and the Student talk about the flowers; the Student tells her the legend of the hyacinth. They hear the Cook coming; the Girl says that she is a vampire like the Old Man and sucks all the nourishment out of the family's food. They have no control over her and cannot make her leave, but are burdened with her for their sins. She says that there are other ordeals in this seemingly beautiful house: a housemaid they have to clean up after; a stove that cannot be lit because it smokes; and all the labor of "keeping the dirt of life at a distance."

The Student says that he would do anything to win her hand, but she replies that that cannot be, because her life is being drained away by the vampire in the kitchen. The Student comments on the many secrets in the house and reflects that sometimes he is overcome with a desire to say all he thinks, though he knows that the world would go to pieces if everyone were completely candid. He remarks that the other day he attended the funeral of the Old Man, his false benefactor; the ceremony was very beautiful and moving, and all the mourners wept. But afterwards the Student learned of the sordid connection between the deceased and the chief mourner, and the next day even the clergyman was revealed to be an embezzler.

The Student picks up the Girl's harp and strokes it, but it gives no sound. He cries that Christ's descent into hell was really His pilgrimage to "this penal colony, to this madhouse and morgue of a world." The Girl droops, and it is apparent that she is dying. Bengtsson comes with the death screen and arranges it in front of her. The Student cries that the Liberator is coming to release this innocent, doomed creature who is suffering through no fault of her own and prays that she may wake in a home without dust, to find friends without faults and love without flaw. The strings of the harp hum softly. The room disappears, and Böcklin's picture of the Island of the Dead is seen in the distance.

AUGUST STRINDBERG

The Great Highway: A Wayfaring Drama

with Seven Stations [*Stora landsvägen*, 1910]

I. In the mountains is a signpost with one arm pointing up, the other down. The Hunter enters and pauses to rest. Although he at first expresses his desire to go upward, he sees the valley below as a cloud parts; he is again drawn back toward earth. The Hermit enters, asking what the Hunter is seeking; he replies that he is looking for the self he lost in the world. The Hermit urges him to return to earth and live out his life among men. The Traveller comes down the path from above, saying he could not stay in the thin air. He asks the name of the country in the distance, and the Hermit replies that it is called the Country of Desires.

II. The Traveller and the Hunter are sitting at a table outside an inn. Two windmills, known as Adam and Eve, stand against a background of sky. Miller Adam and Miller Eve enter, arguing that one mill takes the wind from the other. Each asserts that the other's mill should be torn down. The wife of Miller Adam enters, calling her husband to dinner, and they go out. Miller Eve approaches the Hunter and the Traveller, who regard him suspiciously. He informs them that there is blasting going on nearby and that they are about to get showered with stones. They leap up, but the miller reassures them that the blasters will give the alarm first. He then announces that there are robbers hereabouts, and everyone who has no pass must be examined by the Constable. He leaves, and a Girl enters. The Traveller stops her, guesses that her name is Amelia and that she is the miller's daughter. She asks him where he got this gift of reading people, and he goes on to speculate that she has refused the son of the neighbor miller. She leads him on by agreeing with his guesses and finally says that she will give him something in return for all she has learnt. She tells him that her name is not Amelia and that there is no miller's son; she is the daughter of the manor. After reproving the Traveller for his errors, she tells him to go to the miller and give him her compliments, and the miller will give the Traveller a pass.

The Traveller goes out, and the Girl and the Hunter talk. They remark that guessing riddles is a way to pass the time, because what is said does not mean much. The Hunter agrees that every language is a foreign one, and all are foreigners to one another, travelling incognito even to themselves. A horn sounds, and the Hunter says that it is calling him. He sees the miller and the Traveller fighting and sends the Girl off so she will not be called as a witness. She goes out, and the Hunter complains that he is trapped, allied with a stranger, and involved in a matter that does not concern him. The Traveller enters, saying he hit the miller for making a fool of him; what the miller told him about the blasting and the robbers was a pack of lies. But now they must appear at the autumn assizes, he as the defendant, the Hunter as a witness. In the meanwhile, the Traveller suggests, they should go to the next village, where there is some sort of festivity—an Asses' Gala, at which the biggest dunce in the village is crowned. The name of the next village, he says, is Assesdean, and the village they are in now is called Liarsbourne.

III. The Hunter and the Traveller are sitting on a bench in Assesdean. They remark that for all their travelling together they have not come any closer to one another; the Traveller adds that he hasn't even a clue as to who the Hunter is. The Hunter replies that he is a soldier, always fighting to keep his personal independence. The Schoolmaster appears, and the travellers agree to keep silent so that they will not get involved in anything. The Schoolmaster says that he is the only sane person in the village and therefore pretends to be an imbecile lest others should lock him up. The Blacksmith appears, and the

Schoolmaster puts on ass's ears to disguise himself. The Blacksmith and the Schoolmaster carry on a long and nonsensical conversation. After many complications the Hunter and the Traveller escape with the Schoolmaster, though they have given their word to return and are purportedly just going to the next town to bring back properties for the Gala.

IV. The Hunter and the Traveller are sitting in an arcade in Tophet. The Hunter says that he used to live here many years ago. The Traveller goes into the café, and a Photographer approaches the Hunter and asks to take his picture. Though suspicious, the Hunter consents. The Photographer's wife, his son, and a flower-seller named Klara enter, and all begin to talk at cross-purposes. Klara asserts that the Hunter looks cruel; he kills animals, and she says that this is a sin. The Hunter asks her what she has done with her husband, and she becomes terrified. Then he asks whether Möller has been arrested yet, and all rise in horror. The Traveller comes in, and as the Hunter repeats his question, the others leave hurriedly. The Traveller asks what is going on, and the Hunter replies that it is common knowledge that the last murder was committed by Möller, but no one dares accuse him: there is little evidence against him, and he is the most powerful man in the community. The Hunter says that they must leave at once, but the Traveller refuses, having been overcome by the desire to rescue the pretty café waitress from her degrading job. The Traveller returns to the café and the Hunter walks to the Photographer's showcase and reminisces about his former life, his friends, his child.

An old Japanese comes out of the teashop. He has the appearance of a dying man, and the Hunter goes to him and supports him. The Japanese says that long ago he committed an offense, left his own country, and came here determined to be an honest man. He sold good wares at a reasonable price, but the customers wanted bad wares at a low price, and he was forced to supply them or perish. At first his conscience was quiet, and then one day fifteen years ago he woke up, and ever since has been suffering for his misdeeds. Death alone can liberate him, he says, for the evil is in his very flesh. He says that he will take a sleeping potion and asks the Hunter to have him then put in a coffin and taken to the crematorium. They agree to meet later at the crematorium, and the Japanese goes into his shop.

Möller, the murderer, enters and seems to recognize the Hunter, who tells him that the one he recognizes is no more. Twelve years ago, the Hunter goes on, he committed hara-kiri and executed his old self. Möller remembers that the Hunter put himself in the pillory and publicly confessed all his faults. Now, after he has atoned by years of suffering, the Hunter thinks that he ought to confess Möller's sins as well. He says that Möller made him into a scapegoat, blamed him for the murderer's crimes, and took credit himself for the Hunter's inventions. He then asks about the girl in the café who captivated his companion; Miller replies that she is the Hunter's daughter, whom he raised. The Hunter pales and presses a handkerchief to his mouth; it becomes red with blood.

V. The Hunter enters the arbor outside the crematorium and is soon joined by the Japanese. Now that his life is almost over, the Japanese concludes that the hardest thing to bear is the humiliation of living—the plight of the spirit imprisoned in the flesh. The crematorium furnace begins to glow and casts a light dawn. The Japanese bids goodby to life as a night of heavy dreams.

VI. Two white gates open onto a sandy beach. To one side, in a beech wood, is the Hunter's house. Outside, a table is decorated for a child's birthday party, and a baby carriage stands nearby. The Hunter enters, meditating on the house and its inhabitants and on their innocence and happiness. The Child enters, leads him to the baby carriage, and talks to him about her birthday. She asks his name, and he identifies himself as Ahasuerus—the Wandering Jew. A horn sounds, and the Child goes out, saying her father is coming. The Hunter cries that she is his child and that she did not know him. He bids farewell to the little scene, calling it a sweet vision.

VII. Alone in a dark wood, the Hunter cries that he has lost his way. The voice of a Woman speaks, saying that he who seeks to lose his life shall find it. She says that she knows his voice, and that he was once a lawyer. He replied that he was the defender of the only True One against the idolators. She adds that he was once an evangelist, and he replies that he stopped preaching when he found he could not live up to what he taught, for it was impossible to put those beautiful doctrines into practice. He says that he was also an architect, but when he built well, people were angry because his work was good, and they hired others who built badly. He goes on to say that others blackened him and made him the scapegoat for their sins. The Woman asks why he has no pity for his fellows; he replies that no one ever pitied him. The Woman disappears and the Tempter enters. He says that he comes from the Grand Duke, who admires the Hunter's talents and wants him to become the Court Architect, on the condition that he conduct himself like an ordinary human being. The Hunter replies that the Grand Duke does not want his services, but his soul, and sends the Tempter away. Alone, he soliloquizes on life and wonders what happened to the fair vision of the land of fulfilled desire. He calls on God to bless His creature who suffers so from the gift of life.

A U G U S T   S T R I N D B E R G

Miss Julie   [*Fröken Julie,* 1889]

It is Midsummer Eve, and in the kitchen of a Swedish manor house music can be heard coming from the barn where the peasants are having a dance. Kristin, the cook, is working at the stove when the valet Jean enters, carrying the Count's riding boots. He remarks that on his way back from taking the Count to the station he stopped at the barn to watch the dance and found the Count's daughter Miss Julie dancing with the gamekeeper. Kristin replies that Miss Julie's behavior has been particularly bad ever since her engagement was broken. Jean tells Kristin the real cause of the breakup; he saw Julie making her fiancé jump over her riding whip. After jumping twice and getting smacked with the whip each time, the man took the whip away from her, broke it, and left her. Kristin fusses over Jean and prepares a bit of meat for him. He refuses her offer of beer and brings out a bottle of wine with which to celebrate the holiday. He goes on to talk about Miss Julie, saying that, like her mother before her, she has no proper respect for herself or her position.

Julie comes in to get a concoction Kristin has prepared for her dog. She flirts with Jean and tells him to come and dance with her. Jean demurs, saying that he has promised to dance with Kristin and that in any event people will talk if she shows special favor to one of her servants. Julie begs them to forget about class for tonight and to be just people enjoying a party. She and Jean go out, and after a few minutes Jean returns alone. He asks Kristin whether she is angry with him and fondly puts his arm around her waist. Julie enters and chides Jean for leaving her. She asks why he is wearing his livery on a holiday and tells him to take it off. He steps into his room, and Julie asks Kristin whether Jean is her fiancé. Jean returns and Julie compliments him in French. He responds in French, which he says he learned when he was sommelier at a famous hotel in Lucerne.

Kristin falls asleep. Julie asks Jean to sit down with her and then tells him to get up and get her a drink. He says there is only beer, and Julie replies that her taste is so simple she prefers it to wine. She encourages him to drink with her, makes him offer her a toast, and finally tells him to kiss her shoes. Jean does as bid but says that they should not go on like this lest someone come in and see them—a lady drinking alone at night with a man, and that man a servant. Julie points out that they are not alone, for Kristin is there; she tries to wake her, but Jean tells her to let her sleep, for Kristin has had a hard day and is tired.

Julie is moved by his concern for Kristin and asks him to come out and pick some lilac with her. Kristin gets up and goes sleepily into her bedroom. Jean says that it wouldn't be proper for him to go outside with her, but he finally gives in to her cajoling. At the door he stops, complaining that he has a speck of dust in his eye. Julie makes him sit down and tries to get the speck out with her handkerchief. She acts in a very provocative manner, and he warns her to be careful, saying he has no intention of being her playfellow.

She asks him whether he has never been in love, and he replies shortly that people of his class don't put it that way. However, he says, once he was sick because he couldn't have the girl he wanted. Julie begs to know who she was, and Jean finally admits it was she. He tells a touching story of the poor little laborer's child creeping into the Count's estate to steal apples; trapped when he hid in the outhouse, he was forced to escape through the outlet and emerged covered with dung and muck to see a beautiful little girl in a pink dress. In despair of ever attaining her, he went home and determined to die by sleeping amidst supposedly poisonous elderberry flowers. He concludes that she was a symbol of the hopelessness of his ever getting out of the class he was born in. Now, he says, having spent a good deal of time discreetly listening to the upper classes, he wonders whether there is really as much difference between people as one is led to believe.

Jean asks permission to go to bed, but Julie says she wants him to row her out on the lake to watch the sun rise. He again demurs on the ground of protecting both their reputations and almost begs her to go to bed and leave him alone. He hears people coming toward the kitchen; they will be looking for him, he says, and it will be very bad if he and Julie are found together. The peasants are heard, singing a mocking song. Jean says that there is nothing for them to do but run and that there is no place to go but into his room. Julie is unwilling, but he promises her that she can trust him, and they leave. The peasants enter and begin to carouse. They form a ring and sing and dance. Finally they leave, still singing.

Julie comes in alone, looking at the havoc in the kitchen and wringing her hands. Jean enters, saying that it is not possible for them to stay here; he urges her to run away with him to Switzerland, where he will start a hotel. As long as they are in this house, he says, there are barriers between them—the past and the Count; and the Count so dominates Jean that the very sight of the Count's boots makes him feel small and servile. In another country these class notions can be forgotten, he claims; he will have a hotel, make a fortune, go to Roumania, and buy himself a title.

Julie begs him to tell her that he loves her, but he says harshly that this is no time for sentimentality; they have to settle their future. Though he has professional skill, experience, and a knowledge of foreign languages, Jean admits that he has no money and tells Julie that if she wants to be his partner she must bring the capital. She says that she has no money of her own, whereupon he replies that the whole thing is off. Julie cries out, asking whether he thinks she is going to stay under this roof as his mistress, and begs him to take her away from this shame and humiliation.

He takes out the bottle of wine and fills two used glasses. She accuses him of stealing from her father's wine cellar and goes on to berate herself and calls on God to end her misery. Jean adds cutting taunts and tells her that the story about wanting to die for her was just a lot of talk, the sort of thing that always appeals to women. Turning on him, she calls him a menial and a lackey, to which he responds by calling her a menial's whore and a lackey's harlot. He berates her for her behavior, saying no servant girl would throw herself at a man as she has done. Finally he apologizes for what he has said; he says that there is a certain satisfaction in finding that what he had found dazzling in the upper classes was only moonshine but that nevertheless it hurts to find that what he was struggling so hard to reach isn't real.

Impassioned again, he praises her beauty and tries to pull her to him, but she breaks away. She cries that she loathes him but can't escape from him, and when he suggests that they escape together, she immediately agrees. She asks for a glass of wine and drinks it quickly, though he warns her that it is vulgar to get drunk. If they are to run away together, she says, she had better tell him about her life so that they really know each other. She tells him how her mother, who came from a humble family, was brought up with notions of women's equality and brought her daughter up to excel in boys' skills in order to prove that women are as good as men. Her mother tried to run the whole household in this way, setting women to men's tasks and vice versa, until they were the talk of the neighborhood, and finally her father put his foot down. Later, to revenge herself on her husband for asserting himself and trying to dominate her, the Countess took a lover. Soon there was a scandal in which the lover was financially involved but against whom the Count could prove nothing. It was rumored that the Count tried to shoot himself but failed. From her mother, Julie goes on, she learned to hate and distrust the whole male sex.

Jean asks whether she hates him, and she replies that she would gladly have him killed like a mad dog; but since there is nothing else for them to do, they must go abroad, enjoy themselves as long as they can, and then die. Jean replies that he doesn't want to die, that he is tired of all this, and that he is going to bed. Julie hysterically demands that he owes something to the woman he has ruined; he tosses a coin on the table, saying he doesn't want to be in anyone's debt. Finally he relents and says sympathetically that he doesn't know what she wants him to do; people of his class don't have scenes like this and don't go around hating one another. He suggests that they stay here and keep quiet, since no one knows what has happened between them; but Julie points out that it might happen again, and there might be consequences. Jean then agrees that Julie must go abroad, but alone. She is so tired she cannot act on her own initiative and begs to be told what to do. Jean tells her to go upstairs and dress and get money for the journey. As she leaves, she begs him to speak kindly to her, but he reminds her that orders always sound unkind.

Dawn begins to break, and soon Kristin enters dressed for church. She sees that Miss Julie and Jean have been drinking together and, suspecting the worst, inquires of Jean and receives confirmation of her fears. She states that she won't stay here where she can't respect her employers and goes out. Julie enters carrying a birdcage. She begs Jean to come with her; he agrees to go but refuses to take the finch in the birdcage. Julie says that she would rather have it dead than leave it in strange hands. Jean tells her to give it to him; he puts it on a chopping block and kills it. Julie screams at him to kill her too; she cries that she would like to see his blood on the chopping block and the whole male sex swimming in a sea of blood. Now, she says, she is going to stay and let the storm break when her father finds his desk broken open and his money stolen.

Kristin enters, and Julie flings herself into her arms crying to her to protect her from Jean. Kristin responds coldly, and Jean slips into his room, saying he must shave. Julie begs Kristin to go abroad with them and be their cook in the fantasied hotel. Kristin is righteously indignant at Julie's proposals, but Jean tries to soften her. Before she leaves for church, she delivers a homily on God's special grace, which is not given to all; before leaving, she points out that God is no respecter of persons and that the last shall be first.

Julie wearily asks Jean whether there is any way out for her and what he would do if he were in her place. She picks up the razor and gestures with it, asking whether that is what she should do. She says she would like to, but cannot. The bell rings, signifying that the Count has returned. Jean changes into his livery. Julie begs Jean to order her to do what she ought to do to save her honor, for she has not the strength to do it herself. Jean, having put on his livery, finds himself unable to give orders. Julie tells him to pretend he is the Count and issue orders to his servant. He puts the razor in her hand, tells her to go out to the barn, and then whispers in her ear. She thanks him and says she is going but first asks him to tell her that even the first can receive the gift of grace. He says that now she is one of the last. The bell rings, summoning Jean to the Count. He tells her to go, and Julie walks through the door.

AUGUST STRINDBERG

To Damascus, Part I   [*Till Damaskus,*

written and published 1898; performed 1900]

Scene 1. The play opens on a street corner; there is a bench under a tree, a small church, and a post office and café, both closed. Funeral music is heard in the distance. A Stranger is standing on the corner; he is waiting for the post office to open so he can pick up a letter. A Lady enters and greets him, saying she sensed he wanted her to come; though they met only yesterday, he has aroused her sympathy. He begs her not to leave him, since he is friendless and does not know what to do with himself. Life, he says, has not brought him a single pleasure, and his only religion is the thought that when he can bear things no longer, he can escape into annihilation. A writer, he doubts whether life has any more reality than his books. He says that he does not fear death, but solitude, for then one is not alone but is in the presence of invisible beings. He adds that he believes that the Lady has been sent across his path, either to save him or to destroy him. He tells her of his unhappy childhood, his lonely life, and the persecution he has suffered because of the outspokenness of his writings—persecution that culminated in poverty, divorce, lawsuits, exile, and solitude.

The Lady leaves briefly. A Beggar enters and begins to pick up objects from the gutter. He remarks that he likes to call himself Polycrates, after the man who found the gold ring in the fish's stomach. Life, he says, gave him all he asked for, but he grew tired of success and threw the ring away. Now, being old, he regrets his act and is searching for the ring in the gutters. He leaves and the Lady returns, wearing a Christmas rose. The Stranger asks whether she has read his books; she replies that she has and that they gave her freedom and taught her belief in human rights and dignity. The Stranger observes that she has obviously not read his most recent work and asks her to promise never to read another book of his. She asks him to go into the church with her, but he replies that he does not belong there and that it is as impossible for him to re-enter the church as to become a child again. The Lady goes into the church alone. Six funeral attendants and some mourners enter. The café opens, and the Stranger sits at a table and is served with wine. The Beggar comes in and demands wine, but the Landlord refuses to serve him since he is on the police list for not paying his taxes. The Stranger takes the Beggar's side in the argument that follows; the Landlord looks on his list to see whether the Stranger is on it and finds that the description of the Beggar tallies exactly with that of the Stranger. He tells them both to clear out. The Lady comes out of the church, asking the Stranger why he called her. She says he looks ill and asks him to come with her to a doctor. The Stranger replies that when he is alone he has no strength at all, but with a companion he grows strong. He agrees to go home with her, and she says that perhaps he can free her from the "werewolf," the name she has given her doctor-husband.

Scene 2. In the courtyard of his house, the Doctor waits anxiously to meet the Stranger, and wonders whether he is a former schoolmate of his, nicknamed Caesar, who once got in trouble and put the blame on him. The Stranger enters and asks the Doctor whether they have ever met before, but the Doctor replies that he is sure they have not. The Stranger comments on the large woodpile in the center of the courtyard, which the Doctor says has twice been struck by lightning, and on the Christmas roses that are blooming in the summer, which the Doctor says were planted by a patient who was not quite sane. The Doctor goes behind the woodpile and the Stranger begs the Lady to run away with him. The Doctor reappears and summons the Madman by the name *Caesar*. The Stranger, tormented, again begs the Lady to leave with him, and she agrees.

Scene 3. The Stranger and the Lady are in a dismal hotel room. The Stranger cannot get the money that his publisher owes him, and their only course seems to be to go to the Lady's parents in the country. Though they both feel this is an ignominious and shameful retreat, they agree that they cannot do anything else and leave before the hotel manager comes up to demand their passports and throw them out for being unmarried.

Scene 4. In a hut on a cliff overlooking the sea, after three peaceful days of marriage, the Stranger says that he is again haunted by anxiety. The Lady replies that her parents are reconciled to their marriage and that her former husband has even written a kind letter. The Stranger's mood changes, and he becomes ecstatically happy, crying that he wants all created beings to be happy, to be born without pain, live without suffering, and die content. He shows the Lady a letter, which he believes contains the money they have been waiting for; but when he opens it, he finds that it is only an account showing that nothing is coming to him. He flings imprecations at the heavens. Then an idea of a poem begins to germinate in his mind, and he describes his inward vision of a kitchen in which are an old man and a woman of middle age. The Lady exclaims that he has described her mother and grandfather in their kitchen at home. She longs to go home, and the Stranger agrees to follow her.

Scene 5. The Stranger and the Lady are on the mountain road leading to the Lady's home. On the right there is a chapel, and scattered about the hills are other chapels, crucifixes, and memorials to the victims of accidents. The Stranger and the Lady have no more money and are hungry and ragged. They hear a horn in the distance, which the Lady identifies as her grandfather's hunting horn. They go on in an attempt to reach home before dark.

Scene 6. Between the steep cliffs of a ravine are a smithy and a flour mill. The Stranger comments on the craggy rocks, which seem to resemble giant profiles and in which he sees the profile of the Lady's former husband. Angry at their rags and poverty, the Stranger defiantly throws their last coin into the brook.

Scene 7. The Old Man and the Mother are in the cottage kitchen when the Stranger and the Lady arrive. Though she does not approve of him, the Mother warns the Stranger never to leave the woman who loves him or he will never be happy again. Left alone, the Mother and the Old Man talk of their dislike of the Stranger and their wish to be rid of him. Having read the Stranger's latest book, the Mother determines to get her daughter to read it and know what kind of man she has married.

Scene 8. In the "rose" room of the cottage, which is decorated with rose-colored curtains and furniture, the Mother encourages the Lady to read her husband's last book. The Lady at first refuses, saying she promised not to, but finally she takes the book, looks at it, and hides it just as the Stranger comes in. He is unhappy and complains that the Mother and the Old Man begrudge him their hospitality; in addition, he has received a letter saying he is being sued for child-support payments. He addresses the Lady as Eve, displeasing her, and she says he would not like it if she called him Caesar. Stung, he admits that he is Caesar, the schoolboy for whose misdeed her former husband was punished. He sees that she has been reading his book and becomes more upset. She replies that, having glanced at his book, she has had her eyes opened and she knows good and evil, sees how evil he is, and understands why he calls her Eve. He gets up and leaves, saying he cannot remain here.

Scene 9. In the refectory of an ancient convent sit the Stranger, a woman who resembles the Lady, two men who resemble the Doctor and the Madman respectively, and others. The Abbess tells the Stranger that he was found in the hills three months previously raving in delirium and threatening someone in the clouds with a cross broken from one of the Calvaries. The Confessor comes and tells the Stranger that in his delirium he accused himself of nearly every possible sin and vice. He introduces the other members of the company as Caesar, the Doctor, the Stranger's grief-stricken parents, and so forth. The Stranger turns his back on them, and the Confessor begins reading the Deuteronomic Curse (Deut. 28:15–68). The others listen and join in the curse. The Abbess reminds the Stranger that should he need charity he knows where to find it—in the "rose" room. He rushes out.

Scene 10. In the "rose" room the curtains have been taken down and the furniture covered in brown. The Stranger asks for his wife, and the Mother replies that she has gone away to look for him. He says that his sickness has changed him; he cannot write, cannot sleep, and does not even dare to die since he is no longer sure that his miseries will end with death. The Mother tells him to spend the night in the attic—though she adds that, because of ghosts or for other reasons, no one has ever slept a whole night there.

Scene 11. The Stranger, carrying a lamp, enters the moonlit kitchen. The Mother comes in, and the Stranger tells her he felt a breath of cold air that forced him to get up and that he saw his whole past life unrolled before him. He suffers an attack of angina pectoris, which he construes as an attempt by the Higher Powers to force him to yield and bow down. The Mother counsels him to ask forgiveness and then to try to make amends, but he says he cannot. The Mother advises him to search for his wife.

Scene 12. The Lady enters the ravine, asking whether a man of the Stranger's description has passed through. The Smith and the Miller's Wife shake their heads and refuse her lodging. She goes out, and the Stranger enters, asking whether a woman of the Lady's description had crossed the brook. The Smith and the Miller's Wife shake their heads and refuse the Stranger bread.

Scene 13. On the road in the hills, the Stranger meets the Beggar sitting outside the chapel. The Beggar advises him to follow the road until he comes to the ocean and there to sit down and rest. He adds that the Stranger believes in nothing but evil, which is why he gets nothing but evil, and advises him to try to believe in good. The Stranger goes on his way. The Lady enters, asking whether the Stranger has passed this way. The Beggar points to the print of a boot in the mud and advises her to follow the track.

Scene 14. In the hut on the sea cliff, the Stranger and the Lady meet and embrace. The Stranger tries to take all the blame for what has happened and says that there are times when he feels as if he bears all the sin and sorrow of the world. He tells her of the Beggar's advice to believe in the good; he has tried, and since then things have gone well with him. They agree to go on together.

Scene 15. The Stranger and the Lady are in the dismal hotel room, which the Stranger wanted to revisit in order to suffer. He says he dreamed that her first husband was married to his first wife and was mistreating his children. To know the truth he must go to see the Doctor.

Scene 16. The Stranger enters the courtyard and asks the Doctor whether, with his symptoms, he might be insane. The Doctor replies that the Stranger needs a spiritual healer and that he cannot help him. In any case, he hasn't the time, since he is preparing for his wedding to a widow with two children. The Stranger interprets this to mean his former wife. The Doctor says that he has long since ceased to be concerned about his unjust punishment for the Stranger's boyhood misdeed, but there is no use in forgiving him as long as the Stranger lacks the strength to forgive himself.

Scene 17. The Stranger is sitting beneath the tree on the street corner as in

scene 1. The Lady enters, saying she thinks that their wanderings must be over
now that they are back where they began. The Stranger remembers the expected letter that he never picked up, believing it contained nothing but un-
pleasantness. The Lady tells him to fetch it and believe that what it holds is
good; the Stranger does so and finds that the letter contains money. Before they
start off for the mountains, the Lady wants to go into the church and light a
candle. The Stranger agrees to go in with her.

A U G U S T   S T R I N D B E R G

To Damascus, Part II [*Till Damaskus,*

written and published 1898; performed 1916]

ACT ONE

On the steps below the terrace, the Mother is talking to a Dominican about
her son-in-law. From her description the Dominican recognizes him as the man
who was brought to the convent in delirium the year before and over whom he
read the curse of Deuteronomy, in the belief that it might lead to his salvation.
The Mother says that he was heavily struck by the curse and began to believe
that evil powers were tormenting him. However, he discovered books that
taught him evil spirits could be exorcised, and seems to have overcome them.
The Dominican replies that, not having accepted the love of truth, the Stranger
will easily deceive himself into believing what is false. The Mother complains
that the Stranger is making her daughter evil also; they have separated four
times but have always come back together, and now are expecting a child.

The Stranger appears on the terrace, and the Dominican, demonstrating the
secret hold that the Higher Powers already have over him, makes the sign of the
cross; the Stranger stiffens and cries out. The Dominican makes the sign again,
and the Stranger falls to the ground. The Dominican leaves, and the Lady enters with letters from the post office. She tells the Mother that she reads her
husband's mail in order to know everything about his life, to withhold certain
things from him, and thus to hold his fate in her hand. She says that he is
making electrical experiments to try to harness the lightning and is correspond-
ing with alchemists. She adds that her former husband's plans for marriage
have not turned out, that in his unhappiness he has abandoned his practice,
and that her conscience now torments her about him. She has also heard that
the Stranger's first wife is about to marry again, thus fulfilling his worst nightmare: that his children would have a stepfather. The Mother asks why she
makes the Stranger wear a suit belonging to her former husband. The Lady replies that she has told him the suit belonged to her father and that she likes
tormenting him.

The Stranger enters, asking if she called him and complaining that he sensed she was meddling with his destiny. They see the Doctor coming; the Stranger says he will confront him alone and sends the Lady up the steps. The Doctor, who is dressed exactly like the Stranger, sits down on the other side of the road and does not appear to notice him. When asked what he wants, the Doctor replies that he has come to see this house where he was once happy. He asks whether the Stranger has noticed that they are dressed alike and declares that he is everywhere in the Stranger's house and thoughts and cannot be gotten rid of. In the manner of a curse he claims that he shall confuse the Stranger's mind at his work, lie like a stone in his path so he will stumble, guide him by means of the woman the Stranger stole from him, and speak through the mouth of his child.

ACT TWO

Scene 1. In a laboratory with various kinds of apparatus, the Stranger is telling the Mother that his wife has gone to divorce him. He says that he is trying to make gold, for he believes that gold and scientific honor are the most enduring of all illusions. After the Mother goes, the Lady enters and throws herself at her husband's feet. She cries that she has behaved foolishly; she went to the public prosecutor intending to ask for a divorce but actually gave false information against the Doctor for attempted murder, and because of this she is threatened with jail for bearing false witness. The Stranger assures her that he will take the blame and say that he sent her. He says that he has succeeded in making gold and will use it, not to enrich himself, but to make everyone poor and thus destroy the present order of the world. The face of the Dominican appears at the window; he makes the sign of the cross and disappears. The Stranger feels his presence, and both he and the Lady faintly feel the curse of Deuteronomy being said. The Lady cries that she is in pain and asks to have her mother make up her bed. When she asks the Stranger for his blessing, he is unable to give it. He refuses to come to her until she faints, whereupon he extends her his hand.

Scene 2. In the "rose" room, the walls and curtains are rose-red, the furniture red and white. The Stranger wants to go into his wife's adjoining bedroom, but the Mother refuses, saying that his wife does not want to see him and that in any case the doctor has forbidden his visiting because she is in danger. A maid enters and says the Lady wants her husband to look for a letter in the pocket of her dress. The Stranger finds the letter, addressed to him and opened, but says he will forgive his wife for opening it since he has just received a certificate from the greatest living authority substantiating his claim that he has made gold. The maid says that the Lady asks him to come in, but the Stranger refuses; he says that, since the Mother has tried to make him believe that the child is not his, she has murdered his honor and that there is nothing for him to do but to try to revive it elsewhere. He goes out.

ACT THREE

Scene 1. A hotel room is decorated for a banquet; there are four long tables lavishly set with delicacies. Dessert has just been served, and the guests have golden goblets before them. At the first table are the Stranger and important-looking men in frock coats; at the second and third tables, respectively, are men in morning coats and everyday suits, and at the fourth are Caesar, the Doctor, and others, all in shabby clothes. A Professor at the high table gets up and addresses the company, praising the great discovery of the Stranger, crowning him with a laurel crown, and placing an order around his neck. The band plays Mendelssohn's "Dead March," and during the last part of the Professor's speech, servants exchange the golden goblets for tin ones and take away the delicacies on the table. The Stranger makes a speech saying this is the greatest moment of his life, for it has given him back belief in himself. Everyone rises as he offers the company a toast, and the frock-coated people creep away. The tables are cleared, down to the bare boards, and the ragged people sit down next to the Stranger at the high table. Caesar makes a speech and suggests that the analysis of the Stranger's gold may be wrong. While the company argues the matter, a beautiful screen is taken away, revealing a dingy serving counter, behind which a waitress is dispensing liquor to scavengers and dirty-looking women. The Beggar comes forward and tells the Stranger that he has been feted as a man of science by the Drunkards' Society. The Stranger attempts to leave, but the waitress presents him with the bill for the others' drinks. When he cannot pay, a policeman comes and lays his hand on his shoulder.

Scene 2. The Stranger is in a prison cell; the door opens, and the Beggar brings a newspaper report: the great authority has withdrawn certification of the Stranger's gold and now accuses him of being a charlatan. The Beggar hints that there is other news, and the Stranger seizes on the idea that his wife has remarried and given his children a stepfather. He hears a mournful cradle song in the distance; the beggar says that it is a reminder of all that the Stranger has abandoned in his quest after a chimera.

Scene 3. When the Stranger returns to the rose room, the same occupants are present as before; they act as if no time has passed during his absence. The midwife enters, saying a child is born. The stranger warns them not to let the innocent child near him, for he is already a damned man for whom there is no peace and no forgiveness. The Mother welcomes his decision to leave and tells him to go in peace, a fugitive and a vagabond on earth.

ACT FOUR

Scene 1. The banqueting hall of Act Three is filled with beggars and loose women. The Stranger is telling a woman that he thinks he must be dead but finds it strange to be still walking about. The waitress tells him not to talk so loudly, since there is a dying man in the next room. The Stranger becomes very agitated and cries that the Terrible One is coming. A choir boy comes in ringing a silver bell, and the Dominican enters with the sacrament. All begin to howl like wild beasts. The choir boy and the Dominican go into another room. The Doctor tells the Stranger scandalous stories about his wife's past. The Beggar tries to take the Stranger away, saying that the Doctor is lying, but the Stranger refuses to believe him.

Scene 2. The Beggar and the Stranger enter the ravine; in the foreground is snow, in the background summer. The mill and the smithy are in ruins, and fallen trees choke the stream. The Beggar says the lake in the mountains was drained, causing the river to rise and wash away everything, even the house in the hills. Three children come onto the bridge; the Stranger recognizes them as his children and calls them by name, but they turn away. The Stranger complains that he cannot bear his sufferings, which he believes are eternal.

Scene 3. The Lady is sitting by the cradle in the rose room. The Stranger enters, asks where he is, and says he was told the river had risen and destroyed the house. The Lady asks why he believes everything he hears. He says that the Doctor has lost his wits and is wandering around, penniless and drunken. The Lady replies that they cannot build happiness on the sorrow of others, and so must part. She adds that he should be comforted by having achieved his great goal, for the newspaper reports that gold has been made in England prove that the transformation is possible, and now the chemists want to give a banquet honoring the Stranger. He refuses to believe any of this and goes out. The Lady lets in the Confessor (who is the same character as the Beggar) and tells him that there is nothing left for her husband but to leave the world and enter a monastery. The Stranger returns and recognizes the Confessor, who reminds him that when he lay ill he promised to serve the powers of good, though when he recovered he broke his vow. The Stranger agrees to go with the Confessor but recommends that they go quickly before he changes his mind.

AUGUST STRINDBERG

To Damascus, Part III [*Till Damaskus,*

written 1901; published 1904; performed 1916]

NOTE: In the author's version of the play, there are neither act nor scene divisions.

The Stranger and the Confessor come to the bank of a large river. On the other side is a steep mountain slope on which, high up, the monastery can be seen above the trees. The Stranger is struck by the whiteness of the monastery and thinks of it as his youthful dream of a house in which peace and unity dwell. The Confessor says that they must wait for the pilgrims on the riverbank and asks him whether there is anyone he would like to take leave of; hesitantly, the Stranger says he had a favorite daughter named Sylvia whom he has not seen for many years. The Confessor beckons and a girl appears rowing on the river. She gets out of the boat and runs into the Stranger's arms. Their reunion is happy at first, but they soon antagonize one another, and she leaves. The Confessor says that there are no wine or women where he is going; the Stranger replies that he has had quite enough of women.

The Confessor goes to order the ferry, and the Lady enters in deep mourning for their daughter. She claims to have nothing to live for and nowhere to go; she begs him not to go into the monastery and leave her, for her mother turned her out after the child's death, and she is homeless. The Confessor appears and announces that everything is ready, but the Stranger says he must look after this woman who was once his wife. The Confessor replies that a Sister of Mercy will look after her and draws the Stranger away.

At a crossroads high in the mountains, syphilitics sit around huts and a sulphur pool. The Confessor explains that these Sulphur Springs purify and burn everything rotten. He leaves and the Lady enters. When the Stranger finds her beautiful, she states that he now has a mirror of beauty in his eye. It is apparent that, now that they are on the other side of the river and have left the world behind them, they can see good in one another. The Stranger says that in woman he sought an angel that could lend him wings, but found only an earth-spirit who bound him down and suffocated him. He complains that the hostess is looking at him as if he had the evil eye and brought misfortune. Just then the hostess approaches and tells the Lady that she felt blessed the moment he entered the house and that her luck changed for the better. The Stranger asks how he, who is damned, can bring blessing and falls down and weeps.

The Confessor returns and explains to the Lady that she drew the evil out of the Stranger into herself and then, having become evil, had to suffer. He tells her that her work is ended and that she, too, can find a home up in the monastery. He and the Lady leave the Stranger alone, and the worshipers of Venus form a circle around him, addressing him as "father." The Tempter comes forward and mocks him, saying he is foolish to believe that he taught youth to go in search of Venus, since youth had been doing that long before he was born. The tempter urges him to climb up the mountain with him; the Stranger replies that the Confessor has told him to wait, but finally he agrees to go.

A court is in session on a terrace on the mountain. The Magistrate presents the case: a young man is accused of killing a woman. Asked whether he has anything to say in his defense, the accused says no; but the Tempter intervenes and presents the case as if he himself were the killer. In mitigation of his act, he says that he was young and pure when he met a girl who seemed to him goodness itself. She accepted him, and he worked five years preparing for their marriage, only to discover that she had been unfaithful with at least three men. To free himself from the sinful thoughts her faithlessness brought him, he shot her. The people cry that the dead woman is guilty and the Magistrate agrees that she was the cause of the crime.

The girl's father steps forward and explains that when she was fifteen she fell into the hands of a man who won her heart and then rejected her. Broken by this experience, she spent three years in a mental institution, and when she came out she was two persons, one angel, one devil. When the people cry that the man who abandoned her is to blame, the Tempter again gives his defense: he was a young man of unusual purity who, until he was twenty-five, resisted the enticements of various Potiphar's wives. He succumbed once, and thereafter was drawn only to pure young virgins from whom he fled if they showed any signs of physical attraction to him. The blame, he says, rests on the woman who seduced him. She comes forward, but the Magistrate interrupts, saying if this keeps up they will get back to Eve in Paradise.

The Tempter calls Eve forward and asks her what she has to say in defense of having seduced Adam. She replies that the serpent tempted her. The serpent is called forth, but the Tempter's question is answered by lightning and thunder. All flee except the Tempter, the Stranger, and the Lady. The Tempter reflects that if the serpent is to blame then they are all comparatively innocent. The Lady begs the Stranger to go with her and not to listen to the Tempter, but the Tempter urges him to come and be shown the world. The Stranger stands irresolute between them. Finally the Lady appeals to him as a mother calling an erring and weary child who longs for home; she is transformed into the idealized mother of his dreams who will rock him to sleep on her knees, cleanse him from hate and sin, heal his wounds, and suffer his sorrows. Violently weeping, he goes to where she stands with open arms.

The Stranger and the Lady-Mother are higher up in the mountain. The Lady-Mother climbs until she disappears into the clouds. The Stranger cries out that she is leaving just when his loveliest dream is about to be fulfilled. The Tempter comes forward, and the Stranger tells him of his desire of reconciliation with mankind through a woman. The Stranger meditates on the paradox of how woman, who is evil, can inspire man with the desire to be virtuous and good. The Confessor enters, and after a brief conversation the Tempter leaves. The Stranger confesses he is still tempted by the idea of a reconciliation between mankind and woman, though he has come to realize that the further lovers are apart, the closer their souls can be; yet he feels that happiness can only be found in the Lady's company. The Confessor suggests that they should start a new marriage and he points out a house down by the river in which they could live. The Stranger decides to go down out of the clouds and join the warm mother. The Confessor bids him farewell until the Stranger should again long for what is hard and cold and white.

The Stranger and the Lady, dressed as bridegroom and bride, enter a room in the house on the mountain. They sit down, adoring one another. The candles and lamps go out, leaving only a ray of light from a room adjoining. The Lady takes his hand and leads him into the light.

Some days later, the Lady is sitting bored at the table. The Stranger enters and they quarrel; when apart, they long for one another; when together, they long to part. They agree that they hate each other only because they are bound together, even though that bond is their love. They agree to part. The Lady goes away, and the Tempter appears at the window.

The Stranger and the Tempter talk for some time on the perversities of woman. A woman comes and knocks on the door; she is the Stranger's first wife, who has recently left her second husband. She and the Stranger discuss the failure of their marriage and the inability of men and women to get along together. The Tempter comes in, and all discuss the nature of love. They rise to go, the Stranger saying he is going upward, the Tempter remaining below.

The Stranger meets the Confessor in the chapter house of the monastery. The Confessor tells him that those in the monastery speak as little as possible, for they have so sharpened their perceptions that they are sensitive to one another's thoughts. The Prior enters to question the Stranger and recounts certain events of the Stranger's childhood—how he was blamed for a fault he did not commit and how he later blamed a deed of his own on a schoolfellow out of fear of punishment. The Stranger agrees to forget the history of his own sufferings if only he can be forgiven by the person he wronged. The Prior remarks that he has been, and calls on Pater Isidor (the Doctor of Parts I and II), who agrees that he has forgiven the Stranger; he adds that he himself made a false accusation against another as a boy and that not one of them is without guilt. The Stranger asks to know life's innermost meaning; the Prior tells a story of one of the Paters illustrating the idea that one cannot know, but must believe. The Stranger suggests that no matter what one does, mankind will criticize him; the Prior gives another illustration, showing that worldly fame is a vanity of vanities. The Stranger then asks whether life is worth living, and is told to follow a Pater to the picture gallery.

In the gallery are pictures of people with two or more heads. The Pater explains the portraits: Boccaccio, after a dissolute youth, ended up as a saint in a monastery; Luther, the youthful champion of tolerance, became a supporter of intolerance in his old age; and so forth. The Pater points out that both contradictory parts go into the making of the whole man; he advises the Stranger to develop from his early acceptance and his later negation of everything to a synthesizing outlook that comprehends the whole of life.

An open coffin sits in the monastery chapel. The Confessor leads in the Stranger, who wears the white shirt of the novice. The Confessor asks him whether he is ready and goes out to fetch the others. The Tempter comes forward, asking whether life was so bitter that the Stranger is choosing to leave it. A woman comes with a child to be baptized, and a bridal couple cross the stage. The Stranger tells the Tempter to stop his comments or else they will never reach the end. The Confessor and the others enter, and the Tempter departs. The Confessor wraps the Stranger in the bier cloth and begins the ceremony.

JOHN MILLINGTON SYNGE

The Playboy of the Western World

[1907]

ACT ONE

Margaret Flaherty, known as Pegeen Mike, is sitting in her father's pub near a village in Ireland's County Mayo, making out an order for various articles of women's clothing when she is interrupted by Shawn Keogh, her cousin, a fat young farmer. Shawn asks for the girl's father, Michael James Flaherty, and when Pegeen says that he will be back soon, Shawn awkwardly jokes that after their marriage Shawn won't leave her alone at night. Shawn then reveals that he heard a man groaning in a ditch as he came down the road.

Michael James enters with farmers Philly Cullen and Jimmy Farrell; Pegeen complains to her father that she has been afraid all alone, and Michael teasingly says that her fiancé must stay the night with her in that case. Shawn, far more afraid of the priest's wrath at his sin than the contempt of Pegeen, runs from the room; but he quickly returns and says that the man who was earlier in the ditch is now coming.

Christy Mahon enters the pub and buys a glass of beer. He is tired, frightened, and dirty and says he is on the run from the police. The others, curious, try to find out what Christy has done; suddenly he cries that he killed his father for striking him. Pegeen and the others retreat and look at Christy with respect; Pegeen suggests that a man brave enough to kill his own father would be a good man to have around the pub, and her father eagerly echoes this. Christy, beginning to be proud of the deed, which has excited admiration instead of horror, agrees to work in the pub as potboy.

Pleased, Michael and the two farmers leave to spend the night at a wake. Shawn hesitates and asks Pegeen whether she would like him to stay, but the girl, scornful of her weak fiancé, sends him away. Pegeen flatters the delighted Christy, who in fact is shy and timorous. They are interrupted by a knock at the door, and Pegeen is furious to learn that her fiancé has sent Widow Quin to take Christy to her house for the night. The two women battle over Christy, but finally Pegeen wins and Widow Quin goes. Christy beds down for the night in the bar, and Pegeen goes into a back room.

ACT TWO

Christy is working in the pub the next day. As he is washing himself, he hears someone approaching and runs from the room. Susan Brady, Honour

Blake, Sara Tansey and Nelly, four village girls, enter. Christy returns, and the girls hand over gifts to "the man who killed his own father"—eggs, butter, cake, and a boiled chicken. As the girls stand round giggling and staring at the curiosity, Widow Quin comes in and organizes Christy's breakfast, then asks him to tell his chilling tale. Christy says he struck his father down with a spade because his father wanted him to marry a middle-aged widow. As Christy develops his story, the women make awestruck, flattering comments; Christy grows more confident and swells with pride. Pegeen returns as the widow and Christy are drinking together; furious, Pegeen sends her rivals away.

Pegeen tells Christy that she has been reading the newspapers and saw an account of a hanging. Christy quickly deflates and self-pityingly says he'll have to get back on the road, and Pegeen drops her cutting tone and tells him he is safe at the pub. Shawn and Widow Quin enter and tell Pegeen her sheep are eating cabbages; she goes rushing out. Shawn then anxiously hands Christy a ticket and tells him he will give him trousers and a coat if he will leave. Christy asks why, and Shawn confesses that he is afraid Pegeen will marry Christy if he stays. The widow suggests that Christy at least try on the clothing, and Christy, delighted and flattered, goes out. Shawn and the widow strike a bargain: he will give her animals and various other things if she will help him get rid of Christy.

Christy returns, swaggering with pride in his new attire, and declares that if this is the treatment he can expect he intends to stay. Shawn goes out to let the widow persuade Christy to leave Pegeen to Shawn but Christy, wanting to show himself off to Pegeen, heads for the door. He stops short and staggers back into the room, declaring that the ghost of his father is approaching. Christy hides behind the door as his father, Mahon, enters.

Questioned by the widow, Christy's father reveals that his son gave him a crack on the head after he lost all patience with Christy's foolishness; his son is work shy and clumsy, Mahon says, a silly timorous weakling afraid of girls, unable to drink, and queasy at the smell of tobacco. The widow, very amused, sends the irate father off over the hills, telling him that Christy went that way. Christy reappears, cowed, and fears that now he has lost Pegeen, but the widow offers to take him, saying that they can live together quite happily. Christy answers that all he wants is Pegeen, so the widow promises to keep quiet about Christy's father in return for gifts and concessions when Christy has become the master in place of Pegeen's father. The village girls come to the pub calling for Christy to come to the sports on the sands, and Christy goes off with them.

ACT THREE

Jimmy Farrell and Philly Cullen enter the pub and discuss Christy's success at the sports and his obvious success with Pegeen. As they talk of Christy and the murder he has supposedly committed, old Mahon enters and sits listening. As he is about to tell them the truth, Widow Quin arrives; she gives him a drink and takes the two farmers aside to tell them that the old man is raving: she met him earlier that day and he was then telling how he had killed a man, but when he heard the story of Christy he began saying that his head had been cracked by his son. Jimmy is taken in with the story, but Philly is supicious and tells the widow to ask Mahon what sort of man his son was. The widow slyly asks whether the son was a good sportsman who could beat all others; Mahon replies no, his son is a fool.

Hearing a burst of cheering from the sports going on below, they rush to the window to watch and see Christy coming in first in the mule race; Mahon, not realizing it is his son, cheers with the rest. But as the people below lift Christy up and cheer him up to the pub, Mahon recognizes him. The Widow tells him it can't be his son, for that man is going to marry the daughter of the publican and is the best sportsman in the western world. Mahon, unsure, says he'd better leave and avoid trouble; but Philly, sensing the truth, hurries after him. Left alone with the triumphant Christy, Pegeen proudly begins looking after him; Christy proposes to her, and Pegeen, touched and happy, loses all her stridency and agrees to marry him. Just then her father returns from the wake with Shawn and announces that the dispensation has come and Pegeen will marry Shawn that day. Pegeen declares she will marry Christy and no one else; Christy, using the power of his reputation, challenges Shawn to fight for Pegeen. He seizes a spade, and Shawn runs shrieking from the pub. Michael states that he would rather have a courageous man like Christy than a weakling like Shawn for a son-in-law and gives the couple his blessing.

Suddenly old Mahon rushes in, knocks Christy flat, and tells Pegeen that the boy is his worthless son. Pegeen cries that Christy has been lying all this time about his exploit in killing his father and tells him to go away. Christy, astonished, says he *believed* he killed Mahon even if his father was only knocked out; and haven't his exploits at the sports proved him a man? But Pegeen, near to tears, refuses to listen, and Mahon makes a grab for his son to lead him away back home. Christy, further goaded by the jeers of his former admirers, seizes a spade and chases his father from the pub. He returns, having felled Mahon a second time. Widow Quin tries to persuade Christy to leave by the back door and avoid being lynched, but Christy refuses, believing that Pegeen will marry him now that he is a true hero.

But Pegeen is outside with the others, who are preparing a rope. When no one will volunteer to tie up Christy, Pegeen takes the noose and slips it over him; the men pull it tight about his arms and tell him they are taking him to the police. Christy, outraged by the injustice shown by the people that have been lionizing him, struggles and clings to a table; Pegeen heats up the fire to burn his leg and make him release his grip. More and more angry, Christy swears he will kill others before he is through.

Christy squirms round and bites Shawn's leg; delighted with himself, and, thinking he has nothing to lose, he roars that he will do terrible things. As he shouts, his father crawls in unnoticed and watches. Pegeen has got a sod hot enough and takes it to Christy and burns his leg. Christy screams and looses his grip on the table, and the men begin dragging him to the door.

They start back when they see Mahon, who goes to his son and frees him, declaring that he and Christy will go back home and spread the story of the villainy of the people of County Mayo. Christy agrees to go with his father but says it is rather his father who will go with him. He drives Mahon ahead of him from the pub, and Mahon leaves, smiling happily at his son's new-found courage. Christy turns at the door and blesses all present, saying that from now on he is going to "go romancing through a romping lifetime."

Shawn goes to Pegeen and says that now he and she can be married; but Pegeen boxes his ears, weeping loudly and lamenting her loss of "the only Playboy of the Western World."

J O H N   M I L L I N G T O N   S Y N G E

Riders to the Sea [1904]

In the kitchen of a cottage on an island off the west coast of Ireland, Cathleen is spinning as Nora comes in with a bundle and explains that it contains clothing that they are to examine to determine whether it belonged to their brother Michael, lost at sea nine days ago; the priest gave them to her suggesting that she and Cathleen say nothing about Michael to their mother unless the clothes, taken from a body washed ashore in the far north, turn out to be his. In that case the girls will be able to give their mother the comfort of knowing that her son received a clean burial. They hide the bundle, for their mother, asleep in the next room, might appear at any moment.

Their mother Maurya, old and stiff, enters as her son Bartley comes in from the windy day. He readies himself to take the boat to the horse fair; the weather is bad, and his mother does not want him to go, for she is sure that he, too, will drown and she will have no son left. He must go, he says, for this will be the last boat for two weeks or more, and it promises to be a good fair for horses. He turns in the doorway and looks to his mother for her blessing, but she remains dour and silent and he leaves.

Cathleen chastises her mother for withholding her blessing and suggests that Bartley will die without it. Remembering that he hasn't taken his bread, she wraps it up and urges her mother to hurry down to the wellspring to give it to him along with her blessing. Maurya assents and leaves the house. Cathleen and Nora bring out the parcel of clothes and open it up, examining the shirt and stocking carefully. Nora recognizes her own knitting in the stockings; the clothes are Michael's. They hurriedly put the clothes away again and decide not to tell their mother anything until Bartley returns.

Maurya reappears, the package of bread in her hands. She has seen the most terrible thing: Bartley was riding by on the red mare, and as she began to say to him, "God speed you," the words stuck in her throat, for behind him, on the gray pony, she saw Michael, all dressed up. Bartley blessed her and rode on, and she didn't give him the bread or speak a word. Her daughters tell her that she couldn't have seen Michael, that his body was found up north, and that he has received a clean burial. Maurya then begins to speak softly of the sea that has taken her husband's father, her husband, and five of her six sons; soon it will take Bartley, and she will have no sons. As she reminisces about the deaths and her prayers, some women begin to appear through the door of the cottage; they sit down and keen softly. Then the men come bearing Bartley's body on a plank, covered with a bit of sail cloth; they place him on the kitchen table. The gray pony, they tell Cathleen, kicked Bartley into the sea, and he was drowned in the surf.

Maurya sprinkles holy water on Bartley's body and places Michael's clothes over his feet. She says that she has prayed night after night for him, and for all her sons as well; but now, with all of them gone, she can rest and, even if there isn't much to eat, she'll sleep nights. Her daughters discuss the building of the coffin for Bartley; their mother repeats to herself that Michael had a clean burial in the north and that Bartley will have a fine coffin. "No man at all can be living forever," she says, "and we must be satisfied."

ERNST TOLLER

Man and the Masses   [*Masse Mensch*, 1921]

First Picture. In the back room of a workmen's tavern, a Woman and several workmen are sitting around a table. The Woman speaks passionately of proclaiming a strike and leading the masses to build world peace. There is a knock, and a workman cries that they have been betrayed. The Man enters; the Woman tells the others that there is no danger and asks them to leave. The Man, her husband, says he has come, not to help her, but because his own honor is threatened. He says that she must give up her work; she can fulfill her desire for social service in their own circle by, for instance, founding a home for illegitimate children. The Women replies that she has respect for nothing but her work and that she has taken it on, not out of a mere whim, but because of a deep need to be a human being. The Man tells her that he has taken an oath of loyalty to the state and has informed the authorities about her; otherwise, he says, progress in his career would have been impossible. He adds that her actions give him grounds for divorce. She accepts the blame for their estrangement, though she speaks to him yearningly and passionately. Then her tone changes: tomorrow, she says, she is going to speak to the masses and attack the state to which he has sworn allegiance. He asks whether her decision is final, and she replies that it is. They say good night, and as the Man starts to go, the Woman begs to spend the night with him for the last time.

Second Picture (*dream picture*). Around a desk in a room of the stock exchange sit a clerk, bankers, and brokers. The clerk has the face of the Man of the first scene. Two bankers are bidding on a munition works, and another two discuss the progress of the war, which is going badly. Something is missing, says the third banker; joy and love, replies the fourth. But, he goes on, the trouble will be adjusted; the largest banks will finance an enterprise called Recreation Home: A Place to Strengthen the Desire to Win. In actuality, he reveals, the Recreation Homes will be national brothels.

The clerk announces that a new issue is ready: national bonds for a War Recreation Home. The first two bankers are uninterested, but the third and fourth subscribe to one hundred thousand at par. The second banker receives a telegram saying the drive on the west front has been lost. There are shrieks, and voices begin to offer various war industries. The third banker announces that he will take another hundred thousand, and voices wonder whether the rumor of the lost drive is true. Voices begin to bid. The fourth banker confides to the third that a rise or a fall on the market means nothing; the important thing is to keep the machinery going and the system safe. The Companion, his face a composite of death and life, enters leading the Woman, who addresses them simply as human beings. The third banker asks the fourth whether he has heard that there is a disaster in the mines; the fourth suggests that they have a charity festival and dance on the floor of the stock exchange. Crying that they donate and dance and help the unfortunates, the bankers dance around the exchange.

Third Picture. In a great hall, the Woman is sitting at a long table on the platform. Workers, men and women, are packed closely together in the room. A group of women cry to destroy the factories and machines. The Woman tells them that the factory cannot be wiped out; but the soul of man must master factories to help make a richer life for all. She says that they must strike, and the crowd takes up the cry. The Nameless One emerges from the crowd and hurries to the platform. He calls for more than just a strike, which, he claims, is not peace but merely a pause. War must be stopped entirely, he says, by one final desperate battle. He cries for revolution and enjoins the workers to get arms and to storm the city hall. The Woman tries to interrupt, saying she does not want fresh murders. The Nameless One silences her, saying he is the mass, and mass is destiny and strength. After one bloody battle, he prophesies, there will be eternal peace, the end of misery, and freedom for all people. He tells the Woman that her advice means discord and urges her to keep silent for the sake of the cause. Half-hypnotized, the Woman repeats that he is mass, that he is right. The Nameless One leads the crowd as they storm out of the hall.

Fourth Picture (dream picture). In a walled court lit by a single lantern, the Nameless One appears to the worker guards and begins to play a harmonica. A condemned man enters, a rope around his neck. At his last request, he urges the others to join in a dance. Other condemned men step out of the darkness and dance. The Companion, dressed as a guard, enters, holding the Woman. Another guard brings in a prisoner who looks like the Man; he tells the Nameless One that the Man brought death on himself by shooting at the enemies of the state. The prisoner says that he swore to protect the state. Pushed to the wall, he cries out for life. The Woman tears herself away from the Companion and cries to the guards not to shoot, begging them to forgive the prisoner, her husband, as he has forgiven them. A guard replies that forgiveness is cowardice; he adds that yesterday he escaped from the enemy as they were about to shoot him. The other guards cry, "To the wall!" and the face of the prisoner changes to that of the guard who escaped from the enemy. The Woman tells him that yesterday they stood him against the wall, and now he is standing against the wall again; for he is man. A guard says that mass counts; the Woman replies that the Man counts. The guards, together, rejoin that mass counts. In despair, the Woman stands next to the Man and tells them to shoot.

Fifth Picture. In the hall, the Woman and the Nameless One sit at opposite ends of the long table. A workman comes in and reports on the progress of the war. The Woman speaks sadly of the many who have been killed. The Nameless One replies that in yesterday's war they fought as slaves; in today's battle they are free. The Woman murmurs that in both wars men are human beings. More workmen rush in saying the city is lost and that the enemy is butchering everyone; but their side has hostages that they will shoot if the enemy's shock troops reach them. Mass is revenge, cries the Nameless One; but the Woman pleads that mass should be a band of brothers. She says that she must protect the men outside, because they are men. The Nameless One accuses her of trying to shield those with whom she had grown up. The Woman replies that she shields him, the souls of the workmen, and humanity itself. There are shots outside, and the workers discover that the door is blocked and that they are trapped. Waiting for death, they sing the "Internationale." The doors burst open and soldiers order the workers to hold up their hands. They handcuff the Woman.

Sixth Picture (*dream picture*). Crouching in a cage is a handcuffed person with the face of the Woman. Nearby is the Companion, dressed as a keeper. A headless shadow appears and accuses the Woman of its murder. She says that she is not guilty. Other shadows appear with the same accusation. She says that she did not want bloodshed, and the shadows retort that she kept silent. Finally she asserts that she is guilty. The keeper says her sentimental attitude toward life is foolish. Prisoners enter with tattered rags concealing their faces. The keeper asks who this mass of featureless forms may be; the word "mass" echoes and the Woman cries that mass, being necessity, cannot be guilty. The keeper replies that man cannot be guilty, and to this the Woman cries that God is guilty. When the keeper says that God is within one, the Woman replies that then she will triumph over God. She accuses God and demands that he be brought to justice. The prisoners take up the accusation. The keeper, saying that she is now healed, takes the Woman out of the cage. She asks whether she is free, and he replies that she is fettered and free.

Seventh Picture. The Woman sits at a table in a prison cell. The Man enters and says that the investigation has shown that she is not guilty of the recent shooting; her death sentence, despite her treason, has not yet been confirmed, for nobility of aim, he says, is always respected by right-thinking people. The Woman, murmuring of his respect for good intentions, suddenly sees that he and his state are also guilty of the murders, for it is they who put up prisons, throw the masses into slums, drive them into factories, and sacrifice them in war. The Nameless One enters, saying the masses have sent him to set her free. Everything is prepared; two keepers have been bribed, and a third will be struck down. The Woman hesitates, saying she has no right to win life through a keeper's death. The Nameless One tries to hurry her, but she cries that he murders for humanity just as the deluded *bourgeoisie* murder for the state. She accuses him of having no love for man, and he replies that he loves the principle above everything. The Woman cries for the individual above everything and says that she would betray the masses if she demanded a single life, for no man has the right to kill another to forward any cause. The Nameless One replies that she lacks the power to face the need for action; men, he says, will only be made free through hard facts and harder deeds. He leaves, and a priest enters. The priest states that the Woman thought mankind was good and so allowed outrage against the state and sacred order; but, he tells her, man is all evil. She repeats that she believes in the goodness of mankind and tells him to leave her.

An officer enters to read her sentence. She asks whether they are going to shoot her and says that she is ready. They go out. A few seconds later two women prisoners slip in. One sees bread on the table and leaps at it; then she sees a hand mirror and hides it in her dress. The other finds a silk cloth, which she also hides away. A volley of shots sounds outside. The prisoners, frightened, hurriedly put back the mirror and the silk and sink to their knees, crying.

VSEVOLOD VISHNEVSKI

The Optimistic Tragedy

[*Optimisticheskaya tragediya*, 1932]

ACT ONE

Two sailors of the former Russian Royal Fleet, supported by a chorus, are addressing the theater audience at the dawn of the new epoch created by the Russian Revolution of 1918. Lights dim, and Väinönen, a Finn, is seen standing alone aboard a great battleship. A voice bellows military orders, and Väinönen is joined by Spotty, another sailor, who tells him that Able Seaman Alexei is drilling a naked woman down on deck. When Alexei appears, Väinönen tells him it's "not right" to do that to a woman, and Alexei, who has tendencies to anarchism, asks what *is* right these days. The Finn says everything will be right under socialism, a view that Alexei derides.

Alexei, who has left to send the woman back ashore, suddenly rushes back shouting. A crowd gathers, and Alexei tells them that the new government party, the Bolsheviks, has appointed a commissar to the ship. As the crew discuss the news, a woman appears, perceives that the Chief, an outright anarchist, is the boss of the men, and hands him a paper announcing that she is the Commissar.

As the Commissar stands alone, an officer approaches her; she quickly corrects him for calling himself a lieutenant—he is now a "war seaman." They are interrupted by a commotion, and Väinönen appears, knife in hand, trying to keep back Alexei and another man who want to make love with the woman. More sailors appear, all intending to benefit from the presence of a woman aboard. A half-naked sailor tries to grab the Commissar, who shoots him down with a small pistol. The Commissar orders members of the Communist Party and sympathizers to stay for a meeting, but Foghorn, the Chief's jackal, says that the Chief has already ordered a meeting, and the Commissar is left alone with Väinönen.

In an interlude, the chorus acclaims the ineluctable strength and progress of the Party. Alone, the Chief, Foghorn, and Alexei are discussing the Commissar, but stop short at her arrival. When the boatswain appears, the Commissar sends him to fetch the new Commander, but before leaving, he seeks the assent of the Chief. The Commander arrives and the Commissar tells him to read a new order dissolving the "Free Anarchist Revolutionary Detachment" and organizing a regiment of three battalions under his own orders. The Commissar then announces that the crew leaves for the front the next day. Left together, the Commissar and the Chief, Foghorn, and Alexei discuss anarchism, and the

421

Commissar and the Chief reach an "understanding" which, when the Commissar has left, the Chief describes as "just tactics" to an angry Alexei.

The chorus appears and speaks of those early days of the revolution, a time in which there was "an extra high percentage of traitors," in Lenin's words. The Commander and the bo'sun attempt to get the men assembled. Only a tall sailor, an old sailor, and two others appear smartly; the rest of the crew lounge about insolently. The Chief says he has ordered a rest period, and the bo'sun reluctantly takes his orders from the Chief. Foghorn announces that one of the sailors has robbed an old woman, who enters to identify the thief. Foghorn arbitrarily accuses the tall sailor, and, on the Chief's orders and despite objections from the Commander and the old sailor, the tall sailor is wrapped in a canvas and thrown overboard. Confused, the old woman suddenly pulls out the purse supposedly stolen by the tall sailor. The Chief orders the old woman to be dumped over the side after the sailor.

The Commissar arrives on the scene followed by Alexei, who says the crew wants a farewell dance before leaving for the front. The bo'sun notes that the Chief has ordered rest. Faced with the choice, the Commissar orders the dance to proceed. The chorus sings of the bravery of the forces that fought the White Russians, and the first act ends on the music of the dance, followed by the departure of the men for the front.

ACT TWO

The Commissar's regiment is retreating before the enemy but is rallied by the Commissar and the Commander. Reading over a letter she has just written beginning "my dear . . . ," the Commissar is interrupted by the bo'sun, and assures him that socialism will bring to Russia the order he thirsts for. Väinönen, the Commissar's ally, enters, and the two discuss how to rally all the men to their cause. As Väinönen leaves, the Commander enters and in a frank talk with the Commissar makes known his skepticism of the revolution's chances of success; he is bitter because revolutionaries lined up and shot members of his family. After the Commander leaves, the Commissar tells Väinönen to leave the officer alone, for, if not a communist, he is at least against the anarchists.

The Finn goes out to call Alexei, who enters playing his accordion. Alexei reveals that he voted for the Bolshevik Party in the elections but that his fighting has been for himself rather than for any party; he says that the peasants won't follow the communists; they will always want private property. The Commander and the bo'sun appear as Alexei is about to make a pass at the Commissar; the Commander demands complete control of the regiment. The Chief and Foghorn follow and demand that the regiment be purged of counterrevolutionaries like the officer. Asked to choose between the officer and the anarchists, the Commissar says she is for the regiment. Understanding this to be favorable to him, the Chief leaves to prepare an order for the Commissar to countersign; he tells the others to watch the officer and the bo'sun, who will be dealt with later.

The Commissar sends Väinönen to assemble other Party members. When her allies appear, she tells them that the Chief has sent for anarchist reinforcements and that they have to act quickly. The communists leave to confront the Chief. The chorus quotes an order of the Revolutionary War Council stating that commanders must deal rapidly and severely with anarchy and indiscipline.

When the anarchist group is assembled, two prisoners are brought before the Chief. They reveal themselves as officers who have escaped from a German prisoner-of-war camp; one is shell-shocked, the other has a wounded arm: all they want is to return home. Despite their pleas and the protests of some of the sailors, including Alexei, the Chief orders them to be shot, because they are officers. The Commissar enters with her followers, too late to stop the executions, and confronts the Chief. He fares badly in the ensuing argument, for he has alienated Alexei and some of his men by his arbitrary orders and his refusal to consult them. Seeing her chance, the Commissar announces an order supposedly written by the Chief but in fact made up by herself: it is a death sentence for the Chief for insubordination and for having carried out summary executions. As the sentence is "read," Foghorn quits his boss's side.

The Commissar orders Alexei to carry out the execution. He leads the Chief away, and a shot is heard. The anarchist reinforcements arrive; learning of the Chief's death, they try to fight, but are overpowered by the sailors and pressed into service with them. The bo'sun, with new-found authority, begins drilling the new recruits, who slowly fall in with the spirit of solidarity; with growing enthusiasm they begin marching with the rest of the regiment.

ACT THREE

At a camping place one evening, the Commissar appoints the old sailor commander of a battalion. The Commander announces that the enemy have called up German reinforcements and that a German infantry brigade is moving into the area. The Commissar asks for a battle strategy but rejects the Commander's idea as a textbook plan, wrong for the present circumstances. She decides that the first battalion will hold the present position while the two other battalions will make a flanking move and attack the enemy's rear, all battalions coordinating the attack for five in the morning. The Commander is sent off with two battalions. In an interlude, the chorus eulogizes the long marches of those early days.

Alone with Väinönen on sentry watch, Foghorn sees defeat and death waiting and tries to induce the Finn to run away with him. When Väinönen refuses, Foghorn treacherously stabs him and escapes. The Germans are thus able to take the unguarded regiment by surprise; many Russians are killed and the Commissar, Alexei, and others are taken prisoner. The Commissar impresses on the men that they must at all costs keep quiet about the impending attack by their comrades. A German officer appears and calls for information, but is greeted with silence. Foghorn, captured trying to escape, is led in, and the officer reveals his treachery. He is led away, and the officer orders the Commissar to go with him for questioning; she lets the men understand that she will try to stall for time. A priest enters after a final German plea for information and starts giving last solace to the prisoners, who try to gain time by appearing contrite. Suddenly the Commander's battalions begin the attack from the rear.

The prisoners seize weapons from their guards and join the fighting, shooting down Foghorn as he tries to flee. The Commander arrives at the head of his victorious troops, and the Commissar is carried in, bleeding to death and hardly able to speak after undergoing torture. The men stand around in silent sorrow, and Alexei, in personal grief, quietly plays a revolutionary song on his accordion as the Commissar sinks into death.

Earth-Spirit [*Erdgeist*, written 1895;
performed 1898]

NOTE: Between 1892 and 1895 Wedekind wrote a five-act play entitled *Lulu*. Due to its length and to censorship problems, he later divided it into two plays, *Earth-Spirit* and *Pandora's Box*.

VERSE PROLOGUE

An animal trainer invites the audience to witness the battle between man and beast. Business is bad, he asserts, for audiences now prefer to view more refined versions of animal life, the plays of Ibsen and Hauptmann, at the theater. When he calls for the serpent, a stagehand carries out Lulu. The animal trainer foretells the crimes that Lulu will commit. After she is carried out, he announces that he will confidently face the beast, "the honored public."

ACT ONE

Dr. Schön, a newspaper editor, visits the studio of the artist Schwarz, who is painting a portrait of Schön's fiancée. He accidentally knocks over another portrait, that of a young woman in a Pierrot costume, whom he professes not to know. Schwarz explains that the beautiful girl is always accompanied by her ancient husband when she comes to sit for her portrait. As Schön is departing, the two in question, Lulu and Dr. Goll, arrive and greet Schön, with whom they are obviously well acquainted. Lulu disappears into the bedroom, emerges in a Pierrot costume, and takes her place on the platform. Schön's son Alva arrives to take his father to the dress rehearsal of the ballet that Alva has written. Goll leaves with Schön and Alva, promising to return right after the performance.

Lulu expresses amazement at Goll's departure, for, as she explains to Schwarz, he never leaves her alone. He restricts her life completely and constantly gives her dancing lessons. When she describes her dancing costumes, Schwarz becomes more and more upset and cannot resist trying to seize her hand. She flees and orders him to return to work. As he chases her, she throws an easel at him. When he sees that she has destroyed a portrait, he despairs. Lulu stamps on the portrait and sinks down in dizziness. Schwarz tells her he loves her, though he is puzzled by her strange behavior. When Goll is heard outside, Lulu becomes terrified. Goll breaks down the door, but as he rushes at Lulu and Schwarz, he is unable to breathe and falls to the floor. Schwarz leaves to fetch a doctor. Upon his return Lulu calls him a criminal and a coward. When she goes to change back into her clothes, Schwarz prays for the strength and freedom to be happy, for Lulu's sake. She emerges from the bedroom and asks his help in fastening her dress.

ACT TWO

Lulu is reading in the parlor when Schwarz, now her husband, comes home. The mail arrives, among it the announcement of Schön's engagement. Schwarz's comments upon the beauties of his new wife, who has become his whole life, are interrupted by the bell, which he answers. He returns to say that it was a beggar and goes upstairs. Lulu leads in Schigolch, the beggar, who, it appears, is her father. He asks her for money, which she gives him. He admires her rich surroundings and reveals that things are not going well with him. She admits to him that she does nothing, that she is "an elegant beast."

After the beggar leaves, Schön arrives and reprimands Lulu for visiting his home, threatening to request Schwarz to watch over her. Lulu says that she wants to see him despite his approaching marriage and complains of Schwarz's blind trust. She feels she is going to ruin, for Schwarz loves her without really knowing her. She recalls how Schön took care of her when he caught her, a young girl, stealing his watch. Everything, including her marriages, she owes to him. Schön insists that she stay away from him: he had hoped that her marriage to Schwarz would content her, so that he could safely marry his fiancée.

Schwarz arrives and leads Lulu off, while Schön decides to seek his own freedom by revealing the truth to Schwarz. Upon Schwarz's return, Schön advises him to keep a closer watch on Lulu. Schwarz gradually realizes that his wife is not as innocent as he had thought; he learns of her humble beginnings and of her long association with Schön, whom she wished to marry before she married either Goll or Schwarz. As Schwarz sinks deeper and deeper into despair, Schön advises him to learn to understand Lulu as well as himself in order to save his marriage. Schwarz leaves, saying he will speak with Lulu, but goes into another room and locks the door. A groan is heard. Lulu appears and realizes what is happening. As Alva Schön arrives with news of a revolution in Paris, a death rattle is heard. Lulu brings an ax, with which they force open the door to reveal the body of Schwarz, so ghastly that none can look at it.

Lulu goes to change her clothes, and Schön writes notes to the doctor and the police and sends the maid to deliver them. When Lulu appears, dressed to go out, Schön keeps repeating that the scandal has ruined his engagement and his life; Lulu tells Schön that he will marry her. Escherich, a reporter, enters and snoops around, having heard of the suicide at police headquarters. When he sees the body, however, its throat slit with a razor, he cannot look at it.

ACT THREE

In her dressing room in the theater where she is dancing the lead in one of Alva's ballets, Lulu is joined by Schön and Alva as she is changing costumes.

They discuss Lulu's success, which has been greatly aided by Schön's praise in the newspapers. After Schön leaves, Lulu and Alva recall their youth. Lulu bitterly asserts that Schön aided her career so that she might find a rich husband. She leaves, vowing to dance well for Schön, who has seemed not to notice her despite his praise in the press.

Prince Escerny, an African explorer, enters and chats with Alva. Lulu returns and asks Escerny where Schön is seated. After Alva leaves, Escerny offers Lulu a wealthy life and his devotion, but she pays little attention and leaves for the stage.

Soon after Alva returns, a bell begins ringing, indicating that something has gone wrong. Alva and Escerny run out, and Lulu enters. Alva returns, followed by Schön, who is furious both that Lulu played the scene directly to him and that she broke off the performance. Lulu accuses Schön of humiliating her by appearing with his fiancée. After Alva leaves, Schön tells Lulu that despite his aid she has become as base as her origins, but when she speaks of going to Africa with Escerny, he seems alarmed. She becomes more and more triumphant, and he becomes furious at her confidence in her power over him. He begins to weep, both for himself and for his innocent fiancée. As Lulu dictates, he writes a note to his fiancée, breaking their engagement.

ACT FOUR

In a spacious hall of their home, Lulu and Schön, now married, are visited by the Countess Geschwitz. When Lulu accompanies the countess to the door, Schön mutters about the filth that has infested his house. Lulu returns and asks to spend the afternoon with him, but he informs her that he is busy. After they leave, the countess sneaks back into the room and, hearing voices, hides. Schigolch enters with Rodrigo, an acrobat, and Hugenberg, a schoolboy, whom they tease because of his boyish infatuation with Lulu. They are interrupted by Lulu herself, in a ball dress, who announces that she is expecting company. When Ferdinand, the coachman, announces the arrival of Dr. Schön, the three hide, for they have come without the knowledge of Lulu's husband.

Alva Schön arrives to take Lulu to a matinee. They sit down to lunch, served by Ferdinand. Lulu's comments lead Alva to confess that it is only because they grew up together that he has restrained his feelings for her. Schön peeps through the curtains, and is shocked to see Alva; he also notices that Ferdinand is attracted to Lulu. When Rodrigo's head emerges from his hiding place, Schön also sees him. Lulu knowingly gives her hand to Alva, who kisses it ardently. She leads him to confess his desperate love for her, whereupon she confesses that she poisoned his mother. Lulu spies Schön, who accompanies the dazed Alva out.

Rodrigo emerges, desperate to escape Schön's wrath. He hides as Schön returns and berates Lulu with bitter fury, urging her to kill herself with the revolver that he holds in his hand. Seeking the rest of Lulu's hidden admirers, he comes upon the Countess Geschwitz and locks her in another room. His fury grows, and he offers to kill Lulu himself. She pulls away, holding the revolver down and refusing to take her own life. As Schön forces her to her knees, Hugenberg jumps out from his hiding place and screams for help. As Schön turns, Lulu fires five bullets into him. He calls for Alva, who returns as Lulu calls Schön the one man she loved. Lulu starts to go upstairs, but Alva tells her to stay. As the police arrive, Lulu begs Alva not to surrender her to them, promising to belong to him. Alva, however, will not listen.

FRANK WEDEKIND

Pandora's Box   [*Die Büchse der Pandora,*

written 1895; performed 1904]

PROLOGUE

In the bookshop, the Normal Reader asks to purchase a book from the Enterprising Publisher. The Timid Author enters with a book of poems, followed by the Public Prosecutor, who seeks to protect the Normal Reader from the Timid Author's works by suppressing them. Despite threats of prison, the Timid Author refuses to change his work to suit the Public Prosecutor.

ACT ONE

In a sumptuous drawing room, Rodrigo, an acrobat dressed as a footman, the writer Alva Schön, and Countess Geschwitz discuss the plan by which Lulu, who has been sent to prison for shooting Alva's father, is to escape and wed Rodrigo, who plans to make a trapeze artist out of her. Schigolch arrives and, promising to bring Lulu there shortly, departs with Countess Geschwitz.

Alva expresses admiration for the countess and contempt for the brawny Rodrigo, who retorts that Alva must live on the money from the sale of his father's newspaper. When someone is heard approaching, Rodrigo hides. Young Alfred Hugenberg enters, explaining that he has just run away from the reformatory. He asks Alva for money to further his plan to free Lulu from prison. Rodrigo appears and tells Hugenberg that Lulu died of cholera in prison. When Alva confirms this news, Rodrigo throws the broken-hearted Hugenberg out.

Lulu appears, leaning on Schigolch's arm. Rodrigo, furious at her underfed appearance, denounces her and leaves to visit the police. Schigolch leaves to get the train tickets for himself and Lulu. When Lulu asks to see her portrait, Alva fetches it. Lulu explains the countess's plan to Alva. During the cholera epidemic, the countess took a nurses' training course, nursed cholera victims, and purposely contracted the disease. When she visited Lulu in prison, they exchanged underwear, and Lulu contracted the disease. They were placed in the same hospital ward; the countess used her arts to make them look alike. Just now she came back to fetch something and exchanged places with Lulu. Lulu admits that she feigned an ill appearance when she arrived in order to be rid of Rodrigo.

When Alva tells Lulu that he must either write about her or love her, she becomes amorous and asks him to go with her across the border, assuring him that Schigolch will not come along.

ACT TWO

In an elegant drawing room in Paris, a group of people in evening dress, including Alva, Rodrigo, and Countess Geschwitz, drink a birthday toast to the hostess Lulu, who has assumed the identity of a countess. Several of the guests express an interest in shares in the Jungfrau cable railway. After the others go to the gaming room, the Marquis Casti-Piani informs Lulu that he knows that she has no more money to give him. He gives her a choice: either he will turn her over to the police and receive a reward, or he will sell her to a sumptuous house of ill repute in Cairo. Lulu refuses the latter alternative and assures him that she and Alva still have money. Casti-Piani retorts that they have only shares, which he refuses to accept. He gives her until eleven o'clock to decide and leaves.

The countess enters and accuses Lulu of deceiving her into taking Lulu's place in prison. Lulu says that Rodrigo is in love with the countess despite her Lesbianism. When the countess retorts that Lulu is the slave of Casti-Piani, Lulu asserts that he loves her. The rest of the company pass through on their way to supper.

Rodrigo detains Lulu and demands money from her, threatening to inform the police of her whereabouts. He admits that he has proposed to the countess purely because she is of the nobility. When Lulu asserts that she has no money, Rodrigo repeats his threat and leaves. Several of the company return. Bob, a groom, brings Banker Puntschu the news that shares of the Jungfrau cable railway have fallen. The company proceeds into the dining room. Schigolch arrives and informs Lulu that he needs money. Lulu weeps and tells him of Rodrigo's threat. Schigolch agrees to dispose of Rodrigo; in return, Lulu agrees to give him money. After Schigolch departs and Lulu leaves the room, Casti-Piani pushes Rodrigo into the room and demands to know what he said to Lulu. When Rodrigo reveals his knowledge of Lulu's crime, Casti-Piani leaves.

Lulu enters and tells Rodrigo that the countess will lend her a large sum of money, which she will in turn give him, if Rodrigo will agree to satisfy the countess's burning desire for him. Rodrigo at length agrees and leaves the room, and Lulu calls Countess Geschwitz. She says that Rodrigo has threatened to denounce her to the police unless the Countess Geschwitz will be his that night. At last the countess, out of love for Lulu, agrees to the plan. Rodrigo returns and leaves with the countess for the address that Lulu gives them. Lulu tells Bob, the young groom, that they must exchange clothes and leave immediately; both disappear into the dining room.

The company enters; several, including Alva, bemoan their ruin when Puntschu announces the fall of the Jungfrau shares. One of the two women convinces a journalist to make good his loss by denouncing their friends to the police for a reward. Lulu enters dressed as a groom and informs Alva that the police are about to arrive. They leave together. Only two of the guests are left when Casti-Piani arrives with the police.

ACT THREE

In a shabby attic room in London, Schigolch and Alva are joined by Lulu, who is about to embark upon a career as a prostitute in order to support them all. Despairing over such a fate, Lulu, now Alva's wife, leaves to find a customer.

Alva reminisces about his childhood, recalling the young Lulu, who eventually married and killed his father. When footsteps are heard, Alva and Schigolch climb into a cubbyhole and close the door. Lulu enters with Mr. Hudinei, who gestures strangely and never says a word. She asks him for money; he gives her some, and they disappear into the bedroom.

Alva and Schigolch emerge, and Schigolch goes through Mr. Hudinei's pockets. They return to their cubbyhole as Lulu and Mr. Hudinei emerge from the bedroom. Mr. Hudinei leaves, and Lulu is about to return to the street when Countess Geschwitz, poorly dressed, enters carrying a rolled-up canvas. She announces that she has not been able to secure any money but has brought Lulu's portrait. Despite Lulu's disgust, Alva nails it on the wall and recalls Lulu's beauty at the time it was painted. As Lulu is about to leave, the countess, shocked to learn the purpose of her departure, vows to accompany her wherever she goes.

After Lulu and Countess Geschwitz leave, Alva despairingly reviews memories and reflects that he has not written anything since his father's death. Alva and Schigolch hide as Lulu returns with Kungu Poti, crown prince of Uahubee. When he grabs Lulu, Alva pulls him away. Kungu Poti knocks Alva out and hurriedly leaves.

Lulu sets out again. Schigolch emerges, tries to rouse Alva, and, failing, drags him into the bedroom. Countess Geschwitz returns, and Schigolch goes down to the public house. The countess remains seated as Lulu enters with Dr. Hilti, a young professor. When they disappear into the bedroom, Countess Geschwitz takes out a revolver and holds it to her head. Dr. Hilti rushes in, exclaiming over the corpse in the bedroom. Seeing the countess, he runs out. Lulu rushes after him.

The countess, bemoaning her love for the cruel Lulu, contemplates different forms of suicide. She tries to hang herself but falls to the ground. She is on her knees before Lulu's portrait when Lulu enters with Jack. Lulu bargains unsuccessfully with Jack and leads him into the bedroom.

The countess dreams of going back to Germany and resuming respectable life. Suddenly Lulu, half-dressed, emerges screaming and tries to hold the door shut. Countess Geschwitz takes out her revolver. When Lulu lets the door go, Jack plunges a knife into the countess's stomach. She falls to the floor, and Lulu, terrified, rushes at Jack with a broken bottle. Jack kicks her to the ground and carries her into the other room. Her screaming ceases, and Jack emerges. Before he leaves, he tells the countess that she will not live long either. Thinking of Lulu, Countess Geschwitz dies.

PETER WEISS

The Persecution and Assassination of Marat as Performed by the Inmates of the Asylum of Charenton under the Direction of the Marquis de Sade

[*Die Verfolgung und Ermordung Jean Paul Marats*

dargestellt durch die Schauspielgruppe des Hospizes zu

Charenton unter Anleitung des Herrn de Sade, 1964]

ACT ONE

While a bell rings insistently, the curtain rises on the large, white-tiled bath hall of the asylum at Charenton, an institution that houses not only the insane but also political prisoners and others whose freedom might embarrass the public. A number of white-clad patients are lounging at the back on a platform, before which curtains have been rigged up and are now open. While some male nurses finish their chores and a few patients exhibit rather eccentric behavior, a fat, asthmatic old man of sixty-eight busies himself about the stage. It is the Marquis de Sade, who has been for some years an inmate.

At a sign from the marquis, M. Coulmier, director of the clinic, and his elegantly dressed wife and daughter are escorted in by the male nurses and a group of sisters of a religious order. They are followed by a group of patients in varied costumes. The Coulmiers go to their seats at one side; the others take up positions about an arenalike area at the front center of the stage. After a fanfare, Coulmier welcomes the audience to the amateur theatricals that are about to begin—a part of the hospital's enlightened program of treatment, following the principles of the Declaration of Human Rights. Written and directed by Sade, the play is concerned with the assassination fifteen years earlier of Jean-Paul Marat, a leader of the French Revolution. The marquis takes his place on a dais at one side of the arena; on another dais opposite, the actor who plays Marat steps, wrapped in a sheet, into his bathtub. A patient portraying Marat's mistress, Simonne Evrard, never tires of changing the bandage on his head or the towel about his shoulders.

After some music from the orchestra in the pit, the herald steps forward, a belled cap on his head. Speaking in rhymed couplets, he introduces the actor-patients. Charlotte Corday (a patient who suffers from sleeping sickness); her lover, the Girondist deputy Duperret (an erotomaniac); Jacques Roux, the extremist former priest, most of whose lines Coulmier has censored (a violent patient in a strait jacket); the quartet of singers, three men and a girl (respectively former alcoholics and a prostitute).

The play begins. The quartet sings "Homage to Marat." Four years after the revolution, Marat still writes ceaselessly, demanding an end to the ruling classes. The quartet crowns him with leaves, but the people, played by the patients on the platform, complain that they are still poor; in chorus, they demand their revolution NOW. Urged on by Roux, they call for freedom so noisily that Coulmier has to point out that times have changed and these are outmoded grievances. The male nurses push the patients back and the sisters soothe them by singing a litany.

The herald presents Corday, who is to kill Marat. Aroused from lethargy by the sisters, she declares to music that, though they both believe in change, Marat's methods are too bloody for her; she will kill him to free mankind. As she withdraws, Marat declares to the hovering Simonne that he must write his 14th-of-July call to the people, demanding yet more deaths. The quartet, ignoring Marat, plays cards on the floor while he rages that the people no longer care about the revolution. "I am the revolution," he concludes.

Corday comes to Marat's house and enters, in spite of Simonne's attempt to turn her away. She is about to stab Marat when Sade reminds her that she must come three times before she is admitted. The quartet now sings about the simple girl's arrival in Paris from the country; patients mime the sights she sees. She is confused by the violence in the streets; an execution makes her fearful of her own death. While a gruesome mutilation is mimed, Marat upbraids the audience for its squeamishness, accusing it of forgetting what the people have suffered. Coulmier protests the scene to Sade, but the herald reminds him that they are depicting past events. Sade signals the patients to return to their platform and the curtain is drawn before them as the sisters chant their litany.

Sade begins a running argument with Marat. He says that the aristocrats, deprived of their pleasures, are happy to die to avoid boredom. Although the animating force in Nature is destruction, he hates Nature's indifference; Man should destroy with passion. Sade describes with admiration the protracted public torture of Damiens, who had tried to kill Louis XV—a display far superior to today's machinelike mass executions. Marat says that, unlike Sade, he meets Nature's indifference with action: "The important thing is to pull yourself up by your own hair, to turn yourself inside out and see the whole world with fresh eyes."

The back curtain is opened. Marat leads the patients in a "liturgy," detailing how rich priests have soothed the starving people with pious platitudes. Coulmier protests that this no longer happens. The herald calms him with pretended piety that is marred by a paternoster addressed by an inmate, formerly an abbot, to "our Satan which art in hell."

Sade tells Marat that it is impossible to discover one's own nature. A patient interrupts with a speech declaring that man is a mad animal. Marat seems distressed at this. Denying Sade's claim that "the only reality is the imagination," he complains that men are "still clogged with dead ideas and still oppressed." The quartet and the chorus of patients again demand their revolution NOW. Corday tries to enlist Duperret's support in her venture, but he is interested only in caressing her intimately, a pastime which the herald or the sisters repeatedly try to discourage. Sade declares his scorn of patriotism, saying that it is easy to start "movements that move in vicious circles." He believes only in himself. Marat believes in the revolution but admits that it has overthrown the aristocracy only to establish the role of the bourgeoisie. Roux violently attacks the new rules and their wars. The nurses strap him to a bench.

Sade now gives his opinion of the revolution, while Corday, at his invitation, lashes him with a whip. He had first hoped, he says, for "an orgy greater than all my dreams," but it was only dull. He deplores the revolution as fatal to the individual. Marat is depressed; the quartet sings "Poor Old Marat," and again demands its revolution NOW. Roused with difficulty, Corday orates on the harmony in which Man will one day live. Duperret echoes these sentiments between caresses. Marat orates in turn on economic inequality, to Coulmier's distress. Sade insists that people do not want to be equal; on every level they value their individuality. Marat says that such types must be eliminated. In an access of fear of plots, he flees his bath, but is thrust back by the nurses.

Corday tries a second time to see Marat and is repulsed by Simonne, who, as always, tries to persuade Marat to give up his political concerns and take care of himself. Sade tells him that the people expect everything from the revolution—new shoes, new spouses, better soup. The quartet mocks Marat. In a fevered vision his parents drag onstage a cart bearing generalized figures from his past. A schoolmaster recalls how, as a child, Marat made his playmates fight till blood flowed. His parents recapture their pleasure at his frequent punishments. The schoolmaster, a military man, a scientist, and a member of the nouveaux riches ridicule Marat's greed as a young man for social position; Voltaire and Lavoisier appear and laugh at his revolutionary scientific theories. Together they attribute his radicalism to embittered frustration. Roux defends Marat's motives, the chorus demands its revolution, and the herald declares an intermission.

ACT TWO

In his imagination, Marat, still in his bath, addresses the National Assembly—patients representing the moderate Girondists and the radical Jacobites. He warns them of the corruption of high officials and deplores the failure to carry out the ideals of the revolution. The scene ends in a chaos of boos and cheers. The quartet sings "Poor Old Marat," as Marat keeps calling for his secretary so that he can dictate his call to the people. Sade advises him to give up writing as futile, but Marat says that he has always written with action in mind. Sade predicts that in the France Marat yearns for they will tell him what to write and what work to do and will make endless new laws. Shattered, Marat slumps in his bath.

Corday comes for the third visit. She imagines herself on the scaffold, but, recalling the biblical Judith, refuses Duperret's pleas that she return home. Sade calls Marat's attention to her beauty and remembers his fantasies in prison. "What's the point of a revolution," he inquires, "without general copulation?" The chorus takes up the idea enthusiastically in a song. Corday, obviously impelled by sexual desires, raises her knife.

The herald announces that it is "a part of Sade's dramatic plan to interrupt the climax so this man Marat can hear . . . how the world will go after his death." The singers describe, year by year, the events up to Napoleon's present triumphs. The action continues: Corday at last stabs Marat. He collapses in the posture of Marat in David's painting of his death.

Coulmier makes a short closing speech, reminding all that today there are no oppressors and that the war now in progress can only end in victory. The patients, however, are growing restive. "And if most have a little and few have a lot," the quartet sings, "you can see how much nearer our goal we have got." The patients begin marching, shouting indiscriminately for Charenton, Napoleon, nation, revolution, and copulation. Coulmier's family flee, the nurses are unable to quell the mob, even with the use of violence. Roux, shouting "When will you learn to see? When will you learn to take sides?" is engulfed, for "the patients are fully at the mercy of their mad, marchlike dance." Sade laughs in triumph. The desperate Coulmier signals the curtains to close.

THORNTON WILDER

Our Town [1938]

ACT ONE

The Stage Manager, who remains on stage throughout the play, enters and sets up the tables and chairs that represent Grover's Corners, New Hampshire. He describes the town and some of the people who live there and tells the audience that it is early in the morning of May 7, 1901. Dr. Gibbs enters and walks toward his house, where Mrs. Gibbs is preparing breakfast. He chats briefly with Joe Crowell, who is delivering the morning papers, and with Howie Newsome, the milkman, as they pass by, making their rounds. When Howie disappears, the doctor enters his house and greets his wife.

Next door, Mrs. Webb comes into her kitchen and calls to her children, Wally and Emily, to get up. Mrs. Gibbs also tries to rouse her children, George and Rebecca. When they don't reply, Doc Gibbs calls to George, receives a prompt answer, and leaves the stage. Both the Webb and the Gibbs children enter and sit down to their breakfasts. Domestic conversations go on at both tables: Mrs. Webb asks Wally not to read at the table; George Gibbs asks his mother for an increase in allowance. When the school bell rings, the children join each other in the street and depart for school. Mrs. Gibbs goes outside to feed her chickens and then, while helping Mrs. Webb string beans, gossips about the possibility of using the money from the sale of her old highboy for a trip to Paris.

The Stage Manager comes forward to thank and dismiss the ladies and to call on Professor Willard for a geological, meteorological, and demographic report on Grover's Corners. When the professor retires, the Stage Manager asks Mr. Webb to give a social and political report and to answer a few questions from the audience. Webb leaves as the Stage Manager announces the return of the children from school.

Emily Webb enters and meets George Gibbs, who compliments her on her speech in class and wins her promise for a few hints about the algebra homework. When Mrs. Webb appears, George beats a polite but hasty retreat. Emily and her mother chat, and Mrs. Webb allays her daughter's fears about not being pretty.

Mother and daughter withdraw as the Stage Manager comes forward to give capsule biographies of people like Joe Crowell and Howie Newsome and to describe the broad patterns of life in Grover's Corners. A partially concealed choir under the direction of Simon Stimson begins its evening rehearsal; George Gibbs and Emily Webb start their schoolwork; Dr. Gibbs reads in his kitchen. As Simon rehearses his choir, George calls across to Emily, and they discuss algebra and the moonlight. Dr. Gibbs calls George down to discuss a raise in allowance and the importance of helping Mrs. Gibbs chop firewood. As George returns to his place, his mother, Mrs. Webb, and Mrs. Soames return from choir practice, gossiping about Simon Stimson's drinking habits. Mrs. Webb disappears, followed by Dr. and Mrs. Gibbs. But Rebecca Gibbs joins her brother George at his window, and they stay on, chatting and enjoying the evening.

Mr. Webb and Constable Warren arrive in time to see Simon Stimson walk unsteadily past; the constable departs behind him, and Mr. Webb, after a few words to his daughter Emily, who is enjoying the moonlight at her window, disappears into his house. George and Rebecca Gibbs continue talking in their window until the Stage Manager comes forward to announce the end of the first act.

ACT TWO

The Stage Manager comes on to tell the audience that three years have passed, that it is now early on the morning of July 7, 1904. Mrs. Gibbs and Mrs. Webb begin working in their kitchens; Howie Newsome comes by with the milk, and Si Crowell with the morning papers. Constable Warren joins Si and Howie, and they discuss George Gibbs's imminent retirement from baseball. Si and the constable leave, but Howie delivers his milk and discusses the coming wedding with Mrs. Webb and Mrs. Gibbs before following them off. Dr. Gibbs joins his wife at the table, where they reminisce and discuss George's marriage to Emily, which will take place that afternoon. George enters and, after a brief exchange with his parents, goes over to the Webbs' to see Emily. Much to George's disgust, Mrs. Webb won't let him see his bride, and instead leaves him with Mr. Webb, who enters just in time to get trapped into an awkward discussion of marriage and farming.

As George leaves the Webbs', the Stage Manager interrupts to present a scene from the past, the moment when George and Emily first became aware of their growing love. Both are on their way home from school. They meet, turn into Mr. Morgan's drugstore for a soda—the Stage Manager assumes the role of Mr. Morgan—and their conversation, which begins with a discussion of their personalities, ends with a shy declaration of their commitment to each other.

They depart as the Stage Manager comes forward to call on Dr. and Mrs. Gibbs and to explain to the audience that he wants to show how the parents reacted to the engagement. While Mrs. Gibbs irons, Dr. Gibbs relaxes in a rocker. Their conversation is a mélange of reminiscence and speculation about whether George is old enough to marry. They know the young couple will have their share of trouble, but, since they know that the pain is worth enduring, they consent to the union.

The Stage Manager thanks them as they leave, and while the actors set up their pews behind him, he talks to the audience about the importance of marriage. Mrs. Webb enters but, before going to her pew, expresses sudden concern

437

for Emily. When George comes in, some of his friends from the ball team appear and hoot suggestive comments at him, but the Stage Manager hurries them out. Mrs. Gibbs, noticing the anxious look on George's face, comes to his side. As she talks to him, his momentary doubts fade. Emily enters, dressed in white. She is very doubtful, very frightened. Her father leaves his pew to comfort her. When he has little success, he calls George over, and George and Emily reaffirm their commitment to each other.

The ceremony begins, with the Stage Manager acting as the minister. As the words and the music of the service proceed, one of the guests, Mrs. Soames, comments in a shrill voice on the loveliness of the marriage. George and Emily run joyously off at the end of the ceremony, and the Stage Manager announces the end of the second act.

ACT THREE

Once again the Stage Manager comes on, this time to tell the audience that nine years have passed—it is the summer of 1913. He describes the new setting, a windy hilltop high above Grover's Corners, and points out the graves, the rows of chairs in which Mrs. Gibbs, Mrs. Soames, Simon Stimson, and others are quietly sitting. He talks briefly about death and about what death means to the people of the town but breaks off as Sam Craig enters and approaches Joe Stoddard, the town undertaker, who has been hovering near a new grave. They talk about some of the people who are buried there, and Stoddard adds that Craig's cousin died a week ago in childbirth. Simon Stimson is upset by the presence of the living, and Mrs. Gibbs urges him to be patient. When a funeral procession enters, Mrs. Soames asks Mrs. Gibbs who is coming, and Mrs. Gibbs tells her it is Emily.

The dead reminisce until Emily appears from among the umbrellas of the funeral procession. They greet her, and as she takes her place beside Mrs. Gibbs, she chatters nervously about the new barn and George's new Ford. As the umbrellas leave the stage, Dr. Gibbs comes over and places some of Emily's flowers in front of his wife. The dead are calm and patient while he is there and after he leaves.

Suddenly Emily realizes that she can go back to the world of the living, that she can live her life and watch herself live it. Mrs. Gibbs, Mrs. Soames, and the Stage Manager all advise against it, but Emily is adamant. She chooses her twelfth birthday, February 11, 1899. The Stage Manager accompanies her away from the graves, and she sees the town as it was then. Joe Crowell, Howie Newsome, and Constable Warren pass by on their rounds. Mrs. Webb begins working in her kitchen; Mr. Webb joins her and then departs, calling for his birthday girl. Emily comes in for breakfast and opens her presents—including one from George Gibbs. She tries to talk to her mother from the land of the dead, but her mother hears only the words she said then. When Mr. Webb again calls in the distance for his birthday girl, Emily breaks down. It is too painful. The living do not realize life. Mrs. Webb disappears, and Emily returns to her place among the dead. When George appears and flings himself on her grave, Emily can only comment on how little the living understand.

The Stage Manager comes forward to draw a black curtain over the quiet scene and to tell the audience that almost everyone is asleep in Grover's Corners. "You get a good rest, too," he advises.

THORNTON WILDER

The Skin of Our Teeth [1942]

ACT ONE

A news report, accompanied by slides, tells of the rising of the sun and the approach of a wall of ice. Mr. George Antrobus, discoverer of the lever and the wheel, is pictured, along with his wife, his two children Henry and Gladys, and their maid Lily Sabina. The curtain rises on their home in Excelsior, New Jersey.

Sabina, a heavily rouged blonde, is dusting and awaiting the return of Mr. Antrobus. She speaks of the uncertainty of their lives, for they never know whether the master will return safely from work with food. She adds that, though Henry has accidentally done away with his brother, nevertheless they have somehow survived. When no one appears on the cue line, Sabina becomes flustered and steps out of her role to admit that she hates the play and does not understand the confusing speeches about the trials that the human race has endured. As she longs for the old-fashioned plays, the stage manager reprimands her, and she returns to her role.

Mrs. Antrobus appears on cue, reprimanding Sabina for letting the fire go out, and offers to go and get fire from the neighbors herself, but Sabina realizes they would all perish if she failed to return. Sabina cannot bear the constant uncertainty of their lives, the constant threat of death. Mrs. Antrobus recalls that though Mr. Antrobus brought Sabina home as his new wife, she ended up in the kitchen. Sabina retorts that it was she, not Mrs. Antrobus, who inspired Mr. Antrobus' work.

A knock at the door frightens them into barricading it, but the intruder is only a telegraph boy. After telling about the approaching wall of ice, he relays a message from Mr. Antrobus, who will be an hour late and has sent his wife a singing anniversary message. After the boy leaves, Mrs. Antrobus calls her children in to get warm. Strange sounds outdoors lead them to barricade the door again. It is Mr. Antrobus, swearing loudly, whose return brings joy and relief to the family. As Henry plays with the newly invented wheel, Antrobus celebrates the day of the completion of the alphabet and the discovery of the number one hundred. Sending the children away, Mrs. Antrobus asks her husband the meaning of the cold weather and urges that they flee before the approaching wall of ice: he, in his confusion, can only suggest that they burn everything to keep the fire going.

Refugees appear, asking for food and shelter. Mrs. Antrobus wants to send them away, but Antrobus disagrees. Miss Somerset, who plays the part of Sabina, is suddenly struck by the meaning of this part of the play and steps out of her role to warn the audience not to take the catastrophe seriously. Antrobus finally convinces Mrs. Antrobus to permit his friends to enter, among them Judge Moses, Homer, and nine sisters named Muse. Antrobus is unable to believe that the ice will really put an end to all their endeavors. When, however, Sabina rushes in with the news that Henry has killed the boy next door with a stone, Antrobus wants to give up and put the fire out. Mrs. Antrobus reminds him of all they have survived. Henry recites the multiplication tables, and Gladys tells her father of her achievements in school. Antrobus decides to build up the fire and begins industriously to instruct his children, on the chance that they will survive. Sabina asks the audience to hand up their chairs for the fire to save the human race.

ACT TWO

Another news report tells of the convention of the Order of Mammals, Subdivision Humans, in Atlantic City, at which Mr. Antrobus has been elected president and to which two delegates from each of the rival orders have been sent. After Antrobus makes a speech about the accomplishments of the past and the security of the future, the watchword of which is to be "Enjoy Yourselves," Mrs. Antrobus speaks about the discoveries in the sphere of woman's work, and is congratulated upon her five thousandth wedding anniversary.

On the Boardwalk, Sabina, now Lily-Sabina Fairweather and winner of a beauty contest judged by Antrobus, relates to an old fortune teller her dream of taking President Antrobus away from his wife, taking all men away from their wives, and turning the world upside down. After Sabina leaves, the fortune teller confides to the audience that in the immediate future of the Antrobus family lurks the flood, the deluge which few will survive. She is jeered by the conveneers.

Mr. and Mrs. Antrobus and Gladys appear and perceive Henry threatening a man with a slingshot. Henry sullenly endures the reprimands of his parents. When Gladys wants to take a ride in a roller chair, her father agrees, but her mother berates such a foolish waste of money, prophesying the approach of a rainy day. Amid the arguing, the glamorous Sabina passes by and is greeted by Antrobus. Mrs. Antrobus reacts angrily, but Antrobus defends Sabina. Two black discs appear on the storm signal, denoting a storm. Three discs will mean hurricane; four, the end of the world.

As Mrs. Antrobus leaves to buy raincoats, she suggests that they ride out the storm in the nearby boat. When the rest of the family leave, Antrobus is approached by Sabina, who assures him that she is not the beauty contest type. She invites him to her cabaña, where she suddenly steps out of her role and refuses to play the scene, insisting that it will hurt some people's feelings. After threats from the Stage Manager, it is at last agreed to skip to the end of the scene. Sabina has talked Antrobus into divorcing his wife and marrying her. As the third disc appears on the storm signal, Mrs. Antrobus and Gladys appear on the Boardwalk. Mrs. Antrobus is furious at the sight of Gladys' red stockings.

A broadcast official comes frantically seeking Antrobus, who is shortly supposed to broadcast to the conventions of the world. Antrobus appears with Sabina, announcing his intention of marrying her, and sends the official away. Mrs. Antrobus recalls the promise that constituted their marriage, pointing to Gladys' shockingly worldly stockings as a result of the breaking of such a promise. Antrobus is horrified, blaming Sabina for the stockings. Before she is dragged off by her mother, Gladys tells her father that the police are seeking Henry because he hit a man with a stone. The broadcast official presents a microphone for the scheduled speech, but as Antrobus begins to speak, he is drowned out by thunder. The fortune teller instructs him to take his family and two animals of each kind into the boat. Sabina, begging to be taken along, joins them as the conveneers dance and jeer and the fortune teller hails the new world to be made by Antrobus.

ACT THREE

Sabina enters Antrobus' dilapidated house after the war is over, but she is interrupted by the stage manager and the rest of the company, who explain that seven of the actors have been taken ill and that those who have volunteered to replace them must rehearse the scene, which comes later in the act and in which the hours of the night are represented by philosophers.

The act begins again, with Sabina seeking Mrs. Antrobus and Gladys after the end of the war. As Sabina leaves, Mrs. Antrobus cautiously emerges from a trapdoor, followed by Gladys holding a baby. They meet Sabina, who informs them that the war is over and that Mr. Antrobus, who has many optimistic plans and ideas for his family and for the world, will be there that afternoon. As Henry enters unnoticed, Sabina tells them that Mr. Antrobus will kill Henry if he appears, for Henry is, in fact, the enemy. Henry announces that he has spent seven years looking for his father in order to kill him. Mrs. Antrobus, when she returns from the basement with Gladys, fusses over Henry, who, in the midst of surly protests, falls asleep from exhaustion. As they put the disheveled house in order, Sabina questions the value of renewing the old struggle for existence. Mrs. Antrobus affirms that they cannot back out now and follows Sabina and Gladys to the kitchen.

Antrobus enters and draws a revolver when he hears Henry talking in his sleep about destroying everything. Henry wakes, faces his father, abdicates his position in the family, and announces his plans to go off and start another world, where a man can live as he chooses. Antrobus declares Henry to be the enemy of all his plans. At the approach of Mrs. Antrobus, Antrobus orders Henry to behave. Furious at being thus ordered, Henry moves toward Antrobus.

Suddenly Sabina leaps between them and, stepping out of her role, begs them not to play this scene. Henry admits that he tends to get carried away in this scene because it reminds him of his own bitter, deprived youth with its feelings of emptiness and hate. Sabina muses that they are all wicked and accompanies Henry off the stage.

Resuming the play, Antrobus confesses to Mrs. Antrobus that he has lost the desire to begin building again and wishes, like all the others, merely to settle into the old routine. She tells him that she and Gladys survived the war on the strength of the hope that he would build something better out of the misery. Sabina enters, confessing that she is going to use one of the much-needed beef cubes that she has found to pay her entrance to the movies, though she should give them to the needy. She argues that in such a terrible world one has to take what he can get. At length she surrenders the cubes and assures Antrobus that she is really in favor of any plans he might have to improve the world. After Sabina leaves, Antrobus recalls that his vision, now recovered, has always been based on the needy and confused people, his family and home, and his books. Resolving to begin building once more, he recalls the nights during the war when he would try to remember the words in the books and would give names to the hours of the night. As the whole family gathers, the volunteer actors, as hours of the night, pass by, reciting the words of Spinoza, Plato, Aristotle, and the Bible.

After a blackout, Sabina appears and repeats the opening words of the play. Turning to the audience, she tells them to go home, as the play goes on for ages. She assures them that Mr. and Mrs. Antrobus are as confident and hopeful as at the beginning.

TENNESSEE WILLIAMS

Camino Real [1953]

NOTE: The play is divided into a Prologue and "blocks," rather than acts.

In the foreground of an almost lightless stage is the plaza. On one side is the façade of the luxurious Siete Mares hotel and on the other a Skid Row, housing the Gypsy's stall, the pawnshop, and the Ritz Men Only flophouse. Arches on either side of the plaza lead to dead-end streets. At the back of the plaza is an ancient wall, beyond which a distant range of snow-capped mountains is visible. A flight of stairs mounts to an archway in the wall and leads to "Terra Incognita," the wasteland between the town and the mountains.

Don Quixote, followed by Sancho Panza, advances toward the stage down the center aisle of the theater. As he reaches the stage, Mr. Gutman, a fat man in a linen suit who holds a white cockatoo on his wrist, appears on the balcony of the Siete Mares. He signals a pair of guards, who lower striped frontier-barrier gates. At a word from Gutman, Quixote is let in. Quixote urges Sancho on, but the latter refuses, drawing out a chart and reading that this walled town is the end of the Camino Real and the beginning of the Camino Real, where the spring of humanity has gone dry. Despite Quixote's pleas, Sancho dumps his equipment and goes back up the aisle, saying he is going back to La Mancha. Quixote arranges his blanket on the plaza and prepares to go to sleep. He announces that he will dream and that his dream will be a masque in which old and new meanings will be discovered, and that when he wakes he will choose from among its shadows someone to replace Sancho. The cockatoo cries, and dawn breaks, lighting the plaza. The Gypsy's stall opens. Jacques Casanova comes from the Siete Mares, takes a silver snuffbox from his pocket, and crosses to the loan shark's. Prudence Duvernoy comes from the hotel. Jacques angrily comes from the pawnshop, replacing the snuffbox in his pocket. Prudence accosts him, saying she saw him dining last night with Camille, and asks him to take her a message from an old admirer. Gutman announces Block One on the Camino Real.

Prudence chatters on about the message from a wealthy old gentleman who wants Camille back. Jacques excuses himself and rushes into the hotel. Gutman announces Block Two.

A ragged, sun-blackened figure stumbles into the plaza and toward the dried-up fountain. The old prostitute Rosita laughs, saying there is plenty to drink in the Siete Mares. The Survivor approaches the hotel, and a man in military dress comes out, telling him to stop. When the Survivor stumbles forward, the officer fires at him. Clutching his stomach, the Survivor staggers toward the fountain and drags himself around its rim. Jacques comes out on the terrace and asks

Gutman what happened. He orders a cognac, but Gutman reminds him that his credit has been discontinued and that he will be put out of the hotel if his check doesn't arrive tonight. A blind singer, La Madrecita, enters the plaza, led by a ragged young man called the Dreamer.

Gutman demands to be connected with the generalissimo on the phone. He tells the generalissmo that one of the party of explorers who attempted to cross the desert has come back and that La Madrecita is extending her arms to him and the forbidden word *hermano*—brother—is about to be spoken. While Gutman tells Jacques that the word "brother" is the most dangerous in any human tongue, La Madrecita cradles the dying Survivor in her arms. Suddenly the Dreamer springs up, crying, "Muerto." Gutman, speaking into the phone, informs the generalissimo that the Survivor is no longer surviving and that there had better be some public diversion. A loudspeaker immediately announces that tonight is the Fiesta, at which the moon will restore the virginity of the Gypsy's daughter Esmeralda. Kilroy, a young American vagrant carrying a pair of golden boxing gloves, comes into the plaza. Gutman announces Block Three.

Kilroy says that he was light-heavyweight champion of the West Coast but had to retire because of his heart, which has enlarged to the size of the head of a baby. The Gypsy appears on her roof and, over the loudspeaker, begins her pitch. The street people gather, and one of them picks Kilroy's pocket, whose complaints are ignored by the officer. Kilroy goes to the fountain, notices the body of the Survivor, and cries that the man is dead. The Streetcleaners appear, piping a tune. They stuff the body into their white barrel and trundle off, giggling and whispering. Honky-tonk music begins, and the lights of Skid Row go up for the evening. Kilroy decides to hock his belt with the word "Champ" on it. He enters the loan shark's, and Gutman announces Block Four.

The Baron de Charlus, an elderly, foppish sybarite, crosses from the hotel to the Ritz Men Only and talks to the proprietor about a bed for himself and possibly a friend. Kilroy comes out arguing with the loan shark, his belt unsold. The loan shark wants his golden gloves, but Kilroy refuses to sell. The baron approaches Kilroy and talks to him, but leaves him after deciding that Kilroy is too gentle for his purposes. He goes through an archway, and soon a strangulated cry and a noisy fracas are heard. The Streetcleaners come through the arch with the baron in their barrel. Gutman announces Block Five.

Kilroy and Jacques are talking; Kilroy wants to know how a person can leave the Camino, and Jacques points out the arch in the wall. Kilroy rushes to it but finds the Terra Incognita beyond too fearful to go into alone. Gutman announces Block Six.

Kilroy goes from the wall to the Ritz Men Only to ask about a vacancy but has no money to pay for a bed. From the terrace, Gutman calls him and asks whether he is unemployed. Despite Kilroy's protests and his frantic attempt to escape, Gutman's helpers force him to put on a red fright wig and light-up nose and to play the part of a patsy.

Gutman announces Block Seven. A letter arrives for Jacques, but he is too fearful to open it, and the messenger stuffs it in Jacques's pocket. Lord and

Lady Mulligan talk to Gutman on the terrace; Lord Mulligan complains of his health and is upset because of the way the Streetcleaners point and giggle at him. A hunchback mummer shakes his bells, and one of the side arches begins to shimmer with blue light. Through it Camille—Marguerite Gautier—enters. The street people crowd about her, and Jacques pushes his way through them. Marguerite cries that her purse with her passport in it has been snatched. She and Jacques go to the terrace, and in the course of their conversation Jacques tells her about a nonscheduled airplane called the "Fugitivo" that supposedly lands here sometimes. Gutman announces Block Eight.

The hunchback shakes his bells, and there is a flickering radiance about the hotel entrance. Lord Byron appears in the doorway, dressed for departure. He says that he is sailing for Athens; there is nothing else for him to do but make voyages, or at least attempt them. Marguerite urges Jacques to watch carefully the way Byron goes; perhaps he knows another way out. Byron climbs the steps to the arch in the wall and goes out into the desert. Kilroy follows him to the steps but loses his nerve. Gutman announces Block Nine.

There is a humming sound, and Marguerite excitedly cries that she can see the lights of a plane circling over them. The hotel guests cry that the "Fugitivo" has come, and all rush about, frantically collecting their possessions. There are sounds of the plane landing, and incoming passengers approach the stage down an aisle. The pilot announces that the "Fugitivo" is now loading for departure. Outgoing passengers swarm over him. Marguerite rushes up and gives her name, but the pilot says there is no Gautier on his list. Lord and Lady Mulligan push their way through. Lord Mulligan staggers, crying that he is sick, and the Streetcleaners come down the aisle and seize him as he collapses. Marguerite shrieks that the plane cannot go without her. There is the sound of a plane taking off, and Gutman announces Block Ten.

Jacques comes to Marguerite and comforts her. She says that they are used to one another, like a pair of hawks in the same cage, and that this familiarity is what passes for love on the Camino Real. Nevertheless, she says, tonight she is going to betray him. Gutman announces Block Eleven.

Gutman announces that the Fiesta has begun; the first event is the crowning of the King of the Cuckolds. A spotlight strikes Jacques, and the hunchback rushes forward and places a crown of gilded antlers on his head. After some initial resistance Jacques shouts that on the Camino the greatest lover wears the longest horns. The Gypsy appears on her roof, sounds a gong, and summons Esmeralda, who is told to choose her hero. Kilroy, having sold his golden gloves, emerges from the pawnshop in disguise. Esmeralda calls to him, and the street women strip off his disguise. He breaks away and runs up the stairs of the wall. Esmeralda calls him "Sweetheart" and "Champ"; his resistance crumbles, and he goes back into the plaza; Esmeralda chooses him as her hero, the street people surge toward him and lift him up in the air.

Gutman announces Block Twelve. Kilroy is being interrogated by the Gypsy before being sent up to Esmeralda. The Gypsy reads in the cards that he is on the top of the Streetcleaners' list. Esmeralda is brought in, veiled and reclining on a divan. The Gypsy leaves after relieving Kilroy of the ten-dollar bill he got for his golden gloves. Kilroy asks Esmeralda to lift her veil, but she permits him to lift it only after many coy refusals. Kilroy, suddenly tired, thinks that it wasn't much to give his golden gloves for. The Gypsy comes back and turns Kilroy out. The piping of the Streetcleaners is heard, and Gutman announces Block Thirteen.

Kilroy goes to the Siete Mares and rings the bell, pleading with Gutman to give him a cot in the lobby. Jacques appears and shouts for Gutman, who comes out on the balcony carrying Jacques's portmanteau. Jacques takes the letter from his pocket and opens it, but it contains no remittance, and Gutman heaves the portmanteau into the street. Kilroy and Jacques head for the Ritz Men Only; Kilroy stops, saying he can't make it, for he hears the Streetcleaners' piping. Gutman announces Block Fourteen.

Kilroy climbs to the top of the stairs and looks at the desert beyond. Marguerite comes into the plaza accompanied by a young man wearing a Domino. She thanks him for giving her safe conduct and begins to open her purse. He snatches it, tears off her cloak and her pearl necklace, and leaves her. She sees Kilroy and sits down with him. The Streetcleaners appear; he swings wildly at them and collapses. La Madrecita throws herself over his body before the Streetcleaners can grab it. Gutman announces Block Fifteen.

The body of Kilroy lies across La Madrecita's knees. In the center of the plaza a sheeted figure lies on a table surrounded by a medical instructor and students. The instructor opens the body to determine the cause of death. Kilroy gets up from La Madrecita's lap as the instructor removes from the corpse a solid gold heart as big as the head of a baby. Gutman announces Block Sixteen.

Kilroy rushes forward, snatches his heart, and flees. Esmeralda appears, about to go to bed in her rooftop cot. She drops to her knees and prays to dream of her chosen hero. She crawls into her cot. Kilroy calls to her, but thinking he is just a tomcat in the plaza, she tells him to go away. He rushes into the loan shark's to pawn his gold heart for jewels and furs. He grabs up his loot and rushes back to show it to Esmeralda. Still thinking him a cat, she falls asleep. He pounds on the Gypsy's door, and the contents of a slop jar are thrown at him. Quixote, lying against the wall of Skid Row, stirs and staggers to his feet. He approaches the fountain, which begins to flow, rinses his mouth, and bathes himself. Kilroy complains that the deal on the Camino is rigged, and Quixote advises him not to pity himself. When Kilroy says he was thinking of traveling on, the old knight tells Kilroy to come with him. As they start for the stairs, Marguerite comes out on the terrace. Gutman appears and shouts for Casanova under the windows of the flophouse, saying that Marguerite has guaranteed his bills and is expecting him for breakfast on the terrace. Jacques emerges, shaken but unbowed, and goes toward Marguerite. Quixote goes through the arch into the desert with Kilroy.

TENNESSEE WILLIAMS

Cat on a Hot Tin Roof [1955]

ACT ONE

In the bed-sitting-room of a plantation house in the Mississippi Delta, Brick Pollitt can be heard taking a shower in the adjoining bathroom. His wife Maggie enters to change her dress, on which one of her sister-in-law's five obnoxious children has spilled food. Maggie retails the antics of the children and their parents Gooper and Mae, who have come to celebrate Big Daddy's birthday and, claims Maggie, to do Brick out of his share of his father's estate; the family has just received a medical report that Big Daddy is dying of cancer, though both he and Big Mama have been told he is suffering merely from a spastic colon. Maggie reports that Gooper and Mae are doing their best to influence Big Daddy to make a will in their favor, in view of their five children (with a sixth on the way) and their steadiness and dependability, contrasted with Maggie's childlessness and Brick's heavy drinking and irresponsibility.

Maggie accuses Brick of doing everything to aid and abet his greedy brother and sister-in-law by quitting his job as a sports announcer, by drinking constantly, and by breaking his ankle trying to jump the high hurdles on the high school track the night before. Brick listens with an idle detachment that drives Maggie frantic, and finally his indifference spurs her to ironic comments on how well he has kept his looks, considering how much he drinks, and to a wounding reference to someone named Skipper, obviously a forbidden subject. She speaks of herself as a cat on the hot tin roof of Brick's hostile indifference and thinks of the cat's victory as just staying on as long as she can, which for Maggie means refusing to give up either her love for Brick or her attempts to get him to make love to her again.

They are interrupted by Mae, with whom Maggie spars; after Mae leaves, Maggie locks the door to give them some privacy. They are again interrupted, this time by Big Mama; she wants to bring the happy news that Big Daddy has a clean bill of health, except for a spastic colon. Brick retreats to the bathroom and remains there until Big Mama leaves, at which point he and Maggie begin to taunt one another again, he suggesting that she take a lover or leave him, she bringing up the subject of Skipper again. Brick, infuriated, threatens her with his crutch, saying that the one great thing in his life was his friendship with Skipper and accusing Maggie of calling it dirty. She recalls what happened: after Brick and Skipper, football heroes, graduated from college, they organized their own pro football team so that they could keep on being teammates forever. But Skipper began drinking, Brick was injured, and while Brick was in the hospital, the team lost because Skipper was drunk. Maggie picked that night to

447

tell Skipper either to stop loving her husband or to make Brick let him admit that he did love him; Skipper tried to make love to her to prove that what she said wasn't true. She tells Brick that she destroyed Skipper, who afterward became nothing but a receptacle for drink and drugs, by telling him a truth with which he was unable to live, and which perhaps precipitated his death. Brick strikes at her and misses, then hurls his crutch at her and, losing his balance, pitches forward onto the floor. One of the children bursts into the room firing a cap pistol; as she leaves, the child taunts Maggie for not having any babies. Maggie pleads with Brick to make love to her, since she is now able to conceive, but he rejects her viciously.

ACT TWO

Big Daddy and the rest of the family are arriving in Brick's room for the birthday party. In the conversations that follow, the hostility and rivalry among the members of the family are clearly apparent; Mae informs everyone that the cashmere robe that is ostensibly Brick's birthday present to his father was actually purchased by Maggie; Big Daddy, reprieved from his three-year-long fear that he was dying, reasserts himself as master of his household and bullies and insults all and sundry, including his wife, who is genuinely devoted to him in spite of his crudeness and cruelty. He calls Brick, the only person for whom he has any real affection, and tries to have a serious talk with him, despite interruptions from the perennially eavesdropping Mae and despite Brick's frequent attempts to end their talk. During this scene, as in most of the scenes in which he appears, Brick drinks constantly.

Finally Big Daddy snatches Brick's crutch away from him and demands the reason why he drinks, refusing to get him another drink until Brick tells him. Equivocating, Brick says that he drinks out of disgust at the mendacity of the world; Big Daddy refuses to accept his answer and pins Brick down, pointing out that he started to drink when his friend Skipper died. Brick is immediately enraged and asks whether Big Daddy is suggesting that he and Skipper did "dirty things" together; he is horrified that Big Daddy can talk so calmly about "things like that," which Brick considers unspeakable and disgusting. He goes into a long protest against the world that thinks vile things about exceptional and deep friendship between men and claims heatedly that his relationship with Skipper was absolutely pure. But Big Daddy asks the pertinent question: if so, why did Skipper crack up, and why has Brick become an alcoholic? Brick then accuses Maggie of being jealous of the closeness between him and Skipper and claims that she filled Skipper's mind with the idea that his affection for Brick would not bear careful scrutiny. But Big Daddy will not accept this as the whole story, and forces Brick to admit that Skipper called him long distance and made a drunken confession, on which Brick hung up. When Big Daddy taxes him with being unable to face the truth of Skipper's confession and thereby driving Skipper away from him and into drink and death, Brick retaliates with a truth Big Daddy is not willing to face: he tells him that there will be no happy returns of this birthday. Big Daddy, stunned, goes out, cursing all "lying, dying liars."

ACT THREE

Mae, Gooper, and Big Mama enter, looking for Big Daddy, who is not to be found. They decide that this is the time to break to Big Mama the news that Big Daddy is dying. Mae and Gooper, prepared for everything, have brought along an outline of a trusteeship for Big Daddy's property, but Big Mama, outraged at their easy acceptance of the fact of Big Daddy's death, refuses to look at it and threatens to tear it up if Gooper does not instantly put it back in his briefcase.* Ignoring Gooper, she tells Brick how much Big Daddy would love to see a child of Brick's before he dies. At this, Maggie announces that she is pregnant and Big Mama, overjoyed, rushes off to tell Big Daddy. Mae shrieks that it is a lie, that she has eavesdropped on Maggie and Brick in their bedroom and knows that Brick does not sleep with her. There is a cry of agony from off stage, and Mae and Gooper rush off to see if the pain has struck Big Daddy. Maggie is left alone with Brick, who, having finally drunk enough to achieve a kind of peace, wanders off. When he returns, Maggie has emptied out the liquor cabinet and has taken his pillow from the couch and put it on the bed, promising that she will bring the liquor back and they will get drunk together after they have made the lie she told come true.

TENNESSEE WILLIAMS

The Glass Menagerie [1945]

PART I. PREPARATIONS FOR THE GENTLEMAN CALLER

Scene 1. At the rise of curtain, the audience is faced with the the rear wall of a tenement, flanked on both sides by dark alleys. The wall of the building is transparent, revealing the Wingfield's ground floor apartment, where all the action takes place. On one side of the building is a fire escape, which is the entrance to the apartment. The play is Tom's memory; he appears on stage in a merchant sailor's uniform to introduce the action. He describes all the characters—his mother Amanda, his sister Laura, and his friend Jim O'Connor—and then mentions a fifth, who does not appear except in a large photograph over the mantel: his father, who left them long ago. As the interior of the apartment gradually becomes visible, Amanda and Laura can be seen, seated at a drop-leaf table, eating. Amanda calls Tom, who appears and sits down to eat.

* In the version performed on Broadway, Big Daddy returns to the room at this point and remains until Maggie makes her announcement.

Amanda immediately bombards him with eating instructions, emphasizing the importance of mastication, until Tom, exasperated, stops eating and tells her that he can't enjoy his food. Laura offers to go and get the dessert, but Amanda tells her to stay put, to remain fresh and pretty for her gentlemen callers. Laura says she isn't expecting any. Amanda says you never can tell, they come when least expected; Tom mutters that he knows what's coming as Amanda launches into a reminiscence of her girlhood in Blue Mountain, where on a single Sunday afternoon she had seventeen gentlemen callers. Looking at his photograph, she rues the day she picked their father. She then tells Laura to go and study her shorthand, but to say fresh. Laura says apologetically that she doesn't expect any gentlemen callers, that she isn't popular, as her mother was in Blue Mountain, and that she thinks she is going to be an old maid.

Scene 2. Laura is seated in the front room polishing her glass ornaments, but she quickly thrusts them away and assumes a posture of intense study before a diagram of the typewriter keyboard as she hears her mother's step on the stair. Amanda appears, looking grim. It is clear that something is wrong, and, after many ambiguous gestures and words for dramatic effect, Amanda tears up the diagram of the typewriter keyboard. She tells Laura that on her way to her D.A.R. meeting, she dropped by the business school where Laura is enrolled to tell her teacher that Laura has a cold and to inquire about her progress. She learned from the teacher that Laura has not been to class for six weeks, ever since she became sick to her stomach during the first speed test. Laura explains to her mother that every day for those six weeks, from 7:30 to 5, she has walked around—sometimes going to a museum of the zoo, or, if it were really cold, forgoing lunch and going to the movies—because she can't bear to look at her mother's face when she is disappointed. Angry and shattered, Amanda asks whether Laura intends to play her father's worn-out phonograph records and to amuse herself with her glass menagerie for the rest of her life; she depicts spinsters with no careers as "little birdlike women without any nest—eating the crust of humility all their life." She tells Laura sarcastically that some girls do get married and then asks her whether she ever liked a boy. Laura tells her dreamily of one she liked back in high school—Jim O'Connor. They sat across from one another on Mondays, Wednesdays, and Fridays in the auditorium. He used to call her Blue Roses, because when she had an attack of pleurosis, he thought she said she had "blue roses." He hardly noticed her, though, for he was the most popular boy in the school. Amanda, distracted and not really listening, is suddenly re-energized as she hits upon another plan for Laura: marriage. Laura protests that she is crippled, but Amanda reminds her that she has been told never to use that word, that she has only a slight defect, and that all she has to do is to cultivate charm and vivacity to make up for it.

Scene 3. Tom and Amanda quarrel violently while Laura looks on, panicky. Tom accuses Amanda of confiscating his books; she retorts that she will not have filthy books by Mr. Lawrence in her house. Tom asks her who pays the rent on *her* house. She shrieks at him that no one in his right mind goes off to the movies as often as he does, coming back at 2 A.M., stumbling and muttering to himself and getting up three or four hours later to go to work. She tells him he has no right to jeopardize his job and the security of them all. He tells her that if he were as selfish as she makes him out to be, he'd be where his father is—gone. Announcing his intention to go to the movies, he hurls his jacket across the room: it strikes against Laura's glass collection. There is a tinkle of glass, and Laura cries out as if wounded. Tom drops to his knees to collect the glass.

Scene 4. Later that night, as Tom climbs the fire escape with the unsteadiness of one who has been drinking, a church bell tolls the hour of five. He fishes in his pocket for his keys, removing all sorts of items including a veritable shower of movie ticket stubs. A light shows in the interior of the house and reveals Laura in her nightdress. She lets Tom in; he flops down on his bed in the front room and describes to her the movie, the travelogue, the Mickey Mouse cartoon, and the stage show he has seen. The scene fades out and lights up again as the clock strikes six. Amanda can be heard waking Laura and telling her to tell Tom to "rise and shine." Laura appears, wakes Tom, and begs him to apologize to their mother. Amanda calls out from the kitchenette, tells Laura to go out for some butter, and stands at the window with her back to Tom. After an awkward moment of hesitation, he apologizes to her. Recriminations follow: Amanda weeps that her devotion has made her hateful to her children. Tom comforts her: Amanda tells him that she saw a letter in his room from the Merchant Marine and that she knows what he is thinking but says he can't leave them until Laura is taken care of; after that he can do anything. She pleads with him to bring a nice young man, one that's "clean-living and doesn't drink," home from the warehouse to meet Laura. Tom finally says he will.

Scene 5. A few evenings later, Tom informs his mother that he has invited a young man from work for dinner the next night. Amanda is all in a flurry, planning nothing short of a spring cleaning, new curtains, and a new dress for Laura. Tom tells her not to make such a fuss. He says he didn't mention Laura to his friend at all, but just casually invited him. Amanda barrages him with questions about Jim O'Connor, the young man; he sounds like a very enterprising person from Tom's description, and she thinks he might very well be a good husband for Laura. Tom tells her not to be unrealistic, and above all, not to expect too much from Laura. Laura is peculiar, he says, and they don't notice it because they love her. But to the outside world she may seem very different, he cautions; she is shy, and lives in a world of her own, a world of little glass ornaments and worn-out phonograph records.

PART II. THE GENTLEMAN CALLS

Scene 6. Tom appears as narrator and tells a little about Jim, a high school hero who has not lived up to his promise; Jim is the only person Tom is at all friendly with at the warehouse. He knows that Laura knew Jim in high school and that she had spoken admiringly of him, but he doesn't know whether Jim remembers Laura or not. The scene opens with Laura and her mother getting ready for the gentleman caller. Laura has on a new dress and has her hair done differently, and looks very pretty; Amanda has dug up an old yellow, girlish frock that she used to wear in her brilliant young days at Blue Mountain; she is in a mood of feverish reminiscence. She mentions Jim O'Connor by name, and Laura, already extremely nervous, declares that if it is the same Jim O'Connor she knew in high school, she will not come to the table. When the doorbell rings, Amanda disappears into the kitchenette, and Laura, shaking with nervousness, lets Jim and her brother in. After Tom introduces Jim to Laura, she excuses herself and runs off. Tom and Jim sit out on the fire escape and talk about their respective futures. When Amanda appears, Tom is visibly shocked by her girlish appearance and her flirtatious, Southern charm; but Jim, after an initial bafflement, is won over, and they get along very well together. They sit down to the table and Laura, after some coaxing, appears at the table, but is so weak and faint that Tom has to help her to the front room, where she huddles on the sofa while the other three have their meal.

Scene 7. After dinner, Amanda insists that Tom help her in the kitchenette and tells Jim to keep Laura company in the living room. Jim talks easily and kindly to Laura and draws her out. As soon as she reminds him that they knew each other in high school and that he used to call her Blue Roses, he realizes that she was familiar to him. Basking in Laura's awe and overt adoration, Jim tells her that she has an inferiority complex and that she must have more confidence in herself. He asks her whether she has an interest in something that is more important to her than anything else, and she tells him, haltingly, about her glass collection, taking a little unicorn from the shelf to show it to him. He admires it; he then offers to dance with her to the music floating in from the dance hall across the street. Laura says she can't dance because of her leg, but he will hear nothing of it and dances a waltz with her; they bump into a table and the unicorn falls to the floor, its horn breaking off. Jim then kisses Laura and immediately afterward says he shouldn't have done it; he realizes how much it means to her and explains awkwardly that he is engaged, that he didn't know that Tom brought him home to meet her, and that he is in no position to see her again. Laura, who has been glowing, sinks back into a look of utter desolation. She gives him the unicorn as a souvenir, and when Amanda gaily emerges from the kitchenette, Jim says he has to be off to pick his fiancée up at a train. He says his goodbys and goes. Amanda, crushed, calls Tom in and tells him what happened. Tom says he had no idea that Jim was engaged, and Amanda accuses him of knowing nothing. Tom immediately announces his intention of going to the movies; Amanda calls him selfish to go off to the movies after he has made a fool of them. Tom tells her that the more she calls him selfish, the quicker he will go, and it won't be to the movies. He smashes his glass on the floor and leaves.

During Tom's closing speech, a pantomime takes place in the dimly lit interior of the apartment where, it is evident, Amanda is comforting Laura. Tom tells how he got fired from his job; he left St. Louis and followed in his father's footsteps. He travels constantly and can't stop because he feels pursued; it is the memory of his sister that haunts him and from which he tries to flee. "Oh Laura, Laura," he says, "I tried to leave you behind me, but I am more faithful than I intended to be."

T E N N E S S E E   W I L L I A M S

A Streetcar Named Desire [1947]

Scene 1. On the street corner in a poor but picturesque section of New Orleans is a two-story, rickety house. Eunice, who occupies the upstairs flat, is enjoying the May evening on the steps when Stanley Kowalski and Mitch come around the corner. Stanley stands at the foot of the stairs and bellows at his wife Stella, who comes out on the landing, that he and Mitch are going bowling; Stella asks whether she can come and watch. Soon after they leave, a woman arrives, dressed as if for a garden party, carrying a suitcase and looking with shocked disbelief at her surroundings. She announces herself as Stella's sister Blanche, come to visit; Eunice offers to let her into the flat.

Blanche, left alone in the two-room apartment, spies a whisky bottle and nervously pours herself a drink. When Stella returns, Blanche greets her with feverish vivacity, explaining that she was given a mid-semester leave of absence from her job as a high-school teacher because she has suffered a terrific strain on her nerves. She asks Stella how she looks, confessing that she is as vain as ever about her appearance, even though her beauty is fading. She begins to tell Stella that she has lost Belle Reve, the family plantation in Mississippi, but breaks off to accuse Stella of abandoning the place and leaving her to bear the burden of its debts alone. Stella, reduced to tears by the hysterical attack, goes into the bathroom to wash her face as Stanley enters. He greets Blanche brusquely and peels off his shirt, remarking that he is afraid Blanche will find him the unrefined type. He adds that he has heard she was once married. Blanche replies that she was quite young and that the boy died. In distress, she sinks back into her chair and cries that she is going to be sick.

Scene 2. The next evening Stella tells Stanley that, since he is having his friends in for a poker game, she is taking Blanche out for the evening. She says that Blanche is soaking in a hot tub to quiet her nerves, which have undergone a great strain in the loss of Belle Reve. Stanley is very interested in the disposal of Belle Reve and wants to see the bill of sale, for he thinks Blanche may have swindled Stella—and therefore him—out of her share in the property. Stella insists that the place was lost, not sold, but Stanley jerks open Blanche's trunk and strews about her dresses and furpieces and costume jewelry, demanding to know how she got all those things on a teacher's salary. Stella angrily goes outside, telling Stanley to come with her while Blanche is dressing, but he refuses to move.

Blanche emerges from the bathroom and converses airily with him, trying to wheedle compliments, but he refuses to respond. He demands to know what happened to Belle Reve and to see the papers concerning it. Angrily, she gives him a box, saying that there are thousands of papers stretching over hundreds of years, that her forefathers squandered the land to pay for their "epic fornications"; all that was left to her and Stella was the house and a few acres around it. Stanley declares that a man has to take an interest in his wife's affairs—particularly now that she is expecting a baby. Blanche goes outside, embraces Stella, and tells her that she and Stanley have thrashed everything out and that perhaps, after all, Stanley is the type of man with whom they need to mix their blood now that they have lost Belle Reve. Stanley's friends arrive, carrying a case of beer, and the women leave.

Scene 3. Stanley, Mitch, Steve, and Pablo are still playing poker in the kitchen when Blanche and Stella return. As they go into the bedroom, the women meet Mitch leaving the bathroom; Stella introduces him to Blanche and asks after his mother, who is ill. Blanche is faintly impressed, remarking that he seems more "sensitive" than the other men. Stella goes into the bathroom and Blanche turns on the radio. Stanley shouts at her to turn it off, then leaps up and shuts it off himself. Mitch heads for the bathroom again, but Blanche tells him it is occupied and engages him in conversation. She acts in her most genteel manner and leads him to believe that she is several years younger than she actually is.

As Stella comes out of the bathroom, Blanche turns on the radio and begins to waltz to the music with romantic gestures. Stanley, enraged, stalks into the bedroom, snatches the radio, and hurls it out the window. Stella calls him a drunken animal and pleads with the others to go home. Stanley charges at her and strikes her. The other men rush in and pin him down until he is quiet. Blanche takes Stella upstairs to stay with Eunice, and the men put Stanley in the shower and leave hurriedly. Stanley stumbles out into the street and begins bellowing for Stella, who, despite Blanche's entreaties, soon comes creeping down the stairs, tears in her eyes. They embrace tenderly, and he picks her up and carries her back into the flat.

Scene 4. Early the following morning, Stella is lying down in the disordered bedroom, looking tranquil and at peace. Blanche appears at the kitchen door and rushes to Stella with hysterical tenderness, but Stella very matter-of-factly says that there is nothing to make a fuss about. Blanche, convinced that Stella is married to a madman, wants to help her escape, and is incredulous when Stella insists that she is not in anything she wants to get out of. Trying to think of some way to get money to provide a "way out" for herself and Stella, Blanche remembers Shep Huntleigh, a college boyfriend and now an oil millionaire. She finally abandons her idea of sending him a telegram but cannot get it out of her head that Stella must be unhappy. A train passes outside, and under the cover of its noise Stanley enters the kitchen, unnoticed by the two women. Blanche goes on to say that Stanley is not only common, but bestial and brutal. Another train passes, and Stanley retreats back outside and then calls through the closed door. Stella lets him in and, in full view of Blanche, embraces him fiercely.

Scene 5. Blanche is finishing a letter to Shep Huntleigh, and Stella is dressing when Stanley comes in. He asks Blanche whether she knows a man named Shaw, since a man of that name thought he met her in Mississippi, in a disreputable hotel called the Flamingo. Blanche, with attempted lightness, says that the Flamingo is scarcely the sort of place she would dare to be seen in. Stanley leaves, and Blanche nervously asks Stella whether she has heard any unkind gossip about her. She says Mitch is coming tonight and that she is feeling nervous about their relationship. She has not given him anything but a goodnight kiss and wants him to think she is prim and proper so he will want to marry her. Stanley comes back and Stella goes off with him. Mitch arrives, and Blanche greets him coquettishly.

Scene 6. Blanche and Mitch return about 2 A.M. and go in the apartment for a nightcap. In the course of their conversation Mitch asks her how old she is; he says that he was telling his mother about her, and his mother wanted to know. When he adds that his mother is sick and will not live long, Blanche sympathizes with him gently, saying she knows what it is to be lonely, having lost the person she loved. At sixteen, she says, she married a very talented and handsome boy whom she adored. She sensed that he needed her in a way she did not understand and, after their wedding, felt in some mysterious way that she had failed him. Then, inadvertently, she came upon her husband and an older man in a compromising situation. At first all of them pretended that nothing had happened and drove, drunk and laughing, to a nearby casino. But when they were dancing, she was unable to stop herself and told her husband that she knew what had happened and that he disgusted her. He broke away from her, ran outside, and shot himself. Mitch gets up and takes her in his arms, saying that they both need someone. Blanche huddles gratefully in his embrace.

Scene 7. On an afternoon in mid-September as Stella is setting the table for Blanche's birthday supper, Stanley comes in and says he has found out the truth about Blanche: she not only lived at the disreputable Flamingo Hotel after she lost Belle Reve, but her behavior was so outrageous that the management had to request her to leave; furthermore, she was kicked out of her teaching position after she got mixed up with a seventeen-year-old boy. Stella goes on putting candles on the cake, saying Mitch is coming over for cake and ice cream. Stanley replies that he doesn't expect Mitch will make it; being a buddy of his, Stanley felt obliged to tell him the truth about Blanche. He adds that she is not going to stay here any longer, and just to make sure, he has bought her a bus ticket. Blanche comes out of the bathroom, pretending to be in high spirits, but a look of panic crosses her face as Stanley walks past her. She senses that something has happened, but Stella will not tell her.

Scene 8. Later, Stella, Stanley, and Blanche are finishing a dismal birthday supper. A fourth place at the table is vacant. Stanley presents Blanche with his birthday remembrance—the ticket back to Mississippi. Blanche tries to laugh, then clutches her throat and rushes for the bathroom. Stella accuses Stanley of wanton cruelty; he replies that he and Stella were happy together until Blanche showed up, flaunting her superior ways and describing him as an ape. Stella's labor pains begin, and she asks Stanley to take her to the hospital.

Scene 9. Later that evening, Blanche is sitting in the bedroom, drinking heavily. Mitch rings the bell, and she excitedly lets him in. He observes that it is dark in the room and that he has never had a good look at her in the light. He tears the paper lantern off the light bulb and turns on the light, and she cries out and hides her face. He says that he doesn't mind her being older than she let on; he objects to her lies about her "old-fashioned ideals" and her purity. Blanche cries that after her husband's death panic drove her from one man to another, and that she came here, finally, because she had nowhere else to go. Mitch tries to embrace her but says he doesn't think he wants to marry her any more: she's not clean enough to bring into the house with his mother. She tells him to go away, and when he does not move, she rushes to the window and screams wildly.

Scene 10. A few hours later, Blanche has dragged out her trunk and dressed herself in a crumbled white satin gown and a rhinestone tiara. Stanley comes in, and Blanche announces that she has received a telegram from an old admirer, Shep Huntleigh, inviting her for a Caribbean cruise. Stanley attacks the telegram and the millionaire as being nothing but products of Blanche's imagination. Blanche hysterically tries to call Shep Huntleigh long-distance and, that failing, attempts to send a wire for help. Stanley comes out of the bathroom dressed in brilliant silk pajamas, and Blanche backs away from the phone. She smashes a bottle on the table and threatens to twist the broken end in his face if he comes any closer. He springs toward her and forces her to drop the bottle, and she sinks to the floor. He picks her up and carries her to the bed, saying they have had a date with one another for a long time.

Scene 11. Some weeks later, Stella is packing Blanche's trunk. A poker game is going on in the kitchen. Eunice comes in and asks about Blanche. Stella replies that Blanche has been told that they have made arrangements for her to go to the country; she adds that she doesn't know whether she's doing the right thing, but she couldn't go on living with Stanley if she believed Blanche's story. Blanche comes out of the bathroom, asking whether she has had any phone calls. A doctor and a matron arrive outside. Blanche goes nervously through the kitchen, but outside she stops short, saying the man waiting for her isn't Shep Huntleigh. She rushes back into the bedroom. Stanley and the matron advance on her and Blanche, in panic, cries that she wants to be left alone. She tries to break past the matron, who catches hold of her; when Blanche struggles, the matron pinions her arms, and Blanche falls to her knees. The doctor comes into the room and speaks to her gently, telling the matron to let go of her. He supports her and leads her across the kitchen to the door. Blanche, holding tightly to his arm, says that she has always depended on the kindness of strangers. Stella cries her sister's name as Blanche, the doctor, and the matron go around the corner. Eunice gives Stella her baby, and Stella weeps in complete abandon. Stanley kneels beside her, fondling and soothing her.

WILLIAM BUTLER YEATS

Four Plays for Dancers

AT THE HAWK'S WELL [1917]

Three musicians enter, their faces made up to resemble masks. Singing, they unfold and fold a cloth, hiding the area that serves as the stage. When the cloth is folded, the Guardian of the Well is revealed crouching on the ground; her face is made up to resemble a mask. An Old Man enters, masked. A musician narrates that the Old Man has been watching by the well for fifty years. A Young Man enters, also masked. He says he is Cuchulain and that he has come here seeking a well in which springs water that will give eternal life. This place answers the description of the location of the well, but the Young Man sees only a dry hollow half-full of leaves. The Old Man replies that he has waited for fifty years to find water in it, but that the dancers have deceived him and put him to sleep during the few occasional moments when water has plashed in the spring.

The Girl gives the cry of a hawk, and the Young Man recalls that on his journey here he was attacked by a great hawk which he beat off with his sword. The Old Man replies that the hawk was the Woman of the Sidhe and that men who gaze into her eyes are cursed; he urges the Young Man to leave. The Girl gives the hawk's cry again, and the Old Man says that she is temporarily possessed; her possession is a sign that the water will rise in the spring. The Old Man begs the younger to let him drink first, since he has been watching for so long.

The Guardian of the Well throws off her cloak and rises. She begins to dance, moving like a hawk, and the Old Man falls asleep. As the dance goes on, the Young Man rises and pursues the Girl. He hears the water splash, and he turns. The Old Man wakes and creeps up to the well. He finds it empty, but the stones are wet. The Young Man comes back, saying the Girl has fled from him. There is the sound of a gong, and the Old Man tells him that the Girl has roused the fierce women of the hills, who will pursue Cuchulain as long as he lives. Saying he will face them, the Young Man goes out. The musicians fold up the cloth and sing.

THE ONLY JEALOUSY OF EMER [1919]

Three musicians unfold and fold the cloth, singing. On one side of the stage is a curtained bed on which lies a man, masked and wearing graveclothes. Another man, wearing identical clothes and mask, crouches near the front. Emer sits beside the bed. The musician narrates that the renowned Cuchulain lies dead or swooning; his wife, Queen Emer, has sent for his mistress, Eithne Inguba, and is awaiting her arrival. The girl enters and Emer tells her how Cuchulain came to be lying here like one dead: as the result of a quarrel, he killed a young man who, he then discovered, was his own son begotten on some wild woman. Maddened with sorrow, he ran out into the sea and fought the waves with his sword until he was overcome and washed up, senseless, on the shore. Emer says that an image or changeling might have been put in his place, and Eithne Inguba tells her to call his name so that his spirit, lingering near, may hear and drive the changeling out. Emer replies that it is long since she could call him home and tells Eithne Inguba, his newest love, to call him.

Eithne Inguba says that Cuchulain's love will return to Emer in the end, and Emer confesses that her one hope is that someday she and her husband will sit together at the hearth again. She pulls the curtains of the bed to hide his face from the sea and stirs the fire, saying that enchantments from the sea dread the hearthfire. Eithne Inguba calls him, and Emer urges her to be more bold, saying that they are not rivals but two women struggling together against the sea. Eithne Inguba kisses him but starts back, saying her lips touched some evil thing. She notices that one of his arms is withered. Emer addresses the figure of Cuchulain (which now wears a distorted mask) and asks why it came; it identifies itself as Bricriu of the Sidhe, maker of discord among gods and men. Bricriu says that he has come to bargain with her for the life of Cuchulain; if she will renounce the chance that someday she again will be Cuchulain's favorite, he shall live again. She refuses, saying that that memory and that one hope are all she prizes. Bricriu touches her eyes, and she sees the crouching figure of the Ghost of Cuchulain and calls to him; but Bricriu tells her that he is a phantom and cannot hear or see her.

A Woman of the Sidhe enters and begins to dance around the Ghost of Cuchulain. The Ghost asks who she is and remembers that long ago he met her beside a well that seemed long dry. She fled from him then, she says, but has come now to offer herself. When he replies that memories weigh him down, she tells him to kiss her mouth and memory will vanish; nothing but beauty will remain. About to kiss her, he turns away and murmurs Emer's name. Emer speaks, saying she will be content if the dead will set him free to speak with her by the hearthstone. The Woman, angry at his rejection of her, tells him to ride to the king of Country-Under-Wave and demand his life. The Ghost replies that a man is held to those whom he loved by pain they gave, or by pain he has given. The Ghost goes out, and after a brief conversation the Woman leaves, and Bricriu falls back on the bed. The figure of Cuchulain (now wearing a heroic mask) wakes, crying for Eithne Inguba to take him in her arms, for he has been in some strange place and is afraid. The musicians unfold and fold the cloth, singing.

A somewhat different ending is given "The Only Jealousy of Emer" in the *Collected Plays* (1934). After calling for his lost Emer, the Ghost again cries for the Woman's mouth. She goes out to her chariot, and he follows her. Bricriu urges Emer to cry out that she renounces Cuchulain's love before it is too late and he is in the power of the Sidhe forever. Emer does so, and Bricriu sinks back on the bed. Cuchulain wakes and Eithne Inguba runs to him, claiming that it is she who won him back from the sea.

THE DREAMING OF THE BONES [1919]

Three musicians unfold and fold a cloth, singing that dreams can spring from the dry bones of the dead. The musician narrates that a Young Man with a lantern is stumbling along a path in the hills just before dawn. A Stranger and a Girl, dressed in costumes of a past time and wearing heroic masks, approach him. In response to the Stranger's question, the Young Man says he has fought in Dublin (in the Easter uprising of 1916) and will be shot if captured. The Stranger replies that they know the hills and will hide him safely—though the area is said to be haunted. The three proceed around the stage, and the musician narrates their journey to the summit of the hill. Being near the ruined Abbey of Corcomroe and its cemetery, they talk of ghosts. The Girl tells the Young Man that some ghosts, wandering side by side, have no thought but of love and at the height of their penance can but mingle their eyes—a bitter glance, for though their eyes can meet, their lips cannot. Their awful ghosthood, she says, would be blessed if their lips could meet; but whenever they approach, the memory of their crime flows up between them and drives them apart. The Young Man wonders what crime could be so dreadful. The Girl tells him that the woman's king and lover was overthrown in battle by her husband; and, being blind and in love, the lover brought the Norman army in and sold the country into slavery. The Young Man asks whether she speaks of Dermot and Dervorgilla; the Girl says that she does and adds that they would not be wholly accursed if someone of their race would say he had forgiven them. The Young Man asserts that they shall never be forgiven. They come to the summit, and the Young Man says he can see the Aran Islands and Galway, where the enemy has toppled roof and gable. But for Dermot and Dervorgilla, he says, the town would be untouched and beautiful. The Stranger and the Girl are dancing, and the Young Man asks why they look at each other so passionately and then turn away covering their eyes. The Girl says that for seven hundred years their lips have never met. They drift in their dance from rock to rock and go out. The Young Man reiterates that never shall Dermot and Dervorgilla be forgiven. The musicians unfold and fold a cloth and sing.

CALVARY [1920]

Three musicians unfold and fold a cloth, singing. The first musician narrates Christ's ascent to Calvary, carrying His cross and followed by a mocking crowd. A player wearing the mask of Lazarus approaches the player wearing the mask of Christ. He accuses Christ of taking his death away from him and asks for Christ's death instead. He goes out, and the musician describes the approach of Martha and the three Marys, who clean Christ's feet with their hair and depart. Judas enters and says that he betrayed Christ because He seemed all-powerful; the thought that there was no one not in Christ's power drove Judas wild. But he believed that whoever betrayed Christ would be free, and now he claims that if a man betrays God he is the stronger of the two. Christ asks, what if the betrayal were part of God's plan? He tells Judas to be gone, and three Roman soldiers enter. Judas holds up the cross while Christ stands with His arms stretched out upon it. The soldiers say that they are gamblers and will settle who is to have Christ's cloak by throwing dice. They dance around the cross, moving as if throwing dice, and Christ cries, "My Father, why hast thou forsaken Me?" The musicians unfold the cloth, singing.

WILLIAM BUTLER YEATS

The Words upon the Window-Pane

[1934]

Miss McKenna crosses the room, goes through the door to the entrance hall, and admits Dr. Trench, the president of the spiritualist society, and his young companion John Corbet. She says that Mrs. Henderson is lying down, as she always does before a séance, and goes out to hang up their coats and hats. Dr. Trench explains to Corbet that Mrs. Henderson has given séances that have been marred by the presence of a hostile spirit. Corbet, wandering about, remarks that this is a wonderful room for a lodginghouse. Dr. Trench explains that it was a private house until fifty years ago, and in the eighteenth century belonged to friends of Jonathan Swift—or, more precisely, to friends of Stella. Someone, perhaps Stella herself, cut lines from one of her poems to Swift in a window-pane. Corbet recognizes the poem from which the lines are taken as one that Stella wrote for Swift on his fifty-fourth birthday. He remarks how strange it is that a celibate scholar such as Swift should have been so deeply loved by two women—by Stella, who loved him all her life, and by Vanessa, whom he met at the height of his political career, who followed him to Ireland, loved him for nine years, and perhaps died of love for him. He adds that he is writing an essay on Swift and Stella for his doctorate at Cambridge.

Others come in: Abraham Johnson, a minister who wants to be inspired by the spirit of the great evangelist Moody; Mrs. Mallet, who wants business advice from her departed husband; and Cornelius Patterson, a follower of the dog races. They complain of the hostile influence that ruined the last two séances; two spirits, they say, re-enacted the same situation on both occasions and would not let other spirits through. Dr. Trench explains that sometimes a spirit relives in a séance the pain of its death or some passionate or tragic moment of life; but such spirits do not usually come to séances unless they take place in or near the house where the spirit lived.

Mrs. Henderson comes in and explains that her control is a little girl named

Lulu who will describe the spirits that are present and tell the participants in the séance what spirit wants to speak. The séance begins, and she goes into a trance. Lulu's childish voice describes Mrs. Mallet's husband, but before he can speak, he is driven away by the hostile spirit—an old man—that interfered the last time. Then Lulu sees a young lady bending over the man, and these two spirits take over the séance. The old man is angrily accusing the woman of daring to write to "her" and ask "her" whether she were married to him; from his abusive comments it is clear to Corbet that the spirit of Jonathan Swift is railing at Hester Vanhomrigh, called Vanessa. Vanessa's voice replies that she questioned Stella out of love for him; if he and Stella are not married, why should he not marry Vanessa? Swift replies that he has sworn never to marry; there is something in his blood that no child must inherit. When Vanessa says that her blood would make their children healthy, Swift still refuses, saying he will not add to the rascaldom and knavery of the world. She reminds him that no man in Ireland is as passionate as he and that he needs her and needs children; he is growing old, she says, and an old man without children is very solitary. Swift cries suddenly that he is locked in with his enemy, and Mrs. Henderson, who has risen from her chair, beats on the door. She then slumps to the floor and speaks as Lulu; the control says that her power is almost gone, and the others sing a hymn to bring good influence.

In Swift's voice, Mrs. Henderson now calls for Stella. Swift wonders whether he has wronged her, for because of him she has no children, no lover, no husband. He refers to the poem she wrote him for his fifty-fourth birthday, in which she expressed the thought that women who are loved with a spiritual love keep their beauty better than women loved according to the flesh. He quotes some of the lines, which Corbet cries are the words upon the window-pane. Swift says that he is comforted by the thought expressed in the poem, but sometimes he doubts the truth of it; it is a terrible thing, he says, to be responsible for another's happiness. Mrs. Henderson again speaks as Lulu and then awakens. Dr. Trench tells her not to worry about the séance being spoiled again, for she has done her best.

Corbet, a skeptic about spiritualism, believes that Mrs. Henderson is a marvelous actress and scholar who created the visitation of Swift. He tells her that he has come to the same conclusions as she about the reasons for Swift's celibacy; but he wants to know whether she thinks that Swift refused to beget children because he foresaw a fall from the intellectual heights of his age into the commonness of democracy, or because he was mad. Mrs. Henderson replies that she does not know what he is talking about. She adds that she saw Swift very clearly just before she woke up: he was a dirty, diseased old man. Corbet replies that he looked like that in his old age, long after Stella was dead; his brain was gone by then, and his friends had deserted him. Mrs. Henderson observes that the spirits change from youth to age in a moment, as their thoughts change, and adds that it is sometimes a terrible thing to be out of the body. After the others leave, Mrs. Henderson makes a fire to boil a pot of tea. As she is fussing about, she stops and speaks in Swift's voice, "Perish the day on which I was born!"

CARL ZUCKMAYER

The Captain from Köpenick

[*Der Hauptmann von Köpenick*, 1931]

ACT ONE

Scene 1. Wabschke, the humpback cutter for the military tailor Wormser, is helping Captain von Schlattow into a new uniform in the Wormser shop in late nineteenth-century Potsdam. Wormser enters as Schlattow complains that the uniform buttons are not as specified by regulations, and Wormser calls to his son Willy to bring the measurement book. As they talk, a poorly dressed man, Wilhelm Voigt, hesitates in front of the shop and finally enters, but is driven off by Wormser.

Scene 2. Voigt, thin, stooping, and with a prison pallor, is in a police station, trying to get a residence permit. A policeman checks his record and finds that Voigt has been serving fifteen years for forging a postal order when he was an eighteen-year-old boy. Voigt realizes he won't get the permit, without which he cannot work, and asks for a passport so that he can leave Prussia; he is told to go to another office.

Scene 3. Sitting in the Café National with a former prison friend, Kallenberg, Voigt says he is going to make a last try to get a genuine job: if that fails he has a plan for something else. Schlattow enters in civilian clothing with Dr. Jellinek and sits talking with him. Kallenberg and Voigt count their money to see whether they have enough to pay a prostitute and try to persuade a girl to accept half her usual fee. As they bargain, a drunken soldier roars in with a friend, and the girl goes to sit with him. Kallenberg, annoyed, goes over to the soldier and empties his beer over him. The soldier leaps up, knife drawn, and advances on Kallenberg; Schlattow intervenes, but the soldier refuses to believe him an officer. Schlattow and the soldier come to blows; a policeman arrives, arrests them both, and takes them off to the police station. Voigt tells his friend that the fact that both the soldier and the policeman refused to accept Schlattow's superiority because he was dressed as a civilian, not an officer, proves the point he was making: a man is judged by others according to his appearance.

Scene 4. Voigt tries to get work in a shoe factory but fails because he has a record and no papers.

Scene 5. Captain von Schlattow dismisses his manservant, telling him he has resigned his commission as a question of honor, following his brawl with the soldier. Wabschke enters with the captain's new uniform, and Schlattow tells him to take it back and sell it on commission; he says he will pay the balance if Wormser fails to sell the uniform.

Scene 6. Bedding down for the night in a doss house, Voigt tells Kallenberg he has a plan to break into the Postdam police station and destroy the file on himself; he can also steal work and residence permits. Kallenberg says he will help if he can take the petty cash.

Scene 7. Wormser, in his shop, is reading a newspaper account of two ex-convicts who broke into the police station and have been arrested. Just as Wormser tells Wabschke to put Schlattow's uniform in the window for sale, a newly promoted sergeant enters the shop, tries on the uniform, and is delighted with it. Wormser says he will make the necessary alterations.

ACT TWO

Scene 8. Voigt is in a prison chapel with other prisoners. The governor enters and tells them that it is the fortieth anniversary of the battle of Sedan. Obsessed with military affairs, he orders the men into formation to re-enact the battle, and Voigt proves himself well versed in military affairs, having spent his prison time reading an army manual. The governor states that Voigt is to be discharged the next day.

Scene 9. Voigt, just out of jail, visits his married sister, Marie Hoprecht, and her husband Friedrich, a minor government official. Friedrich tells his wife that Voigt can stay and help her in her shop while he is away on army maneuvers.

Scene 10. Mayor Obermüller of Köpenick is frantically dressing in his bedroom while his wife desperately tries to telephone Wormser's shop in Potsdam to find out why the expected uniform has not yet arrived. Wabschke arrives with the uniform, and Frau Obermüller gives him the mayor's old uniform, telling him to set it off against the bill.

Scene 11. In Rixdorf police station, Voigt vainly tries to get in to see the official—unless he sees him today, Voigt says, it will be too late. But an army officer arrives and says that the office must be closed for the day.

Scene 12. Voigt is sitting in his sister's home with the sick child of a neighbor. As he reads to the child, an officer calls with an order from the police saying that Voigt must leave the town because he has not got his papers.

Scene 13. In the banquet hall of a restaurant, Wormser, his daughter Augusta, and his son Willy are dining with Major and Mrs. Kessler and Dr. Trump. Dressed as an officer, Augusta sings a song in praise of the army, and Wormser reveals that she is wearing the old uniform of the mayor of Köpenick. Captain von Schleinitz enters and proposes a toast to Augusta and to her father, who has arranged the function. The clumsy Willy upsets glasses and dishes over his sister's uniform; Wormser says the uniform is ruined and will have to be sent to an old-clothes shop.

Scene 14. Marie Hoprecht is awaiting her husband's return from maneuvers; when he arrives, she tells him the sick child died. Voigt, deeply upset by her death, returns from the funeral and reveals that he has to leave town. He says he has had enough of being kicked around; he is going to do something about it.

ACT THREE

Scene 15. In Krakauer's old-clothes shop, Voigt bargains over a stained and shabby old captain's uniform. He buys it and hurries out.

Scene 16. Sitting in a park, Voigt overhears a conversation between some officers; later he tells a veteran that he is in the army, imitating the officers' clipped accent.

Scene 17. Voigt goes into the rest room at a Berlin railway station. An official impatiently tries the door several times and finally loses his temper; Voigt emerges in full captain's uniform, and the official jumps to attention. Voigt addresses him as a superior, and the man humbly accepts the admonishment.

Scene 18. Voigt enters the town hall in Köpenick, where minor officials fawn upon him. He orders the soldiers with him to go into the mayor's office.

Scene 19. Voigt arrests Mayor Obermüller and the town treasurer, whom Voigt orders to render an account of the money he is holding. Frau Obermüller arrives, and in Voigt's absence the soldiers tell the mayor that they were requisitioned by Voigt; Obermüller asks on what authority, and they reply they don't know—the fact that Voigt is a captain is enough. The treasurer hands over the town funds to Voigt, who orders that the mayor and the treasurer be taken by carriage to the New Fortress at Berlin. Voigt dismisses his men and, giving them money, tells them to take a train for Berlin and report to the New Fortress.

Scene 20. Voigt is lying in drunken sleep in a beerhouse early one morning, dressed in civilian clothes. A taxi man enters laughing over a newspaper account of an exploit by an impostor who posed as a captain and got away with the town funds. The clients roar with laughter at the story, then rush out to buy a special edition with the latest news on the exploit. Left alone, Voigt reads the story and is saddened to learn that the police think it was the work of a practical joker. The clients rush back shrieking with laughter; they read in the newspaper that a reward is offered for the bogus captain's capture.

Scene 21. In Berlin police headquarters, an inspector is questioning a suspect in the Köpenick affair. A sergeant enters breathlessly and says they have caught the impostor. Voigt is brought in with the passport commissioner, who reveals that Voigt has offered to give the name of the bogus captain in exchange for a passport. When the commissioner promises he will give Voigt a passport, Voigt hands over a left-luggage ticket and says he is the "captain" and that his uniform is at a railway station. Voigt explains that his plan went wrong—he wanted to get a passport at the town hall when he arrested the mayor, but forgot that passports were not issued there. Voigt says that he is ready to serve a jail sentence but afterward plans to leave the country with the promised passport. The police, becoming more and more amused as the story develops, hand Voigt glasses of wine, and Voigt gives them the major part of the money he took from Köpenick town hall.

The uniform is recovered from the left-luggage office, and Voigt puts it on, hotly denying that he has ever stolen from his fellow men—all the time he has been up against the government, he says. Voigt asks for a mirror, explaining that he has never seen himself in the uniform. He stands silently inspecting himself, then begins twitching and shaking and finally explodes in uncontrollable laughter.

Biographical Notes on the Playwrights

EDWARD ALBEE

Born March 12, 1928, in Washington, D.C., Edward Franklin Albee was thirty years old before he made his debut on the American theatrical scene with the one-act *The Zoo Story* (1958). His subsequent output includes four other one-act plays, *The Sandbox* (1959), *The American Dream* (1959–1960), *Fam and Yam* (1960), and *The Death of Bessie Smith* (1960). With the full-length *Who's Afraid of Virginia Woolf?* (1962) Albee established himself as one of America's most promising playwrights. His next full-length play, *Tiny Alice* (1964), a "metaphysical mystery," represented a departure from the mingling of absurdity and acute realism that had distinguished his earlier work. Accused of savagery and pessimism, Albee has claimed that "the responsibility of the playwright is to comment boldly and relentlessly on his time."

MAXWELL ANDERSON

Born December 15, 1888, in Atlantic, Pennsylvania, the son of a Baptist preacher, Maxwell Anderson graduated from the University of North Dakota and spent several years teaching English before turning to journalism in San Francisco and New York. Anderson's first Broadway play, *White Desert* (1923), was followed by three written in collaboration with Laurence Stallings: *What Price Glory* (1924), which brought fame to both writers; *First Flight* (1925); and *The Buccaneer* (1925). Anderson's subsequent plays include *Saturday's Children* (1927); *Gods of Lightning* (1928), an early treatment of the Sacco-Vanzetti theme, written in collaboration with Harold Hickerson; *Elizabeth the Queen* (1930); *Night over Taos* (1932); *Both Your Houses* (1933); *Mary of Scotland* (1933); *Valley Forge* (1934); *Winterset* (1935), a mature treatment, in free verse, of the Sacco-Vanzetti tragedy and a work which attempted to break with the realistic prose drama that had dominated the American stage during the 1920's and early 30's; *High Tor* (1937); *Knickerbocker Holiday* (1938), with music by Kurt Weill; *Key Largo* (1939); *Candle in the Wind* (1941); *The Eve of Saint Mark* (1942); *Joan of Lorraine* (1946); *Anne of the Thousand Days* (1948); *Lost in the Stars* (1948), an adaptation of Alan Paton's *Cry, the Beloved Country*, with music by Weill; *Barefoot in Athens* (1951); and *The Bad Seed* (1955), an adaptation of William March's novel. Equally at home in tragedy, melodrama, or comedy, Anderson was one of the first modern playwrights to achieve commercial success with plays in blank verse. He died February 28, 1959.

JEAN ANOUILH

Born July 23, 1910, in Bordeaux, France, Jean Anouilh studied law and after two years with an advertising firm became Louis Jouvet's secretary at the Comédie des Champs-Elysées. The success of his first play, *L'Hermine* (1932),

467

decided him upon a career in the theater, but he was to write four more plays before achieving popular success with *La Sauvage* (1938). This, with *Le Voyageur sans bagage* (*Traveller without Luggage*, 1937), *Eurydice* (1942), *Antigone* (1943), *Roméo et Jeannette* (1946), and *Médée* (1948), belongs among Anouilh's *pièces noires*, plays dealing with the darker aspects of life. Among the *pièces roses*, treating life in its brighter aspect, are *Le Bal des voleurs* (*Thieves' Carnival*, 1938), *Le Rendez-vous de Senlis* (1938), and *Léocadia* (1939). The *pièces brillantes* include the comedies *L'Invitation au château* (1947), *La Répétition* (*The Rehearsal*, 1950), *Colombe* (1950), and *L'Ecole des pères* (1954). *Ardèle* (1948) and *La Valse des toréadors* (*The Waltz of the Toreadors*, 1952) he labeled "grating" (*pièces grinçantes*). Not categorized are *Ornifle* (1955), *Pauvre Bitos* (1956), *L'Hurluberlu* (1959), and *La Grotte* (1961). *L'Alouette* (*The Lark*, 1953), dealing with Joan of Arc, and *Becket* (1959), dealing with Thomas à Becket, are unorthodox and provocative reworkings of historical themes.

W. H. AUDEN

Born February 21, 1907, in York, England, Wystan Hugh Auden completed his education at Christ Church College, Oxford, working briefly as a teacher and in 1930 joining the young British group of socialist avant-garde poets. He established himself as a poet with *Poems* (1930), *The Orators* (1932), *The Dance of Death* (1933), and *Spain* (1937), the last work based in part upon his experience in the Spanish civil war. With *For the Time Being: A Christmas Oratorio* (1944), *The Age of Anxiety* (1947), and *Homage to Clio* (1960) he turned from the satirical and left-wing viewpoints of his earlier work to cast an eye on the spiritual and moral problems of contemporary man. Though best known as a poet, Auden has written with distinction and versatility for the theater; his dramatic works include the "charade" *Paid on Both Sides* (1933); three plays written in collaboration with Christopher Isherwood, *The Dog Beneath the Skin* (1935), a comedy; *The Ascent of F6* (first performed in 1936); and the melodrama *On the Frontier* (1938); contributions to the reviews *The Pepper Mill* (1937) and *No More Peace* (1938); an adaptation of Webster's *The Duchess of Malfi* (1946); a translation of Mozart's *The Magic Flute* (1956); and, in collaboration with Chester Kallman, librettos for Stravinsky's *The Rake's Progress* and for Hans Werner Henze's *Elegy for Young Lovers*.

JACQUES AUDIBERTI

Born March 25, 1899, in Antibes, France, Jacques Audiberti went to Paris in 1925, mixed with the surrealists, and wrote for newspapers. After attracting attention in a poetry contest, he began publishing poetry and prose and eventually turned to the theater, where his first work to be performed was *Quoat-Quoat* (1946). His plays are often poetic allegories drawing on quasi-medieval symbolism. Others of his works for the theater include *Le Mal court* (1947); *Les Femmes du boeuf* (1948); *La Fête noire* (1948); *Pucelle* (1950); *L'Ampelour* (1950); *Les Naturels du Bordelais* (1953); *Le Cavalier seul* (1955); *Le Ouallou* (1958); *La Hobereaute* (1958); *L'Effet Glapion* (1959); *La Logeuse* (1960); and *La Fourmis au corps* (1961). Audiberti died July 10, 1965, in Paris.

J. M. BARRIE

Born May 9, 1860, in Kirriemuir, Scotland, the son of a weaver, Sir James Matthew Barrie distinguished himself first as an author, producing a series of articles and novels, many of them dealing with his native Scotland in sentimental and whimsical fashion. So great was his success as a playwright, however, that after 1900 he devoted himself exclusively to the theater. His numerous dramatic works include *Jane Annie, or The Good Conduct Prize* (1893), written in collaboration with A. Conan Doyle; *The Professor's Love Story* (1895); *The Little Minister* (1897), a dramatization of his novel; *The Wedding Guest* (1900); *Quality Street* (1903); *The Admirable Crichton* (1902); *Peter Pan* (1904); *Alice Sit-by-the-Fire* (1905); *What Every Woman Knows* (1908); *The Twelve-Pound Look* (1912); *The Old Lady Shows Her Medals* (1916); *A Kiss for Cinderella* (1916); *Dear Brutus* (1917); *Echoes of War* (1918); *Mary Rose* (1920); *Shall We Join the Ladies?* (1922); and two works on biblical subjects that represent a departure from his earlier vein of sentimental comedy, *The Two Shepherds* (1936) and *The Boy David* (1936). Barrie died June 19, 1937, in London.

PHILIP BARRY

Born June 18, 1896, in Rochester, New York, Philip Barry was educated at Yale and at Harvard, where he worked under George Pierce Baker in the "47 Workshop," subsequently writing a play, *You and I*, that was produced in New York in 1922. Among his later plays are *Paris Bound* (1927), *Holiday* (1929), *Hotel Universe* (1930), *The Animal Kingdom* (1932), *Here Come the Clowns* (1938), and *The Philadephia Story* (1939). The bulk of Barry's plays are literate comedies with an occasional serious or mystic note, generally dealing with men and women of wealth and social standing. Barry died on December 3, 1949.

SAMUEL BECKETT

Born in Dublin in 1906, Samuel Beckett completed his studies at Trinity College, Dublin; taught English at the Ecole Normale supérieure in Paris, where he became a close friend and disciple of James Joyce; and, after returning to Trinity to teach French, settled in 1938 in Paris. His first novels, *Murphy* (1938) and *Watt* (1944, published 1953), were written in English, but after 1945 he wrote first in French, subsequently translating into English. His later novels and stories include *Molloy* (1951); *Malone Meurt* (*Malone Dies*, 1951); *L'Innomable* (*The Unnameable*, 1953); *Nouvelles et textes pour rien* (1955); and *Comment c'est* (*How It Is*, 1961). His plays, which, like his novels, constitute major works in the literature of the absurd, include *En attendant Godot* (*Waiting for Godot*, 1952); *Fin de Partie* (*Endgame*, 1957); *Actes sans paroles* (*Acts without Words*, 1957); two English radio plays, *All That Fall* (1957) and *Embers* (1960); *Krapp's Last Tape* (1959) and *Happy Days* (1961), both written in English; and *Comédie* (*Play*, 1963).

BRENDAN BEHAN

Born February 9, 1923, in the slums of North Dublin, Brendan Francis Behan was strongly influenced in his early life by his family's close association with the Irish Republican Army, and at the age of 16 he was arrested by English authorities for the possession of explosives with the intent of blowing up a battleship. From the experience of being sentenced to three years in reform school came his autobiographical novel, *Borstal Boy* (1958). After serving two more prison terms, Behan utilized his jail experience as the basis of his two plays, *The Quare Fellow* (1954) and *The Hostage* (first presented in Gaelic in 1958 and in English in 1961). A third play, *Richard's Cork Leg*, remained unproduced at his death, March 20, 1964. A novel, *The Scarperer* (1964), was published posthumously.

S. N. BEHRMAN

Born June 9, 1893, in Worcester, Massachusetts, Samuel Nathaniel Behrman studied at Clark University, with George Pierce Baker at Harvard, and with John Erskine at Columbia. He achieved recognition with his first play, *The Second Man* (1927), and with his subsequent works established himself as the leading American practitioner of the comedy of ideas, in which the format of drawing-room comedy is adapted to the discussion of serious themes. His plays include *Serena Blandish* (1928), an adaptation of Enid Bagnold's novel; *Meteor* (1929); *Brief Moment* (1931); *Biography* (1932); *Rain from Heaven* (1934), one of the earliest anti-Nazi plays; *End of Summer* (1936); *Amphitryon 38* (1937), an adaptation of Giraudoux's comedy; *Wine of Choice* (1938); *No Time for Comedy* (1939); *The Talley Method* (1941); *The Pirate* (1942); *I Know My Love* (1949); *The Cold Wind and the Warm* (1958), an adaptation of his autobiographical book *The Worcester Account* (1954); and *But for Whom Charley* (1964). Behrman turned witty biographer with *Duveen* (1952) and *Portrait of Max* (1962), a profile of Max Beerbohm. His screenplays for Hollywood include that of the Greta Garbo film *Queen Christina* (1933).

UGO BETTI

Born February 4, 1892, in Camerino, Italy, Ugo Betti studied law, received his doctorate in jurisprudence, and became a judge in 1930; in 1944 he became librarian at the Ministry of Justice. While pursuing his legal career, he managed simultaneously to write a prolific number of plays. His dramatic works include *La Padrona* (1927); *La Casa sull'acqua* (1929); *L'Isola meravigliosa* (1930); *Una bella domenica di settembre* (1937); *I Nostri Sogni* (1937); *Il Paese delle vacanze* (1942); *Notte in casa del ricco* (1942); *Il Deiluvio* (1943); *Marito e moglie* (1947); *Corruzione al palazzo di giustizia* (*Corruption in the Palace of Justice*, 1949); *Irene innocente* (1950); *Spiritismo nell' antica casa* (1950); *Delitto nell' isola delle capre* (*Crime on the Isle of Goats*, 1950); *La Regina e gli insorti* (*The Queen and the Rebels*, 1951); *Il Giocatore* (1951); *Inquisizione* (1952); *La Fuggitiva* (1953); and *Il Fratello protegge e ama*, unperformed when Betti died June 9, 1953, in Rome.

BERTOLT BRECHT

Born February 10, 1898, in Augsburg, Germany, Bertolt Brecht made his initial impact upon the German stage with such plays as *Baal* (1923), *Trommeln in der Nacht* (1922), *Im Dickicht der Städte* (*In the Jungle of*

Cities, 1924), and *Mann ist Mann* (*A Man's a Man*, 1926), which—while imbued with the critical irony toward contemporary society that permeates all his work—were still dependent in large measure upon the techniques of expressionism. With the operas *Die Dreigroschenoper* (*The Threepenny Opera*, 1928) and *Aufstieg und Fall der Stadt Mahagonny* (*Rise and Fall of the City of Mahagonny*, 1930; both with music by Kurt Weill), Brecht simultaneously turned to Marxism and fully exemplified the technique that was to dominate his subsequent production, that of epic theater. Works of this period include *Der Flug der Lindberghs* and *Happy End* (both 1929; both with music by Weill); *Das Badener Lehrstük vom Einverständnis* (1929; with music by Hindemith); *Die Massnahme* (1930); two works patterned on No plays, *Der Jasager* and *Der Neinsager* (1931); *Die Heilige Johanna der Schlachthöfe* (*Saint Joan of the Stockyards*, 1932); and *Die Mutter* (*Mother*, 1932), after Gorki. In 1933 Brecht was driven from Germany by the rise of Nazism and began a fourteen-year exile in Denmark, Sweden, Finland, and, from 1941 to 1947, in the United States. Plays of this period include direct attacks on Nazism, such as *Der Unaufhaltsame Aufsteig des Arturo Ui* (*The Resistible Rise of Arturo Ui*; written 1941); *Furcht und des Dritten Reiches*, 1937; and *Schweyk im Zweitem Weltkrieg* (*Schweyk in the Second World War*, written 1944–1945); plays with historical settings, such as *Das Leben des Galileo Galilei* (*Galileo*, written 1938–1939, performed 1943) and *Mutter Courage und ihre Kinder* (*Mother Courage and Her Children*, 1941); and two Chinese parables, *Der Gute Mensch von Sezuan* (*The Good Woman of Setzuan*, written 1939, produced 1943) and *Der Kaukasiche Kreiderkreis* (*The Caucasian Chalk Circle*, 1948). In 1947 Brecht returned to Zürich and went from there to East Berlin, where in 1948 he founded his own company, the Berliner Ensemble. His works of the last period, which include *Die Tage der Kommune* (*The Days of the Commune*, 1954) and *Der neue Schweyk*, consist to a large extent of adaptations. Brecht died August 15, 1956, in East Germany.

KAREL ČAPEK

Born January 9, 1890, in Male Svatoňovice, Czechoslovakia, Karel Čapek received a scientific training but turned to letters, where his educational background enabled him to devise convincing scientific fantasies. He achieved his first theatrical success with *The Brigand* (1920) and went on to write the internationally acclaimed *R.U.R.* (1921). He subsequently collaborated with his brother Josef on *The Insect Comedy* (1921) and, by himself, wrote *The Makrapoulos Secret* (1922). In 1927 he collaborated again with his brother, this time on *Adam the Creator*; his last plays, written alone, were *The White Plague* (1937) and *The Mother* (1938). His novels include the trilogy *Hordubal* (1933); *The Meteor* (1934); *An Ordinary Life* (1934); and *The War Against the Salamanders* (1936). An ardent defender of, and worker for, the Czech Republic, he was simultaneously founder and director of the Vinohradsky Art Theater, editor on a Prague newspaper, and creative writer. The imaginative moralism and irony of his plays are a marked contrast to the political idealism and optimism of his essays, which include *President Masaryk Tells His Story* (1934) and *The First Rescue Party* (1939). Čapek died on Christmas Day, 1938, in Prague.

PAUL CLAUDEL

Born August 6, 1868, at Villeneuve-sur-Fere-en-Tardenois, France, Paul Louis Charles Marie Claudel entered diplomacy in 1890, shortly after his conversion to Catholicism. He served in consulates as geographically diverse as New York, Shanghai, Rome, and Rio de Janeiro and was ambassador to Tokyo, Washington, and Brussels. In addition to works for the theater, he wrote essays and a vast body of poetry. His theater is of predominantly Christian inspiration and theme, its lyricism derived from the verse of the Bible. Among his plays are *La Jeune Fille Violaine* (written in 1892), rewritten as *L'Annonce faite à Marie (The Tidings Brought to Mary); Tête d'or* (written 1895); *Partage de midi (Break of Noon;* written 1905, performed 1916; revised and performed 1948); *L'Otage* (1914); *Le Soulier de satin (The Satin Slipper;* written 1919–1924, and first performed in a second version in 1943); and *Le Livre de Cristophe Colombe* (1933), which served as a libretto for Milhaud's opera *Cristophe Colombe.* Claudel was elected to the Académie française in 1946; he died February 23, 1955, in Paris.

JEAN COCTEAU

Jean Cocteau was born the son of a well-to-do notary July 5, 1889, at Maison-Lafitte, France, and received his education at the Lycée Condorcet. He distinguished himself not only as a playwright, but as a poet, novelist, film scenarist and director, and artist. Closely associated with the French surrealist movement between the wars, he entered the theater with a series of Dadaistic and satirical ballet librettos. His subsequent dramatic works range from tragedy through psychological drama to comedy and abound in poetic symbolism and technical ingenuity. They include three plays based on tragic Greek themes: *Orphée* (1926), *Antigone* (1922), and *La Machine Infernale* (1934); *La Voix Humaine* (1930), a monodrama; *Les Chevaliers de la Table Ronde* (1937), a humorous treatment of Arthurian legend; *Les Parents Terribles* (1938); *L'Aigle à deux têtes* (1946); and *Bacchus* (1951). Cocteau was elected to the Académie française in 1955 and died in Paris, October 11, 1963.

NOEL COWARD

Born December 16, 1899, in Teddington, near London, Noel Pierce Coward achieved distinction as playwright, actor, composer, and theatrical and film director, but is perhaps most admired as the author of sophisticated stage comedies. He made his stage debut in 1911 as an actor, in 1920 as a comic playwright with *I'll Leave It to You. The Vortex* (1924), a social and psychological drama, brought him success and notoriety; he has written prolifically for the stage, and his subsequent output includes *Fallen Angels* (1925); *Hay Fever* (1925); *Easy Virtue* (1925); *This Year of Grace* (1928), a review; *Bitter Sweet* (1929), a musical; *Private Lives* (1930); *Cavalcade* (1931), a patriotic panorama of thirty years of English history; *Design for Living* (1933); the musical *Conversation Piece* (1934); *Tonight at 8:30* (1936); *Operette* (1938); *Blithe Spirit* (1941); *Present Laughter* (1943); *This Happy Breed* (1943); *Sigh No More* (1945), a musical; *Peace in Our Time* (1947); *Relative Values* (1951); and *Quadrille* (1952). Coward's filmscripts include *In Which We Serve* (1942), *This Happy Breed* (1944), *Brief Encounter* (1946), and *The Astonished Heart*

(1950). His books include two of autobiography, *Present Indicative* (1937) and *Future Indefinite* (1954), and a novel, *Pomp and Circumstance* (1962).

E. E. CUMMINGS

Born October 14, 1894, in Cambridge, Massachusetts, Edward Estlin Cummings was educated at Harvard, receiving his B.A. in 1915 and his M.A. a year later. His World War I experience in a French prison led to the writing of the only one of his books to achieve popularity, *The Enormous Room* (1922). His first collection of poems, *Tulips and Chimneys* (1923), was followed by numerous others, and his collected poems were published in 1954. Though best known for his experiments with language, with poetic forms, and with typographical arrangements, Cummings has also published works for the theater, including two plays, *him* (1927) and *Santa Claus* (1946), as well as the satirical ballet *Tom* (1935). He is the author of a travel diary, *Eimi* (1933); *I, Six Non-Lectures* (1953); and *CIOPW* (1931), a book of drawings and paintings. He died September 23, 1962, in North Conway, Massachusetts.

FRIEDRICH DÜRRENMATT

Born January 5, 1921, in Konolfingen, Switzerland, Friedrich Dürrenmatt studied philosophy and the history of German art and literature at the Universities of Bern and Zurich. His works for the theater include *Es steht geschrieben* (1947); *Der Blinde* (1948); *Romulus der Grosse* (*Romulus the Great*, 1949); *Die Ehe des Herrn Mississippi* (*The Marriage of Mr. Mississippi*, 1952); *Ein Engel kommt nach Babylon* (*An Angel Comes to Babylon*, 1953); *Der Besuch der Alten Dame* (*The Visit of the Old Lady*, 1955), the play which brought him international recognition; and *Die Physiker* (*The Physicists*, 1961). Dürrenmatt has also written several detective novels; like his plays, they are often ironic dissections of contemporary moral dilemmas. Notable among these are *Der Richter und sein Henker* (*The Judge and His Hangmen*) and *Der Verdacht* (*Suspicion*). In 1955 Dürrenmatt published a well-known essay entitled *Theaterprobleme* (*Problems of the Theater*), treating the subject of modern drama.

T. S. ELIOT

Born September 26, 1888, in St. Louis, Missouri, Thomas Stearns Eliot studied at Harvard and at the Sorbonne. He was at Oxford on a traveling fellowship when World War I broke out; he remained in England, teaching, working as a bank clerk, and editing literary reviews, and in 1927 became a British subject. He first attracted attention when his poem *The Lovesong of J. Alfred Prufrock* was published in 1915. When *The Waste Land* was published in 1922, Eliot's position in the avant-garde of young poets was established. Notable among his other works are such poems as *Portrait of a Lady* (1917), *Gerontion* (1920), *The Hollow Men* (1925), *Ash Wednesday* (1930), and *Four Quartets* (1936–1942). With the collections of essays *The Sacred Wood* (1920), *The Use of Poetry and the Use of Criticism* (1933), and *The Classics and the Man of Letters* (1942), Eliot distinguished himself as a leading critic and former of contemporary literary taste. After joining the Anglican church in the late 1920's, Eliot considered social and religious problems in *After Strange Gods: A Primer of Modern Heresy* (1934), *The Idea of a Chris-*

tian Society (1939), and *Notes Toward a Definition of Culture* (1948). In his plays, Eliot has attempted to revive poetic drama for the modern stage; his theatrical works include *Murder in the Cathedral* (1935), written originally for performance in Canterbury Cathedral; *The Family Reunion* (1939); *The Cocktail Party* (1949); *The Confidential Clerk* (1954); and *The Elder Statesman* (1958). Eliot died January 4, 1965, in London.

CHRISTOPHER FRY

Born December 18, 1907, in Bristol, England, Christopher Fry took his mother's surname after the death of his father, Charles Harris. With T. S. Eliot he has led the attempt to restore verse to the British stage, and, like Eliot, he has often dealt with religious themes. He has written for variety, reviews, and operatic spectacles, though his best-known work is in the drama. His works include *Youth and the Peregrines* (1934); *The Boy with a Cart* (written 1937, performed 1950); *Thursday's Child* (1937); *The Town* (1939); *The Firstborn* (written 1945); *A Phoenix Too Frequent* (1946); *Thor, with Angels* (1948); *The Lady's Not for Burning* (1948); *Venus Observed* (1950); *A Sleep of Prisoners* (1951); *The Dark Is Light Enough* (1954); and *Curtmantle* (1961). He has translated Anouilh's *L'Alouette* and *L'Invitation au château* as *The Lark* and *Ring Around the Moon*, respectively, and Giraudoux's *La Guerre de Troie n'aura pas lieu* as *Tiger at the Gates*.

JOHN GALSWORTHY

Born August 14, 1867, in Kingston, England, John Galsworthy was raised in Britain's upper-middle class and was trained as a lawyer, but turned to literature, publishing his first works under a pen name. The year 1906 marked the publication, under his own name, of the first section of *The Forsyte Saga*, as well as his debut as a playwright, with *The Silver Box*. His more than twenty works for the stage, like his fiction, express the development of his own convictions from early championing of the artists, the rebel, and the underdog to later defense of traditional values. His plays include *Strife* (1909), *Justice* (1910), *The Fugitive* (1913), *The Skin Game* (1920), *Loyalties* (1922), *Old English* (1924), *Escape* (1926), and *Exiled* (1929). He refused knighthood in 1918 but accepted the Order of Merit in 1929. He was awarded the Nobel Prize for literature in 1932 and died January 3 of the following year in London.

FEDERICO GARCÍA LORCA

Born June 5, 1898, in Fuentevaqueros near Granada, Spain, Federico García Lorca received his earliest education in music but by the age of twenty had turned to poetry and to the theater. His first published work, *Impresiones y Pasajes* (1918), a series of prose sketches, was followed by the poetic works *Libro de Poemas* (1921), *El Romancero Gitano* (1928), *Poeta en Nueva York* (1930), *Poema del cante jondo* (1931), and the celebrated *Llanto para Ignacio Sánchez Mejillas* (1934). His first dramatic work, *El Maleficio de la mariposa* (1919), was followed by the short play *La niña que riega la albahaca y el príncipe preguntón* (1923) and the farce for puppets *La Tragicomedia de Don Cristobal y la señá Rosita*. His subsequent plays include *Mariana Pineda* (1925); *La Zapatera Prodigiosa* (1926); the three sketches *El Paseo de Buster Keaton,*

Quimera, and *La Doncella, el marinero y el estudiante* (1928); *Amor de don Perlimplín con Belisa en su jardín* (1933); the fragment *El Público*; *Así que pasen cinco años*, unperformed during the poet's lifetime; the three tragedies that placed him in the front rank of Spain's playwrights, *Bodas de Sangre* (1933), *Yerma* (1933), and *La Casa de Bernarda Alba* (1936); and *Doña Rosita la soltera o el lenguaje de las flores* (1935). García Lorca was shot by a band of fascists August 19, 1936, during the Spanish civil war, at the wells near Viznar.

JEAN GENÊT

Born 1910 in Paris, his father unknown, Jean Genêt was abandoned as a baby by his mother and at the age of ten was sent to reform school as a thief. He volunteered in the Foreign Legion and subsequently deserted to become a beggar and professional thief. Threatened with life imprisonment, he was freed by the intervention of Jean-Paul Sartre and Jean Cocteau and was able to devote himself to letters. He has published *Poèmes* (1948) and several prose works, the best known of which are *Notre Dame des fleurs* (*Our Lady of the Flowers*, 1945) and *Journal du Voleur* (*The Thief's Journal*, 1949). His theatrical works include *Les Bonnes* (*The Maids*, 1947); *Haute Surveillance* (*Deathwatch*, 1949); *Le Balcon* (*The Balcony*, 1956); *Les Nègres* (*The Blacks*, 1958); and *Les Paravents* (*The Screens*, 1961).

MICHEL DE GHELDERODE

Born April 3, 1898, in Ixelles near Brussels, Michel de Ghelderode wrote prolifically in Flemish as well as in French. Between the wars he was the official playwright of the Vlaams Volkstoneel, the Flemish theater in Antwerp. After the Second World War his plays were enthusiastically received in Paris. Touched with fantasy and poetry, they are infused with the folklore, liturgy, and fable of the Flemish baroque and reflect the author's sympathy with the Spanish Golden Age. Notable among them are *Escurial* (Flemish, 1927; French, 1930); *Pantagleize* (1930); *Hop Signor!* (1927); *Fastes d'enfer* (*Chronicles of Hell*, 1929); and *L'Ecole des bouffons* (1953). De Ghelderode wrote three works for marionettes: *La Siège d'Ostende* (1933); *Le Mystère de la Passion de Notre Seigneur* (1934); and *La Farce de la Mort qui faillit trépasser* (1952). He died April 1, 1962, in Brussels.

JEAN GIRAUDOUX

Born October 29, 1882, at Bellac in Haute-Vienne, France, Hippolyte Jean Giraudoux established himself as a writer of fiction before turning to the theater at the age of forty-five with *Siegfried* (1928), a plea for Franco-German understanding adapted from his own novel. His subsequent works, less realistic in manner, are notable for their wit, their brilliant and often aphoristic dialogue, and their elegant construction. In *Amphitryon 38* (1929), *La Guerre de Troie n'aura pas lieu* (*Tiger at the Gates*, 1935), and *Electre* (1937), he treated subjects from classical antiquity; in *Judith* (1931) and *Sodome et Gomorrhe* (1943), subjects drawn from the Bible; and in *Ondine* (1939), a subject from folk legend. His works also include *Intermezzo* (*The Enchanted*, 1933), *La Folle de Chaillot* (*The Madwoman of Chaillot*, 1945), and *Pour Lucrèce* (1953), the last two introduced after he died in Paris on January 31, 1944.

MAKSIM GORKI

Maksim Gorki was the pen name of Aleksei Maksimovich Peshkov, born March 16, 1868, in Nizhni Novgorod, Russia; his birthplace is now named Gorki. Orphaned at an early age, he was forced to make his own way in the world from the age of nine; his experiences drove him to a suicide attempt in 1887 but subsequently became material for a series of stories, sketches, and articles published in provincial journals and finally, in 1898, issued in two volumes that brought their author national renown. Gorki's first novel, *Foma Gordeyev* (1899), was a study of a declining merchant family. His first play, *Meshchanye* (*The Petty Bourgeois*, 1901), was followed by his most famous stagework, *Na dne* (*The Lower Depths*, 1902). Gorki was arrested for Bolshevik activities in 1905, and in 1907 published his didactic novel about the revolutionary movement, *Mat'* (*Mother*), while in exile in Italy. From 1913 to 1923 he was engaged upon his three-part autobiography, *Detstvo* (*Childhood*), *V lyudakh* (*In the World*), and *Moi Universitety* (*My Universities*). Permitted to return to Russia in 1913, Gorki worked strenuously for the new Soviet culture and in 1921 returned to Italy to rest; he remained for seven years, producing two novels and the two plays *Yegor Bulychov i drugiye* (*Yegor Bulychev and Others*, performed 1931) and *Dostigayev i drugiye* (*Dostigaev and Others*, performed 1932). Upon his return to the Soviet Union, Gorki, Russia's first great writer to emerge from the proletariat, helped enunciate the literary doctrine of socialist realism, promulgated by the government in 1932. Gorki died in Moscow, June 18, 1936, while undergoing medical treatment.

NORDAHL GRIEG

Born November 1, 1902, in Bergen, Norway, Johan Nordahl Brun Grieg studied in Norway and at Oxford, receiving a degree in philology. He traveled widely as a war correspondent for an Oslo paper, covering the Chinese and Spanish revolutions, and served as a captain in the Second World War, going to England with the Norwegian government-in-exile and flying missions over Germany. His literary career began in 1922 with the publication of a volume of poems *Rundt Kap det Gode Haap* (*Around the Cape of Good Hope*). He published two novels inspired by his experiences in different parts of the world, *Skibet gaar videre* (*The Ship Sails On*, 1924) and *Ung må verden ennu vaere* (*But Young the World Must Be*, 1938). His works for the theater include *Barrabas* (1927), *En ung mans kjaerlighed* (*A Young Man's Love*, 1927), and *Atlanterhavet* (*The Atlantic*, 1932), all three written before familiarity with Russia and with the Russian theater had strengthened his sympathy for the working classes and his interest in social issues; on his return from Russia he produced the plays for which he is best remembered, *Vår aere og vår magt* (*Our Honor and Our Might*, 1935); *Men imorgen—(But Tomorrow!*, 1936); and *Nederlaget* (*The Defeat*, 1937). Before his death on December 2, 1943, in the sky over Berlin, he wrote several war lyrics expressing a deepened love for his country. Three collections of poetry were published posthumously.

MOSS HART

Born October 24, 1904, in New York City, Moss Hart was educated in New York public schools and worked with a variety of little theater groups before his first play, *The Hold-up Man* (1925) was produced, and failed, in Chicago. He achieved theatrical success with the comedy *Once in a Lifetime* (1930), written in collaboration with George S. Kaufman, with whom he wrote the libretto for the musical comedy *Face the Music* (1933) as well as the comedies *Merrily We Roll Along* (1934); *You Can't Take It With You* (1936); *I'd Rather Be Right* (1937); *The American Way* (1939); *The Man Who Came to Dinner* (1939); and *George Washington Slept Here* (1940). Hart also wrote the libretto for Kurt Weill's *Lady in the Dark* (1941); *Winged Victory* (1943); *Light Up the Sky* (1948); and *The Climate of Eden* (1952). He directed the original production of *My Fair Lady* and in 1959 published his autobiography, *Act One*. He died on December 20, 1961.

GERHART HAUPTMANN

Born November 15, 1862, in Obersalzbrunn, Germany, Gerhart Hauptmann studied to be a sculptor but turned instead to letters, producing the romantic epic *Promethidenlos* (1885) and the realistic story *Bahnwärter Thiel* (1887). His first play, *Vor Sonnenaufgang* (1889), initiated the naturalist movement in German literature; with such plays as *Das Friedensfest* (1890) and *Die Weber* (1893), Hauptmann remained in the vanguard of naturalism, but with *Hannele Mattern's Himmelfahrt* (1894) and *Die Versunkene Glocke* (1897) he introduced symbolic overtones into the naturalistic context; the ascendancy of symbolism is marked in such works as *Fuhrman Henschel* (1898), *Der Arme Heinrich* (1902), *Rose Bernd* (1903), *Und Pippa Tanzt!* (1906), *Griselda* (1909), and even in such a naturalistic work as *Die Ratten* (1911). Hauptmann's later theatrical works include *Der Bogen des Odysseus* (1914); *Dorothea Angermann* (1926); *Von Sonnenuntergang* (1932); *Die goldene Harfe* (1933); a monumental trilogy on the House of Atreus, consisting of *Iphigénie in Delphi* (1941), *Iphigénie in Aulis* (1943), and *Agamemnons Tod* (1947); and *Elektra* (1947). Hauptmann's novels include *Der Narr in Christo Emanuel Quint* (1910) and *Im Wirbel der Berufung* (1936), and his epic, *Till Eulenspiegel*, appeared in 1927. He was awarded the Nobel Prize for literature in 1912. He died June 8, 1946, in Agnetendorf, Germany.

LILLIAN HELLMAN

Born June 20, 1905, in New Orleans, Lillian Hellman attended New York University, worked as a reader for a publisher and for a theatrical producer, and eventually took to writing plays herself. Her first performed work, *The Children's Hour* (1934), was based on a Scottish trial and created a furor with its treatment of a Lesbian theme; it was followed by the equally uncompromising *The Little Foxes* (1939) and *The Watch on the Rhine* (1941). Her subsequent works include *The Searching Wind* (1944); *Another Part of the Forest* (1946), dealing with the earlier lives of the characters in *The Little Foxes; The Autumn Garden* (1951); the book for a musical adaptation of Voltaire's *Candide* (1955); *Toys in the Attic* (1960); and *My Mother, My Father, and Me* (1963), adapted from a novel by Burt Blechman. In addition to preparing filmscripts for Hollywood, Miss Hellman has adapted two plays to the American stage: Robles' *Montserrat* and Anouilh's *L'Alouette* (*The Lark*).

Biographical Notes on the Playwrights

EUGÈNE IONESCO

Born November 26, 1912, in Slatina, Rumania, Eugène Ionesco grew up in France but went to Bucharest as a French teacher in 1936. Two years later he returned to France to prepare his thesis and, renouncing the academic life, took up residence in Paris and turned to the theater, establishing himself after some twenty years' effort as the leader of the post-war theater of the absurd. His dramatic works include *La Cantatrice Chauve* (*The Bald Soprano*, 1950); *La Leçon* (*The Lesson*, 1951); *Les Chaises* (*The Chairs*, 1952); *Victimes de devoir* (*Victims of Duty*, 1953); *La Jeune fille à marier* (1953); *Amédée ou Comment s'en débarrasser* (1954); *Jacques ou la Soumission* (1955); *L'Impromptu de l'Alma* (1956); *Le Nouveau Locataire* (*The New Tenant*, 1957); *Tueur sans gages* (*The Assassin*, 1959); *Le Rhinocéros* (1960); *Le Roi se meurt* (*The King Dies*, 1963); and *Le Piéton de l'air* (*The Airwalker*, 1964).

CHRISTOPHER ISHERWOOD

Born August 26, 1904, in England, Christopher William Bradshaw-Isherwood graduated from Corpus Christi, Cambridge, afterwards working as a tutor and studying medicine until he joined his friend W. H. Auden in Germany. His stories collected under the title *Goodbye to Berlin* were based upon his experiences of this period and were later dramatized by John Van Druten as the Broadway play *I Am a Camera*. Isherwood's other books include *All the Conspirators* (1928); *The Memorial* (1932); *The Last of Mr. Norris* (1935); *Lions and Shadows* (1938), an autobiography; *Prater Violet* (1945); *The Condor and the Cows* (1949); *The World in the Evening* (1954); and *Down There on a Visit* (1962). He collaborated with Auden on *Journey to a War* (1939); on the verse plays *The Dog Beneath the Skin* (1935) and *The Ascent of F6* (written 1936; performed 1937); and on the melodrama *On the Frontier* (1938). In 1960 he collaborated with Charles Laughton in a dramatic project based on the dialogues of Plato. After extensive travel Isherwood settled down in Santa Monica, California, turning out filmscripts for Hollywood and editing anthologies on mystical and religious subjects, best known among them *Vedanta for the Modern Man* (1951).

ALFRED JARRY

Born the son of a cloth manufacturer September 8, 1873, in Laval, France, Alfred Jarry was educated at Rennes and Paris; he joined the symbolist group in the latter city, worked with the *Mercure de France*, and eventually founded his own review, *Prehinderion*. His first two plays, *César Antéchrist* (1895) and *L'Autre Alceste* (1896), were unperformed, but in 1896 he achieved a *succès de scandale* with *Ubu Roi*. His subsequent theatrical works included *Ubu sur le butte* (performed 1901), *Ubu enchâiné* (published 1910), and *L'Almanach du Père Ubu* (1899), sequels which never managed to recapture the flavor of the original, as well as *Le Gentilhomme de 1847* (1898), *Par la taille* (1906), *Le Moutardier du pape* (1907), *L'Objet aimé* (produced 1909), and the opera libretto *Pantagruel* (produced 1911). He died November 1, 1907, in Paris.

GEORG KAISER

Born the son of a small business man November 25, 1878, in Magdeburg, Germany, Georg Kaiser lived several years in South America, Spain, and Italy before returning to his homeland to write plays. He first attracted notice with *Die Bürgher von Calais* (*The Burghers of Calais*, 1914) and went on to produce such works as his trilogy on the "new order" of life, consisting of *Die Koralle* (1917), *Gas I* (1918), and *Gas II* (1920); *Von Morgen bis Mitternachts* (*From Morn to Midnight*, 1917), a kind of twentieth-century morality play in which the hero is both a modern Everyman and a Christlike figure who experiences his passion in the seven stations or scenes of the drama; *Der Brand im Opernhaus* (1918); the formal experiment with parallel plot lines, *Nebeneinander* (1923); the antimilitaristic *Lederköpfe* (1928); *Mississippi* (1930); and the children's tragedy, *Das Floss der Medusa* (1945). Kaiser wrote several works on biblical and Greek themes as well as such libretti as *Der Protagonist* (1922) and *Der Zar lässt sich photographieren* (1928), set to music by Kurt Weill. In all, he wrote close to sixty works for the stage. An outspoken opponent of Nazism, he was silenced in 1933 and forced in 1938 to flee to Switzerland, dying in Ascona June 4, 1945.

GEORGE S. KAUFMAN

Born November 16, 1889, in Pittsburgh, Pennsylvania, George Simon Kaufman attended public high school, studied law briefly, and worked at a variety of odd jobs, experience of which he made use in his only play written without a collaborator, *The Butter-and-Egg Man* (1925). After several years spent as a columnist and drama critic for various New York papers, Kaufman collaborated with Marc Connelly on a series of comedies that included *Dulcy* (1921), *To the Ladies* (1922), *Merton of the Movies* (1922), and *Beggar on Horseback* (1924). In 1930 he initiated a collaboration with Moss Hart that produced the comedies *Once in a Lifetime* (1930), *Merrily We Roll Along* (1934), *You Can't Take It with You* (1936), *I'd Rather Be Right* (1937), *The American Way* (1939), *The Man Who Came to Dinner* (1939), and *George Washington Slept Here* (1940). Kaufman's other collaborators, with whom he turned out numerous successful comedies and musical comedy librettos, included Edna Ferber, Morrie Ryskind, Howard Dietz, Ring Lardner, Alexander Woollcott, Nunnally Johnson, and Abe Burrows. Kaufman died June 2, 1961.

W. SOMERSET MAUGHAM

Born January 25, 1874, in Paris, William Somerset Maugham studied at Canterbury, Heidelberg, and London, taking a degree in medicine but renouncing that profession for letters with the publication of his first novel, *Liza of Lambeth* (1897). He consolidated his literary reputation with the partially autobiographical novel *Of Human Bondage* (1915), followed by such works as *The Moon and Sixpence* (1919); *Ashenden* (1928), based on his own wartime experiences as an intelligence agent; *Cakes and Ale* (1930); and *The Razor's Edge* (1944). Maugham also earned popularity as a prolific and skillful short-story writer. He won his greatest success, however, in the theater, above all with his clever and often cynical comedies. His first dramatic work,

Schiffbrüchig, was written in 1897 in German; his first play to be presented in England was *A Man of Honor* (1903), followed by a prodigious number of sophisticated comedies, farces, and melodramas, of which perhaps the most memorable are *Lady Frederick* (1907), *Jack Straw* (1908), *The Noble Spaniard* (1909), *The Tenth Man* (1910), *Loaves and Fishes* (1911), *Our Betters* (1917), *Home and Beauty* (1917), *The Circle* (1921), *The Constant Wife* (1926), and *The Sacred Flame* (1928). Such was Maugham's popularity before World War I that at one point he had four plays running simultaneously in London's West End. His volumes of autobiography and reminiscence include *The Summing Up* (1938), *A Winter's Notebook* (1949), and *The Vagrant Mood* (1952). He was awarded the Order of Merit after his eightieth birthday.

VLADIMIR MAYAKOVSKI

Born the son of a forest inspector, July 7, 1893, in Bagdad, Georgia, Vladimir Vladimirovich Mayakovski moved with his family to Moscow in 1906, when his father died, and there completed his education. In 1912 he joined the cubists and futurists, and when the Revolution came, he supported it enthusiastically, both in action and in poetry. From 1919 to 1922 he directed propaganda for the Soviet wire service ROSTA, and in 1926 he made a trip across the entire Soviet Union, reading his poetry. He distinguished himself in drama as well as in verse: his first work, *Vladimir Mayakovski*, a symbolic monodrama, was staged in 1913, owing its title to the fact that the censor confused the play's and the author's names. It was followed by *Misteriya-buff* (1918); *Radio Oktyabrya* (1926, written with Osip Brik); *Klop* (*The Bedbug*, 1929), his best-known work; and *Banya* (*The Bath*, 1930). He committed suicide in 1930.

ARTHUR MILLER

Born October 17, 1915, in New York City, Arthur Miller began writing plays at the University of Michigan, won several prizes, and returned to New York to publish a novel, *Focus* (1945), based on an unproduced play. His first successfully staged play, *All My Sons* (1947), loosely based on Ibsen, was followed by *Death of a Salesman* (1949), the work which established him as a leading playwright of his generation. His subsequent plays include *The Crucible* (1953) and *A View from the Bridge* (1955). Miller has experimented to a limited extent with flashback and memory devices, but his contribution to American theater has been less in the area of technique than in his attempt to create tragedy for the contemporary stage, with the everyday man as its hero. With the largely autobiographical *After the Fall* (1963) Miller attacked as his theatrical objectives the nature of human responsibility for evil and the pursuit of moral truth. Through *Incident at Vichy* (1964), a work with a similar purpose, his plays have included no comedies; boasting few light moments, they have been deemed skillful, if stern, inquiries into pressing contemporary dilemmas. Miller wrote the scenario for a film, *The Misfits* (1961), which starred his wife Marilyn Monroe.

FERENC MOLNÁR

Born January 12, 1878, in Budapest, Ferenc Molnár studied law in Geneva and in his native city, but turned from the bar to letters, winning success with his first novel, *The Hungry City*, later followed by *The Paul Street Boys* (1907). Molnár's first stagework, the farce *The Doctor* (1902), was followed in 1907 by *The Devil* and in 1909 by the internationally successful *Liliom*, generally reckoned his masterpiece. His subsequent works, many of them ingenious comedies, include *The Guardsman* (1910), *The Wolf* (1912), *The Swan* (1920), *The Red Mill* (1923), *The Glass Slipper* (1924), *The Play's the Thing* (1925), *One, Two, Three* (1928), *The Good Fairy* (1930), *Somebody* (1931), *The Confectioner's Wife* (1933), *The Wedding* (1934), *The Unknown Girl* (1935), and *Delilah* (1937). Molnár spent the last part of his life in New York, where two of his last plays were introduced: *Delicate Story* (1940) and *Miracle in the Mountains* (1947). Few of Molnár's later works achieved the popularity of *Liliom*, which served in 1945 as the basis for Rodgers and Hammerstein's musical *Carousel*. He died April 1, 1952, in New York City.

HENRY DE MONTHERLANT

Born April 21, 1896, in Paris, Henry de Montherlant received his education at Janson-de-Sailly and at Sainte-Croix-de-Neuilly. A volunteer in the First World War, he was seriously wounded in 1918. In 1922 he published his first novel, *Le Songe;* his subsequent works, which included essays, poetry, and such novels as *Les Bestiaires* (1926), *Les Célibataires* (1934), *Pitié pour femmes* (1936), *Le Demon du bien* (1937), and *Les Lépreuses* (1939), earned him election to the Académie française in 1960. His works for the theater include *L'Exil* (1929); *La Reine Morte* (1942); *Fils de personne* (1943); *Un Incompris* (1943); *Malatesta* (1946); *Le Maître de Santiago* (*The Master of Santiago*, 1947); *Demain, il fera jour* (1949); *Pasiphae* (1938); *Celles qu'on prend dans ses bras* (1950); *La ville dont le Prince est un enfant* (1951); *Port-Royal* (1954); *Broceliande* (1956); *Don Juan* (1958); and *Le Cardinal d'Espagne*. From 1926 to 1935 Montherlant lived in Spain and Africa, locales which have served as settings for much of his work.

SEAN O'CASEY

Born March 31, 1880, in Dublin, Sean O'Casey was born and reared in a Dublin slum, so handicapped by poor eyesight that he was unable to read till the age of twelve. Largely self-educated, spending only three years in school, he became active in the Irish revolutionary movement and joined the Gaelic League, learning the Irish language and effecting an entree into the literary world. The Abbey Theatre presented his first three plays, *The Shadow of a Gunman* (1923), *Juno and the Paycock* (1924), and *The Plough and the Stars* (1926), but rejected *The Silver Tassie*, which was produced in London in 1929. O'Casey's subsequent plays include *Within the Gates* (1934), *The Stars Turn Red* (1940), *Purple Dust* (1945; published 1940), *Red Roses for Me* (1946; published 1942), *Oak Leaves and Lavender* (1946), *Cock-a-Doodle Dandy* (1949), and *The Bishop's Bonfire* (1955). O'Casey's six-volume autobiography consists of *I Knock at the Door* (1939), *Pictures in the Hallway* (1942), *Drums under the Windows* (1945), *Inishfallen Fare Thee Well* (1949), *Roses and Crowns* (1952), and *Sunset and Evening Star* (1945). O'Casey died September 18, 1964, in Torquay, England.

CLIFFORD ODETS

Born July 18, 1906, in Philadelphia, Clifford Odets grew up in New York City where, after graduating from high school, he worked for the Theatre Guild and the Group Theatre. He achieved fame with his first two plays, often considered his best, *Waiting for Lefty* (1935) and *Awake and Sing* (1935). His subsequent work adhered to the naturalistic technique and sociopolitical themes that had brought him success, but evinced growing ideological preoccupations. *Till the Day I Die* (1935), *Paradise Lost* (1935), and *I Can't Sleep* (1936) failed to please audiences, while *Golden Boy* (1937) was a success. Following the failures of *Night Music* (1940) and *Clash by Night* (1941), Odets turned out screenplays for Hollywood, voicing his distaste for the film industry in *The Big Knife* (1948). With *The Country Girl* (1950) he abandoned the themes of his earlier work and won a measure of audience approval, and in *The Flowering Peach* (1954) he turned to allegorical fantasy. He died in 1963 while working for television and preparing a musical adaptation of *Golden Boy.*

EUGENE O'NEILL

Born of actor parents October 16, 1888, in New York City, Eugene Gladstone O'Neill received his education at Catholic and private schools, was thrown out of Princeton, and spent most of the three years of his first marriage wandering the world. He became interested in drama during a year spent recuperating from tuberculosis and enrolled in George Pierce Baker's "47 Workshop" at Harvard. His earliest plays, produced by the Provincetown Players, drew on his experience as a seaman and included *Bound East for Cardiff* (1916); *The Long Voyage Home* (1917); *Ile* (1917); and *The Moon of the Caribbees* (1918). He went on to attract the attention of commercial managers and wider audiences with such works as *Beyond the Horizon* (1920); *The Emperor Jones* (1920); *Anna Christie* (1922); *The Hairy Ape* (1922); *Desire Under the Elms* (1924); *All God's Chillun Got Wings* (1924); *The Great God Brown* (1926); the satirical *Marco Millions* (1928); *Strange Interlude* (1928); *Mourning Becomes Electra* (1931); *Ah, Wilderness!* (1933); *Days Without End* (1934); and *The Iceman Cometh* (written 1939; performed 1946). O'Neill's death on November 27, 1953, was followed by posthumous productions of *Long Day's Journey into Night* (1956); *A Moon for the Misbegotten* (1957); and *A Touch of the Poet* (1958). His dramatic production, though largely of a somber cast, ranged from tragedy to lighthearted comedy; in many ways a pioneer, he was one of the first American playwrights to make effective use of Freudian psychology and the devices of the European naturalistic and expressionistic theater, and his revival of the masks, asides, and soliloquies of older drama were innovations for their time. In 1936 he was awarded the Nobel Prize for literature, the only American playwright to be so honored.

JOHN OSBORNE

Born December 12, 1929, in London, John Osborne achieved theatrical success with his first play, *Look Back in Anger* (1956), a work which lent its name to the group of modern English writers known as the "angry young men." His subsequent plays include *The Entertainer* (1957); *Epitaph for George Dillon* (1958, written in collaboration with Anthony Creighton); the musical, *The World of Paul Slickey*, with music by C. Whelen (1959); *Luther* (1961); and *Inadmissible Evidence* (1964). Osborne adapted Fielding's *Tom Jones* to the screen (1963).

LUIGI PIRANDELLO

Born June 28, 1867, Luigi Pirandello spent most of his early career as a professor of literature in an Italian girls' school, but after achieving success as a writer for the stage founded his own theater in Rome and took his own acting company on tours with his plays throughout Europe. As prolific a novelist, short-story writer, and poet as he was playwright, he adapted over twenty of his novels into plays, and these reworkings constitute almost half his dramatic output. His plays, which, like his novels, reflect his preoccupation with symbolism, psychology, and the nature of "truth" and "reality," include *La Morsa* (1910), his first stage work; *Il Dovere del medico* (1913); *Se non così* (1915); *Pensaci, Giacomino!* (1916); *Così è, se vi pare* (*Right You Are, If You Think You Are,* 1917); *Il Piacere dell' Onestà* (1917); *Ma non è una cosa seria* (1918); *L'Uomo, la bestia, e la virtù* (1919); *Tutto per bene* (1920); *Come prima, meglio di prima* (1920); *La Signora Morli Uno e Due* (1920); *Sei personaggi in cerca d'autore* (*Six Characters in Search of an Author,* 1921); *Enrico IV* (*Henry IV,* 1922); *Vestire gli ignudi* (*Naked,* 1922); *La Vita che ti diedi* (1923); *L'Altro figlio* (1923); *Ciascuno a suo modo* (1924); *L'Amico delle mogli* (1927); *O di uno o di nessuno* (1929); *Questa sera si recita a soggetto* (*Tonight We Improvise,* 1930); *Come tu mi vuoi* (*As You Desire Me,* (1934); *Sogno, ma forse no* (1931); *Quando si è qualcuno* (1933); *Non si sa come* (1934); and the uncompleted *I Giganti della Montagna* (1937). Pirandello's nontheatrical works include *Il Fu Mattia Pascal* (*The Late Mattia Pascal,* 1904); *L'Esclusa* (*The Outcast,* 1893); *Uno, Nessuno, e Centomila* (*One, None, and a Hundred Thousand,* 1926); and the vast collection of short stories entitled *Novelle per un anno* (*Stories for a Year,* 1922–1936). Pirandello was awarded the Nobel Prize for literature in 1934, and died in Rome, December 10, 1936.

ELMER RICE

Born September 28, 1892, in New York City, Elmer Rice studied for the bar but abandoned a lawyer's career for that of playwright. His first play, *On Trial* (1914), the earliest stage production to make use of film techniques, was followed by a prolific output that included *The Adding Machine* (1923), a satire in the German expressionist manner; *Street Scene* (1929); *The Left Bank* (1931); *Counselor-at-Law* (1931); and a series of works dealing with the social and political conflicts of the thirties: *We, the People* (1933); *Judgement Day* (1934); *Between Two Worlds* (1934); *American Landscape* (1938); *Two on an Island* (1940); and *Flight to the West* (1940). With *Dream Girl*

(1945) Rice demonstrated his mastery of light comedy, and in 1947, in collaboration with the composer Kurt Weill, he produced an operatic version of *Street Scene*. His subsequent works for the stage include *The Grand Tour* (1951), *The Winner* (1954), and *Cue for Passion* (1958). Rice has also written several novels, including *A Voyage to Purilia* (1930), *Imperial City* (1937), and *The Show Must Go On* (1949), as well as an *Autobiography* (1962).

ARMAND SALACROU

Born the son of a pharmacist, August 9, 1899, in Rouen, France, Armand Salacrou interrupted his medical studies to take a degree in philosophy; long interested in socialism, he was a member of the Communist Party for three years, but broke with it in 1923. His first plays, *Le Casseur d'assiettes* (1923) and *Tour a terre* (1925), testify to his youthful enthusiasm for surrealism. Numerous plays followed, including *Pont de l'Europe* (1925), *Patchouli* (1930), *Atlas-Hotel* (1931), *La Vie en rose* (1931), *Une Femme libre* (1934), *Les Frénétiques* (1934), *L'Inconnue d'Arras* (1935), *Un Homme comme les autres* (1936), *La Terre est ronde* (1938), *Histoire de rire* (1939), *Les Nuits de la colère* (1946), *L'Archipel Lenoir* (1947), *Dieu le savait!* (1950), *Poof* (1950), *Une Femme trop honnête* (1956), and *Boulevard Durand* (1960). Salacrou has also written numerous film scenarios.

WILLIAM SAROYAN

Born of Armenian stock August 31, 1908, in Fresno, California, William Saroyan spent his childhood partly in an orphanage and partly in the care of his widowed mother and attended Fresno Junior High School. In 1934 his collection of stories, *The Daring Young Man on the Flying Trapeze*, brought him widespread recognition. There followed a flood of short stories and novels, including the autobiographical *My Name Is Aram* (1940) and *The Human Comedy* (1942). Two of Saroyan's plays, *My Heart's in the Highlands* (1939) and *The Time of Your Life* (1941), were Broadway successes, and two, *Love's Old Sweet Song* (1940) and *The Beautiful People* (1941), were not. Notable among his subsequent theatrical works is *The Cave Dwellers* (1958). Like his fiction, Saroyan's stageworks blend realism, sentiment, and fantasy.

JEAN-PAUL SARTRE

Born June 21, 1905, in Paris, Jean-Paul Sartre has distinguished himself as a philosopher, novelist, playwright, and film scenarist. The leading French exponent of the existentialist philosophy, he has sought in both fiction and formal philosophy to demonstrate the ethical neutrality of the universe and man's consequent responsibility to create his own ethic and self by means of choice and action. The same theme animates his plays, which range from tragedy to farce and which include *Les Mouches* (*The Flies*, 1943); *Huis-clos* (*No Exit*, 1944); *Morts sans sépulture* (1946); *La Putain respectueuse* (*The Respectful Prostitute*, 1946); *Les Mains sales* (*Dirty Hands*, 1948); *Le Diable et le Bon Dieu* (*The Devil and the Good Lord*, 1951); *Les Faux Nez* (1952); *Kean* (1953); *Nekrassov* (1955); and *Les Séquestrés d'Altona* (1959). Sartre's prose works include the novels grouped under the title *Les Chemins de la*

Liberté and the autobiographical *Les Mots* (*The Words*, 1963). He was awarded the Nobel Prize for literature in 1964 but turned it down.

GEORGES SCHÉHADÉ

Born November 2, 1910, in Alexandria, Egypt, of French-speaking Lebanese parents, Georges Schéhadé studied for the bar, received a degree in law, and became secretary general of the Ecole Générale supérieure des Lettres in Beirut, where he settled. He has published a book of poems, *Poésies*, but is best known as a playwright, a creator of a surrealistic, poetic stage world of dream and fairy tale. His plays include *Monsieur Bob'le* (1951), *La Soirée des proverbes* (1954), *Histoire de Vasco* (1956), *Les Violettes* (1960), and *Le Voyage* (1961).

GEORGE BERNARD SHAW

Born in Dublin July 26, 1856, George Bernard Shaw had written five unsuccessful socialist novels by 1884 when he met William Archer, who urged him to write plays and through whom he became music critic for a London newspaper. He began writing for the stage the following year, but with most of his early plays either banned by the censor or refused production, he sought a reading audience and published his first collection, *Plays Pleasant and Unpleasant* (1898), the pleasant plays being *Arms and the Man*, *Candida* (privately performed in 1895), *The Man of Destiny*, and *You Never Can Tell*; the unpleasant, *The Philanderer*, *Mrs. Warren's Profession*, and *Widowers' Houses*, his first play. It was for this volume that Shaw began his practice of writing challenging, eloquent prefaces to his plays. His next collection, *Three Plays for Puritans* (1900), contained *The Devil's Disciple*, *Caesar and Cleopatra*, and *Captain Brassbound's Conversion*. After the turn of the century, and largely through the efforts of H. Granville-Barker, Shaw began to achieve productions and ultimately acceptance in England. His subsequent plays include *Man and Superman* (written from 1901 to 1903); *John Bull's Other Island* (1904); *Major Barbara* (1905); *Misalliance* (1910); *Fanny's First Play* (1912); *Androcles and the Lion* (1912); *Pygmalion* (1914); *Great Catherine* (1918); *Heartbreak House* (1920); *Back to Methuselah* (1922); *Saint Joan* (1923); *The Simpleton of the Unexpected Isles* (1935); and *Buoyant Billions* (1948), his last full-length play. A member of the Fabian Society from its founding, Shaw wrote many essays on socialism, politics, and economics, and one longer work, *The Intelligent Woman's Guide to Socialism and Capitalism* (1928). He received the Nobel Prize for literature in 1925 and died at Ayot St. Lawrence, November 2, 1950.

ROBERT CEDRIC SHERRIFF

Born June 6, 1896, at Kingston-on-Thames, England, Robert Cedric Sherriff worked in an insurance company and in off-hours wrote for a local theater group, achieving national success when the Stage Society produced *Journey's End* (1928). His subsequent plays include *Badger's Green* (1930); *St. Helen* (1936), written with Jeanne de Casalis; *Miss Mabel* (1948); *Home at Seven* (1950); *The White Carnation* (1953); *The Long Sunset* (1955); *The Telescope* (1957); and *A Shred of Evidence* (1960). For the films, Sherriff wrote

485

the scenarios of *Four Feathers* (1939) and *Storm over the Nile* (1955) and collaborated on the scenarios of *Goodbye, Mr. Chips* (1939); *Odd Man Out* (1947); two films based on short stories of Somerset Maugham, *Quartet* (1949) and *Trio* (1950); and *No Highway in the Sky* (1951).

ROBERT E. SHERWOOD

Born April 4, 1896, in New Rochelle, New York, Robert Emmet Sherwood interrupted his Harvard education to serve with a Canadian regiment in World War I; wounded in France, he returned to this country a bitter opponent of war, attacking the concept of military glory in *The Road to Rome* (1927), his first Broadway production. His subsequent plays included *The Love Nest* (1927); *The Queen's Husband* (1928); *Waterloo Bridge* (1930); *This Is New York* (1931); *Reunion in Vienna* (1931); *Acropolis* (1933); *The Petrified Forest* (1935); *Idiot's Delight* (1936); *Abe Lincoln in Illinois* (1938); *There Shall Be No Night* (1940); *The Rugged Path* (1945); and *Miss Liberty* (1949), a musical comedy with music by Irving Berlin. He was especially preoccupied in the thirties with ideological problems and attempted in his plays to arouse American opinion against European totalitarianism. Under Franklin D. Roosevelt he served as special assistant to the Secretaries of War and of the Navy and as director of overseas operations for the Office of War Information; he described his war services in the book *Roosevelt and Hopkins* (1948). Sherwood published a novel, *The Virtuous Knight* (1931), and collaborated on the filmscripts of *Rebecca* (1940) and *The Best Years of Our Lives* (1946). During the fifties he wrote television plays. He died November 14, 1955.

REINHARD JOHANNES SORGE

Born January 29, 1892, in Berlin, Reinhard Johannes Sorge was a precociously talented dramatist, writing his first play, *Das Unbekannte*, a work heavily influenced by Ibsen, in 1911. From the same period date *Prometheus* (published 1925), *Odysseus* (published 1925), and *Antichrist*. Under the influence of Strindberg's religious plays, Sorge wrote *Der Bettler* (*The Beggar*) in 1912; the work was staged in 1917 by Rheinhardt. During a trip to Rome in 1912, Sorge converted to Catholicism, and his religious preoccupations are apparent in his subsequent works, which include *Guntwar, die Schule eines Propheten* (published 1914); *Metanoeite* (published 1915), and the posthumously published *König David* (1916), *Mutter der Himmel* (1917), *Gericht über Zarathustra* (1921), *Mystiche Zweisprräche* (1922), *Preis der Unbeflekten* (1924), and *Der Sieg des Christus* (1924). Sorge died at Ablaincourt on the French front, July 20, 1916.

AUGUST STRINDBERG

The son of a serving woman and a wholesale merchant, Johan August Strindberg was born in Stockholm January 22, 1849. He first attracted literary attention with his satirical novel *Röda Rummet* (*The Red Room*, 1879). With the publication of the stories in *Giftas* (*Married*, 1884–1886), he brought upon himself prosecution for blasphemy; he was acquitted, but permanently embittered. His first marriage formed the basis for the conflicts in the plays of his realistic-naturalistic period, which include *Fadren* (*The Father*, 1887);

Fröken Julie (*Miss Julie*, 1889); and *Fordringsägare* (*Creditors*, 1889). Strindberg was forced to establish his own short-lived Experimental Theater in Copenhagen in order to stage his works. Emotional disturbances, feelings of persecution, and difficulties in obtaining productions and publishers drove him in 1896 to near psychological collapse, an experience recorded in the autobiographical *Inferno* (1897) and *Legends* (1898) and expressed dramatically in such mystic and symbolic plays as *Till Damaskus* (*To Damascus*, written 1898–1901) and *Brott och Brott* (*There Are Crimes and Crimes*, 1900). It was during this period of crisis that Strindberg began writing the "dream plays," which became forerunners of modern expressionism and which included such works as the mystical *Påsk* (*Easter*, 1901) and *Ett Drömspel* (*A Dream Play*, published 1902, performed 1907). Strindberg also turned to Swedish history and wrote a series of dramas that include *Gustav Vasa* (1899) and *Karl XII* (*Charles XII*, 1902). His subsequent works include five "chamber plays" written for the Intimate Theater that he and August Falck established in Stockholm in 1907, of which the best known is *Spöksonaten* (*The Ghost Sonata*, 1908); the plays written shortly before his death include *Stora Landsvägen* (*The Great Highway*, 1910). Strindberg's collected writings—plays, fairy tales, poems, short stories, sketches, essays, autobiography, and novels—fill more than fifty-five volumes; among them, *The Son of a Servant* (1886), *A Madman's Defense* (written 1887–1888), and *Alone* (1903) are autobiographical works. Strindberg died May 14, 1912, in Stockholm.

JOHN MILLINGTON SYNGE

Born April 6, 1871, at Newton Little, near Dublin, John Millington Synge began his career settling in France and translating French symbolist poetry, but was persuaded by Yeats to return to Ireland, where he became the foremost dramatist of the Irish renaissance. His plays, which he claimed to be literal transcriptions of the speech of western Ireland's peasants, include *In the Shadow of the Glen* (1903); *Riders to the Sea* (1904); *The Well of the Saints* (1905); *The Playboy of the Western World* (1907); *The Tinker's Wedding* (1907); and the nearly completed *Deirdre of the Sorrows* (1910), one of the most distinguished re-creations of Irish myth of the Celtic revival. Synge died in Dublin, March 24, 1909.

ERNST TOLLER

Born the son of a tradesman December 1, 1893, in West Prussia, Ernst Toller studied at Grenoble, Heidelberg, and Monaco and was imprisoned five years for revolutionary activities. His first works were written in jail, the two "chorales" *Der Tag des Proletariats* and *Requiem den gemordeten Brüdern* (published 1920), and in 1923 he published a book of poems, *Das Schwalbenbuch*. His first drama in the conventional sense, *Die Wandlung* (1919), was followed by the idealistic and polemical *Masse Mensch* (1921) and *Die Maschinenstürmer* (1922). With *Der Entfesselte Wotan* (1923) Toller sounded the note of grotesque black farce; the play was followed by *Die Rache des verhöhnten Liebhabers oder Frauenlist und Männerlist* (1928), *Justiz* (1927), *Hoppla, wir leben!* (1927), and *Feuer aus den Kesseln* (1930), as well as other, more minor theatrical works. With the advent of Nazism Toller took refuge in the United States, where he wrote *Pastor Hall* (1937).

He wrote three works of autobiography: *Quer Durch* (1930), *Eine Jungend in Deutschland* (1933), and *Briefe aus dem Gefängnis*. He committed suicide May 22, 1939, in New York.

VSEVOLOD VISHNEVSKI

Born in Russia December 8, 1900, Vsevolod Vital'yevich Vishnevski took part in the Russian revolution of 1917 as a machine gunner with the first cavalry army and first attracted attention with the publication of short stories based on his war experiences. His first play, *Pervaya konnaya* (*First Cavalry Army*), staged in 1930, was followed by *Poslednyi reshitel'nyi* (*The Last Battle*, 1931); *Optimisticheskaya tragediya* (*The Optimistic Tragedy*, 1932), and *Na zapadye boi* (*Fighting in the West*, 1933). Vishnevski wrote the scenarios for the films *My iz Kronshtadta* (*We from Kronstadt*, 1936) and *Nezabyvayemyi 1919–i* (*The Unforgettable Year 1919*, 1951). He died February 28, 1951.

FRANK WEDEKIND

Born of a wealthy family July 24, 1864, in Hanover, Frank Wedekind abandoned preparations for a law career, worked for a while in advertising, and took a job as traveling secretary to a circus, all the while absorbing the influence of playwrights as diverse as Hauptmann, Strindberg, and Büchner. His most famous plays all deal frankly with sexual themes: *Die Junge Welt* (*The Young World*, written 1890, produced 1908); *Frühling's Erwachen* (*Spring's Awakening*, published 1891, performed 1906); *Erdgeist* (*Earth-Spirit*, 1898), and *Die Büchse der Pandora* (*Pandora's Box*, 1903), the last two originally written as one work, *Lulu*, but not produced in that form until 1905. Notable among Wedekind's numerous other plays are *Marquis von Keith* (1901), *Totentanz* (1906; also known as *Tod und Teufel*), and *Schloss Wetterstein* (published 1912). Wedekind and his wife played leading roles in many of his plays, which he produced himself and which are regarded as forerunners of German expressionism in the theater. Wedekind died March 9, 1918, in Monaco.

PETER WEISS

Born August 11, 1916, in Berlin, Peter Weiss left Germany before World War II and eventually settled in Stockholm, becoming a Swedish citizen. An accomplished painter and film director, he is best known as a writer. His first published work was *Från ö till ö* (1947), and he has produced numerous prose works as well as the plays *Nacht mit Gästen* (1963) and *Die Verfolgung und Ermordung Jean Paul Marats dargestellt durch die Schauspielgruppe des Hospizes zu Charenton unter Anleitung des Herrn de Sade* (*The Persecution and Assassination of Marat as Performed by the Inmates of the Asylum of Charenton under the Direction of the Marquis de Sade*, 1964), referred to in its English version as *Marat/Sade*. It was this play which made him the object of international controversy and acclaim and which placed him in the forefront of the most promising post-war European playwrights.

THORNTON WILDER

Born April 17, 1897, in Madison, Wisconsin, Thornton Niven Wilder was educated in China, where his father was American Consul-General, and in the United States, where he graduated from Yale in 1920 and received an M.A. in French from Princeton in 1925. A constant experimenter in unconventional literary and theatrical forms, gifted with a fine prose style and a deeply philosophical outlook, Wilder ranks among the foremost original American writers. His works for the theater include *The Trumpet Shall Sound* (1926); *Our Town* (1938); *The Merchant of Yonkers* (1938), an adaptation of a farce by Johann Nestroy; *The Skin of Our Teeth* (1942), a cyclical history of mankind patterned to some extent on James Joyce's *Finnegans Wake; The Matchmaker* (1955), a revision of *The Merchant of Yonkers;* and a cycle of fourteen one-act plays of which three, *Someone from Assisi, Infancy,* and *Childhood,* were produced in 1962. Wilder has published two collections of one-act plays, *The Angel That Troubled the Waters* (1928) and *The Long Christmas Dinner* (1931), as well as the novels *The Cabala* (1926), *The Bridge of San Luis Rey* (1927), *The Woman of Andros* (1930), *Heaven's My Destination* (1934), and *The Ides of March* (1948). To criticisms of his imitativeness, Wilder has frankly replied that his writing life is a series of infatuations for admired writers. In 1963 *The Matchmaker* triumphed in its Broadway musical reincarnation, *Hello Dolly!*

TENNESSEE WILLIAMS

Born March 26, 1914, in Columbus, Mississippi, Tennessee (Thomas Lanier) Williams held a variety of jobs and worked his way through the University of Iowa before winning a Rockefeller fellowship in 1940 that enabled him to complete the play *Battle of Angels,* unsuccessfully produced the same year. This early failure was followed by *The Glass Menagerie* (1945), his first successful play; *A Streetcar Named Desire* (1947); *Summer and Smoke* (1948); *The Rose Tattoo* (1951); *Camino Real* (1953); *Cat on a Hot Tin Roof* (1955); *Orpheus Descending* (1957), a reworking of *Battle of Angels;* two one-act plays, *Suddenly, Last Summer* and *Something Unspoken* (1958); *Sweet Bird of Youth* (1959); *Period of Adjustment* (1960); *The Night of the Iguana* (1961); and *The Milktrain Doesn't Stop Here Any More* (1963). Williams' stageworks, which have earned him a pre-eminent place in the American theater, also include the comedy *You Touched Me!* (1947), adapted with Donald Wyndham from a story by D. H. Lawrence, and several short plays collected in *Twenty-Seven Wagons Full of Cotton and Other One-Act Plays* (1946). He has also published a novel, *The Roman Spring of Mrs. Stone* (1950); a collection of poems, *In the Winter of Cities* (1955); and two collections of short stories, *One Arm* (1955) and *Hard Candy* (1959), as well as the screenplay for the film *Baby Doll* (1956). Williams has been praised for the lyricism of his language and for his sympathy for the weak and the defeated as well as attacked for his depiction of violence and sexual disorder. He has replied to his critics by stating that the primitivism that underlies the thin veneer of our civilization cannot be ignored.

WILLIAM BUTLER YEATS

Born June 13, 1865, in Dublin, William Butler Yeats was the son of John Butler Yeats, a well-known Irish painter, and he himself studied painting for three years, though he is best known for his achievements in drama and poetry. He published numerous volumes of verse, ranging from romantic and folkloric poems to works of a direct simplicity and others in a more symbolist, stylized vein. In 1896 he became a leader of the Irish renaissance, and with Lady Gregory, George Moore, and others, he founded in 1899 the theater society that was later to become the Abbey Theatre. His numerous works for the theater include *The Countess Cathleen* (1899), *The Land of Heart's Desire* (1899), *Cathleen ni Houlihan* (1902), *Deirdre* (written 1907), *Four Plays for Dancers* (1917–1920), *The Words upon the Window-Pane* (1934), *The Herne's Egg* (written 1938), and *Purgatory* (1939). His prose works include fairy and folk tales, occult writings, collections of essays, and *Autobiographies* (1926). He was elected a senator of the Irish Free State in 1922 and was awarded the Nobel Prize for literature in 1923. He died at Roquebrune, near Monaco, January 28, 1939.

CARL ZUCKMAYER

Born December 27, 1896, in Nackenheim, Germany, Carl Zuckmayer wrote an expressionist play, *Kreuzweg* (1920), and an adaptation from Terence, *Eunuco* (1923), closed for immorality, before hitting his stride with *Der fröliche Weinberg* (*The Merry Vineyard*, 1925) and *Schinderhannes* (1927), both inspired by material from his Rhenish homeland. His subsequent plays include *Katherine Knie* (1928); *Der Hauptmann von Köpenick* (*The Captain from Köpenick*, 1931), his greatest international success; *Bellmann* (1938); *Der Teufels General* (*The Devil's General*, 1946), a serious handling of a theme that had been treated satirically in his earlier work; *Barbara Blomberg* (1949); *Der Gesang im Feuerofen* (*Song in the Fiery Furnace*, 1950); *Das Kalte Licht* (*The Cold Light*, 1955); *Der Trunkene Herkules* (written 1957); and *Die Uhr shlägt eins* (1961). Zuckmayer has also published novels, poems, and short stories. Forced into exile by the rise of Nazism, he moved to Switzerland and, ultimately, made his home in the United States.

Alphabetical List of the Plays